DOSTOEVSKY

DOSTOEVSKY

The Stir of Liberation

1860-1865

JOSEPH FRANK

PRINCETON UNIVERSITY

PRESS

Copyright © 1986 by Princeton University Press
Published by Princeton University Press, 41 William Street,
Princeton, New Jersey 08540
In the United Kingdom: Princeton University Press,
Guildford, Surrey

Library of Congress Cataloging in Publication Data will
be found on the last printed page of this book

First Princeton Paperback printing, 1988

This book has been composed in Linotron Primer

Clothbound editions of Princeton University Press books
are printed on acid-free paper, and binding materials are
chosen for strength and durability. Paperbacks,
although satisfactory for personal collections,
are not usually suitable for library rebinding

Printed in the United States of America by
Princeton University Press, Princeton, New Jersey

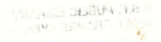

This book is dedicated to
Francis Fergusson
A dear friend and mentor,
whose own works are models
of critical illumination

CONTENTS

CONTENTS

LIST OF ILLUSTRATIONS

Unless otherwise noted, all illustrations are from *Feodor Mikhailovich Dostoevsky v Portretakh, illyustratsiyakh, dokumentakh*, ed. V. S. Nechaeva (Moscow, 1972).

PREFACE

This is the third installment of what has now become a five-volume work dealing with the life and writings of Dostoevsky. My initial plan called for only four volumes, but I was forced to extend it when the present book emerged rather unexpectedly. The time-span covered here (1860-1865) originally formed the closing chapters of volume two, which would thus have included not only Dostoevsky's years in Siberia but also his return and re-entry into literary life. But once I began to investigate these five years more closely in the light of new archival material, recent scholarly studies such as the two volumes on Dostoevsky's magazines by V. S. Nechaeva, and the rich panorama of the activities of the radical intelligentsia contained in Franco Venturi's classic *Roots of Revolution*, I realized that they required a more extensive treatment.

In fact, the pages of the present volume deal with an extremely important period in Dostoevsky's life that has been more or less scanted. Commentators were naturally eager, as I had been myself, to pass over them rapidly so as to reach the major novels that began to appear in the middle and late 1860s. Yet in the early 1860s, as the editor of two important journals, Dostoevsky stood much more directly at the center of Russian social-cultural life than during the remainder of the decade, when he returned to being exclusively a novelist again and lived abroad in self-imposed isolation. It was also during these years, as I hope to show, that his social-political outlook was definitively reshaped.

It was then that he drew the practical conclusions—which would remain essentially unchanged, despite some differences in accentuation, for the rest of his life—from the experiences of his Siberian exile. What he later called the "regeneration" of his convictions did not occur instantaneously but took a certain amount of time; it took, in fact, the amount of time required for the events narrated here to run their course (and even a little beyond). A detailed consideration of these events will help to clarify why Dostoevsky came to the conclusions that he did; and it should also scotch the still widespread notion that he emerged from prison camp blindly prepared to support a tyrannical régime of the most vilely reactionary stripe.

This third volume also brings me back to my initial point of departure. I first began to study Dostoevsky seriously in connection with *Notes from Underground*, and it was my effort to come to grips with this text—an effort whose results are included in the present book—that shaped my whole approach to Dostoevsky's work. For I became persuaded that the issues of his time not only furnished him with external stimulus but entered much more deeply into his creative process than had generally been perceived, and that, for this reason, his creations could not really be understood without a solid knowledge of the social-cultural environment in which he worked. Dostoevsky's response to the ideological conflicts of his society were of course affected by his personality and experiences; but these acquire artistic significance only when they enter into creative symbiosis with the great moral questions posed by the ferment of Russian history in Dostoevsky's lifetime, particularly after 1861.

To comprehend this symbiosis, one must study the many channels through which the social-cultural turbulence of the early 1860s flowed into Dostoevsky's creative imagination. Such channels included a personal involvement that was far from being only that of a spectator or a disabused commentator; Dostoevsky was a participant as well as an observer, who was often on the spot during important manifestations of social unrest. Even when absent, he was heart and soul engaged in following the tumultuous course of events on whose outcome, he was passionately convinced, depended the future destiny of Russia (and hence, ultimately, of humanity as a whole). As we shall see, he also intervened personally, even at the risk of casting suspicion on himself and endangering his interests, when he believed that his intercession might help to ease a turbulent situation heading toward disaster. No book known to me does full justice to Dostoevsky's total immersion in the "unruly sea" (the title of a novel by Pisemsky) whipped up by the storm winds of post-liberation social discontent; and I have felt it important to fill this lacuna in the literature, even if it meant the unanticipated addition of an extra volume to my series.

THE FAVORABLE reception accorded my second volume exceeded all my expectations, and I wish particularly to thank the members of the National Book Critics Circle, who awarded it their annual prize for biography in 1984. Such an accolade, given by a group professionally engaged in evaluating current literary production, is a very great honor, and I am exceedingly grateful for this evidence of widespread appreciation. I take it, however, not merely as a source of personal satisfaction but also as a vindication of the perspective in which I have chosen to write. For it proves that a literary biographer is not necessarily forced to place the purely extrinsic, anecdotal details of the private life of his subject in the foreground, and that these can be presented in terms of the writer's work and strictly subordinated to a fuller delineation of the social-cultural and literary context much more directly linked with creative production.

The dedication of this book is but a small repayment for a debt of inspiration and encouragement contracted during a friendship of over forty years. If an author writes for an ideal reader who represents the standard to which he aspires, then for me this standard has always been embodied in the person and writings of Francis Fergusson; and I have tried as best I could to live up to the example set by his own scrupulousness and integrity.

Once again I am happy to thank the Rockefeller Foundation for its generosity in awarding me a Humanities Fellowship during the academic year 1983-1984, which helped to finance a year's leave of absence from teaching duties at Princeton. Part of that year was spent in the lively atmosphere of the Stanford Humanities Center, which provided congenial working conditions, and whose Director, Ian Watt, created a stimulating intellectual climate in which to exchange ideas with others in various fields. The members of the staff of the Center were very helpful in facilitating the preparation of the manuscript. During the fall term of 1985 I was privileged, as a Director's Visitor, to be a member of the Institute for Advanced Study at Princeton, and I wish to express my warm gratitude to the Director, Harry Woolf, for according me this appointment. Final work on the manuscript and galleys was completed in this ideal atmosphere for scholarly research.

My special thanks go to Edward J. Brown of Stanford University, who put his great knowledge of everything Russian at my disposal and made many suggestions for the improvement of my text. The comments of the seasoned Dostoevskian and loyal friend Robert L. Jackson of Yale University again provided heartwarming reassurance. Nina Berberova, emeritus professor of Russian literature at Princeton University, and an eminent Russian woman of letters in her own right, has again graciously given me her energetic and penetrating comments and her important approval. My colleague Robert Hollander was kind enough to read Chapter 20 and give me the benefit of his knowledge of theology. The chairman of my department at Princeton, Robert Fagles, has been a constant source of intellectual support, personal aid, and practical benevolence for which I am deeply grateful. My colleague Victor Brombert has also helped by the unflagging interest he has always taken in the progress of my work and by the stimulus of his conversation on topics relating to Dostoevsky.

My editor at Princeton University Press, Gretchen Oberfranc, improved my style, straightened out my footnotes, and generally saw to the production of the book with her usual assiduity and skill. Orest Pelech, the former Slavic bibliographer at Princeton's Firestone Library, was unvaryingly attentive to my requests for aid, and I owe to him the illustration of the Petersburg fires. The Princeton Research Council was again very obliging in defraying the costs of typing and other clerical expenses, and the first draft of the manuscript was typed by Carol Szymanski with great care and considerable interest in its contents.

My older daughter Claudine gave the title just the proper snap, and aided her sister Isabelle in reading the proofs attentively. As for the support provided by my wife Marguerite, I can only repeat what I said in my second volume: she serves as my first reader and editor, and I rely absolutely on her

The problem of transliteration is always a difficult one, and I have opted for the simplest solution. For all Russian words, names or otherwise, I use System I in the transliteration chart contained in J. Thomas Shaw, *The Transliteration of Modern Russian for English Language Publications* (Madison, Milwaukee, and London, 1967), 8-9. I have, however, occasionally inserted a "y" to indicate a soft sound where this would not be the natural pronunciation of the transliterated word in English, even though System I does not pay any attention to this feature of Russian. And I have always used English forms, rather than transliteration, where such exist and have become customary (Alexander rather than Aleksandr, for example).

Citations to Dostoevsky's texts in Russian are made to the volumes of the new Soviet edition now in the course of publication: F. M. Dostoevsky, *Polnoe Sobranie Sochinenii* (Leningrad, 1972-); 28 volumes of this planned 30-volume set have so far appeared. For my quotations from Dostoevsky's short stories and novels, I have used the translations of Constance Garnett because she takes fewer liberties with the literal meaning than more recent translators. However, I have not hesitated to alter her version where this seemed indicated. If no source is given for a translation, I have made it myself, and in all cases the translations of Dostoevsky's texts have been collated with the original.

PART I

A Time of Hope

Time makes old formulas look strange,
Our properties and symbols change,
But round the freedom of the Will
Our disagreements center still.

W. H. Auden, *New Year's Letter*

Isolation is the sum-total of wretchedness in man. To be cut off, to be left solitary; to have a world alien, not your world; all a hostile camp for you; not a home at all, of hearts and faces who are yours, whose you are: It is the frightfulest enchantment; too truly a work of the Evil One.

Thomas Carlyle, *Past and Present*

L'immortalité de l'âme est une chose qui nous importe si fort, qui nous touche si profondément, qu'il faut avoir perdu tout sentiment pour être dans l'indifference de savoir ce qui en est. Toutes nos actions et nos pensées doivent prendre des routes si différentes, selon qu'il y aura des biens éternels à espérer ou non, qu'il est impossible de faire une démarche avec sens et jugement, qu'en la réglant par la vue de ce point, qui doit être notre dernier objet.

Ainsi notre premier intérêt et notre premier devoir est de nous éclaircir sur ce sujet, d'où dépend toute notre conduite.

Blaise Pascal, *Pensées*

CHAPTER 1

Introduction

Few great writers in modern literature have been subject to such abrupt and dramatic changes of fortune, both in personal life and literary career, as Feodor Mikhailovich Dostoevsky. Like Byron, whose poetry was so important for Russian literature in the early nineteenth century, Dostoevsky woke up one morning in 1845 to find himself famous—or rather, was awakened at two in the morning by his friend, the young poet Nekrasov, to be told that the influential critic V. G. Belinsky had read the manuscript of his first novel, *Poor Folk*, and praised it to the skies. But this brief period of glory ended quite as suddenly as it had begun after the publication of his next work, *The Double*, a year later.

Now recognized as one of Dostoevsky's early masterpieces, *The Double* brilliantly portrays a schizophrenic consciousness sinking into madness; and Dostoevsky later remarked that here, for the first time, he had caught his initial glimpse of "my extremely important underground type."[1] What Dostoevsky means by this phrase must be interpreted with some caution; when he wrote *The Double*, he could scarcely have been aware of the ideological issues embodied in the character of the underground man—issues that emerge so obviously from the later phase of Russian culture depicted in the present volume. Rather, he meant that the character he created in *The Double*, Mr. Golyadkin, furnished him with a psychological paradigm that he would later constantly re-employ. In 1846, Dostoevsky was preoccupied with the unhappy moral-psychic consequences of a rigidly immutable bureaucratic order in which pretentious subordinates were required to keep their place. The refusal of the "ambitious" Mr. Golyadkin to do so was tantamount to an insurrection against the morality that had been bred into his very bones; and this unaccustomed rebelliousness plunged him into inextricable mental distress. But Dostoevsky's masterful portrayal of the process of Golyadkin's psychic breakdown, and the appearance of a "double" whose ontological status remains ambiguous (did he actually exist, or was he an hallucination?), created difficulties in interpretation that obscured the social import of Dostoevsky's theme: Belinsky cuttingly remarked that such characters belonged in madhouses rather than in works of art. Dostoevsky's artistic reputation was sunk from this moment on, and nothing he wrote during the remainder of the 1840s succeeded in restoring his prestige. All his hopes were finally pinned on a major novel, *Netotchka*

Nezvanova; but this work began to appear just at the moment of his arrest in 1849 as a political conspirator, and it was never completed.

The catastrophe of his imprisonment constituted a much more radical peripety in Dostoevsky's life than his loss of literary reputation. First held in solitary confinement for about a year, he was then subjected to the ordeal of mock execution, and immediately sent to Siberian prison camp for a term of four years. What awaited him after its completion was the daunting prospect of an indefinite stretch of service in the Russian Army. In fact, it was to be ten years from the moment he was taken into custody before he was able to return to St. Petersburg and resume the struggle, now made infinitely more difficult by the lapse of time, to restore his claim to be accepted as a Russian writer of the first rank.

The Feodor Dostoevsky who arrived at St. Petersburg in 1860 was not noticeably changed in external appearance from the one who had left; indeed, he seemed to have gained rather than lost in poise, self-assurance, and physical vigor. But, internally, his experiences had led to a transformation whose momentous consequences would only become visible in the works he was soon producing at a breakneck pace, while at the same time running a monthly "thick" periodical that, in the space of two years, rose to become one of the most important in the country. This inner transformation, as Dostoevsky remarked himself, was far from having occurred all at once, though it can be observed germinating almost from the very beginning of his years of imprisonment and exile. Just a month or so after his arrest, for example, he assures his brother Mikhail that he is very far from being depressed, and that he has now learned how much strength the human personality possesses to create the conditions under which it can survive amidst the worst adversity. One hears in these words a new realization of the power of the personality as an autonomous force—a realization that will ultimately lead to a decisive reshaping of Dostoevsky's vision of human life.

Among the productions of other young writers of the Natural School of the 1840s, Dostoevsky's early work had stood out by that focus on the inner life of his characters whose excessive emphasis had displeased Belinsky. All the same, Dostoevsky had meant this psychology to be taken as a consequence of, and a response to, an inhumane and unjust social order. But what occurred during the next ten years made him excruciatingly aware of other dimensions of the human spirit, and immeasurably broadened and deepened his emotive and artistic horizons. Having stared mortality in the face while awaiting his turn (as he firmly believed) to be executed by a firing squad, and having feverishly assured the skeptical Nikolay Speshnev that they would both soon "be with Christ,"[2] he would never forget his sense of terror and the agonizing questions that assailed him at the daunting prospect that his personality might survive physical extinction. He would never forget either the consolation he had felt at embracing those on the scaffold who stood next to him, or the ecstatic surge of joy at his resurrection from oblivion. "Life is everywhere, life is in ourselves, not in the exterior,"[3] he had written to his brother immediately after his redemption from the grave. Such was his preparation for immersion in the living hell of the house of the dead; and it was this belief that finally enabled him to emerge triumphant from an ordeal that would have crushed anyone of lesser inner fortitude.

It is easy, with the benefit of hindsight, to understand how much the harrowing torment of the mock execution and its aftermath prepared Dostoevsky to resist and overcome the tribulations of prison-camp life. But, plunged as he was from one racking test of endurance to another, matters at first seemed to him only to go from bad to worse. Dostoevsky was horrified at the moral depravity he encountered among the other convicts (the vast majority of whom were peasants) and shocked to discover that they regarded him, solely because he was a member of the educated class, as an alien and an enemy. Moreover, the behavior of his fellow convicts also revealed, with terrible starkness, not only the egoistic drive of the human personality to satisfy its basest instincts, but also, far more unexpectedly, the irrational and self-destructive lengths to which the personality would go if deprived of a sense of its own autonomy. In the future, no view of human life would prove viable for Dostoevsky if it failed to take into account this need of the psyche to *feel* itself free and independent, and thus to assert the dignity of its own self-possession.

What made life possible for Dostoevsky in the camp—and provided the only evidence for any kind of morality he could discern—were the remnants of traditional Christianity still alive in the sensibilities of his fellow prisoners. And when the strain of his alienation and despair finally became too intolerable, when it proved impossible to endure any longer, Dostoevsky underwent a "conversion experience" that enabled him to re-affirm the same truth he had glimpsed after the mock execution—the truth that "life is in ourselves, not in the exterior." According to William James, one of the characteristics of such an experience is that, even though nothing actually changes in the external environment, the *meaning* of everything that surrounds the convert suddenly becomes altered for the better. Such a metamorphosis indubitably took place for Dostoevsky, who, while refusing to gloss over for an instant the manifest harshness, brutality, and backwardness of Russian peasant life, nonetheless became convinced that at its center were preserved the sublime Christian virtues of love and self-sacrifice. Here too we should mention the incalculable effects of his epilepsy, which began during these prison-camp years and which, at the moment of blissful "aura" preceding the attack, filled him with an afflatus of rapturous plenitude and the sense of having made palpable contact with a supernatural principle of world harmony. He thus emerged from prison camp with a set of attitudes (not so much "ideas" as "idea-feelings," to use his own coinage) significantly different from those he had brought with him. And, for the remainder of his life, he would struggle to reconcile these idea-feelings with each other and to use them as guidelines in portraying the momentous issues just then coming to the fore in Russian society.

Shortly after Dostoevsky was freed from captivity, and while he was still serving as a soldier, Russia entered an epochal new stage of its development. Alexander II determined to liberate the serf population that made up the vast majority of the Russian people, and this decision unleashed pent-up forces for social change that soon went beyond the bounds considered permissible by the Tsarist authorities. All the ideals on which previous Russian life had been founded were called into question; influential voices were heard proclaiming that an entirely new moral basis must be sought on which to construct human society. Russian culture thus entered an acute phase of crisis; and the ensuing clash of values, dramatized in the Russian literature of the time, forms the indispensable context within which the works of Dostoevsky must be understood.

Alexander II's initiative was greeted with wholehearted joy by Dostoevsky, whose own ill-fated political activity had been inspired by his revulsion against the injustices of serfdom; and he saw in the impending liberation the fulfillment of the dreams of his youth—the triumph of the cause for which he had paid so dearly. Like the vast majority of the Russian intelligentsia during the "honeymoon period" preceding the liberation of the serfs in 1861, Dostoevsky now became a fervent supporter of the Tsar-Liberator. This mood of unanimity still prevailed to a large extent when he returned to European Russia; and though it changed drastically in the years covered by the present volume, he stubbornly continued to maintain his old allegiance—and did so for the remainder of his life.

Although the Russian intelligentsia were all temporarily united behind the Tsar at this moment in favor of liberation, some of the sources of later conflict had already become visible in the disputes that broke out over aesthetic and more abstract philosophical issues (all, of course, containing social-political implications) between the older literati of the generation of the 1840s and the "new men" of the 1860s who came to the fore during the mid-1850s. Russian culture has labeled this latter group, whose leading representatives were Nikolay Chernyshevsky and Nikolay Dobrolyubov, the *raznochintsy*—those without fixed status or rank (*chin*) in the Russian caste system. Frequently the sons of priestly families, like the two figures just mentioned, the generation of the 1860s attacked the elements of Romantic idealism still remaining in the gentry-liberal culture of their immediate predecessors and replaced such idealism with an all-embracing materialism, an ethics of Utilitarian egoism, and a naive belief in science and rationality as entirely sufficient to unravel the complexities of the human condition. By the time of Dostoevsky's reappearance on the literary scene, these "new men" had assumed a commanding position and won the favor of a devoted young cohort of readers. Like all other established Russian writers, he was forced by them to define his own ideas and values—in his case, more particularly, to determine the significance of everything that had occurred to him during the preceding ten years.

Even though the new doctrines being advocated ran squarely counter to the fundamental credo that Dostoevsky now accepted—a credo he had learned at so painful a cost—his attitude toward the *raznochintsy* was at first by no means hostile. Quite the contrary, and whatever his disagreements, he stressed that the new generation too was inspired by a genuine love for the Russian people. Besides, the memory of his own revolutionary past, when he had cherished hopes very similar to those he now saw springing up once again, made him reluctant to denounce their champions too harshly. It was only when the new generation moved from peaceful arguments in the journals to actual revolutionary agitation that he finally took a hostile stand; but even then he never impugned their motives or the sincerity of their generous—if, in his view, totally misguided—convictions.

As the editor of a journal and a concerned citizen, Dostoevsky was naturally preoccupied with radical ideas on the level of practical politics. As an artist, he was also, and more importantly, meditating on their implications in relation to the vaster moral-spiritual questions posed by the mystery of the human personality and the enigma of human destiny. The result of these meditations began to appear in the larger works he produced during this period, which laid the foundation for his later development.

In his first major post-Siberian novel, *The Insulted and Injured*, Dostoevsky experimented skillfully—if still gropingly—with the form of the *roman-feuilleton* that he would so often later employ, the melodramatic thriller with a mystery or adventure plot that developed out of the Gothic and the historical novel and had been used by Balzac and Dickens among others to portray the modern world. It is in this book that he makes his first tentative and covert attempt to dramatize the moral hazards lurking in radical ideas. The work that succeeded in re-establishing his reputation, the autobiographical *House of the Dead*, created a sensation by its unvarnished though humane portrayal of prison life in a series of interwoven sketches; and it also contains an unprecedented analysis of the irrational lengths to which the human personality will go in quest of a sense of freedom. It is this insight that Dostoevsky will then pit against the radicals, first in his travel articles, *Winter Notes on Summer Impressions*, and then in *Notes from Underground*, little noticed in its own time but since then rightly recognized as the beginning of Dostoevsky's greatest creative phase. Here, for the first time, Dostoevsky creates a work entirely focused on exposing the moral-psychological dangers that he detects hidden behind the innocuous pieties of radical ideology; and when he combined this theme with a flexible adaptation of the form of the melodramatic thriller, he produced the synthesis of his mature masterpieces.

CHAPTER 2

Exile's Return

Feodor Dostoevsky's return to St. Petersburg in mid-December 1859 was not marked by any of the public ceremony that had attended his departure. Ten years earlier, arrested as a political conspirator, he and others involved in the so-called Petrashevsky circle had been publicly exhibited on the enormous Semenovsky Square ordinarily used by the authorities as a parade ground. Ringed by a cordon of Army troops, as well as a large crowd watching from a distance, the Petrashevtsy had been subjected to a mock execution ceremony carefully staged by Nicholas I; only at the very last instant did they learn that their lives had been spared. A few days later, Dostoevsky departed in a convoy of carriages that slid silently through the snowy streets on Christmas Eve. But the cruel spectacle had accomplished its purpose: all Petersburg was talking in frightened whispers about the fate of the Petrashevtsy long after the condemned men had left the capital.

A totally different atmosphere prevailed in 1859; and when Dostoevsky arrived at the Nikolaevsky railway station—accompanied by the wife and foster son he had acquired in Siberia—to step into the outstretched arms of his older brother Mikhail, he was only one among the many returning exiles streaming back to European Russia in those euphoric days of liberalization and reform. Also waiting to greet Feodor Dostoevsky was his old friend Alexander Milyukov, who had come with Mikhail ten years earlier to bid him farewell in the Peter-and-Paul Fortress; and Milyukov's reminiscences of Dostoevsky provide some fleeting impressions of this second encounter: "Feodor Mikhailovich, as it seems to me, had not changed physically: he even looked somewhat healthier than before, and had lost none of his usual energy. . . . I recall that, on this first evening, we exchanged only views and impressions, remembered old times and our common friends."[1]

This last sentence refers to a small celebration held that evening at the apartment Mikhail had rented for his brother's family, and where, inevitably, memories of the past were nostalgically evoked. Dostoevsky was reunited with all those closest to him—such as Apollon Maikov, the poet whom he had once tried unsuccessfully to recruit for the Speshnev secret society in 1849, and who, like himself, had evolved from Russian Westernism toward a much more fervent nationalism. Unexpectedly, too, the man who had been Dostoevsky's evil genius, the "Mephistopheles" who had lured him along the path of revolutionary adventure—the handsome, enigmatic,

8

coolly self-possessed Nikolay Speshnev—also turned up among the guests. He had himself just arrived from Siberia in the suite of Governor-General Nicholas Muraviev, and had dropped in to see his erstwhile fellow conspirator, fellow exile, and now fellow survivor.

Dostoevsky's air of health and vigor, which so struck Milyukov, was by no means attributable solely to the temporarily bracing effects of homecoming. His years at hard labor in the prison camp, as well as the physical exertions required by his six years of drills and parades in the Russian Army, had improved his physical stamina and given him an increased mien of self-assurance. No longer was he beset by the indistinct terrors and apprehensions, the nervousness, timidity, and pathological self-consciousness that had plagued his pre-Siberian years and made him an object of mockery in the merciless literary circles of Petersburg.

What Milyukov could not see at first glance—though it quickly became

1. F. M. Dostoevsky, 1861

common knowledge among Dostoevsky's close friends—was his deep anxiety over the recurrent epileptic attacks that had begun during his years in camp. These weakened him physically for days afterwards, plunged him into bitter moods of black depression, and made him so uncontrollably irritable that he felt as if he had been literally skinned alive and his raw nerves exposed to abrasion by the outside world. To make matters worse, his epilepsy had cast a pall over his marriage ever since, on the honeymoon trip back to Dostoevsky's Army base in Semipalatinsk (the ceremony had been performed in a small Siberian village hundreds of versts away), his new bride had been the horrified witness to a massive seizure with all its frightening and repulsive symptoms. Dostoevsky was then informed for the first time, by a competent local doctor, that the "nervous disease" he had hoped would pass away was actually epilepsy. If, as he disconsolately wrote his brother Mikhail shortly afterwards, he had known this for a certainty earlier, he would never have married; nor, one presumes, would his wife have married *him*.[2] He had subsequently applied for permission to retire from the Army on grounds of ill health; and while eager to return to Petersburg to pick up his literary career, he also wished to consult competent specialists in the capital about alleviating the disquieting malady that crippled him so often both in mind and body.

2

Dostoevsky's presence in St. Petersburg was normally noted by the secret police, who continued to keep a watchful eye on his activities; and it also attracted the attention of the larger literary fraternity in which he was so eager to resume his place. Just a few days after establishing residence, he was elected a member of the newly founded Society for Aid to Needy Writers and Scholars, usually called, more succinctly, the Literary Fund. Up until recently, it was generally believed that Dostoevsky had lent his support to the activities of the Fund only by his participation in the numerous readings and other events (such as amateur theatricals) that the society organized to fill its coffers. Actually, though, he played a much more important and responsible role in its operations. It is difficult to imagine the Dostoevsky of popular conception performing the tasks of an efficient and conscientious administrator; but so he did when elected secretary of the Fund's administrative committee in February 1863. Between 1863 and 1865 he kept the records of the meetings, handled the considerable correspondence of this organization with skill and dispatch, and resigned only when, after having requested a substantial grant for himself, he did not wish to be suspected of exercising any undue influence on the committee's decisions.

One of the main functions of the Literary Fund was to help writers, scholars, and students who, as a result of being arrested or sent into exile, had been deprived of all means of support for themselves and their families. Dostoevsky thus scrupulously came to the aid of many left-wing literati in the course of performing his secretarial duties. Indeed, his first use of the Fund was to sponsor a request (March 28, 1860) for a grant-in-aid to the writer and translator Sergey Durov, an old friend from his days in the Petrashevsky circle, whose social-political opinions, as Dostoevsky very well knew, had remained largely unchanged. Dostoevsky and Durov had served their terms at hard labor in the same prison camp, and there is some evidence that ideological differences had caused a cooling in their friendship during those years. But this did not prevent Dostoevsky from obtaining financial succor for a fellow sufferer whose health had badly deteriorated in Siberia and who was then living out his last days in Odessa as an ailing invalid.[3]

The very first benefit organized by the Fund took place on January 10, a few weeks after Dostoevsky's homecoming, and it is not likely that he would have missed the occasion. Aside from wishing to appear in literary society once more, he would certainly have been attracted by the program, which announced a reading by Turgenev of his newly written, deeply meditative, and highly controversial essay, *Hamlet and Don Quixote*, a work that marked an important moment in the social-cultural debate of the early 1860s. Since Dostoevsky had learned (from a letter of Aleksey Pleshcheev in 1859) that Turgenev had inquired about his welfare very solicitously while he was still in exile, this opportunity to renew his acquaintance with Turgenev would scarcely have been neglected; and an amicable exchange of notes a few months later reveals that the rancorous breakup of their friendship in 1845 had been, at least for the moment, forgotten. Whether or not Dostoevsky was present in the audience, there is no doubt that he thoroughly absorbed the essay, whose ideas left significant traces on his own thinking. For Turgenev's famous pages proved to be a panegyric of the man of faith, Don Quixote, who is held up for admiration in preference to the worldly, skeptical, disillusioned Hamlet, "sicklied o'er by the pale cast of thought." Don Quixote is inspired by an ideal greater than himself (even if a comically deluded one), and this elevates him to a moral superiority that towers over the indecisive and wavering Hamlet.

Turgenev pretended to be dissecting two eternal psychological types, which always had existed, and always would continue to exist, in human nature; but everyone knew that the "Hamlets" of Russian literature were the "superfluous men," the well-meaning but powerless and hopelessly impractical members of the gentry-liberal intelligentsia. The "Don Quixotes," on the other hand, were those who had died on the European barricades in 1848 (like the protagonist of Turgenev's own *Rudin*, a Hamlet who became a Don Quixote) and those members of the younger generation in Russia ready once again to sacrifice themselves for the cause of the people. So as not to leave any doubt concerning the implications of his categories, Turgenev mentions both the Utopian Socialist Charles Fourier and, for good measure, Jesus Christ as examples of the Don Quixote type.

Such an identification, and the moral valuation it implied, brought Turgenev into an uneasy and rather unexpected alliance with younger radical publicists like Nikolay Chernyshevsky and Nikolay Dobrolyubov, who had themselves been carrying on an attack against the Hamlet-type throughout the later 1850s; and it was Turgenev himself, in their view, who had been unduly indulgent toward the feebleness and frailties of his gentry-liberal characters! Perhaps intending to mollify their hostility, Turgenev now indicates agreement with much of their indictment of the Russian Hamlets; but their antagonism to his work was too deeply rooted in the social-cultural situation to be so easily overcome.* As for Dostoevsky, he would, just a year later, add his own voice to the chorus of condemnation: the present social situation, he would then declare, no longer holds any place for the Hamlets of Russian culture. It was time, he told them firmly, to overcome their self-preoccupied egoism and devote themselves to the service of the people.

If Dostoevsky and Turgenev more or less saw eye to eye on this issue, there were other aspects of the essay that eventually stimulated Dostoevsky to work out a differing point of view. For although Turgenev had identified Don Quixote as a Christ-like figure who, in imitation of his sublime original, represents "the exalted principle of self-sacrifice," this principle, he adds, is only grasped "from its comic side" in Cervantes's portrayal.[4] Eight years later, when Dostoevsky came to delineate his own image of the self-sacrificing Don Quixote type in the all-compassionate Prince Myshkin, he stressed very particularly—in obvious contrast to Turgenev—that he did not wish him to be considered a "comic" character.[5]

3

In April 1860, Dostoevsky himself came into prominent public view as a participant in some amateur theatricals organized by the Literary Fund to replenish its treasury. The novelist A. F. Pisemsky had hit on the idea of presenting plays with celebrated literary figures filling all (or most) of the

---

* The radicals, who refused to appreciate the compliment of being compared with Don Quixote, did not openly attack Turgenev's essay; but Dobrolyubov took the occasion of the publication of Turgenev's next novel, *On the Eve*, to express their displeasure. In the course of his article, "When Will the Real Day Come?" he included a long digression on Don Quixote, whom he identified with the liberal reformers bemused by the tempting apparition of radical change but unwilling to face the prospect of revolution. "Many have begun to attack trifles," he writes, "imagining that in them is contained the entire affair, or to fight with shadows and, in this way, showing themselves to be pathetically amusing Don Quixotes despite all the nobility of their strivings." See I. S. Turgenev, *Polnoe Sobranie Sochinenii*, 28 vols. (Moscow-Leningrad, 1960-1968), 8: 563-564.

roles; and Dostoevsky was invited to join in the fun by the well-known journalist Peter Weinberg, with whom he would soon cross swords (though with no permanent hard feelings) over "the woman question." Weinberg offered Dostoevsky his choice of three roles in Gogol's *The Inspector-General (Revizor)*, and he chose that of the postmaster Shpekin, who finally reveals that the flighty young official, Khlestakov, taken at first to be an awesome Imperial envoy, is nothing of the kind. Shpekin regularly opens all the mail that flows through his hands, impelled by an uncontrollable curiosity that also has its "useful" side, and he thus discovers from Khlestakov's letter that the sender is just an impish and impoverished nobody. Dostoevsky, as Weinberg recalls it, was delighted with the role of the postmaster. "It's one of the most comic roles not only in Gogol but in all of the Russian repertory," he said, "and besides, is filled with a deep social significance. . . . I don't know whether I will succeed in measuring up to it, but I will play it with great care and affection."[6]

The evening for the Literary Fund proved to be a howling success: all cultivated Petersburg turned out to see the notorious lions of literature disporting themselves behind the footlights. A high point was the scene in which the local merchants—played by Turgenev, the editor and publisher A. A. Kraevsky, Apollon Maikov, and the novelist and critic A. V. Druzhinin—arrived to present their "gifts" to the supposed inspector-general and to complain about the depredations of the governor. So much laughter and excitement was provoked by their appearance that those who wished to enjoy the play protested publicly against the unseemly uproar—among these indignant spectators being no less a personage than the Grand Prince Konstantin Nikolaevich, the brother of the Tsar, who enjoyed a reputation as a liberal and was known to have worked behind the scenes in favor of the abolition of serfdom. "What happened during several minutes—is difficult even to describe—just let the reader imagine: Turgenev in a long-skirted caftan and carrying a sugar-loaf!"[7] These words are taken from the important memoirs of L. F. Panteleev, then a young student at the University of St. Petersburg who had managed to wangle a place in the audience, and who was soon to be deported to Siberia because of his involvement in revolutionary agitation. Dostoevsky, it would appear, acquitted himself with distinction despite the competition of the better-known celebrities. "Dostoevsky, whom the Petersburg public knew much later as an outstanding public reader," Weinberg writes, "also displayed an excellent gift for the stage. I do not believe that anyone familiar with Feodor Mikhailovich in the last years of his life could possibly imagine him as a comic, even more, a subtle comic, knowing how to stimulate a pure Gogolian laughter; but it was really so, and Dostoevsky-Shpekin was—with a few unimportant exceptions—faultless. . . ."[8] Dostoevsky's gift for the stage had been employed a few years earlier in helping to direct the prison theatricals so vividly depicted in *House of the Dead*. Later, his histrionic abilities, though hardly on the scale of Dickens's triumphs as a public performer, were to be displayed in readings from his own works as well as from those of other Russian authors, and in the sharp dramatic vividness and scenic plasticity of his novels.

Dostoevsky made only one other public appearance during the remainder of the year at a benefit arranged on behalf of the Sunday school movement, an organization that had just sprung up to allow students and members of the educated class, especially wives and daughters, to give free instruction on Sundays to the illiterate masses. The idea had been launched by Professor Platon Pavlov, who taught Russian history at the University of Kiev, and it quickly spread as a result of the enthusiasm and dedication of the budding feminist movement. At a reading in November 1860 to raise funds for the Petersburg branch of this fashionable cause, Dostoevsky shared the platform with the Ukrainian poet Taras Shevchenko, the Russian poets Apollon Maikov and Ya. P. Polonsky, and the novelist A. F. Pisemsky. Also present in the "Passage" (a covered arcade, with rooms for public gatherings) was Elena Shtakenschneider, the sensitive, highly cultivated, and physically deformed daughter (she was a hunchback) of a prominent Petersburg architect and a mother who presided over an important literary salon. Apollon Maikov and Polonsky were close friends of the family as well as of Dostoevsky; and though the latter was not yet a devotee of the Shtakenschneider reunions, he would become one in the 1870s. Elena Shtakenschneider's *Diary*, one of the most valuable sources of information about mid-nineteenth-century Russian culture, records her first glimpse of the still obscure survivor of a vanished era.

Dostoevsky, it would seem, was not able on this occasion to repeat the triumph of *The Inspector-General*. Apparently he had not yet discovered the style of delivery that would make his later readings so electrifying; and the text he had chosen may not have been appropriate. "Dostoevsky read *Netotchka Nezvanova*," notes the diarist, "which was a little too long and dragged-out for a public reading. In addition, Dostoevsky has a weak and monotonous voice, not yet adapted to this kind of reading." He was received with polite applause, but nothing compared to the deafening ovation accorded to Shevchenko. "I think," she speculates, "that this uncontrolled uproar did not so much refer to Shevchenko personally but was really a demonstration. It was meant to honor a martyr, who suffered for the truth [Shevchenko had been sent into exile because of his Ukrainian nationalism]. But Dostoevsky too is an even greater martyr. (Certainly we will consider everything for which he suffered to be truth, though I do not really know very well what he suffered for; enough that he suffered.) Shevchenko was only a soldier, Dostoevsky was in Siberia, at hard labor. Yet Shevchenko receives a stunning ovation, and Dostoevsky a good deal of clapping

but far from the same volume. Just try and make sense of that."9 Whatever
the reason, a year or two later hardly any Russian writer (perhaps only Turgenev) would be received in public with as much acclaim as Dostoevsky.

4

Dostoevsky's passion for the theater unquestionably sprang from a deep
personal inclination that did not need any external stimulus. He had, after
all, initiated his literary career as a young man by writing poetic tragedy;
and on taking up his pen once more in Siberia after prison camp, he had
begun to write a play. All the same, he was particularly drawn to the stage
at this moment because of his flirtation with a gifted actress named Alexandra Shubert. As bad luck would have it—or perhaps good luck, since her
marriage was suffering severe strains—she was also the wife of Dostoevsky's very close friend Dr. Stepan Yanovsky, and the writer played a rather
equivocal role in the affairs of the couple while managing to retain good relations with both.

The whole incident also throws some indirect light on the woeful state of
Dostoevsky's own matrimonial situation, which, there is every reason to believe, was far from happy. The mutual confidence of the pair had been
badly undermined by the shock of discovering that the bridegroom was epileptic; and it soon became obvious that Marya Dimitrievna was suffering
from tuberculosis, a disease that sadly affected both her physical well-being
and the state of her nerves. Convinced that Dostoevsky's family had been
opposed to his marriage and resented her presence in their midst (there is
no reliable evidence to support this suspicion), she made no attempt to bridle an irritable and impetuous temperament not accustomed to concealing
its surges of resentment. As a result, she placed a considerable strain on
Dostoevsky's relations with his beloved older brother and his family. Since
few references to her turn up in the memoirs of the period, we can only infer that the couple rarely appeared in public together; nor is there any evidence that Dostoevsky ever invited people to his home, though he was quite
gregarious and frequented others with great assiduity. In this light, his relations with Alexandra Shubert manifestly reveal a desire to find feminine
companionship elsewhere than at the domestic hearth.

Alexandra Shubert's maiden name was Kulikova, and, though born the
daughter of serf parents, she had made a brilliant debut on the St. Petersburg stage in 1843. Left a widow in 1854 by the death of her actor-husband
Mikhail Shubert, she married Dr. Yanovsky a year later and retired from
the theater to preside over her new household. But in 1858, much to the
displeasure of her husband, she resumed her career; and when offered an
important engagement in Moscow for the 1860 season—a commitment re-
quiring prolonged residence in that city—she accepted despite the doctor's

2. Alexandra Shubert. From Alexandra Shubert, *Moya Zhizn*, ed. A. Dermana (Leningrad, 1929)

opposition. Dostoevsky, who had met her shortly after arriving in Petersburg, obviously found much to admire in this poised, independent, and highly artistic personality, the friend of many well-known writers and the most gifted woman he had ever known closely. (It should be recalled that he had harbored a brief infatuation for another actress, Avdotya Panaeva, whose literary salon he frequented in 1845-1846, and who shortly thereafter became the mistress of Nekrasov and the great love of that poet's life.)[10] Three letters to Alexandra Shubert in the spring of 1860, written in an unusually coquettish tone of flirtatious gallantry, reveal Dostoevsky's respectful passion and his involvement in the intimate affairs of the Yanovsky couple.

The first epistle, filled with expressions of regret at her absence, was sent shortly after the actress had quit Petersburg in March 1860. Just before departure Mikhail Dostoevsky had given a dinner party in her honor, and Dostoevsky recalls that Mme Shubert had found him looking wan and melancholy. Both understood, one suspects, that his mood of distress was linked with her impending absence, and his words appear to confirm such a conjecture: "And how you laughed at my countenance then. I remember that, and [now] I would so much like to see you, talk with you, kiss your little hand."[11] From other passages, we learn that Mme Shubert had confided something personal to Dostoevsky which he had then carelessly revealed to the Maikovs. By this route it had gotten back to Dr. Yanovsky—who abruptly questioned Dostoevsky about the incident, evidently disturbed that his wife had disclosed a family secret to his friend.

That the actress and the writer had become intimate (at least in conversation), and that Dostoevsky had confided some of the miseries of his own marriage to the charming Mme Shubert, is suggested by another passage. "Here with us," he writes, "things are sad, even very much so. The weather is filthy. Small nuisances, and yet one would like to write; in general such dreary nastiness that it's impossible to describe, at least in my case."[12] This last remark could hardly be a reference only to the weather; and it is written to someone who presumably knows what Dostoevsky means when he speaks of "dreary nastiness." In a brighter vein, he assures his correspondent: "If I had the slightest bit of talent for writing a little comedy, even of one act, I would write it for you. I should like to try. If it succeeds (others will decide that) I will offer it to you as a sign of my profound respect."[13]

The next letter, two months later, follows a trip to Moscow, where Dostoevsky had seen Alexandra Shubert perform and spent some time in her captivating company. "The whole excursion to Moscow appears to me as though it had been a dream," he laments; "here I am back again in the dampness and slush of Lake Ladoga, in the tedium, etc. etc."[14] Dostoevsky brought back news to Dr. Yanovsky of his wife's triumph—hardly calculated to rejoice the abandoned husband—and of the friends she had acquired in Moscow, partly with Dostoevsky's help. His old comrade from the days of the Petrashevsky circle, the poet and publicist Aleksey Pleshcheev, had recently joined the editorial staff of a new weekly, the *Moscow Messenger (Moskovskii Vestnik)*, and had introduced her to Moscow society. The letter also contains news of Apollon Maikov, Pisemsky, and a young writer whose talent Dostoevsky appreciated, V. V. Krestovsky, indicating the active interest Alexandra Shubert took in the cultured literary and social milieu that constituted Dostoevsky's own world.

A third letter, on June 12, is the most revelatory of all. By this time, Dr. Yanovsky was thinking of giving up his government post in Petersburg and accepting one in Moscow or, alternatively, of insisting that his wife return to the family fold and limit her activities to private theatricals. In case of refusal, he threatened to assert his legal rights as a husband. "I replied," Dostoevsky informs her, "that in such matters I had not expected him to be capable of appealing to any law. What becomes then, after that, I said, 'of your principles and convictions in practice, were they only words?' " Yanovsky appears to have retreated at this point, insisting that matters would never be carried that far; but the normally mild-tempered doctor, known for his placidity, was so nervous and edgy that Dostoevsky suspected other motives for his irritability: "Perhaps he is jealous, and perhaps his self-love played a large role in our conversation. He is completely convinced, it seems, that we correspond all the time, and that you live according to my advice."[15]

Dr. Yanovsky was unquestionably jealous of Dostoevsky, who reports that, while the writer was gazing at a portrait of Alexandra Shubert, the doctor turned the picture at an angle so that his visitor could no longer keep it in view. Moreover, Mme Shubert had told her husband, for reasons of her own, not really to consider Dostoevsky his friend—presumably because of his relations with her; and she had disclosed to the doctor that Dostoevsky had confided to her, under the pledge of secrecy even from her husband, some of his "domestic circumstances." Even though Mme Shubert had thus undermined Dr. Yanovsky's trust in his old comrade, Dostoevsky takes this betrayal with remarkable equanimity and merely reproaches his correspondent for causing her husband needless pain by her revelations. His advice, finally, is that the couple separate once and for all in their common interest: "There is no life for you [with him], and together it is torture. He would be doing something worthwhile, very worthwhile both for you and for himself. You would, after all, be grateful to him for it and value his humanity very highly. Instead of love (which is finished in any case) he would obtain your heartfelt gratitude, friendship and respect."[16]

Whether or not Dostoevsky's mansuetude was prompted by the hope of eventually replacing Dr. Yanovsky in the favors of Alexandra Shubert, he certainly found her exceedingly appealing, sought emotional solace in her company for his own marital woes, and revealed such woes to her with unaccustomed frankness. He is scrupulous in asserting the disinterestedness of his affection; but he does so in accents that distinctly leave room for other possibilities: "How happy I am that you can confide in me so sincerely and tenderly; that's what a friend is! I tell you frankly: I love you very much and passionately, to such an extent that I have told you myself I am not enamored of you because I valued your just opinion of me, and, my God!, how sorry I was when it seemed to me that you deprived me of your trust; I blamed myself."[17] Such words suggest that their courtly declarations should not be taken too literally; but Alexandra Shubert, so far as we know, was never inclined to test their constancy.

In her rather impersonal memoirs, which focus mainly on her stage career, Mme Shubert remarks only that Dostoevsky "became very attached to me" and says no more;[18] perhaps there was nothing more to tell. All the same, Dostoevsky's abortive romance indicates a search for some relief from his conjugal distress in the companionship of a cultivated woman who could share his artistic interests and ambitions. Two years later he would believe, for a brief time, that he had at last found what he was seeking in

18

the attractive person of a militant young writer and feminist, Apollinaria Suslova, whose first work he would consider promising enough to publish in his magazine.

5

Whatever the complications of his personal life, Dostoevsky's major energies were focused, as they had been ever since leaving prison camp in 1854, on re-establishing his literary reputation. His work had just then begun to appear once more in the Russian periodical press, but the three texts he had published—*A Little Hero* (without his signature) in 1857, *Uncle's Dream* and *The Village of Stepanchikovo* in 1859—had not attracted any favorable public attention. Even the private response had been quite negative, and as sympathetic and kindhearted a friend as Pleshcheev had found both the two latter stories to be failures. Nekrasov, after reading the manuscript of *The Village of Stepanchikovo*—for which Dostoevsky had cherished great hopes—had uttered a chilling verdict: Dostoevsky's literary talents had dried up and he was finished as a writer. Since the novella had been rejected by two journals before being placed, Dostoevsky could scarcely have had any illusions about the fragility of his literary status.

Some consolation was afforded by the publication of a two-volume edition of his works in 1860; but it was necessary for him to live by his pen, and the glories of the past could furnish only a very limited income in the present. Turgenev had been kind enough, on returning from a trip to Moscow (February 1860), to bring Dostoevsky 600 rubles from the publisher as part payment. This sum, however, was only a drop in the bucket of Dostoevsky's expenses; and all his available time in the spring of 1860 thus went into planning and drafting two new books: a major novel, and the sketches that were to become *Notes from the House of the Dead*.

Up to this time, Dostoevsky had always worked as an independent writer who earned his income by selling his work to editors and publishers. But even before his first novel had been printed in 1845, he had dreamed of publishing his own work and reaping all the financial rewards; in later life he *did* succeed in becoming his own publisher. In 1860, though, he and his brother Mikhail were busily engaged in planning another venture designed to allow Dostoevsky to escape, at least partially, from the clutches of the literary entrepreneurs.

Although Mikhail Dostoevsky had lived largely in obscurity during the 1840s, while his younger brother tasted the heady joys and disillusionments of a precipitate exposure to fame, he had, nonetheless, succeeded in carving out for himself a modest literary career. After the arrest and exile of Feodor, however, Mikhail invested a small legacy in establishing a cigarette factory, and in this humdrum occupation managed to earn a secure if modest income for his growing family. Too much a committed member of the Russian intelligentsia to be content solely with a business career, he continued to long for some way of uniting his devotion to the higher life of culture with his domestic responsibilities; and the arrival of a new régime, superseding the draconian era of Nicholas I, provided him with the long-sought opportunity.

On assuming the throne in 1855, one of Alexander II's first measures had been to relax slightly the death-grip of censorship that had prevailed ever since 1848. Public opinion was encouraged, if not to speak out boldly, then at least to raise its voice above a terrified whisper. This new margin of freedom led Mikhail (as it did many others) to think of launching a weekly journal of political and literary news and commentary. Three years later he applied for permission to publish such a journal under the name of *Time* (*Vremya*), and the privilege was granted in October 1858. Dostoevsky had been in correspondence about this project with Mikhail during his last years of exile, and he greeted the prospect with enthusiasm. A few months before returning to Petersburg, he had written his brother: "I am convinced . . . that you and I are much cleverer people, and have more ability and knowledge of the business, than Kraevsky and Nekrasov [editors of two successful "thick" monthly periodicals]. Why, they are just peasants [*muzhiki*] about literature. And yet they get rich, and we are strapped for cash."[19] But the financial risks of such a venture were considerable, and nothing had yet been decided when Dostoevsky set foot in the capital.

It is clear, however, that the two brothers were exploring all the possibilities and attempting to make up their minds once and for all; the chief problem, it may be presumed, was whether Mikhail's business credit was firm enough to raise the necessary funds on acceptable terms. "We wish to do something valuable in the literary way, undertake something," Dostoevsky told Alexandra Shubert as late as May 1860; "this preoccupies us very much. Perhaps we will succeed. At least, all these problems constitute an activity, although only the first step [gap in text]. . . ."[20]

In the same letter, Dostoevsky also speaks of being on the point of beginning intensive work on a novel (presumably *The Insulted and Injured*) and wishing to complete it in the next three months. "I want it to be good," he tells his confidante, "I feel there is poetry there, I know that my whole literary career depends on its success."[21] Four months later, though, he remarks to Alexander Milyukov: "I am getting down to writing"[22]—presumably his novel, which obviously had not made much progress during the summer. By this time, the planned novel had become essential to fill the obligatory slot reserved for the installment of a major fictional work in every issue of a Russian "thick" monthly. As Dostoevsky explained five years later: "I *myself* assured my brother that the plan had been ready for a long time (which was not true), that it would be easy to write, that the first part already had been written, etc." (20: 133).

This deceptive reassurance probably was proffered about the time the final decision was made, sometime in the late spring of 1860, to take the plunge into editing and publishing. On June 18, Mikhail Dostoevsky asked permission of the St. Petersburg Censorship Committee to publish a journal on the basis of the title and program already approved but with one slight change: it would be a monthly instead of a weekly. The Central Censorship Authority approved the request on July 8, and the remainder of the year was occupied by the preparations for publication. During this time Dostoevsky was busily renewing old friendships in the literary world, striking up new ones, and gathering together the contributors who would form the staff of his new magazine.

CHAPTER 3

"A Bit of Liberty,
a Bit of Freedom"

Much of the social life of Russian men of letters in the nineteenth century took place in "circles," which often gathered around publications of differing ideological tendencies and the personalities who dominated their pages. During the 1840s, Dostoevsky had belonged to several such circles: the all-important Belinsky *pléiade*, which included the most promising young writers of the day and whose members worshipped the leading critic, Vissarion Belinsky; the obscure but influential Beketov circle, which leaned toward Fourierism and had established communal living quarters for its members; and the primarily social-political Petrashevsky circle, in whose roundup Dostoevsky's own fate had been sealed.[1] Shortly after resettling in Petersburg, Dostoevsky was invited to spend an evening at the home of Alexander Milyukov, where he met a new circle among whom he was very soon to take a prominent place. Thanks to the accident of Milyukov's friendship and hospitality, he was thus enabled to slip back into the normal structures of Russian social-cultural life without suffering too much from the estrangement of his long exile.

Like the two Dostoevsky brothers, Milyukov had belonged to the Palm-Durov splinter group, a small and more radical offshoot of the major Petrashevsky gatherings; but there is no evidence that he had ever taken any active part in their discussions or plans. He is mentioned only as having, with the encouragement of Feodor Dostoevsky, translated Lamennais's inflammatory *Paroles d'un Croyant* (*Words of a Believer*) into Church Slavonic. This interesting venture, which Dostoevsky may seem to have innocently supported out of friendliness and literary curiosity, contains much more than meets the eye. For Dostoevsky was, as we know, a member of the Speshnev secret society, which had worked underground within the larger Petrashevsky circle and whose aim had been to stir up a peasant revolution against serfdom. The Speshnevites intended to establish a printing press to turn out propaganda, and they probably judged Lamennais's inflammatory appeals to radical Christian egalitarianism—transposed into a hieratic language carrying sacred associations for the peasants—as being ideal for their insurrectionary purposes. This plan was nipped in the bud by the vigilance of the authorities, though Milyukov, whose name was mentioned in the course of the Petrashevsky inquiry, miraculously escaped arrest and was not even called in for questioning. Since he had never visited Petrashevsky, who was considered the center of the presumed conspiracy, his name was not placed on the list of suspects; and this was the reason for his surprising immunity. During the ten years of Dostoevsky's exile, he had continued his career as a schoolteacher and literary publicist, and in 1860 became the editor of a new monthly journal, *The Torch* (*Svetoch*). The contributors to this publication and their friends, who gathered at his home every Tuesday evening, formed the circle in which Dostoevsky immediately began to assert a distinct ascendancy.

2

Nikolay Strakhov, one day to be Dostoevsky's first—and far from entirely trustworthy—biographer, met him at one of these Milyukov evenings. Strakhov was a teacher of natural science in the same secondary school as the host; and when he learned that his colleague was in charge of a new publication, he promptly offered him an essay for consideration on "The Significance of Hegel's Philosophy in our Time." The essay was accepted; and though Strakhov had appeared in print before, he considers this publication to have marked his actual initiation into the world of Petersburg journalism.

Not only was his article taken, but "to my great pleasure . . . A. P. [Milyukov] invited me to his literary circle. On the first Tuesday that I showed up at this circle, I considered myself at last welcome in the society of real men of letters, and was very much interested in everything going on. The most important guests of A. P. turned out to be the Dostoevsky brothers, who were old friends of the host and very much attached to him, so that they were frequently in each other's company."[2] Among the other guests, Strakhov mentions Apollon Maikov, V. V. Krestovsky and D. D. Minaev (two young writers later to make reputations on opposing sides of the social-political barricades), and Dr. Yanovsky. According to Strakhov: "The first place in this circle was taken, of course, by Feodor Mikhailovich; he was considered by all to be the most important writer, and stood out not only because of his reputation but also because of the abundance of his ideas and the passion with which he uttered them. The circle was quite small, and its members very close to each other; so there was no trace of the constraint so usual in all Russian social gatherings."[3]

After this circumspect allusion to the menace hanging over the free discussion of ideas in Russia, Strakhov continues: "Even then, the special style of Feodor Mikhailovich's conversation was noticeable. He often spoke with his interlocutor in an undertone, almost in a whisper, until something particularly stirred him up; then he would become excited and suddenly raise his voice. . . . I still vividly recall his external appearance; he then cultivated only a moustache, and, despite his prominent forehead and fine eyes, distinctly had a military look, that is, the face and features of the common people. I also remember the first time I caught a fleeting glimpse of his first wife, Marya Dimitrievna; she made a very pleasant impression on me because of the pallor and delicacy of her features, although these features were irregular and tiny; one could also see indications of the illness that sent her to the grave."[4]

Dostoevsky had been insistently invited to write for *The Torch*, and D. D. Minaev had even paid him a visit in Tver in the effort to enlist his services for the new literary venture. He had, for a moment, weighed the idea of giving it *The Village of Stepanchikovo* for what even he considered an exorbitant rate per folio sheet; but he finally preferred to receive less from an already established outlet with assured readership. For all his friendship with Milyukov, and though he was listed among the contributors, nothing from Dostoevsky's pen appeared in *The Torch*; or, to be more exact, nothing from the pen of Feodor Dostoevsky. Several early issues, however, did contain contributions by Mikhail Dostoevsky.

The first number of *The Torch* printed Mikhail's translation of Schiller's "Die Götter Griechenlands" ("The Gods of Greece"), and the third a new Russian version of a book that his brother knew by heart: Hugo's *Le dernier jour d'un condamné*. This stunning little work, written out of a profound revulsion against capital punishment, is cast in the form of a diary kept by a man sentenced to die on the guillotine; and it played an extraordinary role in Feodor Dostoevsky's life. He had spoken of it while awaiting his turn to be shot during the mock execution, and a slightly garbled French phrase from the text—*On voit le soleil!*—shows up in the letter that Dostoevsky wrote immediately after this harrowing encounter with mortality. Motifs from Hugo's novel will later be used in both *Crime and Punishment* and *The Devils*, and its technique is referred to in the preface of *A Gentle Creature*.[5] The issue of capital punishment had just taken on a new immediacy for Russians because of the impending reform of their own legal system, and this revival of interest in Hugo's theme probably prompted Mikhail's translation. The same (third) number also contained a long and important essay by Mikhail Dostoevsky on Ostrovsky's *The Storm*, an essay still recognized as a significant contribution to the debate then raging about the play. It also has the additional interest of including some ideas that will soon appear in the pages of the Dostoevsky brothers' own journal.

3

The Torch flared up briefly, feebly illuminated the landscape of Russian letters, and, when it sputtered out after two years, was more or less forgotten for over a century. Recently, however, G. M. Fridlender has drawn attention to its interest as an ideological precursor of the positions that Dostoevsky was soon to enunciate and defend. Milyukov, Fridlender tells us, was "a supporter of the government reforms of the 1860s, [and he] considered that these reforms were the fulfillment of the heritage of the Decembrists and the Petrashevtsy, the realization of their social-political dreams."[6] The optimistic spirit in which Milyukov conducted his journal may be judged from some remarks in his recollections of Dostoevsky. "Our conversations in the small circle of our friends," he writes, "differed a good deal from what it had been in the Durov society. And how could it have been otherwise? Western Europe and Russia, in those ten years, had almost exchanged roles: there, all the humane utopias which had formerly attracted us had crumbled into dust, and reaction had triumphed everywhere; here among us, much of what we had dreamed was beginning to be realized, reforms were being readied, Russian life was being renewed, and new hopes were being born. It is understandable that, in our conversations, the old pessimism no longer had any place."[7]

Dostoevsky shared exactly the same hopes and enthusiasms, and the editorial program that Milyukov announced in the first issue of *The Torch* comes very close to what shortly appeared in the pages of *Time*. The keystone of *The Torch*'s position, wrote the editors, was "the reconciliation of West and East, the Westerners and the Slavophils." Russia was living through "a transitional epoch," and the reforms of its government were leading to "the reconstruction of our social life on solid and rational foundations." In principle, the journal declared itself to be "equally close to the Slavophils and Westerners" and recommended a synthesis of what was best in both. From the first should be taken their "love of the people and the inner link with them"; from the second, "the thirst for progress, and hence a fusion with the enlightenment of the West."[8]

Such words reveal the new situation in Russian culture created by the enormous influence of Alexander Herzen during the 1850s, when Herzen's disillusionment with European politics after 1848 had led him to look longingly back to his native soil and to declare that the Russian *obshchina* (the peasant commune) contained within itself the seeds from which the Socialism of the future could flower. Socialism was still a dream in the West, he had insisted, and could become reality, if at all, only at the price of bitter and bloody struggle; but in Russia it already existed as a trait of the national character and was instinctively accepted by the Russian peasant as the basis of his way of life. Herzen's writings thus led to the widespread acceptance of certain Slavophil ideas among all segments of the intelligentsia (except for the resistance of a few obstinately diehard Russian Westerners). On a trip to London in 1857, Milyukov had paid his obligatory respects to the great publicist in exile, just as Dostoevsky was to do in 1863. During these years, indeed, Dostoevsky yielded to no one in his admiration for Herzen, eagerly reading all the (technically illegal) publications of the

Free London Press that flowed into Russia almost unimpeded, and, when he came across similar ideas in the permitted press, jotting them down in his notebook for future use.[9]

One such jotting, recently published for the first time, contains excerpts from an article, "East and West in Russian Literature," written by I. V. Pavlov (a friend of Turgenev, who, not surprisingly, also shared his ideas) under the pseudonym L. Optukhin. Pavlov argued, like Milyukov, that the extreme positions and exaggerations of both Slavophils and Westerners could not be accepted; but each had contributed something of value that should be amalgamated into a new unity. The Slavophils, whatever their fanaticism, had taught a reverence for the Russian past and the moral-social and spiritual importance of the peasant commune; the Westerners, whatever their alienation from the people, composed that educated minority who sympathized with all manifestations of progress and the advancement of civilization. Pavlov cites Macaulay's contention, in his *History of England*, that "the best people of both parties [the reference was to Whigs and Tories] are found not far from the middle point" (18: 104). Dostoevsky not only copied out this citation but also commented favorably when Pavlov stressed the distinction between the Russian *obshchina* and "communism," that is, the obligatory expropriation of all personal goods and property advocated by certain Utopian Socialist plans for an ideal community. Since no such compulsory abolition of personal property was demanded in the *obshchina* (even though the land was held in common and periodically redistributed), there was no need in Russia for the excessive and arbitrary constraints invented by Western Socialism to attain the same objectives.

If the ambition of *The Torch* to reconcile Westernism and Slavophilism thus provides a general framework of ideas identical with those that *Time* was to proclaim a year or so later, Mikhail Dostoevsky's article on Ostrovsky's play fills in this framework with some details closely anticipating the particular emphases and shadings such ideas will receive at the hands of his brother. To what extent Mikhail was uttering his very own thoughts cannot be determined; but it is safe to assume that he had discussed them with Feodor beforehand, and that the more dynamic Feodor could well have influenced their formulation. Whatever the share of each, Mikhail definitely enunciates a position that Feodor was later to make famous first in Russia and then in the world. For Mikhail unabashedly proclaims that "Russian man possesses the ability to go directly to the truth and to understand it from all sides. With this ability, he also unites the capacity for universal reconciliation, i.e., the ability to pardon even an evil, hostile attitude if only there is truth included in it." This attribute, according to Mikhail, is "endemic in the Russian people" and confirmed by its entire history, not only beginning with Peter the Great but discernible even a good while before. It is also, he asserts, "a possession of the Slavic race" and particularly typical of "Russian man," who is "the most important representative of the Slavic race."[10]

Mikhail's article also contains an interpretation of Katerina, the central female figure of *The Storm*, that runs counter to Dobrolyubov's influential view of Ostrovsky's work. The radical critic had, just the year before, written a lengthy article (almost a small book) examining all of Ostrovsky's production; and he had labeled the Old Russian world that Ostrovsky portrays, the world of the Moscow merchant class, as "a realm of darkness." Any spark of humanity and decency existing among its inhabitants, he had insisted, was inevitably snuffed out by the bigoted religious fanaticism that nurtured its prevailing tyranny and brutality.[11] Mikhail, however, refuses to attribute Katerina's suicide to the pressure of such circumstances; rather, he looks for its source in her own psychology, which is interpreted, however, not in purely personal terms but as revealing significant national traits.

What Mikhail says about Katerina turns her into a character very similar to the male protagonist of Pisemsky's *A Bitter Fate*, another play produced at the same time and one that Feodor greatly admired. In this work, a wealthy peasant, betrayed by a wife who had become the willing mistress of their landowner in her husband's absence, kills her illegitimate child in a fit of blind rage. But, though perfectly able to escape if he had wished to do so, he finally surrenders to the authorities because the torments of his conscience give him no peace and he desires to atone for wreaking his revenge on the innocent babe. The adulterous Katerina too is seen by Mikhail as typically Russian both in the ardency of her passions and her awareness, at the very moment of her fall, that "after her days of ecstasy, long years of tears and repentance will drag themselves along, and that the best way for her to finish this bitter life would be behind high monastery walls or in long and *heart-felt* wanderings to various places of pilgrimage, if not in the slough of some river or the bottom of the closest pond. And yet she yields to temptation all the same."[12]

A particularly "Dostoevskian" note sounds in another passage, where Mikhail stresses the masochistic quality of Katerina's repentance and views such a reaction as a typical feature of the Russian folk character. "Again Russian motifs. She thinks with some sort of sensuality, some sort of boldness, of that moment when all would learn of her fall, and she dreams of the sweetness of punishing herself publicly for her fault. . . . The greater the disgrace, the greater the shame, the lighter will be her soul. . . . We were particularly pleased that this scene [where Katerina confesses her adultery] occurred on the public square, in the presence of outsiders . . . in a word, occurred in the most hostile and uncomfortable circumstances for herself."[13] One recalls, reading such words, the insistence of Sonya in *Crime and Punishment* that Raskolnikov confess not only privately to the police (as he had intended) but also publicly by kneeling down in the street and acknowledging his sin to the passing multitude.

Mikhail's essay ended his collaboration with *The Torch*, and the efforts of the two brothers now became definitively focused on plans for their own journal. Oddly enough, though, instead of reserving all his literary production for *Time*, Feodor Dostoevsky turned to another outlet for the first two chapters of *House of the Dead*. They appeared unexpectedly in an obscure weekly, the *Russian World (Russkii Mir)*, in the fall of 1860; and this curious fact of publication is worth more attention than it has usually received. For it caused Dostoevsky to write a remarkable and little-known addendum to his book—a variant not included in the final text—which is a document of major importance for grasping the inner evolution of his creative sensibility.

4

Why Dostoevsky should have given such a text to the *Russian World*, a magazine of no great stature, remains something of a mystery, especially since he speaks only of working on a "novel" in the letter to Alexandra Shubert already cited. In September, however, the *Russian World* began to publish the introduction and first chapter of *House of the Dead*, and the second chapter was submitted to the censorship shortly thereafter. Dostoevsky had obviously changed his mind, and temporarily set aside the novel for his prison memoirs.

How this came about is recounted in a letter, just recently made available, written by the editor of the *Russian World* within a year after Dostoevsky's death. According to his version, he had been spending the evening in Dostoevsky's company and listening with fascination to the novelist's uninterrupted flow of stories and anecdotes about life in the prison camp. Urged by the enterprising editor, who bears the intriguing name of A. Gieroglifov ("hieroglyph"), to write up such sensational material, Dostoevsky replied that he was reluctant to do so because of the censorship. It is true, as we know from Dostoevsky's letters, that he was afraid the censorship would never permit a book about his prison experiences to see the light of day. But when Gieroglifov offered to take on the brunt of the battle with the censors, such a proposition could well have struck Dostoevsky as being very advantageous; by making a preliminary trial of the censors' response, at second hand as it were, he could learn just how much time and energy it might be worth committing to the project. The result, as Gieroglifov reports, was that "Feodor Mikhailovich decided to make a test, and in one night wrote half the first chapter. . . ."[14] The delighted Gieroglifov, of course, was unaware that Dostoevsky had long made up his mind to write such a book and that, if he was able to dash off half a chapter in one night, it was because a good part of the text already existed in draft. He touchingly continued to believe all his life that *House of the Dead* owed its birth primarily to his prodding; and he may at least be conceded the credit of helping Dostoevsky to overcome the first hurdle standing in the way of its final composition.

Much to Gieroglifov's satisfaction, the first chapter cleared the censorship without any trouble. The second, however, did run into a snag—but not at all of the kind that Dostoevsky had anticipated. It was not, as he had feared, that his account of prison conditions might be considered too harsh; rather, he was accused of painting them in such rosy colors that some enticing details might positively prove an *incitement* to crime. "Individuals who are not morally developed," declared the worried president of the St. Petersburg Censorship Committee, "and whom only the rigor of punishment restrain from crime . . . might conclude from the humanity of the actions of the government that serious crimes are punished by the law only in a feeble fashion."[15] Such an outlandish opinion may appear to be merely another of those countless idiocies that often turn the history of Tsarist censorship into a black comedy; but a brief look at Dostoevsky's pages will show that, in this instance, there was some justification for the response. Early in the second chapter, for example, we come across the following passage: "My first impression on entering the prison was most revolting, and yet strange to say it seemed to me that life in prison was much easier than on the journey I had fancied it would be. Though the prisoners wore fetters, they walked freely about the prison, swore, sang songs, did work on their own account, smoked, even drank vodka (though very few of them), and at night some of them played cards. The labor, for instance, seemed to me by no means so hard, so *penal*, and only long afterwards I realized that the hardness, the penal character of the work lay not so much in its being difficult and uninterrupted as in its being *compulsory*, obligatory, enforced. The peasant in freedom works, I dare say, incomparably harder . . ." (4: 19-20). Dostoevsky also remarks that "the food too seemed to me fairly sufficient," and adds that "our bread was particularly nice, and was celebrated throughout the town" (4: 22).

Such words hardly portray prison life as very forbidding; and the Censorship Committee was not entirely misguided in believing that to a Russian peasant, living under the heel of his landowner and on the edge of destitution, it might even sound very attractive. Of course the possibility of Dostoevsky's pages ever reaching such a reader (even assuming he was literate) was extremely remote—as Dostoevsky hastened to point out in a letter to the president of the committee, Baron Medem. The *Russian World*, he explained, even though a weekly, "was a journal intended primarily for the more or less educated classes and not for the masses. . . ." (The Baron had expressed the opinion that Dostoevsky's prison opus might be more suitable for a less easily accessible monthly.) Dostoevsky, though, did not content himself only with such general reassurances; he decided to write a supplement that could be inserted into the chapter to allay any further doubts: "If the reason for the refusal to allow my article to be printed was the fear that it could serve to create, among the people, a distorted impression of prison life, so now the article [with the supplement] has the goal of creating the impression that, regardless of any alleviations in the fate of the convicts made by the government—the prison camp [*katorga*] does not cease to be a moral torture, which automatically and inescapably punishes crime."[16]

As it turned out, the misgivings of the St. Petersburg Censorship Committee were not shared by the Central Censorship Authority, and Dostoevsky's chapter was approved two months later in its original form. Nothing further was said about the proposed supplement, which was dutifully deposited in the capacious files of the censorship administration and remained there undisturbed for over sixty years until unearthed by A. S. Dolinin in 1922. Dostoevsky never used it in subsequent editions of his book for reasons that can only be surmised. The fragment may have been too intrusive an authorial statement, too much of a break in the tonal impersonality that he wished to maintain; but this only makes it all the more valuable as a clue to what had now become one of Dostoevsky's major themes—a theme that would soon occupy a crucially central place in his creations of the early 1860s.

5

The supplement begins by squarely confronting the objections raised by the censorship and assimilating them into the text. "In a word," Dostoevsky writes, "a total, terrible, genuine torment reigned in the camp without ceasing. And yet (this is exactly what I wish to say) to a superficial observer, or some fine gentleman, at first sight the life of a convict may sometimes seem agreeable. 'But my God!'—he says—'just look at them: there are some (who doesn't know it?) who have never eaten white bread, and who didn't even know that such delicious bread existed in the world. And now, look at what kind of bread he is fed—he, a worthless rascal, a robber! Look at him: how he looks around, how he walks! Yes, he doesn't give a rap for anybody even though he is in shackles! How do you like that!—he's smoking a pipe; and what's that? Cards!!! Bah, a drunk! So he can drink hard liquor in prison camp?! Some punishment!!!' This is what, at first sight, someone coming from the outside will say, perhaps a well-intentioned and kind person . . ." (4: 250).

After dramatizing such a possible reaction, Dostoevsky suddenly confronts this shocked outside observer with a question. Why, if life in the prison camp is so apparently agreeable, are the convicts ready to exchange it at any moment for one of hardship and suffering, for a hazardous and grueling existence as fugitives on the run in the forests and steppes of the Siberian wilderness? The answer is given in a passage that, more powerfully than anything Dostoevsky has written so far, expresses the essence of what he had learned in the house of the dead about the human spirit:

> What is bread? They [the convicts] eat bread to live, but they have no life! The genuine, the real, the most important is lacking, and the convict knows that he will never have it; or he will have it, if you like, but when? . . . It's as if the promise is made only as a joke. . . .
>
> Try an experiment and build a palace. Fit it out with marble, pictures, gold, birds of paradise, hanging gardens, all sorts of things. . . . And step inside. Well, it may be that you would never wish to leave. Perhaps, in actual fact, you would never leave. Everything is there! "Let well enough alone!" But suddenly—a trifle! Your castle is surrounded by walls, and you are told: "Everything is yours! Enjoy yourself! Only, don't take a step outside!" And believe me, in that instant you will wish to quit your paradise and step over the wall. Even more! All this luxury, all this plenitude will only sharpen your suffering. You will even feel insulted as a result of all this luxury. . . . Yes, only one thing is missing: a bit of liberty! a bit of liberty and a bit of freedom. (4: 250)

This remarkable passage reveals, in the first place, an increasingly important trait of Dostoevsky's literary imagination: his tendency to invent an extreme situation, an end-of-the-line set of circumstances, in which he places a character in order to bring out the appropriate moral-psychological reaction that he wishes to exemplify. Clearly, too, we are here at the core of what, just a few years later, will become the underground man's hysterical defense of the irrepressible and indestructible need of the human spirit to maintain the sense of its own freedom—his preference for suffering, if need be, rather than for a life of plenitude in a Socialist Utopia in which such freedom would be eliminated as a matter of principle. Shortly after leaving prison camp, Dostoevsky had compared his years there to living in a world of "compulsory communism";[17] and such words indicate how spontaneously he had identified prison-camp conditions with those that might result if some of the Utopian social worlds dreamed of by the radicals were ever realized in practice. In addition, as if by design, the very latest mutation of Russian radical thought had taken a form which irrefutably confirmed Dostoevsky's instinctive association between the intolerable lack of personal freedom in the prison-camp world and the "scientific" ideas of the Russian Socialists.

Just a few months earlier, *The Contemporary* had printed Chernyshevsky's *The Anthropological Principle in Philosophy*, a work destined to become the philosophical bible of the radical generation of the 1860s; and its appearance had blown up a fierce journalistic storm. The Russian press was very soon filled with attacks on Chernyshevsky's sharply provocative views, and one may assume that Dostoevsky read Chernyshevsky's text the moment it appeared. Whether or not its ideas exercised any immediate effect on his supplement, one thing is clear: the two men could hardly be more opposed in their vision of human life and their conception of the human personality. For Dostoevsky, man's psychic need to feel himself free is so elemental and powerful that it cannot be suppressed even by smothering him in boundless opulence. Chernyshevsky, on the other hand, propounds a simple-minded materialism that sees man as a being totally subservient to the laws of nature (as defined in terms of the sciences of the day, particularly chemistry and physiology), a materialism that—as even a recent commentator sympathetic to the general thrust of his position is forced to admit—"left no room for the irreducible and irrational in human behavior, for all those facts where we deal not with things and objects, but with willing and choosing human beings and their relationships. The problem of freedom was Chernyshevsky's greatest stumbling block, and he would have swept it away into unreality had he not let it reappear by the backstairs in his idea of man as the creator as well as the creature of his environment."[18]

The problem of freedom was indeed one that Chernyshevsky attempted to sweep into unreality; and he did not hesitate to proclaim that nothing such as free will exists, or can exist, as an objective datum. The notion of will or "wanting," he writes, "is only the subjective impression which accompanies in our minds the rise of thoughts and actions from preceding thoughts, actions or external facts."[19] As for ethics and morality, Chernyshevsky adopted a form of Benthamite Utilitarianism that rejects all appeal to any kind of traditional (Christian) moral values. Good and evil are defined in terms of "utility," and man seeks primarily what gives him pleasure and satisfies his egoistic self-interest; but since he is a rational creature, man eventually learns through enlightenment that the most lasting and durable "utility" lies in identifying his own self-interest with that of the vast majority of his fellows. Once this realization has dawned, the enlightened individual attains the level of a selfishly unselfish "rational egoism," which, according to Chernyshevsky, is the highest form of human development.

Such conceptions, which spread very quickly among the younger generation, provided the philosophical underpinnings for the new morality preached by the radical ideology of the 1860s; and no ideas could have set Dostoevsky's teeth more on edge. For if he had acquired any new convictions at all during the searing experiences of his last ten years, if the blows he had suffered at the hands of fate had taught him any lesson, it was to convince him profoundly of two ineluctable truths. One was that the human psyche would never, under any conditions, surrender its desire to assert its freedom; the other was that a Christian morality of love and self-sacrifice was a supreme necessity for both the individual and society at large. The only ray of light shining in the darkness of the prison camp had been kindled for him by the instinctive Christianity of the peasant-convicts. Without these inherited moral values, life among them would have been a literal hell for Dostoevsky, and he shuddered at the thought that it was precisely *these* values the radicals had now set out to undermine and destroy. It was thus inevitable that the Dostoevsky who had written the supplement to *House of the Dead* would sooner or later clash with Chernyshevsky and his followers among the generation of the 1860s. This fateful moment, however, did not arrive until several years later, and only after a great deal of social turbulence had ended all hope of accommodation.

Meanwhile, other difficulties with the censorship delayed the publication of further installments of *House of the Dead* until the new year. In January 1861 the *Russian World* reprinted the introduction and first chapter; three more chapters followed at weekly intervals. At the end of January, a continuation of the work was announced; but this promise was never kept, and Dostoevsky's name abruptly vanished from the list of contributors assembled by the resourceful Mr. Gieroglifov. The reason, of course, was that the first issue of *Time* appeared at the beginning of the new year, and Dostoevsky had no intention of allowing so valuable a literary property to benefit a rival publication.

CHAPTER 4

A New Movement:
Pochvennichestvo

The journals of the Dostoevsky brothers, first *Time* and then its successor *Epoch* (*Epokha*), have taken their place in Russian literature as the mouthpieces of an independent social-cultural tendency called *pochvennichestvo*. (The word *pochva*, whose literal meaning is "soil," also has the accessory sense of "foundation" or "support.")* Besides Feodor Dostoevsky himself, the chief spokesmen for this tendency were the two most important contributors to *Time*, Nikolay Strakhov and Apollon Grigoryev. Strakhov, who was to become an intimate friend of Tolstoy as well as Dostoevsky, was then at the start of a notable career as critic and publicist during which he would advocate philosophical Idealism and defend a moderately Slavophil and eventually Pan-Slavic social-political position. Grigoryev, on the other hand, whose critical essays Strakhov greatly admired and later collected and republished, had long been a well-known man of letters, and by 1861 was almost at the end of a stormy and harried existence as poet, critic, and occasional writer of prose fiction.

Sharp differences of opinion and temper would mark the relation between Dostoevsky and his two main collaborators, and the atmosphere of discord became so intense that the intransigent Grigoryev openly broke with the magazine for a time and refused any further contributions. The pliant Strakhov, who would never have done anything so self-assertive, worked more deviously to incline Dostoevsky's ideas in his own direction. These quarrels, however, were more over literary strategy and tactics than over fundamental principles, though Dostoevsky always preserved a greater personal sympathy for the motives of the radicals, if not for their ideas and activities, than either Strakhov or Grigoryev were able to muster.

The position around which the *pochvenniki* rallied will be traced through the various altercations in which they became embroiled; but some sense of their general tendency can already be gleaned from the announcement of the program of *Time*. This statement of principle—without signature, but carefully composed by Feodor Dostoevsky probably in collaboration

---

* Wayne Dowler, who has written a quite good work in English on the movement (there are none known to me in any other language), prefers to translate the word as "native soil." Wayne Dowler, *Dostoevsky, Grigor'ev and Native Soil Conservatism* (Toronto, 1982).

with Mikhail—was inserted in all the leading newspapers in September, and posters soliciting subscriptions were also distributed in bookstores and other public places. Mikhail's role in the journal, even from an ideological point of view, should not be underestimated; but while Feodor Dostoevsky's name could not be officially displayed on the masthead because he was an ex-convict, everyone recognized that he was the journal's guiding and animating spirit.

2

Even if Strakhov had not certified for posterity that Feodor Dostoevsky wrote the announcement, the characteristic stamp of the writer's fiery temperament would have been immediately apparent in its apocalyptic accents. "We live," declares the first sentence, "in an epoch in the highest degree remarkable and critical." Russia is in the midst of a great transformation, and the important social-political changes being awaited, which will finally resolve "the great peasant question," are only the external symptoms of a more fundamental mutation: "This transformation consists in the fusion of enlightenment, and those who represent it, with the principle of the people's life, and the union of the entire majestic Russian people with all the elements of our current life—the people who, 170 years ago, recoiled from the Petrine reforms, and since that time, torn away from the educated class, have been living their own separate, isolated, and independent existence" (18: 35). The *pochvenniki*, in other words, believed that the social-political issues of the day should be seen as secondary to the larger task of helping to forward a new Russian cultural synthesis—one that would emerge from the fusion of the people and their more cultivated superiors. For the radical intelligentsia, exactly the reverse hierarchy of values prevailed: all other issues were secondary to that of improving the lot of the peasantry in the manner they considered most consonant with social justice.

Another noticeable feature of Dostoevsky's program, which again sets it off sharply from that of the radicals, is his insistence that the transformation must take place *peacefully* and his conviction (or hope) that violence would be avoided. "Undisputably the most important issue [today] is the question of the amelioration of the condition of the peasants. . . . Not the enmity between the classes, between conquerors and conquered, as everywhere in Europe, should lie at the foundation of the development of the future principle of our life. We are not Europe, and among us there will not and should not be conquerors and conquered" (18: 36). Dostoevsky here is by no means, as might be thought at first, badly confusing social-historical fact with wishful thinking when he seeks to deny the existence of class

35

hatred in Russia; he is merely giving voice to a widely accepted theory derived from the writings of the French liberal historian Augustin Thierry.

Thierry had argued that the upper class in most European countries, like the Normans in Sir Walter Scott's *Ivanhoe* (a book whose influence on his own thinking he gratefully acknowledged), had originally ruled over conquered races of alien language and ethnic origin. As a result, the inevitable social-economic class antagonism in Europe was made even more ferocious and intractable because of ingrained racial hatred. The Slavophils immediately seized on this theory to buttress their conviction that the historical and social situation in Russia was fundamentally different from that of Europe; since no such ethnic antagonism existed in their homeland, they concluded that all its problems could be solved peacefully. Nor were the Slavophils alone in accepting such a consoling view of Russian class relations. Just a year before Dostoevsky enunciated it in the announcement of *Time*, Turgenev had expressed the same idea in an unfinished essay on the Russian gentry; and Alexander Herzen, who had translated some of Thierry in the early 1840s, echoed the same opinion throughout the 1850s.[1] Even earlier, Dostoevsky had ingenuously explained to the Commission of Inquiry into the Petrashevsky case that, although he might have expressed some sympathy with the revolutions that took place in Europe in 1848, he had done so only because revolution was the sole possible means for shamefully oppressed lower classes to obtain justice from their racially dissimilar superiors. No such explosion of revenge, he hastened to add, was called for in Russia, where the classes were all of the same stock.[2]

All the same, quite aware that such a thesis smacked of Slavophilism, Dostoevsky is careful in the announcement to separate his own position from that of this unpopular tendency. "We are not here talking about the Slavophils and the Westerners," he declares. "Our era is totally indifferent to their domestic quarrels. We are speaking of the reconciliation of civilization with the principle of the people's life" (18: 37). The *pochvenniki*, at least in this early period, tried very hard to maintain a certain distance from the Slavophils, and they stressed that both parties of the past were totally out of touch with the new social-cultural realities of the 1860s. (Strakhov was much more inclined than either Dostoevsky or Grigoryev to link *pochvennichestvo* with orthodox Slavophilism, and he tried to minimize the distinctions that the two others constantly made between their own views and those of the leading Slavophil spokesmen.)

As the Slavophils saw it, the Russian people had rejected Peter's reforms and valiantly clung to their ancient ways with exemplary stubbornness. For the Westerners, on the other hand, this total rejection of enlightenment, this obstinate desire to preserve the past, only made it more imperative to tear the people away decisively from their ancestral backwardness. Dostoevsky, as could be expected, tried to steer a middle course between these

36

two extremes: "The forms of life offered to them [the people] by the trans-formation did not agree with their spirit, nor with their strivings, were not cut to their measure and came out of season. They called them [the reforms] German, and those who followed the great Tsar, foreigners" (18: 36). But this rejection was not merely a negation of change and development on the part of the people; rather, it had led them to seek change in their own way and on their own terms.

The people "sank into themselves and their situation, tried to create their own outlook, their philosophy, split up into secret and perverted sects, sought new avenues for their lives, new forms. . . . And meanwhile, they have been called the preservers of old, pre-Petrine forms, dim-witted Old Believers" (18: 36). Disdaining the notion that the people were torpid and immobile, Dostoevsky goes back even farther than the reforms of Peter the Great in search of signs of their creativity. These he finds in the religious fermentation of the *Raskol*—the refusal of a substantial portion of the population to accept the Greek-inspired reforms of the Russian liturgy—which had led to a schism (*raskol*) within the Russian Church in the seventeenth century and the proliferation of various dissenting sects of Old Believers. Even though, as Dostoevsky concedes, the results of the schism were "sometimes monstrous" (18: 36), the *raskolniki* nonetheless represent an attempt to create an indigenous Russian culture independent of European influence; and he intimates that the positive values of Russian life for which the *pochvenniki* were seeking so eagerly could perhaps be found among the dissident sects.

Meanwhile, with equal extremism, the upper class had been assimilating European culture through every pore and moving in exactly the opposite direction; so all-consuming was this drive that "sometimes we reproached ourselves for our inability to be European." But in fact, no matter how strenuous the effort made by Russians to become Europeans, such a metamorphosis finally proved to be impossible: "We know now that we cannot be Europeans, that we are not in a condition to squeeze ourselves into one of the forms lived through and worked out by European life on the basis of their own national principle, but to us strange and opposed . . ." (18: 36). This does not mean, however, that in returning at last to Russian life and seeking to create a truly national culture the upper class will simply renounce everything it has acquired. Indeed, such acquisitions have laid the foundation for the great world-historical role that Russia will be called upon to play in the future: "We foresee, and foresee with reverence, that the character of our future activity must be in the highest degree pan-human, that the Russian idea, perhaps, will be the synthesis of all those ideas which Europe has developed, with such persistence and courage, in each of its nationalities; that perhaps everything antagonistic in these ideas will find rec-

onciliation and further development in Russian nationality [*narodnost*]"
(18: 37).

3
————

Dostoevsky's famous doctrine of Russian "pan-humanism," usually associated with a much later stage of his career, is thus expressed here with exemplary clarity in 1861. And though his views will later take on a more pronounced Slavophil cast, their roots undoubtedly go back to a famous article
(partly devoted to Dostoevsky himself) of the arch-Westerner Belinsky,
who in 1846 predicted that "the Russian nationality is foreordained to express the richest and most many-sided essence in its nationality, and that it
is this which explains its amazing ability to adapt and assimilate all alien
elements."[3] Dostoevsky simply expands on this prophecy when, after declaring his belief in "the Russian idea," he continues: "It is not in vain that
we speak in all languages, understand all civilizations, sympathize with the
interests of each European people, understand the meaning and rationale
of events entirely foreign to us." But Dostoevsky adds an important variation of his own when he includes among the characteristics of Russian nationality its capacity for the harshest self-criticism: "It is not in vain that we
have displayed such power of self-condemnation, astonishing to all foreigners" (18: 37). By this qualification, Dostoevsky is able to maintain that even
those among the Russian Westerners who seem most totally alienated from
their native soil are actually displaying a typically Russian national trait;
and he thus evaluates them positively, rather than, as the Slavophils were
wont to do, rejecting them as irredeemably corrupted by European influence. Such a comprehensive attitude toward those whom Dostoevsky
would later call the "Russian Europeans" will always continue to separate
him from the pure Slavophils.

The precise lineaments of the Russian culture of the future that Dostoevsky envisages, which will presumably emerge from the fusion of both these
groups into a new unity, remain alluringly obscure; nor will they gain much
more clarity in his later pronouncements. Most emphasis is placed on the
necessity of fusion, which Dostoevsky urges in accents that manifestly vi-
brate with the pain of the still-aching scars of his prison years. And we can
hear in his words the torments of the man who had written to his brother,
in his very first letter after four years of prison camp: "The hatred of the
upper class among them [the peasant-convicts] is limitless, and they received us, the gentlemen, with hostility and a malevolent joy at seeing our
misfortune. They would have eaten us if that had been allowed. . . . 'You,
gentlemen, iron beaks, you devoured us. Once you were a master, you tortured the people and now you are here, lower than the lowest, just like one

of us.' . . . One hundred and fifty enemies were never tired of persecuting us, it was their pleasure, their distraction, their occupation. . . ."[4]

The memory of such venomous taunts now leads Dostoevsky to insist that the upper class must undertake "the spread of enlightenment, energetically, quickly, and at whatever cost—this is the major problem of our time, the first step toward every activity" (18: 37). The announcement then continues with some further paragraphs on the present state of Russian literature, which is declared to be too subservient to "authorities" of all kind and in need of a truly unfettered organ of opinion. *Time*, of course, is prepared to fill this gap, and proclaims its willingness to do so with more or less belligerent generalities designed to attract subscribers.

4
———

The program of *Time* was broad enough and vague enough to appeal to a large spectrum of opinion among the intelligentsia; and the slogan of *pochvennichestvo*, given the influence of Herzen's ideas, did not have any particularly compromising connotations in the eyes of the radicals at that moment. Dostoevsky's reputation as a returning exile and ex-Petrashevets also served as guarantee that his journal would uphold a liberal and progressive line. Besides, the mood of the literati in those years, as Strakhov recalls, was to emphasize unity rather than to stress divergence. "I still remember," he writes, "the almost friendly feeling which then reigned among writers. . . . It was assumed by everyone that literature was performing some common task and that differences of opinion should fade into the background. In truth, all stood together as one in favor of enlightenment, freedom of speech, the lifting of every fetter and constraint, etc., in a word, in favor of all the usual liberal principles understood in a completely abstract fashion, so that underneath them ran the most diverse and opposed tendencies."[5] Such oppositions would soon come to the surface as a result of the rapidly evolving social-political situation; but *Time* was initially considered to be just another progressive journal, with what would be called, at the end of the decade, a pronounced Populist (*narodny*) slant.

At the same time, Dostoevsky had recruited Strakhov and Grigoryev as his two leading contributors, knowing full well that both were firmly opposed to many aspects of the radical ideology of the 1860s. Both men are important figures in their own right; each played a significant role in Russian culture; and each exercised an undeniable influence on Dostoevsky. But they helped more to enrich and reinforce certain elements already present in his own outlook than to provide the stimulus for a new point of departure.

Strakhov first attracted Dostoevsky's attention through some articles he had printed in *The Torch*: a series on science called *Letters about Life*, and

3. Nikolay Strakhov in the 1850s

a review of P. L. Lavrov's recent *Studies on the Question of Practical Philosophy*. Like many of the radicals he was to confront in print, Strakhov was the son of a priestly family and had been educated in a theological seminary as a youth. Unlike his opponents, though, he had later studied mathematics and natural science and taken an advanced university degree in biology. Such qualifications gave him a scientific competence far superior to that of the average Russian publicist; and he combined these credentials with a devotion to Hegel and German Idealism that made him acutely aware of the limitations of scientific knowledge when confronted with the eternal "cursed questions" of human existence.*

* As illustration, we may cite the following passage from a late work of Strakhov's entitled *On Eternal Truths* (*O Vechnikh Istinakh*, 1887): "Science does not include what is for us the most important, the most essential; it does not include life. The greatest part of our existence is found

40

In his *Letters about Life*, for example, he stresses that the human organism should not be viewed in purely mechanical terms. To understand it properly, one must take into account an inner principle of spiritual development; no approach to human life is really adequate that views it *only* as a product of environment. One can easily see why such an argument, put forward by a writer with a mastery of the latest scientific theories, should have strongly appealed to Dostoevsky, who had once intended to translate a famous treatise on psychology entitled *Psyche* by Carl Gustave Carus. Dostoevsky always took an intense interest in well-informed defenders of a Romantic and Idealist view of nature; and Carus, who was a distinguished German medical doctor and expert in physiology, as well as a painter and man of letters, had continued to maintain his allegiance to Schelling long after that philosopher had fallen out of fashion. In the book that Dostoevsky admired, Carus had staunchly argued that nature, as the creation of a "Divine Idea," could not be considered purely material either in origin or character.[6]

Even closer to Dostoevsky's heart would have been Strakhov's article on Lavrov, who, ten years later, would emerge as a leading spokesman for the ideology of the Russian Populists; but in 1860 he was still only an articulate professor in the Artillery College of St. Petersburg. Chernyshevsky had quickly and slightingly dismissed Lavrov as not being a vigorous enough materialist, and then used his book as the pretext to develop his own ideas in *The Anthropological Principle in Philosophy*. Strakhov, on the contrary, found Lavrov far too *much* of a materialist for his taste, and launched a counterattack in defense of human freedom and moral autonomy against all attempts to make them subservient to material conditions. "The will," he declared, "is subordinate, in an essential and necessary fashion, to one thing only—namely, the idea of its own freedom, the idea of its independent, original and conscious self-determination."[7] For the Dostoevsky who had just written his "supplement" to *House of the Dead*, and who knew with every fiber of his being that a world of sensual and material satiety would be unendurable without moral-psychic freedom, such words must have come as a precious confirmation of his own deepest intuitions.

Strakhov was also of great value to Dostoevsky personally as a philosophical mentor, although in his biography-memoir he rather tends to exagger-

outside science—that part which constitutes our fate, the part that we name God, conscience, our happiness, and our merits. . . . For this reason, not only the contemplation of these subjects in actuality, not only their elevated expression by great thinkers and artists, but even any second-rate novel, any crudely imagined tale, can contain a greater and more accessible interest than the best course in physics and chemistry. Each of us is not a wheel in some great machine; each is mainly the hero of that which we call life." Cited by A. S. Dolinin, "F. M. Dostoevsky i N. N. Strakhov," in *Shestidesyatye Gody*, ed. N. K. Piksanov and O. V. Tsekhnovitser (Moscow, 1940), 246.

Despite his importance in mid-nineteenth-century Russian culture, the literature on Strakhov is quite scanty. A well-informed introductory survey of his career can be found in Linda Gerstein, *Nikolai Strakhov* (Cambridge, Mass., 1971).

ate his friend's lack of intellectual sophistication. To be sure, Dostoevsky once presented him with an uncut copy in German of the first volume of Hegel's *History of Philosophy*; but no one who had actively participated in the ideological debates of the 1840s in Russia, and had mulled over the pages of Belinsky and Herzen, could have helped acquiring a fairly wide acquaintance with the reigning philosophical ideas of the time. Strakhov, however, possessed an impressive culture and a professional mastery to which Dostoevsky could not pretend, and their daily conversations certainly sharpened and refined the novelist's awareness of the implications of his own views and the significance of those of others.

"Our conversations were endless," Strakhov writes, "and they were the best conversations I was ever lucky enough to have in my life." What captivated him about Dostoevsky "was his unusual mind, the speed with which he seized on every idea after just a simple word or allusion. . . . The main subjects of [our conversations] were, of course, journalistic matters, but they touched on all sorts of other themes as well, very often the most abstract questions. Feodor Mikhailovich loved such questions about the essence of matter and the limits of knowledge, and I recall how amused he was when I classified his opinions under the various theories of philosophers known to us from the history of philosophy. It turned out that it was difficult to think up anything new, and he consoled himself jokingly with the remark that at least his ideas coincided with one or another great thinker."

Strakhov also notes another trait of Dostoevsky's intellectual physiognomy that has particular relevance for the ideological character of his great creations. "The most routine abstract thought very often struck him with uncommon force, and would stir him up remarkably. He was, in any case, a person in the highest degree excitable and impressionable. A simple idea, sometimes very familiar and commonplace, would suddenly set him aflame and reveal itself to him in all its significance. He, so to speak, *felt thought* with unusual liveliness. Then he would state it in various forms, sometimes giving it a very sharp, graphic expression, although not explaining it logically or developing its content. Above all, he was an artist, he thought in images and was guided by feeling."[8]

5

If Dostoevsky received a certain intellectual schooling from Strakhov, what he derived from Apollon Grigoryev stirred much deeper levels of his personality. There is no record of any prolonged personal contact between the two men; but Grigoryev was a charismatic presence who exercised his fascination on a whole group of younger contributors, including Strakhov, and the daily editorial meetings of *Time* provided ample opportunity for the exchange of ideas. Traces of such exchanges can be found in Grigoryev's work: one of his last major series of articles, "The Paradoxes of Organic Criticism," is cast in the form of letters to Feodor Dostoevsky, and his important autobiography, *My Literary and Moral Wanderings*, was written at the suggestion of, and dedicated to, Mikhail Dostoevsky.

Dostoevsky would certainly have found the tempestuous and turbulent Grigoryev much more to his taste as a human being than the prudish, finicky Strakhov. For Grigoryev was one of those "broad" Russian natures—much like the young poet I. N. Shidlovsky, the friend and inspirer of Dostoevsky in his youth—who combined the most refined and exalted artistic and spiritual aspirations with sordid and disorderly lives. "Mystic, atheist, Freemason, member of the Petrashevsky circle, artist, poet, editor, critic, dramatist, journalist, singer, guitarist, orator"—these are some of the disparate aspects of Grigoryev as seen through the eyes of his contemporaries.[9] Such lives were felt by Dostoevsky to be typically "Russian," and he wrote that Grigoryev "was, perhaps, of all his contemporaries . . . the most Russian of men as a temperament (I am not saying—as an ideal, that is understood)" (20: 136). In Grigoryev's case, his poetry and criticism were

4. Apollon Grigoryev in the 1850s

held in great esteem by some of the best judges of his time; but he would disappear for weeks on end to indulge in drunken sprees and riotous debauches among the Gypsies, and many of his best essays were written in debtors' prison. "I remember him," writes one of his closest friends, the poet Ya. P. Polonsky, "believing neither in God nor the Devil—and on his knees in Church, praying to the last drop of his blood. I remember him as a skeptic and as a mystic, I remember him as a friend and enemy, fighting with people and flattering Count Kushelev [the owner of a periodical] about his infantile compositions."[10] It has been suggested that traits of Grigoryev, who liked to call himself "the last Romantic," were later embodied in the equally tumultuous and surprisingly poetic Dimitry Karamazov.[11] In any case, both the literary character and his possible real-life prototype are excellent examples of the same chaotically Russian "largeness" of personality.

Grigoryev's intellectual history duplicates that of Dostoevsky in several particulars. For a brief period in 1845 he had attended the gatherings of the Petrashevsky circle, which attracted Dostoevsky two years later; but this flirtation with Utopian Socialism was very short-lived: in the same year he published a verse play, *Two Egoisms*, satirizing both Petrashevsky and a character representing the Moscow Slavophils. Grigoryev himself, though sympathetic to the Slavophils' love of native Russian culture, rejected what he called their infatuation with the "ancient Boyar past"[12] and their refusal to acknowledge anything of value in contemporary Russian literature (with the exception of Gogol). For him, the true values of Russian life were to be found not in any chimerical and idealized Eden before Peter or in the downtrodden peasantry, but rather among those surviving groups—like the Moscow merchant class depicted in Ostrovsky's plays, often staunch Old Believers—who had managed to flourish while zealously clinging to their own mode of existence. Grigoryev was one of the first to hail Ostrovsky as an important revelation of the Russian folk spirit, and he vehemently rejected the accusation that the world portrayed by the dramatist was "a realm of darkness." Although quite willing to concede its less attractive aspects, Grigoryev preferred to seek in it, as Mikhail Dostoevsky had also done, for examples of truly Russian folk traits and redeeming virtues. Grigoryev was himself a great connoisseur of Russian folk culture and of the Gypsy music he found so irresistible, and was famous for virtuoso renditions of such music on the guitar. Some of his best poems, rediscovered and collected at the beginning of the present century by Alexander Blok, attempt to translate the fiery passion and despairing poignancy of his Gypsy revels into words.

Grigoryev's mature essays, which Dostoevsky greatly admired, sketch an original philosophy of Russian culture whose major theses certainly affected the novelist's own opinions on the subject. The central figure in this history is Pushkin, whose writings, as Grigoryev interprets them, mark a watershed in Russian cultural self-consciousness. Until their appearance, foreign influences had been accepted, assimilated, and revered; but in Pushkin, for the first time, one can observe a struggle between the "predatory" types that imitated Western paradigms—the egoistic Romantic and Byronic heroes of his early poetry—and the gently ironical Ivan Petrovich Belkin or the youthfully pure-hearted narrator of *The Captain's Daughter* by whom they are replaced. These are purely Russian characters in their mildness, unaffectedness, and simplicity; and they indicate Pushkin's desire to return to his native soil, with its "truly human, i.e., Christian"[13] values, after succumbing to the seduction of foreign ideals. Grigoryev sees all of post-Pushkin Russian literature in terms of this struggle between "predatory" (*khishchny*) and Russian "meek" (*smirenny*) types, and he works out his cultural typology in a whimsically breathless and involuted style reminiscent of his beloved Thomas Carlyle. His essays contain both broadly impressive generalizations and quite penetrating observations on a whole host of writers up to and including contemporaries such as Turgenev, Tolstoy, and Pisemsky; and he is now generally acknowledged to be the greatest literary critic of mid-nineteenth-century Russia.

6

Dostoevsky was undoubtedly attracted to Grigoryev's ideas because, for one thing, they helped to give a concrete literary-cultural content to his own most intimate experiences. The "return to one's native soil," whose necessity had presented itself to him so agonizingly in the prison camp, now proved to be the path taken by the greatest of all Russian writers—and it was the one destined to be followed by all Russian literature of any stature! Besides the appeal of such views for Dostoevsky, he would also have responded favorably to Grigoryev's contention that "meek" types are the true carriers of Russian moral-social values—an opinion strongly resembling one expressed by P. V. Annenkov in 1859, who had maintained that the "weak person" was the unique upholder of moral standards in Russian society. For the "strong person" demanded by the radicals was all too apt, given the conditions of Russian life, to be a ruthless and merciless oppressor of others.

Such ideas would have been taken by Dostoevsky as precious confirmations of his own artistic premonitions. For his predominant character-types in the 1840s—Devushkin and Golyadkin—can easily be classified as "meek" or "weak," and are filled with timidity and moral compunctions arising from a worried conscience. One of his short stories was even entitled "A Weak [*Slaboe*] Heart," meaning "weak" in the sense of overscrupulousness; and more recently he had depicted a character closer to Grigoryev's conception, Colonel Rostanev in *The Village of Stepanchikovo*, as a slightly ridiculous but nonetheless authentic embodiment of generosity and magnanimity.[14] Much of Dostoevsky's later work may well be seen as a dramatization of the conflict between "predatory" Western (or Western-influenced) types and genuinely Russian "meek" ones—a conflict whose clash of values, portrayed as a duel between moral-spiritual absolutes, he would one day succeed in raising to the level of high tragedy.

It is in Grigoryev's literary essays that we find the most direct and obvious link with Dostoevsky, but there are other points of contact that should also not be overlooked. Like Dostoevsky in his youth, Grigoryev had been strongly influenced by Schelling, and he shared with the novelist a view of art as a means of metaphysical cognition—the chosen vehicle by which the secrets of the Absolute reveal themselves in time and history. Such an exalted conception of art had become very old-fashioned by the 1860s; and Dostoevsky treasured in Grigoryev an extremely valuable ally who could apply such an outlook convincingly to the immediate cultural situation. Both men thus defended the status of art against the mocking onslaught of the radical Utilitarians, and upheld its right to be recognized as an autonomous need and function of the human spirit.

Profoundly sympathetic to Dostoevsky as well was Grigoryev's irrationalism, which had been strengthened and affirmed by his enthusiastic reading of the later Schelling. Kierkegaard too had been strongly influenced by these late works of Schelling, which are now recognized as one of the sources of modern Existentialism, and Grigoryev drew the same conclusion as his Danish predecessor that life could not be contained within rational categories of any kind. "To me 'life' is truly something mysterious," he writes, addressing himself directly to Dostoevsky, "that is, it is mysterious because it is something inexhaustible, 'an abyss which swallows all finite reason,' to use an expression from an old mystic book, a boundless space in which the logical conclusions of the cleverest mind will often get lost, like a wave in the ocean; [life is] even something ironic, but at the same time full of love, in spite of this irony. . . ."[15]

Most striking of all, perhaps, is the temperamental affinity revealed by Grigoryev's reference, in a line of his poetry, to "the mad happiness of suffering," and by his reiteration, in a letter, that "there are sufferings of the soul capable of passing over into a sense of beatitude." How can one not think of Dostoevsky, pertinently asks the Italian Slavist Wolf Giusti, after reading such utterances?[16] And this affinity is further illustrated by their common devotion to the Christian faith as it had developed in their homeland. Just as Dostoevsky had once declared, with reference to the Christian Crusades, that "Europe and its task will be completed by Russia,"[17] so Grigoryev believed that the historical life of Europe was "exhausted, and another is beginning; it will come out of Orthodoxy, a new world lies in this force."[18] But, again like Dostoevsky, he was too much a product of Romanticism and too much a modern to accept either his Christian faith or Orthodoxy without a struggle. "From wherever I begin," he acknowledges, "I always arrive at the same single point: at this deep and sorrowful need to believe in the ideal and the *Jenseits* [the supernatural]."[19] No Russian contemporary of Dostoevsky comes closer than Grigoryev to sharing the same tangled complexity of impulses and attitudes; and a satisfactory study of the relation between these two fascinating figures still remains to be written.*

It was with such comrades-in-arms that Dostoevsky sallied forth to participate in the journalistic wars of the 1860s, and his campaigns are worthy of being followed with the closest attention. Victory certainly cannot be said to have attended his banner; but historians of Russian culture agree that while the *pochvenniki* were in the field, they furnished a quite respectable opposition to the triumph of what has been called (somewhat inaccurately, so far as Chernyshevsky and Dobrolyubov are concerned) Russian Nihilism. Moreover, these wars served to provide Dostoevsky with the materials that he was soon to transmute and elevate, by the power of his genius and personal vision, into the artistic-ideological synthesis of the great novels of the middle and later 1860s.

* One passage from a letter of Grigoryev to Apollon Maikov (January 9/21, 1858), written while Dostoevsky was still in Siberia and hence before the two men could have exchanged ideas, will illustrate this similarity in fundamental outlook: "I do not know what I find more repulsive: Petersburgian progress . . . the dilettantism of orthodoxy, or finally the cynical atheism of Herzen. All these amount to the same thing and have the same value, and 'these three' all come equally from one cause: from a lack of faith in life, the ideal and art. All this results from the *utilitarian* Utopia of sensual felicity or spiritual slavery and Chinese stagnation under the pressure of *external* unity in the absence of inner unity, i.e., Christ, i.e., the Ideal, i.e., *Measure*, Beauty, in which alone truth is contained and which alone can bring truth to man's soul." The identification of Christ in this passage with the Ideal and with Beauty could not be more Dostoevskian. Apollon Grigoryev, *Materiali dlya biografii*, ed. Vlad. Knyazhnin (Petrograd, 1917), 217.

CHAPTER 5

Into the Fray

With the launching of *Time*, the routine of Dostoevsky's life was immutably established for the next five years. All of his energies were absorbed by his work both as editor and contributor, and it is impossible to dissociate his private existence from the quotidian task of running the magazine. Its editorial offices were located in the residence of Mikhail Dostoevsky, and both Feodor and Strakhov lived close by, the latter having moved from another apartment specifically to be nearer at hand. This section of the city was a busy and populous lower-class district, whose grimy and muddy streets, always swarming with hordes of merchants, tradesmen, and laborers, Dostoevsky later portrayed in *Crime and Punishment*. And, as Strakhov recalls nostalgically, "amid these surroundings, which filled us with sadness and repulsion, we all lived through very happy years."[1]

2

Strakhov's memoir helps considerably to fill in the picture of this period of Dostoevsky's life, although his judgments and interpretations must be approached with a good deal of caution. It was, as he describes it, a life of unremitting literary labor, with Dostoevsky working round the clock and taking time off from his desk only for the few hours of sleep needed to recoup his energies. Like Balzac (though drinking tea for stimulation instead of coffee), Dostoevsky invariably wrote at night, starting about midnight and continuing until five or six in the morning; he then slept until two or three, and began his day around that time. The staff of the journal convened regularly at three in the afternoon, probably out of deference to Dostoevsky's unorthodox schedule, "and there [in the offices] we leafed through the newspapers and journals, caught up with everything new, and often then went to dinner together."[2] Very often too Dostoevsky visited Strakhov's daily tea in the early evening, when a group of friends would gather for talk and conviviality. In general, according to Strakhov, Dostoevsky "was oftener at my house than I at his, since I was a bachelor and one could visit me without fearing that anyone would be disturbed."[3] This is a good example of Strakhov's insinuating style, which always suggests much more than it states; here he distinctly hints that Marya Dimitrievna was hardly prone to receive her husband's friends with cordiality.

5. Mikhail Dostoevsky's home and the offices of *Time*

Strakhov also stresses the complete absorption of Dostoevsky and his collaborators in the internecine warfare which, at that agitated moment, imparted so much unaccustomed animation to the Russian periodical press.
To be an editor involved much more than merely reading manuscripts in
the privacy of a study, or carrying on a correspondence with contributors
old, new, or would-be. A journal like *Time* was unavoidably in the center of
a cross fire, and nothing was more important than to know who was a friend
and who a foe. "It was usual in those days," Strakhov explains, "for each
journal to speak of all other journals, so that the impression made by each
article could be seen very quickly. Dostoevsky, Apollon Grigoryev, and I
could be certain that, in each new issue of a journal, we would invariably
come across our names. The rivalry between various journals, the intense
attention given to their tendency, the polemics—all this turned the job of
journalism into such an interesting game that, once having experienced it,
you could not help but feel a great desire to plunge into it again."[4]

Despite such words and his own lengthy career as a publicist, Strakhov harbored a certain unconquerable disdain for the rough-and-tumble of journalistic infighting. He had, as he remarks proudly, belonged to a literary circle of the 1840s for which "the very summit of culture would have been *to understand Hegel and to know Goethe by heart*."[5] These two names (especially the latter) had become symbols for a social-cultural attitude *au-dessus de la mêlée*, of a concern with "eternal" issues and problems far removed from the petty disputes of day-by-day social existence; and Strakhov was shocked, on his first contact with the Milyukov circle, to find himself exposed to a wholly different point of view. The tendency in this circle "had been formed under the influence of French [rather than of German] literature. Political and social questions were thus in the foreground, and swallowed up purely artistic interests. The artist, according to this view, should investigate the evolution of society and bring to consciousness the good and evil coming to birth in its midst; he should, as a result, be a teacher, denouncer, guide. Hence it almost directly followed that eternal and general interests had to be subordinated to transient and political ones. Feodor Mikhailovich was totally steeped in this publicistic tendency and remained faithful to it until the end of his life."[6]

Strakhov's insidious effort to reduce Dostoevsky to the level of a "publicistic" writer shows, at the very least, his total incomprehension of his friend's work if not his own bad faith. It is valuable, all the same, for its emphasis on Dostoevsky's desire to remain in touch with the burgeoning social-cultural issues of his time and to use them for artistic purposes. His passion for journalism derived from the same desire, and he made no distinction, unlike the more pretentious Strakhov, between what Goethe called "the demands of the day" and those of his literary career. "I rather looked at journalism cross-eyed," Strakhov admits, "and approached it with some haughtiness." A little incident reveals the total difference in attitude between the two men even in the days of their closest collaboration. Unused to the slapdash production of journalism, Strakhov spent a good deal of time "over the final polishing of [his] articles," and these efforts usually provoked Dostoevsky's scorn: " 'You're always working for the "Complete Edition" of your writings'—he would say."[7] Such an anecdote, which contains an implicit and wholly unjustified disparagement of Dostoevsky's literary conscientiousness, nonetheless indicates the urgency of his impulse to respond to the moment and helps to explain why his greatest works so often take their origin in such a response.

"It is not surprising," writes Strakhov, as if generously excusing a fault, "that Feodor Mikhailovich loved journalism and zealously served it, even while perfectly well aware, one presumes, of what he was doing, *and to what extent he was betraying the strict forms of thought and art* [italics added]. From his youth he had been raised on journalism, and he remained faithful to it until the end. He fully and unquestioningly belonged to the literature that was in ferment all around him, and never sought for a position removed from it. Ordinarily, what he read were Russian journals and news-papers. . . . Here lay his intellectual interests, and here too lay his material interests."[8] By bringing out, even in this snide and patronizing fashion, Dostoevsky's total devotion to the journalistic world of the early 1860s, Strakhov unwittingly highlights one of the sources of Dostoevsky's genius while intending to deprecate its results. Precisely because Dostoevsky made no distinction between "eternal" issues and those of the current scene—because he could sense the permanently significant in and through the immediate and seemingly ephemeral—he was ultimately ca-pable of writing those ideological novels which constitute his chief claim to glory.

Quite aside from the medium of print, Dostoevsky also came into close personal contact during these years with a wide and diversified range of Russian social-cultural opinion. Indeed, he could see all its nuances em-bodied in the flesh as he spoke to the youthful members of the younger gen-eration who swarmed into the editorial offices of his journal, and who, if they were lucky, were invited to attend the meetings of the circle of editors and contributors where manuscripts were read aloud and final editorial de-cisions taken. *Time* was constantly on the lookout for new young writers and remained unusually receptive to their fledgling efforts. Many names later well-known, some in the annals of the extreme left-wing (such as P. N. Tkachev), published their first work under Dostoevsky's aegis. V. S. Ne-chaeva, the veteran Soviet Russian scholar who has written two valuable books on Dostoevsky's journals, is perfectly right in remarking that "per-haps never again in his life would Dostoevsky have the same chance to come into contact with young people of such diverse backgrounds and sit-uations, but united by an interest in social and literary questions, as when he was at the head of *Time* and *Epoch*. This circumstance should certainly be taken into account in analyzing the novels of Dostoevsky, and the pic-ture they contain of various representatives of the younger generation."[9]

3

Dostoevsky's editorial policy attempted to combine a sympathy for, and an understanding of, the aspirations of the predominantly radical youth for so-cial justice and political reform, with, at the same time, an unremitting hos-tility to the aesthetic, ethical, and metaphysical tenets of radical ideology. This effort to reconcile the irreconcilable led to inevitable tensions between the various groups of contributors; and Dostoevsky's delicate balance was very soon upset by a succession of social-political events which split Rus-sian society into opposing camps and wiped out the middle ground on which he had tried to take his stand.

Strakhov speaks of the contributors to *Time* as having formed two factions. At the center of one was the tempestuous Grigoryev, "who knew how
to gather the young people around him by the attractive qualities of his
mind and heart, and especially by his genuine interest in their literary efforts." The nucleus of the other group, if we are to believe Strakhov, "consisted of Dostoevsky and myself."[10] This firsthand account, long accepted
as definitive, has recently been challenged and replaced by a far more plausible picture of the alignment of forces. Rather than being allied with Dostoevsky, as he later claimed, Strakhov had really been a fellow traveler of
Grigoryev, "though his emotions were not at all stirred by the search for
pochva, but rather by an implacable hatred of materialism and the encouragement of a struggle against it."[11] On the other side, most of the young
radicals gathered round A. E. Razin (not mentioned by Strakhov at all), the
largely self-educated son of a peasant-serf family and the author of a very
popular introduction to a scientific view of the universe for schoolchildren
entitled *God's World*, who was, in addition, a close personal friend of Dobrolyubov. Between the two was a third group, composed of the Dostoevsky
brothers and the survivors of the gentry-liberal circles of the 1840s—Milyukov, Pleshcheev, Apollon Maikov, and others less well-known.[12]

That Strakhov was allied with Grigoryev rather than with Dostoevsky is
perfectly clear from any impartial examination of the facts. When Grigoryev left Petersburg for Orenburg in the spring of 1861 (mostly for personal
reasons, but partly also because of dissatisfaction with the editorial policy
of *Time*), he preferred to carry on his correspondence with the journal
through Strakhov rather than directly with either of the Dostoevskys. In a
letter to M. P. Pogodin, whose ardently nationalistic interpretation of Russian history had played an important role in his own thinking, Grigoryev
wrote about *Time*: "I have there someone who keeps an eye on things, the
young Idealist philosopher Nikolay Nikolaevich Strakhov."[13]

What upset Grigoryev, among other griefs, was Dostoevsky's refusal to
attack the radicals on *The Contemporary*—Chernyshevsky and Dobrolyubov—more vigorously and directly. Strakhov shared the same dislike of
Dostoevsky's caution in this respect, although for the most part he prudently kept his dissenting opinions to himself. Dissatisfied with Dostoevsky's relatively mild rebuttal of Dobrolyubov's views on art (about which we
shall soon have more to say), Strakhov admits: "I could not contain myself,
and I wished to come as quickly as possible into a straightforward and decisive relationship with Nihilist doctrines. I may say that I always had some
sort of organic dislike of Nihilism, and that from 1855 on, when it began to
speak out distinctly, I regarded its appearance in literature with great indignation." Dostoevsky obviously did not share the same animus, as can be
seen from Strakhov's further remark: "The enmity that I felt I tried to impart to Feodor Mikhailovich."[14]

It has sometimes been suggested that the relative "progressivism" of *Time* during its first two years was the result of a deliberate policy of concealment, and that the dyed-in-the-wool reactionary Dostoevsky was shamefully hiding his true views in order to curry favor with a public he knew to be radical and left-wing.[15] There is no reason to deny that Dostoevsky was keenly aware of the direction in which the wind of public opinion was blowing, and that he tried to trim his editorial sails appropriately to avoid being capsized; but this is quite a different matter from intentionally deceiving his readers. All one can say, in reply to this accusation, is that such was not the opinion of his closest collaborators. Strakhov clearly distinguishes Dostoevsky's tolerance for Nihilism from his own deep-seated antagonism; and Grigoryev, in his vehement letters, never suggests that Dostoevsky was anything but perfectly sincere.

There is no hint of any duplicity when Grigoryev writes indignantly to Strakhov of *Time*'s "shameful friendship" with *The Contemporary* and strongly attacks the choice of Razin (whom he dubs "Stenka Razin," the famous leader of a peasant revolt) to take charge of the political section. What is needed, he says, is "not *Stenka*—oops, sorry!—Aleksey Razin, but a new and fresh person, a person who is striving for truth and an independent point of view, and not for a Liberalism *quand même*. . . ."[16] In the letter to Pogodin already cited, in which he could speak more freely than to Strakhov, Grigoryev remarks that he is not writing anything at the moment although the Dostoevskys are urging him to do so. "Let them pine away for a while and sober up a bit from their sympathy with *The Contemporary*," he explains.[17] Evidently he accepts such sympathy as totally genuine, the result of some sort of self-delusion and self-intoxication.

Another source of grievance arose from the unwillingness of the Dostoevskys to link their own doctrine of *pochvennichestvo* too publicly with Slavophilism. One can understand such reluctance on purely tactical grounds: they wished to give the impression of offering something new in the way of ideas, not merely the repetition of a long-familiar position that, to make matters worse, was widely disliked. But in fact, as we learn from Strakhov, Dostoevsky had little or no firsthand acquaintance with old-fashioned Slavophilism and honestly thought his own ideas to be of quite a different stamp. In Strakhov's opinion, which seems in this instance quite accurate, Dostoevsky at this time was "an unconscious Slavophil," whose convictions had emerged from "his encounter with the people and the inner transformation of his mentality," rather than through the direct influence of Slavophil ideas.[18]

Such ideas—or at least the spirit of such ideas—could also be found, as we have already indicated, scattered through Belinsky's essays and more particularly in the post-1848 writings of Herzen. Dostoevsky was so steeped in these latter texts that phrases, expressions, and allusions easily identifiable with Herzen constantly show up in his prose during these years. Strakhov does not mention such sources in speaking of Dostoevsky's "unconscious Slavophilism," but we should remember their existence as a background to his remarks. "Consequently," he writes, "it so happened that Feodor Mikhailovich had acquired a whole series of views and sympathies that were totally Slavophil, and he entered literature with them at first not being aware of his affinity with a long-existing literary party. . . ."[19] Strakhov obligingly undertook the task of raising Dostoevsky's consciousness on this score, and his efforts were rewarded two years later. In a letter to Mikhail from Italy, Feodor asks him to "tell Strakhov that I am reading the Slavophils carefully, and that I have discovered something new."[20]

For the moment, though, the Dostoevskys tried, much to Grigoryev's indignation, to dissuade him from referring so frequently and flatteringly to Slavophil or semi-Slavophil notables whose writings Grigoryev admired despite his disagreements on crucial points. As he sadly complains in a letter to Strakhov: "The words of a very honorable and excellent man such as Mikhail Dostoevsky: 'What sort of profound thinkers are Kireevsky, Khomyakov, and Father Theodore?'*—for a *genuinely* thinking person are a rather terrifying thermometer" of the prevailing social-cultural temperature.[21] Feodor, who was present at this conversation, denies the meaning given it by Grigoryev and explains that his brother was merely conveying the possible reaction of an imaginary reader. Encountering the unfamiliar names and the praise heaped upon them, such a reader would be likely to recall only that "they are retrograde." It was, Dostoevsky agreed, appropriate to acquaint the reader with such thinkers, but "to manage such acquaintance carefully, skillfully, gradually, conveying their spirit and ideas rather than injuring them at that time with resounding and meaningless praises" (20: 34). Dostoevsky here reveals one of the secrets of his own journalistic technique, which he employed with such consummate suc-

* By the reference to "Father Theodore," Grigoryev means Alexis M. Bukharev (1822-1871), who took the name of Theodore when he became a monastic priest. Bukharev was a strange and saintly figure, possessed by the idea that all aspects of human life should be sanctified by Christ, and he found signs of true Christian faith, even if distorted ones, among modern doctrines that were overtly secular and anti-Christian. Bitterly attacked for his unconventional ideas, he renounced his monastic vows, married, and lived in terrible poverty until his death a few years later.

Whether Dostoevsky read him has not been established, but there are quite striking points of similarity. As Nadejda Gorodetsky writes of Bukharev: "Two aspects of the Christian message impressed him: redemption of the world as a whole and the humiliation of Christ." Much the same could be said of Dostoevsky; and Bukharev too believed that a special obligation lay on Orthodox Russia to bring this "Christian message" to the world. See Nadejda Gorodetsky, *The Humiliated Christ in Modern Russian Thought* (New York, 1938), 116-126; also V. V. Zenkovsky, *A History of Russian Philosophy*, trans. George L. Kline, 2 vols. (New York, 1953), 1: 315-319

cess; but Grigoryev interpreted such advice, intended to enable him to circumvent the prejudices of his audience, as an invitation to self-betrayal. This misunderstanding, though finally straightened out, illustrates "the perpetual inner struggle" taking place within the editorial staff of *Time*—a struggle whose competing factions both reflected and shaped the internal conflict being waged among the contradictory elements of Dostoevsky's own world-view.[22]

5

The first number of *Time* contained no less than three contributions from Dostoevsky's indefatigable pen. Readers opening the journal were greeted with an eighty-seven-page first installment of his new novel, *The Insulted and Injured*; the critical section was headed by the first of a series of articles on Russian literature; and the issue was rounded off with a feuilleton jointly composed by Dostoevsky and D. D. Minaev. Since the feuilleton and the novel will be discussed in succeeding chapters, here we shall consider only the article on Russian literature.

Actually, this article is not really about Russian literature at all if we take this to mean a survey of past and present writers. It is, rather, a series of emphatic re-affirmations of some of the themes broached in the announcement of *Time*, and its main thesis is that Europeans do not understand Russia because they are constitutionally incapable of doing so. Since their own countries are racked by class conflict, how can they comprehend a world in which the classes unite peacefully? "It is exactly in this that we are different from you, for you have had to fight to conquer all of your progress, your rights, and your privileges" (18: 50). Moreover, every European nationality is hostile to its neighbors; and while this is a source of strength and individuality, it also pits each of them against the other in a never-ending rivalry that blocks the path to the future. Among Europeans, "the idea of a global humanity becomes fainter and fainter. . . . The bond of Christianity that has united them until now loses its strength every day" (18: 54).

Russia is quite the opposite since "one does not find in Russian man the sharp-edged, closed-off, stubborn quality of the European. . . . He [the Russian] sympathizes with everything human, independently of all differences of nationality, blood and soil. He finds and instantly acknowledges everything reasonable in whatever is, from any point of view, universally human. He has the instinct of the universally human." Hence he is able to reconcile all the inter-European oppositions and enmities "in the Idea which is his own"—that of "a universal, pan-human reconciliation." At the same time, "Russian man manifests the completest capacity for the healthiest self-criticism, the most lucid self-knowledge, and the absence of any self-excuse harmful to the liberty of action" (18: 55). In conclusion, Dostoevsky ad-

duces the work of Pushkin as proof that Russian man, now having assimilated all the benefits of European civilization, has used them to produce the
new and unprecedented "Russian ideal" of universal reconciliation and the
universally human (18: 69).

Expressed baldly in this way, Dostoevsky's ideas sound singularly un-
impressive, and can only strike a modern reader as a deplorable product of
that vogue for political Messianism which, since the early nineteenth century, has seen one or another country proclaimed as the destined instrument chosen by the hand of God to assume the leadership of nations and
create a new and more glorious world order. But Dostoevsky, it should be
emphasized, does *not* express his thoughts baldly at all; he dresses them
up with all sorts of sparkling asides and fills them out with infectious satirical verve. The incapacity of Europeans to understand Russia, for example,
immediately gives rise to a series of thumbnail sketches of the various European types who have set out to unriddle the Russian enigma.

German scholars acquire immortal fame by studying "the Russian bee-
tle," or, out of love for humanity and learning, "translate Kheraskov's *Rossiada* into Sanskrit" (18: 43).* And then there is the typical French traveler, who sometimes comes for the unheard-of duration of "twenty-eight
days . . . in which amount of time he could effectuate and describe a trip
around the world." Dostoevsky is extremely funny about one such French
traveler in Moscow (unmistakably the Marquis de Custine) who "contem-
plates the Kremlin, pensively evokes Napoleon, praises the tea, and celebrates the beauty and health of the people while deploring their premature
demoralization—the fruits of an unhappy transplantation of civilization
and of the gradual disappearance of national customs (of which he finds
fresh proof on the spot in the replacement of the old-fashioned *droshky* by
a new-fangled one closer to the European carriage)." Strongly vituperating
Peter the Great, he immediately "quite à propos, narrates his biography, full
of the most astonishing adventures, for his readers" (18: 44).

Dostoevsky's ideas thus provide only a thin thread of continuity on which
he embroiders in this lively and provocative fashion; and his novelist's ability to dramatize his arguments, to see them being acted out in terms of people and situations, is what still makes his articles so enjoyable and so read-
able. Besides vivifying his theses with such amusing examples, Dostoevsky
also addresses himself directly to the reader and constantly writes as if to
take account of, and respond to, the objections and interjections of an
imaginary interlocutor. He never simply *presents* his opinions as a series of
propositions calculated to convince and persuade by their rational force

* Mikhail M. Kheraskov was a late-eighteenth-century disciple of Russian Classicism, a style
slavishly imitative of French models, and he was chiefly famous for pompous epic poems glo-
rifying the heroic Russian past. His *Rossiada* (1779), based on Voltaire's *Henriade*, contained
a celebration of the conquest of Kazan by Ivan the Terrible.

alone; his arguments always give rise to a process of give-and-take that involves the reader in a dialogue. This stylistic trait has been well noted by Mikhail Bakhtin, who writes that Dostoevsky's "manner of exposing an idea is the same everywhere: he develops it dialogically, not in a dry and logical dialogue, but in the confrontation of global and profoundly individualistic voices. Even in his polemical articles, he does not argue but organizes voices, places one interpretative attitude in face of another, in the majority of cases in the form of an imaginary dialogue."[23]

Most often this argumentative "voice" of the implied reader is given explicit expression in Dostoevsky's text; but even when this is not the case, Dostoevsky always keeps the reader's presumed response in mind in framing his exposition. An excellent example can be found in the paragraphs just preceding Dostoevsky's enunciation of "the Russian idea" and the assertion of his belief in its existence. He knows very well that, to say the least, such a declaration will strike many of his readers as extravagant; and so he goes off on a digression about the fear people seem to have nowadays about expressing their convictions openly. Most of them, he remarks, would rather be accused of being thieves and scoundrels than considered stupid; "and in truth, the moment one wishes to express a truth, according to one's convictions, this immediately has the air of coming from a copybook of maxims!" But an honest man has the obligation to brave ridicule and utter his convictions, "even if they look like copybook maxims, especially if he believes in them." Dostoevsky then sketches the psychology of someone who, like his future character Stavrogin, advocates convictions in which he does not *really* believe and supports them with furious ardor only "because he was trying to convince himself." Such is not his own situation, Dostoevsky assures the reader; he himself genuinely believes in his ideas, "and what does it matter what one may think of us . . . that it [my idea] is false, without foundation, that we exaggerate, that we have too much youthful fire, if not senile feeble-mindedness, that we lack tact, etc., etc." (18: 53). Preparing the ground in this way for his profession of faith, Dostoevsky disarms the reader in advance by turning his enunciation into an act of moral courage whose theoretical merits become secondary in such a context.

6

Dostoevsky additionally enlivens his article with a brilliant evocation of the course of Russian culture, as well as with a running fire of commentary on the current social-cultural scene. Many of his asides are too elliptical to be easily comprehensible now, and may seem to involve obscure and trivial matters hardly worth disinterring from the dustbin of history. But Dostoevsky's sketch of Russian culture contains an analysis of character-types in

Russian literature that foreshadow some of his own creations; and his views on the past, as well as his observations on the current scene, reveal the extremely unstable synthesis he was trying to work out between a sympathetic and a critical attitude toward the radicals.

Beginning his account roughly with the 1840s, Dostoevsky pays a vibrant tribute in passing to the great predecessors Gogol and Lermontov, whose careers had begun earlier (so far as my knowledge goes, this is his first specific reference to Lermontov). The social-cultural impact of both these writers became evident in the 1840s, and was powerfully supplemented by the works of George Sand. Everyone, Dostoevsky recalls, threw themselves on her novels, "and what a rage for reading there was then!" Her works, of course, were one of the main channels through which Utopian Socialist ideas became known in Russia; and "at that period we listened docilely to your opinions about us [he is addressing an imaginary French interlocutor], and we diligently agreed with them" (18: 57).

As a result of this European influence, two new types appeared, "the talented natures" and "the Byronic natures." Both labels are taken from Saltykov-Shchedrin's *Provincial Sketches*, and they reveal Dostoevsky's admiration for an "accusatory" writer much favored by the radicals on *The Contemporary* (though appreciated, if at all, only lukewarmly by the gentry-liberals connected with the same journal).* Saltykov-Shchedrin's "talented natures" are members of the gentry who still retain a spark (or at least an awareness) of decency in their makeup, but constantly give way to temptation and join in the general corruption; they are full of self-hatred and make fun of themselves, "but so to speak out of principle and with a sort of vicious hidden anger. *Everything then* [in the 1840s] *was done according to principle, we lived according to principle, and were terribly afraid to do anything not in conformity with the new ideas*" (18: 58; italics added). These words provide an important clue to the creation of the underground man; and if we are to place that character anywhere in the literary context of the early 1860s, it would surely be as a "talented nature"—although with a much more complex social-cultural and philosophical significance than anything to be found in Saltykov-Shchedrin. The "Byronic natures" are a different breed, who suffer from an acute metaphysical despair that drives them to card-sharping, petty swindling, and gastronomic

---

* Whether *Provincial Sketches* was actually turned down by *The Contemporary* is a matter of scholarly dispute; but we know that Turgenev, shown some of the early sketches, disliked them intensely and probably communicated his distaste to Nekrasov. This may well have discouraged Saltykov-Shchedrin from submitting the manuscript formally for scrutiny. Other members of the gentry-liberal wing of *The Contemporary* such as A. V. Druzhinin, I. I. Panaev, and V. P. Botkin, also considered Saltykov-Shchedrin's work to be "muckraking" journalism and not really literature at all; it was regarded as an inadmissible surrender to the demands of radicals like Chernyshevsky for a Utilitarian art totally dedicated to serving the cause of social progress. See the commentary in M. E. Saltykov-Shchedrin, *Sobranie Sochinenii*, 22 vols. (Moscow, 1965-1977), 2: 483-487.

overindulgence; they too will soon turn up in *Notes from Underground* in a long tirade on the Russian Romantics. Dostoevsky is thus beginning here to block out part of the ideological canvas that he will use for his first great post-Siberian creation.

Turning to the present, Dostoevsky remarks on the happy change that has taken place: "life suddenly became much gayer," and the time for despair and penny-ante Mephistophelianism has vanished for good. Even Saltykov-Shchedrin, Dostoevsky points out approvingly, changed his satirical tone, and his words took on a warm tenderness when he encountered peasant life and its profoundly Christian climate of feeling ("everything happened as if it were only necessary to leave Palmyra [Petersburg] in order immediately to notice all those Arinushkas and sing a new song") (18: 60). Ostrovsky too has pronounced a "new word" by discovering the positive moral values contained in the life of the Russian people. Most attention, though, is given to what Dostoevsky calls "beneficent publicity," that is, the relative freedom of the press that had permitted the rise of an "accusatory literature" exposing abuses and malefactors.

Such writing had recently come under attack from both the right (which did not relish the criticism of existing conditions) and the left (which believed that such criticism did not go far enough). *The Contemporary*, in the person of Dobrolyubov, had made a point of ridiculing complacent liberal journalists who, while pillorying minor bureaucratic misdeeds, refused to utter a word about the system as a whole or to suggest that a total transformation of society was necessary to remedy the outrages they reported. Such hectoring of the reformist "accusatory" literature had, a year or so earlier, called forth a rebuke from the powerful Herzen in London, who had complained that by their mockery of "beneficent publicity" the radicals were playing into the hands of reaction. Indeed, he became so carried away with indignation that, quite unfairly, he suggested the editors of *The Contemporary* might one day receive a well-deserved decoration from the Tsar.* Dostoevsky again tries to steer prudently through these dangerous shoals, indicating his approval of "publicity" on the one hand but without expressing any indignation at the jibes of the radicals on the other. While keeping his distance on all matters of substance, he thus displays in this discreet

---

* Herzen's article, entitled "Very Dangerous!!!" (in English), was published in *The Bell* in June 1859. The editors of *The Contemporary* were very upset, and Nekrasov persuaded Chernyshevsky to make a secret trip to London and attempt to obtain some public retraction. The interview between the two radical leaders was not a success; in a letter to Dobrolyubov, Chernyshevsky wrote of his trip as being "a colossal stupidity." Herzen soon embodied some of their conversation in *The Superfluous and the Bilious*, which will be discussed in Chapter 12.
    A summary account of these events and their results is given in William F. Woehrlin, *Chernyshevsky, The Man and the Journalist* (Cambridge, Mass., 1971), 250-255; for more details, see V. Evgenyev-Maksimov, *Sovremennik pri Chernyshevskom i Dobrolyubove* (Leningrad, 1936), 371-395, and A. I. Gertsen, *Sobranie Sochinenii*, 30 vols. (Moscow, 1954-1961), 14: 492-499.

and allusive fashion at least a sympathetic tolerance for the radical position in the social-cultural skirmishes of the early 1860s.

7

In the last two sections of his *Introduction*, however, the limits of Dostoevsky's agreement with the radicals begin to emerge much more conspicuously. He insists that he does not wish to be understood as approving *everything* uttered by the "golden mediocrities" who join the latest movement out of snobbery and vanity "as soon as it has captured a dominant place in society," and whose stupidity inevitably tarnishes those with whom they are associated. Such people see new ideas only in a completely distorted and vulgarized form that inevitably misses their true significance: "Take an example: thinkers and philanthropists raise the issue, let us say, of woman, of the amelioration of her lot in society, of the equalization of her rights with those of men, of the despotism of a husband, etc. Our 'golden ones' instantly understand all this to mean that marriage has to be abolished *immediately*; most of all: immediately. Even more: every woman not only may, but *must* be unfaithful to her husband, and in this lies the true moral sense of the whole idea" (18: 62). Dostoevsky will have more to say about women's liberation in the very near future; but, as we see already, he is careful to separate himself from those who advocate extreme revisions of the moral norm.

If these remarks can be considered a thrust against the left, Dostoevsky very quickly shifts his ground and attacks the right on the issue of literacy. Even such an "enlightened" expert as the well-known author of peasant stories and famous lexicographer V. I. Dal (whose dictionary of spoken Russian still retains its authority) had expressed fears that the spread of education might have a harmful effect. It was well-known that a large proportion of peasant criminals were literate, and there was some anxiety that the growth of education might increase their number. Dostoevsky joined with the radicals in rejecting such a view, which in any case clashed with the strong emphasis placed by *Time* on the importance of educating the people; and his remarks, which draw on what he had learned about peasant psychology during his prison years, not only anticipate the *House of the Dead*, but supplement it by a shrewd analysis for which he later found no place.

Any peasant knowing how to read, Dostoevsky explains, "enjoys a sort of superiority over the others," and this knowledge "confers on him a greater dignity, more weight, distinguishes him, raises him above his environment." Not that other peasants consider him superior in any substantive sense; but his ability to read gives him more power—a greater capacity to cope with all sorts of circumstances of daily life that leave the others helpless and confused. Naturally, as he becomes aware of this advantage, the literate peasant begins to regard *himself* as a person of some dignity. In a sketch that foreshadows the pious and literate servant Grigory in *The Brothers Karamazov*, Dostoevsky explains how someone of this type will often "give himself an air of importance, be eloquent, emphatic, a trifle pedantic, maintain a disdainful silence when others speak, and speak precisely when all are silent for lack of knowing what to say," and so on (18: 63). With a prescience worth noting, Dostoevsky remarks on the extraordinary influence exercised among the Old Believers by those in the community who could read and, accordingly, served as commentators on the sacred texts. Just a few months later, precisely such a literate *raskolnik*, Anton Petrov, would be responsible for the most important peasant disorder to take place immediately after the liberation of the serfs.

Dostoevsky goes on to argue that the status superiority conferred on a group of the peasantry by their ability to read often adversely affects their character, and leads them to be contemptuous and disdainful of their fellow peasants. The same phenomenon is noticeable among domestic serf-lackeys (such as Vidoplyasov in *The Village of Stepanchikovo*), who have rubbed elbows with the upper classes: "Even though he [a lackey] is far beneath a peasant laborer so far as social position is concerned, it seems to him that he is far superior, and that the uniform, the white collar of his function and his lackey's gloves ennoble him in relation to the *muzhik*, and he despises the latter" (18: 64). Such a sense of superiority, which encourages personal pride, makes it difficult for literate peasants to tolerate being treated like the others; they are apt to lose patience, become insolent, go too far—and land in prison! Not all, of course, as Dostoevsky is careful to note; individual character is as important here as social position; but the social-psychological process constantly exercises its powerful pressure. The remedy is to make education available as quickly and as universally as possible; only the growth of literacy will remove the abnormal prestige that literate peasants acquire, and which sometimes leads to the most harmful results both for themselves and for society.

It is the obligation of the upper class, Dostoevsky insists, to take the lead in making such literacy accessible; and this duty leads him into some reflections on the "superfluous men"—members of the gentry-liberal intelligentsia—who were then, as we have noted, under heavy attack from the radicals. The campaign to undermine their moral prestige and authority, launched by Chernyshevsky in 1859, had initially taken the form of a biting analysis of the pusillanimity of the main character in Turgenev's *Asya*, who had shrunk from the difficulty of marrying a girl whose mother had been a serf. And Turgenev's own recent criticism of the Hamlet-type for its inveterate egoism had not been sufficient to appease the radical critics, who continued to use the characters in his stories and novels as the target of their sarcastic sallies. The attack had been continued, with mounting ferocity and scathing wit, by Dobrolyubov, and had recently reached a crescendo in his sensational article *What Is Oblomovism?*. Listing the most famous examples of "superfluous men" in Russian literature, all the greatest creations of the best-known writers—Pushkin's Onegin, Lermontov's Pechorin, Herzen's Beltov, Turgenev's Rudin—Dobrolyubov had described them without exception as blood brothers of the supine Oblomov, purehearted and noble-minded, but equally incapable of any decisive action. "Weighing heavily upon all these persons," he wrote accusingly, "is the same Oblomovism, which imposes upon them the indelible impress of indolence, idleness, and utter uselessness."[25]

Dostoevsky had very little sympathy with the "superfluous men" in their gentry-liberal incarnation, and shared a good deal of the antipathy of the radicals to this type. Like all members of the generation of the 1840s, though, he still retained a certain tenderness toward them while fully acknowledging their weaknesses and foibles; and his ambivalent attitude was much closer to that of Herzen than to the contemptuous dismissal of the hard-boiled younger generation. The complaint made by the "superfluous men" had always been that conditions in Russia, founded on enslavement and injustice, offered no suitable arena for the employment of their talents and abilities. But everyone now agreed that, with the new situation created by the liberation of the serfs, a life of honorable action inside Russia was possible, and indeed, had become a task devolving on all men of good will; there was no longer any valid reason to strike a pose of nobly reluctant "superfluity" in face of the overwhelming moral morass of Russian life. Even Herzen, who had leaped to the defense of the "superfluous men" against Dobrolyubov's onslaughts, had done so only in relation to the past. For "the day of the Onegins and the Pechorins is over . . . ," he was ready to agree. "One who does not find work now has no one else to blame for it."[26] Dobrolyubov had insisted that the entire class of gentry-liberals should be thrown into the discard and replaced by a new generation nourished on tougher, more realistic values; but Herzen, refusing to take such a sweepingly condemnatory view, had argued that they could still be useful. Essentially, this was also Dostoevsky's opinion; where the two men differed was in their notion of what "work" and "usefulness" implied in the new post-liberation Russia.

Herzen always remained a radical and revolutionary, and "work" for him, while it might involve a temporary truce with Tsarism, did not mean the end of his hostility to a régime that he opposed on principle in the name of democratic Socialism. For Dostoevsky, on the other hand, the time had come for the "superfluous men," those fine flowers of the Russian intelligentsia (among whom he would later number Herzen himself), to abandon their pride and egoism once and for all and devote themselves wholeheartedly to the humdrum task of bettering the lot of their fellow Russians through the patient reconstruction of Russian life. Suppose, Dostoevsky writes mockingly, each of these fine gentlemen undertakes to teach just one child how to read. Such a proposal, of course, would shock their pretensions, and Dostoevsky conveys their horrified response in his ironically dialogic manner: "Is that an activity for people like us! you say with a bitter smile, we who conceal titanic powers in our breasts! We wish to, and can, move mountains; from our hearts flows the purest well-spring of love for all humanity. . . . It's impossible to take a five-inch step when we wish to walk in seven-league boots! Can a giant teach a child to read?" To which Dostoevsky replies in his own voice: "There it is: sacrifice all your titanism to the general good: take a five-inch step instead of a seven-league one; accept wholeheartedly the idea that if you are unable to advance further, five inches is all the same worth more than nothing. Sacrifice everything, even your grandeur and your great ideas, for the general good; stoop down, stoop down, as low as the level of the child" (18: 68).

The intelligentsia is thus enjoined to subdue its pretensions, and to do what it can within the limits of a possibility bounded by the existing (but greatly transformed) social-political situation. Such an injunction will remain a constant of Dostoevsky's thought, and will determine his immitigable opposition to all attempts to stir up what he firmly believed could only be futile and self-destructive revolutionary unrest.

CHAPTER 6

Petersburg Visions

It was rare for an issue of *Time* to appear without one of Dostoevsky's articles or an installment from one of his works in progress; and his presence was also constantly felt in the form of introductions to translations as well as editorial notes appended to the articles of other contributors. Understandably concerned over the impression that would be created by the first issue of the journal, Dostoevsky rewrote almost entirely an article originally assigned to D. D. Minaev. The result was the feuilleton *Petersburg Visions in Verse and Prose*, a unique mixture of Dostoevsky's prose text with Minaev's verses.

Not included in any of the editions of Dostoevsky's work published in his lifetime, this article remained buried in the pages of *Time* until the 1920s. Since then, however, it has been recognized as a work of rare autobiographical value—tossed off on the spur of the moment, perhaps, and certainly written in a tone of offhand casualness, but containing a precious account of how Dostoevsky viewed the process of his own literary maturation in the 1840s. One immediate aim of the feuilleton, as Dostoevsky reshaped it, was certainly to re-introduce himself to the Russian reading public by this evocative résumé of his literary past. But his pages are not limited only to the work of recollection; and when he returns to the present, we catch a first glimpse of the changes that are already faintly discernible in his artistic outlook. Other contributions to these early issues of *Time* also contain hints and suggestions of new creative possibilities that were soon to be realized.

2

Exactly like Dostoevsky's old articles in the *St. Petersburg Gazette* of 1847, the feuilleton begins with complaints about the unhappy lot of a writer of feuilletons, whose job was to provide lively and amusing information about the latest brouhahas in the realm of entertainment. At that moment, the famous Italian actress Adelaide Ristori was performing in Petersburg, "and immediately all the feuilletonists in existence, in all the feuilletons in all the newspapers and journals, with or without tendency, dwell on one and the same subject: la Ristori" (19: 67). Pity the poor feuilletonist, who has to rack his brains to find something new to say about her talent! But there he is, sitting in some damp fourth-floor flat, gnawing at his pen and waiting for inspiration, while right next door, dragging out a miserable existence, huddle together a whole family whose cold and hungry children wail incessantly. Meanwhile, as inspiration about Ristori delays or sputters out entirely, how many "dramas" similar to that of his neighbors are being performed in the vicinity!

Yet the feuilletonist persists in trying to write in the manner of the "New Poet," who devotes his columns in *The Contemporary* to Petersburg high life and dwells on "camellias [kept women] and oysters and coteries" of *bons vivants* (19: 67). The "New Poet" was I. I. Panaev, who, while holding forth in the pages of that progressive journal, incongruously preferred to write about the gilded haunts of Petersburg night life rather than to dwell on the tribulations of its lesser denizens. Minaev's verses also mock Panaev, whose articles had recently been collected and published, and his original text may have been entirely devoted to satirizing this new book. As a well-known editor and journalist, Panaev exercised some power in the literary world; and whatever Dostoevsky's personal feelings about him, which could hardly have been very friendly,* he may have rejected Minaev's piece as too unrelievedly hostile to an important radical publicist. Instead, Dostoevsky's opening jab at Panaev establishes the basic motif of his own feuilleton, which consists of a series of alternating sketches graphically presenting the stark social contrasts of Petersburg existence.

After this debut, Dostoevsky inserts an obvious allusion to *The Insulted and Injured*, or at least identifies its literary origins for the reader: "Here is what I tell myself: if I were a feuilletonist, not only occasionally but for good and all, I believe I would like to turn myself into Eugène Sue in order to describe the mysteries of Petersburg. I am terribly fond of mysteries. I am a dreamer, a mystic, and I confess to you that Petersburg, I do not know why, has always seemed to me some kind of mystery. Even from childhood, almost lost, thrown into Petersburg, I was somehow afraid of it. I recall an event, in which there was almost nothing special, but which struck me with terror. I will tell you about it in all its details; and yet, it is hardly even an event—simply an impression: but, you see, I am a dreamer and a mystic!" (19: 68-69).

The Mysteries of Petersburg could well serve as the title of *The Insulted and Injured*, and every alert Russian reader would have instantly made the connection with Eugène Sue's *Les Mystères de Paris*. Belinsky had written a famous article about this best seller in 1842, and had maintained that Sue's melodramatic and garishly tinted pictures of life in the Parisian lower depths had been redeemed from meretriciousness by his "humanitarian" and "philanthropic" pathos.[1] Dostoevsky thus links his latest work in a direct line with the social preoccupations of his past, as well as with the *ro-*

---

* Dostoevsky had known Panaev fairly well during the 1840s as a member of the Belinsky circle, and the journalist had published an insulting satirical article about the novelist in 1855 without mentioning his name. See, for more details, *Dostoevsky, The Years of Ordeal, 1850-1859* (Princeton, 1983), 236-238. For the speculation about Dostoevsky's reasons for rejecting Minaev's article, see the commentary in *PSS*, 19: 264.

man-feuilleton technique he was now essaying for the first time. It is just after this reference to Sue that Dostoevsky introduces the revelatory passage, lifted (with some slight changes) from his short story *A Weak [Slaboe] Heart* (1848), that has come to be known as "the vision on the Neva."

The writer recalls how, at the beginning of his career, he had once walked across a bridge over the river during a bitterly cold winter day, looking at the frozen expanse sparkling and gleaming in the rays of the setting sun and watching the smoke drift lazily up from the chimneys on both banks, "intertwining and twining as [it] went, so that it seemed as if new buildings were rising above the old, a new town was taking shape in the air":

> It seemed as if all that world, with all its inhabitants, strong and weak, with all their habitations, the refuges of the poor, or the gilded palaces for the comfort of the powerful of this world, was at that twilight hour like a fantastic vision of fairyland, like a dream which in its turn would vanish and pass away like vapor in the dark blue sky. Some strange thought suddenly stirred in me. I shuddered, and my heart was as if flooded with a hot rush of blood that boiled up suddenly from a surge of powerful but hitherto unknown sensation. I seemed to have understood something in that minute which had till then been only stirring in me, but was still uninterpreted; . . . I suppose that my existence began from just that minute. . . . (19: 69)[2]

Dostoevsky attributes an extraordinary importance to this imaginary transformation of the majestic city of Peter the Great, with its medley of imposing palaces and squalid tenement warrens, into a dissolving phantasmagoria that might have been a waking dream. And this fusion of the fantastic and the real, he affirms, marked the beginning of his self-discovery as an artist. Using literary imagery, and still speaking in the fictional disguise of the harassed feuilletonist searching for a subject, he recalls how he had once been in thrall to Romantic influences (Schiller, Hoffmann, Walter Scott), which had given wings to his imagination and lifted him far above his immediate surroundings. Never deigning to cast even a glance at the world around him, he had desired to live "with all my heart and soul in those golden and passionate dreams [of Romanticism] exactly as if from opium." But then, the revelatory impact of the vision made him aware of all those people he had hardly noticed before, "all those . . . strange, astonishing figures, totally prosaic, not at all Don Carlos's or Posa's, fully titular councillors [lower-level bureaucrats] and at the same time, as it were, some sort of fantastic titular councillors" (19: 70). As they emerged into view, they all appeared to be puppets moved by strings; and behind them was the puppet master (Gogol), laughing uproariously himself and provoking everyone else to laughter as well.

But the youthful Dostoevsky did not wish, like the puppet master of genius, to continue to laugh at all the humble creatures surrounding him; instead, he invented another story about them that "tore deeply at my heart" (19: 70). This story, of course, was the sentimental tale of *Poor Folk*—which for the first time in Russian literature, amidst an unsparing depiction of urban seediness and lower-class misery, portrayed those who lived immersed in such conditions as sensitive and suffering souls. Dostoevsky's characters became "fantastic," not because of the comic distortions provided by the oblique prism of Gogolian humor, but through the unexpected delicacy of their feelings and responses. Here, then, was his own literary point of departure—the infatuation with Romanticism, the turn to Gogol, the realization that reality too contained its own kind of visionary strangeness, and the invention of a new variety of such bestrangement.

3

The "vision on the Neva" thus provides a penetrating glimpse into Dostoevsky's pre-Siberian literary evolution; and he insists that the same vision, even if in slightly different forms, has continued to nourish his imagination ever since: "Now, now things are different. My dreams, if you like, are the same, but with other faces, although old acquaintances also sometimes knock at my door." Dostoevsky thus continues to view the ordinary world around him as filled with the strange and uncanny; in the horde of Christmas shoppers flowing through the Petersburg streets, he suddenly sees "just in front of me, in the crowd . . . some sort of figure, not real but fantastic. I, you see, am in no way able to shake off a state of mind disposed to the fantastic. Already in the 1840s they called me a fantasist and ridiculed me for it. Then, all the same, I did not crawl into a hole. Now, it's understood—gray hair, the experience of life, etc., etc., and all the same I still remain a fantasist" (19: 73).

These words are a belated reply to Belinsky's devastating criticism of *The Double* in 1846, and a defiant affirmation of Dostoevsky's refusal to abandon his own peculiar mode of apprehending reality; but Dostoevsky is doing more here than simply defending his past. As an unrepentant "fantasist," he also sees "other faces" that have begun to impinge among his old acquaintances. One is that of a poor impoverished clerk, totally beaten down and subdued by life, so meek that he does not even turn his head when, casually and almost affectionately, he is lashed by a coachman's whip on the Nevsky Prospect: "Neither did he protest nor raise his voice; a totally blameless personage." But one day, overcome by the laments and reproaches of his brood of children and shrewish wife, he suddenly breaks his despondent silence to confess—something totally unimaginable! It turns out that he is really Garibaldi, the notorious bandit and "destroyer of the natural order of things" (19: 71-72). The Russian newspapers and journals, including *Time*, were in those days full of stories about Garibaldi's heroic struggle for Italian independence against Austria, and the Italian patriot had become the darling of the progressive press. Like Poprishchin in Gogol's *Diary of a Madman* (Dostoevsky makes the comparison himself), who landed in a madhouse believing himself to be the King of Spain after reading in the newspapers about the vacancy of the throne, Dostoevsky's clerk becomes obsessed with the idea that he and the great rebel Garibaldi are one and the same person.

To imagine such velleities of insurrection simmering in the breast of the humblest and most resigned of titular councillors is, of course, the very acme of "the fantastic." "And when I dreamed this dream," Dostoevsky admits, "I began to laugh at myself and the eccentricity of my dream" (19: 72). But then the dream turned out to be "true"—or at least confirmed as a possibility by a newspaper story about a similar clerk, retired and living in the direst poverty, who was found at his death to be worth a half-million rubles. An autopsy was to be performed on the corpse, but "it seems to me that no autopsy will elucidate mysteries like this one" (19: 75). In other words, "the prosaic" is shown once again to contain and breed in its bosom the most extravagant behavior and the most baffling psychological enigmas.

Nonetheless, Dostoevsky takes a stab at elucidating the "mystery" with the aid of two alternative psychologies. One is derived from Pushkin's *The Covetous Knight*, and in its light "my Solovyev [the name of the millionaire-derelict] suddenly appeared to me as a colossal figure." Like Pushkin's nobleman, he enjoyed the secret sense of power given by his boundless wealth—"he has only to whistle, and everything he needs will crawl to him obediently." But he does not even whistle; it is power, not satisfaction, that he inwardly craves: "he needs nothing . . . he is above all desires" (19: 73-74). Dostoevsky, however, decides not "to steal from Pushkin" in this instance (though he will not hesitate to do so unashamedly in both *The Idiot* and *A Raw Youth*), and he invents another motivation for Solovyev. In his youth, the clerk had been quite normal, "had known some Luise and gone to the theater," but then something occurred—"perhaps one of those moments . . . when he suddenly caught a glimpse of something, and that something frightened him" (19: 74). From that moment he began to save, in a manner that gradually became deranged, and his niggardliness was an aberrant manner of responding to the terror of whatever existential crisis had abruptly undermined his being.

4

What is striking about these two figures at first sight—and quite contrary to Dostoevsky's emphasis—is not so much their novelty as their quite pronounced resemblance to his characters of the 1840s. Why should he have considered them "other faces" in relation to his early work? Some answer to this question may be ventured if we turn back to analyze the first use of the "vision on the Neva," which occurs in a story narrating the strange history of a poor young copying clerk who, just at the moment when he wins the consent of the girl he loves—just when some genuine personal happiness at last seems to be within his grasp—sinks into madness. The mystery of this anomalous collapse puzzles his close friend Arkady, and it is "the vision" that enlightens him as he broods over his timid friend's breakdown: "He seemed only now [after the vision] to understand all the trouble . . ." (2: 48).

It is the vision which, for the first time, conveys to Arkady a sense of all the grandeur, the terror, and the social inequalities symbolically focused in the city of Peter the Great, which towers over its punier inhabitants (as in Pushkin's *The Bronze Horseman*) and grinds down their spirit by the weight of all the power it embodies. Dostoevsky can only suggest in this way, although he does so unmistakably, what Arkady suddenly understood about the collapse of his friend; he grasps that the tender-hearted Vasya could not endure the prospect of "happiness" because so strong a sense of his own unworthiness and inferiority had been bred into his very bones. In Dostoevsky's early work, then, the "fantastic" had been motivated by the overwhelming and irresistible pressure of the social order incarnated in the majestic splendor of Petersburg. Any deviation from the path of perfect submission and absolute obedience was enough to plunge his characters into psychic derangement; nothing could have been farther from their thoughts than any impulse of willful insubordination.

If we now look more closely at the "other faces" mentioned in the feuilleton, we can see that a certain change has taken place. Although Dostoevsky's downtrodden clerk resembles his earlier characters in every external feature, the obsession with being Garibaldi reveals something new—namely, an obscure recognition that he is harboring truly *rebellious* desires in his breast. Poprishchin, in believing himself to be the King of Spain, only affirms his ambition to rise in the ranks of a world that he accepts with slavish devotion; the same is true of Mr. Golyadkin in *The Double*, whose most exalted aim is to occupy a slightly more important post in the bureaucratic hierarchy and to marry the daughter of his superior. But such desires take on a greatly altered significance when the same character-type, unable to endure his fate any longer, begins to identify himself with Garibaldi and thus acknowledges an urge to destroy the entire world to which he belongs as a revenge for his frustrations. Now, in some hidden and suppressed corner of his psyche, the character himself internalizes the full social-political implications of his resentments, and his consciousness thus contains an explicit, ideologically subversive dimension.

Evidences of such a change can also be found in Dostoevsky's notes for his proposed rewriting of *The Double*, which are contained in his notebooks for 1860-1861: "When you (in Chapter 1) invited Klara Olsufyevna for the polka, you revolted against society—says Junior to Senior, pathetically comforting him." Golyadkin Senior is the "real" Golyadkin, and Junior is his "double," who emerges from and speaks for both his subconscious and his conscience. ("Junior, it turns out," another note reads, "knows all the secrets of Senior, as if he is the personification of Senior's conscience.") Golyadkin thus realizes that his invitation to the daughter of his superior, at a party which he had crashed, was really "a revolt against society"; the motif is enlarged so that a trivial event, pathetically comic in its original form, now becomes a threatening social-political gesture. Similarly, Golyadkin anticipates the underground man in his fantasies of political power, which swing back and forth between revolution and reaction: "Alone with *Junior*, dreams of becoming a Napoleon, a Pericles, a leader of the Russian revolt. Liberalism and revolution, restoring Louis XVI with tears and listening to him (out of goodness)" (1: 434).

These notes are of particular importance because they reveal both the continuity of Dostoevsky's inspiration as well as the danger of confusing one phase with the other. What was only potential in the earlier work is now developed in a fashion that endows his creations with a larger artistic significance, and converts the original comic pathos into a movement of despairing rebellion. Golyadkin's psychology, the split in his personality between "ambition" and fear of the authorities, takes on a new ideological richness; and the same change of scale can be noted in the case of the millionaire-derelict. With him we seem to be back in the world of *Mr. Prokharchin* (1846), who dies in misery while concealing a small fortune and whose avarice had been the result of having "caught a glimpse of something, and that something frightened him."[3] But here too Dostoevsky begins to conceive such a figure as analogous to Pushkin's *The Covetous Knight*, and to portray his miserliness as another manifestation of a perverted will-to-power not unlike that of the clerk whose dreams are haunted by Garibaldi.

Even though this psychology is rejected for the time being, Dostoevsky is clearly moving toward viewing his early characters as more than the sentimental-grotesque miniatures of the past. Now they are magnified to the same level of dignity, and endowed with some of the same elevation of thought and feeling, as Pushkin's great Romantic creations. After first rejecting Romanticism and shrinking its themes and motifs to the level of "the prosaic" in the 1840s, Dostoevsky thus reverses direction to enlarge his "sentimental Naturalism" with some of the grandeur that had once inflamed his youthful literary imagination. More precisely, he is already beginning to feel his way toward the synthesis of his great novels, where a scrupulous depiction of "the prosaic" will be combined with "the fantastic" of psychological extremism, world-consuming ambition, and complex ideological ratiocination.

5

Dostoevsky's feuilleton concludes with a series of sketches of a typical Christmas crowd: an upper-class Russian lady, speaking in French, naturally buys a doll sporting the flamboyant uniform of the French zouaves; another couple carefully chooses among various toys, concerned about their price; unexpectedly, a healthy and well-dressed gentleman, probably cashiered from the Army, asks for alms. Dostoevsky is bitingly sarcastic about this latter personage, whom he cordially despises for his refusal to find honest work: "And would not these demanders of alms make marvelous workmen at a pump or on the railroads! what strength! what health! But—their noble birth stands in the way!" (19: 76).

The final sketch depicts a young lad, twelve or thirteen years old, poorly but neatly dressed and not at all looking like a beggar, who asks for a few kopeks to buy something to eat on the way home. The encounter leads Dostoevsky into some reflections on the demoralizing effects of poverty on a young soul and a bitterly ironic comment on those who dismiss poverty with indifference, or explain it away to comfort their troubled consciences: "Poverty develops a person, it teaches him virtue . . . not so? If the whole world were perfumed, we would not appreciate perfumes" (19: 78). It is clear that Dostoevsky regards this callous utterance of the wisdom of the ages with supreme contempt.

Much of this latter part of the feuilleton, which finally gets around to including Minaev's verses, is devoted to poking fun at various literary luminaries, particularly the "New Poet" and Dostoevsky's old editor, A. A. Kraevsky. Panaev's devotion to "camellias" and elegant Petersburg night life, especially after the poverty evoked a paragraph earlier, stands out in even more condemnatory relief, though Dostoevsky's quips do not go beyond the bounds of permissible satirical jesting. Besides, he scatters his shots so widely that the editors of *The Contemporary* could hardly have felt that he was taking aim specifically at them. Nonetheless, one side remark directed at Dobrolyubov does contain a foretaste of things to come. "One may not agree with Mr. —bov," Dostoevsky writes, "but I think I should die of boredom reading his articles if he changed ever so slightly the character of the commands that he issues to Russian literature" (19: 78-79). This backhanded compliment paves the way for the polemic with Dobrolyubov in the second issue of *Time*, where the ukases of the radical critic will be submitted to prolonged scrutiny.

Time was peppered with Dostoevsky's editorial interventions, and the rewriting of Minaev's feuilleton was only the most drastic and extensive. These interventions ranged from miniature essays to one or two sentences attached to articles as footnotes. Most of the longer items were written as introductions to translated material, much of which Dostoevsky chose himself or approved for publication; and part of *Time*'s considerable success was attributable to Dostoevsky's flair for providing his readers with exciting literary sustenance from a great range of sources. He was constantly on the lookout for material that would interest, instruct, and titillate his regular subscribers and turn casual scanners of the journal into faithful devotees. At the same time, what he chose to print bears the inevitable mark of his own preoccupations; and his editorial comments very often foreshadow his later works or illuminate the manner in which everything he read became grist for his creative mill.

During 1861, *Time* ran a translation of Casanova's account of his escape from the infamous and almost impregnable dungeons of the Venetian Republic. With one eye surely cocked at Chernyshevsky, Dostoevsky describes Casanova's feat as "the story of the triumph of human will over insurmountable obstacles" (19: 86). Dostoevsky also began to run a series of accounts of famous recent murder trials in France, and he recommends these essays as irresistible reading, "more exciting than all possible novels because they light up the dark sides of the human soul that art does not like to approach, or which it approaches only glancingly and in passing" (19: 89). Dostoevsky does not stress the sheerly sensational aspect of such material, the many twists and turns of fate by which clever and audacious criminals are finally brought to justice; what interests him are "the dark sides of the soul" revealed by murder, the psychological motives and behavior of those who kill. With such words, Dostoevsky is anticipatorily staking out the novelistic domain in which he will soon achieve his greatest triumphs. For he will raise the novel of mystery and criminal adventure to new heights by shifting the focus from such external plot action to the psychology (which for him will be inseparable from the ideology) of the criminal.

The first of the series involved the notorious case of Pierre-François Lacenaire, a cold-blooded murderer who wrote poetry and left memoirs, and who fascinated Dostoevsky because of his culture and intellectual attainments. Of Lacenaire himself, Dostoevsky writes that "he is a remarkable personality, enigmatic, frightening, and gripping. Base instincts and cowardice in the face of poverty made him a criminal, and he dared to set himself up as a victim of his century. All this joined to a boundless vanity; it is the type of a vanity developed to the utmost degree" (18: 90). The figure of Lacenaire, whose name later turns up in *The Idiot* and among the notes for *A Raw Youth*, became for Dostoevsky a prototype of the criminal who seizes on the ideas of his time to justify his crime; and his example certainly helped to provide some features for Raskolnikov, Svidrigailov, and Stavrogin.*

Dostoevsky also wrote a few lines introducing a translation of Elizabeth Gaskell's *Mary Barton*, which began to appear in April 1861. Raymond Williams has called *Mary Barton*, which depicts the lives of Manchester textile workers, "the most moving response in literature to the industrial suffering of the 1840s";[4] and the text provides Dostoevsky with an opportunity to illustrate the contrast between social conditions in Russia and those (as he believed) much harsher ones reigning in capitalist and industrialized Europe. "We print this interesting novel," he writes, "because it starkly portrays the life and sufferings of the English working class. Of all European states, only Russia can look with brotherly sympathy on all this misfortune, all this class hatred, thank God totally unknown [here]. The granting of land to our peasants rescues us forever from that terrible abscess now appearing everywhere—which is known as pauperism or *proletarianism*" (19: 211-212).

Besides furnishing Dostoevsky with the welcome occasion to point such a moral, *Mary Barton* probably affected him more creatively as well. Elizabeth Gaskell, the wife of a Unitarian minister, approaches the lives of her upright but impoverished characters in much the same spirit of social-Christian compassion as prevails in Dostoevsky's pre-Siberian work. Moreover, her novel centers on a murder committed solely to revenge the crying injustice of the plight of starving workers, a murder committed purely out of a painful sense of humanitarian obligation. Ultimately unable to endure the torments of his conscience, the murderer voluntarily confesses to save the life of an innocent victim accused in his place; and the climax occurs in a very effective courtroom scene. Without pressing the point too hard, it seems clear that Dostoevsky's familiarity with such a book nourished the process of artistic gestation that fed most immediately into *Crime and Punishment* and, later, into *The Brothers Karamazov* as well.[5]

A lengthier preface in the first issue precedes three stories by Edgar Al-

---

* The enigmatic and sinister figure of Pierre-François Lacenaire has never ceased to exercise its fascination since his execution in 1836. A new edition of his memoirs, published in 1968, was accompanied by documents of the epoch relating to his trial and execution. A poem by Théophile Gautier, reprinted in the volume, celebrates the hand of Lacenaire, which had been stuffed and mounted and adorned the salon of Maxime du Camp, the friend of Flaubert. See *Mémoires de Lacenaire*, ed. Monique le Bailly (Paris, 1968); for the poem, 293-294.

Many people have seen an artistic reincarnation of Lacenaire without being fully aware of the aura surrounding his life and death. In the French film masterpiece of Marcel Carné, *Les Enfants du Paradis* (1945), set in the early nineteenth century, the character of the poet-murderer played by Marcel Herrand is based on the career of Pierre-François Lacenaire and bears his name. See Georges Sadoul, *Histoire Générale du Cinema*, vol. 6 (Paris, 1954), 68-70.

len Poe, and both Dostoevsky's text and the translations can be linked even more closely than *Mary Barton* with his creations in the next few years. Some of Poe had been translated into Russian previously; but since he had not attracted much attention, Dostoevsky's preface, in the words of a Soviet Russian scholar, contains "the first serious and penetrating evaluation of the American writer made in Russia" (19: 282). Indeed, according to an American specialist, Dostoevsky's preface of 1860 includes "the most perceptive observations yet made in any language specifically on Poe's artistic technique."[6]

What struck Dostoevsky in Poe was "the vigor of his imagination," which he defines as "the power of specific detail": Poe will invent the most extraordinary and even impossible situations, but in his "stories you will so clearly see all the details of the form of the existence presented to you" that the reader is absolutely convinced of their verisimilitude. Unlike Baudelaire, whose translations of Poe (including the prefatory essays) Dostoevsky had certainly read, he does not view him as a *poète maudit* condemned by the reigning vulgarity of American life; rather, he suggests quite brilliantly that the outstanding feature of Poe's imagination is typically American. Materialism was presumed to be the dominating aspect of American civilization, and "if there is the fantastic in Poe, it has, so to speak, something material about it. Clearly, he is fully an American even in his most fantastic stories" (19: 88-89).

Whether Dostoevsky himself chose the stories of Poe that he printed is not known, but they can all be related to the great works he will write in just a few more years—his *Notes from Underground*, as well as the slightly later *Crime and Punishment*. Even the least of Poe's stories in *Time*—*The Devil in the Belfry*, hardly more than a broad comic anecdote—is an allegory of the intrusion of the irrational into an orderly world that has always run in accordance with its immutable laws. When the devil gets into the belfry of the sleepy town of Vondervotteimittis, the lives of the sedate burghers are thrown completely out of kilter because the belfry clock at noontime does not stop at twelve but goes on to chime thirteen. The two other stories, *The Tell-Tale Heart* and *The Black Cat*, contain features that can be linked even more concretely with Dostoevsky's artistic future.

Both are written in a first-person mode by a narrator unable to suppress a sense of guilt about his crimes, and whose conscience finally bursts forth in self-betrayal. Both also illustrate the same irresistible pressure of the irrational to thwart the best-laid and most cunning calculations of the rational mind. The narrator of *The Tell-Tale Heart*, a motiveless murderer who kills because of a pathological obsession, believes he has committed the perfect crime; but he finally blurts out a confession because he thinks that others as well as himself hear the thunderous noise of the victim's heart continuing to beat through the floor under which the corpse lies buried.

The Black Cat is also the story of a crime executed in secret, and ultimately discovered because of an oversight caused by panic and terror. Above all, *The Black Cat* contains the narrator's comment on his inexplicable sadism toward the cat he supposedly loves. Such behavior is attributed to "the spirit of PERVERSENESS. *Of this spirit philosophy takes no account* [italics added]. Yet I am not more sure that my soul lives, than I am that perverseness is one of the primitive impulses of the human heart—one of the indivisible primary faculties, or sentiments, which gives direction to the character of Man. Who has not, a hundred times, found himself committing a vile or stupid action, for no other reason than because he knows he should *not*? Have we not a perpetual inclination, in the teeth of our best judgment, to violate that which is *Law*, merely because we understand it to be such?"[7] This passage may surely be seen as one of the sources leading to the philosophical-psychological dialectic of the first part of *Notes from Underground.*

Yet, for all his admiration of Poe's talent, Dostoevsky does not consider him the equal of another "fantasist," E.T.A. Hoffmann, whose work had exercised a strong influence on Russian literature in the 1830s and whom Dostoevsky had read as an adolescent with reverent attention. What gives Hoffmann the upper hand, he maintains, is that the supernatural and unearthly interpenetrate and fuse in his work with the commonplace and the verisimilar; sometimes Hoffmann "even seeks his ideal outside the earthly, in some sort of extraordinary world that he accepts as superior, as if he himself believed in the existence of this mysterious enchanted world. . . ." Poe is inferior to Hoffmann, not so much as a writer, but as a "poet," since the German Romantic constantly infuses his work with aspiration toward "an ideal"—and in such aspiration Dostoevsky locates "the purity, and the real, true beauty inherent in man" (19: 88-89). Dostoevsky's own best post-Siberian creations, one might say, attempt to strike a balance between the two writers, rivaling Poe for vividness and verisimilitude but never losing Hoffmann's sense of the unearthly and the transcendent as a controlling force in human life.

Dostoevsky thus tried to be both a writer like Poe and a poet like Hoffmann; for him these two aspects of literature could not, or at least should not, ever be separated. Indeed, the necessity of keeping the two united was an issue very much on his mind precisely at this moment, and it was one that continued to preoccupy his thinking about art and life. For the most important function of art, he believed, was—and always had been—to inspire man by providing him with an ideal of transcendence toward which he could eternally aspire. This was the very position he asserted when, in the second number of *Time*, he launched his first open attack against the radical camp.

CHAPTER 7

An Aesthetics of
Transcendence

The founding of *Time* aroused diverse echoes in the world of Petersburg journalism, but in general its reception was quite friendly. *Notes of the Fatherland*, which had been singled out for some acerbic thrusts, responded with a sharp riposte; but *The Contemporary*, whatever the personal sentiments of its editors, rallied to the support of this new literary enterprise directed (as everyone knew) by a returning exile who "had suffered for a good cause." Old enmities were forgotten or laid aside as Panaev saluted the announcement of *Time* in his influential column, congratulating the new periodical on the boldness of its rejection of all "literary authorities" and its resolve to occupy a totally independent position. Nekrasov also welcomed *Time*'s denunciation of "authorities" in a four-line verse published in *Svistok* (*The Whistle*, a satirical supplement to *The Contemporary* founded by Dobrolyubov); and the same publication also contained a jesting "Hymn to *Time*" from the poet's pen to greet the new arrival: "Welcome to thee, new comrade!" ran the first line.[1]

Chernyshevsky, who also greeted *Time* in a survey of periodicals, was more reserved. He commented on the latent hostility that Panaev and Nekrasov were willing to overlook, and expressed pique at Dostoevsky's barbed allusions to Dobrolyubov despite their relative mildness. Noting that *Time* was living up to its announced program of independence, and expressing its opinions unceremoniously on all and sundry (including *The Contemporary*), he remarks that this attitude might give offense "if we were inclined to get on a high horse when someone judges us as sharply as we often judge others." But such asperities were within the rules of the game, and their appearance "in no way lessens our inclination to support *Time*." Nonetheless, with a touch of annoyance, Chernyshevsky adds that "if it should occur to us to quarrel with *Time*, we would remark that it errs when it speaks of the essays signed with the abbreviation —bov as if they laid claim to being taken as authorities."[2]

Chernyshevsky also made no attempt to conceal his displeasure at much that he disliked in the program of *pochvennichestvo*; but for the moment he was willing to assume that such disagreements were only theoretical and did not preclude a mutual dedication to the common social cause. "So far as we can judge from the first issue," he writes diplomatically, "*Time* differs from *The Contemporary* in its ideas concerning many of those questions about which there can be a difference of opinion in polite society."[3] This Aesopian phrase indicates Chernyshevsky's desire not to alienate a possible social-political ally, while putting the *pochvenniki* on notice that certain limits could not be overstepped. Such an uneasy alliance continued through most of 1861, and was not ruptured even by the second of Dostoevsky's series of articles on Russian literature, *Mr. —bov and the Question of Art.*

At first sight, Dostoevsky's text appears to be only a response, tossed off in the heat of the journalistic fray, to two recent articles of Dobrolyubov (mainly one devoted to the stories of the Ukrainian-Russian authoress Maria Markovich, who wrote under the pseudonym of Marco Vovchok). In reality, however, Dostoevsky's article is much more than a casual product of journalistic necessity; it contains the results of long meditations on the question of art that extend from the beginning of his literary career through his Siberian years. During the mid-1840s, he had disagreed with both Belinsky and Petrashevsky over the problem of the social function of art, and had argued that while art played an important social role, especially in Russia, the artist should be accorded absolute freedom to accomplish his task in any manner he saw fit. He had told Belinsky that "art has no necessity to have a tendency, that art is an end in itself, that an author should concern himself only with artistic quality and the idea will come by itself . . ." (18: 128-129). The "idea" was of crucial significance; but it should not be tailored according to any preconceived notion of what the social mission of art should be in a given historical situation.

Several years later, exactly the position that Dostoevsky had rejected as a young writer was codified into an influential theory by Chernyshevsky in *The Aesthetic Relation of Art to Reality.* Artists, insisted the radical critic, had the obligation to subordinate their inspiration to "life," and "life" was defined essentially in terms of the immediate task of obtaining social justice. Chernyshevsky's ideas stirred up a huge controversy in Russian criticism, which then became stylized into an opposition between Gogol and Pushkin. The first was elevated by the radicals into an exemplar of what they wished literature to be, an accusation and exposé of the evils of Russian society; the second was celebrated by their opponents as the image of the serene Olympian dedicating his divine gifts to the "eternal" entanglements of the human condition. Both were praised and denounced with equal fervor and equal lack of discrimination; and Dobrolyubov particularly enjoyed heaping scorn on what he called Pushkin's "anthology-pieces" and "toy rattles."[4]

All this began during Dostoevsky's years in prison camp; but he caught up with the polemic once he emerged and began to read the periodicals.

Indeed, since we know that he then started to work on a series of *Letters on Art*, whose subject would have been "essentially, about the significance of Christianity in art,"[5] there is some evidence that he wished to add his own voice to the raging debate. This work, if ever actually written, has not survived; but some glimpse of its ideas may surely be obtained in the texts we are about to discuss.

2

In line with the general policy of *Time*, Dostoevsky tries to dissociate his polemic from any invidious personal connotations. It must frankly be recognized, he writes, that Dobrolyubov "is almost the only one of our critics who is now being read" (18: 72), and it is for this reason that his opinions and judgments are worth the closest attention. Such words, undoubtedly meant to cushion the blow, are also a sincere tribute of admiration for Dobrolyubov's brilliant journalistic talent. At the same time, Dostoevsky also tries to cover his flanks with a broadside against one of the bulwarks of the "Pushkinian" camp, the *Notes of the Fatherland*, as well as with a celebration of the importance of Belinsky. Ironically noting the self-praise of that publication in its announcement for 1861, he singles out for comment a deprecating reference to Belinsky as not having given enough importance to the "historical" study of Russian literature. "In the first place," Dostoevsky retorts, "it is not true, and even if it were, in two pages of Belinsky (an edition of whose works is now in the course of being completed) more is said about the historical aspect of Russian literature than in all the pages of the *Notes of the Fatherland* from 1848 up to the present" (18: 71). No quarter is given to the critic of that journal, S. S. Dudyshkin, who might have been considered one of his allies against Dobrolyubov. Dostoevsky thus publicly aligns himself with the radicals, for whom Belinsky was an unsurpassable master, and establishes his credentials as a nonpartisan commentator who, even if picking a quarrel with Dobrolyubov, can hardly be considered to belong to the party of the enemy.

To begin, Dostoevsky sets the two extreme positions in confrontation with each other and demonstrates that both are self-contradictory. The partisans of the freedom of art, who insist that "art is an end in itself" and hence does not tolerate constraints and directives, at the same time object to "accusatory" literature and its themes. As a result, they infringe the very principle of the freedom of art they presumably wish to defend. The radical Utilitarians demand that art be useful; but, since they are indifferent to artistic quality, they too find themselves in contradiction with their own leading principle: "A work without artistic value can never and in no way attain its goal; moreover, it does more harm than good to its cause; hence the Utilitarians, in neglecting artistic value, are the first to harm their own cause . . . since they seek for benefit and not harm" (18: 79).

Even though both poles are thus rejected as being internally inconsistent, it is obvious that Dostoevsky believes the mistake of the partisans of art to be only a venial sin, while that of the Utilitarians implies a denial of the very right of art to exist. It is true, Dostoevsky acknowledges, that Dobrolyubov does not specifically go to such lengths; but Chernyshevsky *had*, after all, compared art to school texts whose "purpose is to prepare the student for reading the original sources and later to serve as reference books from time to time."[6] And even if the Utilitarians do not openly reject art, they not only hold it in very low esteem but seem to harbor an irritable resentment against artistic quality as such; if not, why do they "detest Pushkin, and label all his inspiration as affectations, grimaces, hocus-pocus and grace-notes, while his poems are considered trifles fit only for anthologies?" (18: 79).

As proof of the ultimate contempt of the Utilitarians for art, Dostoevsky singles out Dobrolyubov's praise of Marco Vovchok, whose stories had been translated from Ukrainian into Russian by no less a personage than Turgenev.* Dostoevsky concentrates his fire on one of her stories, *Masha*—a work Dobrolyubov had cited at length with approval—which portrays the inner resistance of a young serf girl to her enslaved condition. Apathetic and slothful as a serf, her character changes and displays the fiercest and most determined energy once her freedom has been purchased by her brother. For Dobrolyubov, this story illustrated the depth of the Russian common people's longing for freedom; it stood as a lesson for all those who, in some obscure corner of their minds, still continued to believe that the Russian peasant was too undeveloped as an individual to harbor any such desire for emancipation. Outraged at such a demeaning conception of the Russian people, Dobrolyubov argued that they were really full of initiative, courage, and energy, and he turned to the statistics of crime to prove his point. In words that startlingly anticipate those Dostoevsky will soon use in *House of the Dead*, he writes: "the strength which lies in them [the Russian common people], finding no free and proper outlet, is compelled to force an unconventional way for itself . . . often in a way fatal to itself."[7]

An authoritative Soviet Russian commentator has argued that Dostoevsky attacked Dobrolyubov because the reformist *pochvennik* refused to accept such a "revolutionary" image of the Russian people; but exactly the opposite happens to be true. Dostoevsky emphatically affirms that, far from

* In view of Turgenev's efforts on behalf of Marco Vovchok, Dostoevsky's criticisms of her may also seem to reflect indirectly on her patron. This is probably why Dostoevsky goes out of his way in the text to render a personal homage to Turgenev. Among the evidence he adduces to prove Dobrolyubov's disdain of art, he mentions that "Mr. —bov has begun to express himself with some sort of special displeasure about Mr. Turgenev, the most artistic of all contemporary Russian novelists." *PSS*, 18: 79-80.

6. N. A. Dobrolyubov, ca. 1860

having any quarrel with Dobrolyubov's opinion of the Russian people, he approves of it wholeheartedly, and he even expresses surprise at Dobrolyubov's conviction that such ideas are not generally accepted.* The tendency of Marco Vovchok's work, Dostoevsky declares firmly, is worthy of the highest praise, "and we are ready to rejoice in [her] activity" (18: 92). But it is one thing to approve of her intentions; it is quite another to overlook the glaring artistic deficiencies of her stories, which, in Dostoevsky's opinion, ruin whatever persuasive power the worthy ideas embodied in them might have exercised.

To prove his point, Dostoevsky simply reprints the extracts from the story given by Dobrolyubov himself; he does not think it necessary to argue the case in detail, allowing the stilted sentiments and casebook reactions to

* "The stories of Marko Vovchok," writes G. M. Fridlender, "were, for Dobrolyubov, an important symptom in Russian literature of the historically significant upswing that could be noted in the life of the people. The *pochvennik* Dostoevsky did not share Dobrolyubov's political position: this was the cause of his heated controversy with Dobrolyubov. . . ." See the otherwise valuable article on Dostoevsky's aesthetics in G. M. Fridlender, *Dostoevsky i Mirovaya Literatura* (Moscow, 1979), 62-100; quotation from p. 93.

speak for themselves. Masha, he comments, is "a tent-show heroine, some sort of bookish creature of the study, not a woman" (18: 90). And if Dobrolyubov thinks that reading *Masha* will cause supporters of serfdom to change their minds, then he is woefully mistaken. How can an author prove that a particular sentiment (for example, a hatred of serfdom) exists among the Russian common people when she lacks the artistic ability to portray characters who resemble Russians at all? The characters of *Masha* are "some sort of supernumeraries out of a ballet dressed up in Russian *caftans* and *sarafans*; they are *paysans* and *paysannes*, not Russian peasant men and women" (18: 92-93). Hence, Dostoevsky informs Dobrolyubov, "artistic form is in the highest degree useful, and useful precisely from *your* point of view" (18: 93). For the falsity of *Masha* will have the very opposite effect from that intended by the author. It will only persuade those who already hold a contemptuous opinion of the Russian peasant that, since no alternative image can be convincingly projected, the time-honored one they still cling to must be accurate.

<hr />

3

If Dostoevsky had been concerned merely to indict the absurdities of both the partisans of art and the radical Utilitarians, and to establish his own independent position in this literary controversy, then he might well have terminated his article after disposing of Marco Vovchok. But he was hunting for bigger game, and his real (though unmentioned) quarry was Chernyshevsky's Feuerbachian aesthetics, with its devaluation of the whole realm of the supernatural and the transcendent and its ultimate aim of exposing art as a substitute religion. No more than Chernyshevsky could he make his argument in any explicit and overt form; but the drift of his words is unmistakable when placed in this context.

For Chernyshevsky, art is merely a deceptive alternative for the material satisfactions of real life and serves as an imaginary surrogate just so long as these satisfactions are withheld. "If a man is obliged to live in the tundras of Siberia . . . ," Chernyshevsky had written, "he may dream of magic gardens with unearthly trees with coral branches, emerald leaves, and ruby fruit, but on transferring his residence to, say, the Kursk province, and being able to roam to his heart's content in a modest but tolerable orchard with apple, cherry, and pear trees. . . . The dreamer will forget not only about *The Arabian Nights* but also about the orange groves in Spain."[8] Dostoevsky, however, categorically rejects the notion that art exists only as an imaginary replacement for the lacks and frustrations of man's material needs. Man has other needs as well, and, Dostoevsky affirms, "art is for man just as much a need as eating or drinking. The need for beauty, and the creations embodying it, are inseparable from man, and without it man would perhaps have no wish to live. Man thirsts for [beauty] . . . and it is perhaps in this that lies the greatest mystery of artistic creation, that the image of beauty which emerges from its hands immediately becomes an idol *without any conditions*" (18: 94).

Dostoevsky, it is clear, is no longer talking about literary criticism and whether Marco Vovchok is or is not a good writer; here he is touching on the relations of art and religion. The images of art have traditionally provided the objects of religious reverence because man has a need to worship such objects—a need to worship something entirely transcending the bounds of human life as he knows it. Man has always displayed an unconditional need for beauty inseparable from his history; without it, as Dostoevsky poignantly suggests, he would perhaps not wish to go on living at all. The creations of art thus immediately become "idols," objects of worship, "because the need for beauty develops most strongly when man is in disaccord with reality, in discordance, in struggle, that is, *when he lives most fully*, for the moment at which man lives most fully is when he is seeking something, when he wishes to attain something; it is then that he displays the most natural desire for everything that is harmonious and serene, and in beauty there is harmony and serenity" (18: 94). For Dostoevsky, as well as for Chernyshevsky, this quest is the result of a lack in the real world of human struggle and deprivation; but there can be no question for Dostoevsky of bridging the gap between the real and the ideal merely by material means. Since man "lives most fully" in Dostoevsky's universe only when he in *disaccord* with reality, it is evident that the novelist's vision of what is ultimately important in human life totally differs from that of Chernyshevsky. Indeed, the idea that man could ever attain entire and total contentment with his life on earth is linked by Dostoevsky with images of the death of the spirit and of moral decadence. At such moments, Dostoevsky writes, "it is as if life slowed down, and we have even seen examples of how man, having attained the ideal of his desires, not knowing what to strive for any longer, satisfied to the gills, fell into some kind of melancholy, even provoking such melancholy in himself; how he sought for another ideal in his life, and, satiated beyond measure, not only failed to value what he enjoyed but even consciously diverged from the proper path, stimulating in himself tastes that were eccentric, unhealthy, stinging, discordant, sometimes monstrous, losing the feel for, and the aesthetic sense of, healthy beauty and demanding the exceptional in its stead." To adopt, as an ideal for mankind, the aim of the fullest material satisfaction is thus the equivalent of encouraging moral perversity and corruption. For this reason, a genuine "beauty" embodying the "eternal ideals" of mankind—ideals of harmony and serenity far transcending the human realm—is "an indispensable exigence of the human organism" (18: 94). Only such ideals, which man continually struggles to attain and to realize in his own existence, can prevent him from sinking into apathy and despair.

4

This conception of beauty as some form of transcendent expression of mankind's eternal ideals provides Dostoevsky with a vantage point from which to combat the narrow definition of "usefulness" in Utilitarian aesthetics. For if art is entrusted with the task of expressing mankind's eternal ideals, then to prescribe a particular role for it in terms of "utility" implies that one knows in advance the outcome of the entire historical destiny of the human race. But such knowledge, of course, is outside the human ken: "How, indeed, can one determine clearly and independently exactly what must be done to arrive at the ideal of all our desires, to achieve everything that humanity wishes and toward which it aspires?" Since we cannot do this, "how [can we] determine *in full certainty* what is harmful and useful"; indeed, we cannot even tell how, and in what degree, art has been "useful" to humanity in the past.

Who would have predicted, for example, that the works of two "old fogies" such as Corneille and Racine could play "a decisive and unexpected part in the circumstances of the historical life of a whole people" (that is, during the French Revolution) (18: 78)? The manifold ways in which art interacts with society are impossible to foresee; works that seem to have no direct social relevance at all may well, under certain circumstances, exercise the most powerful and direct influence on the life of action. But if we are not able to understand exactly how this comes about, "it is very possible that we also delude ourselves too when we strictly and imperatively dictate mankind's occupations and show art the normal path of its usefulness and its genuine mission." The Utilitarians wish to limit art to the social needs of the present, and regard any concern with the past—such as an admiration for *The Iliad*—as shameful escapism, a retreat into self-indulgent enjoyment and idle dilettantism. Dostoevsky recognizes the moral concern motivating such a position, and says that "this is why we feel so much sympathy for them [the radicals] and wish them to be respected" (18: 95-96); but their ideas are erroneous all the same and must be rejected.

In the first place, since Russian culture has now become part of European civilization as a whole, it is only natural for Russian writers to draw freely on the common treasures of "the historical and universally human" (18: 99). Moreover, a contemporary writer can use the past to express the most burning issues of the present—a point Dostoevsky illustrates by a brilliant analysis of a poem, *Diana*, written by the *bête noire* of the radical critics, the lyricist A. A. Fet. This finely chiseled little work, quite Parnassian in feeling, describes a moment of disappointed expectation: the poet suddenly imagines that a statue of the goddess Diana will come to life and descend from her pedestal to walk through the streets of Rome. But, alas! "the motionless marble / whitely gleamed before me with unfathomable beauty" (18: 97).

Dostoevsky interprets the poem, especially these last two lines, as "a passionate appeal, a prayer before the perfection of past beauty, and a hidden inner nostalgia for that same perfection which the soul is seeking, but which it must long continue to seek, while long continuing to be tormented with birth-pangs before it is found" (18: 97). The "hidden inner nostalgia" that Dostoevsky discerns in this text is surely a longing for a new theogony, a new apparition of the sacred that would come to replace the beautiful, though lifeless, pagan idol; it is a longing for the birth of Christ, for the God-man who was indeed one day to walk on earth and supplant the immobile and distant Roman goddess. And since Dostoevsky has described his own time as one of "striving, struggle, uncertainty, and faith (because our time is a time of faith)," he interprets Fet's poem as expressing the most urgent of contemporary themes.*

These reflections on art conclude with a single sentence that, Dostoevsky believes, resolves the conflict between the two entrenched misunderstandings, and which he prints as an independent paragraph in italics: "*Art is always actual and real, has never existed in any other way, and, most important, cannot exist in any other way*" (18: 98). This idea was first expressed in Russian criticism by Valerian Maikov, Dostoevsky's close friend in the 1840s (whose untimely death is mentioned briefly and with great regret at the beginning of his article); and Dostoevsky now reiterates it as the cornerstone of his own doctrine. If it sometimes seems that art deviates from reality and is not "useful," this is only because we do not yet know all the ways through which art serves mankind, and because we are, even if

* Dostoevsky's imaginative reading of this poem, which at first may seem somewhat forced, receives some indirect confirmation from the remarks of Roman Jakobson about the symbolic meaning attributed to sculpture in the Russian tradition. "It is important to see," he writes, "that in his poems [those of Pushkin] the statue is most often called *idol*, something which had greatly surprised Tsar Nicholas I in *The Bronze Horseman*. Whether it is Pushkin the atheist, Blok the heretic, or the antireligious poetry of Mayakovsky, Russian poets had been raised in the world of Orthodox customs, and their work, whether intentionally or not, is steeped in *the symbolism of the Eastern Church*. It is the Orthodox tradition, which vehemently forbade sculpture, did not allow it inside churches, and considered it a pagan or diabolic sin (the two notions were the same for the Church), which suggested to Pushkin *the close link uniting statues and idolatry, diabolism and magic*."

Jakobson then quotes Gogol to prove that, "from the Russian point of view, sculpture and the image of paganism" are inseparable. "It [sculpture] was born at the same time as the finite pagan world," Gogol had written, "it expressed [that world] and died at the same time. . . . It was, in the same degree as pagan belief, separated from Christianity by a frontier." Jakobson's article, originally published in Czech, is here quoted from the French translation of his selected criticism. Roman Jakobson, "La Statue dans la Symbolique de Pouchkine," in *Questions de Poétique*, trans. by several hands, ed. Tzvetan Todorov (Paris, 1973), 186-187.

for the most laudable reasons, too narrowly focused on the immediate and the common good. Of course artists themselves sometimes stray from the proper path, and in such cases the efforts of Dobrolyubov and his brethren to call them to order are quite legitimate. But Dostoevsky makes a sharp distinction between criticism, admonition, exhortation, persuasion, and the issuance of what are in effect dictates and ukases as to how artists should create.

All such efforts to regiment art are in any case doomed to futility; no true artist will obey them, and art will go its own way regardless of attempts to bridle its creative caprices. Such attempts are based on a total misunderstanding of the nature of art, which always has responded to, and has never separated itself from, the needs and interests of humankind. Dostoevsky thus defends the liberty of art, not because he rejects the criterion of "utility," but "precisely with the certainty that the freer art will be in its development, the more useful it will be to the interests of humanity" (18: 102). Once again he takes up a totally original position, arguing both for the liberty *and* the utility of art, but—most important of all—defining such "utility" in terms of man's eternal striving to incorporate within his life the inspiration of a supernatural religious ideal.

This crucial aspect of Dostoevsky's argument has been relatively neglected, but it is of fundamental importance for an understanding of his own gradually evolving view of life. It is significant, for example, that the instances of sane and healthy "beauty" he refers to—*The Iliad*, the *Apollo of Belvedere*, the poem of Fet—all have religious connotations, if only pagan ones, and he even goes out of his way to stress this point in a remark. "This marble is a god," he says, speaking of the *Apollo*, "and spit at it as much as you like, you will not rob it of its divinity. . . . There are, of course, thousands of impressions in the world, but surely it is not for nothing that this sort of impression is a special one, the impression of a god" (18: 78).* Even though Dostoevsky limits himself to examples from classical antiquity, this line of reasoning could easily culminate in an affirmation of the importance of "Christianity in art." Shortly after leaving prison camp in 1854, Dostoevsky had written that nothing in the world was "more beautiful" than the figure of Christ;[9] and it was this beauty that provided moral inspiration for the modern world just as the gods of Greek and Roman mythology had done for antiquity.[10] Probably for reasons of ideological strategy, he deliberately underplays this Christian aspect of his argument and takes refuge in the Greco-Roman past; but it was not from the religion of the Greeks and Romans that Dostoevsky expected any answer to the anguishing questions confronting both modern Russia and modern man.

---

* Dostoevsky is here paraphrasing a famous poem of Pushkin, "The Poet and the Crowd," in which the poet scornfully tells the benighted mob: "The Apollo Belvedere is for you an idol. / In him no usefulness—usefulness—do you discern." For the Russian text, *PSS*, 18: 289.

What Dostoevsky says only by implication in this article is expressed quite
openly in another essay written several months later. At this point, he is no
longer polemicizing with Dobrolyubov and the radicals but with that
staunch pillar of the régime, the editor of *The Russian Messenger* M. N.
Katkov, and the issue at stake is not aesthetics but women's liberation.
More will be said about this quarrel in the next chapter; here we shall only
focus on a striking analysis of Pushkin's poem *Egyptian Nights* (included
in a story with the same title) that Dostoevsky offered in support of his
views.

The poem, one of his old favorites, describes Cleopatra offering to spend
a night with any male member of her entourage who will agree to forfeit his
life at dawn in return for enjoying the supreme privilege of her favors.
Pushkin paints her challenge in voluptuous detail as she dwells on the delights awaiting the man (or men) intrepid enough to accept her fatal invitation; and Katkov had spoken censoriously of the work as inadmissibly giving voice to "the ultimate expressions of passion," as brazenly uncovering
a secret that "should never see the light of day" (19: 134). To Dostoevsky,
however, such a view was appallingly short-sighted and indicated a total
incapacity to appreciate poetry. Undertaking to enlighten Katkov as to the
real significance of the poem, he returns to some of the issues raised in his
debate with Dobrolyubov; and one has the distinct impression that this
reading is another fragment of his lost treatise on the role of Christianity in
art.

Far from being immoral, as Katkov suggests, the poem exudes for Dostoevsky an expression of "frightful terror . . . the illustration of a perversion
of human nature reaching such a degree of horror . . . that the impression
left by it is no longer scabrous but frightening." For Dostoevsky, the poem
vividly embodies the moral-psychic disorder induced by satisfaction and
satiation—by that absence of any spiritual ideal whose effects had already
been diagnosed in his earlier essay. Cleopatra's world is one in which
"all faith has been lost," and since "the future offers nothing, everything
must come from the present, life must be nourished only by what exists."
This is manifestly the universe as Chernyshevsky would have wished it to
be, existence shorn of whatever splendors of the imaginary or transcenden-
tal it may once have contained. In such a world, "everything takes refuge
in the flesh, everything is thrown into fleshly debauchery, and, to supply
the lack of higher spiritual impressions, the nerves and the body are goaded
with everything capable of arousing the sensibility. The most monstrous
perversions, the most abnormal acts, little by little become customary" (19:
135-136).

Cleopatra is "the representative of this type of society," and the poet depicts her in a moment of boredom (*skuka*) when only a "violent sensation" can relieve her tedium. She has already exhausted all the byways of eroticism, and "perhaps the Marquis de Sade would only be a child by comparison." Now something extra is needed, and what stirs in her soul is "a fierce and ferocious" irony—the irony of her contempt as she watches her subjects tremble at her challenge, an irony spiced with the dreadful joy of anticipation as she mingles sensuality with the cruelty of an executioner. Never had she known anything so savagely exciting, and her soul gloats with the repulsive delight of the female spider "who, it is said, devours the male at the instant of sexual union" (19: 136). Of the three men who aspire to Cleopatra's couch, two—a hardened Roman warrior, and a young disciple of Epicurus, ready to trade his life for a night of pleasure—do not arouse any particular response in the queen's breast. But the third, a nameless boy, his face alight with "the violence of a virgin passion," does not leave her unmoved: "On him the scornful queen permitted / Briefly a grieving look to rest."[11]

These lines are not cited, but Dostoevsky translates their emotion into the fleeting awakening of a spark of moral feeling: "He looked into the queen's countenance, and there was so much ecstasy, so much limitless happiness, so much radiant love in his eyes, that a human being suddenly awoke in the hyena, and the queen looked at the youth with a glance of sympathy. She was still capable of being stirred by compassion!" Pushkin, Dostoevsky surmises, was not able to bear the picture he had himself painted. The poet could not rest content with Cleopatra as monster, and "for an instant he makes her human"; but this instant passes as quickly as it came, and only adds an additional *frisson* to the unholy joys that she anticipates. "You understand much more clearly now," Dostoevsky explains to his readers, "what sort of people it was to which our divine redeemer descended. And you understand much more clearly the meaning of the word: redeemer" (19: 137).

If we transpose this remarkable reading from the classical past to mid-nineteenth-century Russia, we immediately obtain the outlines of much of Dostoevsky's own world, with some of his major themes and his entire psychology of decadence. Indeed, in the novel he was then writing, *The Insulted and Injured*, Dostoevsky was in the course of making this transposition himself; his villain, Prince Valkovsky, is the first Russian embodiment of the psychology of the Cleopatra-type, which will reappear in such figures as Svidrigailov, Stavrogin, and the elder Karamazov (who says of himself, "I've got quite the countenance of an ancient Roman patrician of the decadent period") (14: 22).* It is no accident that, three years

---

* In her excellent study of the poetics of *The Brothers Karamazov*, V. E. Vetlovskaya cites this curious remark and links it with her view that an important influence on the narrative perspec-

later, Cleopatra turns up in *Notes from Underground* sticking gold pins into her slave girls for amusement.

Since Pushkin's poem is set within the period of the Greco-Roman decline, and the imagery of Fet's poem can easily be linked with this period of history, Dostoevsky's preoccupation with decadence is justified in both cases by the texts themselves. It should be pointed out, however, that the late Greco-Roman world had also just then taken on a symbolic contemporary meaning as a result of the ongoing social-cultural debate. All through the 1850s, Herzen had compared the state of western Europe after 1848 with that of Rome in its decline; and he spoke of Europe's eventual revitalization by the impending Russian social revolution as parallel to the moral rejuvenation provided for the ancient world by the arrival of Christianity. To counter this Slavophil-colored prognosis, Chernyshevsky had taken up the cudgels on behalf of the West; and in a resounding article, *On the Reasons for the Fall of Rome* (1861), he had tried to demonstrate that the Roman Empire had been brought to its knees by the attacks of the barbarians rather than through inner spiritual decay. Dostoevsky and Herzen thus shared much the same historical-philosophical vision of a declining European civilization destined to be redeemed by Russian Christianity. But while Herzen was simply using an historical analogy (though he did believe that the morality of the Russian peasant was purer and more Christian than that of the rapacious European bourgeoisie), Dostoevsky accepted this historical imagery as containing a literal truth. The loss of a religious ideal in the West had turned Europe into a society similar to that of Rome in its decadence, where various forms of moral disorder and perverted sensuality pullulated uncontrollably; and the Western ideas now being propagated by the radicals would have exactly the same effect in Russia.

6

Nothing more on art of comparable importance to the article on Dobrolyubov appeared from Dostoevsky's pen in *Time* during 1861 or later. Nonetheless, in 1861 the journal did print two unsigned pieces on aesthetic matters that are usually attributed to Dostoevsky.* One is a review of the

---

tive of the novel was the hagiographic pattern of the life of St. Aleksey, the man of God. St. Aleksey was supposed to have been born in Rome at the end of the fourth century, the son of a wealthy Roman notable.

My own remark is not intended to contest this observation, but rather to strengthen it by showing how often, and how early, Dostoevsky's imagination linked moral decadence with this late Roman period and saw his own times as assailed by very similar problems. V. E. Vetlovskaya, *Poetika Romana "Bratya Karamazovy"* (Leningrad, 1977), 169.

* These two essays were not included by N. N. Strakhov in the list of unsigned articles by Dostoevsky that he gave to Mme Dostoevskaya after her husband's death. Ever since, there has been continuous controversy over whether they should be included among his works. After careful consideration of the opposing arguments, the most recent student of the sub-

annual exposition of the Academy of Art in Petersburg for 1860-1861; the other is devoted to the sketches of a new writer, N. V. Uspensky, who belonged to a group of young plebeian authors encouraged by *The Contemporary*. Neither article rises to the heights of the controversy with Dobrolyubov, and the issue both raise—that of realism versus naturalism, of what it means to depict "reality" in art—is approached more on the level of artistic practice than of theory. Still, both help us to come somewhat closer to Dostoevsky's own conception of realism.

Dostoevsky did not often write on the plastic arts (only one later article of the same kind is included in *The Diary of a Writer*), but he was capable of responding very strongly to their appeal. Not a connoisseur (if by this we mean someone sensitive to the purely sensuous or plastic appeal of the visual media), he considered them solely as a means for conveying impressions and ideas; and his attention always focuses on the human meaning or content of the works he is considering. Within these limits, however, he is a very acute observer, and his forceful comments indicate the intensity with which he reacted—an intensity that later inspired him to use Holbein the Younger's *Descent from the Cross* as a key symbol in *The Idiot*, and Claude Lorrain's *Acis and Galatea* both in the suppressed chapters of *The Devils* and later in *A Raw Youth*.

The big hit of the Academy show in Petersburg that year was the painting of a young artist named V. I. Yakobi (who later became very well-known and quite academic) depicting a party of prisoners resting at one of the way stations along their route to Siberia. Such a canvas would have been impossible to exhibit earlier, and the subject alone was enough to attract the attention of a socially conscious public; but the artist had also done his best to draw out the full political pathos of his theme. At the center of the picture lay the still-shackled corpse of a convict on a broken-down peasant cart; one hand of the dead man, dangling over the side, bore a ring with a precious stone visible on a finger. It was clear, Dostoevsky observes, that "he was not a vagabond, an assassin or a thief" (19: 152); evidently he was an upper-class prisoner—hence a political one—who had reached the end of his thorny road. A repulsive-looking fellow convict, crouching under the cart, is stealthily removing the ring from the lifeless hand. The officer in charge of the way station, with a completely impassive expression and still smoking his pipe, checks on the death by raising the eyelid of the corpse. Other prisoners are scattered around the cart, some playing cards, all utterly unconcerned with the tragic demise of their comrade.

Dostoevsky, who knew whereof he spoke in such matters, approves of the picture as unquestionably verisimilar: "everything was just so in nature as the artist presents it on the canvas, if, that is, you look at nature only on the surface" (19: 153). The picture, he agrees, presents the scene as it

---

ject, G. M. Fridlender, concludes that the weight of the evidence warrants assigning them, either in whole or in large part, to Dostoevsky. See the lengthy discussion in *PSS*, 19: 314-321.

7. A detail from V. I. Yakobi, *A Halt of the Convicts*, 1861. From
Istoria Russkogo Iskusstva (Moscow, 1960)

might have been viewed through a photographic apparatus or reflected in
a mirror; but such a reproduction is "the absence of art" rather than its accomplishment. Dostoevsky misses a distinctly personal response of the artist to the scene, some reaction inspiring a deeper grasp of the diverse characters he was portraying: "In antiquity, it would have been said that he
should look with the eyes of the body, but above all with the eyes of the soul,
or the eyes of the spirit. Let him see the 'unfortunates' under arrest as human beings, and let him show this to us" (19: 154). Although the officer of
the way station had been toughened to such sights by his job, it would still
not have been impossible to depict him in a different light—as, for example,
in the poem by N. I. Ogarev, "The Tale of a Way Station Officer," published
in Herzen's *The Polar Star* (*Polyarnaya Zvezda*) in 1859. (Since the author
was, like Herzen, a political exile in London, Dostoevsky mentions only the

title of the poem, not the name of the poet or the banned publication in which it had appeared.)

Why, Dostoevsky asks, such a deplorable lack of inner substance in Ya-kobi's picture? No doubt because of the training that art students received in the Academy, a training that emphasized only the surface duplication of reality. "This is a very useful and necessary effort," he admits, "and very praiseworthy for a student of the Academy. But this is still only the me-chanical side of art, its alphabet and orthography" (19: 154). Something more is needed to turn a copy into a work of art, and what is lacking can be supplied only by a more determined attempt of the artist to grasp the hu-man significance of what he has observed. The same criticism, also made of other pictures in the exhibition, is obviously related to Dostoevsky's own early literary work, which had reacted against the external portrayal of lower-class types in the physiological sketches of the 1840s (called daguer-rotypes), as well as against the comic, puppetlike grotesques of Gogol's Petersburg stories. His own ambition had been to portray such types from the inside—to see and depict them as fully sentient human beings rather than as stereotypes.

Two other painters also lead to reflections directly linked with Dostoev-sky's own artistic concerns. Criticizing a well-known specialist of sea-scapes for overdoing his effects, Dostoevsky finds a literary analogy for this defect in the works of Alexandre Dumas. It is true, he acknowledges, that "all art consists in a certain amount of exaggeration, but with this reserva-tion, that one should not overstep a certain limit" (19: 162). Where this limit should be drawn was a question that continued to plague Dostoevsky all his life. Another painting, beautifully executed, is marred by an impos-sible subject; it depicts a young girl, evidently soon to die of tuberculosis, surrounded by her sorrowing family. "Death in itself is a repulsive affair," Dostoevsky comments, "but waiting for it is even more repulsive"; and no one has "ever succeeded in making the repulsive beautiful" (19: 167). The picture enshrines an unrelieved agony that most people will find unendur-able, and Dostoevsky cannot imagine who would wish to hang such a can-vas on the wall. Grappling with this same artistic problem himself in *The Idiot*, where he portrays the tubercular young Ippolit also in the process of dying, Dostoevsky tries to solve it by dramatizing the revolt of the dying character against his fate. For the moment, though, he remarks only that "the truth of art is not at all the same as—it is something entirely different from—the truth of nature" (19: 167).

7

The article on Uspensky's stories also involves the question of realism, and the degree to which true artistry differs from a simple attempt at literal mi-mesis. Chernyshevsky had written an enthusiastic piece about Uspensky called *Has Not the Change Already Begun?*—the "change" being a shift in the attitude of Russian literature toward the peasantry as previously reflected in the works of such gentry writers as D. V. Grigorovich, Turgenev, Saltykov-Shchedrin, and others. These authors had tended to idealize the peasantry, or at least to soften and smooth over the more repellent aspects of its cultural backwardness. As the son of a poor country priest, Uspensky made no attempt in his sketches of peasant life to conceal the ignorance and uncouthness of the people. "The public considers the small pieces of Mr. Uspensky to be worthy of notice," wrote Chernyshevsky. "Why is this so? It seems to us that the reason is not solely because of his unquestionable talent. . . . Mr. Uspensky possesses another quality that strongly pleases the best part of the public. He writes the truth about the people without any adornment."[12]

While by no means hostile to Uspensky, and giving quite a sensitive and discriminating analysis of his quality as a writer, Dostoevsky thinks that Chernyshevsky's praise is exaggerated. In the first place, he refuses to agree that Uspensky brings anything *new* to the portrayal of the people not already present in Ostrovsky, Turgenev, Pisemsky, and Tolstoy. And though he is ready to concede that the gentry writers did not yet see *all* the truth about the people (Dostoevsky does not think that the time has yet arrived for this to be possible), it was a momentous event when they began to see *some* of the truth: "They were the *first* to look at the people, to look from a new and in many respects correct point of view, and to announce in literature the consciously new idea about the people held by the upper class of our society; and this, for us, is what is most noteworthy about them. For in these views everything is contained: our development, our hopes, our history" (19: 178-179). These views led, in other words, to the liberation of the serfs, and are the harbinger of the future fusion of the classes that Dostoevsky so ardently desired.

Consequently, Dostoevsky does not believe that Uspensky is "*the founder* of some sort of new view in the description of the people's existence"; even one of the best stories in his book (*Grushka*) "is only a drop squeezed from a third-rate character of Ostrovsky." Uspensky's technique is compared to that of someone setting up a camera on a public place without choosing any particular point of view. "As a result, everything that happens in any corner of the place will be reproduced accurately, just *as it is*." If, at that moment, an aerial balloon descended (as might happen) or if the tail of a dog intruded for a moment from beyond the frame, both would be reproduced, even though they had nothing to do with the picture "or, better, the idea of this picture." Criticizing Uspensky for an excess of such superfluous and irrelevant detail, Dostoevsky refuses to accept the argument that such an approach guarantees accuracy. "This is confusion, not accuracy," he insists (19: 179-180); and even though Uspensky's admirers praise his presumably objective and "unbiased" view of his material, in fact no such view can possibly exist.

Every artist, Dostoevsky declares, raises to consciousness some aspect of life that had previously existed in unremarked obscurity; it is only the artist who calls this aspect of the world to our attention and gives it a name. "Of course, the most important thing here is what the artist himself is capable of seeing, what constitutes his own particular point of view—is he humane, discerning, civic-minded, and finally, is he an artist?" (18: 181). Dostoevsky thus once again vigorously rejects any notion that the artist simply reproduces nature in some slavish and passive fashion. Every artist has his own angle of vision; what he offers is inevitably a product of his subjectivity; but its value is not simply a function of the peculiarities of his temperament. Dostoevsky insists both on the importance of an artist's personal contribution (what he calls, in relation to himself, "fantasy"), as well as on the necessity for such "fantasy" to be oriented toward the society of its time, that is, "realism." It is precisely as such a "fantastic realism" that he will later define his own artistic quintessence.

Despite all his reservations, Dostoevsky's ultimate judgment on Uspensky is generally favorable. Although refusing Chernyshevsky's attempt to elevate this writer above his gentry-liberal predecessors, he agrees that Uspensky's pitiless portrayal of the peasantry does not spring from any hostility. For the young writer "loves the people, not for this, that, or the other reason, but he loves them as they are. For him everything in the people is precious, every trait; this is why he values every trait." Seeming to be cold and impassive, he neither brings out the good sides of the people nor blames the bad; it is up to the reader to draw his own conclusions; but, Dostoevsky adds, "there are indications that his impassiveness does not arise from indifference or inner insensibility" (19: 182-183). On the contrary, Uspensky loves the people with all their faults; and since this laudable emotion triumphs over the manifold artistic weaknesses of his work, Dostoevsky finally joins Chernyshevsky—though from quite a different point of view—in praising this promising new recruit to the ranks of Russian literature.[13] He will be much less diplomatic, as we shall see in the next chapter, when taking issue with representatives of other currents of Russian social-cultural opinion.

CHAPTER 8

Polemical Skirmishes

Written with a good deal of verve, but not at all in a hostile tone, Dostoevsky's essay did not elicit any immediate riposte from *The Contemporary*. Dobrolyubov was then in Italy struggling against the last stages of the tuberculosis that killed him a year later; Chernyshevsky was devoting all his literary energies to social questions; and Dostoevsky had, after all, stressed his agreement with the radical image of the liberty-loving Russian people. Most of the other journals, also engaged in arguments with *The Contemporary*, commented favorably on Dostoevsky's article; even a committed progressive like Aleksey Pleshcheev, a personal friend of Dobrolyubov, greeted it with approval. Writing to Turgenev, then in Europe and eager for the latest literary news from home, he remarks that Dostoevsky had published a long article discussing "the views of *The Contemporary* on art" and "containing a sensible protest against such views."[1]

Dostoevsky's notebooks for 1861-1862, which have only recently become available in their entirety, include some entries indicating that he planned to continue sparring with *The Contemporary* on the same issue. Under the title of *Utility and Morality*, he sketched a series of essays elaborating on his objections to the Utilitarian approach to art: "Shakespeare. His uselessness. Shakespeare was a backward person . . . (the opinions of *The Contemporary*)" (20: 152).[2] Chernyshevsky had indeed questioned whether Shakespeare had really done anything to improve the life of the society of his time; and his crushing answer had been: "As a poet, he did not give this any thought."[3] Even though these projected essays were never written, Dostoevsky did not forget this particular outrage against the English dramatist he revered. Later, he would place an impassioned defense of Shakespeare in the mouth of his marvelous Stepan Trofimovich Verkhovensky—the embodiment of the gentry-liberal ideals of the 1840s—when he replies in *The Devils* to the jeering, yelling mob shouting the slogans of the 1860s derived from such remarks as Chernyshevsky's.

Despite the attack on Dobrolyubov, and the efforts of Strakhov and Grigoryev, *Time* generally managed to preserve its progressive reputation during the first year of publication; nor is this surprising if we glance at its position on most of the vital questions of the day. When confronted with the swarm of problems arising from the liberation of the peasantry, and within the limits permitted by the censorship, *Time* invariably favored the interests of the peasants against those of the landowners and the bureaucracy. *Time* also highlighted the plight of the proletariat in Europe and strongly defended Engels's *Condition of the Working Class in England*, with its terrible pictures of proletarian misery, against the criticisms of the German economist Bruno Hildebrand. In one of the earliest references to Engels's work in the Russian press, the writer of the *Time* article calls him "the most gifted and learned of all German Socialists"; and Socialism as an economic theory (euphemistically called "association") was unambiguously championed in *Time* against *laissez-faire* doctrines. Proudhon, known to be close to Herzen, was always referred to with great respect.[4]*

Dostoevsky also directed his brisk polemical fire primarily against non-radical publications, and even aligned himself with the radicals against what he considered excessive severity on the part of their opponents. Without wishing to be identified with their particular opinions, he strove to preserve the status of a disinterested and understanding ally who sympathized with their ultimate moral-social aims while deploring the regrettable excesses to which they were prone. At the same time, he defended the achievements of Russian literature, both past and present, equally against the Russian Westerners and the Slavophils; and while acknowledging his admiration for the Slavophil conception of Russian nationality, he also sep-

---

* Among the other indications of *Time*'s progressivism, and in view of Dostoevsky's later anti-Semitic utterances, it is worth noting the defense of the Jews contained in the February 1862 issue of the journal. A new law stipulating that Jews with university degrees were eligible for posts in all branches of the civil service prompted the Slavophil *Day* to protest against opening administrative positions to "a handful of individuals, thoroughly denying Christian teachings, Christian ideals and ethics . . . and professing an inimical and antagonistic doctrine. . . ."

Time responded immediately by charging that those who defended Christianity by attacking the Jews were "pitiable friends who do more harm to Christianity than do its enemies!" The writer then goes on to argue that, "if there is, within Judaism, something inherently harmful to Christianity, then the preservation of Christian society from this evil can be found only within its faith." But *Day* wishes to protect Christianity with legal safeguards; "and before you know it, it will be seeking it by fire and sword!" The author concludes: "It is not this spirit, it seems to us, that inspired the teachings of Him in whose name *Day* is apparently speaking. The teachings of peace, love, and concord should have prompted other thoughts and other words."

Whether Dostoevsky wrote this article has never been established. Various scholars have also attributed it to Strakhov and, more recently, to a younger contributor, M. I. Vladislavlev, who later married Dostoevsky's niece and had a distinguished academic career as a philosopher; but Dostoevsky certainly gave it his approval as editor-in-chief. David Goldstein, who has written the best work on the question of Dostoevsky and the Jews, believes that he did so only to curry favor with a radical readership.

Such a "skeptical and cynical interpretation of *Time*'s utilization of the Jewish question for its own ends" (these are Goldstein's own words) must of course be accepted as a possibility. But this does not rule out the alternative possibility that *Time* genuinely meant what it said. After all, Dostoevsky *did* believe that Christianity, particularly its Eastern Orthodox variety, was a religion of spiritual freedom that excluded persecution—even though, as time went on, he found this conviction more and more difficult to reconcile with his increasing antipathy to the Jews. The question seems to me less black and white than Goldstein tends to make it; there is no reason to assume that Dostoevsky, whose feelings were constantly shifting about so many other matters, was always a firm and immutable anti-Semite. Whatever the motive, the fact remains that, in the chronicle of internal affairs in *Time*, the Jews were constantly defended against the attacks being made against them. See V. S. Nechaeva, *Zhurnal M. M. i F. M. Dostoevskikh, "Vremya," 1861-1863* (Moscow, 1972), 272-273; David I. Goldstein, *Dostoevsky and the Jews* (Austin, Tex., 1981), chap. 3; also my own remarks in the foreword to that book, ix-xv.

arated himself sharply, just as Herzen had done, from the more retrograde aspects of their social-political views.

2

Dostoevsky's "progressivism," with all its hesitations and reservations, was very much in evidence in the position he took regarding a quarrel that burst out in the spring of 1861 over the explosive "woman question." The uproar began, innocently enough, with a newspaper account of a literary evening in the provincial town of Perm. As part of the festivities, Pushkin's *Egyptian Nights* had been read aloud by the wife of a local official whose rendition created a small scandal. A worthy and heavily bemedaled officer had loudly protested against such an immoral poem being declaimed in public by a member of the female sex, and the indignant recitalist stoutly defended both Pushkin and women's rights with equal, if not greater, vehemence and volume. Peter Weinberg—the same who had organized the theatrical presentation for the Literary Fund—then decided to liven up his rather dull journal *The Century* (*Vek*) by reprinting passages from the newspaper dispatch dealing with the incident. What stirred up the additional fuss, however, was his facetious embellishment of the newspaper account.

Some members of the Perm audience, he insinuated, listening to Mme Tolmachev with rapture, may possibly have stood in the same relation to her as "the admirers of Cleopatra." To make matters worse, he affirmed that the writings of John Stuart Mill and M. L. Mikhailov (who had recently begun to publicize the issue of women's rights in *The Contemporary*) had now been put in the shade, and that perhaps "the campaign for the emancipation of women" had really begun with the bold Mme Tolmachev, in the guise of Cleopatra, passionately declaiming her offer of an incomparable night of love.[5] Weinberg's patently offensive remarks led to a general journalistic donnybrook, and Dostoevsky's comments reveal his very cautious approach to this extremely delicate subject. For while castigating the malicious damage caused by Weinberg's innuendos to the reputation of an innocent lover of Pushkin, he also suggested that Mme Tolmachev might have gone too far and acted "a bit flightily and inopportunely." He strongly defended her right to read the poem in public, and declared himself in favor of women's rights "with all my heart"; but perhaps Russian society was not yet ready to accept such behavior, and its sensibilities should not have been ruffled while progress was being made in wiping out prejudice (19: 102-103).

Dostoevsky did not contribute any further to the exchange of unpleasantries over Mme Tolmachev, but he was not allowed to forget her even if he had wished to do so. His intervention on behalf of a "progressive" cause identified with *The Contemporary* distinctly irritated the powerful M. N. Katkov, a bitter enemy of the radicals, whose journal *The Russian Messenger* then proceeded to pillory *Time* and its collaborators with the epithet of "emancipators" (a word that, in Russian, had taken on the meaning of advocating sexual license).

Dostoevsky replied to Katkov's calumny by explaining that his own conception of female emancipation did not mean "the right of every woman to provide horns for her husband each time that the occasion was propitious for doing so." So far as he personally was concerned, Dostoevsky continues, the entire question of emancipation comes down to that of "a Christian love of mankind, to the education of oneself in the name of mutual love—of the love that the woman also has the right to demand for herself" (19: 126). Such a relation between the sexes, which can result only from a proper evolution of society, will be realized naturally in the course of time. Meanwhile, there is nothing wrong—quite the contrary, it is imperative—to debate the issue publicly even if this gives rise to "erroneous theories." At least, Dostoevsky retorts, the "emancipators" are "animated by principles of love of mankind and worthy of sympathy and respect" (19: 127).

3

That Dostoevsky long remembered Mme Tolmachev is indicated by the cynical roué Svidrigailov, who, several years later, smacks his lips in *Crime and Punishment* at the recollection of her provocative performance (6: 216). But the lady's major contribution to Russian culture, besides having elicited from Dostoevsky the interpretation of *Egyptian Nights* discussed in the last chapter, is to have initiated his quarrel with Katkov. Female emancipation, however, was only one among the many subjects hotly disputed between the two all through 1861.

The Russian Messenger at this period was the organ of a moderate liberalism within the Russian social-political spectrum. Katkov greatly admired Tocqueville, praised the English political system as a model, and supported *laissez-faire* economics in the name of individual freedom. Whatever Dostoevsky's reservations about *The Contemporary*, his instinctive democratic populism made him far more hostile to Katkov's advocacy of Western bourgeois liberalism than to the Socialism of the radicals, who at least were defenders of the Russian commune along with the Slavophils. Even though Dostoevsky, as a supporter of the régime, was a political ally of Katkov, his social sympathies were much closer to those of Chernyshevsky. The social-economic articles of *Time* thus resembled those in *The Contemporary* far more than they did those in Katkov's journal; and Katkov's intransigent Westernism also provoked Dostoevsky in other ways—as can be seen from a furious dispute between the two over the present state of Russian culture.

This quarrel arose because *The Contemporary*, unable directly to manifest its increasingly intransigent radicalism, took recourse in the Aesopian tactic of expressing its supreme contempt for those representatives of European liberalism whom Katkov most admired. Such articles drove him into a frenzy, and he tended to look with supreme disdain and detestation at a Russian culture in which the stupidities of *The Contemporary* could gain so wide a following. What could be at the root of the evil if not the whole unhappy past of Russia itself? As a result, Katkov was given to uttering disabused reflections about the so-called achievements of Russian culture, and about the wonders of Russian nationality, that stirred Dostoevsky to a fighting fury.

What they argued about has now mainly an antiquarian interest; but one or two remarks of Dostoevsky are distinctly worth salvaging. In reply to Katkov, he stresses the experiential source of his own convictions about "Russian nationality," which were not derived from theory but from his compulsory contact with the Russian people in Siberia, and his discovery, at that time, of their true nature. To know what "Russian nationality" means, he tells his opponent, "circumstances must have forced you to live with the people, "to share their ideas and interests, at least temporarily, in a practical, immediate fashion, and not solely from a position of superiority." It is only then, "when you will have lived with them [the people], that their character will impress itself on your soul so strongly, so palpably, that you will no longer be able to lose faith in them" (19: 113). In the course of this rebuttal, Dostoevsky also defends *The Contemporary* (and its satirical supplement, *The Whistle*) against Katkov's imprecations, though he does so only indirectly by refusing to concede that all of Russian culture had culminated in the doctrines of the radicals.

Another article also displays Dostoevsky taking sides with *The Contemporary* against Katkov's broadsides. Once again, however, he is exceedingly careful to indicate his rejection of the radicals' "ideas" while defending their right to speak out despite the obvious contradictions in which they become entangled. Dostoevsky's words here are worth the closest attention because they so clearly foreshadow the dialectic of Part I of *Notes from Underground*. Katkov had argued, with a good deal of logic, that in view of the doctrines propounded in Chernyshevsky's *Anthropological Principle in Philosophy*, the radicals were completely inconsistent when they appealed to moral principles and ideals as the basis of their complaints against the existing order: "Whoever sees in man only salts, acids, and chemical alkalis, with the same degree of meaning and force that they have for us in a test tube," has no right to speak "of the rights of man, of his well-being, and of the amelioration of his condition." To which Dostoevsky replied: "I can assure you that I, who write these lines, do not at all think or believe myself to have emerged *entirely* from a test tube. I cannot believe this. But even if this were my conviction, why should this forbid me to speak of the rights of man, of his well-being, and of the amelioration of his condition?" (19: 131).

Dostoevsky thus clearly differentiates his own views from Chernyshevsky's "scientism," and presumably would agree with Katkov that Chernyshevsky was inconsistent in appealing to morality while also reducing mankind to the status of a chemical compound. But he refuses to agree further that such an error deprives Chernyshevsky of the right to raise his voice and be heard on moral-social matters. Instead, exactly as the underground man would soon be doing, Dostoevsky shifts the question from the level of logic to that of psychology and of the ineradicable needs of the human personality. Men, he writes, are required to live together even if only for their mutual advantage; no society is possible unless the obligations of its members toward each other are recognized; and since men cannot escape behaving in their own lives according to some code of morality, they should not be denied the right to discuss its principles.

"Whatever their convictions," Dostoevsky writes, "men must nonetheless remain men, they are not able to destroy their own nature; the instinct of conservation would remain unchanged in them, and besides, man, because he is man, would feel the need to love his neighbor, the need to sacrifice himself for his neighbor, because love is unthinkable without self-sacrifice, and love, we repeat, cannot be destroyed. Man would then have to hate what is his own nature. Can you believe that?" (19: 131-132). Four years later, arguing this time *against* Chernyshevsky, Dostoevsky will dramatize these reflections as a split in the psyche of the underground man. For although the underground man accepts Chernyshevsky's ideas as the very latest word of modern "science," he cannot humanly live with their consequences; it turns out to be impossible for him "to hate what is his own nature" and *entirely* to suppress his moral awareness.

Even in springing to the defense of the radicals, as we thus clearly see, Dostoevsky always does so from his own position and never conceals his disagreement with their theories. But he also never loses sight, at least at this stage of his career, of what he genuinely believed to be the purity of their dominating aim—the aim of bettering the lot of the downtrodden Russian peasant. Dostoevsky, after all, could not so easily forget that he had stood in their ranks just eleven years before; nor could he endure seeing the radicals maligned by those like Katkov, who had never shared their passionate revulsion against injustice and yet now read them lessons in morality. "You began to abuse our 'progressives,' our 'scribblers,' our 'shriekers,' " he tells Katkov, "not only for their enthusiasms and shallowness—let that pass!—no, you had to demonstrate that they are dishonorable people, that they are *dishonest*" (19: 172).

"Really," Dostoevsky retorts, "is a man who makes a mistake necessarily a scoundrel? And sometimes, as a matter of fact, the more deformed the manifestation of life seems to be, the more frantic, the more ugly, the more uncontrolled it is, the more this means that life wishes to appear at any cost—and you say there is no life there. Here is anguish, suffering—but what is that to you?" (19: 175-176). In another passage, he remarks that where Katkov perceives only egregious error and futility, he observes something quite different. "We see there suffering and torments without relief. . . . In the painful search for a way out, [such a person] stumbles, falls. . . . Yes, such people stumble. But why blacken them with the epithet of dishonest?" (19: 173). In Dostoevsky's refusal to accept such insults, we can already catch a glimpse of how he will treat some of his erring characters misled by radical ideologies.

4

The Russian Messenger was by no means the only nonradical journal with which Dostoevsky exchanged potshots during 1861. A favorite target for his ire was *Notes of the Fatherland*, whose literary critic, S. S. Dudyshkin, had had the temerity to declare that Pushkin was not really a "national" poet. For Dostoevsky, such an opinion was not only the height of absurdity but equivalent to sacrilege, and he set out to destroy it in a slashing article that contains a brilliant reading of *Evgeny Onegin.* Just as he had felt called upon to prove to Katkov that *Egyptian Nights* was not "immoral," so now, in another inspired excursus, he sets out to refute Dudyshkin's contention that Pushkin's hero was not "a historical type."

Dostoevsky's furious words almost leap off the page: nothing, he maintains, could be more "national," nothing more "historical," than the personage of Onegin! For "he sums up, with a blinding clarity, all the traits that only a Russian could exhibit at a certain moment of Russian life—namely, the moment when we felt civilization as life itself, not as a capricious foreign transplant, while at the same time all the surprises, all the strange questions—unanswerable in the terms of that period—began for the first time, arising everywhere, to assail Russian society and to force the doors of its consciousness." It was then that the Russian national psyche, feeling perfectly at one with its acquired European civilization, "suddenly began to open its eyes and to see in the Russian life surrounding us some strange phenomena, which did not fit in with our so-called European elements; and we did not know if this was good or bad, monstrous or magnificent" (19: 10).

Dostoevsky interprets Pushkin much as Apollon Grigoryev had done (and was just then doing again) in an important series of articles published by *Time* during 1861 on *The Development of the Idea of Nationality in Russian Literature.* Pushkin incarnated the moment when Russian culture, having assimilated Europeanism through every pore, became conscious that it could never be truly European and was confronted with the problem of its historical destiny. "This was the first beginning of the epoch," Dostoevsky writes, "when our leading people brutally separated into two parties, then entered into a furious civil war. For the Slavophils and Westerners are also a historical phenomenon and in the highest degree national" (19: 10). Common to both Grigoryev and Dostoevsky, this vision of the history of Russian culture would later furnish the novelist with part of the social-cultural groundplan of *The Devils*, where Stavrogin, a reincarnation of the Onegin-type, inspires both Slavophil (Shatov) and Westerner (Kirillov) ideological offshoots.

Indeed, some traits of Stavrogin already begin to emerge as Dostoevsky transforms Grigoryev's sweeping panorama—the history of the coming-to-consciousness of the Russian national psyche—into a complex drama of inner self-discovery. "Onegin's skepticism carries something tragic in its very principle," he writes, "and sometimes sounds with a ferocious irony." He is caught, like Matthew Arnold's traveler in "Stanzas from the Grande Chartreuse," "Wandering between two worlds, one dead, / The other powerless to be born, / With nowhere yet to rest [his] head,"[6] in search of a new ideal to replace the old European one in which, like the entire highly civilized society to which he belongs, he is no longer able fully to believe: "For at bottom, his soul is thirsting for a new truth" (19: 11).

It is impossible here to follow all the subtleties of Dostoevsky's analysis of Onegin's existential anguish, which he sees composed of both a "bitter irony" and a total lack of self-respect because "his conscience murmurs to him that he is a hollow man"; and yet he knows that "he is also not a hollow man: is one hollow when one can suffer?" (19: 11). In any case, he is "a child of his epoch" and represents "an entire epoch which *for the first time* looks at itself." This Onegin-type, becoming part of the consciousness of Russian society, has been reborn and re-elaborated in each new generation: "In the personage of Pechorin [the protagonist of Lermontov's *A Hero of Our Time*] it reached a state of insatiable, bilious malice, and of a strange contrast, in the highest degree original and Russian, of a contradiction between two heterogeneous elements: an egoism extending to self-adoration, and at the same time a malicious self-contempt" (19: 12).

Dostoevsky sees "the jeering mask of Gogol" as revealing the same dilemma, and implies that Gogol "allowed himself to die, powerless to create and precisely to determine an ideal at which he would not be able to laugh." The final stage of the process is found in Turgenev's Rudin and the Hamlet of the Shchigrovsky District (a character in a short story of the same name), who "no longer laugh at their own activity and their own convictions: they believe, and are saved by this faith." Both figures, in other words, are inspired by the humanitarian ideals of the 1840s, particularly by a deep compassion for the people, and hence have been rescued from despair: "they are almost no longer egoists" (19: 12). In this impassioned sketch of the history of the "superfluous man" in Russian literature, the intricacies of Dostoevskian psychology begin to merge with the course of Russian social-cultural development, and the conquest of egoism and the search for faith and an ideal become identical with a rediscovery of the values of the Russian common people.

5
———

These articles are part of the running battle that Dostoevsky waged with the representatives of Russian Westernism, unable to comprehend the treasures of their own culture because blinkered by European ideas of decorum and outmoded literary standards. In a milder and more conciliatory tone, he also fought the same battle in another article devoted to one of the numerous projects then being proposed for an anthology of readings designed to further the education of the people. This problem was much on everybody's mind, and Tolstoy, after writing on the subject in 1861, moved into action a year later to found his school for peasant children in Yasnaya Polyana. *Time*, incidentally, followed Tolstoy's experiments very closely and commented on them with considerable sympathy. Chernyshevsky, while paying due tribute to Count Tolstoy's noble purposes and beneficent aims, scornfully dismissed his educational theories as rubbish.

The project that Dostoevsky examines at length was published in *Notes of the Fatherland*; but since Dostoevsky respected the author and was in sympathy with his purpose, his manner is much less combative than when dealing with Dudyshkin or Katkov. In essence, however, his criticisms—nourished by his own unique exposure to Russian peasant life in Siberia—add up to much the same indictment. The Westernism of the Russian educated class, even those among them with the best will in the world, has incapacitated them for any understanding of how Russian peasants really feel and behave; most of all, they are incapable of approaching their fellow countrymen as fully sentient human beings. The author of the project, for example, laudably stresses that it is essential to appeal to the people as far as possible from *their own* point of view and not from that of their superiors. Yet he explains very carefully that his anthology is organized so as to impart gradually all sorts of useful knowledge, whose diffusion is calculated to eradicate ignorance and prejudice among the regrettably backward denizens of the Russian countryside. Such a noble purpose, Dostoevsky objects, simply condemns the project to be still-born; the people would understand this intention immediately, consider it insulting and derogatory, and shun the book like a plague whatever its other merits. "There is nothing," Dostoevsky insists, "of which a man becomes so quickly aware as the tone you take in speaking to him, your attitude toward him" (19: 28).

For Dostoevsky, the main aim of a reader for the people should not be to instruct or to reform but solely to entertain; what is important is to inculcate a taste for reading, and for this purpose all means are permissible. Instead of filling the book with useful and instructive material like the *Song of Igor* (was this included, Dostoevsky asks caustically, so as to make the Russian people more Russian?) or Russian proverbs—of which the peasant certainly had a greater store than the editor himself—Dostoevsky suggests that the selections should appeal to the imagination and to the people's well-known taste for the strange and the marvelous. Nor was it necessary to limit such choices to Russian sources; extracts from the voyages of Captain Cook and even—horror of horrors!—from the novels of Alexandre Dumas could also be used. At this point, Dostoevsky includes an engaging personal reminiscence that may throw some light on why, when he resumed his literary career, he chose to try his hand at the *roman-feuilleton*, and continued to favor those tightly knit, melodramatic plots that so many of his contemporaries considered evidence of a deplorable literary taste.

"I have personally, in the barracks, listened to a public reading (one soldier read, the others listened) concerning the adventures of a certain Chevalier de Chevarny and the Duchess of La Vergondière. . . . When the action arrived at the moment at which the Duchess renounces her wealth and gives the several millions of her annual revenue to Rose, a lowly *grisette* whom she marries off to the Chevalier, and when she herself becomes a *grisette* to marry Olivier Durand, a simple soldier but of good family, who refuses to become an officer solely so as not to have recourse to dishonorable protectors, the impression produced on the listeners was extraordinary." Dostoevsky adds that, having often read such material aloud himself to similar audiences, "I have always produced an effect by my reading, and this gave me great pleasure and delight" (19: 53). The euphoric impression created by such occasions may well have left Dostoevsky with a desire to captivate his invisible audience of readers by similar literary devices.

One aspect of the project that particularly horrified Dostoevsky was the suggestion that the book be distributed, with the help of the local authorities, at the annual meeting of the commune, and be given as a gift by the elder of each village to all peasants who had learned to read. Dostoevsky can hardly contain his sarcasm at this "patriarchal" notion, taken from the sentimental *contes* of Karamzin about rococo Russian peasants painted on porcelain. And he dashes off a caustic little sketch depicting the bewilderment of a genuine peasant receiving such a "recompense," and wondering, with the help of his equally suspicious fellow villagers, what new deviltry of the authorities lay behind such an incomprehensible event. Any subsidy for such a book, Dostoevsky argues, should be carefully concealed; the work should be sold to the peasant just as any other piece of merchandise because only by such a subterfuge will his mistrust be allayed. Otherwise, he will invariably feel that he is being admonished, lectured at, or hoodwinked in some way and treated as a member of an inferior species.

6

During 1861, Dostoevsky made a clean polemical sweep of the existing so-cial-political ideologies in Russia. Not only did he take on the radical left (*The Contemporary*), the liberal left (*Notes of the Fatherland*), and the liberal center (*The Russian Messenger*), but he also had his word to say about the new Slavophil publication *Day* (*Den*), which represented inde-pendent conservative opinion as distinguished from official government publications. And one may tentatively define his relation to Slavophilism as being the exact obverse of his attitude toward the radicals: while personally unsympathetic to the social biases of the Slavophils, he nonetheless found in their writings a justification for many of his own most intimate idea-feel-ings.

During the 1840s, Dostoevsky had belonged to the camp of the Russian Westerners, who, with Belinsky at their head, had carried on a belligerent campaign against Slavophil ideas. His first novel, *Poor Folk*, praised to the skies by Belinsky, had been considered one of the finest products of the Natural School of young writers; and since the Slavophils looked down with fastidious distaste at the productions of this Westernizing literary tend-ency, Dostoevsky had been severely manhandled in Slavophil literary crit-icism. "Dostoevsky is not an artist and will never be one," wrote Konstantin Aksakov in 1847, curtly dismissing *Poor Folk* with this irrevocable condem-nation.[7] Dostoevsky thus had very good personal reasons for keeping his distance from the Slavophils; but he had always been a Russian nationalist, even at the very height of his Westerner phase, and some of his utterances in the Palm-Durov circle reveal an early stage of that amalgam of Slavophil and Westerner ideas that now dominated the Russian social-cultural scene.[8]

Since the 1840s, like the majority of his contemporaries, Dostoevsky had come to accept certain essential elements of Slavophilism as self-evident truths. One such truth, unflaggingly proclaimed by Herzen and equally ac-cepted by Chernyshevsky, was that the Russian commune—and hence the peasantry who lived according to its precepts—embodied a moral-social principle superior to Western individualism and egoism. Dostoevsky gives the Slavophils full credit for discovering this truth when he declares that they possess "a strong sentiment, perceptive and accurate, of several of the elements (but certainly not all) that lie at the basis of the Russian national personality. There is not a Westerner who has better understood and better described the *mir*, the Russian commune, than K[onstantin]. S. Aksakov in one of his last writings, unfortunately left unfinished" (19: 59). What text of Aksakov Dostoevsky is referring to remains unclear; but it may well be one first published in 1861, and which since then frequently has been cited as classic.

Aksakov here characterizes the ethos of the Russian commune by means of a musical analogy which, as Andrzej Walicki has written, depicts this institution as "the most perfect incarnation of the community principle as a universal norm of human relations."[9] Aksakov writes:

> The commune is an association of people who have renounced their personal egoism, their individuality, and express common accord: this is an act of love, a noble Christian act which expresses itself more or less clearly in its various other manifestations. Thus the commune is a moral choir, and just as each individual voice in the chorus is not lost but only subordinated to the overall harmony, and can be heard together with all the other voices—so too in the commune the individual is not lost but only renounces his exclusivity in the name of general accord and finds himself on a higher and purer level, in mutual harmony with other individuals motivated by a similar self-abnegation; just as every voice contributes to the vocal harmony, so in the spiritual harmony of the commune every personality makes itself heard, not in isolation but as part of the group—and thus you have the noble phenomenon of the harmonious coexistence of rational beings (consciousness): you have fellowship, the commune—the triumph of the human spirit.[10]

Such a specifically Slavophil-Christian interpretation of the commune would hardly have been accepted by either Herzen or Chernyshevsky, who preferred to regard the institution rather as a home-grown and embryonic variety of peasant Socialism that could easily be transformed into a modern Utopian cooperative. All the same, whatever disagreements existed concerning the larger meaning to be attributed to the continued existence of the commune in Russia, or as to what it might portend for the future, everyone concurred that the Russian folk character had not yet been corrupted by individualism. Russian peasant life still contained a certain moral harmony reflected in the democratic egalitarianism of the commune, and the Slavophils had been the first to discern the social-political importance of this providential survival. As we shall see in Chapter 16, Dostoevsky fully shared Aksakov's exalted image of the moral elevation displayed in the quotidian workings of Russian communal life; and there are striking resemblances between what Dostoevsky would later say about the Russian people and the ideal vision of them projected by Aksakov.

This is very far from saying, however, that Dostoevsky should now be considered a convert to Slavophilism. His acceptance of Aksakov's notion of the commune did not mean that he shared the Slavophil position on other questions, and he allows himself the freest rein to formulate his often caustic criticisms. The backward-looking aspects of Slavophilism, its nostalgia for a mythical pre-Petrine past, he simply dismisses as a lament for the lost Boyar privileges of the landed gentry, now living off its vanished glories and clinging to a few faded tintypes ("the panorama of Moscow seen from the Sparrow Hills . . . the siege of Kazan . . . the monastery caves of Kiev, and other historical tableaux depicted in the French style by Karamzin," etc.) (19: 60). This unhealthy devotion to the past is what causes the Slavophils to reject everything flourishing and vital in the Russia of the present—such as, for example, the new Russian literature, the voice of the national conscience, which they continue to malign so viciously and unjustly.

Dostoevsky's indignation was especially aroused by the charge, leveled by the same Konstantin Aksakov he had just praised, that contemporary Russian literature had renounced its nationality "not stirred by a passionately indignant love, but rather by a total impiety, instinctively hostile to all the sanctity of honor and duty" (19: 58). This accusation was tantamount to a personal attack on the integrity of Dostoevsky's own work, and he lashes back with the countercharge that the Slavophils are woefully blinded by prejudice. They do not understand that the Russian literature they castigate—"that passionately negative literature, inspired by a power of derision and voluntary self-criticism without previous precedent in any literature" (19: 60)—is itself a reaction against the excesses and injustices created by that very Westernism the Slavophils also abhor. Russian literature too was now returning to its native soil, but first it had to clear the ground by a ruthless scrutiny of Russian life in the period of "the disintegration of the reforms of Peter the Great" (19: 58). Whatever its defects, modern Russian literature has always been on the side of life, of movement, and of change, and for this reason has succeeded in winning the favor of the public. The Slavophils have remained stagnant and immobile, fixed in their eternal pose of rejection, and thus have never been able to obtain any influence over the mass of Russian opinion.

Another source of outrage was a passage from the pen of the editor of *Day*, Ivan Aksakov, who had attempted to argue that the relations between the Russian serf and his master, unjust though they may have been, were still morally superior to those between the indentured peasants of Western Europe and their feudal overlords. Dostoevsky explodes with fury at such cant and picks Aksakov apart relentlessly word for word: "You say that there was nothing comparable among us to the feudal relations of the Occident? No sir, one was truly no better than the other. Ask the *muzhiki*" (19: 66). This penchant of the Slavophils for defending the morally indefensible out of respect for Russian traditions (though their main spokesmen had been favorable to the liberation of the serfs) displayed that complacent gentry psychology which always continued to grate on Dostoevsky's nerves despite his growing sympathy for so many Slavophil ideas.

7

It should be amply clear by now why *Time*, during its first year of life, acquired the reputation of belonging to the camp of *The Contemporary*, and why Strakhov and Grigoryev were chafing at the bit. Doing what he could to right the balance, Strakhov kept up a steady sniping fire against the radicals in the form of articles written as letters addressed to the editor. Lacking the combative temperament of a true polemicist, he contented himself mainly with pointing out various crudities and absurdities in an amused and superior manner, employing an irony that often made his meaning obscure and was soon to have disastrous consequences for the journal.

Some of his remarks, though, are worth attention both as illustrations of his shrewdness in spotting significant social-political trends and as indications of the touchy nature of his relations with Dostoevsky. In one article (June 1861), he singles out the explosive début of a new young radical publicist, Dimitry Pisarev, who had excitedly announced in *The Russian Word* that all the philosophy of the past was just "useless scholasticism." Strakhov comments that "Pisarev has gone further than all" his fellow radicals on the path of negation: "He rejects everything in the name of one general authority, in the name of *life*, and life he obviously understands as *the alluring variety of lively and unlimited pleasures*."[11] In this very acute observation, Strakhov picks out an important turn of radical ideology toward an unrestrained individualism which, in the very next year, would lead to a schism among the radical intelligentsia of decisive importance for Russian culture in the 1860s.

Another of Strakhov's articles (August 1861) contains some animadversions against "whistling," though he does not mention any names.[12] Much to his annoyance, Dostoevsky appended a footnote: "Voltaire whistled all his life, and not without sense and not without results. (And how furious they were at him, precisely for the whistle.)" (19: 139). Clearly, as the editor of *Time*, Dostoevsky wished to dissociate himself from Strakhov's condemnation of Dobrolyubov and other contributors to *The Whistle*.[13] The reference to Voltaire could have only one meaning: the Russian radicals too were using the lash of satire to further the cause of progress and enlightenment.

It may be thought, perhaps, that Dostoevsky's footnote was only an editorial maneuver prompted by expediency; but a glance at his notebooks is enough to prove that he was genuinely expressing his own point of view. For these private remarks do not reveal any objections to the radicals *in principle*, or any expressions of a personal and deep-rooted animosity. This agreement in substance comes out very clearly in some lengthy notes Dostoevsky made for an article intended to take part in the controversy, then in full swing, over N. I. Pirogov, a remarkable personality who was a famous surgeon as well as a social activist. Pirogov had been a strong and important voice for liberal reform in Russian society, and in the past had been praised by *The Contemporary* for his progressive ideas; but he had recently come under attack for yielding to expediency on the issue of disciplinary flogging for students.

Dostoevsky wished to speak out in Pirogov's defense, but not because he disagreed with Dobrolyubov (Pirogov's implacable assailant) on the main issue. He too believed that Pirogov had been mistaken in having consented, no matter how unwillingly, to retain flogging as a possible punishment in the school district under his supervision. "In everything, you [Dobrolyubov] are completely just," he jots down. "Except for the malice and the tone." What displeased Dostoevsky was the failure to respect Pirogov as an individual: "You pounced on Mr. Pirogov as on a man completely lost, bespattering him with mud, and in the person of Mr. Pirogov you insulted everyone; society is more noble than you thought. It is able to forgive a man. You did not forgive, i.e., you do not value a man, people without humanity" (20: 101). And when Dobrolyubov asked sarcastically in print why Pirogov "did not direct all his efforts toward a *decisive and fundamental* change," Dostoevsky replied: "probably due to the fact that he would have accomplished nothing. . . . Consequently, Pirogov reasoned that it was better to do at least *something*, if not everything. Are you not satisfied with that 'at least something' Mr. —bov? After all, it is better than nothing" (20: 164).

Here is the heart of the disagreement between Dostoevsky and the radicals in 1861. What he reproached them for—much more openly in his notebooks than in public print—was their hastiness and impatience, their desire to leap over history and to bring about changes that could be realized only at a much later stage of Russian social development. "Where are you hurrying?" he asks Chernyshevsky in one note. "Our society is positively not ready for anything. The questions stand before us. They have ripened, they are ready, but our society is not ready in the least. It is disunited" (20: 153). Dostoevsky's tolerance for the radicals, as we can see from these jottings, was already beginning to stretch a bit thin; and it snapped in the following year, when the contributors and readers of *The Contemporary* turned from intellectual disaffection to active political agitation.

The basis for all further progress in Russia, as Dostoevsky saw it, was to work peacefully in favor of the advances newly made possible by the immense achievement of the liberation of the serfs and the further impending reforms that Alexander II had announced. *Time* printed the full text of the manifesto announcing the liberation and referred to it as a "sublime event" initiating a glorious new phase of Russian history comparable to its most magnificent moments—the defeat of the Tartars, the reforms of Peter the Great, the war of 1812. *The Contemporary*, on the other hand, let the occasion pass without uttering a single word: the radicals had been bitterly disappointed by the terms of the liberation, which they considered imposed too great a tax burden on the peasantry in favor of the idle and undeserving landowners.

This painful disillusionment of the radical intelligentsia soon gave rise to their first open attempts at protest; and it was as a result of such overt efforts to stir discontent that Dostoevsky's attitude toward them began to alter. He could only consider as futile and deluded any such attack on the very foundations of the Russian state, and he feared, with some reason, that it would lead to the reimposition of those repressive measures whose recent easing had at last allowed Russian society to breathe a little more freely. Such a fear is openly expressed even in the novel he was then writing, *The Insulted and Injured*, the first large-scale work of his post-Siberian period.

CHAPTER 9

The Insulted
and Injured

Everyone knew that the considerable success of *Time* was attributable, not only to Dostoevsky's flair as an editor and his vigor as a cultural publicist, but in even larger measure to his talents as a writer. His novel *The Insulted and Injured* began to appear as a serial in the first (January) issue and ran through seven numbers of the journal. The work encountered a mixed critical reception; but it was read with avid attention and achieved its purpose of making readers impatient for the next installment. Even as severe a judge as the novelist Evgenia Tur, who declared bluntly that the work "could not sustain the slightest criticism as art," was forced to admit that "the external interest does not flag to the very last line . . . of Mr. Dostoevsky's captivating, enchanting story."[1] Dobrolyubov devoted his very last essay "Downtrodden People" (*Zabitye Lyudi*)—a classic of Russian criticism—to a penetrating survey of the entire corpus of Dostoevsky's writings up to and including *The Insulted and Injured*. In an obvious reply to Dostoevsky's attack some months earlier, he remarked that the book was "beneath aesthetic criticism"; but, he acknowledged, everyone had been reading what stood out as the most interesting Russian novel published in 1861.[2]

Our contemporary view of Dostoevsky can hardly be that of Evgenia Tur or Dobrolyubov, but there is no reason to disagree with their verdict: *The Insulted and Injured* is by far the weakest of Dostoevsky's six major post-Siberian novels. The passage of time has not revealed complexities in the text indiscernible to its first readers—as is the case, for example, with *Notes from Underground*, hardly noticed at all when it appeared and considered a curiosity until the end of the century; nor did Dostoevsky himself have any illusions about the quality of his own creation. "I recognize fully," he publicly admitted several years later, commenting on some remarks made by Apollon Grigoryev, "that in my novel there are many characters who are puppets and not human beings, perambulating books and not characters who have taken on artistic form (this really requires time and a *gestation* of ideas in the mind and the soul)." He maintained, nonetheless, that even though he had produced "a bizarre book, in it are some fifty odd pages of which I am proud" (20: 134).

Whatever its manifest flaws, *The Insulted and Injured* still makes very good reading; and for the student of Dostoevsky it retains a particular fascination. For it allows us to catch the author in a stage of transition, trying his hand for the first time at mastering the technique of the *roman-feuilleton* and also giving shape to new character-types, themes, and motifs. Many of these will later become quite familiar; but here they appear in embryonic and not yet fully realized embodiments. Indeed, one sometimes has the curious impression that *The Insulted and Injured* is really an anthology culled from several of Dostoevsky's masterpieces, and put together by an ignorant compiler who has failed to grasp all the complexities of the originals. The truth is, though, that whether for lack of time (as he believed) or because of a more deeply rooted uncertainty (as is more likely), Dostoevsky himself does not yet appear to know exactly how to use the artistic ideas he was experimenting with and to which he was giving their initial, inchoate expression.

From our modern point of view, what is most interesting about *The Insulted and Injured* is its anticipations of future masterpieces. To appreciate its place in Dostoevsky's evolution, however, requires some sense of how it appeared to its first readers; only from such an awareness can we properly understand both the impression it created and the scarcely noticed promises for the future that we can now so easily discern. The book will thus be discussed from both these points of view: first in the perspective of 1861, and then, using this as a point of comparison, in the light of our present comprehension.

2

The origin of what was to become *The Insulted and Injured* can be traced to an idea that Dostoevsky mentions in a letter from Siberia in 1857, while he was still serving in the Russian Army. "I am writing a novel of Petersburg life," he tells Mikhail, "similar to *Poor Folk* (but the idea is better than *Poor Folk*)."[3] Unfortunately he fails to offer any further information concerning this "better idea"; but *Poor Folk* plays a very important symbolic role in the later text, and we cannot go far wrong in viewing the relation between the two as crucial. Scholars have worked diligently over the years to provide a more detailed genealogy for the book, and analogies have been noted, more or less plausibly, with Schiller (*Kabale und Liebe*), Goethe (*Wilhelm Meister's Lehrjahre*), Dickens (*Old Curiosity Shop*), as well as with Laclos, Rousseau, and the Marquis de Sade. The construction of the plot and the general stylistic tonality bear the strong imprint of *Les Mystères de Paris* and other *romans-feuilletons* of the same kind, mixed with a dash of E.T.A. Hoffmann in the opening pages. All such comparisons are suggestive and, if nothing else, indicate the breadth of Dostoevsky's literary culture. Such exploration of possible "sources," however, tells us little about what Dostoevsky made of them; and for this we must turn to a closer examination of the text.

The Insulted and Injured is composed of two interweaving plot lines, which at first seem to have little to do with each other but then gradually draw together as the story unfolds. The first, typical of the sentimental romantic novel, concerns an impoverished gentry family, the Ikhmenyevs. Their daughter, Natasha, falls in love with Alyosha, the son of a wealthy neighbor, Prince Valkovsky; and when the Prince frowns on their romance because he has destined Alyosha for a wealthy heiress, the two young people run away and live together out of wedlock. As a result, Natasha is renounced by her outraged father, Nikolay Sergeevich Ikhmenyev, not only for having disgraced the family escutcheon but also because Prince Valkovsky, once a friend and supposed benefactor, has now become his deadly personal enemy. The crux of this plot line is the mutual unhappiness of Natasha and her father, who love each other deeply despite her lethal blow to the family pride and his furious condemnation of her scandalous behavior.

The second plot line introduces the *roman-feuilleton* Gothic element of mystery, secret intrigue, and venal betrayal. It focuses on the figure of little Nellie, a thirteen-year-old Petersburg waif, whom the narrator, a young novelist named Ivan Petrovich, meets by chance. Intrigued by the eccentric appearance and behavior of an old man in a St. Petersburg coffeehouse, the young observer of life follows him into the street and, when the oldster collapses and dies on the spot, moves into his dingy room. The deceased man was the grandfather of little Nellie, who comes to visit him without knowing of his death and finds Ivan Petrovich occupying his quarters. Little Nellie is rescued from the clutches of a procuress by her new acquaintance and his friend Masloboev, an ex-schoolteacher leading a shady existence on the edge of the Petersburg underworld but still retaining some traces of the moral idealism of his youth. Ivan Petrovich, a foster-son of the Ikhmenyevs who had once been engaged to Natasha, takes Nellie in to live with him, looks after her welfare, and gradually pieces together the pathetic story of her appalling existence.

By a coincidence typical of the *roman-feuilleton* form, she turns out to be—as we learn at the very end of the book—the Prince's abandoned daughter. Valkovsky had seduced her mother, persuaded his infatuated young wife to rob her wealthy father, Jeremy Smith, and then had discarded her and their child once having obtained possession of the money. The two plots finally come together when, in order to reconcile Natasha with *her* father, and at the prompting of Ivan Petrovich, Nellie tells the heart-rending story of her life. Painting in dismal colors the refusal of her grandfather to forgive her mother even as she lay, destitute and dying, on the floor of a dank Petersburg hovel, Nellie's piteous tale brings about the forgiveness of Natasha and defeats the plan of the villainous Valkovsky to throw the unprotected girl into the arms of the lecherous old Count Nainsky.

Dostoevsky works out this complicated machinery with a good deal of technical skill, interweaving the story of Nellie's life gradually with that of the Ikhmenyevs, revealing portions of the past through her own words and those of Masloboev, and carefully preparing for the highly emotional and embarrassingly bathetic climax. All the events are seen through the eyes of Ivan Petrovich, who is an obvious physical link between the two plots just as Valkovsky is a more covert one. The time of writing is about a year after the events have taken place, and an additional element of pathos is provided by the situation in which Ivan Petrovich finds himself as he takes pen in hand to tell his story. "It had all ended in my being here in the hospital," he explains, "and I believe I am soon going to die. . . . I want to write it all down, and if I had not found this occupation I believe I should have died of misery" (3: 177). The tale he recounts is of the shipwreck of his own life (the magazine version bears the subtitle "From the Notes of an Unsuccessful Writer"), and he is about to perish with a sense of waste and despair. But he has nonetheless succeeded in rescuing others (the Ikhmenyevs), in surrounding the last days of Nellie with loving tenderness, and in remaining true to himself and the values of kindness and compassion in which he believes.

This brief sketch of the cumbrous intrigue shows Dostoevsky making use of the tritest material—the wrath of a loving but angry and heartbroken father against an erring daughter; a rich, powerful aristocrat, cynical and corrupt to the core, who wreaks his will on the innocent and pure-hearted; a virtuous young man (the narrator) in love with the heroine and ready to sacrifice himself unstintingly on her behalf; a poor waif exposed to the unspeakable evils of the Petersburg underworld, snatched from perdition by a generous rescuer, and who carries the secret of Valkovsky's scandalous past. All these motifs are the most threadbare ingredients of the *roman-feuilleton*, and Dostoevsky exploits them unashamedly for their maximum capacity to pluck the heartstrings.

Any doubt on this score can easily be allayed by citing a passage like the following about Nellie's mother, inserted at the conclusion of Part II to whet the appetite for what lies ahead: "It was a fearful story. It was the story of a woman abandoned and living on the wreck of her happiness, sick, worn out and forsaken by everyone, rejected by the last creature to whom she could look—her father, once wronged by her and crazed by intolerable sufferings and humiliations. It was the story of a woman driven to despair, wandering through the cold, filthy streets of Petersburg, begging alms with the little girl whom she regarded as a baby. . . . It was a gloomy story, one of those gloomy and distressing dramas which are so often played out un-

113

seen, almost mysterious, under the lowering sky of Petersburg, in the dark corners of the vast town, in the midst of the giddy ferment of life, of dull egoism, of clashing interests, of gloomy vice and secret crimes, in that lowest hell of senseless and abnormal life . . ." (3: 299-300). Dostoevsky here thickens the atmosphere with as heavy a hand and as murky a palette as Eugène Sue or Frédéric Soulié, and his overwrought sentimentality of tone conveys much of what provoked the contemptuous references of its first critics to the book's lack of artistic quality.

3

All the same, if we place the novel back in the context of 1861, it is not too difficult to understand why it was a popular success. For one thing, since its depiction of the literary career of Ivan Petrovich contains obvious references to Dostoevsky's own life—his initial celebrity as a result of Belinsky's backing, and then his decline in critical favor and popularity—it had the gossipy merit of being a *roman à clef*. These events are now much better known from the reminiscences that Dostoevsky later confided to his *Diary of a Writer*; but then they had the flavor of novelty and gave the reader a sense of being introduced behind the scenes into the coulisses of Russian literary life. Dostoevsky's use of such autobiographical material, just as in the case of his "Petersburg Visions," once again served to refresh the literary memory of his readers and to bridge the gap created by his long absence. Besides, a deliberate "autobiographism" has been noted as a new trait of the Russian prose of the 1850s, and can be seen equally in Tolstoy's *Childhood, Boyhood*, and *Sevastopol Stories* as well as in S. T. Aksakov's *A Family Chronicle*. Dostoevsky had read these new publications shortly after his release from prison camp and was thus, in his own work, following the current of the moment.

The Insulted and Injured also contained a considerable social-cultural relevance and was perused partly as a tract for the times devoted to the burning issue of woman's liberation. Its heroine, Natasha, whose sterling moral qualities are never questioned, leaves her respectable family openly and voluntarily to become the mistress of her lover. And while she suffers as a result of her misstep, not a trace of a shadow is ever cast on her character because of this deliberate defiance of conventional morality; indeed, Ivan Petrovich defends her indignantly against any attempt to defame her reputation. The action, moreover, is organized so as to bring out the importance of her being forgiven *unconditionally* by her outraged father, that is, of being forgiven with no requirement that she renounce or repudiate her past. The book can thus be considered a moderate plea for sexual liberation, and particularly for the elimination of a double standard of morality.

In addition, even though Dostoevsky assigns his own literary past of the

1840s to his character Ivan Petrovich, the novel is actually set twenty years later; and the book is filled with allusions that give it an almost journalistic topicality. One scene in particular involves a conversation referring to the liberation of the serfs and other reforms just then in the offing, and the passage illustrates both Dostoevsky's use of current issues to liven up his text as well as revealing some of his own anxieties.

The place is an aristocratic salon, and the speaker "a diplomat" who banefully welcomes the growing restiveness created by the policies of the new régime: "He kept insisting that the whole spirit of reform and improvement would only too soon bring forth certain results, that seeing those results 'they would come to their senses,' and that not only in society (that is, of course, a certain part of it) would this spirit of reform pass away, but they would learn their mistake from experience, and then with redoubled energies would return to the old traditions . . . and that consequently it was to be hoped that the extreme limit of recklessness would be reached as soon as possible." The motto of the people for whom the diplomat is speaking, he says, is: "*pire ça va, mieux ça est!*" (the worse the better). Naturally, Dostoevsky's Satanic villain, Prince Valkovsky, smiles "with revolting sympathy" at the reactionary import of these words (3: 345).

4

Such a "liberal" social-political attitude is also reinforced by many other aspects of the novel, which was universally seen as a direct continuation of Dostoevsky's writings of the 1840s. Even though he had never before used the ingredients and technique of the *roman-feuilleton*, this type of novel had long been identified with the propagation of "progressive" and Socialist ideas (*Les Mystères de Paris* had dramatized a number of Fourierist notions). Dostoevsky's use of the form was thus considered perfectly congruent with his subversive past and, even more, as indicating a reinforcement of the social-humanitarian principles for which he had suffered hard labor and exile. "The sympathy for the weak and the oppressed which had been expressed . . . in the first novel of Mr. Dostoevsky [*Poor Folk*]," wrote one critic, "has now, with his latest novel *The Insulted and Injured*, reached the apogee of its significance."[4] This was also the opinion of Dobrolyubov, who saw no marked difference between the Dostoevsky of the past and the present, and even attacked the novelist precisely for this reason. Dostoevsky, the critic pointed out, continued to depict "weak" characters unable to assert themselves in any effective fashion; and while these are not "superfluous men," Dobrolyubov nevertheless chides him, as both he and Chernyshevsky had done in the case of Turgenev, for failing to realize that Russian life has entered a new phase in which literature is called upon to depict protagonists with more strength of will.[5]

This impression of continuity with Dostoevsky's early work was particularly augmented by the repeated evocation of *Poor Folk* throughout the new text. In one touching, half-comic scene Dostoevsky describes the proud young author Ivan Petrovich, his first novel hot off the press, reading it aloud to his admiring foster-family. The old-fashioned provincial Nikolay Sergeevich can only conceive of literature as something highly bombastic and intensely patriotic, something in the style of official panegyrics and "infinitely lofty." Frankly baffled by Ivan Petrovich's unpretentious little tale of a poor copying clerk and a dishonored maiden, he instinctively responds, all the same, to the emotional appeal of its call for sympathy with the suffering and downtrodden: "There it is, it's simply a little story but it wrings your heart . . . and one learns that the most downtrodden, humblest man is a man, too, and a brother." Natasha also is moved to tears: "all at once she snatched my hand, kissed it, and ran out of the room" (3: 188-189). Shortly afterwards, she and Ivan Petrovich become engaged to be married.

Poor Folk is used in this manner throughout as a touchstone of moral sensibility; all the "good" characters respond to it in an appropriately compassionate fashion, and even the disreputable and hard-drinking Masloboev confesses that "when I read it, I almost became a respectable man again" (3: 265). The scoundrelly Prince Valkovsky reacts in quite a different manner—not with a quickening of conscience, but rather with an outburst of scorn at the literary mode of which it was a product and whose inspiration had been revived and intensified in the more recent "accusatory" literature. "Poverty is all the fashion with you now," he says contemptuously to Ivan Petrovich, "lost coats, government inspectors, quarrelsome officers, bureaucratic clerks, old times, dissenters, I know, I know." (These allusions begin with Gogol and take in more recent writers, such as Saltykov-Shchedrin and Melnikov-Pechersky, the last known for stories about the dissenting religious sects.) He admonishes Ivan Petrovich, for the benefit of his career, to move in "higher" circles, "if only that you ought to know what you're describing, and in novels we have counts and princes and boudoirs . . ." (3: 355). Sound literary advice though this may be, it clearly reveals the Prince's exclusive interest in wealth and position and his total indifference to the life and fate of those at the mercy of his depredations.

Prince Valkovsky is so stagey and melodramatic an aristocratic villain that it is difficult for us now to take him at all seriously. If any character deserves to be labeled a "perambulating book," it is certainly the Prince; but our reaction is not that of Dostoevsky's initial readers, who considered the Prince a plausible and quite familiar social type. As Evgenia Tur wrote, without blinking an eyelash, "everyone having some acquaintance with the world has met many such people, but happily, that is, happily for our society, such people as Prince Ivan [Valkovsky] are dying out year by year and are no longer being born."[6] Since his power to oppress could thus be taken as more than a fictional convention, Dostoevsky's portrayal of the Prince was accepted as a searing exposé of the depravity of an entire social class. Moreover, the author's "sympathy with the weak and the oppressed" was clearly indicated—just as it had been during the 1840s—by the presentation of his humble folk as infinitely superior to the Prince from a moral point of view and, indeed, as the living refutation of his witheringly contemptuous view of his fellow humans.

For a Russian reader of the time, accustomed to regard "weak" characters as doomed to inevitable defeat by the very excess of their moral merits, the Prince was a thoroughly unmitigated scoundrel while the battered but unblemished Ikhmenyevs—not to mention the all-suffering Ivan Petrovich—were exemplars of sterling worth and integrity. No power at the Prince's command could shatter the indestructible bonds of their love and devotion to each other, as becomes clear in Ikhmenyev's ecstatic but badly overstrained declaration terminating the climactic reconciliation scene:

> Oh Lord, I thank Thee for all, for all, for Thy wrath and for Thy mercy!
> . . . And for Thy sun which is shining upon us again after the storm!
> . . . Oh, we may be insulted and injured, but we're together again, and now the proud and haughty who have insulted and injured us may triumph! Let them throw stones at us! Have no fear, Natasha. . . . We will go hand in hand and I will say to them, "This is my darling, this is my beloved daughter, my innocent daughter whom you have insulted and injured, but whom I love and bless for ever and ever." (3: 422)

The Insulted and Injured thus contains the same structure of moral oppositions as Dostoevsky's "sentimental Naturalism" of the 1840s, even though the Ikhmenyevs are gentry rather than bureaucratic clerks and the power that attempts to crush them is no longer the vague and anomalous might of Petersburg but a thoroughly corrupt and depraved member of the ruling class. If, therefore, we read the book through the eyes of its original audience—familiar only with Dostoevsky's past, which he had just brought vividly back to life, and naturally inclined to interpret his new work in this context—it is perfectly comprehensible why they should have considered it only as a more sensational example of his long-familiar "humanism" and compassion for the "poor folk" of a heartless Russian society.

5

Without the benefit of our hindsight, it was impossible for Dostoevsky's readers to see the future novelist germinating amidst the more or less tolerable clichés of *The Insulted and Injured*. One or two critics were uneasily aware of something "new" in the book; but this awareness took the form of negative criticism. Protests were uttered against the "implausible" passivity of Ivan Petrovich, and, even more pertinently, objections were raised by one critic against the title because it had led him to expect a genuine social novel. In fact, as he rightly points out, the characters behave in such a bizarre fashion that most of their difficulties are caused by their own blindness and folly; the intrigues of Prince Valkovsky, on closer inspection, play only an accessory part in their dilemmas. "Cannot we find enough instances in our society of insult and injury occurring all the time," he asks impatiently, "not exceptions as in the novel of Mr. Dostoevsky, but directly arising from our manners and customs?"[7] Such a legitimate reaction, which stems partly from the excesses of the melodramatic intrigue, also arises more fundamentally from Dostoevsky's handling of his characters so as continually to *undercut* the supposed social-humanitarian significance of the book. What determines their fate, in the final analysis, are the traits of their own personalities, not the external mechanism of the *roman-feuilleton* plot; and this creates a continual dissonance between the workings of the plot machinery and the deeper causes of their predicaments, which are rooted in themselves and their personal values. The inordinate mawkishness of certain passages is probably an attempt to compensate for this discrepancy and to pump up emotions of facile pity not justified by the text.

One may of course attribute such dissonance to artistic oversight (and Dostoevsky's own admission that he wrote the book too hastily seems to confirm such a judgment), but it can also be diagnosed as part of an internal evolution that had not yet completed its course. For it is now obvious that, within the framework of his hackneyed plot, Dostoevsky was perceptibly beginning to grope his way toward his later novel-tragedy of ideas. What we can glimpse in *The Insulted and Injured*, through the interstices of the clichés, is a premature novel about a young writer who represents the "philanthropic" ideology of the 1840s, and whose world and life are shattered because his convictions prove inadequate to cope with the deeper forces of human passion and egoism that overwhelm his well-meaning innocence. All the characters who initially share his views undergo and suffer the same experience; but only he is dealt a mortal blow. His convictions had been the basis of his life and work as a writer, and, once they have been destroyed, there is no reason left for him to live.

This theme of innocence and its self-deceptions is struck very early by some semi-ironic remarks about Ikhmenyev, whose relation to Valkovsky derives from a warm-hearted self-delusion analogous to that of the unselfish Colonel Rostanev toward the malevolent Foma Fomich in *The Village of Stepanchikovo*. Ikhmenyev was, we learn, "one of those very simple-hearted and naively Romantic men who are, whatever else one wishes to say about them, so charming among us in Russia, and who, if they once give their affection to someone (sometimes only God knows why) surrender themselves heart and soul, sometimes stretching their attachment to comic lengths" (3: 181). He refuses to believe any of the discreditable rumors circulating about the Prince and declares that "he [the Prince] *was incapable of a mean action*" (3: 182; italics added). Ikhmenyev thus prefers to live in a world where moral imperfection does not exist; and he takes much the same attitude toward his daughter Natasha, whom he steadfastly continues to regard as an angelic child even though she has reached marriageable age. Another example of such "naive Romanticism," less instinctive and more literary in character, is found in Nellie's mother, who ran off with Valkovsky because "from the very beginning she dreamed of something like a heaven upon earth, of angels; her love was boundless, her faith limitless, and, I am convinced, she went mad not because he ceased to love her and threw her over, but because she had been deceived by him, *he was capable of deceiving* and had thrown her over, because her angel had turned into dirt, had spat on and humiliated her" (3: 437).

When Romantics of this type are betrayed by life, as invariably occurs, their response is to fall back on outraged pride, regardless of the suffering this may cause to those they presumably love the most. Just as Ikhmenyev execrates his beloved daughter when she publicly dishonors his name by becoming the mistress of Valkovsky's son, so Nellie's mother condemns her daughter to a life of terrible misery and torment because "in her horror and, above all, her pride, she drew back from him [Valkovsky] with infinite contempt" (3: 438) and refused to use the documents in her possession proving their marriage. The proud and hence egoistic reaction of such frustrated Romantics leads to a masochistic intensification of their own misery and a certain sadism with regard to others (Natasha, Nellie). In the case of Ikhmenyev, this inner conflict is finally overcome by a movement of love that vanquishes pride and conquers the rankling resentment created by betrayal. It also involves the acceptance of a world where good and evil are inextricably intermingled, and where "the shattering of idealism" (to use K. Mochulsky's apt phrase)[8] is an unavoidable and even salutary precondition for forgiveness and reconciliation.

6

Much the same conflict occurs in the Natasha-Alyosha relationship, even though Natasha is not specifically called a Romantic; but she is still an integral part of the *Poor Folk* world, and has responded lovingly to its message and its author. Additionally, she is described as having "that characteristic of good-natured people, *perhaps inherited from her father*—the habit of thinking highly of people, of persistently thinking them better than they really are, warmly exaggerating everything good in them" (3: 270; italics added). What she feels for Alyosha, however, destroys her "innocence" both literally and figuratively, and reveals aspects of her character that bewilder and frighten her by their unexpected complexity.

Natasha, it should be understood, is very far from being the innocent victim of a typical aristocratic seducer à la Steerforth in *David Copperfield*; on the contrary, it is she who forces the issue and decides to live openly with her lover. Indeed, her passion for the weak-willed, frivolous, and inconstant Alyosha has reached such a pitch that she is willing to submit to any degradation so as to cling to him and "to be his slave, his willing slave" (3: 200). But she is fully aware that her infatuation is "abject" and abnormal, springing more from a desire for domination than from a genuine love between equals. It is her pride that has been wounded by Alyosha's philandering, and her pride impels her not only to humiliate her father but also to plunge herself into an abyss of masochistic abasement and self-torment. Once again her conflict is resolved as the result of a successful inner struggle: Natasha conquers her egoism and regains her self-respect by voluntarily surrendering Alyosha to her far more suitable rival, the young heiress Katya.

In the case of little Nellie, Dostoevsky brings this type of moral-psychological conflict, with its characteristic swing from wounded sensibility to masochistic self-laceration and sadism, into its sharpest focus. Among all the "insulted and injured," Nellie has the most right to claim such a designation; and she has acquired a savage pride and a mistrust of humanity initially encouraged by her mother's fierce intransigence. Nellie's personality thus combines a youthful need for affection and love with suspicion and hatred, and she refuses at first to respond even to generosity or kindness. Dostoevsky's depiction of her shifting moods, and of the gradual softening and taming of her spirit, are among the best sections of the book; one suspects that these are among the fifty or so pages of which he remained proud. The self-tormenting depths of Nellie's psychology are brought out in one crucial scene, when all the embittered memories of her past have surged back in a flood and she rushes out of Ivan Petrovich's sheltering room to beg in the streets as a gesture of defiance. Tears come to Ivan Petrovich's eyes when he chances upon her:

> Yes, tears for poor Nellie, though at the same time I felt great indignation; she was not begging through need; she was not forsaken, not abandoned by someone to the caprice of destiny. She was not escaping from cruel oppressors, but from friends who loved and cherished her . . . she had been ill-treated; her hurt could not be healed, and she seemed purposely trying to aggravate her wound by this mysterious behavior, this mistrustfulness of us all; as though she enjoyed her own pain, by this *egoism of suffering*, if I may so express it. This aggravation of suffering and this revelling in it I could understand; it is the enjoyment of many of the insulted and injured, oppressed by destiny and smarting under the sense of injustice. (3: 385-386)

It is Dostoevsky himself who italicizes the phrase "egoism of suffering," highlighting its importance, it seems to me, because it contains the internal thematic link uniting three main centers of action: Natasha–Ikhmenyev, Natasha–Alyosha–Katya, Nellie–Ivan Petrovich. In each case, one or more of the characters responds in this fashion to some indignity or humiliation; in each, the conflict is resolved when, in an act of outgoing love, the egoism of suffering is overcome. So far as Nellie is concerned, the resolution occurs when she agrees to tell her heart-rending story, at the urging of Ivan Petrovich, in order to bring about the reconciliation of Natasha and her father. And, since Nellie knows that the emotional strain of recalling her past may prove fatal, her victory is achieved at the greatest cost of all. When Ivan Petrovich makes his plea, she looks at him with "a strange, prolonged gaze," and he writes that "there was something like reproach in that gaze . . . I felt it in my heart" (3: 407). All the same, Nellie makes the supreme sacrifice for those she has come to love, and, as the doctor had predicted, her heart gives way shortly afterward. It is not by chance, of course, that this scene takes place during Easter week.

What we find in all these episodes, then, is the emergence of an entirely different kind of novel, which has little or nothing to do with the original *roman-feuilleton* intrigue. Dostoevsky tries as best he can to stitch the two together, but the seams are very visible and sometimes form a contradictory patchwork. Natasha's decision to give up Alyosha, for example, which in one pattern is clearly meant as a noble gesture, in another actually *helps* the dastardly Valkovsky obtain access to the fortune of Katya; and the suggestion that Masloboev may make life difficult for Valkovsky in the future, with the help of the papers proving him to be Nellie's father, is canceled out a page or so later with Nellie's death. Dostoevsky is manifestly caught between two types of motivation for his action, and unable to integrate them in any consistent fashion. The most interesting parts of the novel, however, derive from the same attack on "naive Romanticism" and sentimental idealism, as well as the continuing exploration of the psychology of the "egoism of suffering," that Dostoevsky had already initiated in *Uncle's Dream* and *The Village of Stepanchikovo*.[9] Dostoevsky's interest, it is clear, had moved away from the social-humanitarian thematic of his *roman-feuilleton* plot and was taking on a decisively moral-psychological orientation. But what his "humanism" had now come to mean was a faith in the power of the human personality to struggle successfully against the self-destructive consequences of its own resentments and frustrations.

7

Even though Dostoevsky had not yet decisively abandoned his old philanthropic ideals and values in *The Insulted and Injured*—and none of his contemporaries imagined that he was doing so—there are still definite indications that he was continuing that revision of his past already initiated. As we shall see in a moment, such a revision is the explicit purpose of the finest scene in the book; but an earlier passage concerning Ivan Petrovich, and describing what he calls a state of "mystic terror," anticipates the more explicit undermining to which he will soon be subjected. When overcome by such a mood, Ivan Petrovich is assailed by an indefinable fear of something unknown, and his mind becomes sharply divorced from his feelings. "It is," he writes, "a most oppressive agonizing state of terror of something which I don't know how to define and something passing all understanding and outside the natural order of things, which yet may take shape this very minute, as though in mockery of all the conclusions of reason, and come to me and stand before me as an undeniable fact, hideous, horrible, and relentless. This fear usually becomes more and more acute, in spite of the protests of reason, so much so that although the mind sometimes is of exceptional clarity at such moments, it loses all power of resistance" (3: 208).

Such a condition of hallucination and dissociation probably conveys sensations connected with Dostoevsky's own "nervous illness" in the mid-1840s, which is usually considered the forerunner of his epilepsy. In the text, this apprehension of "mystic terror" induces a lucid paralysis of the will in the face of looming monstrosity, and prefigures the helplessness of Ivan Petrovich when confronted by the turbulent passions he is called on to cope with among the other characters. More generally, it also foreshadows Dostoevsky's great theme of the impotence of reason to contend with the dark mysteries of human existence—with all those mysteries symbolized by the fear of the unknown, and which Ivan Petrovich tellingly compares to "the anguish of people who are afraid of the dead" (3: 208).*

Dostoevsky is not yet ready to develop this larger theme, but he does not hesitate to underscore the ineffectuality of Ivan Petrovich when openly challenged by Prince Valkovsky; and the scene in which this challenge occurs allows Dostoevsky to present Ivan Petrovich from a more objective and critical point of view. The setting is a fashionable restaurant, to which Valkovsky invites Ivan Petrovich for a little private conversation—the first of many such dialogues, usually taking place in taverns, during which Dostoevsky's characters thrash out their differences. Towering head and shoulders above the level of the remainder of the text, this scene, for the first time, allows us to catch a glimpse of the great Dostoevsky to come. By elevating the theme of egoism to its full metaphysical dimension, Dostoevsky momentarily lifts his soap-opera plot to a new height of dignity; and by

---

* What Dostoevsky is describing here fits very well with the analysis given by Rudolf Otto of the primitive roots of all religious feeling. The affective source of the birth of the numinous is what Otto calls the sense of the *mysterium tremendum*, one of whose elementary forms is " 'daemonic dread' (cf. the horror of Pan), with its queer perversion, a sort of abortive offshoot, the dread of ghosts. It first begins to stir in the feeling of 'something uncanny,' 'eerie,' or 'weird.' It is this feeling which, emerging in the mind of primeval man, forms the starting point of the entire religious development in history." Rudolf Otto, *The Idea of the Holy* (London, 1952), 14.

covertly fusing the theme of egoism with that of radical ideology, he at last strikes the vein that will soon provide him with a new source of inspiration.

Valkovsky's long and gloating "confession" to Ivan Petrovich serves a number of functions. In the first place, it amply confirms the earlier suggestions that he is a shameless reprobate and libertine; not only does he harbor a taste for the usual forms of vice, but he particularly enjoys the self-conscious desecration of the moral norms of society (Dostoevsky here draws on Laclos's *Les Liaisons Dangereuses* for an example of this proclivity).* Valkovsky unmasks himself to Ivan Petrovich for the sheer pleasure of shocking his idealistic young interlocutor, and he compares his pleasure in doing so to that of a sexual pervert exhibiting himself in public (manifestly referring to Rousseau's *Confessions*). Much of this self-exposure, of course, was calculated to discredit Valkovsky in the eyes of the reader, but it also functions to disclose some of the "irrational" depths of personality equally exhibited in the behavior of the other characters. Nothing gives Valkovsky more delight, he explains, than deliberately to provoke "some ever-young Schiller," first by pretending to take seriously "all those vulgar and worthless naivetés and idyllic nonsense," and then "suddenly distorting my ecstatic countenance into a grimace, putting out my tongue at him when he is least of all expecting such a surprise" (3: 360).

Valkovsky, as we see, thus criticizes Ivan Petrovich in much the same terms as the young author himself uses for Ikhmenyev and Nellie's mother. The actual creator of *Poor Folk* is now unmistakably placing his previous artistic self, and the values inspiring his early work, among the manifestations of that "naive Romanticism" whose shortcomings his new novel had set out to expose. And this debunking of Ivan Petrovich becomes even more pointed when Valkovsky displays his familiarity—as it were, from the inside—with the idea-feelings of his interlocutor. For it turns out that the Prince is not simply an inveterate blackguard but himself a disillusioned idealist, who "ages ago, in the golden days of my youth," as he sardonically explains, once too had had "a fancy to become a metaphysician and philanthropist, and came round almost to the same ideas as you." He too had "wanted to be a benefactor of humanity, to found a philanthropic society,"*

---

* The Prince speaks of an old acquaintance of his, "a beauty of the first rank," who "was reputed to be as cold as the driven snow, and frightened everyone by her immaculate, her menacing virtue." In reality, however, "my lady's sensuality was such that even the Marquis de Sade might have taken lessons from her." What she enjoyed the most was "this jeering [in private] at everything which in public the Countess preached as being lofty, transcendent and inviolable . . . in that, above all, lay the keenness of the gratification" (3: 364). Valkovsky is well informed on such matters because, for a year, he had participated in her secret pleasures.

Dostoevsky here is evidently alluding to the character of the Marquise de Merteuil in Laclos's novel. This relation to Laclos has been noted in Soviet Russian criticism, but has not been seen as part of the attack on egoism underlying Dostoevsky's conception. R.G. Nazirov, "Tragediinoe Nachalo v Romane F. M. Dostoevskogo 'Unizhennye i Oskorblennye,' " *Filologicheskie Nauki*, 4 (1965), 35-37.

* Dostoevsky's choice of terms unmistakably links Valkovsky's words with his own past. Fif-

and had even constructed a model hospital on his estate. But boredom had finally gotten the better of him—boredom, and a sense of the ultimate futility of existence. "We shall die—and what comes then!" he exclaims; and "well, so I took to dangling after the girls." The protesting husband of "one little shepherdess" was flogged so badly that he died in the model hospital (3: 361).

Face-to-face with metaphysical ennui and the ineluctability of extinction, Valkovsky discovers that the "pleasures" of philanthropy are hardly powerful enough to compensate for the vacuity of existence; and like Cleopatra he begins to search for stronger stimulants. Besides, the ideology of social-humanitarianism was now terribly out of date, and what had replaced it, Valkovsky appreciatively informs Ivan Petrovich, comes very pat to the Prince's purposes. On being reproached for his "beastliness," by the indignant narrator, the Prince retorts that all such estimable remonstrances are "nonsense." Moral obligations are a sham because, "What isn't nonsense is personality—myself." For his own part, he proclaims, "I . . . have long since freed myself from all shackles, and even moral obligations. I only recognize obligations when I see I have something to gain by them. . . . You long for the ideal, for virtue. Well, my dear fellow, I am ready to admit anything you tell me to, but what can I do if I know for a fact that at the root of all human virtue lies the completest egoism. And the more virtuous anything is, the more egoism there is in it. Love yourself, that's the one rule I recognize" (3: 365).

By asserting a doctrine of absolute egoism against Ivan Petrovich's "philanthropic" self-abnegation, Valkovsky thus objectifies and justifies, as a sinister philosophy of evil, the very same drives and impulses against which the "good" characters have been carrying on a moral struggle. It was once traditional in Russian criticism to trace Valkovsky's tirade back to Max Stirner (with whose ideas Dostoevsky was unquestionably familiar), and to view them as a denunciation of Western egoism, individualism, and capitalism. More recently, it has been reluctantly conceded that Dostoevsky is also parodying Chernyshevsky's "rational egoism," and that Valkovsky is in fact Dostoevsky's first artistic reaction to the radical doctrines of the

teen years later, in his *Diary of a Writer*, he will use exactly the same expression to characterize his youthful radicalism.

On a trip from Moscow to Petersburg, at the age of sixteen, Dostoevsky witnessed the routine beating of a peasant coachman by a government courier. "This disgusting sight," he wrote, "has remained in my memory all my life. Never was I able to forget it, or that courier. . . . This little scene appeared to me, so to speak, as an emblem, as something which very graphically demonstrated the link between cause and effect [he is referring to the cruelty of Russian life]. In the late forties, during the period of my most unrestrained and fervent dreams, it suddenly occurred to me that should I ever happen *to found a philanthropic society* I would by all means engrave this courier's troika on the seal of the society as an emblem and warning sign" (22: 29; italics added). For more details, see *Dostoevsky: The Seeds of Revolt, 1821-1849* (Princeton, 1976), 69-73.

1860s.* For Dostoevsky uses Valkovsky to follow out the logic of Chernyshevsky's position to the end—without accepting the proviso that reason
and self-interest would ultimately coincide, and that egoism would miraculously convert itself into beneficence through rational calculation. Dostoevsky knew very well that Chernyshevsky was anything but a disciple of
Stirner; but he also remembered the irrational frenzies of frustrated egoism
that he had witnessed in the prison camp, and he had read Laclos and the
Marquis de Sade. Like them, he was persuaded that to base morality on
egoism was to risk unleashing forces in the human personality over which
Utilitarian reason had little control. Indeed, Dostoevsky's allusions to these
two writers indicate his awareness of an indebtedness to the libertine tradition of the French eighteenth-century novel, in which characters similar
to Valkovsky (could his name be related to that of Valmont in *Les Liaisons
Dangereuses?*) also dramatize, whether with approval or dismay, the possible consequences of putting into practice the logic of an egoism unrestrained by moral inhibitions. †

Like his eighteenth-century prototypes, when Valkovsky yields to the

* In her preface to an edition of *The Insulted and Injured*, L. M. Rosenblyum remarks: "Although, in the uncovering of Valkovsky's views, no direct association is visible with the materialism of [the generation of] the 1860s, one may, all the same, assume that they contain, of
course in a covert form, an onslaught against Chernyshevsky's *The Anthropological Principle
in Philosophy*—the work in which the ethical principles of the radical democrats are set forth.
The Anthropological Principle was published a year before *The Insulted and Injured.*"
The commentary to the novel in the new Academy edition of Dostoevsky's collected works,
while calling special attention to Rosenblyum's preface in a footnote, cautiously circles round
this issue and links Valkovsky's ideas directly only with Max Stirner. See F. M. Dostoevsky, *Unizhennye i Oskorblennye*, ed. L. M. Rosenblyum (Moscow, 1955), 25; *PSS*, 3: 527-528.
† Turgenev, in two letters written shortly after Dostoevsky's death, refers to him as the Russian ("our") Marquis de Sade. He did so with approving reference to a famous and still influential article by N. K. Mikhailovsky, "A Cruel Talent," which focuses on Dostoevsky's use of
sadism in his novels and suggests that he was attracted to such material by his own unhealthy
inclinations. Many years later Mario Praz, in his classic *The Romantic Agony*, included Dostoevsky among the writers who may be considered followers and disciples of Sade.
Dostoevsky's own references to Sade indicate his familiarity with that writer's work, though
he never mentions any titles by name. The only properly libertine novel he refers to is *Thérèse
philosophe*, whose author is unknown (usually it is attributed to the Marquis d'Argens). Although not sadistic in content, the book anticipates Sade philosophically in its advocacy of a
complete liberty, restrained only by considerations of prudence, in the relations between the
sexes; and Sade himself referred to the book approvingly in *Justine*. A recent student affirms
that "*Thérèse philosophe* is the first libertine novel in which the erotic and philosophic elements
are totally integrated," and is superior to its predecessors because "there is an attempt to present consistent, systematic opposing views, even if the goal is to prove them utterly wrong—in
bed or at the discussion table." Barry Ivker, "Towards a Definition of Libertinism in 18th Century French Fiction," *Studies in Voltaire and the Eighteenth Century*, ed. Theodore Bester-
mann, 73 (1970), 231; see also William Brumfield, "*Thérèse Philosophe* and Dostoevsky's Great
Sinners," *Comparative Literature* 32 (1980), 238-252.
As Robert L. Jackson points out, those who have written about Dostoevsky's relation to Sade
and sadism have remained more or less faithful to Mikhailovsky's hostile bias and have used it
to draw highly questionable inferences about Dostoevsky's character. It is unforgivably crude,
however, to confuse an artist's selection of certain material with the manner in which he employs it and the meaning it assumes in his work. Dostoevsky always uses sadism for specific
artistic and ideological purposes, and invariably to illustrate the possible horrors, as Jackson
well shows, of a world without God and hence without morality and moral restraints of any kind.
For more information, see Jackson's excellent article, "Dostoevskij and the Marquis de Sade,"
Russian Literature, 4 (1976), 27-46.

temptations of sensuality, and the sadistic pleasures of desecration and domination, he finds it very convenient to have a doctrine of egoistic self-interest at hand providing a philosophical rationale for his worst instincts. Since everyone possesses such instincts, even the "good" characters, who believe firmly in a morality of love and self-sacrifice, can quite easily become prey to the passions of "egoism"; and Prince Valkovsky illustrates what might well happen if "egoism" were to be taken seriously as the prevailing norm of behavior. Valkovsky, as has long been accepted, is the prefiguration of such later characters as Svidrigailov and Stavrogin; less well-known is that he is also Dostoevsky's first attempt, inspired by the radical ideology of the 1860s, to portray the futility of "reason" to control the entire gamut of possibilities contained in the human psyche.

Ivan Petrovich does not play a very effective role in the confrontation scene any more than he does in the novel as a whole; but since he manages to fling a few insults at the Prince, these are presumably enough to establish his moral authority. Dostoevsky, however, lamentably fails to use the potentialities offered by such a scene in the manner that he would later perfect. Such exchanges in the future would reveal hidden aspects of the characters to each other and lead to decisive peripeties in the action; but nothing of the sort happens here—neither Ivan Petrovich nor the Prince is fundamentally altered by their talk. True, Ivan Petrovich at one moment regrets the "cursed weakness and delicacy" (3: 355) that prevent him from being more aggressive, but this is as far as Dostoevsky goes in allowing Valkovsky to strike a spark. Ivan Petrovich is not impelled to revise his values under the assault, nor does he attain any new insight into their shortcomings; it is as if Dostoevsky, whether consciously or not, was still refusing to discredit his own past too overtly.

Part of that function, however, is assumed by the sympathetic if disreputable Masloboev, who serves as an alter ego for Ivan Petrovich and treats his callow friend with patronizing pity rather than Valkovsky's contempt. Masloboev, who has knocked about the world and has few illusions, tells his old friend some of the same home truths that we hear from the lips of Prince Valkovsky and displays exactly the same scorn for "Schillerism" and "naive Romanticism." Similarly, a critical note is also struck when Dostoevsky, although portraying Ivan Petrovich as largely immune from jealousy (and hence from the torments of the "egoism of suffering" when Natasha leaves him for Alyosha),* refuses to exclude him entirely from the burden

---

* There is a bit of evidence that Dostoevsky felt Ivan Petrovich's lack of reaction to be a weakness. In some notes for the novel, scribbled on the back of a notice for a rehearsal of Gogol's *The Inspector-General*, he wrote: "Less indulgence and love for Alyosha on the part of the poet (Ivan Petrovich)." Again: "Poet more independent toward Alyosha—(hatred)." Dostoevsky evidently began to have some second thoughts about Ivan Petrovich's total absence of resentment at the loss of Natasha; but he never managed to incorporate these suggestions into the text. See *PSS*, 3: 448.

of guilt incurred by all the others. For Ivan Petrovich knows that his desire to reconcile Natasha and her father has been instrumental in hastening the death of little Nellie; even he is tainted with the stain of evil, despite the purity of his intentions and his desire to sacrifice himself for all those who suffer.

8

Other aspects of the novel also suggest that Dostoevsky had now come to regard his past attitudes as lamentably and unforgivably naive. There is talk of a "circle," again linked with the *Poor Folk* world, that meets once a week and to which the hare-brained Alyosha has been attracted. 'They all know you, Ivan Petrovich," he burbles. "That is, they have read your works and expect great things of you in the future" (3: 308-309). What Alyosha reports of their discussions brings the group within the orbit of the "progressive" ideas of the 1840s (with a little updating). They converse, he confides, "of everything in general that leads to progress, to humanity, to love, it's all in relation to contemporary questions. We talk of the need of a free press, of the reforms that are beginning, of the love of humanity, of the leaders of today, we read and discuss them" (3: 310). It is generally accepted that Dostoevsky is here drawing, more or less amiably, on his own experiences in the Petrashevsky circle; and he handles all this as part of the same universe of illusory innocence represented by Ivan Petrovich and, at a farther extreme, by Alyosha.

Since the report of the circle is conveyed by the giddy and flighty Alyosha, his words immediately characterize it as just another of his evanescent enthusiasms, engagingly youthful and refreshing and filled with the exuberance of adolescent inexperience. "We all talked of our present," he says, "of our future, of science and literature, and talked so well, so frankly and simply. . . . There's a high-school boy who comes too" (3: 309). The implications of this last bit of information are not lost on Prince Valkovsky, who listens to his son "with a malignant sneer; there was malice in his face"; and the Prince breaks into convulsive laughter "simply to wound and to humiliate his son as deeply as possible." But Alyosha, for the only time in the book, manages to stand up to his father and to answer him "with extreme sincerity and a sort of severe dignity." Yes, he replies, "I am enthusiastic over lofty ideas. They may be mistaken, but what they rest upon is holy" (3: 311).

Such words, we may surmise, indicate precisely how Dostoevsky himself felt about the ideals of his radical past—the ideals he had just brought back to life again in the pages of *The Insulted and Injured*. There was no question in his mind that they had been "mistaken," or at least lamentably shortsighted in their view of the human condition; but he still continued to believe that what they had rested upon—the values of compassion and love—were sacred. What now prevented such values from being realized, however, was no longer primarily the deformations of character caused by an oppressive and unjust social system and a crushing political tyranny. It was, rather, the hidden forces of egoism and pride slumbering in every human breast.*

9
———

All through *The Insulted and Injured*, then, we can see Dostoevsky poised on the brink of a new phase of creation but still hesitating to take the leap. All the same, as we have already had occasion to remark, time and again in this novel we can catch suggestions of character-types and motifs that serve as unmistakable harbingers of the masterpieces to come. Some of these intimations have been noted in passing; and we may conclude with a few others that help to document the seminal importance for Dostoevsky of this abortive but richly promising attempt to come to terms with his past and open the way into the artistic future.

Dostoevsky's characters often bear a family resemblance, if not externally then at least in their psychology, and it is not too far-fetched to point out a connection between the ragged little waif Nellie in *The Insulted and Injured* and the gloriously beautiful Nastasya Filippovna in *The Idiot* surrounded by all the luxurious appurtenances of wealth. Both are consumed by the "egoism of suffering"—Nellie as a response to the torments of her frightful existence, Nastasya because she had been entrapped against her will into a life of shame. Both exhibit a fierce pride, a drive toward masochistic self-abasement, and an undying hatred of their persecutors and oppressors. Nellie finally overcomes her egoism at the cost of her life; so does Nastasya by offering herself as a victim to Rogozhin's knife. What is only tearful in the early novel, however, becomes tragic in the later one.

The same difference of level can be noted in the case of Alyosha Valkovsky, who turns out, quite unexpectedly, to be a first draft of Dostoevsky's most touching effort to portray his moral ideal in the figure of Prince Myshkin. The yawning gap between the impression produced by the two char-

* Nietzsche's admiration for such works of Dostoevsky as *House of the Dead, Notes from Underground* and *Crime and Punishment* is well-known; less widespread is the knowledge that he also read *The Insulted and Injured* with great appreciation. Indeed, according to an account given by a friend, he told her that he had perused it with "his eyes overflowing" with tears. Such a reaction indicates that the formidable Nietzsche was quite capable of yielding to facile emotion, and that he surrendered completely to Dostoevsky's all-too-evident efforts to pluck the heartstrings of his readers. As Wolfgang Gesemann has suggested, the German philosopher may also have been intrigued by Dostoevsky's attack against the sentimental idealism of the "schöne Seele," as well as "the excitement of the encounter with the creatively genial refinement of Stirnerism" in Prince Valkovsky. See Wolfgang Gesemann, "Nietzsche's Verhältnis zu Dostoevskij auf dem europäischen Hintergrund der 8oer Jahre," *Die Welt der Slaven*, 6 (July 1961), 135, 147-150.

acters illustrates how Dostoevsky can employ almost identical traits to obtain very different types of significance; for while the lineaments of Myshkin are faintly profiled in Alyosha, there is no trace in him as yet of Myshkin's supreme saintliness. On the contrary, he shows "some of the bad habits characteristic of aristocratic society: frivolity, self-complacency and polite insolence" (3: 201). Such disobliging features, all the same, are greatly overshadowed by his candor and ingenuousness, and by a goodness of heart that compensates for his inability to understand the full consequences of his conduct. The most striking attribute of Alyosha, and one that most clearly stamps him as Myshkin's predecessor, is his capacity—or weakness, depending on the point of view—for living so totally in each moment of time, or in each experience and encounter, that he lacks any sense of continuity or consequence. It is thus impossible to hold him responsible for anything, or even to take offense at the chaos in other people's lives that he unwittingly creates; he behaves completely like a child and is characterized as being one: "he was too simple for his age and had no notion of real life" (3: 202).

Alyosha is thus a pure *naif*, existing outside the categories of good and evil and of social responsibility. He is genuinely unable to choose between Natasha and Katya, just as Myshkin will be unable to decide between Nastasya Filippovna and Aglaya Epanchin, and the two women also meet here to decide the future of the indecisive love object. But the conflict between love-as-passion and love-as-compassion, which is one day to tear Prince Myshkin apart, is totally absent in the case of Alyosha, who flits lightly from girl to girl and is in love with them all. Alyosha is a Myshkin, as it were, still lacking a religious aura and motivated solely by ordinary human drives and instincts—a Myshkin whose childlike purity is mixed with so much self-indulgence that Dostoevsky has trouble projecting him as favorably as his role in the plot requires.

The Insulted and Injured also contains the first use of a thematic motif indissolubly connected with Dostoevsky's major novels. "We shall have to work out our future happiness by suffering," says Natasha, referring to her relations with her father, "pay for it somehow by fresh miseries. Everything is purified by suffering. . . ." Nothing is more important for a proper understanding of Dostoevsky than an accurate grasp of what these words mean, and a close look at their first use may help to avoid some widespread errors. Natasha here is responding to a question put by Ivan Petrovich: Why does she not simply return home to her father and throw herself on his mercy? Her reply is that he will insist on an "impossible atonement" (3: 230), will require her to renounce her past and her love for Alyosha—and to this she will not submit. Her father, in other words, is still consumed by his wounded resentment, and only the prolongation of his unhappiness may ultimately soften his heart to genuine forgiveness. Natasha, it is clear, is not referring to material hardship or physical deprivation, but rather to the process by which the ramparts of pride, egoism, and wounded self-esteem are battered down and the way left open for forgiveness and love. It is only in this sense that Dostoevsky will ever maintain "suffering" to be a good.

Indeed, as if to obviate any misunderstanding, he pointedly makes clear that nothing is more despicable than to exhibit insensibility or indifference to the suffering of others, or worse, callously to impose suffering for the sake of self-advantage. For Dostoevsky, the nadir of human perversity is to justify a base or vicious act on the ground that the suffering it causes is "good" for the unwilling victim. Prince Valkovsky takes exactly this line in explaining his behavior toward Nellie's mother: "I reflected that by giving her back [her] money I should perhaps make her unhappy. I should have deprived her of the enjoyment of being miserable *entirely owing to me*, and cursing me for it all her life. . . . This ecstasy of suffering can be found in Schilleresque natures, of course; perhaps she will have nothing to eat, but I am convinced that she was happy. I did not want to deprive her of that happiness and did not send her back her money" (3: 367). The underground man, with somewhat less conviction, will use exactly the same reasoning to justify his odious humiliation of the repentant prostitute Liza in the closing scene of *Notes from Underground*.

These considerations should be enough to illustrate both the interest and the shortcomings of Dostoevsky's first major post-Siberian novel. Such deficiencies will only be surmounted when, a few years later, he places the theme of egoism squarely at the center of his action and portrays the radical ideologies of both the 1860s and the 1840s as having encouraged the growth and spread in Russia of this noxious moral plague. For the moment, such a possibility is only adumbrated in *The Insulted and Injured*, where it remains buried under the lachrymose trivia of a *roman-feuilleton* plot that focuses on the behavior of irate fathers toward their erring daughters. Dostoevsky will continue to employ the technique of this kind of melodramatic thriller, derived from the Gothic novel by way of Scott, Dickens, and Balzac (the "urban Gothic," as George Steiner has called it),[10] and to rely on its effects of suspense and dramatic surprise to rivet the attention of his reader. But he will recast it completely to eliminate its usual motivation, or better, to subordinate such motivation firmly to his own creative explorations of the ultimate moral consequences of radical beliefs.

PART II

The Era of Proclamations

CHAPTER 10

The First Leaflets

In the fall of each year, it was the custom for Russian periodicals to print a declaration of their plans and intentions and to appeal for subscriptions. *Time* carried such an announcement, written by Feodor Dostoevsky, in its issue of September 1861—and it was not only a statement of principles but also a legitimate paean of triumph. "The public has supported us," Dostoevsky declared; "it has responded to our announcement of publication made last year, and thus has reinforced us in our certitude that the idea in whose name we have launched our journal is correct. We can say without boasting that the support shown us by the public has been of a degree quite unprecedented for a long time in our journalism" (19: 147). Dostoevsky then goes on to state the general principles of *pochvennichestvo* in his usual sprightly fashion, offering numerous ingenious illustrations of the necessity for Russians to create a culture of their own rather than accepting any of the ready-made European models: "Can one really not agree that even in our past existence, old-fashioned as it was, there were many phenomena that we measured with too narrow a yardstick? . . . Even in many events that we have traced back directly to 'the realm of darkness,' we have neglected to notice the strength coming from the soil, the laws of evolution, love" (19: 148).

Dostoevsky again asserts *Time*'s policy of independence from all existing currents of Russian opinion, and continues to battle with all those journals against which hostilities had already been declared. Only the Slavophils are spared because, as Dostoevsky now affirms, Russian thought has been irresistibly moving in their direction at least since the late 1840s. "If Belinsky had lived one more year," he asserts, echoing an idea of Grigoryev's, "he would have become a Slavophil, which means that he would have fallen out of the frying pan into the fire; nothing else remained for him; and besides, in the development of his thought, he did not fear any fire. He loved man too much for that!" (19: 149). Dostoevsky thus attempts to enlist the sacred name of Belinsky for the cause of *pochvennichestvo*—not in order to accentuate the elements it had absorbed from Westernism, but rather to enhance its Slavophil component with the aureole of the great critic's prestige.

Despite this clear indication of a more pronounced Slavophil tendency, Dostoevsky tried to maintain *Time*'s good (or at least not yet overtly hostile) relations with the radical progressives of *The Contemporary*. Accordingly, he expresses regret at the sharpness of some of his polemics against "opinions which perhaps were in radical disagreement with our own"; those polemics perhaps offended the public by their harshness and excessive self-assurance, "but [they] were honest opinions, uttered without fear and inspired by noble motives" (19: 149). If he cherished any hopes that such words would have a soothing effect, he was sadly mistaken; before 1861 was out *The Contemporary* printed its first attack on *Time* from the pen of the young critic M. A. Antonovich, soon to become famous for the intemperance and coarseness of his polemical manner and his total lack of literary judgment. This skirmish marked the beginning of a war of words and ideas that continued throughout the life of Dostoevsky's two journals.

Becoming more strident and embittered with time, this polemic played its part in turning Dostoevsky decisively against the radicals and ending whatever tolerance for them he yet retained. Still more crucial in this respect was the social-political conjuncture of 1861-1862, the years that marked the beginning of outright revolutionary agitation aimed at dethroning Alexander II and stirring up a peasant revolution. The events of these years convinced Dostoevsky that all hopes of political compromise with the radicals were futile, and that, even worse, their hopeless endeavors would only strengthen the reaction he had prophesied in the words of Prince Valkovsky. As a result, he would see no other possible course but to align himself definitively with the anti-radical opposition—though not, it should be added, with the measures of repression taken by the government to silence radical opinion.

2

The one or two years immediately following the liberation of the serfs on February 16, 1861, are known by Russian historians as "the era of proclamations." For the first time since the Decembrist uprising in 1825, open agitation was carried on against the régime in the streets of Petersburg and Moscow. Proclamations mysteriously surfaced everywhere, and Dostoevsky remembered eleven years later how "one morning I found at the door of my apartment, on the handle of the lock, one of the most remarkable proclamations among those which had been appearing at the time, and there had been a good many of them" (21: 25). Other people had much the same experience: inflammatory leaflets turned up not only in doorhandles and mailboxes, but also lying scattered along main streets such as the Nevsky Prospect. Before discussing the content of these documents, one should note, as a highly significant and unprecedented event, the sheer fact of their appearance—not to mention the boldness of those who wrote and distributed them at the risk of extremely severe penalties. The sudden explosion of this propaganda campaign reveals the rancorous discontent of the radical intelligentsia with the Tsar whom, just a few years before, they had been hailing in adulatory terms for his intention to bring an end to serf-dom.

Even before the issuance of the liberation decree, the radical progres-sives had become convinced that the economic terms proposed would prove disadvantageous to the peasantry and, in the long run, lead to their impoverishment. The peasants themselves were simply bewildered by the complicated terms of the manifesto, which, of course, most of them could not read; and rumors swept the vast countryside that the "true liberation" supposedly proclaimed by the Tsar was being concealed by the rapacious landed gentry. Such a "true liberation" had long been cherished in the apocalyptic imagination of the Russian peasants, who dreamed that they would be granted, without any required repayment, *all* the land they deemed to be their own. Such claims did not, except in a few instances, in-clude the land ordinarily considered to be the landlords' property. "What the peasants meant by their dreams of 'true liberty,' " Franco Venturi has written, "was mainly the complete separation of their community from the landlord, the breaking of all ties between them, and hence the *obshchina* closing in on itself."[1]

Various literate peasants or people of peasant stock, who set up as "inter-preters" of the floridly written and ambiguous liberation decree in the sense desired by the people, gained a wide following among credulous listeners only too willing to believe in the treachery and mendacity of their overlords. Refusal to obey the local authorities occurred in several districts, and the most widespread disorder of this kind took place in and around the small village of Bezdna in the province of Kazan. At this spot, a *raskolnik* named Anton Petrov acquired an immense authority over the peasantry of the re-gion when, on the basis of an aberrant reading of the manifesto supposedly inspired by divine illumination, he proclaimed the "true liberation" which pretended to disclose the genuine intentions of the holy Tsar. Troops were finally sent in during April 1861 to arrest the agitator, who was telling the peasants not to comply with any of their obligations to the landowners; and when his followers refused to surrender him on command, several salvos were fired into the unarmed and peaceful mass. The official casualty fig-ures listed fifty-one dead and seventy-seven wounded, but word-of-mouth reports spoke of several hundred casualties. A requiem mass for the peas-ants killed at Bezdna was organized in nearby Kazan by the students of the University and the Ecclesiastical Academy, and a popular young clergy-man who taught history at the Academy made a speech declaring Anton Petrov to have been "a new prophet . . . and he too has proclaimed liberty in the name of God."[2]*

* Dostoevsky refers to "the Anton Petrov affair" in *The Devils* and ridicules his archetypal lib-eral, Stepan Trofimovich Verkhovensky, for having been thrown into a panic when similar

This clergyman, Afanasy Prokofievich Shchapov by name, had already achieved some notoriety for a Slavophil interpretation of the religious schism in the Russian Church. He depicted the schismatics as a native form of defiance against the imposition of foreign customs and ideas; and when the *raskolniki* later rejected the alien state reforms imposed by Peter the Great, even declaring the Tsar himself to be nothing less than the dreaded apparition of the Antichrist, Shchapov considered such a reaction to be a continuance of the same struggle for cultural independence. Taken into custody for his subversive speech at the Kazan service, he was tried, deprived of his chair, and sentenced to confinement in a monastery. But Alexander II intervened to lighten the sentence, and ordered Shchapov to be given a post in the branch of the Ministry of Internal Affairs dealing with relations with the Old Believers.

A year later he began to issue his most important work, *The Land and the Schism (Zemstvo i raskol)*, the second part of which, probably through the recommendation of Apollon Grigoryev, was published in *Time*. Much of this text was devoted to the sect of the *Beguny* ("Runners," or "Wanderers"), whose beliefs Shchapov interpreted not as an exclusively religious phenomenon but as a form of social protest. The *Beguny* refused to carry an internal passport, as required by law, because they believed the world to be ruled by Antichrist; and they wandered through the Russian land as wayfarers, stubbornly rejecting all the obligations imposed on them by the godless state. They were, as Abbott Gleason has recently put it, "religious and unself-conscious anarchists" who were escaping from state constraints, and they served "to lend an apocalyptic religious sanction to the previously existing phenomenon of peasant flight" from servitude.[3] Shchapov's theories certainly contributed their share to Dostoevsky's own assessment of the dissenting sects as a positive manifestation of Russian social-religious protest against the domination of Western ideas and values; and he sought in the heretical theology of the sects an insight into the indigenous essence of the Russian folk character. A bill from a bookstore dated August 1862 shows him to have ordered, among many other works, five books on the *Raskol*, including the major historical study by Shchapov.[4]

3

The growth of peasant unrest within the country also stirred the intelligentsia into action. Three months after the fusillade at Bezdna, the first leaf-

events occurred closer to his own province: "He cried out at the club that more troops were needed, that they ought to be telegraphed for from another province. . . . Fortunately it all passed over very quickly and ended in nothing, but I was surprised at Stepan Trofimovich at the time" (10: 32).

One may perhaps surmise from this remark that Dostoevsky believed the government had needlessly used force to cope with a problem that might have been resolved peacefully.

let of what was to become a veritable blizzard made its appearance in Petersburg and then in Moscow. Called *The Great Russian* (*Velikoruss*) and quite moderate in tone, it was clearly addressed to the educated classes and inspired by some of the fears aroused by events in Bezdna and elsewhere in the countryside. Two other numbers were circulated at the beginning and end of September, just preceding the outbreak of student disorders at the University of St. Petersburg.

"The government is bringing Russia to a Pugachev revolt," declared the first issue. "We must reexamine the entire peasant problem and solve it in some other way."[5] The government itself, it was suggested, should pay the redemption fees for the land allotted to the peasants, and at the same time free the nationalities of the Russian Empire or at least give them the choice of freedom. No clear political change was advocated, and the leaflet even appealed to Alexander II to bypass the bureaucracy that was stifling his reforms; a national assembly should be convened to help the Tsar come into more direct contact with the nation as a whole. The author or authors of *The Great Russian* still remain unknown, but the suspects all belonged to the circle of students and young Army officers grouped around Chernyshevsky and *The Contemporary*. V. A. Obruchev, an ex-officer who had joined the staff of *The Contemporary*, was caught distributing the leaflet and sent to Siberia for a number of years (a setback that did not prevent him from subsequently ending his career as a major-general in the Army).

Simultaneously with the second and third numbers of *The Great Russian*, which circulated in the fall of 1861, another proclamation appeared, entitled *To the Young Generation* (*K Molodomu Pokoleniyu*). Its author is now known to be N. V. Shelgunov, an official in the Pedagogical Institute for Forestry who also contributed social-economic articles to *The Contemporary*. The leaflet was revised by the same M. L. Mikhailov who had gained fame as a defender of woman's rights, and Herzen printed it in London, with considerable reluctance and foreboding, at his Free Russian Press. Mikhailov was imprudent enough to show one of the smuggled copies to Vsevolod Kostomarov, a young writer who had come to Petersburg with a letter of introduction from Aleksey Pleshcheev and had contributed both to *The Contemporary* and to *Time* (the second issue of *Time* contained his Russian version of one of Longfellow's *Poems on Slavery*). When the authorities began to investigate Kostomarov, he was denounced by his younger brother; the suspect in turn denounced Mikhailov, already under surveillance; and the latter was arrested on September 14, 1861. He was the first well-known member of the intelligentsia to have been personally touched by the repression mounted in response to the leaflet campaign, and his imprisonment in solitary confinement, his trial, and his sentence to Siberia for six years in December 1861 produced an enormous wave of indignation.

To the Young Generation was only one of a series of leaflets written by Mikhailov, Shelgunov, and perhaps Chernyshevsky (the others, addressed to peasants and soldiers, were never printed), and it took a much harsher line than the moderate *The Great Russian*. No question now remained that a political change was envisaged, and that the authors had broken with Tsarism once and for all: "We do not need a power that oppresses us; we do not need a power that prevents the mental, civic, and economic development of the country; we do not need a power that raises corruption and self-seeking as its banner." What Russia needs is "an elected leader receiving a salary for his services," and Alexander II should be told that the greatest achievement of his reign—the liberation of the serfs—had created a new order in which he had become superfluous: "If Alexander does not understand this and does not wish voluntarily to make way for the people—so much the worse for him." The general dissatisfaction can still be kept within bounds if the Tsar gives up the throne; but "if to achieve our ends, by dividing the land among the people, we have to kill a hundred thousand of the gentry, even that will not deter us."[6]

Noticeable in *To the Young Generation* is the strong influence of Herzen's "Russian Socialism," with its Messianic vision of a social-political future for Russia without precedent in the history of Europe. The failure of the revolutions of 1848, the leaflet declares, "is a failure for Europe only. It tells us nothing of the possibility of other changes here in Russia." Europe is weighed down by the burden of its heritage, but Russia's very backwardness, the absence of traditions and of a true "political past" of its own, constitutes its chance for the future: "This is why, unlike Western Europe, we are not afraid of the future. . . . We believe in the forces of Russia because we believe that we have been destined to bring a new principle into history, to hand on our own message and not to haunt the old gardens of Europe."[7] A full democracy was envisaged; all land belonging to the nation would be divided into *obshchinas*; everyone would be a member of a self-administered commune, and whether a state of any kind would continue to exist is left unclear.

Dostoevsky mentions *To the Young Generation* by name and was certainly familiar with its contents, whose willingness to contemplate the prospect of mass slaughter would probably have sent shivers down his spine (though he had not flinched from the same prospect himself twelve years before). But he would surely have responded with a certain sympathy to the declaration that Russia would introduce a totally new principle into the historical destinies of mankind. Indeed, some passages of the text bear a striking resemblance to Dostoevsky's stress in *Time* on the necessity for Russians to create their own indigenous culture. The leaflet, for example, attacks "the constitutionalists" and "economists" who desire "to turn Russia into England and impregnate us with English maturity. But does Russia

138

have anything in common with England as regards its geographical position, its natural riches, the conditions of its soil, the quality and quantity of land? Would the English on Russian soil have developed as they did on their island? We have aped the French and Germans quite enough, do we need to ape the English as well? No, we do not desire English economic maturity, Russian stomachs will not be able to digest it."[8] Whatever his objections to the political aims of the proclamation, Dostoevsky would hardly have been able to suppress a twinge of approval for such sentiments.

4

In view of the events at Bezdna and their aftermaths, which noticeably increased the mood of tension and uncertainty in the country, the government decided to tighten restrictions and regulations in all areas where they had been relaxed in recent years. Nowhere had they been more liberal than in the universities, where students had acquired the right to set up their own libraries, establish mutual-aid funds, publish newspapers if they wished, and more or less run their own affairs. Limitations on admission had also been lifted, and lectures were thrown open to all who wished to attend. When this freedom led to manifestations of displeasure against unpopular professors that sometimes assumed a political character, authorities took these as indications of a rebelliousness they no longer wished to tolerate.

New regulations drawn up for the universities abolished all the corporate liberties of the students and reimposed fees that had been eliminated for the poorer ones just a few years earlier. These regulations, approved by the Tsar in May 1861, were instituted at the beginning of the fall term; but the students refused to accept them, and, to the unfeigned delight of a large crowd of onlookers enjoying the unprecedented spectacle, organized a protest march through the streets despite the presence of police and waiting Army troops. After delegates were chosen to see the rector and present the students' demands, the marchers peacefully dispersed on being assured that no action would be taken against them. But many were treacherously arrested the same night, other arrests followed later, and, when agitation continued, the universities were closed for a full year. A number of the students who participated in these events later became well-known in the ranks of the Russian revolutionary movement.

The sympathies of most of the intelligentsia, including Feodor and Mikhail Dostoevsky, were on the side of the students against the authorities. When those arrested were incarcerated in the Peter-and-Paul Fortress (though some had to be taken to Kronstadt because of the overflow), Dostoevsky surely recalled his own long months of solitary confinement in the same forbidding prison. But the students were not suspected of any criminal political conspiracy, and times had changed since the sinister days of 1849. The student-prisoners were lodged in common quarters, visitors could come and go as they pleased, and gifts from friends and well-wishers poured in to make their lot more comfortable. A large slab of beef was grilled in the apartment of Mikhail Dostoevsky and sent, along with bottles of cognac and red wine, to help the captives pass the time agreeably and to supplement their prison rations. Strakhov, who supplies this information, writes that the provisions were dispatched in the name of "the editorial bureau of *Time*," thus giving this manifestation of sympathy a wider significance as a public declaration of the liberalism of the editors and contributors of the periodical.[9]

By the fall of 1861, Dostoevsky had already published several installments of *House of the Dead*, and these sketches provided the Russian public with its first terrifying image of what lay ahead for those sentenced for a political crime. "At that time we knew about Siberia through *Notes from the House of the Dead*," wrote Shelgunov many years later, "and this, of course, was quite enough to make us fear for the fate of Mikhailov."[10] No writer was now more celebrated than Dostoevsky, whose name was surrounded with the halo of his former suffering, and whose sketches only served to enhance his prestige as a precursor on the path of political martyrdom that so many members of the younger generation had begun to suspect they might be forced to tread themselves. As a result, he was often asked to read from his works by student groups and for the benefit of worthy causes such as the Literary Fund and the Sunday-school movement. As the novelist P. D. Boborykin later recalled, in the author of *The Insulted and Injured* the radical youth saw, "a fighter for social justice and an exposer of all those who, in Russia, crushed every freedom and extinguished every ray of light."[11]

Dostoevsky invariably accepted such invitations, both then and later, because he believed it of first importance to keep in touch with his potential readers. As his fame increased, he also hoped that it might be possible to exercise some influence on public opinion through his personal interventions. Besides, he also looked with a good deal of sympathy on the initiative of the Sunday-school movement, which had spread like wildfire since its founding. Professor Pavlov had come from Kiev to St. Petersburg in 1861 and now guided his followers from his new post in the capital. The government, with disarming innocence, at first reacted favorably to this display of initiative and enterprise by the intelligentsia, and classrooms were placed at the disposal of the movement with official approval. Two years later, an investigation showed that Pavlov's favorite slogan, "la révolution par l'école," had been taken quite literally and that some teachers had used the classroom to indoctrinate their pupils in favor of atheism and subversion. The thought may possibly have crossed Dostoevsky's mind that the instruction in such schools, given the social-political complexion of the majority of the teachers, might not be restricted to penmanship, simple arithmetic, and the rudiments of geography. But he was an ardent advocate of educating the people as rapidly as possible, and he probably believed them quite impervious to "dangerous" ideas with a Western flavor and expressed in Western terms. Certainly, from his point of view, the masses were far more in need of instruction of any kind than of being protected from contact with possibly seditious mentors.

5

Nothing untoward occurred at the various benefits in which Dostoevsky participated up through the spring of 1862; but matters were very different at a sensational "literary-musical evening" on March 2, which took place in the large salle Ruadze before an excitable crowd of three thousand people. The event, which Dostoevsky later enshrined in the masterly *fête* scene of *The Devils*, was organized on behalf of the Literary Fund; but arrangements had been confided to a special section set up to help needy students and run by students themselves—many of them among the leaders of radical agitation in the University. Even without such clearly partisan sponsorship, this massive assemblage of the Petersburg intelligentsia in the heavily charged atmosphere created by the massacre at Bezdna, the student demonstrations, the proclamations, the arrests, and the recent sentencing of Mikhailov could hardly have avoided taking on the significance of a public protest. Everyone knew, as Shelgunov wrote in his memoirs, that among the "needy students" for whom the flower of the cultured public wished to raise money were Mikhailov and Obruchev,[12] and the social-political character of the evening was accentuated by many details.

The literati invited to participate were all of a progressive or radical complexion: Dostoevsky, Professor Platon Pavlov, Chernyshevsky, Nekrasov, and V. S. Kurochkin (editor of the radical satirical journal *The Spark*). Henrik Wienawski, Anton Rubinstein, and the leading soprano of the Italian opera had agreed to take charge of the musical interludes, and an ensemble made up of the wives and daughters of participants and their friends (including Dostoevsky's niece) were scheduled to perform on four grand pianos in the finale. The choice of music on the program was also probably not without significance. The prima donna sang a *lied* of Schubert followed by the Neapolitan folksong "Santa Lucia"; and one suspects that this sequence was understood as a tribute to the struggle of the Italian people for independence against Austrian rule. If Rubinstein played his piano transcription of Beethoven's "The Ruins of Athens" (1811), it was because this work, as was well known, had been composed in honor of the Greek revolt against the Turkish Empire. Rubinstein had recast it under the inspiration of the revolutions of 1848 throughout Europe, and a series of uprisings in

Greek cities just the month before (February 1862) had given the piece a new immediacy. Glinka's "Kamarinskaya," a symbol of peasant earthiness and self-assertion, had been arranged for the ensemble as the final musical offering.[13]

Dostoevsky was chosen to open the program, and he read from some still unpublished chapters of *House of the Dead* describing the death of a soldier from consumption in the prison hospital. By what may have been only chance, though the coincidence is really too good to be true, the name of this soldier also turned out to be Mikhailov. "He was quite young, not more than five-and-twenty, tall, thin, and of extremely attractive appearance . . . [he] was strangely silent, always gently and quietly melancholy, as though he were 'drying up' in prison." The death scene is embellished with those Dickensian details that Dostoevsky always loves to employ: "I remember the glowing slanting rays of the sun piercing through the green frozen panes of our windows. The sunshine was streaming full on the dying man" (4: 140). Mikhailov tears off his prison rags during the convulsions of his death agony, and Dostoevsky dwells on the terribly emaciated body, the cross dangling from his neck, and the iron fetters that prison regulations would not allow to be removed. The grizzled sentry on duty, summoned to carry out the corpse, is so moved by the piteous sight that he takes off his helmet and sword belt and crosses himself. A gray-haired convict gestures toward Mikhailov at the same time and mutters: "He too had a mother" (4: 141). One can well imagine the intensely moving effect of this passage, with its constant repetition of the name, on those many people who knew *the other* Mikhailov well and were filled with ominous premonitions about his future.

Yet the audience response to Dostoevsky was as nothing compared to the veritable hurricane aroused by the intervention of Professor Platon Pavlov, who had announced a lecture on the topic of "A Thousand Years of Russian History." The millennium of Russia had been celebrated that very year with a great display of official pomp, and Pavlov's speech, duly submitted to the censorship, had been approved for delivery. But the nervous and highly volatile Pavlov, who is mentioned in the memoirs of the left-wing L. F. Panteleev as "not a completely normal person,"[14] whipped the audience into hysteria by his manner of delivery. Speaking in a quavering voice that sometimes rose to a shriek, he accentuated the words of his text so as to turn them into an implacable indictment of Russian history under its thousand years of autocratic rule. Shelgunov provides this firsthand report: "In the hall one could hear a growing rumble, there were shouts of furious exhilaration, seats were rattled, heels were pounded. I was sitting on the platform with others, among them Nekrasov, awaiting his turn. The agitated E. P. Kovalevsky [the president of the Literary Fund] ran up, and, turning to us, said: 'Stop him! Stop him! To-morrow he'll be sent away!' But it was impossible to get Pavlov off the platform; more and more carried away, he finished his talk amidst the deafening shouts of the public and left the platform."[15] The audience had been worked up to an indescribable pitch of enthusiasm, and the applause was not only ear-shattering but climaxed by a ringing chorus of the "Marseillaise." Kovalevsky's prediction proved correct: the next day Pavlov was sent into provincial exile and only allowed to return to the capital several years later.

Dostoevsky recalled this memorable outburst of long-suppressed public resentment in the turbulent *fête* scene of *The Devils*—an occasion also organized, it will be recalled, for the charitable purpose of aiding the needy governesses of the province. Pavlov is parodied in the figure of the professor who strikes the narrator by his peculiar comportment as he walks back and forth in preparation for his entry on stage: "Short, bald, with a graying beard, decently dressed, he seemed to be about forty years old. But most curious of all was that, each time he swung around, he lifted his right fist and waved it over his head, only to lower it abruptly as if he were crushing some adversary. This gesture was regularly repeated" (10: 365). Later in the proceedings, in the midst of general uproar and confusion, he leaps on the stage and takes control of the unruly multitude: "He absolutely looked like a madman. His face lit up with a smile of triumph, filled with an immense conceit, he contemplated the hall and seemed overjoyed at the disorder reigning there." Once launched into his speech, "he lifted his fist, brandished it furiously over his head, and brought it down with a sharp blow as if pulverizing some adversary. Frantic shouts broke out everywhere; half of the hall applauded with all their might. The most timid allowed themselves to be swept away: Russia was being covered with mud; how could one refuse to shout with enthusiasm?" (10: 374).

Unlike Dostoevsky's *fête* scene, however, which terminates in pandemonium, the audience in the salle Ruadze eventually calmed down. Pavlov's performance was followed by Nekrasov, who read some of his "civic" poems, and then the prima donna sang and Rubinstein played "The Ruins of Athens." As his contribution to the program, Chernyshevsky offered some reminiscences eulogizing the recently deceased Dobrolyubov and defending him against charges of coldness and personal abrasiveness. Many found the text inappropriate, the delivery dull, and Chernyshevsky's casual manner even vaguely insulting to the public; hisses were heard from time to time, although they were drowned out by the applause of his partisans. He was succeeded by Kurochkin, who read his translations of some of Béranger's explicitly radical poems in praise of revolution and Socialism, and the evening ended with a rousing version of the "Kamarinskaya." The music enjoyed a great success throughout, and so many encores were requested that a well-bred agent of the secret police, in the report he submitted, indignantly commented on the "indelicacy" of dragging out the evening for so long that ladies had been pinned to their seats for seven hours.[16]

6

The repercussions caused by this literary-musical evening affected much more than the personal fortunes of Professor Platon Pavlov. Despite the closing of the University earlier in 1861, the faculty had organized public lectures to replace the regular classes; but Petersburg students, as a protest against Pavlov's exile, now decided to boycott these informal courses. Professors were asked to join the movement by canceling their lectures, and those who refused were mercilessly harassed. The authorities themselves finally decided to terminate the de facto university, which had been given permission to use certain official buildings for its courses. "The reason for the destruction of the [free] university," Strakhov wrote nineteen years later, "was the famous 'literary-musical evening.' . . . That evening was undertaken with the aim of providing, as it were, a showing of all the leading progressive literary forces. . . . The noise and enthusiasm were enormous, and it has always seemed to me since that the evening was the highest point reached by the liberal movement of our society, as well as the culmination of our cloud-castle revolution."[17]

After this scandalous demonstration, Strakhov goes on to explain, it became clear that "every liberal measure arouse[d] a movement in society that used such a measure for its own ends, which were not liberal at all but entirely radical."[18] In all probability, this is the conclusion that Dostoevsky also began to draw from the same riotous sequence of events; but he did not swing round to sharing Strakhov's implacable hostility toward the radicals and all their ilk. Instead, rather than joining in the hue and cry against them that shortly ensued, he urgently tried to warn them against the consequences of their own folly.

CHAPTER 11

Young Russia

Historians do not agree with Strakhov's judgment that the "literary-musical evening" was the highest crest reached by the pounding wave of social-political unrest during the spring of 1862. Actually, the true peak of the "era of proclamations" arrived two months later, in mid-May, when a leaflet entitled *Young Russia* was circulated. It is this remarkable document that brought the revolutionary ferment of the time to its convulsive climax.

The Tsarist authorities never discovered that its author was a twenty-year-old youth, P. G. Zaichnevsky, who already had acquired a considerable underground past despite his tender years. On entering the University of Moscow in 1859, his first move had been to set up a clandestine printing press and publish works by Herzen, Nikolay Ogarev, Feuerbach (*The Essence of Christianity*), and Büchner (*Force and Matter*). Making no secret of his radical sympathies, he attempted to organize peasant resistance to the terms of the liberation during the summer of 1861, and he was arrested after openly proclaiming his revolutionary ideas in a letter intercepted by the secret police and brought to the attention of the Tsar. All the same, Zaichnevsky enjoyed the same astonishingly lax conditions of imprisonment in Moscow as had been accorded the Petersburg students. Friends could visit him without hindrance, supply him with fresh fruit and food to augment his prison rations, and bring books, magazines, and newspapers (some of them illegal) to keep him in touch with the political scene. Zaichnevsky wrote the proclamation in his cell with the help of a small group of friends, all regular visitors, who had taken an active part in Moscow student demonstrations in the autumn of 1861. The manuscript, smuggled out with the help of a guard, was printed by Zaichnevsky's comrades on their own press; and they decided to make Petersburg the center of distribution so as to divert attention from the real source.

Young Russia burst like a thunderclap over the country, and, combined with the other disturbances of the time, created an atmosphere of confusion and panic. Both as an individual citizen distressed by social disarray, and as the editor of a journal required to take a stand on public issues, Dostoevsky was deeply involved with the crisis symbolized by the *Young Russia* proclamation; and his behavior at this crucial moment may be considered emblematic of the social-political stance he would always maintain in the future. For what he did, so far as possible, was to intervene in the turmoil with the hope of calming the extreme passions that were leading the blindly reckless radicals to disaster and might provoke the frightened government to measures of severe repression. He attempted, in other words, to play the role of a conciliator; and it was in such a capacity that he would continue to define his own role in the desperate struggle that tore Russian society apart during his lifetime.

2

A vivid sense of the first reactions caused by *Young Russia* may be given in Dostoevsky's own words, written eleven years after he found a copy wedged into the door handle of his apartment: "One could not have imagined anything more nonsensical and stupid. Its contents were most shocking, and expressed in a most ludicrous form; such as only a scoundrel could have invented in order to write them down. I was very much annoyed, and all day I felt bad. All this was still novel, and so close that even to gain a clear view of these men was still difficult." What overcame Dostoevsky most of all, even despite himself, was a strange sense of exasperation: "And here I, who heart and soul disagreed with these people, and with the meaning of their movement—I became suddenly vexed and almost ashamed, as it were, of their incompetence: 'Why is everything so stupid and ignorant about them?' " He found himself greatly upset "by the educational, mental level, and the lack of even a minimal comprehension of reality—this, to me, was terribly oppressive. Even though I had lived in Petersburg some three years and had observed certain events, this proclamation that morning stupefied me, as it were, and came as an altogether new and unexpected revelation: never before that day had I experienced such nullity!" (21: 25).*

Why Dostoevsky should have responded so violently to the leaflet becomes quite comprehensible once we glance at its contents. *Young Russia* minced no words in declaring its aims, and exhibited none of the reluctance to go to extremes still discernible in the other two proclamations. *To the Young Generation*, which had also contemplated violence, did so only as a last resort and far preferred a peaceful abdication; but *Young Russia* took exactly the opposite tack. It demanded "a revolution, a bloody and pitiless revolution, a revolution which must change everything down to the very roots, utterly overthrowing all the foundations of present society and bringing about the ruin of all who support the present order."[1] And this would require not only a social-political revolution; it would mean the total transformation of a system in which "a small number of people who own

---

* In his article, Dostoevsky mistakenly cites the title of the proclamation he had read as *To the Young Generation*. But from other details and a collocation of all the evidence, it is clear that he could only have been speaking of *Young Russia*. There is no argument on this score among the specialists. See *PSS*, 21: 393-394.

capital control the fate of the rest" and in which, consequently, "everything is false, everything is stupid, from religion . . . to the family."[2] Accordingly, the leaflet demanded the total emancipation of women, the abolition of marriage (as "immoral"), the suppression of the family (as a barrier to the full development of the individual), the dissolution of convents and monasteries (as "centers of debauchery"), and the secularization of all church property.[3]

The ultimate objective of *Young Russia* was a democratic republic, and its economics, similar to that of the other proclamations, was based on strengthening and extending the operations of the *obshchina*. But Zaichnevsky was less interested in the future than in the immediate task of preparing the revolution, which, like so many others, he was convinced was on the point of breaking out because of the peasantry's discontent with the terms of liberation. The first step was thus to attack all those, such as Herzen and the authors of *The Great Russian*, who advocated some sort of liberal compromise; and in his critical analysis of the policy of Herzen's *The Bell*, Zaichnevsky joins forces with the polemic against "the superfluous men" of the 1840s initiated by Chernyshevsky and Dobrolyubov. All thought of compromise is rejected because, *Young Russia* declares, revolutions in the past had failed through lack of determination, and "we will go further, not only than the poor revolutionaries of 1848, but also than the great terrorists of the 1790s [in France]."[4] The ultimate aim, of course, was to give power to the people, who would eventually rule themselves in a perfect democratic fashion; but such a transfer of sovereignty could occur only after the triumph of the revolution had been secured. Till then, it would be necessary to place all power in the hands of a revolutionary dictatorship, which would "stop at nothing" to establish "new foundations of society and the economy." Well-read in the history of revolutions, Zaichnevsky himself gave the appropriate label to his own political outlook: Russian Jacobinism.

Such generalities pale into insignificance, however, beside the description of what might occur if the victorious revolution encountered any resolute resistance: "The day will soon come when we will unfurl the great banner of the future, the red banner. And with a mighty cry of 'long live the Russian Social and Democratic Republic,' we will move against the Winter Palace to wipe out all those who dwell there." Bloodshed would, so far as possible, be restricted to the Tsar and his immediate entourage; but if the "whole imperial party" rose in defense of the royal family, then "we will cry 'To your axes' and then we will . . . destroy them in the squares, if the cowardly swine dare to go there. We will destroy them in their houses, in the narrow streets of the towns, in the broad avenues of the capital, and in the villages. Remember that, when this happens, anyone who is not with us is against us and an enemy, and that every method is used to destroy the enemy."[5] Such indulgence in fantasies of mass carnage and total extermination, coupled with a direct threat against the royal family, imparted a sinister aura to *Young Russia* that horrified most of its readers and caused Dostoevsky to despair of the mental capacities of its authors.

His own reactions, though, were so mixed that he pretended to find them baffling. Why should he have identified himself with such gory predictions to the extent of passing a technical judgment of "incompetence" on *Young Russia*? Was he not heart and soul opposed to everything that the leaflet so ferociously advocated? My own opinion is that he was not half as puzzled as he suggests; he knew very well why he had responded in so peculiar a fashion, but the explanation was hardly one he could admit to the readers of his weekly column, *The Diary of a Writer*, in 1873. For if he could so easily place himself in the position of those who had composed the leaflet, it was for the simple reason that its implacable words brought back all too indelible recollections of his own revolutionary past. Dostoevsky too had once been a member of a group of conspirators—the Speshnev secret society—whose aim had been to stir a peasant revolution; he and his comrades had also coolly contemplated the possibility of mass slaughter; and they too had foreseen that the revolution would require guidance and control by the dictatorship of a small council of all-powerful leaders.

Young Russia was thus exposing to public view the very same ruthless revolutionary outlook that Dostoevsky had struggled so stubbornly, and so successfully, to conceal in the investigation of the Petrashevsky affair. And his reaction to the leaflet, it may be surmised, had been prompted by the shock of seeing all this *openly* expressed; it was as if his buried past had risen up to confront him, and the secret he had so carefully guarded all these years—and would continue to guard for the remainder of his life—had finally been brought to light. Moreover, while such a program might once have seemed justified as a desperate last resort in a period of black reaction, its bold disclosure at the present time, *after* the liberation of the serfs, could only have struck him as catastrophic. Its effect on society, as he must have instantly foreseen, would inevitably be to precipitate a general revulsion against the radicals and *all* their objectives.

3

Bloodcurdling passages like those cited above from the text of *Young Russia* provided good grounds for the suspicion that its authors and their friends (the proclamation spoke in the name of a "Central Revolutionary Committee") were somehow linked with and responsible for the series of fires that began to flame in Petersburg almost simultaneously with the pamphlet's circulation. The fires, which raged for two weeks, broke out in various places at the same time as if according to a pre-arranged plan. Whole areas of the city were devastated, including many of the poorer districts; thousands of victims were left homeless and in need of food and shelter. Destructive fires were of course a very common occurrence in Russia, where most construction was of wood; "it is well known that our provincial towns burn down every five years," notes Turgenev laconically in *Fathers and Children*.[6] But the Petersburg fires in the spring of 1862 surpassed anything known till then in the extent of damage and the mysterious inability to control the blazes. No one has established to this day who, if anyone, was responsible for the disaster, whether it was the work of incendiaries or simply of chance. Public opinion, which the authorities did nothing to counteract, immediately connected the catastrophe with the call for total destruction trumpeted by *Young Russia*; and such an association was all the more inevitable because fire, called by peasants the Red Rooster, had always been one of their traditional weapons against the landowners.

An atmosphere of gloom and apprehension reigned throughout the city. "I recall once going with Feodor Mikhailovich for relaxation somewhere on the outskirts of the city to get some fresh air," Strakhov writes. "From the steamer we could see thick clusters of smoke rising in three or four places. . . . We went into some sort of garden park, where music was being played and gypsies sang. But no matter how much we tried to amuse ourselves, our dejected mood did not pass off, and I was soon ready to go home. It is

8. St. Petersburg in Flames. From *L'Illustration*, vol. 40 (Paris, 1862), 4

hard not to believe the fires the work of incendiaries, but this affair, like so many other awful evils of that epoch, for some reason remained totally covered with darkness."[7]

Another impression of the same catastrophe is probably conveyed in Dostoevsky's description of a fire in *The Devils*, a book that contains many allusions—transposed into his own artistic terms—to these crisis-ridden days of the early 1860s. As in the Petersburg fires, several blazes break out simultaneously and a whole quarter begins to burn: "In the neighboring streets there was a terrible confusion. Before the menace of the approaching flames, the inhabitants moved out their furniture, their belongings; but not being able to make up their minds to leave their homes, they settled down in the streets on the chests and feather quilts, each one under his window. The men were occupied with a backbreaking task: they pitilessly tore down all the wooden fences and even the shacks when they were within reach of the flames and the wind was blowing in that direction. The small children, wakened from sleep, were crying; the women, who had already gathered together all their belongings, broke into lamentations; but others went about vacating their homes in silence. Sparks and burning embers flew off into the distance, and were somehow smothered." Crowds came to watch, and Dostoevsky comments that a nighttime fire "produces in the spectator (except if something of his own is destroyed, of course) a sort of nervous commotion, wakes in him the instincts of destruction which, alas!, slumber in every soul, even the soul of the most timid and respectable of functionaries . . ." (10: 394).

From the letter of a young student of philosophy and contributor to *Time*, M. I. Vladislavlev (who later married one of Mikhail Dostoevsky's daughters and rose to become rector of the University of St. Petersburg), we catch a glimpse of how various members of the Dostoevsky family reacted to the fright created by the widespread fires. To Mikhail Dostoevsky's son, then absent from the city, he writes: "Now, really, times are such that wherever you look something is always burning right under your nose. The number of watchmen have been increased. In our house one gate—that leading to the apartment of Feodor Mikhailovich—is closed all the time, and in the other a porter is always sitting to ask people where they are going. I am not at all afraid of the fires because I can almost say: *omnia (mea) mecum porto*; it's a shame about the books if they burn up. Feodor Mikhailovich, I have heard, has insured his possessions. Marya Dimitrievna, I believe, is terribly afraid of the fires and, I think (I myself have not seen them since your departure, and in general don't visit them), wanted to move to Tver for the summer but then for some reason changed her mind. Mikhail Mikhailovich is very philosophical about the fires. I asked him one day: 'and what would you do, Mikhail Mikhailovich, if a fire broke out in your house?' 'Nothing,' he said, 'what can one do?—just keep from being burned alive.' "

Vladislavlev also comments on the rumors: "Everybody throws the blame for setting the fires on the students who are supposed to have printed *Young Russia*. Of course this is nonsense."[8]

Vladislavlev's view represented a minority opinion, and some notion of the frightened anecdotes that were circulating may be gleaned from a letter of Ivan Aksakov to another prominent Slavophil, Yury Samarin. Every store clerk, Aksakov tells him, had read *Young Russia*, and "this proclamation (even before the fires) had filled the people with *horror* in the literal sense of the word. . . . It made even more suspicious, in the eyes of the people, literacy, science, enlightenment—gifts coming from our hands, those of the gentry." The Tsar was reported to have told the lower ranks of the Army and the noncommissioned officers of a plot against his life, and explained that he relied on them but not on the officers because the upper ranks no longer believed in God. Aksakov continues: "The people, of course, did not understand the proclamation [*Young Russia*], but made out only that it preaches impiety, disrespect for '*one's father and mother*,' holds marriage in contempt and wishes to slit the throats of the royal family. . . . Turgenev told me (he was at the fire in the Shchukin Market)—that he heard with his own ears how the most ordinary grizzled *muzhik* shouted: 'The *professors* burned this down.' 'Professors, students'—these words have already become known to the people!"[9]

Young Russia thus brought on a rising tide of resentment against the educated class and everything it represented in the country; literacy and enlightenment itself were threatened because of the menacing and seemingly uncontrollable situation. More than any other of his contemporaries, Dostoevsky had suffered at first hand from the split between the mentality of the people and that of the educated class and had dedicated his journal to the task of creating the unified Russian culture made possible at last by the liberation. Nothing would have seemed to him more ominous for the future, more of a setback for everything he hoped to advance, than the intensifying enmity that he saw swelling all around him between the two groups. And since, just as in the 1840s, he was temperamentally incapable of remaining a mere spectator, he decided to see what he could do personally to ward off the impending disaster. Sometime during these days (the exact date is uncertain, but it was in late May or early June), he unexpectedly paid a call on Chernyshevsky to have a talk with him about the calamitous events threatening to tear apart the fabric of Russian society.

4
———

Two accounts have been left of this incident: one by Dostoevsky writing in 1873, the other by Chernyshevsky setting down his reminiscences ten years later. Both confirm that such a visit took place, but differ in their account of what was said and meant to be understood. One thing, however, is clear: Chernyshevsky's version contains some distortion of the facts. He pretends, for example, that he had never before encountered Dostoevsky in person and recognized him, as he stood in the doorway, only because "his face was somewhat known to me from portraits";[10] but both had appeared on the same platform two months earlier during the famous literary-musical evening. Dostoevsky, on the other hand, recalls having met Chernyshevsky in 1859, just after returning to Petersburg, and claims that later they "would meet sometimes, but very rarely." Since the two would certainly have bumped into each other occasionally in the small, closed world of the St. Petersburg literati, his version seems much more plausible.

As Dostoevsky tells it, he went to see Chernyshevsky at about five in the afternoon on the very day that he found the *Young Russia* proclamation attached to his door handle; it was thus the leaflet that stirred him into action, not, at least in his version, the fires. When he arrived, Chernyshevsky "opened the door with extreme cordiality and led me into the living room." Dostoevsky did not beat around the bush, and their conversation ran as follows:

> "Nikolay Gavrilovich, what is this"—I handed him the proclamation.
>
> He took it as something quite unknown to him and read it. There were only about ten lines.*
>
> "How, what?"—he asked me, with a slight smile.
>
> "Is it possible that they are so stupid and ridiculous? Is it possible that they can't be stopped and that an end can't be put to this abomination?"
>
> He answered very weightily and impressively:
>
> "Do you really suppose that I am in sympathy with them and that I could have taken part in the compilation of this scrap of paper?"
>
> "Indeed, I do not suppose it."—I answered—"and I even deem it unnecessary to assure you of this. But at any rate they should be stopped by all means. Your word carries weight with them, and they are certainly afraid of your opinion."
>
> "I know no one among them."
>
> "I am also convinced of this. However, one doesn't have to know them at all or speak personally to them. It would suffice if you would express aloud somewhere your reproof. This will reach them."
>
> "Maybe it will have no effect. Besides, these, as side facts, are inevitable."
>
> "And yet they are damaging to everybody and everything."
>
> (21: 25-26)

* Here Dostoevsky's memory has played him false again, just as it did about the title of the proclamation. *Young Russia* was longer than ten lines; perhaps he meant that the nature of its contents could be seen after ten lines. A copy of the text is printed as an appendix in B. P. Kozmin, *P. G. Zaichnevsky i "Molodaya Rossiya"* (Moscow, 1932), 157-170.

The conversation ended when someone else arrived for a visit (Dostoevsky discreetly does not mention any names), and he took his leave. "I deem
it my duty to remark," he adds, "that I spoke to Chernyshevsky sincerely,
and I believed, as I also believe now, that he was not 'in sympathy' with
these leaflet distributors." (Since Dostoevsky published his article while
Chernyshevsky was still in punitive exile, convicted of having written revolutionary propaganda intended for distribution among the peasantry, his
words could be taken as an implicit criticism of the sentence.) Chernyshevsky, Dostoevsky continues, repaid his call shortly afterwards, staying for
an hour or so: "I confess that I have rarely met a more kindhearted, cordial
man, so that even then I felt puzzled over certain comments on his alleged
harsh, uncongenial character" (21: 25-26).

An innocent reader might presume that Chernyshevsky's return call was
simply a matter of courtesy; but in fact he had dropped in for a very specific

9. N. G. Chernyshevsky, ca. 1859

153

purpose, wishing, as we now know, to obtain Dostoevsky's permission to use certain extracts from *House of the Dead* in one of the readers for the people then being assembled on all sides. The chief editor of the proposed book was a Colonel Putyata of the General Staff College, who also happened to be a member of the secret revolutionary group known as Land and Liberty (*Zemlya i Volya*) that had begun to form around this time. The history of this underground organization, the first of many that sprang up during the 1860s, is still very obscure; but its active members are all known to have been friends or acquaintances of Chernyshevsky and to have circulated within the orbit of *The Contemporary*. (Whether Chernyshevsky himself was an official adherent has never been established and is a matter of dispute among specialists.)[11] Just then on the point of leaving for his first trip to Europe, Dostoevsky gave full authority to Chernyshevsky to make a selection from *House of the Dead* or to authorize someone else of his choosing to do so. If nothing else, Dostoevsky's willingness to give Chernyshevsky a free hand with the disposition of his work goes a long way to confirm his account of the personal friendliness he felt toward the radical leader.

Chernyshevsky's sentiments are more difficult to estimate, but they may have been less icily ironic than would appear from the tone of his words many years later. He had been close to members of the Petrashevsky circle as a young man, some of them intimate friends of Dostoevsky, and he had read Dostoevsky's early work, if not with unqualified admiration then at least with some appreciation.[12] By 1883, however, after long years of crippling exile, he had become understandably embittered. Echoes of Dostoevsky's increasing glory had certainly reached him even in the godforsaken arctic wilderness to which he had been sent to freeze, and this ascension had been crowned by the apotheosis of Dostoevsky's state funeral two years earlier. The portrait he offers, at any rate, seems deliberately calculated to cast a cloud over Dostoevsky's refulgence.

He depicts Dostoevsky as having entered his flat frantically several days after the monster fire in the Old Clothes Market, and to have blurted out: "I have come to you on a very important matter with an urgent request. You are well acquainted with the people who burnt the Old Clothes Market and have an influence on them. I beg you, stop them from any continuation of what they have done." Chernyshevsky pretends to have received this overwrought plea as the utterance of someone under extreme mental stress, and to have recalled that Dostoevsky was known to suffer from a nervous disorder bordering on derangement. Adopting the tactic recommended by doctors in such situations, who agree with patients in order to calm their agitated condition, he replied: "Very well, Feodor Mikhailovich, I will do as you wish." At this, Dostoevsky "grasped my hand, pressed it as hard as he could, and in a voice choking with joyful emotion expressed, in ecstatic phrases, his personal gratitude that out of consideration for him I was pre-

serving Petersburg from the fate to which the city had been condemned—
that of being burned down."

Once this assurance had quieted Dostoevsky, Chernyshevsky then
adroitly shifted the conversation to less dangerous subjects such as
whether *Time* was doing well and would be able to meet the expenses of
publication. Happily distracted from his obsessions, Dostoevsky turned to
this topic and spoke for two hours, while Chernyshevsky, listening with one
ear, impatiently awaited his departure.[13] As for the return visit, Chernyshevsky disingenuously writes as if he had not known Colonel Putyata at all,
referring to him, without using his name, only as "a gentleman of modest
and honorable appearance," who had presumably just dropped in out of the
blue to enlist Chernyshevsky's aid in a worthy cause. Impressed with his
plans for a reader, Chernyshevsky agreed to help this gentleman, a stranger
to literary circles, with the problem of obtaining permissions for his anthology. Dostoevsky's name happened to be on the list of contributors, and
Chernyshevsky decided to use the occasion to repay his call. Once Dostoevsky had quickly given his consent to publication, the remainder of the conversation, of no importance, was devoted to regaling his guest with praises
of his brother and Strakhov. "I remained with him as long as politeness required," Chernyshevsky concludes with heavy sarcasm, "probably more
than five minutes and, in fact, less than four hours, and then I said good-
bye."[14]

5

—————

If we were to accept Chernyshevsky's version of Dostoevsky's visit, then it
would appear that he had come to talk about the fires, and, in addition, considered the incendiaries to be people who would heed Chernyshevsky's admonition. Even though Dostoevsky does not mention the fires in his account, it is likely that, on this detail, Chernyshevsky's memory did not play
him false; the leaflet and the fires were so closely connected in everyone's
minds that both probably entered their conversation. Chernyshevsky implies, however, that Dostoevsky believed the fires had been set by radicals
over whom Chernyshevsky could exercise control; and here he is contra-
dicted by some evidence that has recently been published. For on the very
day of his visit (according to one authoritative reconstruction of the sequence of events),[15] either Dostoevsky or his brother Mikhail (probably
both in collaboration) wrote an article for *Time* flatly asserting that there
was not a scrap of evidence to link the blazes with *Young Russia* or to imagine that the students as a body sympathized with the gory ideas advocated
in the proclamation. When this first article was rejected by the censorship,
the Dostoevskys wrote another with no better success. Neither article could
be published; but the proof sheets, which contain an annotation in the

hand of the Tsar, were extracted several years ago from the cavernous (and miraculously intact) files of the Ministry of Internal Affairs and made available for scrutiny. If we assume the Dostoevskys to be giving their honest opinion (and we know from Vladislavlev that this was the view of their entourage), then it is difficult to give credence to Chernyshevsky's report of Dostoevsky's words.

The first suppressed piece begins with an account of the fires and discusses the popular supposition, which is found quite credible, that they could not *all* have been accidental. As a result, the most fantastic rumors have begun circulating; and *Time* makes the extremely provocative suggestion that such gossip, rather than originating with the people themselves, "very probably came to them from outside."[16] Why should the people by themselves suspect the students of setting the fires? "It is said that the people who printed *Young Russia* are capable of anything, that they will use any means, that the fires are the first symptoms of their activity." Perhaps so, although it is difficult to understand what they hope to gain by such a tactic, which is compared to patting a friend (the people) on the back with an iron gauntlet studded with nails. "But has it been established, in the first place, that the people causing the fires are connected with *Young Russia* . . . and has it been established—this is the principal, the most important circumstance of all—that the existing young generation, and particularly the students, are supporters of *Young Russia*?" No facts have been offered to confirm any such connection, and the article accuses all those who suggest it (reference is made to the *St. Petersburg Gazette* and the *Northern Bee*) of committing crimes themselves. "Do you realize what a terrible crime it is to stir up the enmity of one group in society against another?" Such a crime is all the more terrible because it incites the people— "who, for all their excellent and truthful qualities, are perpetually kept in darkness and ignorance"—against a small handful of students who have themselves been perpetually insulted and are now injured by almost everybody.

"Three scrofulous schoolboys, of whom the oldest is in fact not more than thirteen," writes *Time* jeeringly, "printed and distributed the stupidest leaflet, not even being able to cope very well with the foreign books from which they stole everything and of which they made a mockery. This stupid leaflet should have been greeted with a salvo of laughter."[17] Instead, various decrepit gentlemen suffering from advanced cases of gout, and with the mentality of old peasant women, were thrown into a panicky, paralytic fear and immediately started a campaign of wild tittle-tattle that has now infected everybody. *Time* concludes that public opinion can be reassured only if all the facts at the disposal of the government are given the fullest publicity; otherwise, silence may be taken as confirmation of what the people already erroneously believe to be true. The second article, a much shorter and less vehement version of the first, makes the same points: "We demand a public trial, and immediately, let there be martial law if the city is threatened and if (which we absolutely deny) these fires have something in common with a political movement."

By their protest against attributing the fires to the criminal arson of radical students, and their bold intimation that such talk had been inspired "from outside," these two articles represent a considerable act of political courage in view of the lynch-mob mentality of the moment.[18] Indeed, after being forbidden by the censorship, the articles were sent, by special order of the Tsar, to the secret police and then to the commission set up to investigate the cause of the fires. One phrase that attracted particular attention was the reference to "three scrofulous schoolboys"; and when Mikhail Dostoevsky was called in for questioning on June 8, as the responsible editor of the publication, he was asked to identify them by name and to give any further information at his disposal. Poor Mikhail had to explain laboriously that the reference was only a "literary expression" and did not refer to actual schoolboys known to the editors of *Time*. "I have nothing at all to do with people who write such things as *Young Russia*," he declared with firm dignity.[19] This ended the matter so far as the Dostoevsky brothers were aware, although in fact *Time* narrowly escaped being prohibited for eight months. A decision to this effect was taken secretly and then withdrawn, with the proviso that *Time* should be kept under close observation. The sword of Damocles had thus already begun to swing invisibly over the heads of the hapless Dostoevskys, and it was to fall exactly a year later.

6

From Chernyshevsky's scornful little memoir recalling Dostoevsky's impetuous visit, we are obviously intended to gather that the novelist's behavior had been a misguided waste of time. But, among the scanty annals of the revolutionary underground during these agitated months, there is some indirect evidence that Dostoevsky's attempt to intervene may not have been entirely in vain. If his visit was not decisive, then at least it may have reinforced Chernyshevsky's initial negative reaction to *Young Russia*—a reaction that made him speak of the Moscow group who had produced the document as "extremely overexalted," and to refuse to help in its distribution.[20] Aside from the exaggeration of its rhetoric, he could hardly have sympathized with its vision of a revolution in which the people were assigned only the role of shock troops and cannon fodder to be manipulated by a small, all-powerful revolutionary committee. Clearly disturbed as well by the wave of hatred against students and radicals induced by the proclamation and the fires, and perhaps more impressed than he cared to admit later by Dostoevsky's remonstrances, he sent one of the members of Land

and Liberty to contact the Moscow group and ask for some public effort to quell the rising storm. This messenger was dispatched shortly after the probable date of Chernyshevsky's conversation with Dostoevsky.[21]*

So far as is known, the emissary from Petersburg was not allowed to visit Zaichnevsky in prison; but on June 5 another student, P. D. Ballod, the possessor of a "pocket printing-press," was arrested in Petersburg. Among his belongings were copies of *Young Russia* and, in manuscript, another proclamation entitled *A Warning*, whose purpose was to explain that the revolutionaries should not be confused with whoever was responsible for the fires. "To think that a revolution is not too high a price to pay for an amelioration of the fate of the common people," this proclamation declared, "is not at all the same as burning the houses and workstalls of the poor."[22] *A Warning* was of course never published, and its author still remains unknown; but specialists suggest Chernyshevsky himself, or one of the leaders of the Petersburg student movement who was also an active member of the inner circle of Land and Liberty.

Encouraged by the popular outrage directed against the suspected revolutionary destroyers of the capital, the government decided to strike while the city was still smoldering. On June 15 the Petersburg censorship committee suspended publication of both *The Contemporary* and the equally left-wing *Russian Word* for eight months. The authorities were told on June 27 to refuse a foreign passport to Chernyshevsky if he requested one, and on July 7 he was taken into custody along with an important member of Land and Liberty, Nikolay Serno-Solovievich. By this time Dostoevsky was far away, embarked on his first trip to Europe during the summer of 1862; but we shall see that his thoughts turned constantly to home, and that the situation there filled him with anxiety and dismay.

He left, however, knowing that he had done what he could to avert the worst. As an ex-political prisoner, he had risked bringing himself under suspicion again by his visit to Chernyshevsky, whose apartment, as he had good reason to surmise, was kept under close surveillance by the secret police. He had endangered his journal *Time* on the same occasion by his simultaneous attempt to counteract the rumors about the fires. He had tried to tell the young revolutionary hotheads through Chernyshevsky to tone down the incendiary words that lent credence to the slanders of their enemies; and he had struggled to defend them and the students against the popular fury by which they were threatened. For he knew very well, as he had indicated in *The Insulted and Injured*, that the reactionaries close to

---

* A connection between these two events has also been suggested by a Soviet Russian scholar: "When Chernyshevsky sent Sleptsov to Moscow, with the aim of putting pressure on the authors of *Young Russia* to take some sort of measures to soften the impression left by several superfluous points in their proclaimed demands [?] was this not precisely what Dostoevsky had asked Chernyshevsky to do?" N. G. Rosenblyum, "Petersburgskie Pozhary 1862 g. i Dostoevsky," *LN*, 86 (Moscow, 1973), 40.

the seats of power were eagerly waiting to take full advantage of the menacing situation. His one aim, even if unsuccessful, had been to prevent events from reaching the point of no return—to check the increasingly reckless and defiant extremism on the one side and the increasingly blind and indiscriminate reaction on the other. It was an aim he was never totally to abandon, and to which he would always return the moment he saw a ray of hope.

CHAPTER 12

Portrait of
a Nihilist

It is customary for Soviet Russian historians to speak of "the revolutionary situation" that existed in the early 1860s. There is no reliable evidence that the stability of the régime was ever seriously threatened; but amidst reports of one peasant mutiny after another repressed by armed force, and with inflammatory leaflets mysteriously appearing everywhere—people even found them lying on theater seats, along with the programs—the fear of revolution was in everyone's mind during the turbulent months following the liberation of the serfs. All of the proclamations assumed revolution to be imminent because of peasant unrest, and many conversations were being carried on similar to the one that took place at a gathering of the editorial staff of *Time*.

A young contributor, N. F. Bunakov, then at the beginning of a modest literary career (he had been a member of a radical circle in his hometown of Vologda, and the next year was to enter the ranks of Land and Liberty), has preserved it for posterity. "F. M. Dostoevsky," he writes, "invited me to an evening at which I met the entire circle of the journal except Apollon Grigoryev, who was not then in Petersburg. Naturally, I behaved somewhat shyly in the presence of these 'real' writers and listened much more than I spoke. I recall a lively argument over whether Russia was ready for a revolutionary movement and if such was possible—a topic then making the rounds everywhere. . . . The majority of people in the *Time* circle denied the seriousness of the revolutionary proclamations [*The Great Russian* and *To the Young Generation* had already appeared] and the possibility of a revolutionary movement of the Russian people."[1]

A young poet, Platon Kuskov, differed with the others and held his ground against A. E. Razin, the political authority of *Time*, and "the compliantly good-natured Strakhov, who supported an undefined middle ground." At last, "the inflammable Feodor Mikhailovich, who had been scurrying around the room with little footsteps for some time without mixing in the conversation, suddenly began to speak under his breath—and everyone became silent. He, obviously, was the prophet of the circle, before whom everybody bent their knee. And this prophet spoke of humility, of the purifying role of suffering, of the pan-humanity of the Russian people, of the impossibility for them of taking any self-willed action on behalf of their own welfare, of their aversion for any violence, of the unnaturalness of any kind of unity between them and their self-designated benefactors, who had taken their revolutionary ideas from books or directly from a Western life that is the opposite of Russian life and cannot serve it as a model."[2]

Since Bunakov wrote his memoirs at the end of the century, the terms in which he presents Dostoevsky's remarks may well be colored by his later knowledge of the writer's views. But whatever the reasons Dostoevsky may have given for his convictions, his years in Siberia had convinced him that the Russian peasantry was not "revolutionary" in the Western sense of desiring a new form of government to replace Tsarism; and he knew in his bones that no "unity" was possible between the peasants and the intelligentsia who might try to exploit their grievances for revolutionary ends. As things turned out, the predictions of Dostoevsky and his *Time* circle proved far more accurate than the overheated expectations of the young radicals: no revolution occurred, or anything that could really be considered a revolutionary threat. Peasant discontent with the terms of the liberation, at Bezdna and elsewhere, was remarkably peaceful, nonviolent except for a few isolated cases, and inspired by unbroken loyalty to the Tsar; the violence came entirely from the government.* Dostoevsky's opinion on how the authorities behaved at this critical juncture may perhaps be surmised from a scene in *The Devils* that can be read as a comment on their lack of judgment. When a loyal delegation of factory workers comes to protest, on behalf of their comrades, against a rascally overseer who had swindled them of their wages, Governor-General von Lembke is terrified out of his wits and orders them flogged. Mistakenly assuming their appeal for justice to be a revolutionary uprising, von Lembke responds with force; and his deluded severity only serves to unleash all the social chaos that then breaks loose.

2

Even if no genuine revolution was on the point of taking place in Russia during the early 1860s, however, the events we have been chronicling

---

* Just how "revolutionary" the Russian peasant was at this time continues to be a hotly disputed issue even among Soviet Russian historians. But one of the most highly respected of them, who enjoys the equal esteem of his Western colleagues, would seem to agree with Dostoevsky and the *Time* circle.

After a survey of the most important movements of peasant protest immediately after the liberation decree, he writes: "Notwithstanding the scope and vigor of the peasant movement, it remained spontaneous, disorganized, loyal to the Tsar, and lacking in a political program. The peasants refused to recognize the authenticity of the 'Statutes of 19 February,' assuming that the gentry and officials had 'substituted' the Statutes for the 'real freedom' granted by the Tsar. . . . This new myth illustrated the power of the artless monarchical illusions of the peasantry and doomed the peasant protest mainly to passive forms of resistance." Peter A. Zaionchkovsky, *The Abolition of Serfdom in Russia*, ed. and trans. Susan Wobst (Gulf Breeze, Fla., 1973), 118.

mark a moment of great social-cultural importance. What they signify is the sensational advent on the Russian historical scene, in full force and as a dominating group, of a new generation of the intelligentsia largely different in social composition from the previous one and bringing with it a whole new set of ideas and values. Everyone was aware of the change, and it was stated in telling words at the beginning of the next decade by N. K. Mikhailovsky, who now occupied the place of Belinsky and Chernyshevsky as the leading radical publicist: "What happened?—The *raznochintsy* arrived. Nothing further happened. Nonetheless this event, however it may be judged, and whether one sympathizes with it or not, is an event of the highest importance, which created an epoch in Russian literature; and the dominating importance of the event absolutely had to be acknowledged on all sides."[3] Mikhailovsky confines his remarks to literature because to speak too openly of politics in this connection would have been dangerous; but of course his readers would take his meaning without any trouble.

Who and what were the *raznochintsy*? They were the sons of priests, petty officials, impoverished landowners, sometimes serfs enfranchised or not, all of whom had managed to acquire an education and to exist in the interstices of the Russian caste system. They had been nourished on the writings of the older generation of gentry-liberals and gentry-radicals like Herzen, Granovsky, Ogarev, Turgenev, but recognized as their only real ancestor and predecessor the stormy figure of "furious Vissarion" Belinsky, a *raznochinets* like themselves, who had assimilated the rich literary and philosophical culture of the gentry but whose intransigent social behavior both shocked and delighted his noble friends by its defiance of hypocritical convention.* The young Count Tolstoy, an impenitent upholder of gentry values, instantly objected in 1856 to the *tone* of Chernyshevsky's criticism in a letter to Nekrasov; and he accurately traces the degeneration of literary manners back to its source: "All this is Belinsky! He spoke at the top of his voice, and spoke in an angry tone because he was angry, and . . . this one [Chernyshevsky] thinks that to speak well one has to speak insolently, and to do so one has to stir oneself up."[4]

At first, this new generation had vented their anger against existing con-

---

* A typical incident is recounted in the memoirs of Alexander Herzen: "Once he [Belinsky] went in Holy Week to dine with a literary man, and Lenten dishes were served. 'Is it long,' he asked, 'since you became so devout?' 'We eat Lenten fare,' answered the literary gentleman, 'simply and solely for the sake of the servants.' *'For the sake of the servants,'* said Belinsky, and he turned pale. 'For the sake of the servants,' he repeated, and flung down his dinner napkin. 'Where are your servants? I'll tell them that they are deceived. Any open vice is better and more humane than this contempt for the weak and uneducated, this hypocrisy in support of ignorance. And do you imagine that you are free people? You are on the same level as all the tsars and priests and slaveowners. Good-bye. I don't eat Lenten fare for the edification of others; I have no servants.!' " Alexander Herzen, *My Past and Thoughts*, trans. Constance Garnett, rev. Humphrey Higgins, 4 vols. (New York, 1968), 2: 412.

This section of Herzen's epoch-making work helped to shape the image of Belinsky that appealed to the young *raznochintsy*.

ditions in the pages of literary journals; now they had moved on not only to distributing more or less violent proclamations but also, it was widely thought, had set Petersburg ablaze. And just at this very instant, by an extraordinary stroke of historical fortune, a great novel appeared portraying a *raznochinets* hero in all his self-proclaimed rebelliousness and irresistible strength. Turgenev's *Fathers and Children*, written during the previous two years and dedicated to the memory of Belinsky, was printed by Katkov's *Russian Messenger* in March 1862, just between the first two proclamations and *Young Russia* and simultaneously with the literary-musical evening. Turgenev's central figure, Bazarov, the son of a humble Army doctor like Belinsky (and like Dostoevsky as well, although his father acquired noble rank), was immediately accepted as a verisimilar literary image of the new social type of the 1860s. "I shall not enlarge on the impression this novel has created," Turgenev wrote seven years later. "I shall merely say that when I returned to Petersburg on the very day of the notorious fires in the Apraksin Marketplace, the word 'Nihilist' had been caught up by thousands of people, and the first exclamation that escaped from the lips of the first acquaintance I met on the Nevsky Prospect was: 'Look what *your* Nihilists are doing! They are setting Petersburg on fire!' "[5]

Turgenev's novel immediately became the exclusive storm center of social-cultural controversy; and the debates over the character of Bazarov, who personified the split between the gentry-liberal intelligentsia of the 1840s and the radical *raznochintsy* of the 1860s, led to a *new* rift between two factions within the radical camp itself. These debates set the terms that dominated Russian social-cultural and literary life for the remainder of the decade, and they form an indispensable background for understanding some of Dostoevsky's most important thematic concerns. Moreover, *Time* took an active part in the furious controversy over Turgenev's novel and made a contribution that Turgenev himself considered crucial. Dostoevsky communicated his personal appreciation of the book in a letter, and Turgenev replied by expressing not only his gratitude but also his admiration for Dostoevsky's penetrating understanding of his artistic aims. All these are matters that call for more ample elucidation.

3
———

Both Chernyshevsky and Dobrolyubov, as mentioned earlier, had conducted a steady campaign all through the late 1850s aimed at ridiculing the prestige of the gentry-liberal types. In addition, they had attacked the reverence for art so characteristic of the older generation, and tried to replace all the high-flown moral principles of the past with a sober and simple—far too simple—ethics based on "rational egoism." Such ideas, not to mention the personality and manners of the stiff-necked and bristly *raznochintsy*, were quite repugnant to most of the eminent members of the older generation. An early sample of their displeasure can be found in a rather nasty short story by D. V. Grigorovich, *The School of Hospitality* (1855). This work depicts a character named Chernushkin, a slimy journalist, who is clearly meant as a takeoff on Chernyshevsky: "His appearance struck one so much by its venomousness that, basing himself on this alone, one editor hired him as a critic for his journal; the editor also particularly counted on the fact that Chernushkin suffered from liver pains and had bilious attacks." Chernushkin trumpets the opinion that the writers he knows do not occupy themselves with serious matters, and "he concluded by very wittily comparing literature to a cup of coffee after dinner."[6]

Grigorovich's spiteful attack already reveals two of the traits that will invariably be attributed to the *raznochinets* type: an offensive and aggressive tone, and a depreciation of art. These same traits, along with the reference to the liver, appear in Herzen's far more important *The Superfluous and the Bilious* (1860), written after the secret visit by Chernyshevsky to London in the summer of 1859. The impressions garnered by Herzen during this interview, as well as from other visitors with the same background, are sharply conveyed when he describes the attitude of the new generation toward the one of which he was so eminent a representative. His "bilious" interlocutor, he says, "looked on us [the "superfluous" gentry-liberals] as on the fine skeleton of a mammoth, as at an interesting bone that had been dug up and belonged with a different sun and different trees."

For his part, Herzen comments acidly on "the depressing faces of the Daniels of the Neva, who gloomily reproach men for dining without gnashing their teeth, and for enjoying pictures or music without remembering the misfortunes of the world." And he professes himself rather frightened by "the ease with which they [the bilious] despaired of everything, the vindictive pleasure of their renunciation, *and their terrible ruthlessness*" (italics added). For Herzen believed that "the denial of every personal right, the insults, the humiliations they had endured" had left all of "the bilious" with "a devouring, irritable and distorted vanity."[7] These pages are a preliminary sketch for Turgenev's fuller and less ironically hostile treatment of the same type, whom he called, in a letter to Katkov, "the real hero of our time," adding: "What a hero and what a time—you will say. . . . But that is how things are."[8]

Turgenev's earlier writings had often been used as a target for the attack on "superfluous men," and such attacks had been all the more galling because they appeared in the same journal, *The Contemporary*, that provided the main outlet for his own creations. The normally mild-mannered and amiable Turgenev was also personally offended by the unceremonious fashion in which he was treated by the members of what came to be called "the consistory" (a reference to the clerical origins of many of the new staff of *The Contemporary*), and Dobrolyubov in particular did not conceal his dislike. Matters came to a head in the spring of 1860, when Dobrolyubov's article about *On the Eve* was printed over Turgenev's protests, and he found an insulting remark in another article a few months later stating that his depiction of Rudin (a character partly based on Bakunin) had been purposely turned into a caricature to satisfy "his wealthy friends."[9] At this time he decided to break all relations with *The Contemporary*, and notified Nekrasov to this effect in October of that year. It was during the summer of 1860 that he began to sketch his plan for *Fathers and Children*.

Turgenev later denied that his novel was inspired by any desire to attack the new generation in general and Dobrolyubov in particular; and if he meant that he did not wish merely to indulge in ridicule or satire, then he may be taken at his word. His sense of life was too lyrical and too melancholy to be content merely with mockery, even though, as is quite likely, he may have begun the book with a feeling of intense outrage. There is ample

10. I. S. Turgenev, ca. 1865. From Turgenev, *Polnoe Sobranie Sochinenii*, vol. 9 (Moscow-Leningrad, 1965)

evidence that, during the early stages of composition, his sentiments toward the *raznochintsy* were far from tender. The articles of Dobrolyubov, he declared to an acquaintance in Paris during that winter, are "a decoction of bile which only those can find pleasing who have neither taste nor good sense, or whose taste is depraved, like that of an anemic girl who devours chalk and plaster and has lost her wits."[10] He spoke of those guiding *The Contemporary* as "Huns and Vandals who hate every kind of civilization. They do not have, it is true, the external, material strength of our old oppressors the Mongols, but they are worth no more and far surpass them in cunning."[11]

The premature death of Dobrolyubov in November 1861 (he was only twenty-five) softened Turgenev somewhat, and his remarks in a letter indicate how his feelings about the *raznochintsy* had evolved: "I felt sorry about the death of Dobrolyubov, although I did not share his point of view: he was a gifted man—young. . . . It's a pity that such strength is destroyed and squandered in vain!"[12] This elegiac note conveys some of the modulation that Turgenev was now bringing to the creation of Bazarov, for whom, in the course of composition, he admits having come to feel "an involuntary attachment."[13] And it was probably around this time that the incident occurred of which he later spoke to the Norwegian-American novelist Hjalmar Boyesen: "I was taking a walk and thinking of death. Just then, before my eyes, rose the picture of a man who was dying. It was Bazarov. The picture produced a strong impression on me, and then the other characters of the novel and the action itself began to evolve."[14] Once his subject was seen in this perspective, it was impossible for Turgenev to refuse to sympathize with his character in some degree. By the time the book was finished, he probably really could not say, as he admitted ten years later, what his personal feelings about Bazarov actually had been: "Whether I loved him or hated him, Lord only knows!"[15]

Turgenev, however, did much more than merely "imagine" his central character; he also carefully studied the writings in which the new generation expressed its contemptuous rejection of the old, and he drew on the ideas he found there with remarkable precision. All the social-cultural issues of the day are reflected so accurately in the book that one Soviet Russian critic has rightly called it "a lapidary artistic chronicle of contemporary life."[16] Nonetheless, the shading that Turgenev gave to these issues was determined by his own artistic aims and ambiguous attitudes; like Dostoevsky, he could simultaneously sympathize with the ardent moral fervor of the young, deplore their intemperance, detest their ideas, and lament over their fate. Many of the positions that Bazarov advocates are not so much echoes of *The Contemporary* as subtle deformations and exaggerations calculated to reveal their ultimate implications and thus their dangerous potentialities. It is hardly surprising that partisans of these ideas should have found Turgenev's rendition unacceptable; much more unexpected is that even one radical spokesman should have proclaimed Bazarov to be the beacon lighting up the path to the future.

4

One of Turgenev's best-known plays is called *A Month in the Country*, and the novel *Fathers and Children* might well have been given the same title. The entire action takes place in the summer of 1859, just on the eve of the liberation, when two college friends, freshly minted graduates of the University of St. Petersburg, come to spend their holidays in the countryside. One is Arkady Kirsanov, the scion of a gentry family, who has invited his slightly older classmate Evgeny Bazarov—originally of peasant and clerical stock, although his father is a retired Army doctor—to visit the by no means flourishing Kirsanov estate. There Bazarov meets Arkady's father, Nikolay Petrovich, a soft-hearted and sensitive Romantic type of the 1840s, who reads Pushkin, communes with nature, plays the violoncello for recreation, and has placed his peasants on quit-rent as an expression of his liberalism.* Arkady's uncle, Pavel Petrovich, is quite another gentry type—an elegant dandy who affects English manners and mannerisms, admires Western (particularly English) aristocratic liberalism, does not have an ounce of sentiment in his makeup, and belongs to the period of the 1830s with its Byronic Onegins and Pechorins rather than to the Romantic-sentimental and humanitarian 1840s. Pavel Petrovich and Bazarov, humanly speaking, are both the same kind of commanding personality, and each demands respect for his individual dignity with unyielding stubbornness. The exchanges between them contain most of the explicit ideological substance of the book, and their duel of words eventually becomes one of pistols at ten paces.

Such a parallel between Bazarov and Pavel Petrovich is brought out by the very structure of the action: what Bazarov learns about the past of Pavel Petrovich from Arkady distinctly foreshadows his own fate. For Pavel Petrovich's life had been ruined by an infatuation with an enigmatic woman, who became his mistress for a time but whom he could never fully possess. When she left him, "he no longer expected anything special of himself or of others, and he undertook nothing" (8: 233-224).† Like a good materialist of the 1860s, and as a student of medicine who spends his time dissecting frogs, Bazarov does not believe in love. "And what about all those mysterious relations between a man and a woman?" he asks Arkady scornfully.

* Quit-rent (*obrok* in Russian) meant that the peasant could discharge his obligation to the landlord in dues or rent and was no longer responsible for labor service (*barshchina*) on the landlord's estate.

† Page references throughout this section and the next are to *Fathers and Children* in I. S. Turgenev, *Polnoe Sobranie Sochinenii*, 28 vols. (Moscow-Leningrad, 1960-1968).

"We physiologists know what these relations are." Of Pavel Petrovich's story he says: "Still, I must say that a man who stakes his whole life on one card—a woman's love—and when that card fails, turns sour, and lets himself go till he's fit for nothing, is not a man but a male animal" (8: 226). Bazarov thus reduces so-called love to pure sensuality, and expresses only contempt for someone who has allowed his life to be determined by such desires, not because he has any objection to sensuality himself, but because on that level (the only one he recognizes) all women are alike.

He learns, however, that love is much more than the momentary contact of one epidermis with another when he falls under the spell of the superb, wealthy, and supremely self-possessed Mme Odintsova, and begins to realize that with her he might not be able to "gain his ends" as he had done so easily with others. What upsets him is not that he might be (and is) repulsed, but that "he found, to his own bewilderment, that it was beyond his power to turn his back on her." Bazarov discovers himself to be a victim of the very Romantic passion whose existence he had refused to acknowledge; "he could easily have mastered his blood, but something else was taking root in him, something he had never admitted, at which he had always jeered, at which all his pride revolted" (8: 287). Up until this time, Bazarov had been certain that the reductive rationalism of his "scientific" view of life, which dissolved all "higher values" into purely material drives and reflexes, was vastly superior to the old-fashioned Romantic folderol that he treated with such contempt. But now he realizes that what he had considered pure illusion, "romanticism, nonsense, rot, artiness," could triumph over his own most deep-seated convictions. This blow to his pride shatters the whole framework of values that supports his supreme self-confidence and deprives his life of meaning—just as it had done with Pavel Petrovich. Bazarov dies accidentally from a cut made by a slip of the scalpel while dissecting an infected corpse; but it is clear that by this time he has lost all interest in life.

Fathers and Children thus inaugurates what will become the dominant theme of the Russian novel of the 1860s: the conflict between the narrow rationalism and materialism upheld by this new generation, and all those "irrational" feelings and values whose reality they refuse to acknowledge. But if Turgenev exposes the shortcomings of the world-view of the *razno-chintsy* in this way, he nonetheless delineates Bazarov as someone far superior in energy, force of character, and promise for the future to any of the gentry characters by whom he is surrounded. Both of the older Kirsanovs are quite clearly relics of the past, unable to cope with the new Russian society on the point of bursting its old bounds. Pavel Petrovich finally goes to settle abroad for good and, though much admired "as a perfect gentleman" by his English friends in Dresden, lives a life of quiet desperation (8: 400). Arkady and his father flourish in contented mediocrity on their estate, but the towering image of the rebellious Bazarov definitely places their "family happiness" (to use a Tolstoyan tag) in the shade. "Your sort, you gentry," Bazarov tells Arkady, when the two erstwhile friends come to the parting of the ways, "can never get beyond refined submission or refined indignation, and that's a mere trifle. You won't fight . . . but we mean to fight . . . we want to smash other people!" (8: 380).

5

All through the novel, Turgenev's portrait of the relations between the two generations deftly captures, in incisive dialogues and shrewd authorial observations, the full range of the opposition that had been building up both in personal contacts and in journalistic exchanges; and his delineation of this conflict sets the ideological terms in which the polemics of the immediate future would be carried on.

Bazarov's casual and self-confident behavior with the Kirsanovs very quickly grates on Pavel Petrovich's nerves, and his reaction conveys some of the objections already cited to the *tone* of the *raznochintsy*: "He [Pavel Petrovich] was beginning to feel a secret irritation. His aristocratic nature was revolted by Bazarov's absolute nonchalance. This surgeon's son was not only unintimidated, he even gave abrupt and indifferent answers, and in the tone of his voice there was something coarse, almost insolent" (8: 218). The obsolescence of the older generation is revealed by Nikolay Kirsanov's fondness for Pushkin and his amateur efforts on the violoncello. "It's time to throw up that rubbish," Bazarov says, referring to Pushkin, and he counsels Arkady to give his father "something sensible to read." The two friends condescendingly decide that Büchner's *Force and Matter* would be suitable as an introduction to more serious intellectual fare because it "is written in popular language" (8: 238-239).

Bazarov's attack against art is carried on vigorously and, for an informed reader of that time, with obvious reference to Chernyshevsky's thesis; but while Chernyshevsky had merely argued that art should be subordinate to life, and had not denied it a certain secondary usefulness, Turgenev pushes the opposition between the "aesthetic" and the "useful" into a total negation. When Pavel Petrovich complains that young Russian artists regard "Raphael as a fool," Bazarov retorts: "To my mind, Raphael's not worth a brass farthing; and they are no better than he" (8: 247). No distinction is made between different kinds of art as more or less useful, and another remark of Bazarov illustrates the point with epigrammatic terseness: "A good chemist is twenty times as useful as any poet" (8: 219).

So far as more general ideas are concerned, Bazarov evidently exemplifies Chernyshevsky's conviction that the physical sciences, with their theory of a universal material determinism, furnish the basis for a solution to

169

all problems, including those of a moral-social nature. "We know approximately what physical diseases come from," Bazarov informs the skeptical Mme Odintsova; "moral diseases come from bad education, from all the nonsense people's heads are stuffed with from childhood; from the deformed state of society; in short, reform society, and there will be no diseases" (8: 277). But this faith in science, which still implies a belief in general principles of some sort, is then splintered by Bazarov into particular sciences. "There are sciences," he declares, "as there are trades and vocations; but abstract science doesn't exist at all" (8: 219). Ultimately, even science itself becomes reduced to "sensations," and it is these, in all their infinite variety, that have the last word. "There are no general principles—you've not made even that out as yet!" Bazarov exclaims to Arkady with some astonishment. "There are feelings. . . . Why do I like chemistry? Why do you like apples?—also by virtue of our sensations." The "feelings" referred to here by Bazarov are purely physical sensations, not psychic or emotive ones, and Bazarov insists that "men will never penetrate deeper than that" (8: 325). Chernyshevsky's scientism thus ends up as a solipsistic empiricism or sensationalism in which all general principles or values are dissolved (much as in Max Stirner) into a matter of individual taste or preference.

It is this attack on *all* general principles that forms the basis of what Turgenev labels Bazarov's "Nihilism"—a term that had just come into usage in connection with the radicals and was destined, as a result of Turgenev's novel, to a great career.* A Nihilist, Arkady eagerly explains, "is a man who does not bow before any authority, who does not take any principle on faith, whatever reverence that principle may be enshrined in" (8: 216). In the most famous passage in the book, Bazarov explains the universal scope of this rejection to the incredulous elder Kirsanovs:

"We act by virtue of what we recognize as useful," observed Bazarov. "At the present time, negation is the most useful of all—and we deny—"
"Everything?"
"Everything!"
"What, not only art and poetry . . . but even . . . horrible to say . . ."
"Everything," repeated Bazarov, with indescribable composure.
Pavel Petrovich stared at him. He had not expected this; while Arkady fairly blushed with delight.
"Allow me, though," began Nikolay Petrovich. "You deny every-

---

* There has been considerable discussion over the antecedents of this term in Russian criticism, and whether or not Turgenev borrowed it from some articles of Katkov, who had used it in polemics with the radicals of *The Contemporary* during 1861. Turgenev's uncorrected manuscript, which has only recently been studied in detail, does not bear out this supposition. The word "Nihilist" appears in parts written before the publication of Katkov's articles; it was not added later in the margin or above the line. See the commentary in I. S. Turgenev, *Polnoe Sobranie Sochinenii*, 8: 588-589.

thing, or, speaking more precisely, you destroy everything. . . . But one must construct too, you know?"

"That's not our business now. . . . The ground has to be cleared first." (8: 243)

To be sure, Arkady immediately leaps in to say that "the present condition of the people requires it"—thus linking such negation with the aim of a revolutionary social transformation. But this distant aim, so far as Bazarov is concerned, remains clearly subordinate to the work of negation and destruction, to a personal emancipation from all inherited principles and prejudices and the encouragement of such emancipation among others. Turgenev here thus reverses the actual order of priorities among the followers of *The Contemporary*, whose goals were much more social-political than personal. Very probably, though, he had already become aware of another radical current in the essays of Pisarev and other contributors to the *Russian Word*, who, as Strakhov had noted, put a much stronger accent on self-assertion and self-liberation, and whose philosophical preferences were in fact quite close to Bazarov's "sensationalistic" empiricism.

Bazarov's attitude toward "the people" is also a mixture of conflicting ideas which, without representing any single prevalent point of view, finally again puts the emphasis on a solitary individualism. On the one hand, he is proud of his plebeian origins; and when Pavel Petrovich, shocked at his utterances, accuses him of not being "Russian," he replies, "My grandfather ploughed the land," and points out—what is true—that the peasants feel much more at home with him than with the gentry. But he is also an inflexible Westerner, who refuses to idealize the peasants in any way and ridicules their backwardness and superstition: "The people imagine that when it thunders the prophet Elijah's riding across the sky in his chariot. What then? Are we to agree with them?" (8: 244). Even that holy of holies, the village *obshchina*, does not escape the lash of Bazarov's iconoclasm; and in this he reflects primarily the opinion of his creator, the Western liberal Turgenev, but also a viewpoint just beginning to make its appearance in *The Russian Word*.[17]

No scene in *Fathers and Children* is more prophetic than the one in which Turgenev brilliantly dramatizes all the ambiguities of Bazarov's love-hate relation to the people—the internal clash between his self-assertive ideas, which express an aching need for personal self-fulfillment, and the obligation imposed by history on his generation to devote their lives to bettering the lot of the backward peasantry. Bazarov recalls that once, while walking past the *izba* of a prosperous peasant, Arkady had piously remarked that Russia would "attain perfection when the poorest peasant had a [clean and comfortable] hut" and that "every one of us ought to work to bring [that] about." Such an obligation impels Bazarov to confess to a feeling of intense "hatred for this poorest peasant, this Philip or Sidor, for whom I'm to be ready to jump out of my skin, and who won't even thank me for it . . . and what do I need his thanks for? Why, suppose he does live in a clean hut, while nettles are growing out of me—well, what then?" (8: 325).

Turgenev penetrates here, with consummate insight, to the anguishing dilemma of the young Russian radical of the 1860s, heart and soul dedicated to serving a people from whom he is totally alienated by his culture—a people on whose behalf he must surrender all claims to happiness, and yet who cannot even understand the nature or meaning of his self-sacrifice. Such an awareness of the tragic isolation of the intelligentsia—an isolation that had been one of Dostoevsky's most shocking discoveries during his years in the Siberian prison camp—had hardly been fully grasped yet as an objective datum of the Russian social-cultural situation. It was to become much more widespread in the next few years, partly because the people did not behave in the manner that the intelligentsia had anticipated, partly because Turgenev had raised the issue to the level of consciousness. As a result, Bazarov's sense of indomitable will and strength as an *individual*, as well as his realization that he stands alone above and beyond the people, will come to the foreground and shape the guiding attitudes of the *raznochintsy* intelligentsia throughout the remainder of the 1860s.

6

Even before the publication of *Fathers and Children*, rumors had been making the rounds in Petersburg that Turgenev's new novel was a revengeful lampoon of Dobrolyubov. Chernyshevsky, as a matter of fact, continued to believe this to his dying day and repeated the accusation as late as 1884;[18] nor can one deny that certain aspects of the book place the radicals in a highly unflattering light. Depending on how the text was read, it could be taken either as an "apotheosis" of Bazarov (to cite the scandalized reaction of Katkov)[19] or as a condemnation and exposure of the type he incarnated. The second view was that of the majority of readers, and is echoed in a report of the secret police surveying the cultural scene in 1862 with a good deal of perspicacity: "With this work . . . Turgenev branded our adolescent revolutionaries with the caustic name of 'Nihilists,' and shook the doctrine of materialism and its representatives."[20] To make certain that Turgenev would receive the proper chastisement for his audacity, Chernyshevsky entrusted the review of the novel to the twenty-two-year-old M. A. Antonovich, a protégé of Dobrolyubov known for his belligerence.

Antonovich's essay, "The Asmodeus of Our Time," is not so much an article about Turgenev's novel as a headlong onslaught intended to destroy whatever credit it might be given as a picture of the aims and ideals of the young generation. Denying any artistic value to the work and bizarrely misinterpreting some of its scenes (Antonovich thinks that Bazarov, on his deathbed, wishes to see Mme Odintsova once again only to receive a last sensual thrill), he declares the book to be "nothing better than a pitiless and even destructive criticism of the young generation."[21] Bazarov, in his view, is depicted "not as a human being but as some kind of terrifying being, simply a devil, or, to put it more poetically, an Asmodeus."[22] This name is used because Antonovich wishes to place *Fathers and Children* in the same contemptible category as a novel published in 1858, *An Asmodeus of Our Time*, whose author was the ill-famed V. I. Askochensky. The name of this gentleman, who also edited a journal devoted to defending the cause of the Russian Orthodox faith, had become a "byword for obscurantism" in mid-nineteenth Russian culture.[23]

Most of Antonovich's article is devoted to defaming Turgenev by every possible means; there is even an allusion, which could hardly be misunderstood, to his well-known love affair with the French-Spanish prima donna Pauline Garcia-Viardot. Since Bazarov is considered only the grotesque caricature of a radical, Antonovich does not waste much space taking issue with his particular utterances and declarations. He does point out, all the same, that Bazarov's contempt for art goes much too far: "We negate only your art, your poetry, Mr. Turgenev . . . but we do not negate, and we even demand, another art and poetry."[24] But Antonovich then ineptly mentions the totally apolitical Goethe as the kind of poet *he* considers acceptable, which prompted Dostoevsky to remark in his notebook: "We are ready to bet that he [Antonovich] will not open Goethe in his life, and perhaps has not opened him yet" (20: 153). Antonovich also observes that Bazarov, in negating all principles, actually accepts the principle of negation; and when he says, "we act according to what we consider useful," he is of course accepting the principle of utility. Why, then, portray him as making negation "a matter of taste," and claiming that the young generation does not act in terms of *any* principle?[25] Antonovich is here defending the actual position of *The Contemporary* against Turgenev's cunning manipulations; but whatever the justice of such remarks, they are drowned in the flood of abuse that has made Antonovich's article a synonym for critical malpractice.

Quite opposite was the reaction of Dimitry Pisarev, the chief critic of *The Russian Word*, a journal which, until that time, had been considered a staunch ally of *The Contemporary*. Pisarev's work, as we know, had already attracted the ironic attention of Strakhov; and just a month or two before his article on Turgenev appeared, Strakhov had focused on him once again in the January 1862 issue of *Time*. "Mr. Pisarev must be read," he insists; "Mr. Pisarev, in my opinion, is the very latest and the most striking manifestation of our contemporary literature, in him its deepest secret comes to the surface. . . . Mr. Chernyshevsky is the foundation and principle, Mr. Pisarev—the consequence and conclusion."[26] Although Pisarev was supposedly a follower of Chernyshevsky, Strakhov noted in the young critic a tendency to draw the extremest conclusions from the lessons of the Master—the very same "Nihilist" conclusions that Bazarov would soon be proclaiming in Turgenev's pages. "If authority is deceitful," Pisarev had written in the swashbuckling essay to which Strakhov refers, "doubt will destroy it, and properly so; if it is necessary or useful, then doubt will turn it over, examine it from all angles, and put it back in place. In a word, here is the ultimatum of our camp: what can be broken should be broken; what resists the blow is worth keeping, what flies to pieces is rubbish; in any case, strike right and left, no harm can come of it and no harm will come."[27] No wonder that Dostoevsky also jotted down in his notebook the laconic observation: "Now Pisarev has gone further" (20: 156).

The author of this little hymn to destruction naturally found Turgenev's hero completely to his taste, and he welcomed precisely those aspects of Bazarov considered defamatory by Antonovich as distinctive of the new "hero of our time." Bazarov, Pisarev declares without hesitation, is "a representative of our younger generation; in his person are gathered together all those traits scattered among the mass in a lesser degree." Chief among these traits is his immense superiority to everyone else he encounters. "Bazarov is extraordinarily conceited," Pisarev acknowledges, "but his conceit is inconspicuous precisely because of its immensity. He is not occupied with the trifles that make up the relations of ordinary people; he cannot be insulted by obvious scorn, nor gladdened by signs of respect; he is so full of himself, he considers himself to stand so securely on such a height, that he is almost completely indifferent to the opinion of other people." Pavel Petrovich once refers to Bazarov as possessing a "Satanic pride," and Pisarev hastens to agree that "this expression is very felicitously chosen and is a perfect characterization of our hero."[28]

Not only does Bazarov exhibit a "Satanic pride," but he also trumpets a world-view based on an "empiricism" that reduces all matters of principle to individual preference; and Pisarev blithely accepts such a doctrine as the very last word of "science." "Thus Bazarov everywhere and in everything does only what he wishes, or what seems to him useful and attractive. He is governed only by personal caprice or personal calculation. Neither over him, nor outside him, nor inside him does he recognize any regulator, any moral law, any principle." Such people as Bazarov, Pisarev explains, can be honest or dishonest, good citizens or thorough scoundrels, all depending on circumstance and personal taste. "Nothing except personal taste prevents him from murdering and robbing, and nothing except personal taste stirs people of this stripe to make discoveries in the field of science and social existence."[29] Pisarev concedes that the Bazarovs also act by "calculation," and are quite aware that in committing crimes they might be caught and punished; breaking the law can be disadvantageous and is hence to be avoided. But Bazarov, as Pisarev sees him, is far above feeling any *moral* compunction against committing crimes: the new hero of the younger generation would hardly subordinate his will to any such antiquated prejudice. Three years later, Raskolnikov in *Crime and Punishment* will show what might occur when this interpretation of the Bazarov-type is taken seriously and put to the test.

All through Pisarev's article, particular stress is placed on Bazarov's grandeur as an *individual*, who towers not only above all other members of the educated class but even more above the people. As a result, Pisarev is quite sensitive to Bazarov's moral-spiritual isolation and even casts it in the form of a universal social law:

> In every period there have been people in the world dissatisfied with life in general, or with some special form of life in particular; in every period these people have made up an insignificant minority. The masses, in every period, have lived contentedly, and with their inherent placidity have been satisfied with what was at hand. Only some sort of material catastrophe . . . jolts this mass into uneasy movement, into the destruction of its customary, dreamily tranquil, vegetative existence. . . . This mass does not make discoveries or commit crimes; *other people think and suffer, search and find, struggle and err on its behalf—other people eternally alien to it, eternally regarding it with contempt, and at the same time eternally working to increase the amenities of its life.*[30] (Italics added)

Pisarev thus draws a sharp line between ordinary and extraordinary people, between the mass and those self-conscious individuals who resemble Bazarov in their lonely loftiness. Nothing similar can be found in *The Contemporary*, where the intelligentsia and the people were invariably considered to be united in the attainment of a common social-political goal (however "backward" the peasantry might be, and however much in need of enlightenment). This image of the transcendent *raznochinets* hero who acts alone, and cannot help but feel *contempt* for the people whose lives he wishes to ameliorate and elevate, was something genuinely new on the Russian social-cultural scene. And there can be little doubt that it set Dostoevsky's imagination working along the lines eventually leading to Raskolnikov and his famous article "On Crime," which also separates the world into "ordinary" and "extraordinary" people and claims for the second category the *right* to "step over" the moral law.

More immediately, Pisarev's article consoled Turgenev somewhat for the hail of abuse raining down on him from all sides. Whoever reads Turgenev's novel, Pisarev affirmed, and understands to what extent he has presented Bazarov favorably even *against* his own convictions, "cannot help but express to him a deep and lively gratitude, as a great artist and an honorable Russian citizen."[31] At the time this accolade appeared, it was still only a minority opinion on the left; and while Turgenev called it "very remarkable," he had no illusions that it would calm the roar of outrage. "My novel, at the present time, has simply poured oil on the fire," he writes Annenkov. "I do not regret that the majority of the young are angry at me; I even have the boldness to believe that I have been useful."[32] But whatever the satisfaction afforded by Pisarev's praise, Turgenev could hardly have recognized his own complex conception in this celebration of a Bazarov beyond good and evil, a type who had become glorified almost to the dimensions of a Nietzschean superman.

7

Just before the publication of *Fathers and Children*, a rumor made the rounds that Turgenev had decided to publish his novel in *Time* rather than in *The Russian Messenger*. This bit of literary tittle-tattle, probably inspired by Katkov's widely known demands for extensive revisions of the text, was given some credence by being printed in *The Book Messenger*, a journal devoted to news about the literary world. An exchange of letters between Turgenev and Dostoevsky clarified the matter, and Dostoevsky seized the occasion to solicit a contribution for *Time* from Turgenev's prestigious pen. Dostoevsky also sent copies of the journal to Turgenev in Paris, and was rewarded by the assurance of a future contribution as well as some compliments on *House of the Dead*. "The picture of the *bath*," Turgenev wrote, "is simply Dantesque—and in your characterization of various figures (for example, Petrov)—much fine and truthful psychology."[33]

Dostoevsky read *Fathers and Children* immediately on its magazine publication, at the beginning of March, and conveyed his admiration to Turgenev without delay. He received a reply before the month was out expressing Turgenev's gratitude and satisfaction: "Dear Feodor Mikhailovich, it is useless to tell you how happy you made me by what you said about *Fathers and Children*. It is not a question here of the gratification of vanity, but rather the assurance that one, after all, has not made a mistake and has not entirely missed the mark." Dostoevsky's original letter has unfortunately been lost, but Turgenev's reply assures him that he has perfectly understood the significance of the book: "You have so fully and sensitively grasped what I wished to express in Bazarov that I can only raise my hands in astonishment—and satisfaction. It is as if you had slipped into my soul and intuited even what I did not think necessary to utter. I hope to God that what you have said is not only the sharp penetration of a master but also the direct understanding of a reader—that is, I hope to God everyone sees even a part of what you have seen!"[34]

Turgenev was especially impressed because, at a point where a cut had been made in the text (it was later restored), Dostoevsky had sensed that something was missing;* and he refers to Dostoevsky's letter with admiration in his other correspondence. One of his lengthiest efforts at self-defense was written to K. K. Sluchevsky, who had addressed him on behalf and at the urging of the Russian students at Heidelberg. They had been much incensed at Turgenev's slighting reference, in his final chapter, to the Russians studying at this center of scientific research, who "astounded" their German professors at first "by the soundness of their view of things" and then "no less by their complete inactivity and absolute idleness." Replying to a long list of their objections, and particularly to the charge that he had "rehabilitated" the gentry, Turgenev remarks in conclusion: "Up to the present only two people have fully understood Bazarov, that is, understood my intention: Dostoevsky and Botkin."[35] A month later, he writes to Dostoevsky again: "The rumors reaching me about *Fathers and Children* only confirm my expectations: except for yourself and Botkin, it seems, no one has taken the trouble to understand what I wished to do." A few sentences later he explains: "no one, it seems, suspected that I tried to present him [Bazarov] as a tragic figure—and everyone says: why is he so bad?—or—why is he so good?"[36]

Even though it is impossible to know exactly what Dostoevsky had written, a hint is given in a few sentences that he set down a year later in *Winter Notes on Summer Impressions*. In this passage Dostoevsky is elaborating ironically on how superior the Westernized Russian intelligentsia feel to the people, and how susceptible they are to any kind of criticism that places such superiority in doubt. "With what self-centered satisfaction did we repudiate and punish Turgenev when he dared not to be satisfied with us, did not find his happiness in our majestic personalities, and went elsewhere to look for something better than we are. . . . Better than we are, God in Heaven! . . . And thus he got what he deserved for his Bazarov, his restless and tormented Bazarov (the mark of a great heart) in spite of all his Nihilism" (5: 59). Bazarov here is grasped precisely as the kind of tragic figure that Turgenev had wished to portray, a hero whose tragedy lies in the conflict between his Western ideas (his ideology) and "the great heart" whose impulses and longings he could not suppress or deny.

It may be assumed that Dostoevsky discussed Turgenev's novel with Strakhov when assigning him to review it for *Time*; and Strakhov's analy-

---

* The passage in question, which Turgenev tells Dostoevsky he regrets having cut, is from Chap. 25: " 'Yes, my dear fellow,' he [Bazarov] commented, 'you see what comes of living with feudal people. You turn feudal yourself, and find yourself taking part in knightly tournaments. Well. . .' " The reference is to the fact that Bazarov had fought a duel, in due and proper form, with Pavel Petrovich. I. S. Turgenev, *Polnoe Sobranie Sochinenii*, 8: 587.

sis, one of the finest contemporary reactions to the book, undoubtedly conveys a good deal of Dostoevsky's own ideas. Appearing in the April issue, Strakhov's article takes into account the responses of both Antonovich and Pisarev; and he agrees with Pisarev that Bazarov's ideas are those of the young generation. "The enthusiasm of Mr. Pisarev," he observes, "fully demonstrates that Bazarovs exist, *if not in reality then in possibility*, and that they are understood by Mr. Turgenev at least to the degree that they understand themselves" (italics added).[37] But, in his view, both the enthusiasm of Pisarev and the hostility of Antonovich are equally mistaken for the very reason given by Turgenev himself: each poses the problem of the book in terms of whether the author was really a partisan of the "fathers" or the "children," the past or the future. To approach the work on this level, however, is thoroughly to misunderstand its true significance; its real meaning lies much deeper and is concerned with a far different problem.

"Never," Strakhov writes, "has the disaccord between life and thought been felt as intensely as at the present time."[38] It is this disaccord that Turgenev dramatizes, and it is here, rather than in the conflict of generations, that the book's ultimate moral lesson can be located. Bazarov, as Pisarev had rightly said, is manifestly superior as an individual to all the other people in the book, fathers included. But it turns out that he is not superior to the forces of life which they embody, no matter in how paltry a form; he is not superior to the forces that he vainly strives to suppress in himself because they do not jibe with the theory about life that he accepts. Bazarov disapproves of responding to the blandishments of nature, and Turgenev depicts nature in all its beauty; Bazarov does not value friendship or romantic love, and Turgenev shows how real both are in his heart; Bazarov rejects family sentiment, and Turgenev portrays the unselfish, anguished love of his doting parents; Bazarov scorns the appeal of art, and Turgenev delineates him with all the resources of a great poetic talent. "Bazarov is a Titan revolting against his mother-earth,"[39] Strakhov writes; but no Titan is powerful enough to triumph over the forces which, because they are immutably rooted in man's emotional nature, provide the eternal foundations of human life.

Shortly after Strakhov's article appeared, Turgenev arrived in Petersburg from Paris and hastened to pay a visit to the editorial offices of *Time*. "He found us assembled," Strakhov recalls, "and invited Mikhail Mikhailovich, Feodor Mikhailovich, and myself to dine with him in the Hotel Clea. The storm which had blown up against him obviously upset him."[40] Lionized by the reactionaries, vilified by the majority of the radicals, praised by Pisarev for having glorified Nihilism—Turgenev made a particular point of seeking out the company of the editors of *Time* at the first opportunity. For it was only among them, and nowhere else in Russia, that he had found any informed sympathy with and comprehension of the greatest novel of his literary career.

CHAPTER 13

"The Land of
Holy Wonders"

During the animated dinner-table talk at the Hotel Clea, Turgenev entertained his guests with all his accustomed liveliness and charm; but the subject on which he held forth was not, as might have been expected, his novel and its repercussions. Rather, he dwelt on the dangers that awaited unwary Russians who innocently entrusted themselves to the tempting delights of European residence. His main topic, Strakhov reports, "was the attitude of foreigners to Russians living in Europe. He recounted, with artistic vividness, what clever and sneaky tricks foreigners employed to fleece Russians, to get hold of their possessions, to have wills made in their favor, etc. I often recalled this conversation later, and I regretted that these shrewd observations, and of course many more like them, collected in the course of a lengthy residence abroad, were never committed to print."[1]

Turgenev was famous for his affability as a conversationalist, and he may simply have been catering to the prejudices of his interlocutors against those Russians who, like himself, so often abandoned the harsh birthright of their native soil for the sophisticated seductions of Europe. But perhaps the conversation proceeded along these lines because some mention had been made of Dostoevsky's impending first trip abroad. Such a trip was a great event in the life of any self-conscious and educated Russian, particularly those who had grown up in the first half of the nineteenth century; and we know that Dostoevsky had long desired to see with his own eyes those fabulous lands which, ever since his boyhood, had inflamed his imagination.

Just the year before, Dostoevsky had expressed all his own yearning in an envious question included in a letter to the poet Ya. P. Polonsky. Will the fortunate voyager, then pausing in Austria, be able to resist the temptation to pass over the Alps and descend into the Italian plain before returning home? "Happy man! How many times, starting with the days of my childhood, have I dreamt of being in Italy. Ever since the novels of Anne Radcliffe, which I read when I was eight years old, all sorts of Catarinas, Alfonsos, and Lucias have been running around in my head. As for Don Pedros and Doña Claras, I still rave about them even now. Then it was the turn of Shakespeare—Verona, Romeo and Juliet—the devil only knows what magic was there! Italy! Italy! but instead of Italy I landed in Semipalatinsk, and before that in the Dead House. Will I never succeed in getting to Europe while I still have the strength, the passion, and the poetry? Is it possible I will go only in another ten years, to warm my old bones against rheumatism and roast my balding pate in the Southern sun?"[2] Such wistful words, thrown out in the midst of a business letter to a contributor of *Time*, reveal all the passionate eagerness with which Dostoevsky awaited the opportunity to catch a glimpse of the enchanted world beyond the Russian confines.

The financial situation of *Time* was now promising enough to allow him to realize this long-cherished dream; and he also desired to consult specialists in Europe about his epilepsy. His application for a passport was made for reasons of health, and he writes to his brother Andrey, just a day before setting off, that he is going abroad essentially for medical treatment. He further explains that he is traveling without his wife, partly for lack of funds, partly because Marya Dimitrievna wished to stay with her son Pasha to supervise his preparation for the entrance examinations to the *gymnasium*. The plan was for Dostoevsky to join up with Strakhov, also making a first trip to Europe, in mid-July. Departure was arranged so that he could take part in a reading for the benefit of the victims of the Petersburg fires, and then, on June 7, 1862, he left for the first of what were to be many *Wanderjahren* in Europe.

2

The first leg of Dostoevsky's trip took him from Russia through Germany, Belgium, and France to Paris, where he planned to spend a month. Some of the observations he garnered along the way can be found in his *Winter Notes on Summer Impressions*, written the following year and published in *Time*. This series of articles, despite its title, contains far more than a kaleidoscope of hasty impressions and the wayward observations of a passing tourist. They are, in fact, filled with the most serious cultural and social-political reflections, even though such ideas appear in the midst of casual travel sketches whose pert and light-hearted tone communicates a deceptive air of frivolity. Such weightier aspects of *Winter Notes* will be dealt with later; here we shall select only those features that help to fill out the account of his voyage and bring us closer to his first spontaneous reactions to the spectacle of European life.

Some of the anticipatory eagerness so evident in his letter to Polonsky swept over Dostoevsky even more strongly as his train approached the small border town of Eydkühnen on the Russian-German frontier. His heart suddenly began to beat faster at the thought that he was finally to catch his first longed-for glimpse of life on European soil: "And so I am at last going to see Europe, I, who have so vainly dreamt about it for almost forty years, I, who when I was scarcely sixteen, very seriously, 'wished to Switzerland to flee,' like the Belopyatkin of Nekrasov, but did not flee; and now at last I am about to enter 'the land of holy wonders,' the land I had so often longed for and languished after, in which I had placed so stubborn a faith!" (5: 51).

As night fell in the swaying railroad car, and while Dostoevsky was mulling over in his mind the many images of Europe acquired from his lifelong immersion in its culture, he also contemplated his neighbors in the compartment. There was an elderly couple, solid and inoffensive Russian landowners, making a quick trip to see the London World's Fair that Dostoevsky would visit himself. There was a Russian businessman from London, who had been back in his homeland for two weeks to settle some matter and was now returning abroad. And there was a typical Englishman, "redhaired, with an English haircut and intensely serious. All through the trip he did not address to any of us the slightest bit of a word in any language; during the day he read, without stopping, some sort of book, printed in the tiny English type that only the English can tolerate and even praise for its convenience; and exactly at ten o'clock in the evening, he hastened to take off his shoes and put on slippers. Such, probably, had been the habit of his lifetime, and he did not wish to change it even in the railroad car" (5: 53). Clearly, Europeans were not people whose way of life could easily be altered!

Dostoevsky unfortunately does not give us his reactions to crossing the border, but we know that his journey from there to Berlin was very far from a joy ride. He arrived in the German metropolis "ill, suffering from a liver complaint, jolted for two entire days in the train through rain and fog . . . deprived of sleep, yellow, harassed, exhausted." His first observation, in such a disabused state of body and soul, was that "Berlin bore an incredible resemblance to Petersburg. The same streets, all in a straight row, the same smells, the same . . . (really, there would be no end to enumerating all such similarities)." Had it been worth all the trouble and the two racking days and nights in the railroad car, only to find in Berlin what he had been escaping from at home? Even the famous linden trees of Unter den Linden—commented on approvingly by Karamzin in his famous *Letters of a Russian Traveler*, a book well-known to Dostoevsky since childhood—"did not succeed in pleasing me, and yet, to look after them properly, the Berliners would sacrifice everything they hold dear, perhaps even their Constitution; and what could be more precious to a Berliner than his Constitution!" (5: 47). Debates over the Prussian Constitution were then in full swing, and Dostoevsky's dig alludes to the constantly reiterated charge that the Constitution was being violated by the Prussian Crown.

To make matters worse, it suddenly dawned on him that all the people in

Berlin had a terribly German look about them; this upset him so much that he decided to push on immediately to Dresden, without even stopping to admire the famous frescoes of Kaulbach (still being painted), which adorned the staircase of the new Berlin Art Museum. "I nourish the profound conviction," he admits, "that one has to practice getting used to Germans, and without such practice it is hard to tolerate them in large doses." In Dresden, Dostoevsky found that it was not so much Germans in general as the female of the species that put him out of countenance: "Scarcely had I gone into the street when it suddenly struck me that nothing could be more unattractive than the women of Dresden, and that even the singer of love Vsevolod Krestovsky, the most dedicated and joyous of our Russian poets, would be totally lost here and even, perhaps, have doubts about his vocation" (5: 47).

Faced with such discouraging sights, he pinned the remainder of his hopes for a happier outcome on the cathedral of Cologne. Ever since his days as an engineering student, when he had sketched this venerable edifice in his architecture class, it had filled him with awe; but even such a time-tested attraction did not succeed in stirring him to the requisite response: "It seemed to me that it was just lace, lace and nothing but lace, a trinket somewhat along the lines of a paperweight for a writing desk, but one hundred and forty meters high" (5: 48). On returning through Cologne a month later, he looked again and changed his mind—and even wished to ask pardon of the monument "on his knees," as Karamzin had done with the Rhine waterfall whose splendor he had failed properly to appreciate on first approach.

Dostoevsky attributes his humiliating lapse in Cologne to two disturbing factors, which had combined to prevent him from mustering the proper aesthetic reaction. Just beside the cathedral was the headquarters of Jean-Maria Farina, the Italian chemist who had invented *eau de Cologne*, and Dostoevsky could not succeed in shaking off the vendors who hawked this local product on him with infuriating persistence: "I cannot affirm with complete certainty that they hail you exactly in such terms—'*eau de Cologne* or your life!'—but, who knows, it could be so." He also found himself terribly put out—to such a point that he became "exasperated and unjust"—by a new bridge that was the pride of the city. The bridge, he concedes, was certainly an impressive achievement, but the conceit of the natives concerning it was more than he could bear. It seemed to Dostoevsky—although he admits having no ground whatever for his suspicion—that he was known to be a Russian, and that the haughtiness evinced by the petty official to whom he paid a *groschen* at the entrance was an allusion to the inferiority of Russia so far as bridges were concerned! In consequence, he hastily bought a bottle of cologne and rushed on to Paris, "in the hope that the French would be kinder and more interesting" (5: 48-49).

Before arriving in Paris, however, he paused along the way—very probably at Wiesbaden, with its inviting roulette casino—to try his luck at gambling. What happened on this first fling remains obscure; but Strakhov believes that Dostoevsky quickly acquired eleven thousand francs, and suggests that this easy win pushed him along the path to perdition.[3] A later letter from Mikhail, informing his brother that he was forwarding some money from a publisher, indicates that Dostoevsky was again short of cash and probably had lost his winnings as he was so often to do in the future. "For God's sake, don't gamble any more," his brother pleads. "How can you gamble considering our luck?"[4] This episode is the first symptom of Dostoevsky's addiction to roulette, which was to grip him so strongly in the future but only, oddly enough, while traveling or living abroad.

3

Paris was the Mecca for all Russian tourists—whether those, like Herzen and Bakunin, who came to worship at the hallowed shrine of revolutionary upheaval, or those, more numerous, who hastened to kick up their heels at the Bal Mabille and chase *grisettes* in the Latin Quarter. There were also, of course, those who did not allow one source of interest to exclude the other. What Dostoevsky has to say about France naturally focuses on Paris; but even before actually setting foot in the capital city he caught a disturbing whiff of the prevailing political climate in the Second Empire. He and a Swiss gentleman had been carrying on a pleasant conversation in their empty carriage as the train crossed the border when, at a local stop, four Frenchmen came aboard and took seats in their compartment. Dostoevsky's voluble Swiss friend abruptly fell silent and refused to respond to further prompting. The new arrivals, Dostoevsky noticed, carried no baggage and were dressed with an affectation of chic and bravado; but their clothes had distinctly seen better days, and their linen was of dubious cleanliness. The four passengers, ostentatiously paying no attention to the two other occupants, did not exchange a single word and descended at the next station. The Swiss gentleman then regained his previous animation, and revealed to Dostoevsky that the four unsavory Frenchmen had been police spies patrolling the frontier; their assignment was to inspect all entering foreigners and telegraph descriptions to the proper authorities. Since Dostoevsky himself, as he knew very well, was kept under the vigilant scrutiny of the Russian secret police, his surprise at this bit of information seems rather disingenuous.

It was mid-June when he reached Paris, and he remained there for two weeks—long enough to soak up the atmosphere that he depicts in this tableau of the crowd in the Palais Royal peacefully disporting itself of a summer's evening. "Countless husbands are taking a walk with countless wives on their arm, while their charming and well-behaved children frolic around them as the fountain gently splashes, and its monotonous ripple evokes something tranquil, quiet, permanent, eternal, Heidelbergesque" (5: 75-76). What especially struck Dostoevsky in Paris was the reigning sense of order and propriety, and he labels the city—jestingly, of course— "the most moral and virtuous city on the face of the earth" (5: 68). In reality, he claimed, what the French admire above all is money, though they will scarcely admit to anything so demeaning for a single moment: "The Parisian loves to do business, but it seems that even in doing business and in skinning you alive in his shop like a chicken, he skins you not, as in the old days, for the sake of profit, but out of virtue, in the name of some sacred necessity" (5: 76).

Following in the footsteps of Herzen, who had diagnosed the essence of the French bourgeoisie as reflected in the plays of Eugène Scribe, Dostoevsky also hastens to the theater to investigate how this image has evolved. He observes that "the bourgeois particularly likes vaudeville, but he likes melodrama even more"; melodrama is now beginning to gain the upper hand in public taste "over the unpretentious and good-humored vaudeville." This change is not simply a matter of mode but has a deeper reason: the bourgeois "needs the sublime, he needs some unutterable nobility, he needs sentimentality, and he finds all this in melodrama" (5: 95). The plots of various plays by Dumas *fils*, Augier, Sardou, and the indefatigable Scribe are then summarized in a burlesque fashion, and in all of them Dostoevsky finds the same traits. All contain characters of unutterable nobility and impeccable virtue (whatever might be suspected privately by a cynical observer); all concern a young man who, in the first act, renounces a fortune for the highest motives (whatever they are), only to end in the last act by invariably marrying a poor girl who suddenly inherits incalculable wealth (unless it finally turns out that he, instead of being a penniless orphan, is really the legitimate son of a Rothschild). For all his mockery, though, Dostoevsky would not scruple a few years later to allow *his* impoverished Prince Myshkin unexpectedly to inherit a fortune.

Much intrigued by the French love of eloquence, Dostoevsky probably paid a visit to the Chamber of Deputies to observe some of the debates. He is amusingly caustic about the flights of rhetoric, the ritual exchange of flowery compliments, and the handful of deputies allowed to speak for the opposition. Every year, he explains, the Parisian is filled with an expectant emotion while awaiting the debates about public affairs "because he knows they will be eloquent, and he is content. He also knows very well that there will be only eloquence and nothing else, that there will be words, words, words, and that absolutely nothing will result from them. But that is enough to make him as content as can be" (5: 86). Such ridicule of the parliamentary system as nothing but a school of rhetoric was calculated to ap-

peal to a wide gamut of readers: those progressives who would appreciate
the exposure of the sham democracy of the Second Empire, but also those
Russians who preferred an unabashed and benevolent autocracy—one capable of abolishing serfdom with the stroke of a pen—to hypocritical and
class-biased constitutions and the windy futility of party debate.

Wandering one day into the *salle des pas perdus*, Dostoevsky stumbled
on a civil case being tried concerning a will made in favor of a Catholic monastic order. This bone of contention provides him with the opportunity to
indulge one of his favorite obsessions: the treacherous machinations of the
Roman Catholic Church, always ready to use any means to fill its coffers.
"It turned out, from the case in question, that the good fathers, by a prolonged, clever, and well-studied pressure (they have a science for that)
gained control over the soul of a very beautiful and wealthy lady, whom
they had seduced into living with them in their monastery, and whom they
had frightened with various terrors to the point of illness and hysteria—all
this with calculated purpose, and in a careful progression." The fathers, in
this instance, lost the case because their opponent happened to be represented by the great legal orator Jules Favre; nothing and no one could resist
the overwhelming effect of his majestic perorations. "It was thus that I was
fortunate enough," Dostoevsky comments dryly, "to become acquainted
with the flower of French eloquence, so to speak, at its principal source" (5:
88-89).

He noted the same taste for lofty language on a much lower social level
when he stepped into the Pantheon one day and followed his guide into the
crypt. The voice of the guide, probably an invalided war veteran, rose to a
sort of chant as he pointed out the tombs of Voltaire and Rousseau and began to declaim his set piece: "*Cî-git Voltaire . . .* he attacked prejudices, destroyed ignorance, battled against the angel of darkness, held high the
torch of enlightenment." Rousseau, if we are to believe Dostoevsky, was
called "*l'homme de la nature et de la vérité*"—a garbled citation from a passage in the *Confessions*, which appears in exactly the same form in Karamzin's *Letters of a Russian Traveler*. Seized by a sudden fit of laughter
at hearing such exalted phrases emerging from the lips of his humble
guide, Dostoevsky kept interrupting him teasingly until silenced by a protest made with quiet dignity. Thereafter Dostoevsky wonders whether all
the oratory that had washed over the French people since the Revolution,
and which was presumed to have led to their re-education, had not really
brought about only one result: "the love of eloquence for the sake of eloquence" (5: 89-90).

After spending his time seeing the sights, and consulting various medical authorities about his epilepsy, Dostoevsky summed up his impressions
in a letter to Strakhov a day before leaving for London. "Ah! Nikolay Nikolaevich," he writes, "Paris is a very boring city, and were there not a number

of truly remarkable things, one could die of boredom. By God! The French are a nauseating people. You have told me about the self-satisfied faces, complacent and unctuous, that flourish among us at the mineral spa [outside Petersburg]. But I swear to you that the faces here are just as bad. Ours are simply carnivorous scoundrels, and, most of the time, know it, but here they are completely convinced that this is how one must be. The Frenchman is pleasant, honest, polite, but false, and money for him is everything. No trace of any ideal."[5] One might be inclined to attribute such words merely to Dostoevsky's personal spleen and his well-known xenophobia; but since they coincide so perfectly with the portrait of the French given by the much more urbane and cosmopolitan Herzen in his sparkling *Letters from France and Italy*, we may view them as just another example of a recurring Russian reaction to bourgeois French life.*

It would be amusing, if it were not so predictably chauvinistic, to see Dostoevsky complaining that "the general level of culture is extremely low (I am not speaking of certified scholars. But they are not very numerous; and anyway, is scholarship culture in the sense we are accustomed to give this word?)."[6] The judicious Strakhov, Dostoevsky realizes, might well doubt such a judgment, especially when based on so short a stay in Paris (where the severe critic had no cultural contacts at all, although he could speak the language with some facility), and he hastens to add that all one needs is "a half-hour to observe and understand certain facts which clearly indicate whole aspects of the social situation, namely, that these facts are possible and that they exist." All the same, Dostoevsky concedes that "there is much to see and study" in Paris; and since "I am obliged to remain here for some time . . . I wish from now on to visit and study the city without wasting time, so far as this is possible for the simple tourist that I am. I do not know whether I will write anything."[7] Dostoevsky, of course, did eventually exploit his travels for literary purposes in *Winter Notes* and very probably jotted down some first impressions; but for the moment he went no further.

4

If what absorbed Dostoevsky in Paris was the stifling sense of bourgeois order and propriety, what overwhelmed him in London was the clamorous vitality of the city in all the nakedness of its clashing discords: "Even externally, what a contrast with Paris! This city day and night going about its business, enormous as the ocean, with the roaring and rumbling of ma-

---

* Compare, for example, Dostoevsky's words with Herzen's cutting judgment: "The [French] bourgeois . . . has invented a morality based on arithmetic, on the power of money, on the love of order." Or another comment of the same kind: "The bourgeois weeps in the theatre, moved by his own virtue as portrayed by Scribe, moved by his mercantile heroism and the poetry of shopkeeping." Cited in A. S. Dolinin, "Dostoevsky i Gertsen," *Poslednie Romany Dostoevskogo* (Moscow-Leningrad, 1963), 220-221.

chines, the railroad line constructed above the houses (and soon under-neath the houses), that boldness in enterprise, this apparent disorder which is, in essence, a bourgeois order to the highest degree, this polluted Thames, this air filled with coal dust; these magnificent parks and squares and those terrifying streets of a section like Whitechapel, with its half-na-ked, wild and starving population. The City with its millions and the com-merce of the universe, the Crystal Palace, the World's Fair . . ." (5: 69). We shall return in Chapter 16 to Dostoevsky's impressions of the World's Fair; here it is only necessary to note its place in the panorama of oppositions that make up his vision of London.

For a socially conscious Russian, London was the capital city of the clas-sic land of the dispossessed proletariat, and Dostoevsky's attention is riv-eted by this aspect of lower-class life. In London, he says, "one can see the masses in such proportions and in such circumstances as nowhere else in the world." Someone had described to him (and who could it have been if not the London resident Herzen?) how every Saturday night a half-million workers, with their wives and children, swarmed through the downtown streets to celebrate the beginning of their one day of leisure: "All of them bring their weekly savings, what they have earned by hard labor and amidst curses." Everything remains open, all the butcher shops and the eating places continue to do business, and night is transformed into day as the streets are lit by powerful gas lamps: "It is as if a ball had been organized for these white negroes. The crowd pushes into the open taverns and in the streets. They eat and drink. The beer halls are decorated like palaces. Everybody is drunk, but without gaiety, with a sad drunkenness, sullen, gloomy, strangely silent. Only sometimes an exchange of insults and a bloody quarrel breaks the suspicious silence, which fills one with melan-choly. Everyone hurries to get dead drunk as quickly as possible, so as to lose consciousness." Dostoevsky wandered among such a crowd at two o'-clock one Saturday night, and, he says, "the impression of what I had seen tormented me for three whole days" (5: 70-71).

On another evening he wandered among the thousands of prostitutes plying their trade in the Haymarket; and he marveled both at the luxuri-ousness of the cafés, where accommodations could be rented for the night, and the attractiveness of some of the women. "Nowhere in the world is there a more beautiful type than the Englishwoman"; some he saw had "faces truly fit for a keepsake." Like the Romantic artist Piskarev in Gogol's *Nevsky Prospect*, Dostoevsky was quite overcome by the exquisite delicacy of some of these countenances and haunted by the image of their fate. One passage outlines the beginning of a story about a young girl whom he no-ticed sitting at a table in the gallery of a casino and drinking gin. "I have never seen anywhere anything that came close to this ideal beauty"; with her was a young man, "apparently a rich gentleman, evidently not used to frequenting casinos." They spoke slowly, interrupted by long pauses, and to Dostoevsky, from a distance, her expression appeared to be sad, dreamy, withdrawn; he imagined her superior in intelligence and sensibility to the other unhappy creatures around her, "otherwise what meaning would there be in a human face?" At last the two shook hands, the young man left, "and she, with the spotty color that the alcohol had given to her pale cheeks, lost herself in the crowd of women for sale" (5: 71-72).

Dostoevsky was accosted not only by prostitutes but also by other women engaged in the charitable labor of trying to redeem these poor lost souls. A lady dressed in black, and whose bonnet almost entirely concealed her face, pressed a page on him while uttering a few words in unintelligible French. The paper contained verses in French from the Bible, evidently prepared for foreign tourists who might show up in the Haymarket throng. Later, Dostoevsky was told that he had seen Catholic propagandists at work, but the costume suggests rather some early volunteers of the Salvation Army which became formally organized three years later. Whether accurate or not, Dostoevsky seized on this information to nourish his anti-Catholic prejudices. "The [Catholic] propagandists, men and women, are legion," he writes. "It is a subtle and well thought-out propaganda. The Catholic priest himself searches out some miserable worker's family and gains their confidence. . . . He feeds them all, gives them clothes, provides heating, looks after the sick, buys medicine, becomes the friend of the family, and finally converts them all to Catholicism" (5: 73). The idea of Roman Catholicism has thus already become identified with that of a betrayal of the true spirit of the Christian faith, which substitutes for Christ's message of charity and love the temptation of worldly goods and comforts.

5

The most important event of Dostoevsky's stay in London was his meeting with Herzen, whom he probably visited several times during the eight or so days of his English sojourn. The two had met once long before (in 1846) at the home of I. I. Panaev, at a time when Dostoevsky had been suffering from acute feelings of persecution. Terribly upset by the decline of his literary reputation, he had regarded the fast-rising star of Herzen with jealous envy; and his behavior must have betrayed some of his anxieties if we are to judge from Herzen's acid remark in a letter: "I saw Dostoevsky today. . . . I cannot say that he made a very pleasant impression."[8] Since then, Dostoevsky had not only gained a new assurance but now found himself spiritually closer to Herzen than to any of his major contemporaries. Herzen's writings, in which he had found so many anticipations and echoes of his own return to his native soil, had played a crucial role in his recent development, and his admiration for Herzen was very well-known. As Strakhov observes, Dostoevsky's "relation to Herzen then was quite tender, and his *Winter Notes* smacks of some of the influence of this writer."[9]

Certainly, conditions could not have been more auspicious for the two men to meet again just at this time. Herzen had often referred to the Petrashevsky circle in glowing terms during the 1850s, and in his masterly *On the Development of Revolutionary Ideas in Russia* (1851), had listed Dostoevsky among "the most noble and outstanding" people who had been condemned to Siberia for their political idealism. *Poor Folk* was singled out as evidence of the Socialist turn taken by Russian literature during the 1840s, and more recently Herzen had exhibited the liveliest interest in *House of the Dead.* As for Dostoevsky, he wholeheartedly shared Herzen's view that the very backwardness of Russia, the continued existence of the peasant *obshchina*, was in reality an enormous advantage; it meant that Russia would open the way to the Socialist future and was destined to take over the leadership of mankind from a faltering and decadent Europe. Like Herzen too, he had become increasingly exasperated with the intransigent radicalism of *The Contemporary*, whose pitiless scorn for any sort of compromise with existing conditions had succeeded in eroding Herzen's once enormous and uncontested influence. Significantly, the word "bilious" turns up in Dostoevsky's notebooks to refer to Chernyshevsky almost immediately after Herzen's *The Superfluous and the Bilious* had appeared in *The Bell* (20: 155).

Recent events had also given Dostoevsky and Herzen a good many urgent matters to talk about—the Petersburg fires, *Young Russia*, and the arrest of Chernyshevsky just a short while before. Unfortunately, we have no account of what they said to each other on those two occasions (probably the 11th and certainly the 16th of July.[10] That they touched on Chernyshevsky we know indirectly because, as Dostoevsky later wrote, "Herzen told me that Chernyshevsky made a disagreeable impression on him, that is, by his appearance and manners. For my part, I liked Chernyshevsky's appearance and manners" (21: 35). On another issue, that of *Young Russia*, the two men saw eye to eye. Evidence for this can be found in Herzen's article, "Young and Old Russia," printed in the issue of *The Bell* for July 15, just a few days after the first visit; and if the manuscript were not dated July 5, it might be thought to betray some of the influence of their exchange of ideas.

For Herzen points out, just as Dostoevsky had done, that the proclamation *Young Russia* was unquestionably the product of overheated youthful impetuosity ("for us there is no doubt that the leaflet was written by very young people"), and as such should not be given any earthshaking importance. He too speaks with some irony of the panic that it provoked: "Weak people of faltering faith! How little is required to frighten your womanish nerves, to cause you to run backward, and to grasp at the coattails of the local police officer. . . ." Echoing Dostoevsky's comment that the youthful authors of *Young Russia* were unable to cope with the Western revolutionary sources they had so hastily ingested, Herzen also asks amusedly: "Is there really any possibility that the Russian people will rise in the name of the Socialism of Blanqui, proclaiming aloud the cry ['Long live the Russian Social and Democratic Republic'], when three of the longest words will be incomprehensible to them?"[11]

Most striking of all is a paragraph in which, sounding for all the world like a *pochvennik*, Herzen attributes the excesses of *Young Russia* to the separation of the educated class from the people. "Having said all this," he writes, referring to his criticism of the pamphlet, "we shall add that their [the authors'] fearless logic is one of the most characteristic traits of the Russian genius *estranged from the people*. Our history has left us nothing sacred, we do not possess those *honored relics of the past* which restrain European man but which he holds dear. As a result of the slavery in which we lived, the alienation from ourselves, our break with the people, our impotence to act, there remained for us a painful consolation but a consolation all the same—the nakedness of our negation, our logical ruthlessness, and it was with some sort of joy that we pronounced those final, *extreme* words which the lips of our teachers have barely whispered, turning white as they did so and looking around uneasily." But, Herzen concludes—much like Dostoevsky—now "times have changed," and "to speak in foreign phrases, to utter foreign slogans—this is to misunderstand both the business at hand as well as the people, and to show disrespect for both" (italics in text).[12] Dostoevsky would certainly have read such words with great approbation, even though he would not have shared Herzen's tolerant opinion that the exaggerations of the youthful firebrands could not possibly cause any harm.

Only one other subject of their conversation is definitely known from Dostoevsky's later account. He was a great admirer of Herzen's brilliant part essay, part dialogue, *From the Other Shore*, and he praised it very highly when he had the chance to talk to its author. Indeed, few other writings of Herzen would have been as close to Dostoevsky's heart as this bitter indictment of the illusions of Utopian Socialism, this denunciation of European civilization as hidebound to the social-political forms of the past and incapable of going beyond their limits, this torrent of scorn poured on the radical European intelligentsia for imagining that the masses would really pay attention to their high-flown lucubrations. All these aspects of the work had found a vibrant echo in Dostoevsky's "idea-feelings" after his Siberian years, and helped to crystallize them into conscious political positions. Other elements, however, in which various facets of Herzen's multifarious mind enter into debate with each other, did not appeal to Dostoevsky in the same degree. Although a total pessimism about the future of mankind seems most prominent, and is generally taken to represent Herzen's own view at the time, other voices in the text eloquently rebut such gloomy conclusions; and Dostoevsky aligns himself with these more hopeful augurs. As he remarked to Herzen, "your opponent is also very clever. Admit, that in many instances he pinned you to the wall." Herzen laughed, and recalled an earlier occasion when Belinsky had once read him a similar dialogue article. But Belinsky had incautiously given himself all the best arguments, and, when Herzen was asked for his opinion, he replied jestingly that the piece was "very, very good, and one can see that you are very clever. But did you really want to waste your time with such a fool?" (21:8).*

Regrettably we have no further information about this exchange of ideas; but Dostoevsky's reference to the cleverness of Herzen's opponents, whose position in *From the Other Shore* he obviously prefers, may perhaps furnish a clue and justify a speculation. Herzen had gone on, after writing this work, to develop his theory of "Russian Socialism," in which his disillusionment with the European working class and its leaders gave way to a hope for the future founded on the traditional egalitarian Socialism of the Russian peasant and his native *obshchina*. Would not Dostoevsky have indicated his agreement with Herzen on *this* point—and to such a degree that the ever skeptical Herzen even recoiled somewhat from the fervency of Dostoevsky's words? Such would seem to be the sense of Herzen's own reference to their conversation in a letter to N. I. Ogarev, whom Dostoevsky had probably met a day or so earlier. "Dostoevsky was here yesterday—he is a naive, not entirely lucid, but very nice person," he writes. "He believes with enthusiasm in the Russian people."[13] Would not Dostoevsky's "naiveté" have consisted precisely in an excess of such enthusiasm?

If such had been the tenor of their conversation, and if Herzen had given only lukewarm assent to Dostoevsky's exaltation of the Russian people, then we can well understand why, in the portrait he furnished of Herzen eleven years later, Dostoevsky should have placed such stress on the inner divisions of Herzen's temperament. "He was an artist, a thinker, a brilliant writer, an extraordinarily well-read man, a wit, a wonderful conversationalist (he spoke even better than he wrote), and superbly self-reflective. Self-reflection—the faculty of turning a most profound personal sentiment into

---

* There is some conflict among the authorities on Herzen as to exactly when he spoke with Dostoevsky about *From the Other Shore*. The commentator in the Academy of Sciences edition believes it occurred during the meeting in London. The editors of the third volume of a chronicle of Herzen's life assign the conversation to October 13/November 1, 1863, when the two men met accidentally aboard a boat going from Naples to Livorno (see chapter 18). No conclusive evidence is cited that would clinch the case for either thesis.

In view of this uncertainty, one can only appeal to common sense and plausibility. It seems more likely that the conversation would have taken place at the formal visit in London, during the first opportunity that Dostoevsky had personally to express his admiration for Herzen's work, rather than later on shipboard where Dostoevsky was also distracted and embarrassed by other concerns. See *PSS*, 21:374; *Letopis Zhizni i Tvorchestva A. I. Gertsena, 1859–Iyun 1864* (Moscow, 1983), 566.

an object which he set before himself, which he would worship, and which, a minute later, he would ridicule—that faculty was highly developed in him. Unquestionably, this was an unusual man, but whatever he may have been . . . invariably everywhere and all his life, he was above all a *gentilhomme russe et citoyen du monde*, a mere product of former servitude which he hated and from which he descended, not only through his father, but precisely as a result of the severance from his native land and its ideals" (21: 9). These final words recall the terms Herzen had used himself for the authors of *Young Russia*, and the entire passage, in its mélange of admiration and rejection, reveals some of the later ambiguity of Dostoevsky's relation to the man whose ideas and values he had once so esteemed. This image of Herzen was sketched in 1873, just at the time Dostoevsky was beginning to jot down ideas in his notebook for *A Raw Youth*; and he was soon to pour such recollections into the character of Versilov, a Russian-European type whose psychology is very similar to the one pictured here and who also possesses some of the charm and brilliance invariably attributed to Herzen's personality.

Dostoevsky must surely have been aware that in visiting Herzen he was taking a step which might endanger him even more than his precipitate call on Chernyshevsky in Petersburg. The Third Section kept a very sharp eye on the activities of the Herzen household, and Chernyshevsky had been arrested after spies reported that Herzen was imprudently sending a letter to Nikolay Serno-Solovievich offering to print *The Contemporary* in London. Dostoevsky's presence did not escape the vigilant operatives who kept Herzen under surveillance, and information was sent back to Russia that in London Dostoevsky "had struck up a friendship with the exiles Herzen and Bakunin."[14] The flamboyant Bakunin, then also living in London, had recently made a sensational escape from Siberian exile by way of the United States.

A good deal of ink has been spilled over whether or not Dostoevsky actually met Bakunin, and the question has been given some importance because L. P. Grossman has argued that Bakunin was the direct prototype for Stavrogin in *The Devils*.[15] Dostoevsky's imagination, however, though it certainly worked from prototypes, invariably fused all sorts of suggestions into a representative image; he never took only a single personage as an exclusive source of inspiration. Whether the two men ever met thus becomes a minor question so far as Dostoevsky the artist is concerned, though it may well have occurred because Bakunin so assiduously attended Herzen's Sunday afternoon receptions. In any event, Dostoevsky's name was placed on the list of those persons who visited Herzen not simply out of curiosity but because they sympathized "more or less with his criminal intentions."[16] A special command was issued to search his luggage very thoroughly on his way home; fortunately no severer measures were taken.

Strakhov, also making his first trip to Europe during this summer, expected to join Dostoevsky in mid-July. Mikhail had been particularly eager for his brother to have a traveling companion because he feared some accident or injury caused by an epileptic crisis. Dostoevsky complained of his loneliness in letters both to his brother and Strakhov ("you cannot believe," he writes the latter, "to what extent the soul here falls prey to solitude. A feeling of sadness and oppression!"), and looked forward gratefully to having an accompanying friend. "What will it be like when I come down from the Alps into the plains of Italy!" he asks Strakhov. "Ah! if we were together: we could see Naples, we could wander in Rome, God willing we could caress some young Venetian in a gondola (eh! Nikolay Nikolaevich!). But 'nothing, nothing, silence!' as Poprishchin says in this situation."[17]*

Dostoevsky and Strakhov joined forces in Geneva in late July and traveled together through Switzerland and the north of Italy to Florence. Elaborate plans had been worked out as to how the two should meet; but Strakhov simply walked along the lake shore and found Dostoevsky sitting in the first large café. The noisy encounter of the two overjoyed Russians attracted unfavorable glances from the sedate Swiss reading their newspapers, and the strangers hastened into the street. Dostoevsky found Geneva "in general depressing and dull," and the two friends traveled to Lucerne, where Strakhov was eager to sample the beauties of the Lake of Four Cantons. A steamer trip on the lake in fine weather was a great success, and they then left for Florence by way of Turin, Genoa, and Livorno, traveling by boat and train. In Florence they spent a week in a modest *pensione* on the Via Tornebuoni, which Strakhov praises for its old-fashioned simplicity and "patriarchal customs." These, alas, had entirely vanished when he returned thirteen years later, having been replaced by an affectation of luxury, by pilfering, and by insolence.[18]

The two Russians were naturally inseparable, and Strakhov has left an engaging image of Dostoevsky in his unaccustomed role as tourist. "Feodor Mikhailovich was not a great master in the art of voyaging," he writes; "he was not particularly taken up with nature, nor with historical monuments, nor works of art (with the exception of the most notable); all his attention was focused on people, on grasping their nature and character, and on the general impression of life going on around him in the streets. He excitedly explained to me that he despised the usual prescribed manner of looking at the various noteworthy sights of the locality according to the guidebook." This account more or less agrees with Dostoevsky's own remarks in *Winter*

* This is an allusion to Gogol's story *Memoirs of a Madman*, in which a lowly office clerk imagines that the daughter of his superior is in love with him and admonishes himself in this way to keep the secret.

Notes, but one wonders whether he was as little interested in the Uffizi as Strakhov pretends (casting himself, of course, in the role of civilized art lover). On later trips, Dostoevsky was, as we know from the diary of his second wife, an interested and assiduous museum-goer. The two men read Hugo's *Les Misérables* (just then coming out), with Dostoevsky eagerly buying volume after volume and passing them on to Strakhov. Most of all they walked and talked, and Strakhov paints an idyllic image of these leisurely conversations: "Most pleasant of all were our evening talks, as the sun was setting, over a glass of red wine" in one café or another.[19]

Until a few years ago, this portrait of an amicable exchange of ideas between two friends, delighted to be in each other's company, was accepted as accurately depicting the quality of the relationship. A recently published document, however, throws an entirely new light on their conversations and uncovers some of the tensions that eventually led Strakhov, shortly after Dostoevsky's death, to denounce his erstwhile friend in a scurrilous letter to Tolstoy. This document, the undated draft of an unfinished article entitled "Observations," is dedicated to Dostoevsky and composed in Strakhov's favorite form of an open letter. Found in the Strakhov archives, it seems to have been composed in Florence or shortly thereafter, and it begins by recalling one of those dialogues that its author later depicted with such accents of nostalgia. "In one of our walks through Florence," he writes, "when we came to the Piazza della Signoria and stopped for a moment, since we were going in opposite directions, you [Dostoevsky] declared to me very heatedly that there was in the tendency of my thought a defect that you hated, despised, and would persecute until your dying day. Then we shook hands firmly and parted."[20] So much for the carefully chiseled cameo of unruffled concord that Strakhov later offered to a gullible world!

What was the cause of the dispute? Why should Dostoevsky have reacted so heatedly and, it must be conceded, insultingly? Although Strakhov's text remains largely in the realm of vague generalities, it is not hard to infer what was at stake if we recall the background of the time in Russia and remember that Dostoevsky and Strakhov did not see eye to eye on how to treat the radicals. Strakhov had always been in favor of a hard line, and his remarks seem to refer to this position. No one, he argued, should be permitted to escape the logical consequences of his convictions and actions; no excuses should be made on the ground that people did not understand the full implications of their own ideas. "And by the way—do you recall clearly what the question was?" he asks Dostoevsky. "You found unbearable and repugnant my partiality for that kind of proof which in logic is called indirect, or a *reductio ad absurdum*. You found unpardonable that I often led our reasoning to the conclusion which, in the simplest fashion, can be expressed as: 'but really, it is impossible that 2 plus 2 do not equal 4.' "[21]

Strakhov was thus insisting that the radicals be made to assume the full onus of their beliefs and not be given the benefit of any doubt. Dostoevsky, on the other hand, did not as yet wish to pin them against the wall, and he argued that their seeming inconsistency should be given a more charitable interpretation. No one, he had replied to Strakhov, *really* wished to affirm that "2 *plus* 2 *equals* 3, or 2 *plus* 2 *equals* 5, and that . . . if something like this is said, then it is strange on my [Strakhov's] part to take this with complete seriousness, since obviously the people who say 2 *plus* 2 *does not equal* 4 do not at all intend to say this, but, without question, think and wish to express something else." For Dostoevsky, illogicality is not a proof of error but the indication of a conflict between what is said and what is actually meant; the error is a clue to something hidden and concealed under the idea that must be understood as its *real* meaning. With a good deal of justice, Strakhov argues that such a postulate puts him at a disadvantage with everyone "because, whatever they say and however they say it, I am obliged, on your view, without fail to understand what they *wished* to say, and whether or not this desired meaning has some sort of hidden foundation."[22] These words reveal the basis on which, so far, Dostoevsky had refused to condemn the radicals *in toto*; no matter how hostile he was to their expressed ideas, underneath these he sensed a desire for the good that should be recognized and acknowledged.

Another passage in Strakhov's allusive text comes close to revealing the social-cultural dimension of their disagreement: "Was our dispute in Florence anybody else's affair? But I am not alone in hating stupidities, and you are not alone in condescendingly pardoning them for what you assume underlies them." In fact, Strakhov goes on, these attitudes have now turned into opposing parties in Russian literature: "they had to be formed, and the clash between the two sides was inevitable, and will inevitably recur." Curiously, Strakhov characterizes both camps in a fashion quite unflattering for the one to which he belongs. On one side (Dostoevsky's) there is "often youthfulness, always ardor, a passion for preachment, carelessness about form and any kind of accuracy, but on the other hand live feeling and thought, not infrequently talent, sometimes flashes of genius. . . ." On the other (his own), there is "a certain coldness, the habit of strict and accurate thought, the absence of a great passion for preachment, the silence of the most living strings." Even though capable of sympathy for the first side, as shown by the terms he chooses, Strakhov nonetheless declares that "willy-nilly I will support the second. Such is my unhappy fate. . . ."[23]

At this juncture the text takes a sudden leap from the realm of social politics to that of the ultimate basis of morality. "Is man really good?" Strakhov asks abruptly. "Are we really able boldly to deny his rottenness?" His answer to this question is emphatically negative; and he supports his conclusion by an appeal to the testimony of the Christian faith: "The ideal of the

195

perfect man, shown us by Christianity, is not dead and cannot die in our souls; it has grown together with it forever. And thus, when the picture of contemporary humanity is unrolled before us and we are asked: Is man good? we immediately find in ourselves the decisive answer: 'No, rotten to the core!' "[24] The fragment breaks off at this point, but it contains enough for us to understand why Dostoevsky was stirred to such anger and hostility.

Despite a widely held and erroneous belief to the contrary, Dostoevsky did not at all share Strakhov's "Christian" view that man is "rotten to the core" (which represents the view only of an extreme Augustinian or Reformation Christianity). On the contrary, Dostoevsky believed that since man, and Russian man in particular, was capable of remorse and repentance, the hope of his redemption should never be abandoned; no doubt Strakhov understood this to be the root cause of Dostoevsky's refusal to renounce all sympathy with the radicals once and for all. And if Strakhov expressed his own view of man to Dostoevsky as candidly as he exposes it in the article, we can see why his friend should have been so indignant, and why he responded with the furious declaration that he "would hate, despise, and persecute" such a cast of mind for the remainder of his days. Strakhov was indeed striking here at Dostoevsky's deepest pieties—at the truths he felt he had glimpsed amidst his sufferings in the house of the dead, and at the revelation vouchsafed him in the sacred memory of the *muzhik* Marey,who had once consoled and comforted him as a child.[25] He was striking at Dostoevsky's fundamental faith in the treasures of Christian love concealed in the soul of the ignorant and unenlightened Russian people; and such a sacrilege Dostoevsky could not forgive.

After their week in Florence together the two men parted company, Strakhov to go on to Paris and Dostoevsky intending to journey south to Rome and Naples. For unknown reasons he changed his mind, and by the beginning of September was back in Petersburg ready to take up his post again as de facto editor and chief contributor to *Time*.

CHAPTER 14

Time:
The Final Months

On returning to Petersburg in the fall of 1862, both Dostoevsky and Stra-khov took up their work on *Time* again with renewed vigor. Apollon Grigo-ryev had also returned from self-imposed exile in Orenburg and was once again a rallying presence and an active contributor. "Everyone began to work as hard as they could," Strakhov informs us, "and the affair went so well that there was cause for rejoicing."[1] By mid-year, *Time*'s subscription list had gone over the four thousand mark, thus reaching the level of such long-established publications as *Notes of the Fatherland*.

Security was thus at last in sight for the hard-pressed Dostoevskys, who had worked like galley slaves to establish their publication on a sound fi-nancial footing. Even more encouraging, their editorial portfolio was over-flowing with manuscripts that kept pouring in from all corners of Russia and testified to the growing prestige acquired by *Time* in the brief span of two years. Feodor Dostoevsky could certainly have allowed himself to feel some satisfaction, not only with the success of his own contributions, but also with the skill he had demonstrated as a managing editor. These fair prospects for the future, however, proved to be only a momentarily gratify-ing illusion. The meteoric rise of *Time* was abruptly ended when—partly as a result of error, but mainly because of its political temerity—it was sup-pressed by the government in May 1863.

During the last nine months of its existence, *Time* continued to bear wit-ness to Dostoevsky's indefatigable literary and editorial activity. New chap-ters of *House of the Dead* were published at irregular intervals (the series had begun during the first year), and, at the beginning of 1863, he com-menced his *Winter Notes on Summer Impressions*, which ran through three installments. In addition, Dostoevsky managed to append a flood of editorial notes to various contributions, dash off a short story, and maintain a steady drumfire of polemical articles. Since separate chapters will be de-voted to the two longer works completed at this period, the present one will concentrate on his shorter pieces and the journalistic exchanges.

2

Dostoevsky, as we know, had read *Les Misérables* during his stay in Florence, and the publication of this powerful epic-novel had brought Hugo's name once again to the forefront of world literature. Ever the canny editor, Dostoevsky seized the moment to commission for *Time* the first Russian translation of Hugo's earlier masterpiece, *Notre Dame de Paris*, and he introduced the first chapters with a brief preface. Like so many others, Dostoevsky had read the book in his youth, when it captivated all of literate Russia by its grandiose evocations of medieval Paris; and Dostoevsky had revered its author as a poet whose "childlike Christian tendency" expressed the noblest and most sacred ideals of the modern world. Indeed, as his preface indicates, he continued to admire Hugo as the greatest contemporary spokesman for a social Christianity whose values were still very much alive in his own sensibility, even though he no longer accepted them, as he had done in the days of serfdom, as a guide to political action. The ideal inspiring Hugo's work, he writes, "is the fundamental thought of all the art of the nineteenth century, and it is a thought of which Victor Hugo as artist was probably the first herald. This thought is Christian and highly moral: its formula is the raising up of the fallen human being, crushed by the unjust pressure of circumstances, a centuries-old stagnation, and of social prejudices" (20: 28).

Although declaring that "allegory is not conceivable in a work of art such as *Notre Dame de Paris*," Dostoevsky nonetheless proceeds to give an allegorical significance to the character of Quasimodo. "But who," he asks, "can escape the idea that Quasimodo is a personification of the French people of the Middle Ages, oppressed and despised, deaf and deformed, gifted only with a frightening physical force, but in whom awakens finally a love and a thirst for justice simultaneously with a consciousness of its legitimate right and of its infinite, still undeveloped powers?" What Dostoevsky finds in Hugo's novel is thus "the idea of raising up the lowly"; but this idea is far more than merely a personal pecularity of Hugo's talent. It is, Dostoevsky affirms "the historic testament of modern times, so often unjustly accused of contributing nothing to compare with the great literary works of the past." And perhaps, he prophesies, "at the end of the century it will become embodied, completely, clearly, and powerfully, in some great work of art that will express the profound character of the time as fully and lastingly as, for example, *The Divine Comedy* expressed its epoch of medieval Catholic beliefs and ideals" (20: 28-29). Dostoevsky's own *Brothers Karamazov*, though "raising up the lowly" is only one of its many themes, comes closer than any work at the end of the century to fulfilling this prophecy of a great masterpiece of Christian art.

Actually, Dostoevsky was giving this theme its most forceful expression in the work he was just then in the process of writing, *House of the Dead*. Nowhere more directly than here was he engaged in "raising up the lowly" by teaching his Russian readers to look with new eyes at the "unfortunates" penned up behind the stockades of prison camps in the wastes of Siberia. To attain this new vision, however, it was first necessary for the Russian educated class to overcome the estrangement, the total alienation, that separated them from the Russian peasant—an estrangement Dostoevsky himself had felt as the greatest torture he had been forced to endure during his convict years. Remarks on this subject, as we have seen, crop up continually in his articles, and he is particularly sensitive to the difficulties involved in overcoming the deeply rooted mistrust nourished by the peasant.

"One must speak the truth: we do not know how to go to the people," Dostoevsky had written a month or two before publishing his preface to Hugo's novel. "In this respect, we do not know the proper middle way. Either we exhibit a coarseness beyond all belief, or the pitiful, sugar-sweet manner of a Manilov [a character in *Dead Souls*]." Elsewhere in the same article, Dostoevsky remarks that "we have to transform ourselves morally in a certain degree. We have to renounce our class prejudices and our egoistic points of view." Just as the people detest the fists that had formerly beaten them into submission, so too they "will not tolerate either a politeness *à la française* which they take as an insult. One must love the people, but not with a sentimental love acquired in the study" (20: 16, 20).

3

These words exactly define the theme of a satirical short story, *A Nasty Tale*, written in the same year*—a story highlighting the difficulties experienced by a young and elegant general in the Civil Service named Ivan Il-yich Pralinsky when he tries to put into practice the spirit of the new liberalism that had become the prevailing social-cultural fashion of the early 1860s. In this instance, "the people" are not the Russian peasantry but the lower ranks of the bureaucracy and a motley assortment of Petersburg student youth. They include the inevitable medical student à la Bazarov and a young contributor to a satirical journal, *The Burning Brand* (obviously *The Spark*), who had published all of "four bad verses and thus obtained a reputation as a liberal" (5: 30). Still, the problem that Dostoevsky dramatizes— the difficulty of overcoming the distrust between the upper and lower rungs of the social hierarchy—is much the same as with the peasantry; and the "philanthropic" General Pralinsky learns, in a most mortifying manner,

* In Constance Garnett's translation, the story is called *An Unpleasant Predicament* and is better known in English under this more decorous title.

that it is no easy task to bridge the class barrier between his exalted rank and the world of ordinary mortals.

Pralinsky himself, whose name ("praline," a French candy) sufficiently indicates a rather weak and self-indulgent character, is a young man who had risen in the Civil Service without any particular effort or distinction. Of very good family and imposing appearance and manners, he combines an overweening vanity (at times he dreams of becoming a great statesman) with occasional feelings of depression and a sense that his life has really been *une existence manquée* (he naturally thinks in such French phrases): "In short, he was a good-natured man and a poet at heart." The period of reforms inspires him with great enthusiasm and helps to conquer an increasing sense of morbidity and futility. "He talked about the new ideas, which he very quickly and unexpectedly made his own, drove about town, and in many places succeeded in gaining the reputation of a desperate Liberal, which flattered him greatly" (5: 7-8).

One evening, after having drunk a considerable quantity of champagne with two older colleagues of equal rank, Ivan Ilyich finds himself unexpectedly walking through a lower-class district of Petersburg. He had tried out some of his ideas about "humanity" on his older, more hard-bitten companions, but had met with a very skeptical reaction: "We won't be able to bear it," one of them said suddenly. Pralinsky had felt a surge of personal resentment at this disclaimer and left the apartment with a rankling sense of grievance. But then he hears the noise of a celebration, discovers it is the wedding party of one of his clerks, and decides to put his theories to the test. What if he were to drop in unexpectedly and enchant the assembled company with his awesome presence and democratic behavior? "Humanity . . . the love of one's kind," he muses inwardly. "Restore a man to himself, revive his personal dignity, and then . . . when the ground is cleared, get to work." For, once the ground *is* cleared, then "the man's mine, the man is caught, so to speak, in a net, and I can do what I like with him, that is, for his own good" (5: 9, 11). Such thoughts, of course, uncover the patronizing and self-serving roots of such "humanity."

The consequences of Pralinsky's *beau geste* are exactly what might have been expected—except that he had not anticipated them at all. The unconcerned merrymaking at the wedding is immediately cut short by the appearance of so august a personage. The poor bridegroom, who bears the ludicrous name of Pseldonimov (a play on "pseudonym"), is so shocked that he remains frozen in a servile bow, and the whole company is plunged into a situation of embarrassed conjecture and confusion. Pralinsky had imagined himself gracefully and amiably explaining his unannounced visit, and so winning all hearts by his magnanimity. But his efforts at conversation, so successful in various *salons*, here fall completely flat, and he becomes increasingly irritated by the failure to elicit the flattering response he had envisaged.

As time goes on, he notices the company becoming more relaxed and the dancing starting up again; word had gotten round that the General, after all, was only "a little top-heavy," and this explanation clears up the whole question. But while a bit earlier Pralinsky had been praying for such a relaxation of the atmosphere, he now finds himself more upset than by the previous chilly restraint: "How was it? They had held back and now they were so quickly emancipated! One might think it nothing, but this transformation was somehow strange; it indicated something. It was as though they had forgotten Ivan Ilyich's existence." Poor Ivan Ilyich becomes more and more troubled, perplexed, and confused, swears to himself a thousand times to cut the experiment short, and finds himself somehow leading the company to the dinner table. Once there, he tosses off a glass of vodka without thinking; as a scion of good society "he had never drunk vodka before," and the fiery people's drink finishes him off completely (5: 24, 27, 28). He becomes more and more maudlin, begins to dribble at the mouth, tries to make a speech about "humanity" to redeem the situation, but is met only by hoots and catcalls of derision.

The ideological climax occurs during a head-on clash between the young radical journalist, who had gloomily pronounced Pralinsky "a retrograde" the moment he set eyes on him, and the drunken General. Reduced to despair, the latter asks the company whether he was "greatly lowered in [their] eyes or not" for having come to the wedding. To which the young radical, who had been helping himself liberally to the vodka, replies furiously: "Yes, you came to show off your humanity! You've hindered the enjoyment of everyone. You've been drinking champagne [hastily bought for the General] without thinking that it is beyond the means of a clerk at ten rubles a month, and I suspect you're one of those bureaucrats who have a weakness for the young wives of their subordinates. . . . Yes, yes, yes!" (5: 33-34).

This tirade destroys Pralinsky completely, and the story ends with a crescendo of comic catastrophes. Falling flat on his face in a sodden stupor, he is naturally given the only decent bed and thus ruins the consummation of the nuptials. After a night of misery and retching discomfort, during which he is nursed by the mother of the bridegroom with the tolerant stolidity of the common people, he flees at the crack of dawn. For eight days he refuses to set foot in his office, haunted by fear that his misadventure might have become common knowledge; but he notices no change when he finally decides to confront the world. Dispatching the usual business with more than usual decision and authority, he greets with relief the blessed news that Pseldonimov has asked for a transfer to another bureau—the very one headed by the general who had been most ironic about Pralinsky's progressive ardors. In his heart of hearts, and overwhelmed by a terrible sense of shame, Pralinsky now admits that such doubts had been quite warranted. "No, severity, severity, nothing but severity"—these are his final words as he renounces once and for all the treacherous pitfalls of "humanity" (5: 45).

A Nasty Tale is an amusing satirical grotesque in the broad manner of Saltykov-Shchedrin and reveals the influence of that social satirist on Dostoevsky's style. It speaks eloquently for itself as a disabused comment on the times, but it can also be taken as a self-reflexive comment on Dostoevsky's own past. For in one of the crucial scenes of his first novel, *Poor Folk*—a scene that had much impressed Belinsky—an equally enlightened and equally philanthropic General, out of the goodness of his heart, gives a threadbare subordinate a hundred rubles. Since Dostoevsky had depicted this generous gesture with unconcealed sympathy, *A Nasty Tale* can well be read as a debunking in maturity of such youthful naiveté. By placing in Pralinsky's mouth the clichés about humanity that had been so popular among progressive circles in the 1840s, and which had just taken a new lease on life in the early 1860s, Dostoevsky now unmasks the condescending class psychology that all too often lay behind such noble professions of benevolence.

Written in a slapstick style of considerable comic vigor, the scenes of feasting and dancing foreshadow such later episodes as Marmeladov's wake in *Crime and Punishment* and the masterly fête scene of *The Devils*. But the good-humored gaiety of tone is rather unusual in Dostoevsky, and so is his tolerant and amused depiction of the lively and irreverent Petersburg youth whom he treats with considerable sympathy; he clearly preferred their breezy iconoclasm to the fatuous and self-complacent likes of a Pralinsky. It is the ideological clash that raises the story above the level of a farcical sketch, and we should note that Dostoevsky did not hesitate to use a character whose ideas he certainly disliked—the young radical journalist—as his spokesman in a particular artistic context to discredit another character whose attitudes he disliked even more. One of the most striking aspects of Dostoevsky's genius is this willingness to acknowledge the *relative human validity*, in concrete situations, of points of view with which he did not at all agree in other contexts, and to bring them to the most vivid and forceful artistic life.

4

During most of the first year of *Time*, Dostoevsky had managed to indicate his objections to various aspects of radical ideology without arousing any hostile response. Such invulnerability was partly a token of respect for his status as an ex-political prisoner, who had paid a heavy price for attempting to free the Russian people from slavery; and the installments of *House of the Dead* had made clear just how heavy the price had been. No such respect was accorded Strakhov, however, and at the end of 1861 *The Contemporary* finally replied to his politely phrased but exasperating pinpricks through the pen of M. A. Antonovich. This article marked the beginning of an increasingly harsh polemic between the radicals and *Time* that eventually involved Dostoevsky himself; and it led, in the second half of 1862, to a total deterioration of the previously amicable relations between *Time* and those of its contributors and readers who belonged to the radical intelligentsia.

Antonovich may have been a blundering and imperceptive literary critic, but Chernyshevsky was not wrong in thinking him an effective social-cultural combatant at close quarters. Chosen for the task of replying to Strakhov, his attack on *Time* skillfully hits its target within the limits allowed by the censorship. There is something incontestably cloudy about the idea of *pochvennichestvo*, he claims, and *Time*'s contributors would find themselves in great difficulty if prohibited from endlessly repeating the usual phrases about *pochva*: "there would be nothing left for them to say." Greatly concerned with the gulf that exists between the educated classes in Russia and the peasantry, they attribute this gulf to the reforms of Peter the Great. But Antonovich cleverly points out that "even aside from this [cause], they [the classes] would have split apart of themselves as a result of general social causes, not historical ones only, which everywhere, and not only among us, have produced and will produce such a split."[2] The real cause of the rift is thus social-economic and not primarily cultural; nor is the division between the haves and have-nots a peculiarly Russian phenomenon.

In addition, Antonovich is sharply ironical about the exalted notions held by the *pochvenniki* (primarily Dostoevsky, although he is not mentioned by name) regarding the world-historical mission of the Russian people. Whether such ideas make sense or not, they can in any event refer only to a far distant future; if one asks what the *pochvenniki* advocate in the present, it turns out to mean only one very simple thing: literacy. Literacy, however, has not solved the social problems of more advanced countries such as England and Germany, and there is no reason to believe it will have any happier effect in Russia. "For, you see," Antonovich writes with provocative crudeness, "everywhere in first place is the stomach. First of all it is necessary to manage to obtain a crust of bread and to eat, and then one can be occupied with whatever other matters one pleases: literacy, science, art, etc. What is to be done?, unhappily this is what human nature demands."[3]

Strakhov replied to this broadside the next month with another of his so-called letters to the editor. Not wishing to rehash the same slogans that Antonovich had ridiculed, he snipes away rather feebly for several pages before tackling the main issue. Is the satisfaction of material needs mankind's first priority? Strakhov vigorously objects to such an idea in the name of idealism, and in doing so anticipates what will soon become a crucial Dostoevskian theme. If mankind has not yet constructed a society in which hunger has been eliminated, he argues, it is not because of incapacity to do so; the real reason is that "mankind has always wanted *more*; it has been eternally attracted to other goods, other desires . . . more important and gratifying than the simple *absence of suffering*" (italics in text).[4] The cause of material deprivation is thus mankind's unquenchable idealism, its desire for an aim and a goal for life higher than material well-being alone; and such a desire can never be suppressed, no matter what efforts are made to tear it out of the human character.

Indeed, it is not only impossible but absolutely undesirable to eliminate the innate idealism of mankind; the true task is not that of reducing man to the level of his material needs but, rather, to make sure that his imperishable longing for the ideal is guided in the proper fashion. And this direction, as Strakhov indicates, has long been established by the message of Christ: "The question of material well-being and, in general, of the elimination of the suffering to which humanity has been exposed, is, as is well-known, the most vital contemporary question. But it was posed long ago; it is spoken of in the Gospels, and there, precisely, the following is said about it: *Seek first the Kingdom of God and all things shall be given unto thee.* It seems to me that, even today, there is no need to alter this pronouncement."[5] Such words offer no response at all to Antonovich's arguments, and they are uttered in a tone of unctuous complacency all too revelatory of Strakhov's sensibility. Reinhold Niebuhr, writing about more recent advocates of a very similar position, has commented appositely that "the introduction of [Christian] perfectionist ideas into politics for the sake of reinforcing counsels of submission to injustice smells of dishonesty."[6] Such an unpleasant odor distinctly emanates from this Strakhovian defense of idealism.

Must one say the same about Dostoevsky, who saw the issue in terms very similar to those of Strakhov? Not entirely, it seems to me, although he too maintained that there are more exalted aims in human life than satisfying hunger, and he too wished to believe that mankind, when faced with the alternative, would choose suffering over satiation. Yet just a month after Strakhov's article appeared, and perhaps prompted by some dissatisfaction with its tenor,* Dostoevsky took up some of the same issues. Most

---

* Dostoevsky appended a lengthy editorial note to Strakhov's article, which declared that "we find this letter quite unsatisfactory, and are surprised at the frivolity and one-sidedness of our collaborator." It is difficult to know how literally to take this assertion; but Strakhov does complain about Dostoevsky's editorial footnotes to his articles during the magazine's first year. Another passage from this footnote is worth quoting because it casts some light on Dostoev-

of what he says covers familiar territory, but now he links *Time*'s advocacy of education and literacy with an *improvement* in the well-being of the peasant class. "If our people are poor and hungry," he writes, "it is not because they lack the means to gain their daily bread. We have ample land, and the lack of people to work it means that it is not difficult to obtain a surplus. Our people are poor and hungry because, as a result of particular circumstances, their moral level is low, and they do not know how to make a profit from the immense natural riches at their disposal. It is thus necessary, first and foremost, to become concerned with their intellectual development" (20: 20). How accurate Dostoevsky was in his estimate of the economic situation need not be decided here; but such words reveal that he did not wave aside the material needs of the people as casually as Strakhov was inclined to do.

Moreover, even though Dostoevsky may coincide with Strakhov on the level of ideas and formulations, there is a considerable difference in the human resonance of his affirmation (or his hope) that mankind would always display an irresistible inclination to choose suffering in preference to the satisfaction of material need. To Dostoevsky, the dilemma of such a choice inevitably evoked memories of the frantic outbursts of his fellow inmates in the house of the dead, trying, at terrible cost, to assert the autonomy of their personality. The idealism of mankind thus did not mean a vague Christian piety or a superior disdain of worldly goods: it meant, rather, a defense of man's inner freedom and the affirmation of his dignity as a fully human being; it meant that men were willing to sacrifice every material satisfaction, and even life itself if need be, for the sake of this supreme value. Dostoevsky had no sniffish distaste for the idea that material needs require gratification, and he could never rest content with Strakhov's smug acceptance of the human suffering that results when such needs are neglected. But he refused to give them absolute priority, and to barter away in exchange that moral autonomy which he considered the very essence of man's humanity. The acceptance of suffering over earthly bread involved an agonizing choice, as Dostoevsky saw it, between two values recognized as equally legitimate and powerful; and there is a huge gulf, both in moral substance and human sensitivity, between the tragic dignity of his position and Strakhov's sanctimonious reflections.

---

sky himself. Antonovich had asked what *Time* meant by idealism, and Dostoevsky cites in reply a passage from Strakhov's text with which he obviously agrees. "Does not all evil arise," Strakhov had written, "because we give too much honor to what should not be honored, that we consider important what has no importance? That we so eagerly accept truth where there is no truth, that we so easily sacrifice ourselves, so easily create for ourselves everywhere false idols and false gods?" Idealism is thus the inherent need of the human personality to believe in truth and God, which also inevitably involves the capacity to be misled. This helps explain why even Dostoevsky's most negative heroes are "idealistic" in their own way and, in the end, sacrifice themselves to one or another version of a false god. *PSS*, 20: 225.

After the exchange between Antonovich and Strakhov, direct polemics between *Time* and the radicals ceased for the moment. In July 1862 *The Contemporary* was banned for an eight-month period; and this event, along with the simultaneous arrest of Chernyshevsky, caused a sharp shift in the social-cultural climate that placed *Time* in an exceedingly awkward predicament. It was no longer possible to continue to criticize radical ideas—no matter how respectfully, or with how many qualifications—without seeming to support the repressive measures of the government. To cease to argue with the radicals would have meant to abandon *Time*'s very reason for being; but to continue with the same editorial policy was to court disaster and even execration. The treacherous crosscurrents created by this new situation left very little room for maneuver, and Dostoevsky—perhaps still believing that his personal history, and the spirit of his recent work, would guard him against being taken as an advocate of reaction—persisted in speaking his mind as freely as in the past. He soon discovered, however, that words which previously might have been overlooked or shrugged off now provoked a fiercely hostile rejoinder.

The seemingly innocuous announcement to subscribers for 1863, published in the September issue, immediately stirred up a fracas. Again attacking the "theoreticians," as he had done so often before, Dostoevsky now went on imprudently to question the motives of those "whistlers who whistled for bread and for the sole pleasure of whistling," and who, he added for good measure, spurred themselves on with "the little whips of a routine liberalism" (20: 208, 211). The phrase "whistlers who whistled for bread" justifiably stirred whatever remained of the radical press (especially *The Spark*) to a livid rage, and relentless attacks now began to rain down on *Time* with unceasing vehemence. The insulting thrust also had a more serious practical consequence as well. One of *Time*'s most promising young contributors, N. G. Pomyalovsky, who had already published two chapters of his *Seminary Sketches* in its pages, refused any further collaboration because, as he wrote Mikhail Dostoevsky, he no longer agreed "with the program of your journal in principle."[7]

A further disquieting sign of the times was a letter from Nekrasov to Dostoevsky explaining why another promised contribution would not be forthcoming. Some notion of the tense and suspicious atmosphere then reigning in literary circles may also be gathered from Nekrasov's astonishing frankness. Rumors were circulating, he admitted, "that I *betrayed* Chernyshevsky [to the authorities] and walk around freely in the open air in Petersburg. . . . In view of all this, I must not, for the time being, give any further cause for ambiguous rumors."[8] Dostoevsky was quite upset by the implications of this letter, and replied in an aggrieved tone: "How could collaboration with our journal compromise you and justify gossip such as, for example, that you betrayed Chernyshevsky? Is our journal reactionary? No, not even in the eyes of our enemies. We can be accused of anything, but not of being reactionary."[9] Such words affirm the neutral position that Dostoevsky was still trying desperately to maintain, but which was becoming more and more impossible to defend.

Dostoevsky, all the same, had every reason to take umbrage at Nekrasov's insinuation that *Time* might be considered reactionary. Even though his articles during 1862-1863 reveal his growing disenchantment with the radicals and an increasing tilt toward Slavophilism, *Time* had not become conservative in any sense that would have gained favor with the authorities. It continued to refer to the *Raskol*, which was officially illegal and rejected the whole apparatus of the Russian state, as proof of the capacity of the Russian people to create their own indigenous forms of culture; and Dostoevsky repeatedly adduces the communal system of landholding as additional evidence of such capacity. "Western publicists, after lengthy researches," he writes, "have finally stopped at the principle of association [a code word for Socialism], in which they see the salvation of labor from the despotism of capital. But, in Western life, this communal principle has not yet become a part of life; it will make its way in the future. . . . In Russia, it already exists as a given of life itself, and only awaits favorable conditions to develop further" (20: 21). He could hardly have declared in clearer words his agreement with the basic tenets of Herzen's "Russian Socialism."

Moreover, Dostoevsky did what he could to counteract the journalistic clamor—led in large part by Katkov, now repenting of his previous tenderness toward English liberalism—that called for the suppression of all the new forces making for progress in Russian society. It is useless, Dostoevsky retorted, to look for scapegoats in attempting to explain the events of the disastrous spring of 1862 because, really, there is no guilty party at whom one can point an accusing finger: "Just as guilty are, in this respect, Pushkin, Fonvizin, Kantemir, and Lomonosov. We will go further: just as much, exactly as much, if not even more guilty are Laplace, and Galileo, and Copernicus" (20: 34). Evidently, nothing less than the whole history of Russian enlightenment and Western science must be held accountable, and it is thus absurd to indict the sinister influence of one or another individual or group. As every Russian reader would understand, Dostoevsky was insisting that the progress of enlightenment could not be reversed; and he was suggesting that to remedy the threatening situation educated Russian society should be allowed more (rather than less) freedom of initiative and expression.

Other articles show Dostoevsky becoming personally involved in the controversies occasioned by his reference to "whistlers for bread," which rapidly began to take on an unpleasantly acrimonious tone. Such pinpricks, however, were soon replaced by a much more serious and sustained assault when *The Contemporary* resumed publication at the end of February 1863. This reappearance brought into the field against *Time* a new and exceedingly formidable foe, the scathing satirist Saltykov-Shchedrin, who had now joined the editorial staff of the revived journal; and he was promptly assigned the task, formerly entrusted to the bellicose but inept Antonovich, of carrying on the fight against the *pochvenniki*. Saltykov-Shchedrin, whose *Provincial Sketches* had appeared in Katkov's *The Russian Messenger*, and some of whose sketches had also graced the pages of *Time*, had not previously been known as a flaming radical. And since Dostoevsky had frequently expressed great admiration for his talents, his sudden intervention as a prominent antagonist was bitterly resented.

The initial exchanges between these two masters of contumely did not involve any issues of substance; and though the argument was carried on anonymously, each recognized the inimitable stamp of the other's style and tone. The second passage at arms was much more serious, with Saltykov-Shchedrin labeling *Time*'s contributors as "meek little birds," constantly living in fear and trembling even though "no one has injured you. No one opposes you, no one even thinks about you." There was much more in this condescending vein, including the prediction that *Time* would soon "Katkovize," that is, wholly join the antiradical camp; but meanwhile, it is trying to maintain an impossible position: "What is the guiding thought of your journal? None. What have you said? Nothing. You have continuously striven to utter some sort of truth on the order of 'soft-boiled boots' [a Russian expression for nonsense], you always have sat between two stools, and your naiveté extends so far that you have not wished to notice that you have tumbled to the ground."[10]

Dostoevsky responded to this telling assault with a counterattack aimed at disproving the insulting charge that *Time*'s acknowledged success could be largely attributed to the temporary disappearance of the two radical journals. Dates are cited to prove that Saltykov-Shchedrin himself had been a contributor to *Time* before *The Contemporary* had been suspended, and Dostoevsky maintains that the supposedly anonymous author of the article is "an artistic temperament above all, and whatever you do in literature, it is never anything other than art for art's sake. . . . When you wrote your accusatory works, you did so, not in the grip of some indignation or conviction, but simply because accusatory literature was in some sense a modish tendency." There is also a malicious allusion to Saltykov-Shchedrin's sudden political metamorphosis: "from the quite ordinary liberal that you were has emerged a newly baked Nihilist" (20: 92).

No direct reply was made to these taunts; but in the next issue of *The Whistler*, Saltykov-Shchedrin listed the mock titles of a number of his intended contributions; and these all contain allusions that ridicule either *Time* in general or Feodor Dostoevsky in particular. One such title, which Dostoevsky long remembered, was "Self-Satisfied Fedya, A Tale for Children in Verse," a sample extract of which runs as follows:

> Fedya did not pray to God,
> "Things are all right," he thought, "just so!"
> He idled his time away . . .
> And really put his foot in it!
> Once lightheartedly he played
> With Gogol's "Overcoat"—
> And with the usual long-winded tripe
> Filled up *Time*.[11]

The controversy ceased with this lampoon because, the very next month, *Time* vanished from the literary scene; but matters did not end there by any means. This was only the beginning of an increasingly fierce exchange between these two major figures which, a year later, would culminate in a brilliant burst of parodistic dialogue skits on both sides. Nor did Dostoevsky forget to include two satirical barbs against Saltykov-Shchedrin in his very next work, *Notes from Underground*.

Before taking leave of *Time* entirely, a few words should be said about Strakhov's contributions to these concluding issues—not so much for their own sake, but because they help to fill in the ideological background against which Dostoevsky was to create *Crime and Punishment*. Two of these articles deal with the issue of personal charity, a virtue which *The Spark*, invoking the authority of Adam Smith and Malthus, had attacked as outmoded and even harmful, arguing that all such individual initiatives should be replaced by public institutions dispensing aid to the needy. Strakhov ridiculed the ignorance of the contributors to *The Spark*, who seemed unaware that English economics, based on the principle of maximizing individual self-interest, could not be in favor of *any* kind of charity; this moral conception derives from a totally different view of human relations and the needs of a human community.[12] Raskolnikov will later invoke such theories of English economics, consistent with Strakhov's interpretation, as an excuse for attempting to suppress his own charitable impulses.

Strakhov's scientific competence and philosophical culture also gave him a special vantage point from which to write on Darwin's *Origin of Species*, and he provided the first informed Russian commentary on the book for the pages of *Time*. In a piece called "Evil Auguries," he hails the work as "a mighty step forward in the evolution of natural science." But he takes strong objection to the preface of the French translator, who had eagerly accepted Darwin's struggle-for-life idea as a *social* theory, and had argued that once the existence of "superior" and "inferior" races is admitted, all sympathy for the weak, the suffering, and the inferior was misplaced and undesirable. "The secret of human life," Strakhov replies, "is contained in itself, and we lose its significance as soon as we do not separate man from nature, as soon as we place him on the same level with [nature's] creations and begin to judge him from the same point of view as animals and plants."[13]

Social Darwinism, whose moral danger Strakhov instantly foresaw, never became an integral part of Russian radical ideology in the mid-1860s; but, two years later, it was momentarily defended in *The Russian Word* by V. A. Zaitsev (with some support from Pisarev), and it blended very easily with some of the arrogant individualism already expressed in Pisarev's defense of Bazarov. This fleeting, if not inconsistent, reinforcement of Russian Nihilism by Social Darwinism did not escape the penetrating vigilance of Dostoevsky, who dramatized it unforgettably in Raskolnikov's ambition to prove to himself that he was of the "superior" race of the "Napoleons."

7

It is a sad irony that Dostoevsky's journal should have been shut down at the very moment it was battling most ferociously with *The Contemporary*. Russia, however, was then occupied by events far surpassing in immediate importance the internal squabbles of its native intelligentsia. January 1863 marked the outbreak of still another Polish revolt against Russian hegemony, and *Time* was swept under in the vortex created by this courageous and defiant, though ultimately doomed, challenge to the might of the Russian Empire.

If Russian opinion had been more or less favorable, up until that moment, to the Polish desire for more local independence, feelings quickly shifted after the uprising began with a massacre of sleeping Russian soldiers in their barracks. The Poles also demanded, in addition to independence, a restoration of the Polish borders of 1772, which included Lithuania, White Russia, and much of the Ukraine. The pressure exerted by France and England on behalf of these claims only succeeded in whipping up Russian nationalism to a fever pitch, and the support of the radicals for the Polish cause (some young Russian officers even deserted and fought with the Poles) ended whatever influence the extreme left still may have had in society at large. Herzen's support for the Poles, assumed much against his better judgment (he was won over by the volatile Bakunin, always spoiling for a revolution), dealt a deathblow to *The Bell.*

The radicals within the country could hardly express support for the Polish cause in the Russian press, and Strakhov notes, as a telling sign of the times, that very little utterance of opinion about the uprising appeared in the Petersburg journals. Of course an event of such gravity did not pass unnoticed; but coverage was limited—as in the case of *Time*—to a more or less neutral summary of official dispatches and an account of the international diplomatic maneuverings. In Moscow, however, Katkov was carrying on a blistering campaign against the Poles and the Russian radicals, whom he threw together (not without some justification, as we have seen) into one unsavory heap; and he became the much-applauded man of the hour, the admired voice of Russian patriotic indignation. The failure of the Petersburg press to raise its voice with equal vehemence was bitterly resented in Moscow. The Muscovites were all too ready to take the relative silence as a sign of treason, and they did not hesitate to hurl such an accusation against the first available target offering itself to their fury. Unfortunately for *Time*, this target turned out to be an article by Strakhov which, although intended as a public avowal in favor of the Russian cause, was written in such tortuous and elusive terms that it could easily be misread as a justification of the desperate Polish revolt.

Dostoevsky explains what happened in a letter to Turgenev a month after the axe had fallen. "You know the orientation of our journal: it is an orientation essentially Russian and even anti-Western. Would we have the idea of defending the Poles? Yet we are accused of antipatriotic convictions, of sympathy for the Poles. . . ." Strakhov's article, he admits, had contained "certain awkwardnesses of exposition" and "suffered from certain lacunae," but Dostoevsky explained that he had, mistakenly, counted on the general position of the journal to prevent erroneous interpretations. "The idea of the article (Strakhov wrote it) was as follows: that the Poles despise us as barbarians to such a degree, are so boastful to us of their 'European' civilization, that one can scarcely foresee for a long time any moral peace (the only durable kind) with us. But, as the exposition of the article was not understood, it was interpreted as follows: that we affirmed, *of ourselves*, that the Poles have a civilization so superior to ours, and we are so inferior, that obviously they are right and we are wrong."[14]

Such a charge was indeed instantly made by a writer in the *Moscow Gazette*—a newspaper edited by Katkov in addition to his monthly journal— and it was echoed elsewhere. When Dostoevsky wrote a reply, the censorship banned its publication, and, as he indignantly reports to Turgenev, "certain journals (the *Day*, among others) have seriously undertaken to prove to us that Polish civilization is only a surface civilization, aristocratic and Jesuitical, thus not at all superior to ours,"[15] when this was the very point of Strakhov's article. Strakhov, however, does paint Polish civilization in such glowing colors that the misunderstanding is quite comprehensible; even as well-informed a Frenchman as Charles de Mazade, who kept an eye on Russian affairs for the *Revue des Deux Mondes*, translated the article as a symptom of internal Russian support for the Polish cause.[16] The Tsar, already ill-disposed toward *Time*, decided that the moment had come to put an end to this persistent journalistic nuisance once and for all. The order to ban the publication, handed down on May 24, 1863, was justified not only on the basis of Strakhov's article but also because of "the harmful tendency of the journal."[17]

So ended the life of *Time*, just as the joint enterprise of the Dostoevsky brothers had begun to raise its head above water financially, and its demise left Mikhail saddled with a huge load of debt. The event was disastrous from every point of view and produced a further strain in the relations between Strakhov and Dostoevsky. To be sure, Strakhov could not be held entirely to blame because, as editor in charge, Dostoevsky had read and approved his essay; but some words were spoken that were probably less restrained than Strakhov indicates. "After the banning of the journal," he writes, "Feodor Mikhailovich mildly reproached me for the dryness and abstractness of my exposition, and I was then mildly offended by his observation; but now I willingly acknowledge its justice."[18] The two remained on ostensibly friendly terms, although the whole affair left a festering resentment that came out much later in the remarks each made about the other in private.

was: his *House of the Dead* created the genre in Russia, thus responding to an immense and apprehensive curiosity concerning the conditions of life of those "unfortunates" (as they were invariably called by the commonfolk) who ran afoul of the state, especially those convicted of political rather than common-law crimes. The politicals usually came from the ranks of the educated, and any public allusion to *their* fate—as, for example, in the painting of Yakobi mentioned earlier—was certain to excite the liveliest interest. Many years later the Populist critic A. M. Skabichevsky, who had been a student in the early 1860s, recalled "the sensation caused by the *House of the Dead* when it first appeared in the pages of *Time* during 1861-1862."[1]

Dostoevsky had thought of writing such a book ever since his imprisonment and had sketched preliminary versions over the years in accordance with the idea he had outlined in October 1859. "These *Notes from the House of the Dead*," he had written to Mikhail, "have now taken shape in my mind according to a complete and finished plan. . . . My figure will disappear. These are the notes of an unknown; but I guarantee their interest. They will have the very greatest interest. There will be the serious and the gloomy and the humorous, and peasant conversation with a particular convict coloring (I have read you several expressions recorded by me *on the spot*), and the depiction of characters *unheard of* previously in literature, and the touching, and finally, the most important, my name. . . . I am convinced that the public will read this with avidity."[2] Dostoevsky's reference to the importance of his "name" indicates that he counted on his readers to accept the work as an accurate report of his prison years. But his presence as a political convict would pervade the book as a whole rather than being placed in the foreground ("my figure will disappear"). This double perspective is very carefully maintained, and must constantly be kept in mind if we are to avoid the error of taking the work as either an unadorned memoir or a purely fictional construct; in fact, it is a unique combination of both.

According to his intention, Dostoevsky's sketches were generally accepted as a reliable account of documentary value, and later researches have tended to confirm this instinctive assessment. What Dostoevsky records about his fellow convicts has recently been checked against the records of the Omsk prison contained in the central historical archives of the Russian Army, and all of the people he mentions have been identified. Most of the information given about them has also been verified, although there are some discrepancies between the documents and Dostoevsky's version. A tendency has been noted to make the crimes of his companions more severe than the record indicates, and, it has been suggested, he did so in order implicitly to justify the extreme harshness of the punishments. But since he had no way of knowing what the facts really were, relying only on what he was told, he may not knowingly have distorted at all. It is also possible that what Dostoevsky learned came closer to the truth than what the authorities had been able to verify from the testimony of sullenly hostile peasant informants.

The publication of *House of the Dead* immediately unleashed a huge debate in the press about Russian justice and the system of imprisonment: all sorts of reforms were suggested or advocated as a result of the information it provided. The scene in the prison hospital, where the dying prisoner had to remain shackled until his last breath, aroused particular indignation, and the necessity for such senselessly cruel regulations was angrily challenged. Also widely discussed was Dostoevsky's plea that the motivation for a crime should be taken into account in determining the severity of the sentence. "For instance," Dostoevsky wrote, "two men may commit murder; and in both cases almost the same punishment is given. Yet look at the difference between the crimes. One may have committed murder for nothing, for an onion. . . . Another murders a sensual tyrant in defense of the honor of his betrothed, his sister, his child. Another is a fugitive [a runaway serf], hemmed in by a regiment of trackers, who commits a murder in defense of his freedom, his life, often dying of hunger; and another murders little children for the pleasure of killing, of feeling their warm blood on his hands, of enjoying their terror, and their last dovelike flutter under the knife. Yet all these are sent to the same penal servitude" (4: 42-43).

Aside from such legal and administrative issues, what predominated in the public reaction was a recognition of the warmhearted humanism that pervaded the book. Dostoevsky had succeeded in "redeeming" a whole class of criminals and outcasts (not all, to be sure, but the vast majority), whom he had returned to the human fold, as it were, by depicting them with sympathetic insight. Each of these figures was presented as an individual, with his own history, temperament, and psychology, and Dostoevsky often allows his people to tell their stories in their own words. Time and again, too, he unobtrusively sketches in a background revealing that the violence for which the peasant convicts had been condemned had been, more often than not, a reaction provoked by intolerable humiliation and mistreatment. Such an attitude toward a group of men who would all previously have been considered outside the pale of the morally redeemable was seen as an extension of the ethos of Dostoevsky's work in the 1840s; and Alexander Milyukov stated this point very forcefully in the pages of *The Torch*. "The reader knows," he wrote, "what sort of a world this is [i.e., the prison camp]. But see how the author looks at it. He has known how to illuminate it with such a radiantly human light, warm it with such a kindly feeling. . . . In each criminal he searches for the human being, and each of his portraits is a warmhearted sincere question addressed to society in the name of truth and love of humanity."[3]*

* The genuineness of Dostoevsky's "humanism" has sometimes been questioned by calling attention to the demeaning manner in which he depicts the Jewish convict Isay Fomich Bum-

For many years to come *House of the Dead* would continue to be regarded in this light, and long preserved for Dostoevsky his reputation as a progressive even when his novels were explicitly directed against the very foundations of Russian radical ideology. Those aspects of life in prison camp which, as we can now see, had helped to convert him from the radicalism of his youth were simply overlooked or subordinated to the more prominent overall impression. It was the humanitarian note that rang out above all others for contemporary readers, and this was sufficient to silence the rest. At most, as I. I. Zamotin has written, his contemporaries recognized that "the initial humanism of Dostoevsky, which in the 1840s had been based on foreign sources identical with those of Russian Westernism, had now crystallized in a much more concrete form—that of the humanitarian analysis and illumination of Russian reality."[4] But such an evolution could be observed everywhere in Russian literature during the late 1850s and early 1860s, and the particular nuances of Dostoevsky's own development were not immediately apparent.

3
———

House of the Dead obviously owes its origin to the accidents of Dostoevsky's existence, but also fits quite neatly into a genre much cultivated in Russian literature at that moment. Many accounts of personal experience written in a loose, sketchlike form, and tied together in a seemingly haphazard fashion, were then being produced; and Dostoevsky was quite familiar with them all. On leaving prison camp, he had read Turgenev's *A Sportsman's Sketches* and the very popular sketches by S. T. Aksakov about hunting and fishing. Tolstoy's *Sevastopol Stories* were also published shortly after Dostoevsky's release, and he hastened to read these too, as well as everything else that came from Tolstoy's pen. Herzen's masterly memoirs, *My Past*

---

shtein. There are many problems connected with the treatment of this character, not least the fact that the only convict of Jewish origin among Dostoevsky's fellow prisoners, Isay Bumshtel, is listed in the prison records as a convert to the Orthodox Christian faith. Yet Dostoevsky shows him as a practicing Jew, who performs his prayers faithfully and much to the amusement of the other inmates. There are, in addition, numerous inconsistencies and exaggerations in Dostoevsky's portrayal of this ritual observance; some of these may be simple mistakes, but others are evidently used to increase the ludicrousness of Isay's behavior in the eyes of his audience.

Dostoevsky's supposedly comic portrait of Isay, whatever its relation to what he may have actually seen, cannot be said to transcend the contemptuous treatment of the Jew prevalent in Russian literature for most of the nineteenth century; and it stands in sharp contrast to the favorable light in which some other convicts are depicted. Yet the attitude of the narrator toward Isay Fomich is by no means entirely unfriendly or hostile. He even says they were "great friends"; and, as David Goldstein has written of the bath scene, "it is with sympathy, if not affection, that he evokes 'the blissful countenance of my prison comrade and barracks mate, the unforgettable Isay Fomich.'" Such touches, which for us are quite inadequate to redeem the distastefulness of the overall image, were probably sufficient guarantees of "humanism" to Dostoevsky's first readers, accustomed to seeing Jews treated only in a manner that excluded *any* sense of personal identification with them as individual human beings. See *PSS*, 4: 283-284; Joshua Kunitz, *Russian Literature and the Jew* (New York, 1929), esp. chap. 2; David I. Goldstein, *Dostoevsky and the Jews* (Austin, Tex., 1981), 21, and chap. 14.

and Thoughts, had begun to appear during the mid-1850s in *The Bell*, and new installments were published throughout the remainder of the decade.

The sudden emergence of this semi-journalistic literary mode may be attributed partly to a relaxation of the censorship, which encouraged writers to speak more freely and personally than they had done in the past without the protective disguise of "fiction" (Herzen, living in exile, did not have to worry about the censorship at all). Writers thus instinctively turned back to the form of the "physiological sketch," much favored during the 1840s—another period of relative literary freedom—which had emphasized the accurate observation of social types embedded in their material environment, and aimed at depicting people in the routine of their everyday existence. Most early sketches of this type had focused on urban characters and city life, whether in Petersburg or Moscow; but the renaissance of the form in the 1850s extended its thematic range to take in the life of the peasantry.

Since the aim of such sketches was to convey an impression of truthfulness, they were not linked together by any sort of novelistic intrigue that might arouse suspicions concerning the verisimilitude of the life being portrayed. Such relative plotlessness then became a distinctive feature of the Russian novel when writers like Turgenev and Tolstoy went on to more complex genres than the sketch and the short story. Dostoevsky stands out as the great exception to this tendency of Russian nineteenth-century prose, and had already begun to experiment with the elaborately plotted *roman-feuilleton* technique that he would soon raise to new heights. But *House of the Dead*, among many other things, is also a tribute to his literary versatility and proves that he could adapt his technique to his material and to whatever artistic purpose he chose. It was important, above all, that the reader have no doubts about the veracity of his account; and so Dostoevsky eschewed all "novelistic" effects, and developed his own original variation of the larger sketch forms used by the Russian writers he admired.

4
___

Dostoevsky's sketches, unlike those of either Turgenev or Tolstoy, reach the reader through the interposition of two frame narrators. The first is the presumed editor of the book, who appears in the Introduction and gives the impression of being a well-educated, curious, and observant person; not a native of Siberia, he has spent a considerable time there—probably in some official capacity like Dostoevsky's friend Baron Wrangel, who met him shortly after the completion of his sentence at hard labor. This first narrator supplies a tongue-in-cheek picture of life in that remote region ("the inhabitants are simple folk and not of liberal views; everything goes on according to the old-fashioned, solid, time-honored traditions") which drips with polite sarcasm, and indicates to the Russian reader that the region was really a sink of iniquity (4: 5). His words are also an invitation to look carefully beneath the surface of the prose for hidden meanings, and this signal was surely meant to alert the reader not to take completely at face value the information provided by the first narrator about the second. The nominal author of the sketches is a former landowner, Alexander Petrovich Goryanchikov (the name suggests someone who has suffered greatly: *gore* in Russian means "grief" or "misfortune"), who has served a ten-year sentence for murdering his wife in a fit of jealous rage during their first year of marriage. Goryanchikov lives in complete seclusion, earns his scant living by giving lessons to local children, and shuns all contact with the world, presumably unable to adjust to normal life after his years in penal servitude.

When Goryanchikov dies suddenly, the first narrator manages, in the nick of time, to rescue some of the dead man's papers from being torn up and thrown away. The documents prove to be mostly exercises written by his students, but one bundle contains a "disconnected description of the ten years spent by Alexander Petrovich in the prison camp." These pages break off occasionally and are interspersed with passages from another story, "some strange and terrible reminiscences, jotted down irregularly, spasmodically, as though by some overpowering impulse. I read these fragments over several times, and was almost convinced that they were written in a state of insanity." Such "strange and terrible reminiscences" probably refer to the murder, which haunts Goryanchikov and gives him no inner peace; on St. Catherine's Day (his wife's name was Katya) "he always had a requiem service sung for someone." Hence this portion of the posthumous text is not reproduced (though it may be considered an anticipation of things to come in Dostoevsky's work), and the editor decides that only Goryanchikov's account of his prison years is "not devoid of interest." For Goryanchikov reveals "an absolutely new, till then unknown world," and for this reason the editor decides to offer his sketches for public scrutiny (4: 8).

Just how seriously this second narrator should be taken has been a continual matter of dispute. Some critics, both Russian and others, are disposed to take him very seriously indeed, and the ever-iconoclastic Victor Shklovsky has tried to make out a case for giving the fate of Goryanchikov a central place in the interpretation of the book.[6] But if we regard him as the genuine narrator of *House of the Dead*, rather than Dostoevsky himself, then it is impossible not to charge the author with unforgivable carelessness. In Chapter 2, for example, when Akim Akimich tells the convict narrator that the peasant inmates "are not fond of gentlemen . . . especially politicals," he is clearly addressing someone included in this latter category; and there are other allusions to the same status of the narrator scattered through the book (4: 28). Moreover, if we are supposed to accept Goryanchikov as more than a convention, then Dostoevsky can be accused of allowing a disturbing clash to occur between his theme as a whole and the frame narration in which it is contained. For none of the consoling truths that the narrator has learned in the house of the dead; none of his discovery of the people and his triumph over his initial despair; none of the exuberance, the sense of hope, the possibility of beginning a new life that he felt on his release—none of these events are in accord with the character and fate of the Goryanchikov who is presumed to have written the manuscript we read.*

The accepted view, which seems to me more convincing, is that Dostoevsky introduced Goryanchikov primarily as a means of avoiding trouble with the censorship, and that he did not expect his readers to take him as more than a convenient device. Nor, in fact, did they do so: the book was universally accepted as a more or less faithful account of Dostoevsky's own past as a political prisoner, even though, as he remarked much later with a touch of humor, he still came across people who believed he had been sent to *katorga* for having murdered his wife (22: 47). Such a device, as a matter of fact, was practically obligatory for a book of this kind under Russian conditions, and was also employed by another survivor of the Petrashevsky circle, F. N. Lvov, who published his souvenirs of Siberia almost simultaneously.

Like Dostoevsky, Lvov concealed himself behind a fictitious narrator cast as a Romantic seeker of justice: an Army officer who, unable to endure the brutal treatment of the lower ranks by his superior, had shot his tyrannical colonel in the hand. A later exile, P. F. Yakubovich—whose memoirs, published at the end of the century, betray Dostoevsky's influence—explained in a letter how important it still was to adopt a "disguise" while making it as transparent as possible. "You yourself must understand," he tells his correspondent, "that if the author vanishes from his work, this does not depend on his own volition. . . . That perhaps it may be done unsuccessfully— that's another question; but the author does not try to make his disguise more successful: on the contrary, he wishes to use an obvious and well-worn stereotype."[7] It is thus preferable to allow for the pressure of external circumstances, and not to impose more of an "artistic" pattern on the narrative structure of *House of the Dead* than the evidence supports; there is artistry enough, but of a different kind.

Even if we agree, however, that Goryanchikov is more of a device than a narrator, and that it is Dostoevsky himself who unmistakably speaks in the

---

* With his usual ingenuity, Shklovsky tries to circumvent this awkward inconsistency by suggesting that the reader is expected to perceive a connection between the final removing of the shackles as Goryanchikov steps free and the scene in which the shackles are removed from the dead body of Mikhailov. But, even if such a connection is made, the effect could just as well be one of contrast rather than identification. Moreover, as V. A. Tunimanov has written, for the reader "it is not Goryanchikov who emerges from prison but the author-narrator, that is, Dostoevsky. The 'conclusion' of the book is not at all despairing, and one should not, evidently, exaggerate the pessimism of the *Notes*. . . ." See Victor Shklovsky, *Za i Protiv* (Moscow, 1957), 102; V. A. Tunimanov, *Tvorchestvo Dostoevskogo, 1854-1862* (Leningrad, 1980), 80.

body of the book, R. L. Jackson has perceptively suggested that the invention of this figure may have had a deeper significance all the same. The image we receive of Goryanchikov, who shuns almost all human contact and seems to be living in a state of shock—as if under the effect of a traumatic experience too severe to be overcome—certainly represents one aspect of Dostoevsky's own reaction to his prison-camp encounters. Very little reflection of such an attitude can be seen in the book itself—or rather, we detect its gradual transmutation into feelings of comprehension and friendliness, although there is no portrayal of the inner process through which this change occurs. Jackson believes that, by placing the distraught Goryanchikov at the threshold of the work, Dostoevsky was in a sense eliminating him from the remainder, and in so doing "freed *Notes from the House of the Dead* from the tyranny of a deeply personal, misanthropic subjectivity, a tormented ego driven to the limits of malice and despair, to almost complete moral exhaustion by years of forced existence in the 'human herd.' "[8] Such a conjecture seems to me quite plausible, and Goryanchikov could well have served some such cathartic function during the course of creation.

5
———

It may appear at first as if Dostoevsky's *House of the Dead* has no organization whatever, and merely contains a straightforward, somewhat disorganized, and inevitably cautious and circumspect account of his prison years. But while the book has no plot in the obvious sense, it is, all the same, more unified than either of its two most notable rivals, *A Sportsman's Sketches* and *Sevastopol Stories*. Turgenev's sketches are, in fact, totally independent of each other and united only by the loosest of narrative links: the rambles of a huntsman in search of game bring him into contact with Russian life all along the social scale, and he conveys to us the curiosities of his observations. The sketches thus have a unity imparted by the sensitive and humane personality of the teller, a cultivated Russian gentleman of liberal tendencies, but no other overall organization. Tolstoy is closer to Dostoevsky because his *Stories* are at least held together by unity of place; but they too are more or less independent and lack any ambitious structural integration. What unifies his narratives is their evolution from the initial glorification of the heroism of the defenders of Sevastopol to a muted protest against the futility of the incessant carnage; and they acquire a slight epic movement because the fall of the city, whose defense they describe, terminates the last of the four stories.

House of the Dead is organized much more carefully, and its overarching pattern reflects the narrator's gradual penetration into the strange and disorienting world of the prison camp—his attainment, as he slowly overcomes his prejudices and preconceptions, of a new understanding of the

intense humanity and particular moral quality of those he had at first regarded only with loathing and dismay. The plan of the work, shaped by this
process of discovery, is thus "dynamic" in character, and reproduces the
movement of moral-psychological assimilation and re-evaluation that Dostoevsky himself underwent.

The first six chapters depict his first disorienting impressions of this
strange new world to which he had been exposed. Only after this initiation,
when he has overcome his bewilderment at the appalling spectacle he sees
before him, do individuals begin to stand out with any clarity, and it is then
that the names of persons appear in the chapter titles. This aspect of the
form has been well defined by K. Mochulsky, who remarks that, in the beginning, Dostoevsky "is an external observer, grasping only the most glaring and striking features"; it is only later that "he penetrates into the mysterious depths of this world" and "perceives anew that which had been
seen, re-evaluates his first impressions, deepens his conclusions."[9] Jacques
Catteau has also sensitively remarked on the significant shift in the principles of the organization of chapters between Parts One and Two. At first,
what is accentuated is the shock of initial contact ("First Impressions"), or
the sudden perception of individual character ("Petrov"), while the second
part spreads out into chapters held together by spatial contiguity ("The
Hospital") or by loose subject groupings ("Prison Animals," "Comrades").[10]
In other words, the personality of the narrator, quite prominent in the perspective of earlier chapters, fades into the background as he merges into
the everyday life of the community.

Critics have often commented adversely on the "repetitions" of the book,
without realizing that such returns of character and motif form part of the
structure by which the negative first impressions are deepened and transformed. Such repetitions also act on the reader to reinforce the sense of living in an enclosed world of immutable routine, a world in which people,
and time itself, constantly revolve in an endless cycle allowing for no real
change. Indeed, Dostoevsky's handling of time is particularly subtle and
unobtrusive, and works to shape the perceptions of the reader underneath
the seeming artlessness of the sketch form; he thus anticipates many of the
experiments of our own day in correlating the shape of narrative time to accord with subjective experience. Time literally comes to a stop in the early
chapters as the narrator concentrates gropingly on the unfamiliar perceptions that he is forced to cope with; but it speeds up gradually until, at the
end, we find it hard to believe that ten years have actually elapsed.* Much

---

* In this respect, one can compare *House of the Dead* with Thomas Mann's *The Magic Moun-
tain*, which is constructed along very similar lines. "Through the organization of the novel,"
writes one critic, "the reader is led to experience time in a variety of ways. The principle upon
which the organization of chapters is based is anything but profound: it is the simple perception
that our attention, when first we enter a new situation, is focused upon myriad details that are
gradually, as we adjust to the new surroundings, simplified into an accustomed routine of even

of the book is also structured around the cycle of the seasons (essentially the cycle of the first year of imprisonment, although Dostoevsky plays fast and loose with the literal sequence of events),† and this too imparts a unity and continuity lacking in the usual collection of sketches.

It is probably this greater sense of unity achieved by Dostoevsky that has led to so much speculation regarding the genre to which *House of the Dead* should be assigned. Is it a series of sketches, a personal memoir, or, as Victor Shklovsky has insisted, "a novel of a special type,"[11] a documentary novel about a collectivity rather than about a single individual or family? The attempt to answer this question has led to much ingenious analysis without any response clearly emerging as victorious. The reasonable conclusion is that it is a mixed form combining aspects of all three types, and that it is less important to classify it properly than to understand the unique mixture that Dostoevsky created. The basis is unquestionably that of the sketch form, as in Turgenev; there is also a strong element of the personal memoir, as in Tolstoy (the history of an encounter with, and adaptation to a strange, bewildering, and frightening milieu); but Shklovsky is also right in calling attention to the importance accorded the collectivity. For what distinguishes *House of the Dead* from all works of a similar kind is this unprecedented effort by an educated Russian to grasp and portray the moral-spiritual essence of a peasant world that he has been forced to *accept* provisionally as his own.

Dostoevsky conveys this apprehension of group life, the sense of living in a self-contained and unified world, by various means. One is the reappearance of characters, who first are seen in one context and then turn up again in others to exhibit new facets of their personality; this technique is an adaptation in miniature of the similar effect created by such reappearances in Balzac's *La Comédie Humaine*. In addition, Dostoevsky also reshapes the Russian sketch form to strengthen the atmosphere of self-enclosure. In his

---

texture. . . . Thomas Mann has constructed this temporal sequence with supreme artistic consciousness. It is quite apparent how, at the end of each chapter, the rhythm of time (hours, days, weeks, months, years) begins to blur into the rhythm of the succeeding chapter, gradually producing the effect of 'eternal sameness' that is mentioned in the various digressions on time. The tendency of the novel 'to be constantly present' is enhanced, of course, by Thomas Mann's much-discussed use of leitmotif." Theodore Ziolkowski, *Dimensions of the Modern Novel* (Princeton, 1969), 90-93.

Much the same effect is created by Dostoevsky, who also uses leitmotifs, though in a much less self-conscious fashion. Mann was a great reader of Dostoevsky, and we can only speculate on how much he may have learned from the technique of *House of the Dead.*

† Dostoevsky wished to give the impression that the Christmas celebrations, which included the convicts' visit to the bathhouse and the theatrical spectacle, had taken place during the first month of his arrival. Hence he advanced the date of his entry into prison to December, although he actually entered on January 25th. Pierre Pascal notes that, in the first chapter of the text printed in *The Russian World*, the date is given originally as "during the month of January," and then, in the second chapter, is moved back to December. Readers were asked to change the first date, which was attributed to a typographical error. Additionally, we know that the theatrical spectacle occurred in November 1851, during the second year of Dostoevsky's imprisonment, not at all at the time specified by the book. See Pierre Pascal's valuable edition and translation of *Récits de la Maison des Morts* (Paris, 1961), lxxvi-lxxvii, 17.

classic study of the young Tolstoy, B. M. Eikhenbaum has pointed out that, in the typical sketch, "a characteristic compositional device" was to use "a lyrical landscape as a frame." This device, "especially canonized by Turgenev" in *A Sportsman's Sketches*, is also used by Tolstoy in his *Sevastopol Stories*; and in both writers the lyrical evocation of nature provides a welcome release from the oppressive limits of the central situation.[12] Nature offers an escape into an innocent world of peace and serenity by contrast with the routine brutality of the treatment of peasant serfs or the unending slaughter at Sevastopol. An occasional poignant release of this kind can also be observed in Dostoevsky's sketches, as he turns his eyes to the sky overhead, feels the quickening effects of spring freshness, or gazes at the steppe fading into the distance through the slats of the prison stockade. But since such instants rarely if ever are used to frame and punctuate a sequence, they never function implicitly to offer some alternative to the world being portrayed.

Much more often the frame in Dostoevsky's sketches is provided by the constraints of prison life—the life he shares with the collectivity. Time and again in *House of the Dead*, after the description of some holiday or other event (such as the prison theatricals) that has broken the stifling tedium of routine, this enclosing and constricting type of frame terminates the chapter. "But why describe this Bedlam! The oppressive day came to an end at last. The convicts fell asleep on the plank bed. They talked and muttered in their sleep that night even more than usual. Here and there they were still sitting over cards. The holiday so long looked forward to was over. Tomorrow the daily round, tomorrow work again" (4: 116). Here we have the "nature" of the prison world, which does not allow man to dissolve his heartache in its limitless and consoling expanse; rather, it only sinks the individual, who may have felt a momentary upsurge of liberation, more despairingly back into the imprisonment of his mass-fate.

Still another aspect of *House of the Dead* distinguishes it markedly from the similar works of Turgenev and Tolstoy. All three writers share the same overriding theme—the encounter of a member of the upper, educated class with the Russian people—and each treats it in his own distinctive way. Turgenev stresses the spiritual beauty and richness of Russian peasant life, the poetry of its superstitions and customs, and by so doing makes the serf status of the peasant and the casual cruelty of his treatment all the more unforgivable. Tolstoy discovers the Russian peasantry amidst the besieged bastions of Sevastopol, and is astonished at the calm tranquillity of its unassuming heroism—so much at variance with the vanity occupying the consciousness of upper-class officers dreaming of decorations and promotions. "You understand that the feeling which actuates them [the peasant soldiers] is not the petty ambition or forgetfulness which you yourself experienced, but something more powerful. . . ," and this understanding in-

223

spires Tolstoy with "a joyous conviction of the strength of the Russian people."[13] Such strength, however, is demonstrated exclusively by their imperturbable and almost cheerful acceptance of death out of instinctive loyalty to God, the Tsar, and Mother Russia.

Only Dostoevsky depicts the Russian people *in revolt* against their enslaved condition, implacably hating the gentlemen who have oppressed them and ready to use their knives and axes to strike back when mistreatment becomes unbearable and they are driven beyond endurance. Even more, it is precisely such peasants—whose crimes, for the most part, were a violent protest against the refusal to consider them as fully sentient human beings—whom Dostoevsky singles out as the finest specimens of the Russian people: "After all, one must tell the whole truth; these men were exceptional men. Perhaps they were the most gifted, the strongest of our people. But their mighty energies were vainly wasted, wasted abnormally, unjustly, hopelessly. And who was to blame, whose fault was it? That's just it, who was to blame?" (4: 231). There can be no doubt of the answer: the abhorrent institution of serfdom, and the whole complex of social customs that had led to the treatment of serfs as members of an inferior species. No wonder that Dostoevsky's portrait of the Russian peasantry—his image of them as indomitable and unyielding in their ceaseless struggle against the most brutal subjugation—became, above all others, a favorite of the Russian radicals in the midst of the revolutionary aspirations of the early 1860s.

6

From a purely artistic point of view, *House of the Dead* is probably the most *unusual* book that Dostoevsky ever produced—unusual not so much in Russian literature, despite the novelty of its depiction of prison life, but rather in the context of his own production. One would be hard put to recognize the prison memoirs and his purely creative work as coming from the same pen. The intense dramatism of the fiction is here replaced by a calm objectivity of presentation; there is very little close analysis of interior states of mind; and there are marvelous descriptive passages that reveal Dostoevsky's ability as an observer of the external world, even though dialogue and monologue manifestly dominate in his novels over the depiction of scenery and locale.

These "non-Dostoevskian" qualities of *House of the Dead*, as it were, are one reason why a number of his great contemporaries preferred his prison memoirs to all those other works to which we now assign a much greater value. In a letter to A. A. Fet, Turgenev spoke of the "smelly self-laceration" of *Crime and Punishment* (he was referring to the second part); but he called the bath scene in *House of the Dead* "simply Dantesque."[14] Herzen made the same comparison with Dante, and added that Dostoevsky "had created out of the description of the customs of a Siberian prison a fresco in the spirit of Michelangelo."[15] Tolstoy too admired the book, considering it one of the most original works of Russian prose; in *What Is Art?* he placed it among the few works in world literature that could be taken as models of a "lofty religious art, inspired by love of God and one's neighbor."[16]

The bath scene singled out for praise by Turgenev is indeed an impressive example of Dostoevsky's ability to present a mass tableau with broad strokes and to paint a picture worthy of the battlescapes of Tolstoy himself. It is too long to quote in full, but a few passages will convey the flavor:

> There was not a spot on the floor as big as the palm of your hand where there was not a convict squatting, splashing from his bucket. ... On the top shelf and on all the steps leading up to it men were crouched, huddled together washing themselves. But they did not wash themselves much. Men of the peasant class don't wash much with soap and hot water; they only steam themselves terribly and then douche themselves with cold water—that is their idea of a bath. Fifty birches were rising and falling rhythmically on the shelves; they all thrashed themselves into a state of stupefaction. ... As a rule the steaming backs of the convicts show distinctly the scars of the blows or lashes they have received in the past, so that all those backs looked now as though freshly wounded. The scars were horrible! A shiver ran down me at the sight of them. They pour more boiling water on the hot bricks and clouds of thick, hot steam fill the whole bathhouse; they all laugh and shout. Through the clouds of steam one gets glimpses of scarred backs, shaven heads, bent arms and legs. ... It occurred to me that if one day we would all be in hell together it would be very much like this place. (4: 98)

Even in what seems a purely descriptive passage, Dostoevsky carefully and quietly selects the symbolic detail ("all those backs looked now as though freshly wounded") that reinforces one of his main motifs—the terrible inhumanity of flogging, with its degradation of the human spirit and its devilish temptation to unleash the sadistic instincts.

It is impossible to go through the book in detail and analyze how Dostoevsky skillfully weaves together all the seemingly casual events and accidents of prison life through this type of symbolic accentuation. But another famous episode, which clearly has an emblematic significance, is part of the relatively lighthearted chapter about prison animals that reveals a side of Dostoevsky's sensitivity rarely observable elsewhere. Here he describes a crippled eagle, whose lair was in the farthest corner of the stockade, and who, exhausted and unable to fly because of a broken wing, had been brought into camp by a work party. "I remember how fiercely he glared at us, looking about him at the inquisitive crowd, and opened his crooked beak, preparing to sell his life dearly" (4: 193).

Refusing to be tamed, at first disdaining even to eat, the eagle finally accepts food—but only in solitude, never in the presence of others. The convicts soon tired of his novelty, "yet every day there were pieces of fresh meat and a broken pot of water near him." Someone was evidently looking after him on the sly, but Dostoevsky's own efforts to approach him were unavailing: "All the time I was near him he used to stare intently in my face with his savage, piercing eyes. Fierce and solitary he awaited death, mistrustful and hostile to all." Even though the other convicts appeared to have forgotten about him, sometime in late autumn his unconquerable spirit moved them to set him free: "They said that they must take the eagle out. 'Let him die if he must, but not in prison,' they said" (4: 193-194).

All their own instinctive yearning for freedom receives poignant expression in the clipped conversation that Dostoevsky records (or re-creates) in the superb scene depicting the eagle's release:

> He [a convict] threw the eagle from the rampart into the plain. It was a cold, gloomy day of late autumn, the wind was whistling over the bare plain and rustling in the yellow, withered, tussocky grass of the steppes. The eagle went off in a straight line, fluttering his injured wing, as though in haste to get away from us anywhere. With curiosity the convicts watched his head flitting through the grass.
> "Look at him!" said one dreamily. "He doesn't look round!" added another. "He hasn't looked round once, lads, he just runs off!"
> "Did you expect him to come back and to say thank you?" observed a third.
> "Ah, to be sure, it's freedom. It's freedom he sniffs."
> "You can't see him now, mates. . . ."
> "What are you standing for? March," shouted the guards, and we all trudged to work in silence. (4: 194)

One can well understand why Tolstoy, with his intense empathy for sheer animal vitality—the Tolstoy who created Uncle Eroshka in *The Cossacks*, and described so feelingly the death of the mare Froufrou in *Anna Karenina*—should have greatly admired this scene and included it in a volume of readings he edited as late as 1904.

7

If the eagle episode unforgettably symbolizes the motif of freedom that runs through *House of the Dead*, the remarkable *skaz* narrative, "Akulka's Husband," is equally emblematic of another major theme. It dramatizes the survival in the Russian common man, even in the midst of his worst ex-

cesses, of a strain of deep and pure humanity which, if not capable of redeeming his behavior, at least indicates a remorseful awareness of his own
degradation. Such awareness always provided Dostoevsky with an all-important ray of hope in the midst of moral darkness: "Sometimes one would
know a man for years in prison and despise him and think that he was not
a human being but a brute. And suddenly a moment will come by chance
when his soul will suddenly reveal itself in an involuntary outburst, and you
see in it such wealth, such feeling, such heart, such a vivid understanding
of its own suffering, and of the suffering of others, that your eyes are open
and for the first moment you can't believe what you have seen and heard
yourself" (4: 197-198). In truth, Dostoevsky provides only one, relatively insignificant example of such a "sudden revelation of the soul"—the meek
and harmless convict Sushilov, who worked for him as a body servant, one
day broke into tears and refused to accept money after suffering a rebuke.
But "Akulka's Husband" offers an additional and far more sensational illustration of exactly such an "involuntary outburst" of the Russian soul.

"Akulka's Husband," a story told in the hospital by one peasant convict
to another, is retold by Dostoevsky in the narrator's own uneducated speech
style; and the interpolated comments of the listener, an older peasant playing the role of Greek chorus, are pitched in the same stylistic key. The tale
is a somber one of passion, pride, revenge, and finally murder, notable for
its unsparing depiction of the terrible savagery of Russian peasant customs; but peasant life is also portrayed, without an instant of incongruity,
as manifesting the same desperate passions that elsewhere have furnished
the subject for high tragedy. Several years later, Dostoevsky would print
Leskov's classic novella *Lady Macbeth from Mtsensk* in *Epoch*, the successor to *Time*; but Dostoevsky had anticipated Leskov by finding peasant versions of Romeo and Juliet and Othello in the godforsaken village where the
events of his *skaz* take place.

Filka Morozov is a young daredevil of the Russian type, a "broad" nature,
who quarrels because of some money matter with the father of eighteen-
year-old Akulka whom he had been more or less expected to marry. To spite
the old man, he claims to have slept with his daughter already; and the response of the dignified and wealthy village notable, when he learns of this
presumed defilement of his family, lights up the whole milieu in a flash. "In
ancient years," says the old man, "in the time of the worthy patriarchs, I
should have chopped her to pieces at the stake, but nowadays it's all darkness and rottenness." Her parents beat Akulka unmercifully ("sometimes
the neighbors all along the street would hear Akulka howling"), and Filka
gloats over his revenge. "I've made them feel it," says he, "they can't forget
it." Akulka, to cover the family disgrace, is married off to the impoverished
narrator, a weak-willed and sniveling young man completely under the
domination of the more powerful Filka. The bridegroom finds her a virgin

on her wedding night, and realizes that she has been maligned. But then, publicly abused and humiliated by Filka, he too begins beating Akulka without any obvious reason—because, as he admits to his interlocutor, who solemnly disapproves, "it was insulting. . . . Besides, I got into the habit of it . . ." (4: 168-171).

Meanwhile, Filka Morozov sells himself to a wealthy family as a substitute for a son scheduled to be drafted into the Army and leads a riotous life. During the period of waiting, the substitute was traditionally allowed to indulge his every whim, and so "Filka was having a rare time at the shopkeeper's, sleeping with the daughter, pulling the father's beard every day after dinner, and doing just as he liked." On the day of his departure, as he was being driven through the streets and waving farewell, he saw Akulka. "Leaping out of the carriage, he bowed down before her and confessed: 'You are my soul . . . my darling. I've loved you for two years, and now they are taking me for a soldier with music. Forgive me,' said he, 'honest daughter of an honest father, for I've been a scoundrel to you and it's all been my fault.' " Akulka bowed down before him too, and in the same formal accents of folk poetry replied: " 'You forgive me too, good youth, I have no thought of any evil you have done' " (4: 171-172).

Questioned by her angry husband, she tells him: "Why, I love him now more than all the world." This is more than the resentful spouse can bear: after a sleepless night he quietly drives with her to a forest the next day, seizes her thick braids, and slits her throat. "She screamed, the blood spurted out, I threw down the knife, flung my arms round her, lay on the ground, and the blood was simply streaming, simply streaming on my face and hands." He runs home, takes refuge in an old bathhouse, and is found still crouching there a day or so later frozen in panic terror. Dostoevsky characterizes him as "a cowardly, mawkish youth" who was treated in the prison camp "with contempt" by everyone, and "could very easily be made to do anything. It was not that he was especially docile, but he was fond of making friends and was ready to do anything to please" (4: 172-173, 166).

Dostoevsky's mastery of the *skaz* form, and the subdued, laconic, impassive tone of his narration—so contrary to the usual nervous rhythms of his prose, particularly his monologues—can hardly be admired enough; they show that, if he had chosen, he could have been an entirely different kind of writer. Most remarkable of all is the successful transplantation of a typical "Dostoevskian" situation—the "underground" hatred of Filka Morozov, with all its dreadful consequences, and then his confession and repentance—into a peasant setting. How many critics have affirmed, as an indisputable truth, that the conflicts of Dostoevsky's characters could only arise in a complex and highly sophisticated culture and were the product of an urban environment! In any event, the poetic exchange between Filka and Akulka at the climax does succeed in redeeming for a moment, with a flash of the purest and most exalted sentiment, the appalling world of peasant ferocity amidst which the action is set.*

8
_____

Since there are several allusions in *House of the Dead* to recent changes for the better in prison-camp conditions, every reader would understand, even though no dates are given, that the work deals with events that took place during the reign of Nicholas I. The first narrator writes as someone who, in the early 1860s, is looking back at a recent but by now almost legendary past. Besides such references to prison reforms, several other passages also introduce the point of view of the present. The most dramatic is the episode involving "the parricide Ilinsky," whose story is told in the very first chapter. A riotous young officer, a merry and lightheaded fellow, Ilinsky had been convicted of murdering his wealthy father in cold blood so as to obtain money for his debauches; and his history later furnished the nucleus for the plot involving Dimitry Karamazov in *The Brothers Karamazov*. Despite the supposedly irrefutable evidence piled up against Ilinsky, Dostoevsky never quite believed him to be guilty because something in his easygoing and carefree personality suggested that his claim of innocence might be justified.

Ilinsky more or less vanishes from sight until the seventh chapter of the second part, when the first narrator suddenly intervenes to make a declaration:

> The other day the editor of the *Notes from House of the Dead* received information from Siberia that the criminal really was innocent and had suffered ten years in penal servitude for nothing; that his innocence had been established before a court, officially, that the real criminals had been found out and had confessed, and that the luckless fellow had already been released from prison. The editor can feel no doubt of the truth of the news. There is nothing more to add. There is

* In the brooding and powerful opera that he based on *House of the Dead* and completed in 1927, the Czech composer Leoš Janáček made very effective use both of the eagle episode and the narrative of Akulka's husband. Indeed, in his libretto both Goryanchikov and the crippled eagle arrive in camp at the same time and their stories are fused into one. Both are released at the climax and, unlike the book, the eagle's wing has been healed; the bird (and, presumably, Goryanchikov) leave the camp not to die but rather to soar away into a new life.

The story told by Akulka's husband is also embellished with some new details. After its recital, which is quite faithful to the original, another prisoner (Mikhailov) dies in the hospital and is recognized to be Filka Morozov. Such a plot coincidence is precisely the sort of novelistic effect that Dostoevsky wished to avoid; but it works very well in the operatic context. This grim scene, the lowest point of the work, is immediately followed by the news of Goryanchikov's release, which comes very unexpectedly. He does not simply complete his term, as in the book, but rather, as happened to another prisoner, is given his liberty by special order of the Tsar. The opera concludes with an intensely moving chorus of convicts intoning a word for freedom that is the same in Czech as in Russian (*svoboda*). One wonders if this masterpiece is ever performed these days in its native country.

no need to enlarge on all the tragic significance of this fact, and to speak of the young life crushed under this terrible charge. The fact is too impressive, it speaks for itself. (4: 195)

Whether Dostoevsky actually received such news while in the course of composition, or whether he reserved it for the effect of surprise that it creates, cannot be determined; the second alternative seems more plausible because, as V. A. Tunimanov has remarked, the revelation of Ilinsky's innocence has been carefully prepared for by the doubts expressed earlier.[17] But the result is certainly to jolt the reader into an awareness of the present, and to remind him that many of the convicts he had read about were still serving their sentences. More importantly, the incident dramatizes the shortcomings of "facts" as indices to the depths of human character, and confirms Dostoevsky's reliance on the truth of his own perceptions in preference to the so-called proofs gathered through judicial inquiries. This opposition between external data and the clues derived from intuitive observation would later become an important motif in both *Crime and Punishment* and *The Brothers Karamazov*. Razumikhin, in the first novel, heatedly argues that the housepainter suspected of the murder could not have been guilty simply because of the way he had behaved shortly after the crime was known to have occurred; and all the proofs accumulated against Dimitry Karamazov do not lead to truth but to a judicial error, which could have been avoided if the straightforwardness of his impetuous character had been given some consideration.

Other indications of the time of writing, if less sensational, evidently reflect Dostoevsky's response to the social-cultural situation of the early 1860s. Indeed, it can well be argued that the entire book was written as a response to this situation, and that Dostoevsky's portrayal of the instinctive Christianity of the peasant-convicts, as well as of their hostile alienation from the educated class, was intended to reveal the patent futility of revolutionary hopes inspired by a radical ideology that the peasants would reject with abhorrence if they understood it at all. The chapter entitled "The Complaint," in which the peasant-convicts refuse to allow the narrator to join their protest against the deteriorating quality of prison food, speaks for itself as a warning against the delusions of the radical intelligentsia that they could lead a peasant revolution. And the natural leaders of the people thrown up from their ranks were too headstrong, impetuous, and ignorant to accomplish anything except precipitate their followers into disaster.[17] Such aspects of the book stand out much more clearly for us, in the light of Dostoevsky's later evolution, than they did for his contemporaries.

A few passages, however, can hardly be read except as manifest thrusts against some of the notions, strenuously propagated by Chernyshevsky, which had now attained the status of irrefutable truth among the younger generation. There was a firm belief, for example, in the overwhelming power of environment to determine human behavior—a theory that Dostoevsky rejects when, after speaking of the unaffected humanity of the doctors in the prison hospital, he then mentions cases in which some doctors take bribes, make profits, and neglect their patients. Reprehensible conduct of this kind, he remarks, has sometimes been pardoned as a consequence of the corrupting effects of "environment"; but he will have none of such paltry excuses. "It is high time," he declares, "we gave up apathetic complaints of being corrupted by our environment. It is true no doubt that it does destroy a great deal in us, but not everything, and often a crafty and knowing rogue, especially if he is an eloquent speaker or writer, will cover up not simply weakness but often real baseness, justifying it by the influence of 'environment' " (4: 142). Dostoevsky thus is perfectly willing to acknowledge the pressure of environment, but not to the point of eliminating individual moral responsibility altogether; and he is particularly alert to the danger of a cynical misuse of such views to justify the most arrant knavery.

An even more overt sally against Chernyshevsky is contained in another passage describing a widow who lives in the vicinity of the prison camp and devotes her life to helping the convicts. "There are in Siberia, and practically always have been," he remarks, "some people who seem to make it the object of their lives to look after the 'unfortunates,' to show pure and disinterested sympathy and compassion for them, as though they were their own children." One such lady named Nastasya Ivanovna had nothing remarkable about her and was, indeed, quite unremarkable: "All that one could see in her was an infinite kindness, an irresistible desire to please one, to comfort one, to do something nice for one." Dostoevsky recalls a modest cigarette case of cardboard she had made for him, covered with colored paper trimmed with gilt around the edges; she knew he smoked cigarettes and thought the case might give him pleasure. "Some people maintain (I have heard it and read it)," Dostoevsky continues, "that the purest love for one's neighbor is at the same time the greatest egoism. What egoism there could be in this instance, I can't understand" (4: 68).

Dostoevsky could hardly have rejected with more firmness the attempt of Chernyshevsky to establish a new ethics on the foundation of egoism. But while such passages are a clear challenge to the intention of recasting the moral code in Utilitarian terms, a more subtle and powerful rejection— one that will soon provide the inspiration for *Notes from Underground*— can be found elsewhere in the book. It is contained in the pages describing the frenzied desire of the convicts to express the freedom of their personalities, even if in doing so they sacrifice all self-interest in the usual sense to attain only the momentary, irrational illusion of moral-psychic autonomy. What the prisoners value more than anything else, as Dostoevsky un-

CHAPTER 16

Winter Notes on
Summer Impressions

The last important work that Dostoevsky published in *Time* was *Winter Notes on Summer Impressions*, a series of articles in which he launches a full-scale assault on the major pieties of the radical credo. This text has already been used to follow Dostoevsky on his first journey through Europe; but to view it only as an ordinary travel account hardly does justice to its importance. For Dostoevsky seizes the occasion to explore the whole tangled history of the relationship between educated Russians and European culture. Within this framework he also discusses the larger issues then being posed by radical ideology: the basis of a new moral-social order; the question of Socialism; the future destiny of mankind. By the time he finishes, he will have discovered both the literary and the ideological stance that will lead within two years to the composition of his first post-Siberian masterpiece. *Winter Notes on Summer Impressions* may thus be viewed as a prelude to, or better, as a preliminary draft of *Notes from Underground*; and it is primarily as such that we shall discuss it here.

2

Winter Notes fits into an important genre of Russian literature—the travel diary or journal, which would now be called cultural reportage—and Dostoevsky follows in the footsteps of illustrious predecessors. Two well-known works, Fonvizin's *Letters from France* and Karamzin's *Letters of a Russian Traveler*, are referred to in Dostoevsky's text; Herzen's *Letters from France and Italy*, of equal if not greater importance, could not be mentioned for reasons of censorship. Yet, as A. S. Dolinin has amply shown, Herzen's *Letters* were ever-present in Dostoevsky's memory, and probably on his writing-desk as well, as he was setting down his own reflections on the same subject.[1] Much like Americans such as Hawthorne, Emerson, and Henry James, cultivated Russians felt a need to define their own national individuality by comparing themselves with Europe; and Dostoevsky's *Winter Notes* takes its place in a long line of works through which Russians have examined the roots of their own culture as it had evolved, since Peter the Great, under the successive waves of European influence. Only by making the prescribed pilgrimage to the West, only by ceasing to regard Europe through the haze of distance as some enchanted land, could a Russian best discover what aspects of European influence in his homeland he might wish to preserve and what discard. As a result, the travel diary has always been one of the chief means by which Russian self-consciousness has been sharpened and affirmed; and Dostoevsky's *Winter Notes*, true to type, thus gives us a fuller and franker expression of his convictions than any so far encountered in public print.

Like the vast majority of travelers from whatever country to a foreign land, much of what Dostoevsky saw and felt corresponded gratifyingly to many of the expectations he had entertained before leaving. Roman Jakobson has amusingly pointed out the astonishing similarity in the reaction to Europe, and particularly to France, that can be observed over the time span of a century and a half in the writings of the widest and most diverse variety of Russian visitors. Whether in 1800 or 1900, whether a Socialist radical, a patriotic Slavophil, a diehard reactionary, a moderate liberal, or a completely apolitical Symbolist aesthete—Russians have invariably responded to a homogeneous "myth of France" well represented in one of the letters by Dostoevsky already quoted.[2] A few sentences may be cited again: "You have spoken to me," he remarks to Strakhov, "about the dismal faces, insolent and complacent, that flourish among us at the mineral spa [outside Petersburg]. But I swear the ones here are just as bad. Ours are simply carnivorous scoundrels, and, most of the time, know it, *but here they are completely convinced that this is how it must be* [italics added]. The Frenchman is pleasant, decent, polite, but false, and money for him is everything. No trace of any ideal."[3]

Long before he departed on his journey, Dostoevsky had been persuaded that Europe was a dying culture—a culture that had lost the spiritual bond of unity it had once possessed. He also firmly believed that Russia and the Russian people represented a fresh source of moral-social inspiration through whom a new world order would come to birth. It was thus a simple matter for him to pierce through the illusions of the glittering European surface, and instantly to detect the corruption lying concealed underneath. True, some manifestations of this corruption might appear to be similar in Paris and Petersburg; rogues and scoundrels existed as surely in the one place as in the other. But Dostoevsky's letter shows the tactic that he will use time and again in *Winter Notes* to evade the consequences of such awkwardly impartial reflections. Russians are *conscious* of their moral delinquency; they feel it as such, even if only as a vaguely troubling disquietude; and hence they have preserved the indispensable basis of morality. Europeans have become so depraved that the very meaning of their own conduct escapes them completely and they complacently take evil for good. This insistence on the moral stultification of Europe runs as a leitmotif all through *Winter Notes*, and emerges as its ultimate conclusion. But such a generalization, hardly unexpected for the regular readers of *Time*, is of less interest at the moment than the manner and means by which it is expressed.

Written in the first person, *Winter Notes* is a continuous dialogue with those whom Dostoevsky addresses as "my friends." They have been urging him to communicate his impressions of Europe to them, and the "winter notes" he is finally composing are his answer to their pressing demands. Dostoevsky never loses sight of these friends all through his articles and, indeed, professes to be rather worried about *their* reactions to *his* reactions. Will they not consider him terribly irresponsible because he tried to see too much too quickly? Can he really tell them anything they do not already know—and know far more thoroughly than he does? Dostoevsky finally decides that his friends are not requesting the sort of reliable information anyone can obtain from a guidebook; what they desire instead is someone "who would not be afraid to reveal a personal impression or adventure of his— *even one that did him little credit*"; and he would not arrange to verify his personal opinions with the renowned authorities. "In a word, you desire only my own personal but sincere observations" (5: 49; italics added).

Very well! Dostoevsky determines to dedicate himself to conveying his "sincere observations," though he is certain that they will "do him little credit." But why such an unflattering assumption? Because he knows that his friends will have a predetermined attitude toward Europe—one of admiration and awe—which he does not find in accord with what surges up in his own reactions. His first contacts with European life in Germany, as we have seen, had been quite upsetting and unpleasant, and had violated all the rules and regulations of the "renowned authorities." Nothing—neither Unter den Linden, nor German women, nor the Cologne cathedral— had aroused the proper desire to genuflect! All this was terribly disturbing, even inexplicable, until he returned to his hotel room one day feeling ill and examined his symptoms: "My tongue was yellow and malignant. . . . I thought, 'Can it be, can it really be that man, this lord of all creation, is dependent to such a degree on his liver? What baseness!' " (5: 48).

If for no other reason, this reference to the liver inevitably recalls the opening sentences of *Notes from Underground*; and while the anatomical allusion may seem, at first glance, only a casual coincidence, closer scrutiny reveals a deeper relation. Indeed, the rhetorical strategy used here is an anticipation of the one so masterfully deployed in the fictional work, where the author, again writing in the first person, also dramatizes a split in his consciousness between a pattern of behavior that might be considered normal and reasonable and an unexpected emotive reaction that surges up from some instinctive and visceral level of the personality. Both works, in addition, maintain the same extremely close "dialogical" relation with the reader ("my friends"), who becomes an implicit and invoked presence *within* the text and is constantly appealed to as an interlocutor.

In this first chapter of *Winter Notes*, precisely the same situation exists between Dostoevsky and his readers as he will later recreate for the underground man. These readers anticipate an attitude of wide-eyed reverence before the glories of Europe; and the author shares this expectation sufficiently so that, when his own involuntary responses fail to correspond, he can only laugh at himself for his incapacity. But, at the same time, he feels his irreverence to be a more genuine and authentic reaction than the automatic obeisance that his readers expect. Hence his irony cuts two ways, being directed both against himself (for having somehow failed to measure up to Europe) and against the reader (for being unable to tolerate any but a hackneyed and conventional point of view). Such an "inverted irony," which turns back on the writer as a means of turning *against* an imagined judge and critic in the person of the reader, is precisely the one that will be used in *Notes from Underground.*

3

Dostoevsky initially employs this technique to convey only what seems a purely personal and individual response to the panorama of European life; but he wishes the reader to understand that his reaction is by no means as exclusive or aberrant as may appear. Quite the contrary, it springs directly out of the whole ambivalent relation of the Russian psyche to European culture. It expresses the adoration of Europe induced by education, the self-hatred provoked by such adoration (since it inevitably produces a sense of inferiority), and then the irrepressible need to assert independence even if only in a self-mocking manner. Accordingly, two chapters of *Winter Notes* are devoted to a very lively illustration of the intricacies of this relation, which Dostoevsky runs over in his mind as his train clanks and whistles through the night on its way to the European border. Was he finally going to see Europe, "the land of holy wonders," about which he had dreamed ever since, as a boy, his parents had read to him from the novels of Anne Radcliffe before bedtime? Was he really going to see France, the nation before which Belinsky and his *pléiade* had bowed with such reverence? "Then France was all the vogue—in 1846," Dostoevsky recalls. "It was not only that such names as George Sand, Proudhon, etc., were idolized, or others like Ledru-Rollin and Louis Blanc, etc., were honored. No, quite simply all sorts of pipsqueaks, the most insignificant names, who immediately blamed themselves when things got around to them [i.e., who renounced their radicalism]—even these were held in high esteem" (5: 50).

On the one hand, then, Russians are filled with the most servile and uncritical veneration for Europe; but Dostoevsky also found a sentence from

Fonvizin constantly intruding into his thoughts. "The French," Fonvizin had written, "lack good sense, yes, and if they acquired it, they would consider this the worst misfortune that could befall them." Moreover, the very phrase that had popped into his head—"the land of holy wonders"—came from a poem written in 1834 by the Slavophil Aleksey Khomyakov as a dirge for a dying civilization: "Oh how sorrowful, sorrowful am I! / A thick darkness falls / On the faraway West, the land of holy wonders."[4] The poem is much more a lament for the death of the West than a panegyric of its achievements, and both Fonvizin and Khomyakov illustrate the critical distance from European culture which, for all their admiration, continues to exist in the subconscious of every educated Russian. Fonvizin's heart, Dostoevsky remarks knowingly, probably tickled with delight when he wrote his irreverent phrase about the French; and for three or four generations, "all such phrases berating foreigners, even if we run across them now, contain something irresistibly pleasing for us Russians. . . . But of course only in the deepest secret, even sometimes in secret from ourselves" (5: 50). This Russian refusal to acknowledge the secret of its ambivalent relation to Europe is reflected by Dostoevsky's inverted irony, which jestingly anticipates such outraged reactions and overcomes them at the same time.

Such meditations on the anomalies of the Russian attitude toward Europe naturally lead Dostoevsky to think back on the origins of this fateful relationship, and he sketches its history in a chapter which, though labeled "completely superfluous," contains the very heart of the matter. "I began to ponder," he says, "on this theme: how Europe has, at various times, been reflected in us and constantly broken in on us with its civilization, and to what extent we have become civilized, and how many of us now are really civilized through and through?" (5: 55). In the past, despite the brilliant French surface of the court of Catherine the Great—in spite of the perukes, the lace cuffs, the curtsies, and the dress swords dangling at the waist—the Russian landowner and apprentice courtier had still kept his old habits and feelings. These were admittedly brutal, barbarous, and revolting, but they were still his own, they were still Russian; and the people felt more at home with this generation than with their more "humane" offspring. Then came Chatsky, the hero of Griboyedov's comedy *Woe from Wit*, who had assimilated the culture of Europe and, on returning home to Russia, found life there unbearable. The first of the "superfluous men," Chatsky flees back to Europe to solace his wounded sensibility, lamenting that there is no longer any place for him in his homeland. "One thing I cannot understand: Chatsky was after all a very intelligent man," Dostoevsky writes. "How could it happen that an intelligent man could find nothing here to do? All of them found nothing to do, for a period of two or three generations" (5: 62).

The latest Russian type, the progressive and radical, neither acts out a farce like Catherine's courtier nor is troubled by self-doubt; he has become completely and complacently European. "For how self-assured we are now in our civilizing mission, how haughtily we settle problems! Why even talk about problems! There is no such thing as a native soil, as a people. Nationality?—only a certain system of paying taxes! The soul?—a *tabula rasa*, a bit of wax, out of which you can paste together on the spot a real man, a universal general man, a homuncule—all that's necessary is to apply the fruits of European civilization, and read two or three books!" (5: 59). One can already hear the jeering, provocative voice of the underground man in these sentences, which contain exactly the inflections of his tone: a partial identification ("we") with ideas he really abhors and implicitly rejects through the very sarcasm by which they are affirmed. Visibly, Dostoevsky's meditations on the manner in which Europe has been assimilated into the Russian psyche, and his attempt to dramatize this symbiosis through his own reactions as a *representative* figure, have led him stylistically to the very threshold of his next creation.

4

With the fourth chapter of *Winter Notes*, Dostoevsky finally crosses the French border and, as we recall, discovers that his railroad compartment has been invaded by police spies between stations. No doubt he wished his Russian readers to feel the proper shudder of horror at such surveillance, and to conclude that the vaunted liberties of the West were simply so many shams: Russians had no reason to be envious of European "liberty." But Dostoevsky could not let the matter rest, and reinforces this exposure of European hypocrisy by contrasting the presumed Russian reaction with the European (in this case French) violation of the norms of political decency. The elderly couple who ran one of the hotels at which he stayed in Paris, and who requested information about him for the police, anxiously explained that all this documentation was absolutely "ne-cess-ary"—and a very respectable and worthy couple they were, the essence of bourgeois propriety. "But the word 'ne-cess-ary,' far from being pronounced in any apologetic or derogatory tone, was uttered, rather, precisely in the sense of the completest necessity to the point of being identical with their own personal convictions" (5: 67-68). Such, presumably, would not have been the case in Russia, where people bowed to force and the pressure of historical necessity without allowing it to obliterate their moral awareness.

Dostoevsky then quickly moves on to London, the city in which the soullessness and heartlessness of Western life—its crass materialism, its unashamed contempt for anything other than the sordid pursuit of worldly gain—was mirrored in the most arrogantly brazen fashion. The chapter on London bears as its title the single, flamboyant name of the false god of the flesh execrated in the Old Testament: "Baal." It is this god, transposed into a symbol of modern materialism, before whom all of Western civilization now bows down in prostrate worship; and the results can be seen in the canvas that Dostoevsky brushes in with a palate even darker in hue than that of Dickens, the inspired native poet of the city's sordidness and mass misery. London is nothing but a pitiless wilderness of wild, half-naked, besotted proletarians, gloomily drowning their despair in debauchery and gin. And over all this chaos of restless, preoccupied crowds, of whistling and roaring machinery, of heart-rending scenes of brutalized degradation, reigns the great idol to whom all render homage—the spirit of Baal embodied in the resplendent and majestic London World's Fair.

During his eight days in London, Dostoevsky paid an obligatory visit to the famous Crystal Palace to see the second London World's Fair, which had opened in May 1862 and was dedicated to exhibiting the latest triumphs of science and technology. A monument of modern architecture originally constructed for the first London World's Fair in 1851 by Sir Joseph Paxton, the huge cast-iron and glass building, covering nineteen acres and located on high ground just outside the city, had since been transformed into a museum. The Crystal Palace thus became for Dostoevsky an image of the unholy spirit of modernity that brooded malevolently over London; and in his imagination this spirit takes on the form of the monstrous Beast whose coming was prophesied in the Apocalypse:

> Can this really be the accomplished ideal?—you think;—is not this the end? is not this really the "one herd." Will we not have to accept this really as the whole truth and remain silent once and for all? All this is so majestic, victorious, and proud that it takes your breath away. You observe these hundreds of thousands, these millions of people, obediently flowing here from all over the world—people coming with one thought, peacefully, unceasingly, and silently crowding into this colossal palace; and you feel that something has been finally completed and terminated. This is some sort of Biblical illustration, some prophecy of the Apocalypse fulfilled before your eyes. You feel that one must have perpetual spiritual resistance and negation so as not to surrender, not to submit to the impression, not to bow before the fact and deify Baal, that is, not to accept the existing as one's ideal. . . . (5: 69-70)*

Dostoevsky thus acknowledges the power of this idol by his awe-struck

---

* Dostoevsky was by no means the only writer to use religious imagery in speaking of the Crystal Palace. Walter Houghton remarks that the World's Fair of 1851 was generally greeted by "the identification of progress with the spirit of God," and he cites a passage from Charles Kingsley, who wrote that "he was moved to tears; to him [entering the Crystal Palace] was like going into a sacred place." A few days later, Kingsley preached a sermon in which he saw everything that the Palace symbolized as "proofs of the Kingdom of God, realizations of the gifts which Christ received for men, vaster than any of which they [our forefathers] had dreamed." Walter E. Houghton, *The Victorian Frame of Mind, 1830-1870* (New Haven and London, 1957), 43.

11. Main Hall of the Crystal Palace. From *Scientific American*, March 19, 1851

description of its shrine, but his words are equally plangent when he portrays the fate of its victims and sacrifices. Any vestiges of human feeling among them seemed to have been obliterated; all he could detect was a frantic search for sensual pleasure and for oblivion. "The people are always the people," Dostoevsky observes after sketching some London street scenes, "but here everything was so colossal, so striking, that you seemed to grasp tangibly what up to now you had only imagined. Here you no longer see a people, but the systematic, submissive and induced lack of consciousness" (5: 71). What lay at the bottom of all this external splendor, attained at the price of so much human misery, was "the same stubborn, dumb, deep-rooted struggle, the struggle to the death between the general Western principle of individuality and the necessity of somehow living together, of somehow establishing a society and organizing an ant-heap. Even turning into an ant-heap just so as to organize something, just so as not to eat each other up—otherwise, one turns into a cannibal!" (5: 69).*

English (Western) society was thus dominated by the war of all against all, which at best, since some form of social order had to be created, could lead only to the "ant-heap"—to the total, unthinking compliance of human volition with the commands of the social Moloch. How different, we can well imagine Dostoevsky thinking, with the spirit that ruled in the Russian village, no matter how backward and meager in resources! Had he himself not written, just a year before, that the West was incapable of putting the principle of communality into practice because there it "has not fused with life," while in Russia it already existed as an accepted social fact and only awaited further favorable development? Shortly after his meeting with Dostoevsky, Herzen once again stated much the same conclusion more sweepingly in a series of open letters addressed to Turgenev entitled *Ends and Beginnings* (Europe was at the end of its historical life, Russia at the beginning). "Petty-bourgeoisiedom," Herzen states bluntly, "is the final word of the civilization based on the unconditioned rule of property," and Russia would be able to utter a new "word" in world history because it had never accepted this principle of property as sacrosanct.[5] The radical Russian Socialist Herzen and the *pochvennik* Dostoevsky, as we have already

---

* It is striking to observe the similarity of Dostoevsky's remarks about London with those of Friedrich Engels in his *The Condition of the Working Class in England*. "Hundreds of thousands of people from all classes and ranks of society crowd by each other [on the streets]. . . . Meanwhile it occurs to no one that others are worth even a glance. The brutal indifference, the unfeeling isolation of each individual person in his private interest becomes the more repulsive and offensive, the more these individuals are pushed into a tiny space. We know well enough that this isolation of the individual, this narrow-minded self-seeking—is everywhere the fundamental principle of modern society. . . . From this it follows that the social war—the war of all against all—has been openly declared. As in Stirner, men here regard each other only as useful objects." Cited in Steven Marcus, *Engels, Manchester and the Working Class* (New York, 1975), 147. As already mentioned, one of the earliest Russian discussions of Engels's book appeared in *Time* in 1861. Geoffrey C. Kabat makes a detailed comparison between this work of Engels and *Winter Notes* in his *Ideology and Imagination* (New York, 1978), 74-91.

observed more than once, thus shared the same aversion to Western society and placed the same hopes in the presumed Socialist proclivities of the Russian peasant. But for Dostoevsky these Socialist proclivities were rooted in an exalted conception of Christian self-sacrifice which the enlightened atheist and liberated man of the world Herzen would hardly have been willing to accept as an ideal.

5

The last three chapters of *Winter Notes* are devoted to Paris, and these pages come closest to giving Dostoevsky's readers some of the ordinary fare contained in Russian accounts of Europe. French was the only foreign language that Dostoevsky spoke fluently, and he was much more at ease in Paris than in London. All his impressions, however, are highly stylized in the manner of the famous French satirist of the bourgeoisie, Henri Monnier, whom Dostoevsky had read with great appreciation as a young man. Monnier's most famous phrase—*ma femme et mon parapluie!*—had been cited by Dostoevsky in a letter seventeen years earlier;[6] and the image of the complacent, self-satisfied, pompously ridiculous French bourgeois whom Monnier pilloried reappears in Dostoevsky's pages sketched even more acidly by a pen dipped in caustic contempt.

In general, the image that Dostoevsky conveys is of a society rotten to the core with greed for gold yet consumed with vanity at its own moral perfection. "The bourgeois," he writes, "is a curious fellow: he frankly proclaims money as the highest virtue and human obligation, and at the same time he is frightfully fond of pretending to be the most virtuous of men." All of French life under Napoleon III is seen as a sinister comedy, staged exclusively for the purpose of allowing the bourgeoisie to enjoy *both* their continual accumulation of wealth and the spectacle of their ineffable virtue. Dostoevsky ironically celebrates the order, propriety, and security of Paris, which form such a contrast to the roaring chaos of London; yet he detects, underneath the seeming stability of the surface, a curious uneasiness and hidden fear. But what can the French bourgeoisie fear, Dostoevsky asks. Is France not the very acme of perfection, the final, incarnate ideal of Western man? Certainly it cannot fear the working class because, following the lead of Herzen, Dostoevsky writes that "the workers are all in their souls property owners; all their ideal is to become property owners and to possess as many things as possible; this is their nature" (5: 76, 78). Hence, while the bourgeoisie fears everyone—the working class, the Communists, the Socialists—all such apprehensions are the result of a ludicrous mistake. No group in the West really represents any threat to the hegemony of the *spiritual* principle embodied in the bourgeoisie.

What, after all, has become of the ideals of the French Revolution under the Second Empire, the ideals of *liberté*, *égalité*, and *fraternité*? Dostoevsky answers that, so far as the first two are concerned, they have vanished like soap bubbles. In momentary accord with Karl Marx and the Socialists, Dostoevsky views political freedom and legal equality, unaccompanied by economic equality, simply as repulsive fictions invented by the bourgeoisie to delude the proletariat. As for *fraternité*, this, Dostoevsky says, is in the most curious position of all. Europe is always talking about brotherhood and has even raised it to the status of a universal ideal; yet brotherhood is the very antithesis of the European character:

> In the French nature, indeed, in the Western European nature in general, brotherhood is not present. Instead, we find the personal principle, the principle of isolation, a vigorous self-concern, self-assertion, self-determination, within the bounds of one's own ego. This ego sets itself in opposition, as a separate, self-justifying principle, against all of nature and all other humans; it claims equality and equal value with whatever exists outside itself. (5: 79)

Dostoevsky then goes on to describe what brotherhood *really* is; and though he speaks in purely moral terms, every Russian reader would instantly fill in the social reality to which he was referring. This reality, of course, is the Russian peasant *obshchina*, with its land held in common and its democratic administration for the good of all. True brotherhood, as in the *obshchina*, is an instinctive mutual relation between the individual and the community in which each desires only the welfare of the other. The individual does not, as in the West, insist on his exclusive rights as an isolated ego; he freely brings these rights to the community in sacrifice without even being asked to do so. Reciprocally, the community, without making any demands or *imposing* any conditions on the individual, guarantees him equal protection and status with all.

Dostoevsky illustrates this ideal situation in the form of a dialogue between the individual and the community. "My greatest joy," the individual says, "is to sacrifice everything to you, without hurting you by so doing." But the community, as Dostoevsky sees it, then responds: "You offer us too much. . . . Take everything that is ours too. Constantly and with all our might, we shall struggle to increase your personal freedom and your individual fulfillment. . . . We are all behind you; we guarantee your safety; we watch eternally over you." And then, turning back to the skeptical reader once more, Dostoevsky falls into the jeering tone of the underground man: "There's a Utopia for you, gentlemen! Everything is based on feelings, on nature, not on reason. Why, this actually humbles the reason. What do you think? Is this a Utopia or not?" If by Utopia one means a not-yet-realized ideal, then for Dostoevsky the exchange he had just sketched was not Utopian at all; he firmly believed that such a ballet of moral sublimity actually *existed*—though in forms that were often imperfect and distorted—at the heart of Russian peasant life. And this state of social harmony was not only impossible for, but even incomprehensible to, the European personality, which could not conceive of obtaining anything for itself without a struggle against others. "Its demands are made belligerently, it insists on its rights, requires an equal status—and that is the end of brotherhood" (5: 80-81).

When the Slavophils had glorified the *obshchina* in similar terms, the Westerners had always responded with one standard objection: the Russian commune did not allow for the full development of individual personality. Significantly, this is the very argument that Dostoevsky imagines his Russian readers advancing against his definition of true brotherhood.[7] " 'Yes, but,' you will say, 'is it necessary to be without character in order to be happy? Is salvation really to be found in "characterlessness"?' " To which Dostoevsky replies that, on the contrary, brotherhood requires a much higher development of personality than has been attained in the West: "Understand me: a voluntary, totally conscious sacrifice of oneself in the interests of all, made under no sort of compulsion, is in my opinion a sign of the highest development of the personality. Voluntarily to sacrifice one's life for all, to die on the cross or at the stake, is possible only with the very strongest development of personality" (5: 79).

This sacrifice, moreover, must be made without the slightest suggestion or thought of recompense; if such an idea is present, then it ruins everything by destroying the underlying moral nature of the act of self-sacrifice and turning it into a utilitarian calculation. Even the slightest estimate of advantages to be obtained is the "one little hair" that, if it gets into the machinery, can destroy the delicate balance of renunciations. "One must make the sacrifice," Dostoevsky explains, "so as to give all and even desire that nothing can be given in return, so that nobody is deprived of anything on your behalf." From which it follows that true brotherhood cannot be artificially established or created: "it must live unconsciously in the nature of the entire race, in a word: to have the brotherly principle of love—one must love. One must instinctively be drawn to brotherhood . . . despite the age-old sufferings of a nation, despite the barbarous crudity and ignorance that has taken root there, despite age-old slavery and the invasion of foreign races—in a word, the need for brotherly communion must be in the nature of a people, must be born with them or have been assimilated as a way of life from time immemorial" (5: 80). It is thus only the Russian people who are capable of brotherhood; all attempts to establish this principle in the West, as an alternative to the horrors of the war of all against all, are doomed to failure.

6

This is the context in which Dostoevsky raises the question of Socialism, which had just then ceased to have much importance in Europe but was still crucial in Russia.* It was the Socialists, Dostoevsky concedes, who really took the ideal of *fraternité* seriously and tried to find ways of putting it into practice. They proclaim: "All for one and one for all!"—and nothing better than such an ideal, Dostoevsky agrees, can possibly be imagined, especially since, as he slyly observes, "this formula is taken unchanged from a book everyone is familiar with" (it is the epigraph of Cabet's famous Utopian Socialist novel, *Voyage en Icarie*). But when the Socialists confront as their major obstacle the nature of European man, to whom the principle of brotherhood is spiritually alien, they appeal to his reason, and try to convince him that brotherhood will be to everyone's advantage once it is established. The Socialists argue, preach, explain, draw up plans and projects, and point out with great specificity just what benefits will accrue and "just how much each [individual] must freely contribute, at the detriment of his personality, to the commune [*obshchina*]" (5: 81).

Dostoevsky, to do him justice, does not accuse the Socialist ideal of involving any compulsion. On the contrary, he explicitly recognizes that the Socialists desire an entirely voluntary acceptance of their goals; yet he accepts as axiomatic that Socialism—the Utopian Socialism of the mid-nineteenth century, with its endeavor to establish ideal communities and entirely to transform human relations—involves an encroachment on the rights of personality. This postulate, so self-evident for Dostoevsky that he does not take the trouble to explain it, must be understood in the perspective of his implicit comparison with the Russian commune. The Russian, for whom brotherhood is a vital instinct, experiences no inner conflict as the result of the self-sacrifices demanded by life in his village. But the European, whose primary instinct is egoistic self-interest rather than brotherhood, can only feel the demands of the Socialist commune as an infringement on the complete autonomy of his individual personality. For this reason, the rational motive of self-interest—the motive that the Russian radicals, following Chernyshevsky, were in the process of making the cornerstone of their world-view—is the "hair" that will destroy the innate Russian instinct of true brotherhood once it gets into the machinery.

To buttress this conclusion, Dostoevsky mentions a few incidents from the checkered history of Socialist communities (those of Cabet and Victor Considérant), about which he was obviously well informed. Most such attempts quickly fell apart as a result of internal bickering and disagreement, and Dostoevsky draws what seems to him the pertinent lesson:

* See the remark of Herzen, in his *Ends and Beginnings, 1862-1863*, that "it is easier to picture Europe returning to the Catholicism of the time of Gregory Hildebrandt at the invitation of Donoso Cortés and Count Montalembert, than as a socialist republic on Fourier's or Cabet's pattern. But who speaks seriously of socialism nowadays? The European world may rest easy on that score; the shutters are put up, there is no heat-lightning on the horizon, the thunder is far away. . . ." Alexander Herzen, *My Thoughts and Past*, trans. Constance Garnett, rev. Humphrey Higgins (New York, 1968), 4: 1736.

Naturally there is something very tempting about living, if not fraternally, then at least on a purely rational basis, i.e., it is fine when all protect you and require of you only work and agreement. But here a mystery arises: it seems that man is completely protected, promised food, drink, and work, and for all this he is asked in return only a small drop of his personal freedom for the good of all, the tiniest, tiniest drop. But no, man does not like to live by such calculations, even this tiny drop is burdensome. It seems to him, stupidly, *that this is prison* and that he is better off by himself because—he is completely free. And, you know, even though he is flayed alive for this freedom, obtains no work, starves to death, and his free will is equal to nothing—all the same, it seems to this eccentric fellow that his free will is better. (5: 81; italics added)

In this momentous passage, we can observe the bitter lessons of Dostoevsky's prison years, with their nightmarish proof of man's ineradicable need to *feel* free, combining with his reflections on Socialism, on the Russian commune, and on the relations of Russia with Europe, to create the outlines of the underground man. For the "eccentric fellow" (*chudak*) who materializes in this quotation, and refuses to give up the tiniest drop of his freedom as the price for joining the Socialist commune, clearly provides the first glimpse of this memorable character.

Faced with the choice of preserving the full autonomy of personality or surrendering part of it in order to obtain some self-advantage, mankind, Dostoevsky firmly believed, would instinctively choose suffering and hardship for the sake of freedom. This is why rational Socialist communes are doomed to failure, and why the acceptance of European ideas by Russian radicals—ideas that accentuate the self-regarding elements of the human psyche—is so disastrous. Dostoevsky thus considers the revolt of the *chudak*, under such circumstances, as inevitable and even salutary (which explains his seeming identification with the similar revolt of the underground man against the laws of nature). In both instances, we have a defense and assertion of the positive value of moral-psychic freedom. But, as Dostoevsky also indicates, the consequences of such behavior *without* any possibility of reconciliation between the individual and society will inevitably be self-destructive; and only a world governed by the Christian moral-social ideals still alive in the Russian commune can thus ward off chaos. Only in such a world will the freedom of the personality be respected and recognized; only here will the individual be inspired by the spirit of love to surrender his personality, not for the sake of a presumed self-advantage, but for the good of all.

As for the Socialists, they will inevitably consider the stubbornly irrational resistance of "eccentric fellows" to their benevolent plans as totally absurd and abuse them with scornful contempt. They will "spit and tell him [whoever refuses to join] that he is a fool, a child, has not grown up yet and does not understand his own interest; that an ant, some insignificant, speechless ant, is more intelligent, because after all in the ant-heap everything is so fine, so controlled, everyone is fed, happy, each knows his job, in a word: man has still not caught up with the ant-heap!" And when the appeal to reason and self-interest finally proves a failure, the Socialists will fall back on their ultimate slogan: *"liberté, égalité, fraternité ou la mort!"*; but the bourgeoisie, who so far have had the heavier artillery, will then win an easy victory as in 1848. Dostoevsky thus concludes that "if Socialism is possible anywhere, it can only be somewhere that is not France" (5: 81).

Clearly, this "somewhere" is Russia, the country in which the principle of communality exists as an age-old heritage of the Russian folk psyche. But this principle is rooted in a Christian ethic of self-sacrifice rather than in a Utilitarian doctrine of self-interest, and the effect of propagating the second can only be to destroy the first—and thus, paradoxically, to destroy the very basis of the possibility of a successful Socialism in Russia and the world. From Dostoevsky's point of view, then, whatever we may think of its plausibility, his opposition to the philosophy of "rational egoism" was a defense of the Russian commune; and this commune was the destined foundation, singled out by the hand of Providence, on which the Christian-Socialist society of the future would be built. He was convinced that, once realized in Russia, it would blossom into a new and glorious phase of world history.

7

Dostoevsky's *Winter Notes* thus brings us right to the threshold of his great creative period, which begins with the composition of *Notes from Underground* two years later; and while these articles have been sadly neglected by students of his work, we have tried to show how intimately they are connected with the process of artistic gestation that occurred at this time. It is not so much that *Winter Notes* contains some of the major symbols and motifs of *Notes from Underground*—the liver complaint, the ant-heap, the Crystal Palace, the "stupid" recalcitrance of the "eccentric fellow" to surrender even the tiniest drop of his freedom to the artificial and rational Socialist community. Even more important is the rhetoric of inverted irony, which the underground man will simply internalize at a much higher level of philosophical and psychological self-awareness. For he will concentrate within himself *all* the contradictions arising from the ambivalent Russian attitude toward Europe as represented by the two radical ideologies that Dostoevsky had so far encountered in his lifetime: the rational egoism and materialism of the 1860s and the philanthropic and Romantic Utopian Socialism of the 1840s.

In *Winter Notes*, too, we can catch very perceptibly the way in which an artistic character emerges in Dostoevsky's creative imagination as a result of his reflections on the consequences of an ideological attitude. The "eccentric fellow" suddenly appears as a living incarnation of the refusal of the human personality to surrender an iota of its personal freedom even in exchange for quite substantial practical benefits. Other examples of the same process have already been noted: the paradisial prison imagined for the unpublished supplement to *House of the Dead*, and the character of Prince Valkovsky, in whom Dostoevsky depicts an "ideological" personality carrying the theory of egoism to an extreme in practice. Dostoevsky's artistic sensibility has now begun to operate more and more along such lines—through the imaginative dramatization of the absolute limits of an idea, and by the intuitive realization of the concrete human behavior appropriate to existing in such "fantastic" (though perfectly verisimilar) situations. This growing tendency toward what may be called ideological eschatology, combined with the psychological genius that Dostoevsky has already so amply demonstrated, will open up to him the path to his great works.

PART III

Polina

CHAPTER 17

An Emancipated
Woman

Despite the severity of the permanent interdiction of *Time*, its editors and chief contributors could not believe that the fatal misunderstanding on which it was based would long continue. Strakhov, whose reputation was personally at stake, hurriedly wrote letters to Katkov and Ivan Aksakov explaining his loyalty and devotion to the Russian cause. He even thought of appealing directly to the Tsar, but was dissuaded from doing so by an influential friend, the censor A. V. Nikitenko, who made some discreet inquiries in court circles. The censorship would not even allow Strakhov's letters to be printed in the journals to which they were addressed; but Katkov, magnanimous to a repentant foe, replied that he did not doubt the sincerity of his explanations and would try to clarify the matter in an article.

Hopes thus revived, as Dostoevsky wrote to Turgenev in mid-June, that the situation could be rectified and the decision of the authorities reversed. "We have some hope that the banning of our journal is only temporary. There is no certainty, but we have good reasons to believe so; all this will become clearer in September."[1] A week or two later, Katkov's article lifted the dire accusation of pro-Polonism from *Time*'s shoulders; but he continued to take sharp objection to the principles of *pochvennichestvo*, whose cloudiness he decried as being at the root of the trouble. Still, this article paved the way for the authorities to change their mind, although they took longer to do so than Dostoevsky had anticipated.

Meanwhile, he had taken a firm decision to travel abroad again during the summer months, although funds were now extremely tight and he could no longer count on *Time* to finance the journey. According to Strakhov, however, Dostoevsky believed that his first trip abroad had greatly improved his health, and his epileptic attacks had become less frequent during his European stay. Dostoevsky himself told Turgenev that he was coming to Paris and Berlin primarily to consult specialists in epilepsy (he gives the names of two doctors). "If you knew the depressions I have after my attacks," he writes despairingly, "and which sometimes last for weeks!"[2] There is no reason to doubt the genuineness of such declarations; but Dostoevsky was also eager to go abroad for another motive that he could scarcely avow in public. Waiting for him when he arrived in Paris would be his new traveling companion, also a contributor to *Time* like Strakhov but, in this instance, a female and a very attractive one: the twenty-three-year-old Apollinaria Suslova, the second great love of Dostoevsky's life.

2

Very little is known about Dostoevsky's conjugal existence with Marya Dimitrievna after his return to Petersburg from exile. But the very absence of information, the lack of any but the most fleeting references to her in Dostoevsky's letters and in memoirs of the period, already tells us something if only by inference. It would suggest that she lived largely in seclusion, whether by necessity or choice; and she often spent long periods of time in other cities with a milder climate than Petersburg. It is typical that young Vladislavlev—housed right next door and an admirer of her husband, as well as almost a member of the family—should have seen her so infrequently and noted laconically: "I do not usually go there." Her tuberculosis had continued to worsen, and it is likely that she had crises of hysterical rage similar to those of the equally tubercular and equally embittered Katerina Ivanovna of *Crime and Punishment*. The terrible disappointment expressed by that character in her marriage may correspond to feelings also voiced, in moments of despairing fury, by Marya Dimitrievna.*

Dostoevsky had earlier sought relief from such domestic tribulations in a flirtation with the cultivated and talented Alexandra Shubert. It is also quite possible that he had relations with other women of which we know nothing; he was not at all averse to such casual encounters when the occasion made them feasible. There are some shocked remarks by Strakhov—a perennial bachelor, apparently terrified of women—that may be taken as referring to such indulgences, although they are prudently extended to characterize the attitude of the Milyukov circle as a whole. "People who were extremely sensitive in moral relations, who nourished the most exalted kind of thought," he writes, "and who, for the most part, were far removed from any sort of physical dissoluteness, nonetheless looked quite calmly on all disorders of this kind and spoke of them as amusing trifles, which it was quite permissible to surrender to in moments of leisure."[3]

Dostoevsky's own view of such questions is illustrated in a letter to Baron Wrangel, who had been engaged in a desperate love affair with a coquettish

---

* Among the mass of material left by Anna Grigoryevna Dostoevsky concerning her husband's private life, there is only one—though quite lurid—allusion to his relations with his first wife. Terribly upset by some reproaches made to her for having been harsh, the truly all-forbearing Anna Grigoryevna, now aggrieved, jotted down in her journal: "Really I was beside myself. That's all the thanks I get for never grumbling at him. It isn't worth controlling oneself. *Marya Dimitrievna never hesitated to call him a rogue and a rascal and a criminal, and to her he was like an obedient dog.*" *Dnevnik A. G. Dostoevskoi 1867* (Moscow, 1923), 326; italics added.

and promiscuous older woman in Siberia. In his diagnosis of the lady's character, Dostoevsky reveals some of his own far from priggish attitude toward such temptresses. Wrangel's inamorata, he explains to the younger man, is incapable of fidelity and of "a complete and continuous love. She can give a minute of voluptuousness and total happiness, but only a minute; she cannot promise anything more than that, and if she does, she is deceiving herself and ought not to be blamed; that's why one should accept that minute, be infinitely grateful for it—and that's all. You will make her happy by leaving her in peace." A few sentences later, Dostoevsky adds: "If the man is resigned and content, these creatures are capable (according to my memories) of maintaining a sincere and intimate friendship with him, and even, on occasion, to recommence the love affair."[4] Such words, especially the reference to "memories," would suggest that Dostoevsky had had affairs of this kind himself.

All the same, Dostoevsky was not a libertine who could be satisfied with purely sensual and fleeting satisfactions; nor would he, like Baudelaire, separate the flesh and the spirit as sources of two entirely different kinds of pleasure. He had been attracted to Marya Dimitrievna not only physically but also because of her qualities of mind and the nobility of her character, and he sought a similar combination in other women. It may be that he met Apollinaria Suslova—as Dostoevsky's daughter reports in her extremely unreliable memoirs—after the hero-worshipping young girl had sent a declaration of love to the admired author.[5] More likely, if letters were exchanged, they dealt at first with less romantic matters. A story by Suslova was published in the tenth issue of *Time* (October 1861), and she would hardly have missed the chance to visit the editorial bureau of the journal: the intrepid Miss Suslova, then all of twenty-one, was not someone to hesitate taking a step then considered bold for a respectable young lady. Her story, *For the Time Being*, depicts a young woman who determinedly runs away from an unloved husband to escape boredom and depression, and earns her own meager living by giving lessons. Soon dying of tuberculosis brought on by the hardships of her life, she regrets nothing, and is proud of having remained true to herself. No better or worse than scores of others, the story is a typical product of the Russian movement for female emancipation in the 1860s; and Suslova intended her own life to be a living incarnation of such a protest.

3
———

What do we know about Apollinaria Suslova—Dostoevsky's beloved Polina—before she entered his life? Not very much, and that little due largely to her remarkable younger sister Nadezhda, who became the first Russian woman to obtain a medical degree and whose life has thus been investigated as a pioneer of women's liberation. Both girls came from a family of peasant-serf stock, and their history is an excellent illustration of the rise of the *raznochintsy* intelligentsia. Their father, an enterprising serf of Count Sheremetev, had managed to buy his freedom even before the liberation; and he then became one of the managers of the count's estates. Apollinaria Suslova spent her early years in the countryside growing up among the peasantry, and prideful references to her closeness to the *muzhiki* appear in her *Diary*.

The family moved to Petersburg when she was fifteen, and the sisters were sent to a private school where they learned foreign languages but apparently little else. They soon took full advantage of the opening of the University of St. Petersburg to the public, and attended the lecture courses offered there by various noted professors. Apollinaria is known to have worked as a teacher in the Sunday-school movement, and both girls also tried their hand at literary composition. Apollinaria led the way by her contributions to *Time*; the younger Nadezhda later published two stories in *The Contemporary* during 1864, but her interests shifted shortly thereafter to medicine. This useful scientific profession was then all the rage among the youth, who took as their models Bazarov and the medical heroes of another popular novel, Chernyshevsky's *What Is To Be Done?* (1863). Apollinaria, however, continued for a much longer time to cherish the hope of pursuing a literary career.

It is impossible to establish the exact moment when she and Dostoevsky became lovers; the most likely date is sometime during the winter of 1862-1863. Nothing reliable is known about the intimate details of their relationship, although the imagination of biographers has not been loath to invent the most titillating conjectures about Dostoevsky's presumed sexual demands on a young and inexperienced mistress. The documents at our disposal do not provide the slightest support for such flights of lubricious fancy; and Suslova's own attitude toward him, as seen in her *Diary* and other papers, does not justify any notion that he had assaulted and outraged her virgin sensibilities by any sexual excesses or perversities.

On the contrary, in a letter to Dostoevsky written shortly after the publication of *Notes from Underground* (about which she had evidently heard some comment), Suslova remonstrates: "What sort of scandalous story are you writing? We [she and her friends in Paris] are going to read it. . . . But I don't like you to write cynical things. Somehow, it is not in keeping with you; at least not as I imagined you to be earlier."[6] These are hardly the words of a maiden who had discovered, to her horror, that Dostoevsky was a sexual monster. Moreover, for all her emancipation, Suslova also had a good dose of Russian radical highmindedness and would have found any abnormality to be acutely distasteful. "The theater presents some awful filth!" she notes in her *Diary* about French vaudeville. "Dirty things are

12. Apollinaria Suslova. From Dominique Arban et al.,
Dostoïevski (Paris, 1971)

said on the stage and the actresses make gestures that one is embarrassed to look at."[7]

Speculations of sexual abuse can thus be dismissed. But there is ample evidence that the Dostoevsky-Suslova liaison did not go smoothly after the first excitement of possession and novelty had worn off, and whatever strains began to appear could, very plausibly, have had a sexual aspect. After all, there was a twenty-year difference of age between the two; and Dostoevsky, in addition, was weighed down by worry over Marya Dimitrievna, drained by his crushing editorial and literary obligations, and compelled to cope with the depressing and enervating effects of epileptic attacks recurring at this time with shorter and shorter intervals of respite. It is difficult to imagine that he could have made a very satisfactory lover for an ardent and inexperienced young girl, and one suspects that he aroused Suslova's sensuality without being able to satisfy it entirely. When she was offhandedly seduced a few months later by a young and handsome Spanish medical student seeking some diversion in the Latin Quarter, she responded to his caresses with a rapturous intensity that argues a previous gnawing sense of sexual dissatisfaction.

Such inferences, however reasonable, can only remain hypothetical; but another source of conflict between the two soon cast a pall over the idyll of their romance. Suslova was a young Russian feminist of the 1860s, who scorned conventional public opinion and despised the views held by such opinion regarding the relations between the sexes. Indeed, she regarded herself precisely as a person courageous enough to defy old-fashioned prejudices for the sake of her convictions. "All my friends are kind people," she notes in her *Diary*, "but weak and poor in spirit; they are abundant in their words, but poor in their deeds. I haven't met a single one among them who would not be afraid of the truth, or who wouldn't have retreated before the conventions of life. . . . *I cannot respect such people*. I consider it a crime to talk one way and act another" (italics added).[8]

These words are contained in the draft of a letter to her Spanish lover, Salvador; and Dostoevsky is certainly included among the "friends" that Suslova mentions here with such disdain. For if we try to imagine the conditions of their intimacy, it will be easy to see why her respect for him was inevitably bound to decline. Dostoevsky's romance was no secret from his brother Mikhail, but he made strenuous efforts to keep it hidden from others. He was terrified that gossip might get back to Marya Dimitrievna and make their common life together even stormier than it was; we may also assume, more charitably, that he did not wish to cause the consumptive invalid any extra suffering. He was thus forced to meet Suslova on the sly and to hide their love affair from the prying eyes of the world—exactly the sort of kowtowing to social bigotry that would have revolted her to the core. Inevitably too, with all his other pressing duties and responsibilities, he was compelled to relegate her to a comparatively minor place in his life and to see her only during those brief periods he could snatch from more urgent concerns. Such a demeaning situation would have upset even an ordinary young girl involved in the first great love affair of her life. With the high-spirited and mettlesome Suslova, uncompromising in her belief that actions should be entirely consonant with words (such as, for example, professions of love), the result could only have been to create a strong sense of resentment against the man she had surrendered to and idolized, and who, she could not help feeling, had betrayed her trust.

Among her papers was found the undated draft of a letter intended for Dostoevsky but, so far as we know, never sent; and what she says there provides the best confirmation of the picture we have just sketched. "You asked me not to write you that I am ashamed of my love for you," she says. "Not only will I not write this, I can [even] assure you that I have never written such a thing or thought of writing it [because] I was never ashamed of my love for you: it was beautiful, even grandiose. I might have written you that I blushed on account of our earlier relations. But there can be nothing new to you in this, for I have never concealed them [?], and how many times I wanted to break them off before I left for abroad."[9] The terms used to characterize her love for Dostoevsky ("beautiful," "grandiose") indicate some of the exalted expectations she had cherished on entering the affair. But what had ruined everything was the nature of their "relations"; and while this word can be given a sexual connotation, the context indicates it should not be taken exclusively in such a sense.

As Suslova explains, Dostoevsky "could never understand" that their "relations" were not "proper" because he always felt them to be so from his point of view: "You behaved like a serious, busy man, [who] understood his obligations after his own [fashion], but would not miss his pleasures either; on the contrary, perhaps even found it necessary to have some pleasure, on the grounds that some great doctor or philosopher once said that it was necessary to get drunk every month." Such words surely suggest a malaise, but one deriving from a sense of occupying a distinctly secondary place in Dostoevsky's life—of having simply become part of a routine that included the physical release provided by their secret liaison. What inspires her sarcasm is a suspicion of being "used" for Dostoevsky's convenience, his failure to reciprocate her own "beautiful" and "grandiose" sentiments in an appropriate manner. The same attitude is expressed in one of her short stories (unpublished), which is obviously based on her affair with Dostoevsky. Here the heroine tells her ex-lover: "The conditions under which our relationship developed, owing to the circumstances, were unbearable to me because of their ambiguity, yet I could not renounce you either."[10]

Twenty years later, Suslova's second husband, the noted philosophical essayist V. V. Rozanov (whose first important book was a classic study of Dostoevsky, *The Legend of the Grand Inquisitor*), once asked her why, in the end, she and Dostoevsky had become estranged. He reports their conversation in a letter to a third party:

"Because he did not wish to divorce his wife, who was tubercular and dying."

"You say she was dying. . . ."

"Yes. She was dying. She died six months later. But I was no longer in love with Feodor."

"Why did you stop loving him?"

"Because he would not get a divorce. . . . I gave myself to him, out of love, without asking anything. He should have behaved in the same way! He behaved otherwise and I left him."[11]

To make matters worse, when quarrels began to break out between them, Dostoevsky could do little more than wring his hands in anguish and guilt; he proved incapable of behaving according to Suslova's conception of what it meant to be a man. In an entry in her *Diary* made a year later, while mulling over her previous relations with her ex-lover Salvador (she had just caught an accidental glimpse of him in the street), she writes: "And what is it I want of him now? That he should confess his guilt, be remorseful, that is, be a Feodor Mikhailovich?"[12] Dostoevsky's name, as we see, has now taken on the deprecating meaning of someone who can do nothing but cravenly acknowledge his contrition.

Such was the mood in which Suslova preceded Dostoevsky to Paris in the early spring of 1863, there to await his arrival; and he certainly looked forward all the more eagerly to joining her because, at last, he would be able to devote himself to her with the exclusive attention she so much resented not having received. Why she left beforehand is unclear, though perhaps the editorial affairs of the banned periodical were in such disarray that Dostoevsky, not knowing for certain when he could leave, did not wish to make her wait indefinitely. Perhaps, unhappy over the situation we have described, she wished to precede him with the obscure presentiment that some new adventure might await her on European soil, the traditional Russian locus for what Stendhal calls *amour-passion.* Whatever the reason, she went on ahead while Dostoevsky attempted to raise funds by offering his next work to another journal (*The Library for Reading*) and, when this failed, obtaining a loan of 1,500 rubles from the Literary Fund. In return, and as guarantee, he offered the rights to all his already published works in perpetuity if he failed to repay his debt by February 1864. The risks involved in such a guarantee were of course enormous, and they indicate how determined he was, at whatever price, to manage what would be a honeymoon trip with his adored Polina through France and Italy.

4

When Dostoevsky finally left Petersburg in mid-August, one might have thought he would hasten to Paris by the fastest route. Instead, he delayed his trip to make a four-day stopover in Wiesbaden for a fling at the gaming tables. His first try at roulette the year before had netted him 11,000 francs, and this initial success, if we are to believe Strakhov, was the fatal lure that led him on and nourished the gambling fever by which he was soon to become possessed.[13] At Wiesbaden he began by winning 10,400 francs, and he had enough self-control to take his windfall away, put the money in his suitcase, and make a vow not to return to the casino. But, as was so often to happen in the future, he could not sustain such a reasonable resolution; he returned to the hypnotic lure of the spinning wheel and lost half his winnings. In a letter to his wife's sister, V. D. Constant, written shortly thereafter from Paris, Dostoevsky explains that he is keeping part of what is left for himself, sending part to Mikhail for safekeeping, and enclosing another part to her for the expenses of Marya Dimitrievna. The latter was spending the summer in Vladimir, and taking some kind of cure that might call for extra outlays.[14]

This pause at Wiesbaden may be considered the true beginning of the gambling mania that invariably swept over Dostoevsky whenever he came to Europe during the 1860s (there is no evidence that any significant gambling occurred in Russia). Much—far too much—attention is usually devoted to these gambling interludes in standard accounts of his life; one would think that no other Russian writer of equal stature had ever indulged a similar propensity. In fact, Tolstoy was a madcap plunger as a young man, and Nekrasov won and lost huge amounts (he mostly won) on the turn of a card. Dostoevsky differed from them only in not being able to afford his losses (he could not sell an estate like Tolstoy, including all its "souls," to pay off a debt) and in always losing rather than gaining a fortune as did Nekrasov. Moreover, the fitful and sporadic character of his gambling, as well as the fact that he firmly stopped once having attained a little emotional and financial security, strongly argues against overestimating the importance of this addiction in the total picture of his life. He was not a congenital and incurably pathological gambler—like the character he depicts in his famous novella, *The Gambler*, too often taken for a self-portrait—but only a repetitive one, subject to recurring episodes and capable of abstention for the greater part of his life. The psychiatric literature draws a clear distinction between these two types.

The immediate cause of Dostoevsky's gambling, at least as he explained it to his intimates, was always the banal one of hoping to win enough money to rescue him from difficult situations; and though he usually ended by losing every penny, it cannot be said that his aim was *entirely* unreasonable. He frequently *did* win large sums, which he then proceeded to lose either immediately or soon thereafter—exactly as at Wiesbaden—because he could never stop in time. All the same, his winnings always convinced him that success—and a solution to all his material needs and worries—lay within tantalizing reach of his grasp. Telling Mikhail how he had quickly racked up gains of 3,000 francs at Wiesbaden, he writes: "Tell me: after that how is it possible not to be carried away, why should I not believe that happiness is in my grasp if I stick rigorously to my system? And I need money, for myself, for you, for my wife, to write a novel. . . . Yes, I have come here in order to save you all and to save myself."[15] Nonetheless, gambling quite obviously satisfied some deep psychic need for Dostoevsky, and its hold over him cannot be attributed solely to such pragmatic motives. It is equally clear, however, that this need became a *dominant* force in his personality only during special periods of stress. One such condition was evidently a sharp worsening of his economic situation, such as the disappearance of *Time* and, along with it, his sole reliable source of income. The influence of other conditions, which equally placed him in precarious emotional straits, will soon become clearer.

There is no general agreement among neuropsychiatrists as to the causes of a gambling obsession, and a recent authoritative survey of the question warns against accepting any of the too-hasty and too-sweeping generalizations propounded in psychoanalytic treatments of the subject. The attempt to link gambling with specific sexual maladjustments has not proven successful, and, as Dr. Harvey R. Greenberg wryly remarks, "it must be deemed moot whether they [compulsive and repetitive gamblers] are truly suffering from a defensive displacement of libido from bedroom to bookie."[16] Freud's connection of gambling with "conflicts . . . centered around masturbation" has met with skepticism even among Freudians themselves: Otto Fenichel has honestly admitted that such an etiology "hardly suffices to explain the specific passion for gambling."[17] Fenichel's own classification of gambling among the impulse-neuroses has received more widespread acceptance, and some of his other observations are also helpful in coming close to Dostoevsky's situation.

Quite surprisingly, Fenichel speaks of gambling not so much in the perspective of its presumed sexual origins as in relation to its *significance* for the anxiety-ridden gambler, using a phenomenological rather than a strictly Freudian approach. "Gambling, in its essence," he writes, "is a provocation of fate, which is forced to make its decision for or against the individual." Such words are reminiscent of the more traditional "metaphysical" and Romantic view of gambling expressed by, among others, a writer whom Dostoevsky greatly admired, E.T.A. Hoffmann. Another observation by Fenichel is even more relevant in this context: "The gambler dares to compel the gods to make a decision about him, hoping for their forgiveness; but even to lose (to be sentenced or killed) seems to him preferable to a continuation of the unbearable superego pressure."[18] Fenichel does not mention Dostoevsky at all in his discussion of gambling neurosis, but his views dovetail almost exactly with what we know of Dostoevsky's own situation.

Nothing is more obvious, in the first place, than that Dostoevsky was overcome with particularly acute feelings of guilt each time he went abroad. Just before his first trip he writes his younger brother Andrey: "Now I am going off [alone], I leave my brother and I say to myself: how will he manage by himself (with *Time*)? I was after all a zealous collaborator."[19] In his letter to Strakhov from Paris, on the same journey, he speaks of his feelings of depression and sadness and implicitly attributes them to guilt: "One feels that he [the traveler] has broken the attachments with his soil, his essential, native routine, the current cares of one's own family."[20] For the *pochvennik* Dostoevsky, personal concerns blend naturally with his ideology of devotion to his native land; the very act of going abroad was thus in itself a source of increased emotional perturbation.

On his second trip, Dostoevsky left Mikhail in the lurch to grapple single-handedly with the desperate problems caused by the suppression of *Time*. And he went to meet his young mistress fully realizing that Marya Dimitrievna was at death's door, while he had already taken a very risky gamble on his ability to repay his debt. To make matters worse, he had left his refractory and ne'er-do-well stepson Pasha in the tutelage of a young radical contributor to *Time*, and he became increasingly worried during his trip about Pasha's behavior and the absence of any word about Marya Dimitrievna's condition. A letter to Mikhail from Turin expresses more explicitly the same sentiments as a year earlier (when he was traveling with Strakhov), and thus cannot be entirely attributed to the difficulties of his relations with Suslova at this moment: "To seek happiness in leaving everything, even in that in which I might have been useful, is egoism, and this thought now poisons my happiness (if there is such a thing as happiness at all)."[21]

The burden of Dostoevsky's superego as he embarked on this second trip to Europe must surely have been crushing, and it was increased even further by the tensions that had already developed in his affair with Suslova. His pause to play roulette at Wiesbaden before going on to meet her thus becomes perfectly comprehensible as an effort to find some release from the oppression of his anxiety and guilt, and, in effect, to appeal to the gods for a sign of forgiveness. Nor should we forget in this context that Dostoevsky was unashamedly superstitious and genuinely believed in signs, omens, and portents. His friend Baron Wrangel had already remarked on this trait of his character in Siberia; and more recently, in a letter to an unknown correspondent containing drawings of Old Church Slavic characters that Dostoevsky had seen in a dream, he excitedly asks for some interpretation of what he obviously considered to be a prophetic message.[22]

Of course Dostoevsky hoped to win—and thus to assuage his guilt by compensating those he had abandoned and betrayed (Mikhail and Marya Dimitrievna), while receiving reassurance and absolution at the same time for his adulterous relation with Suslova. What usually happened, though, was that he atoned for his sins by being justly punished and suffering agonies of humiliation when he lost, although in Wiesbaden he did not go under completely. Psychoanalytic interpreters of Dostoevsky's character, lacking Fenichel's breadth of vision, tend to stress only this masochistic component of his gambling obsession. But to reduce it simply to a search for self-punishment seems to me totally inadequate as an account of Dostoevsky's oscillating hopes and fears, and his genuine conviction of the possibility of a miraculous solution to all his financial anxieties.

Whatever the psychic origins of Dostoevsky's gambling mania, its most interesting feature was the theory he developed about it—a theory that links it firmly with the themes of his great novels. For what Dostoevsky calls his "system," in the letter to Mikhail already cited, is not really a system at all. It is merely the conviction that, if he could entirely succeed in mastering his emotions, if he could impose an iron self-control on his feelings—if, in other words, he could suppress the whole irrational part of his psyche—why, then he would certainly win! "Do not believe that I am boasting in saying that I know the secret of winning in my joy at not having lost," he tells V. D. Constant. "This secret, I really know it; it's terribly stupid and simple and consists in holding oneself in at every moment and not to get excited, no matter what the play. And that's all; it's then absolutely impossible to lose, and one is sure of winning."

As Dostoevsky above all was in a position to know, however, human beings are not exclusively creatures of reason and self-control; to dominate oneself to the extent demanded is an almost impossible task. There were people at the gaming tables (he mentions "a Frenchwoman and an English lord" at Wiesbaden) who had mastered the art, and he could evidently do so himself for all-too-brief periods. But, the letter to Constant goes on, "however clever you may be, with a will of iron, you will succumb all the same. Even Strakhov the philosopher would succumb. So, happy are those who do not gamble and look on roulette with the utmost distaste and as a vast stupidity."[23] Gambling for Dostoevsky thus implicitly involved an attempt to raise oneself above the level of the human; and in these unpretentious and apologetic remarks Dostoevsky is actually touching on one of the great themes of Western literature—a theme that he would shortly take up himself. For one cannot help thinking here of Marlowe's *Dr. Faustus*, as well as of the Machiavellian villains of Elizabethan tragedy, who pit a cold and calculating reason against all the moral dictates of conscience standing in the way of an unbridled pursuit of self-interest. In the tradition of European literature, such attempts to put into practice this dream of the icy self-domination of reason have invariably been depicted as a source of sacrilege and of monstrous moral disorder. For they signify mankind's attempt to set itself up as a rival of, and a replacement for, the will of the Christian God, who had endowed the human species with a middling rank and an ambiguous status in that great chain of being which ruled the imagination of Western man for so many centuries. Something of this traditional view still persists in Dostoevsky, and in *Crime and Punishment* he will soon portray the consequences of a similar belief in the supremacy of the power of naked human reason to supplant the workings of conscience.

Gambling may thus also be regarded as a continual testing by Dostoevsky of his overriding conviction of the power of the irrational in human existence; he was not only seeking to relieve his guilt feelings, but also, at the same time, engaged in deciding whether his deepest beliefs about human life were justified. As a result, he could not win without losing (since his success negated his own highest values), or lose without winning (since his defeat confirmed the ultimate roots of his view of man and human life). This inner contradiction helps us to understand why, in the long run, he was doomed to gamble away his winnings in uncontrollable excitement. For by doing so he was paradoxically affirming his acceptance of the proper order of the universe as he conceived of it, and learning the same lesson as the underground man and all of his great negative heros beginning with Raskolnikov who deludedly believe they can master and suppress the irrational promptings of Christian conscience. After each such episode, in any case, Dostoevsky always returned to his writing desk with renewed vigor and a sense of deliverance.

5

By the time Dostoevsky arrived in Paris on August 14, 1863, the unhappy fate of his romance with Suslova had already been sealed. Just a few days before, she had fallen into the masterful Spanish arms of the irresistible Salvador; and since her *Diary* begins at this very moment, we can follow the course of events in some detail. At first, she explains, "I had wanted to see him [Dostoevsky] so that I could tell him everything." But then she made up her mind to break the news in a letter that she confides to her notebook; and this document discloses so much about their past relations, and about Suslova herself, that it must be cited in full. It begins brutally:

> You are coming too late. . . . Only very recently I was dreaming of going to Italy with you, and I even began to learn Italian; everything has changed within a few days. You told me one day that I would never surrender my heart easily. I have surrendered it within a week's time, at the first call, without a struggle, without assurance, almost without hope that I was being loved. I was right to get angry with you, when you began to sing my praises. Don't think that I am shaming you, but I want to tell you that you did not know me, nor did I know myself. Good-bye, dear!
>
> I would like to see you, but what would it lead to? I would very much like to talk to you about Russia.

Such words were certainly meant to wound to the quick, and they convey the impression that Suslova's easy acquiescence may have been partly prompted by a desire to take revenge on Dostoevsky. In any case, her attitude toward him as a person, if not as a lover, is obviously quite ambivalent and will remain so. The text of her *Diary* continues: "At this moment I am very, very sad. How generous, how high-minded he is [evidently Dostoevsky]. What an intellect! What a soul!"[24]

Whether or not Suslova had really abandoned herself to Salvador "almost without hope that I was being loved," she was already aware that his flaming Latin passion had cooled considerably after conquest. Upset by her lover's offhand remark that he might be going to South America soon on family business, and his persistent inquiries as to when she was leaving for Italy, Suslova begins to despair and falls back on her pride. "Today I have been thinking a great deal," she writes, "and I almost felt glad that Salvador loves me so little; it makes me freer. I feel like seeing Europe and America, going to London for some advice [to visit Herzen, whom she had not met so far], and then joining the *beguny* sect."[25] Exactly what she thought life would be like among the "runners" may be left to conjecture; but Shchapov's depiction of them in *Time* as an enticing symbol of the spirit of democratic libertarianism among the Russian people had clearly caught her fancy. This entry was made four days before Dostoevsky was scheduled to step off the train.

In the interim, Salvador had failed to keep an appointment and added insult to injury by leaving unanswered a letter deposited in his room. Suslova continued to fight against admitting the awful truth, but was too lucid not to recognize her abandonment. Dostoevsky turned up in the midst of this drama, having first, as per agreement, notified her by mail that he was in Paris. She replied by sending off the letter drafted in her *Diary*; but he was too impatient to wait for word and left his hotel room to call on her before it arrived. The account of their meeting, as depicted by Suslova, is too long to quote, but some extracts are indispensable for a proper understanding of their relationship.

On seeing her emerge to meet him, trembling and upset, he instantly asked what was wrong, and she blurted out awkwardly that he should not have come "because it's too late." Dostoevsky then "hung his head," almost as if having expected the blow, and said: "I must know everything, let's go somewhere, and tell me, or I'll die." The two left in a carriage for Dostoevsky's hotel, and both stared blankly into space as he kept shouting to the startled cabman to drive faster; but he "kept hold of my hand all the way, pressing it hard from time to time and making some sort of convulsive movements." Once in Dostoevsky's room, a scene occurred that Suslova later used verbatim in a short story: "He fell at my feet, and, putting his arms around my knees, clasping them and sobbing, he exclaimed between sobs: 'I have lost you, I knew it!' Then, having regained his composure, he began to ask me about the man. 'Perhaps he is handsome, young, and glib. But you will never find a heart such as mine!' "[26] Dostoevsky, it seems evident, had all along feared losing her to a younger and handsomer rival, and he now saw his worst forebodings as having come true.

He soon realized, however, that Suslova herself was by no means happy with his replacement. Indeed, she finally broke down and began to weep herself, explaining that her own love was unrequited. "Oh, Polina, why must you be so unhappy," Dostoevsky is quoted as responding. "It had to happen that you would fall in love with another man. I knew it. Why, you fell in love with me by mistake, because yours is a generous heart, you waited until you were twenty-three, you are the only woman who does not demand of a man that he obligate himself in any way, but at what price: a man and a woman are not one and the same. He takes, she gives."[27] At this point, Dostoevsky's own sense of pain is overcome both by gratitude to Suslova for the past, and by a desire to warn her of the dangers incurred by her "emancipated" unwillingness to protect herself against the consequences of her "generosity." Dostoevsky's view here was dramatized later in *The Devils*, where Shatov's emancipated wife, who had become the mistress of Stavrogin, is forced to suffer the agonies of childbirth while the indifferent Stavrogin pays no attention at all to the results of his dalliance.

Suslova then went on to describe "what kind of man the other was," and Dostoevsky "said that he experienced a feeling of disgust at that moment: that he felt better knowing that he was not a serious person, no Lermontov."[28] Probably encouraged by what must have been Suslova's unflattering picture of her seducer, Dostoevsky revived and began to hope that all was not lost. After all, he had been in much the same situation with Marya Dimitrievna over Vergunov, the young schoolteacher who had been his rival, and he had managed to redress the balance in his favor.[29] "He told me," Suslova continues, "that he was happy to have met a human being such as I was in this world. He begged me to remain his friend. . . . Then he suggested that we travel to Italy together, while remaining like brother and sister." Her response to this proposal gives us a glimpse into one of the previous sources of her discontent. "When I told him that, most probably, he would be writing his novel, he answered: 'What do you take me for? Do you think that all this is going to pass without leaving an impression?' " The conversation concluded with a promise of further meetings, and an acknowledgment by Suslova of Dostoevsky's continued hold over her affections: "I felt relieved after I had talked with him. He understands me."[30]

6
———

For the next week, matters remained in this indecisive stage. Suslova saw Dostoevsky regularly (she mentions in one entry "coming home from F.M. rather late"), while at the same time writing letters, both proud and pleading, to Salvador, unable to make up her mind whether or not to send them.

On September 1, she found a letter in her room from a "friend" of her Spanish cavalier, explaining that he was ill with typhus and being cared for by family connections who would become suspicious if she paid him a visit. The poor girl, completely taken in by this cruel ruse, immediately penned "an answer . . . telling him [the letter writer] that I considered it barbaric that I could not see Sal[vador], thinking him on the edge of the grave." Whether Dostoevsky accepted the initial letter at face value is doubtful; but he tried to reassure her, and "told me that what with the air they have here, and the medical care available, it shouldn't be dangerous."[31]

An obscure reference suggests that Suslova then moved to Salvador's hotel, probably to be able to nurse him through his convalescence, and expected to receive a visit from his "friend" with some news. But while taking a walk in the streets adjacent to the Sorbonne, she unexpectedly ran into Salvador himself, large as life, although looking pale and flushed. He offered an embarrassed explanation, told her that his illness had not been typhus at all, barely looked at the letter she asked him to read, and found an obviously false pretext to quit her company as rapidly as possible. "Once alone," she writes, "I quickly understood what had happened. When I found myself alone in my room I became hysterical. I screamed that I was going to kill him." Apparently she decided to carry out her resolution: "I made everything ready, burned some of my notebooks and letters (those letters that would compromise me). *I felt wonderfully well*" (italics added). Not having slept all night, Suslova rushed to Dostoevsky at seven in the morning the next day. Opening the door for her in his nightclothes, the startled Dostoevsky then "went back to bed wrapping himself up in his blanket. He looked at me with astonishment and apprehension. . . . I told him that he should come to my place right away. I wanted to tell him everything and ask him to be my judge."[32]

By the time Dostoevsky arrived, Suslova's mood had changed completely: she came to meet him munching a piece of toast, and declared with a laugh that she was now much calmer. "Yes," he said, "and I am very glad about that, but who can tell anything for sure when it concerns you?" Now for the first time Suslova told him the whole story, concealing nothing, and Dostoevsky advised her to forget about the unhappy betrayal. "I had, of course, sullied myself, but . . . it had only been an accident. . . . Sal[vador], being a young man, needed a mistress, and I happened to be available so he took advantage of me, and why shouldn't he have done so? A pretty woman, agreeable to all tastes." Suslova now admits that "F.M. was right, I understood perfectly well, but how hard it was for me!"[33]

Dostoevsky was still afraid that Suslova might "come up with some foolishness," and warned her against doing anything rash. Her reply tells us a good deal about herself, as well as about her future relations with Dostoevsky and the portrait he was to paint of her later in *The Gambler*. " 'I would not like to kill him' I said, 'but I would like to torture him for a very long time.' " Another passage in her *Diary* elaborates on this impulse: "Right now I suddenly feel a desire to avenge myself, but how? By what means?" Suslova finally decided to send Salvador a sum of money in payment for the "service" he had rendered her, hoping by this gesture to wound the *hidalgo* dignity that had previously impressed her in his character. Dostoevsky opposed this idea because he believed that "subconsciously, I was using this as a pretext to get in touch with Sal[vador]," and also because "he finds I ought to suffer (renounce my vengeance) for my stupidity. . . ."[34] The insulting letter was sent nonetheless, but the new missive elicited no more reply than all the others.

A few days later, Suslova and Dostoevsky departed on their long-planned trip to Italy in response to Dostoevsky's proposal that they undertake the journey as "brother and sister." He would have been less than human if he had not hoped that his role of friend and counselor would eventually return again to being that of lover; but Suslova was seething with an unappeased desire for vengeance, and in the absence of Salvador she turned on the hapless Dostoevsky instead. He too, after all, was an ex-lover who had betrayed her expectations; and while grateful for his continued sympathy and solicitude, she also took a sadistic pleasure in treating him as she no doubt imagined herself treating Salvador if he had been within her reach.

CHAPTER 18

A Tormented Lover

Dostoevsky and Suslova left Paris sometime during the first week of September, although their plans for travel remained uncertain until the moment of departure. "My health isn't very good," Dostoevsky writes his sister-in-law on September 1. "I do not think I shall remain in Paris much longer. Perhaps I will go to Italy. Everything depends on circumstances."[1] Since an entry in Suslova's *Diary* for the 5th of September was made in Baden-Baden, the pair must have left a day or two earlier; and what Suslova jots down about her feelings on this first stop along the way hardly bodes well for the future of their journey. In Paris, she confesses, "I lost a great deal [of hope]. It seems to me that I shall never love anybody. A thirst for revenge burned in my soul for a long time after [?], and I decided that, if I do not become distracted in Italy, I will return to Paris and do as I had planned" (presumably kill Salvador).[2]

Dostoevsky, on the other hand, was in very high spirits on leaving, buoyed up by Suslova's encouraging decision to depart and the conviction that half of the battle to win her back had already been won. His exuberance was well displayed in an incident that Suslova refers to amusedly as "a row at the Papal Embassy."[3] Rome, in those years, was within the diplomatic jurisdiction of the Vatican, and it was necessary to obtain a visa from the Papal authorities to visit the territory. The two Russian subjects accordingly presented themselves at the Papal Embassy in Paris, and Dostoevsky later used what occurred there as the basis of a scene in *The Gambler*.

Negligently told to wait "by a little Abbé, fiftyish, all dried up and with a frosty expression on his face," Dostoevsky sat down and began to read *L'Opinion Nationale*, which, like most French journals of the period, was strongly anti-Russian. Noticing very soon that various other arrivals were being admitted to the Monsignor in charge, he became terribly annoyed and asked to be taken care of "since the Monsignor was receiving callers." But he was told—with, as he felt, an answering stare of unutterable contempt—that the Monsignor could not be disturbed over coffee on *his* account. At this, Dostoevsky flared up: "Let me tell you that I spit on your Monsignor's coffee," he shouted, and threatened to invade the chambers himself unless some action were taken. He was, he thundered, "a heretic and a barbarian," and "did not care a bit for all [the] Archbishops, Monsignors, etc., etc." (5: 211). The frightened Abbé, believing Russians capable of anything, hastened out of the room, and a moment later Dostoevsky obtained not only his visa but the additional satisfaction of having successfully revolted against being treated as an inferior. Never a patient or placid person, Dostoevsky's anti-Catholicism would have provided ample provocation for his unseemly outburst; but the temptation to impress Suslova probably gave an extra fillip of bravado to his performance.

2

During the trip from Paris to Baden-Baden, the conversation between the pair turned to Lermontov (whose name decidedly seems to have haunted their relationship), and Suslova recalled a line from one of his most famous poems, *The Demon*, in which the poet pronounces anathema on the entire world. Suddenly, her own misfortunes "appeared so petty, so unworthy of any serious attention"—why indeed give them any thought at all? Lermontov's demon, she decided, was right in assuming a complete indifference to the universe; but Suslova herself could not attain such a superior level of all-embracing scorn. "I feel sick," she writes. "That would be too unjust. It seems to me that certain laws of justice exist in nature."[4] If such laws of justice do exist, then she logically and implacably refuses to surrender her idea of obtaining revenge for everything she has suffered.

Another diary entry reveals her ego in the process of obtaining satisfaction for the painful wounds inflicted by the unhappy past: "While we were enroute here, he [Dostoevsky] told me he had some hope, though he had earlier insisted that he had none. *I did not say anything to this, but I knew it was not going to happen*" (italics added).[5] Suslova clearly did not wish to discourage Dostoevsky too severely, but she had, all the same, firmly made up her mind not to resume their previous relations; her behavior thus continued to inflame his passion while frustrating its satisfaction. There can be no doubt that she was deliberately playing with his emotions; but she was probably less cold and calculating than her own journal might lead one to believe. Certainly she derived some consolation from the ardency of Dostoevsky's wooing; and there were occasional moments of tenderness, such as the one she describes when, lying on her bed, she summoned Dostoevsky to sit close by and hold her hand. "I felt good," she notes. "I took his hand and for a long time held it in mine. . . . I told him that I had been unfair and unkind to him in Paris, that it may have seemed as though I had been thinking only of myself, yet I had been thinking of him, too, but did not want to say it, so as not to hurt him."[6]

No wonder Dostoevsky suddenly leaped to his feet, stumbled, explained that he wished to close the window, but then admitted, "with a strange expression" on his face, that he had just been on the point of bending to kiss her foot. Desiring then to undress and go to bed, Suslova indicated as much indirectly; but Dostoevsky invented various excuses for not leaving the room immediately and then came back several times on one pretext or another. When it became clear that Suslova would remain adamant, he finally closed his door (the two had adjoining rooms). The next day he apologized for his behavior "and said that he had been drunk [actually they had only been drinking tea]. Then he said that I must probably find it unpleasant, the way he was annoying me. I answered that I didn't mind, and refused to be drawn into a discussion of the subject, *so that he could neither cherish hope nor be quite without it*" (italics added).[7] Suslova later excerpted this particular scene from her notebook and used it, dialogue and all, in a short story, although without including her private commentary on the action.

The evening after this incident, she reflects on her behavior and wonders about the change that has taken place in her character. Her conduct toward Dostoevsky certainly did not conform with her old ideals, and the pure embodiment of these ideals now appears before her mind's eye: "I just remembered my sister; she would have censured me for my trip to Italy, but I don't feel that way myself." Suslova consoles herself with the reflection that, after all, she "has a passion for traveling" and learning. Why should she not see the world while she has the chance? But this feeble justification only touches the surface, and she admits that something far more basic is taking place: "And actually, that catechism which I had made up for myself, which I was so proud to have lived by, now seems very narrow to me. It was an involvement that would lead to narrowness and dullness of spirit." The "catechism" in question probably refers to that credo of absolute equality, sincerity, and honesty in personal relations advocated by the radicals of the 1860s, and which Suslova had now found to be so treacherous and inadequate. "I have my peace of mind now," she writes. "I notice that a revolution is taking place in my thinking."[8]

Dostoevsky was forced to bear the emotional brunt of this inner revolution, although at first not fully aware of what was taking place. His mood at the start was light-hearted and ebullient, and Suslova writes that "the journey here [to Baden-Baden] with F.M. was rather entertaining . . . he spoke in verse during the entire trip, and finally, here, where we had some trouble finding two rooms with two beds, he signed the guest register 'officer' at which we had to laugh a lot. He plays roulette all the time and is generally very carefree."[9] Dostoevsky was, legally speaking, a retired officer of the Russian Army, and he had every right to the designation. But Russian officers were also the traditional darlings of the ladies, and he was surely casting himself for such a conquering romantic role in the very near future.

Dostoevsky's gaiety, however, did not continue for very long; and though Suslova's evasiveness was surely a major factor in the darkening of his disposition, his severe losses at roulette contributed their share as well. At the start, he tells Mikhail, "I came to the table [at Baden] and in *a quarter of an hour* had won 600 francs. That fired me up. Suddenly, I began to lose, I couldn't stop, and I lost everything, down to the last kopek."[10] Suslova mentions casually that "F.M. has lost some money gambling and is a bit worried about not having enough money for our journey."[11] Her nonchalant tone indicates that Dostoevsky was trying to put a good face on his difficulties for her benefit, but his letters home tell quite a different story. He pleads with Mikhail to scrape together whatever he can and send it immediately, and he asks his sister-in-law to retrieve for him one hundred rubles from the amount dispatched earlier for Marya Dimitrievna. The diplomatic maneuvers involved in such a task were extremely intricate, and Dostoevsky takes several pages to explain how the feat might be accomplished without arousing Marya Dimitrievna's stormy susceptibilities.

As if all this were not enough, Dostoevsky's agitated stay in Baden-Baden was further complicated by the obligation to call on Turgenev, who had settled there recently in a *ménage à trois* with Pauline Viardot, her husband, and family. Turgenev would have been offended if he had heard of Dostoevsky's passage by accident; but Dostoevsky also knew that, if he caught sight of Suslova, tongues would immediately start to wag in Petersburg. "At Baden I saw Turgenev," Dostoevsky reports to Mikhail. "I visited him twice and he came to see me once in return. He did not see A.P. I did not want him to know. He is depressed, although he has been cured thanks to Baden. . . . He spoke to me of all his moral torments and his doubts. Philosophic doubts, but which undermine life. A bit fatuous. I did not hide from him that I gambled. He gave me *Phantoms* to read, but gambling prevented me from reading and I returned it unread. He said that he wrote it for our journal and that if, once in Rome, I ask him for it, he will send it there. But what do I know of the journal?"[12]

The sensitive Turgenev was still suffering from the uproar caused by *Fathers and Children*, especially from the unrelenting hostility of that portion of the radical press (*The Contemporary* and *The Spark*) which continued to consider the work a defamation of the younger generation. Moreover, he had quite recently come under the dispiriting influence of Schopenhauer, and, just a few months earlier, Herzen had written him: "With your Schopenhauer you've become a Nihilist"—not of course a Russian one, imbued with combative spirit and faith in the future, but a Schopenhauerian variant weighed down by the belief that existence is only a realm of unrelieved suffering.[13] Such were the "philosophical doubts" that Turgenev confessed to a Dostoevsky hardly in the frame of mind to be a receptive listener, and who, having fought his own way back from hopelessness, would scarcely have sympathized with such ideas under any conditions. The failure to read *Phantoms*, destined for *Time* or whatever journal replaced it, was of course a terrible *faux pas*, and Mikhail's cry of anguish when he read the above passage can be heard in his response. "Do you know what Turgenev means for us *now*?" he wails to his brother.[14] Nothing could have been a greater affront to Turgenev's considerable literary vanity, especially at this troubled moment of his career. But *Phantoms* did appear, all the same, in the first number of *Epoch*, thus testifying to the good will Turgenev continued to nourish for the defenders of *Fathers and Children*.

3

Dostoevsky had asked that the money he so urgently requested be forwarded to Turin, where it would await them once the ill-matched pair, alternating between tenderness and tantrums, had crossed the Alps by way of Switzerland. On arrival, however, they found nothing, and both lived in constant fear of being summoned to pay their hotel bill and dragged to the police. "Here, that's how things are done," Dostoevsky informs Mikhail; "no arrangement is possible . . . and I am not alone here. It's horrible!" But such an awful eventuality did not occur, and the eagerly awaited funds finally came to the rescue. Meanwhile, Dostoevsky had not been idle and even tried to do some writing—perhaps a travel article, perhaps some notes for *The Gambler*; but, he tells Mikhail, "I tore up everything I had written in Turin. I have had enough of writing on order."[15]

Despite the harassments attendant on his joyless wanderings, Dostoevsky still found the time seriously to further his education. "Tell Strakhov that I am carefully reading the Slavophils," he instructs Mikhail, "and that I have found something new."[16] These words confirm that Dostoevsky's previous knowledge of Slavophilism had largely been acquired at second-hand. A reference in Suslova's *Diary* indicates that she too was probably leafing through some of the texts that her ex- and would-be lover was perusing. "Yesterday, in Turin, I read something about philosophy, and, contrary to my expectations," she writes with engaging candor, "understood a thing or two."[17] What she understood was that Kant had said that things-in-themselves could not be known, while Hegel arrived at the idea that things exist only in the concept. Since Slavophil thought was steeped in German Idealism, it is likely that she had come across this distinction in one of their works.

Another entry in Suslova's *Diary* once more discloses those erratic oscillations of her sentiments that made Dostoevsky's situation so emotionally confusing and vexatious. "I feel once more a tenderness toward F.M.," she confides. "It happened that I was upbraiding him, and later I felt that I had been wrong, so I wanted to make up for it and I became tender with him. He responded with such joy I was moved by it, and I became twice as tender. When I was sitting next to him, looking at him caressingly, he said:

'There is that familiar look, it's a long time since I saw it last!' I let my head fall on his chest and began to cry." Most of Suslova's jottings are taken up with such fluctuations of her own unstable emotions, but occasionally she gives us a glimpse of a Dostoevsky concerned with other matters than regaining his place in her affections. At Turin, we suddenly see him musing over the iniquities of absolute power and anticipating one of the motifs of *Crime and Punishment*: "As we were having dinner, he said, looking at a little girl who was doing her lessons: 'Well, imagine, there you have a little girl like her with an old man, and suddenly some Napoleon says, "I want this city destroyed." It has always been that way in this world.' "[18]

4
———

After a stormy sea voyage from Genoa, with a stopover in Livorno, the two arrived in Rome to spend some time in the Eternal City. Dostoevsky wrote a number of letters from Rome, but they are all concerned with practical matters and singularly lack any personal reactions to the grandiose spectacle spread before him by the ruins of the ancient capital and the majesty of the modern seat of Papal authority. "Strange: I write from *Rome*, and not a word about Rome," he cannot help remarking to Strakhov in a postscript. All the same, he does make one brief comment: "Yesterday morning, I visited St. Peter's! The impression is very strong, Nikolay Nikolaevich, and gives one a shiver up the spine."[19]

The shiver, one presumes, was not caused by aesthetic appreciation but rather by the mighty power for evil that Dostoevsky always associated with the Roman Church. A sentence or two later, surely not by accident, Dostoevsky again refers to the Slavophils. "The Slavophils, naturally," he tells Strakhov, "have pronounced some *new words*, and of such a kind that even the initiates have not yet been able to adjust to them. In solving social questions they put on astonishingly well-fed airs: satiated aristocrats."[20] Dostoevsky has not really changed his mind, and continues to view the Slavophils as obdurately reactionary on social issues; but he has now discovered something original in them of fundamental importance. What can this possibly be that he had not been aware of before?

Dostoevsky's apparent Slavophilism in the early 1860s, as we have seen, had been assimilated through Belinsky and Herzen, from whose writings he had absorbed a rejection of Russian Europeanism as well as an echo and confirmation of his own Messianic hopes for a Russia destined to provide mankind with the future form of its social organization. But what he could not have discovered through them was the systematic *theological* basis that the Slavophils had provided for such ideas. Slavophil theology was bitterly anti-Catholic, and traced all the evils of mankind, past and present, back to the Roman Catholic pope's assumption of the temporal power once possessed by the Roman emperors.* St. Peter's, in Dostoevsky's eyes, could only have been seen as the living embodiment of such un-Christian claims to worldly grandeur, and his visit to Rome thus coincided with a very important phase in the evolution of his ideas. Dostoevsky had of course long been anti-Catholic, and had believed that the Orthodox Christianity of Russia would provide a principle of renewal for the modern world; but he had held such notions more in the form of prejudices than of doctrines. Slavophil thought now gave them a wide-ranging conceptual foundation, and it was only after Dostoevsky's second trip to Europe that he begins to express the opposition between Russia and Europe in primarily religious terms. "The Polish War," he confides to his notebook during the winter of 1863-1864, "is a war of two Christianities—it is the beginning of the future war between Orthodoxy and Catholicism, in other words—of the Slavic genius with European civilization" (20: 170).

The fluctuations of Dostoevsky's affair with Suslova seem to have reached a new phase in Rome, and her diary entries, which reveal the strange duel in which the pair now engaged, already prefigure some of the situations of *The Gambler*. Dostoevsky now openly begins to protest against Suslova's attitude toward him, and bluntly accuses her of moral sadism. "Yesterday F.M. was importunate again," she writes during their Roman stay. "He said I took too serious and stern a view of things that really were not worth it." More important, "he had the notion that it [her behavior] was just a caprice, a desire to torture him. 'You know that,' he said, 'you can't torture a man this long, for he will eventually quit trying.' " Dostoevsky also accused her of still being in love with Salvador (she admits this to be true in her *Diary*, but refuses to acknowledge it to him). Again, she notes that "when he [Dostoevsky] woke up he became unusually free and easy, cheer-

* In an article which has had a major influence on the history of Russian thought, Ivan Kireevsky declared that "the classical world of ancient paganism, which Russia lacked in her inheritance, represented in its essence a triumph of formal human reason over everything that is to be found inside and outside of it." This triumph of formal human reason led, among other disasters, to "the pope [becoming] the head of the church instead of Jesus Christ, then a temporal sovereign, finally infallible; the existence of God was being proved by a syllogism throughout the entire Christendom; the whole totality of faith was supported by syllogistic scholasticism; the Inquisition, Jesuitry, in one word, all the peculiarities of Catholicism developed through the power of the same formal process of reasoning, so that Protestantism itself, which the Catholics reproach with rationalism, developed directly out of the rationalism of Catholicism. A perspicacious mind could see in advance, in this final triumph of formal reason over faith and tradition, the entire present fate of Europe, as a result of a fallacious principle: Strauss and the new philosophy in all of its aspects; industrialism as the mainspring of social life; philanthropy based on calculated self-interest; the system of education accelerated by the power of aroused jealousy; Goethe, the crown of German poesy, the literary Talleyrand, who changes his beauty as the other changes his governments; Napoleon, the hero of our time, the ideal of soulless calculation; the numerical majority, a fruit of rationalistic politics; and Louis Philippe, the latest result of such hopes and such expensive experiments!"

These words illustrate some of the suggestive sweep of Slavophil thought, which coincides with Dostoevsky's ideas in so many ways. See, for the above citation and more information, Nicholas V. Riasanovsky, *Russia and the West in the Teaching of the Slavophiles* (rpt. Gloucester, Mass., 1965), 96.

ful and pressing. It was as though he wanted in this fashion to conquer his own inner hurt and sadness, and spite me." But, a little while later, he dropped the game of jocosity and admitted "I am unhappy"—at which "I embraced him with ardor," and the merry-go-round began once again. That evening, leaving Suslova's room at one in the morning, with his temptress lying fetchingly undressed in bed, Dostoevsky said "that it was humiliating for him to leave in this fashion. . . . 'For the Russians never did retreat.' "[21] Here we catch some of the serio-comic flavor of the contest between the two, which is quite close to the tonality of *The Gambler.*

It was in the midst of such scenes that *The Gambler* was originally conceived, and its first mention occurs in a letter to Strakhov from Rome. Dostoevsky continued to remain critically short of funds, and tried to raise some by asking his friend to offer magazine editors a new story idea in return for an advance. What Dostoevsky outlines is the first version of *The Gambler,* which at this stage was much more ambitious than the final redaction:

> The subject of this story is the following: a type of Russian man living abroad. Just remember: the newspapers this summer have often raised the question of Russians abroad. All this will be reflected in my story. It will be the mirror of the national reality, so far as possible of course. I imagine an impulsive character, but a man very cultivated nonetheless, incomplete in all things, having lost his faith *but not daring not to believe*, in revolt against the authorities and fearing them. He consoles himself by saying that he has *nothing to do* in Russia; at this point, a severe criticism of people in Russia who resemble our Russians abroad. But it is impossible to tell you everything. . . . The essential is that all his vital powers of life, his violences, his audacity are devoted to *roulette*. He is a gambler, but not an ordinary gambler—just as the Covetous Knight of Pushkin is not a simple merchant. . . . He is a poet in his fashion, but he is ashamed of that poetry because he profoundly feels its *baseness*, although the need of *risk* ennobles him in his own eyes. The story retraces how, for three years, he drags himself through the gambling houses and plays *roulette.*[22]

This is of course Dostoevsky's first stab at expressing his idea, and it contains a thematic complexity going far beyond what would ultimately be included in the finished composition. Indeed, the passage contains a motif manifestly pointing toward *Notes from Underground* and which will be appropriated for this earlier work. The conception of a character who has lost his faith but does not dare *not* to believe recalls the Golyadkin-type of *The Double,* terrified at his own audacity in stepping over the divinely sanctioned boundaries of the Russian caste system. Dostoevsky had continued to make notes for a revised version of this text all through 1860-1864; and a year after his letter about *The Gambler* he turned this type into the underground man, who also suffers from not daring *not* to believe in certain ideas that he finds incompatible with his moral sensibility. These ideas are no longer those that prop up the Russian bureaucratic system, but rather the essential tenets of the Western European ideologies that have invaded and reshaped the Russian moral-social psyche. What remained for *The Gambler* was the national theme, the delights and dangers of the "poetry of risk," and the emotional difficulties of Dostoevsky's tortuous involvement with Suslova (though only their psychological essence will be employed, not any of the actual circumstances).

5

The peregrinations of the pair, by turns quarreling and embracing (though Dostoevsky never regained his previous place as lover), next took them to Naples. By this time he was becoming thoroughly sick of the whole escapade, and longed to be back in Russia. From Rome, once again admonishing his stepson Pasha to pay more attention to his studies and less to hanging around the Yussopov Gardens (an amusement park on the outskirts of Petersburg), he adds: "I am well, and have not had any epileptic attacks; and though there is much here to see, to visit, and to be amused with, I still have a great desire to return to Russia. So much so that at certain moments it is painful for me to be here among strangers."23

How Dostoevsky had now begun to look on the trip may be inferred from a later letter to Turgenev that apologizes for not having provided a forwarding address to which *Phantoms* could be mailed. "I remained everywhere only for a brief time," he explains, "and it generally happened that, leaving one city, I scarcely knew in the evening where I would be the following day. Certain circumstances caused all these movements not always to depend on me; it was rather I who depended on circumstances."24 Even allowing for a certain exaggeration, Dostoevsky probably felt himself to have become a plaything of Suslova's whims and caprices, since the couple's destination more or less was decided by her changing moods from day to day. He thus firmly made up his mind in Rome that Naples was to be the last stop on their swing southward; from there he planned to go north again and return home via Turin and Geneva.

Nothing noteworthy occurred during their week-long stay in Naples: Suslova's *Diary* merely mentions that they were assailed by beggars and that a whole crowd gathered when they asked a question. But, as they were embarking at the port for the return trip to Livorno, they were, much to Dostoevsky's consternation, unexpectedly confronted with Herzen and his entire family also mounting the gangplank. It was impossible for Dostoevsky to conceal Suslova, and, she writes amusedly, "F.M. introduced me as a relative in very vague terms. He conducted himself in their presence as though he were my brother, or even closer [?], which must have puzzled H. somewhat. F.M. told him a great deal about me, and H. listened attentively."[25] Unfortunately, Suslova does not record Dostoevsky's words; but one imagines him dwelling on her literary ambitions and achievements and improvising frantically on the spur of the moment.

A rather amusing situation arose (not, of course, for Dostoevsky) because Herzen's oldest son, later to become a physiologist of renown, was also a member of the party. The twenty-four-year-old Alexander Jr. found Dostoevsky's young "relative" quite attractive, and the two soon became engaged in lively conversation. Suslova solemnly records that Alexander Jr. was "a kind of desperate young man," who, when she ventured the opinion that "I had found more or less the same disgusting situation everywhere" abroad, sweepingly "went on to prove that it was not 'more or less' but equally disgusting everywhere." As this agreeable meeting of minds was taking place, poor Dostoevsky was pacing up and down the deck, pretending as best he could to be highly gratified at the sight of his charming relative being diverted by an extremely eligible young man. Suslova, however, finally took pity on her distraught companion. "As I was conversing with [Alexander Jr.]," she writes, "being quite animated myself, F.M. walked by without stopping, and I asked him to join us, which made him quite glad."[26]

Discovering that Suslova was to be in Paris that winter, Alexander Jr., who planned to be there himself, said that he would look her up and asked for an address, but then remarked he could undoubtedly obtain it through a mutual acquaintance. To keep up appearances, Dostoevsky insisted that Suslova give Alexander Jr. her card "so as to show him more attention." Later, in private, "he told me nervously that I absolutely must write him if H. were to see me. This I promised to do. And in general, he did not discuss young H. with me at all, though when I brought up his name first, in a rather casual manner, he responded and spoke of him, not entirely in favorable terms."[27] The coquettish Suslova clearly could not resist teasing Dostoevsky just a little about young Herzen's attentions.

Suslova's diary provides no further details of the meeting between Herzen and Dostoevsky, but there is a fleeting reference to it in the recently published draft of an article that Dostoevsky wrote many years later for his *Diary of a Writer*. The article was prompted by the suicide of Herzen's youngest daughter Liza, and Dostoevsky initially intended to bring in some of his reminiscences of the family that he finally discarded. The variant, however, records a conversation on the boat from Naples with Olga, Herzen's second daughter, who "grieved over her father because everyone in Russia had turned away from him, considered him a traitor to Russia (this was the year of the Polish uprising); but she did not launch into a defense of him for me, did not explain his convictions" (23: 324). Evidently nourishing no such sentiments, Dostoevsky did not allow Herzen's support of the Poles to exclude personal relations and to overshadow all his other great services in stirring Russian consciousness and awakening Russian thought.

Traces of this incident can also be found in a work that Herzen wrote a year or so later, *Letters to an Adversary*, addressed to a prominent Slavophil, Yury Samarin. An old friend of Herzen's from his early Moscow days, Samarin had more recently emerged as a prominent Slavophil spokesman; as an important government functionary, he had also taken a leading role in furthering the emancipation of the serfs. During the course of his controversy with Samarin, Herzen recalls that "a year ago I met, on a boat between Naples and Livorno, a Russian who was reading the works of Khomyakov in a new edition. Since he was on the point of falling asleep, I asked him to hand me the book and read a good part of it." The Russian in question could only have been Dostoevsky, who thus gave Herzen the opportunity to renew his acquaintance with Slavophil thought at one of its most important sources.

What Herzen says about Khomyakov indicates to what extent his own ideas and those of his political adversaries still converged on essential issues. "I clearly saw that on many points, we [Khomyakov and himself] had understood the Western question in the same way, despite the differences in explanations and deductions. . . . The same is true as regards his appreciation of the specific elements of the life of the Russian people, which serves as the starting point of our own evolution." Herzen thus agreed with Khomyakov's negative evaluation of Western civilization and with the hopes placed by the Slavophils in the *obshchina*; but he refused to accept the Slavophil explanation, then in the course of impressing itself on Dostoevsky, of why Europe had gone astray.

Khomyakov affirms, Herzen writes, "that the entire history of the Occident, that is, almost *all* the history of fifteen hundred years, has not succeeded because the German-Latin peoples adopted the Catholic faith and not that of the Greek Orthodox religion. . . ." To which Herzen replies ironically that "in general, I have not been able to understand, either earlier or at present, why Christianity *is not Christian* outside the walls of the Oriental Church, nor why Russia represented the doctrine of liberty (not in practice, naturally . . .), and the Occident a doctrine based on necessity."[28] One cannot help wondering whether the two men discussed such reactions when Dostoevsky awoke and the volume was returned; but perhaps the conversation remained confined to those anti-Western sentiments about which Herzen and the Slavophils, as well as Dostoevsky, were in complete accord. On landing in Livorno, Dostoevsky made a particular point of accompanying the Herzen family to their hotel; and he went to lunch with them the next day, probably unaccompanied by Suslova since she fails to record any such visit.

This stimulating encounter with the representative of free Russian thought in Europe, which perhaps drew their minds away from their personal imbroglio, seems to have had a mollifying effect on the increasingly acrimonious relations between Dostoevsky and his recalcitrant beloved. "On the day of our departure from Naples," Suslova states, "F.M. and I quarreled, but on board ship, that same day, under the influence of our meeting with H., which animated us, we had a heart-to-heart talk and made up again (it was about the emancipation of women). From that day on we no longer had any arguments. I was with him almost [?] as I had been before, and I felt sorry having to part with him."²⁹ Whether Dostoevsky's feelings were exactly the same is difficult to judge; but while no longer under any illusions as to her character, his passion for Suslova had by no means abated, and it was painful for him to contemplate giving her up entirely. The two travelers thus parted on a note of reconciliation; and the alluring image of the tempting Apollinaria, who had never *completely* excluded the possibility of a resumption of their love affair—who always seemed to remain just ever so slightly, but not entirely, beyond his grasp—continued to haunt Dostoevsky for several more years to come.

6

By the time he reached Turin, on the road home, Dostoevsky's thoughts were preoccupied with other concerns, and he sketches for the benefit of Turgenev the discouraging prospect that he foresees awaiting him but which, all the same, he is eager to rejoin: "A difficult task awaits me in Petersburg. Although my health has infinitely improved, in two or three months it will, without doubt, be entirely destroyed. Nothing can be done about it. The journal has to be remade from scratch. It must be more up-to-date, more interesting, and at the same time it must respect literature—incompatible aims according to a number of Petersburg thinkers. But we have the intention of fighting fiercely against this contempt leveled at literature. We hope that we shall not lag behind. Support us I beg of you [by sending *Phantoms*], join us."³⁰

The same letter also contains an apology for Dostoevsky's impossible behavior at their last meeting in Baden, which he vaguely attributes to "the tumult of passions" (his gambling, although certainly thinking of Suslova as well) in which he was then caught. "If I had not the hope of doing something more intelligent in the future," he writes wryly, "really, I would be very ashamed now. But after all! Am I going to ask pardon of myself?"³¹ Far from doing so, Dostoevsky gambled once more in Hamburg, once more was stranded without a penny, and was forced to appeal to Suslova in Paris for help. A loyal friend, if not a docile mistress, she was about to pledge her watch and chain but managed to raise three hundred francs without this ultimate recourse. A chastened Dostoevsky limped home in early November to find matters still undecided so far as the journal was concerned, and his personal affairs in more disarray than he had anticipated.

Passing through Petersburg very rapidly, by November 10 Dostoevsky was in Vladimir with Marya Dimitrievna, whose condition obviously gave him a shock. "The health of Marya Dimitrievna is *very* bad," he wrote her sister in Petersburg. "She has been terribly ill for two months now. She was very badly looked after by her doctor; now she has a different one. She has been particularly worn out, for these past two months, by a continual fever."[32] Her situation was so grave that Dostoevsky decided not to return with her to the harsh climate of Petersburg and planned to live in Moscow, renting a small apartment in the northern capital where he could stay from time to time when looking after the affairs of the journal. A few days later, he writes her sister again "that Marya Dimitrievna, it seems, can become well again in Moscow. [Could he really have believed this?] We are running around, looking for a place to live, etc., etc."[33] Dostoevsky punctiliously introduced his wife to his Moscow relatives, obviously hoping they would look after her during his planned absences; and the financial pressures on him eased for the moment because his wealthy Moscow uncle, who had recently died, left him a bequest in his will. But this windfall provided the only bright spot in a situation that rapidly became more and more gloomy and tormenting.

PART IV

The Prison of Utopia

CHAPTER 19

Epoch

All during the summer and fall, Mikhail had been busily engaged in writing endless petitions to the authorities asking for permission to resume publication; and in mid-November his efforts were finally crowned with success. Permission was given, not to revive *Time*, but to publish a new journal, and Mikhail informs his brother that "I am now writing the announcement. And all this I must do without consulting with you. This, my friend, is very painful for me, and though I am a person of decision who does not falter in moments of difficulty, it is still very sad to have to act alone in a matter involving us all."[1] The loss of the previous name of the journal may seem insignificant, but was actually quite an important setback. It meant that the new publication could not benefit from the prestige already acquired by *Time* in the past two years, and would have to begin anew to establish itself in the eyes of the reading public. Mikhail's letter also bluntly reveals one of the key problems that the new journal faced from the outset: the absence of Feodor's guiding editorial hand and brilliant journalistic pen at the crucial moment when a new start was being made.

2

Dostoevsky nonetheless took as active a part as he could in the preparations, and there was a steady flow of correspondence between the two cities. The first matter on the agenda was that of a name, and the initial one proposed by Mikhail was *Pravda (Truth)*. Dostoevsky liked its feel and was quite enthusiastic: "So far as the title *Truth* is concerned, it is, in my opinion, perfect, astonishing, and to have hit upon it does us honor. . . . It includes *our most exact* idea, fits the circumstances, and especially, there is a kind of *naiveté*, of *faith*, about it which exactly corresponds to our spirit and our orientation because our review [*Time*] was always extremely naive, and who knows? perhaps it caught on through its naiveté and its faith." Dostoevsky suggested that the two titles be linked together in the announcement by some such slogan as "the Time demands the Truth," so that the second title could be seen as a natural outgrowth of the first. He also suggests that the announcement should be original and striking, even eccentric if need be, so as to attract attention; nothing could be worse than the usual rodomontade that everybody reads with a yawn. It should, he says, be "laconic, abrupt, proud," and "should not make any allusion [presumably to the unhappy past]; in a word, give evidence of the most complete assurance."[2]

The title that Dostoevsky found so perfect was unfortunately not accepted by the authorities, and objections were also made to *Pochva* (*Soil*) as more suitable for an agricultural publication. *Epokha* (*Epoch*) was finally hit upon; *Epoch* it remained; and the first public announcement asking for subscriptions was placed in the *St. Petersburg Gazette* at the end of January 1864. Since subscription announcements were usually made in the early fall, this delay in obtaining permission to publish meant that *Epoch* got off to a very bad financial start; most potential subscribers had already sent their money elsewhere. Also, the hope of publishing immediately in February proved impossible, and the first issue (a double one), which came off the presses only in April, created a regrettable impression of editorial disorganization and unreliability. Strakhov uncharitably blames Mikhail Dostoevsky for lacking energy at this crucial moment, forgetting to mention that Mikhail's youngest daughter Varya died of scarlet fever in February and that the poor father was prostrate with grief.

In the same letter that waxes eloquent over the title *Truth*, Dostoevsky also mentions three possible contributions he might be able to make to the first issue, although adding that "affairs [concerned with relocating in Moscow] do not leave me a moment for writing." To make matters worse, his epilepsy had returned, and "I have already had two attacks, one of which (the last) was very strong." Still, Dostoevsky believed that he would be able to write a lead article establishing the position of the journal, and he mentions two others as well: "A critique of the novel of Chernyshevsky and the one of Pisemsky would create a considerable effect, and especially would fit our affair. Two opposed ideas and both demolished. As a result, the truth."[3]

Pisemsky's *The Unruly Sea* (1863), which had been published in *The Russian Messenger*, was among the first of the important so-called anti-Nihilist novels that form a subcategory in Russian prose fiction of the nineteenth century. Such books differ from Turgenev's *Fathers and Children*, or Dostoevsky's *Crime and Punishment*, by depicting the Nihilists as outright scoundrels and villains moved only by the basest and most unsavory personal motives. Even the one novel of Dostoevsky that might be included in this class, *The Devils*, does not really go that far: Peter Verkhovensky is totally unscrupulous, but he does act out of principle (even if a totally perverted one) and not for sordid, purely private reasons. On the opposing side, Chernyshevsky's Utopian novel, *What Is To Be Done?* (1863), gave a glowing picture of the extraordinary moral virtues of the "new people" whom Turgenev had maligned with the label of Nihilist; and it also includes an enticing tableau of their future Utopian Socialist paradise. Just as he had done in the past, Dostoevsky wished to steer a middle ideological course between the slanders of the reactionaries and the daydreams of the radicals, aiming at a "truth" independent of both while doing justice to each at the same time.

Chernyshevsky, it will be recalled, had been arrested on July 7, 1862, and it may cause some confusion to see him mentioned now as the author of a novel legally published in 1863—a novel, moreover, whose subversive content is plain to the eyes of any intelligent reader. But the book, astonishingly, did appear with the official imprimatur of the censorship while Chernyshevsky was tightly under lock and key; and its publication is perhaps the most spectacular example of bureaucratic bungling in the cultural realm during the reign of Alexander II. It may also seem surprising that the literary essayist, philosophical commentator, historian, and economist Chernyshevsky should have turned his hand to fiction. But when imprisonment cut him off from his usual literary labors, he decided, with undaunted determination, to take a leaf from two writers he greatly admired, William Godwin and Harriet Beecher Stowe, and carry on his work as ideological mentor of the radicals by means of the novel. The result was *What Is To Be Done?*, which, for all its obvious artistic weaknesses, ranks as one of the most successful works of propaganda ever written in fictional form. Few books have had so direct and effective an impact on the lives of so wide a mass of people, beginning with the efforts of Chernyshevsky's immediate disciples to form Socialist cooperative communes similar to those he depicted, and continuing up to V. I. Lenin, whose admiration for Chernyshevsky's novel was unbounded and for whom it was a source of personal inspiration.*

3

What Is To Be Done? reached the pages of *The Contemporary* by a circuitous and often risible route, all of whose twists and turns have still not been charted. The journey began when Chernyshevsky sent the first installment

---

* Numerous testimony abounds as to the enormous importance of Chernyshevsky's novel in Russian social-cultural history. "The issues of *The Contemporary* in which it [the novel] had been printed," writes Andrzej Walicki, "were preserved with immense piety, as though they were family heirlooms. For many members of the younger generation the novel became a true 'encyclopedia of life and knowledge.' In her memoirs, Lenin's wife, Nadezhda Krupskaya, relates that her husband recalled the work in every slight detail. Plekhanov was not exaggerating when he declared that 'since the introduction of printing presses into Russia no printed work has had such a great success in Russia as Chernyshevsky's *What Is To Be Done?*'" Andrzej Walicki, *A History of Russian Thought*, trans. Hilda Andrews-Rusiecka (Oxford, 1975), 190.

Nikolay Valentinov, who knew Lenin very well, recalls in his memoirs a conversation in which he criticized the novel as being artistically deficient. "His [Lenin's] face stiffened and he flushed around the cheek-bones—this always happened when he was angry. . . . 'I declare,' he said, 'that it is impermissible to call *What Is To Be Done?* crude and untalented. . . . My brother, for example, was captivated by him [Chernyshevsky] and so was I. *He completely transformed my outlook.*" Nikolay Valentinov, *Encounters with Lenin*, trans. Paul Rosta and Brian Pearce (London, 1968), 63-64.

285

of the novel to Prince Golitsyn, who was the head of a commission appointed to investigate the charges against him. Finding nothing "political" in what he read (as indeed there is nothing *overtly* political in the novel as a whole), the Prince considered his obligations at an end and meticulously dispatched the manuscript to the censorship for more detailed inspection. The censor, impressed by the "stamp and wrappings" of the commission, assumed it had been approved and promptly passed it on to the journal. Whereupon Nekrasov, in a fit of absent-mindedness, left the pages of the first installment in a cab and advertised for its return in the newspaper of the St. Petersburg police. When it was retrieved, the police themselves dutifully turned over one of the most subversive texts in Russian literature to the anxious editor. These facts explain how the first installment was published; but why the remainder slipped through the censorship net, even after the revolutionary drift of the work was clear for all to see, still remains a mystery.

Printed in three issues of *The Contemporary* beginning in March 1863 (and partly overlapping with the publication of *Winter Notes*), the work created an indescribable commotion, much of which derived from its polemical relation to *Fathers and Children*. Chernyshevsky, as we know, staunchly believed that Turgenev's masterpiece was nothing but a dastardly caricature of Dobrolyubov; and his own book undertakes to present a more accurate image of the "new people" whom Turgenev had supposedly defamed (Dobrolyubov had first called the young radicals "new people," and Chernyshevsky picks up this phrase for his subtitle: "Tales About New People"). The two chief male characters, Lopukhov and Kirsanov, are both *raznochintsy* and medical students when the book opens—perfect analogues of Bazarov—but Kirsanov later succeeds in becoming one of the leading lights of international medicine. Both are part of a romantic triangle involving the heroine, Vera Pavlovna; but while Bazarov is destroyed when his fatal attraction to Mme Odintsova proves stronger than his will, quite the opposite occurs to Chernyshevsky's characters. Since they follow the precepts of "rational egoism," they are able to untie the woefully tangled love-knot without a quiver of the outdated romantic *Weltschmerz* that undoes Bazarov, or even a trace of such primitive emotions as resentment or jealousy. Chernyshevsky's heroes easily surmount all the obstacles that brought Bazarov to an untimely grave, and demonstrate, with crushing clarity, how badly Turgenev had distorted the true lineaments of the "new people."

This refutation of Turgenev would have been enough to guarantee the book its enormous success; but it gripped the imagination of its young readers even more strongly by offering solutions to the whole range of problems that preoccupied the radical intelligentsia in the 1860s—solutions which, it reassured them, could be put into successful practice with miraculous ease. Rational egoism was the wonder-working talisman that provided the final key to all human complexities—whether the relations between the sexes, the establishment of new social institutions, the attainment of success in private life, the hoodwinking of the stupid Tsarist authorities, or the total transformation of mankind both physically and spiritually in the future Earthly Paradise. All one had to do was accept a rigorous egoism as the norm of one's behavior, and then believe that a "rational" egoism compels one, by the sheer force of logic, always to identify self-interest with that of the greatest good of the greatest number.

It is hardly possible to suppress a smile as Chernyshevsky's virtuosos of virtue solemnly argue themselves into the conviction that a strict egoism alone determines all their actions. In reality, although ridiculing the ethics of self-sacrifice at every opportunity, they behave in perfect accordance with its precepts. But such behavior is not *felt* by them as self-sacrifice because, according to Chernyshevsky's image of human nature, once the principles of rational egoism are internalized, obsolescent reactions of "nonrational egoism" simply cease to exist. The passions and the emotions will thus *always* respond in a manner compatible with the injunctions of enlightened reason, which has proven once and for all that to benefit others is in reality the highest degree of self-concern. Nothing more self-renunciatory could possibly be imagined; but this display of the purest virtue is masked as the most arrant and egregious selfishness.

As an example, we may take Lopukhov's decision to marry Vera Pavlovna immediately, and so rescue her from familial oppression rather than waiting, as had been planned, until he obtained his medical degree; he thus throws up for Vera's sake the chance of a brilliant academic and medical career. Chernyshevsky is well aware that a corrupt and cynical "average" reader may well consider this to be very strange behavior for an "egoist." And he hastens to explain that Lopukhov had "made up his mind, conscientiously and resolutely, to renounce all material advantages and honors, so as to work for the benefit of others, finding that the pleasure of such work was the best utility for him."

Armed with this conviction, Lopukhov now finds it quite easy, even child's play, to give up everything he had striven all his life to attain. What worries him is only whether he is being perfectly consistent. Might he really be giving in to the enemy and making a sacrifice? Lopukhov reassures himself, as he is mulling over his decision, by the consoling reflection that "the notion of sacrifice is a false term; a sacrifice is equivalent to such nonsense as 'top-boots with soft-boiled eggs!' One acts in the way that's most agreeable." Instead of interpreting his own actions as a sacrifice, he uses them, on the contrary, to prove the omnipresence of egoism. "What a hypocrite!" he says of himself. "Why should I take a degree? Can't I live without diplomas? Perhaps, with lessons and translations, I'll make even more than a doctor."[4] On the basis of such reasoning, the troubled Lopukhov quiets his fears that he might be infringing the miraculous tenets of rational egoism.

The most finished illustration of this control of the will by the reason is the revolutionary Superman Rakhmetov, whose underground activity as an organizer is very skillfully conveyed by euphemisms. Rakhmetov is a monster of efficiency and self-mastery, who leads the life of a total ascetic while himself being in favor of the completest enjoyment and even of the liberation of the senses. Toughening himself by sleeping on a bed of nails, he subordinates all concern about other people to the attainment of his great unnamed purpose: revolution. Rakhmetov is a Bazarov wholeheartedly absorbed in his cause, unshakable and unconquerable in his strength, and deprived even of the few remaining traits of self-doubt and emotional responsiveness that make his predecessor humanly sympathetic. This ideal of the steel-nerved rationalist-revolutionary, who destroys all vestiges of personal sympathies and inclinations so as to comply with the icy logic of social utility, forms an intermediate link in the line leading from Bazarov to Raskolnikov.

4

For the Dostoevsky who had just written *House of the Dead* and *Winter Notes*, Chernyshevsky's novel, with its touchingly naive faith in Utilitarian reason, could hardly have been felt except as a direct challenge. And the challenge was all the more provoking because, in the famous fourth dream of Vera Pavlovna, one of Dostoevsky's own key symbols is used with a significance directly opposed to his interpretation. In this climactic passage, Chernyshevsky brushes in a tableau of the evolution of humanity in the pseudo-epical style used by French Social Romantics like Ballanche and Lamennais at the beginning of the century—an evolution that culminates in the advent of the Socialist Utopia. Not surprisingly, this Utopia turns out to resemble the life that Fourier had imagined for his ideal phalanstery; and it would certainly have brought back for Dostoevsky memories of his days in the Petrashevsky circle, where Fourier's ideas had been passionately revered and debated in an atmosphere of candid exaltation. Even then, however, the details of the Fourierist blueprint for the future had seemed to him rather ridiculous, and he had agreed with his friend Valerian Maikov that the phalanstery hardly left any leeway for the freedom of the individual.[5] Fourteen years later—and what years for Dostoevsky and Russia!—the resurgence of such fantasies could only have appeared to him as the height of absurdity. Once again he was confronted with this dream image of a future in which man had completely conquered nature, and established a way of life allowing all desires to be freely and completely satisfied. No gap exists in this world between every appetite and its satisfaction; all conflict, all unhappiness, all inner striving and spiritual agitation have totally vanished. This is the literal end of history, whose attainment marks the final stasis of mankind in an unending round of pleasure and gratification. For Dostoevsky, the ideal of such a world immediately called up images of Greco-Roman decadence and the inevitable growth of the most perverse passions in an effort to escape from the sheer boredom of total satiation.

To make matters worse, Chernyshevsky had selected as an icon of this glorious world of fulfillment the Crystal Palace of the London World's Fair—precisely the same edifice that Dostoevsky had seen as the monstrous incarnation of modern materialism, the contemporary version of the flesh goddess Baal. But, to Chernyshevsky's bedazzled eyes, this structure represented the first hint of what would become the gleaming visual embodiment of the Socialist Utopia of the future, the manifest goal of all human aspirations:

> A building, an enormous, enormous building, such as are now in but a few capitals and those the very largest—or no, there is not a single one like it now! It stands in the midst of fields and meadows, gardens and woods. . . . And that building, that kind of architecture is already hinted at in the palace that stands on Sydenham Hill. Glass and steel, steel and glass, and that is all. No, that is not all, that is only the shell of the building, that is its exterior walls. But there, inside, there is a real house, an enormous house. It is covered by this crystal and steel building as by a sheath. It is surrounded by broad galleries on every floor. . . . But how rich all this is! Aluminum everywhere, and all the spaces between windows are hung with mirrors. And what rugs on the floor! . . . And there are tropical trees and flowers everywhere. The whole house is a huge winter garden.[6]

The "palace that stands on Sydenham Hill," as everyone knew, was the Crystal Palace, which Chernyshevsky had probably visited on his secret trip to London to consult with Herzen, and which, in any event, he had written about sight unseen in 1854. In Chernyshevsky's pages, then, Dostoevsky once again encountered all the old Utopian dreams of the 1840s with which he was so familiar, now allied with the new faith in Utilitarian reason that ran so squarely counter to the sense of human life he had so painfully acquired. One can well see why, when it became necessary to supply an artistic text for *Epoch*, his initial intention of writing an article partly devoted to Chernyshevsky's novel should have blossomed into the idea of providing a more imaginative and artistic response.

5

The Dostoevskys were counting on being able to print Turgenev's *Phantoms* in their first number, and were thrown into consternation when its author began to have some second thoughts about publishing it at all. Since the prose poem *Phantoms* is a lyrical rhapsody playing variations on the theme of cosmic disillusionment and world-weariness, Turgenev thought, with some reason, that a work of this nature might be badly received in a period of rabid literary realism. In a letter to P. V. Annenkov, who looked after his affairs in Russia, he also expressed doubts as to whether the Dostoevskys really wanted his text or were only hoping to use his name as an advertisement on the cover of their journal. This disabused reflection, one suspects, was inspired by Dostoevsky's negligent attitude in Baden-Baden. To repair the damage, Mikhail urgently asked Feodor to write Turgenev, and the guilty party hastened to do so from St. Petersburg, where he was then on a visit to confer about editorial matters. The letter is of great interest, not only for the troubled history of the Dostoevsky-Turgenev relationship, but also because it enables us to glimpse some of the dialectic of *Notes from Underground* already germinating in Dostoevsky's sensibility.

Dostoevsky admits frankly that it would be a great asset to have Turgenev's name adorn the cover of *Epoch*; but, he assures the reluctant writer, "I give you my word of honor that we have much more need of your story than to dress up the cover of our review with your name." As for Turgenev's concern about the advisability of publishing a text of this nature, Dostoevsky responds with a tirade against the prevailing cultural trend. What is needed is precisely something different because "the mediocrities who for six years now have imitated the masters have sunk the real so low that a purely poetic work (eminently poetic) will even cause rejoicing. As for those who understand nothing, why worry about them? . . . A narrow Utilitarianism—that's all they ask for. Write the most poetic work for them; they will put it aside and take up one that describes somebody being flogged. *Poetic truth* is considered nonsense."[7]

Such words, seemingly not very diplomatic, might well have reinforced Turgenev's fears; but Dostoevsky hastens to reassure him that readers are aching for a change, and stresses the inner contradiction between the ideas the Nihilists espouse and their genuine feelings: "I know . . . the case of such a Utilitarian (a Nihilist) who, although dissatisfied with your story, agreed nonetheless that he could not tear himself away from it; that it left a strong impression. We have too many Nihilists who are so only on the surface."[8] Whether any such reader of *Phantoms* was numbered among Dostoevsky's acquaintances may be left undecided; more important is to note his focus on a figure of this kind, so obviously at odds with himself, and who, like the underground man, finds it impossible to square his emotive reactions with his convictions.

Describing *Phantoms* quite accurately, Dostoevsky goes on to tell Turgenev that his prose poem expresses "*the anguish of a cultivated and self-conscious being living in our time.*" A sentence or two later, he compares the work to music: "In my view . . . [music] is the same language [as literature], but expressing what consciousness has not yet captured (not rea-soning, but the whole range of consciousness); thus, this language brings a positive benefit, but our Utilitarians do not understand this; those among them who love music though have not *given it up* and continue to play it."[9] Once more we see Dostoevsky dwelling on the discrepancy between reason (in its Russian Nihilist form) and the full range of human consciousness; the figure of the Nihilist music lover, unable to abandon his passion despite his philosophy, again reveals Dostoevsky groping his way toward his next important fictional creation.

6

Dostoevsky's letter succeeded in allaying Turgenev's fears, and *Phantoms* was solidly secured for *Epoch*; but the journal still needed more prose fic-tion. ("To appear only with the story of Turgenev is pretty thin," Dostoevsky comments to Mikhail.)[10] Probably at the beginning of the new year, pressed by editorial necessity, he decided to try himself to supply a new artistic work for the February deadline even though the conditions of his life were any-thing but propitious for artistic creation. Some image of these conditions may be gleaned from a letter in January: "At every instant Marya Dimi-trievna sees death before her eyes: she is afflicted and becomes desperate," he writes her sister. "Such moments are very painful for her. Her nerves are completely worn out. Her chest is very bad, and she is thin as a nail. It's terrible! It's awful to see this!"[11]

Pasha Isaev had been dispatched to console his mother, but his presence only stirred the agonizing realization that her condition was hopeless, and he was sent home sooner than planned. "I pity her very much," Dostoevsky writes, "and my life, all in all, is not cheerful. But it seems that I am indis-pensable to her, so I remain."[12] A rare outside glimpse of the Dostoevskys appears in a letter of Apollon Maikov, who dropped in for a visit sometime in January on a trip to Moscow. "It is terrible," he tells his wife, "to see how much worse Marya Dimitrievna looks: yellow, nothing but skin and bones, the very image of death. She was very, very happy to see me, asked after you, but her coughing placed a limit on her talkativeness. Feodor Mi-khailovich diverts her with various trifles, little handbags, piggy-banks, etc., and she seems very pleased with them. They both present a very sad picture: she with tuberculosis, and he with epilepsy."[13]

Nevertheless, Dostoevsky tried as best he could to work on a story which, though unnamed, was manifestly the first part of *Notes from Underground*. Yet his own health was also badly deteriorating, and he tells Mikhail at the beginning of February that he has been ill for the past two weeks, not only with epilepsy ("that would not be important," he remarks stoically), but with an infection of the bladder that has prevented him from either sitting or lying down comfortably. As a result, he pushes the deadline of the story ahead to March and adds: "I won't hide from you that my work is going badly. My novella, suddenly, has begun to displease me. However, it's my own fault, I have messed up something in it. I don't know what it will give." His failure to meet his deadline and, even more, his dissatisfaction with what he had written, depressed him terribly, and he remarks that "I shall never forgive myself that I was not able to finish earlier." He was also worried that he might have written himself out, and confesses to being "terribly nervous about my health."[14]

In mid-February, Dostoevsky traveled to Petersburg (Mikhail's little Varya died during his stay there), and on his return to Moscow on February 29 he wrote both to console his bereaved brother and to outline further plans and projects for *Epoch*. He thought it would be a good idea to revive the old practice of briefly reviewing *all* the books and magazines that appeared each month, thus providing readers with a handy literary service; he also mentions "the idea for a magnificent article on the theoreticism and the fantastic among the theoreticians (of *The Contemporary*)."[15] Although never developed as such, this idea probably became absorbed into *Notes from Underground*, the first part of which was completed sometime around the end of February. Approved by the censorship on March 20, it appeared in the first double number of *Epoch* several weeks later. The information already given exhausts all we know reliably about the genesis of this work, but some speculations may tentatively be ventured.

It is quite likely that, in setting out to write his article on *What Is To Be Done?*, Dostoevsky had begun to compose in the familiar first-person style of *Winter Notes* and using the same sort of persona—a Russian more or less accepting Western ideas, but emotionally and subconsciously in revolt against them. In this case, of course, the "Western" ideas would be those of the radicals of the 1860s, as exemplified not only by *What Is To Be Done?* but also, more theoretically, by *The Anthropological Principle in Philosophy* with its outright denial of free will. When confronted a bit later with the need for a "story," Dostoevsky retained the original form but gave the "I" of the narrative more social specificity by drawing on his plans for the revision of *The Double*. The conception of Golyadkin, as we know from Dostoevsky's notebooks, had been evolving steadily in the direction of an inner assimilation of radical ideology; and the narrator of Dostoevsky's new work thus becomes a development of the Golyadkin-type. This supposition—the fusion of the underground man with Golyadkin at a certain stage—is supported by a small detail in the work: both men serve under the same bureau chief, Anton Antonovich Setotchkin.

There is some indication, too, that Dostoevsky intended to write a series of episodes with the underground man as central figure; but he never developed the plan beyond the two parts of the existing text.[16] And just as Part

I grew out of an article about *What Is To Be Done?*,* absorbing along the way some of the material for a rewriting of *The Double*, so Part II probably emerged from Dostoevsky's intention to write a work called *A Confession* (the title had been announced in *Time* at the beginning of 1863 as Dostoevsky's next contribution). First mentioned in October 1859, this project is described in a letter to Mikhail as "a *confession*—a novel that I wished to write after everything, so to say, I have had to live through myself. . . . I conceived it in *katorga*, lying on the plank bed, in painful moments of sorrow and self-criticism."[17]

Judging from the last phrase, this confession would, at the very least, have contained a disillusioned contemplation of Dostoevsky's ideological past in the 1840s. Since this is precisely what we find in Part II, we can plausibly assume that this scheme was also embodied in *Notes from Underground*; nor would such an amalgamation have been entirely fortuitous. Despite all its coldly calculating terminology of egoism and Utilitarianism, Chernyshevsky's novel had revived much of the sentimental, idealistic atmosphere of the 1840s and shared its philanthropic reveries of a redeemed and purified humanity. Dostoevsky could thus easily integrate such material from his own past, both ideological and personal, into his new creation; and it is surely no coincidence that the underground man in Part II is exactly the same age as Dostoevsky at the time of his success with *Poor Folk* in 1845. Whatever autobiographical elements are contained in this second part, however, are all assimilated into, and integrated with, the overriding artistic thrust of the text as a whole.

7

On March 20, 1864, Dostoevsky wrote to Mikhail that he was following a severe regimen, taking innumerable precautions with his diet, and that his infectious condition was on the mend. Marya Dimitrievna's sister had also providentially arrived from Petersburg to take charge of the household. "Without her," he comments, "I don't know what would have become of us." Marya Dimitrievna was growing weaker every day, and Dostoevsky had been told that her death might occur at any moment; but she contin-

---

* Some confusion may well be caused by the remark of the commentator to the Academy edition of Dostoevsky's work that "the conception of *Notes from Underground* took form, probably, at the end of 1862, in the period when he was thinking over and writing *Winter Notes on Summer Impressions*: in these travel sketches, Dostoevsky concisely formulated one of the basic points of the philosophical confession of the hero [?] of *Notes*—the idea of the impossibility of constructing human life 'on rational foundations.' " *PSS*, 5: 374.

This assertion, in my view, regrettably confuses a general ideological position, which in fact goes much further back than *Winter Notes*, with the genesis of a particular and concrete artistic embodiment of this position. Even though, as we have seen, there are close connections between *Winter Notes* and *Notes from Underground*, no evidence exists that Dostoevsky thought of writing a *work* of the kind that finally emerged until a year later and in close connection with his proposed article on Chernyshevsky's *What Is To Be Done?*.

ued desperately to cling to life, and was still pathetically making plans for the summer months and choosing her place of residence in future years. The emotional drain of this heart-rending situation must surely have been enormous; but Dostoevsky assures Mikhail that "I have gone back to my work on my novella [Part II of *Notes from Underground*]. I am trying to free myself from it as quickly as possible, and at the same time to succeed with it as best I can. It's much more difficult to write than I had believed. And yet, it is absolutely necessary that it be successful; it is necessary *for me*. It has an extremely bizarre tone, brutal and violent; it may displease; poetry will have to soften it all through and make it bearable. But I hope that this will get better."[18]

One week later, Dostoevsky was sent the first issue of *Epoch* hot off the presses and was anything but pleased with the result. Having re-read *Phantoms*, he now offers this judgment: "In my opinion, there is a good deal of rubbish in it; something rotten, morbid, senile, *disbelief out of impotence*, in a word, all of Turgenev and his convictions, but the poetry compensates for a good deal."[19] Several years later, *Phantoms* would provide part of the inspiration for his brilliantly wicked take-off on Turgenev's lyrical-elegiac manner in *The Devils*.

Much more vehement was his reaction to his own contribution, which he could scarcely recognize in what he saw before him. Not only had it been very badly proofread (as was the entire issue), but his conception had also been seriously mutilated by the censorship. "It would have been better," he says, "not to have published the next-to-last chapter at all (where the essential, the very idea of the work is expressed) than to publish it like that, that is, *with phrases that are garbled and contradict each other* [italics added]. Alas! What is to be done? Those swinish censors: in passages where I mocked at everything and sometimes blasphemed for the sake of appearances—that is let by, and where I concluded with the need for faith and Christ—that is censored. What are the censors doing? Are they conspiring against the government, or what?"[20] These comments are of major importance for the interpretation of Part I, and we shall return to the problems which they pose.

Meanwhile, Dostoevsky was working away at the second part valiantly, but finding it increasingly difficult to surmount the crushing burden of his almost impossible circumstances. "My friend," he writes Mikhail at the beginning of April, "I have been ill a good part of the month [March], then convalescent, and even now I am not yet entirely well. My nerves are shot and I have not been able to get back my strength. I am so grimly tormented by *so many things* that I don't even wish to speak of them. My wife is dying, *literally*. There is not a day when, at such and such a moment, we do not believe that we see her going. Her sufferings are terrible and this works on me, because. . . ." The sentence trails off in this fashion, and Dostoevsky evidently assumes that Mikhail will understand what he leaves unsaid; perhaps he was thinking of the affair with Suslova, whose secret only Mikhail was supposed to have known. Yet, Dostoevsky continues, "I write and write, every morning, . . . [and] the story is getting longer. Sometimes I imagine that it is worth nothing, and yet I write with enthusiasm; I do not know what it will give."[21] Dostoevsky hopes that he can perhaps send half of the second part soon to be set up in type, but insists that it can only be published as a whole and not in installments.

Several other letters to Mikhail in early April contain urgent requests for money because the last stages of Marya Dimitrievna's illness had led to a flood of extra expenses; and he also outlines an elaborate strategy for extracting a loan on behalf of *Epoch* from their wealthy and old-fashionedly pious Moscow aunt. On April 9, Dostoevsky again comments that Part II is getting longer, but he now seems to have become more intimately involved with his creation. "In my heart of hearts I count on it quite a lot," he confesses. "It will be something sincere and powerful; it will be true. Even if it's bad, it will produce an effect. I know it."[22] Four days later, he again describes his lamentable condition ("I am in a frightening state, nervous, morally ill"), but provides additional information about his story. He now sees it comprising three chapters: the first is almost finished; the second is drafted but chaotic; the third is not yet begun. Dostoevsky wonders whether the first chapter could not be published by itself and expresses his willingness to make such a sacrifice, though convinced it would injure the effect of the whole: "I will be made fun of, all the more since, deprived of the sequel (the two others are essential) it [the first chapter] loses all its juice. You know what a *transition* is in music. This is exactly the same. The first chapter seems to be nothing but chatter; but suddenly this chatter in the last two chapters is resolved by a sudden catastrophe."[23] These words, the last in Dostoevsky's correspondence referring to the composition of *Notes from Underground*, were written six days before Marya Dimitrievna breathed her last.

CHAPTER 20

"Will I Ever
See Masha Again?"

One of Dostoevsky's most moving stories, *A Gentle Creature*, is composed entirely in the form of an internal monologue. It depicts the thoughts of a husband pacing back and forth in the room containing the remains of his dead wife, who had committed suicide by throwing herself out of a window clutching an icon in her hand. The story took its origin from a newspaper account of such a suicide, and nothing allows us to draw any parallel between Marya Dimitrievna and the humble ex-seamstress whose pathetic end inspired Dostoevsky. All the same, the desperately groping ruminations of the husband irresistibly recall what occurred when Dostoevsky was keeping a vigil at the bier of *his* dead wife. For he too pored over their life together as he sat beside her corpse, and such thoughts led him on to ponder as well the great issues of good and evil, of life on earth and its meaning, and of the possibility of an eternity beyond the grave. He brooded over all those questions which, since the dawn of human consciousness, have plagued mankind in the face of death; and in such a severe and solemn moment of self-scrutiny, he tried to unriddle his own answers to these perennial enigmas.

To justify the technique of his short story, Dostoevsky asks the reader to assume that some invisible but omnipresent stenographer has taken down the words of his character. Luckily, no appeal to any such fiction is required in order to insert ourselves into Dostoevsky's own mind; he allows us to do so very easily because, while sitting in the eerie stillness, he threw open his notebook and, by the dim light of the flickering candles, jotted down his reflections. This text has long been known from a copy of the original, and the original itself has recently been edited and published. Yet surprisingly little attention has been paid to this crucial document, even though nothing else from Dostoevsky's pen takes us so directly to the heart of his religious idea-feelings—those adumbrations of the absolute in which he tried to give shape and form to his beliefs.* Nowhere else does he tell us so unequivo-

---

* Despite the richness of the commentary in the new Academy edition of Dostoevsky's works—for which, whatever differences may exist on points of interpretation, one can only be grateful to Soviet Russian scholars—there is very little information proffered on this crucial document. Nor is the situation any better in the volume of *Literaturnoe Nasledstvo* in which

cally what he really thought about God, immortality, the role of Christ in human existence, and the meaning of human life on earth.

2

The fragment begins with a direct statement and a poignant question: "Masha is lying on the table. Will I ever see Masha again?" (20: 172).[1] This was not, of course, the first time that events had impelled Dostoevsky to peer beyond the limits of earthly existence. He had asked the same question, much more agonizingly, fifteen years earlier, when he had awaited his turn before a firing squad during the mock execution staged by Nicholas I. If we accept the account of these moments that he later included in *The Idiot*, what Dostoevsky had felt then was a "terrible" sense of incertitude and "repulsion before the unknown" (8: 52). Another survivor reports that, in a brief conversation with his atheistic friend Nikolay Speshnev, who was stoically resigned to turning into "a handful of dust," Dostoevsky had fever-ishly affirmed that they would soon both "be with Christ."[2] Dostoevsky thus refused to accept the bleak prospect of total extinction and clung to the hope of a Christian afterlife—a hope that is reiterated in the fragment. But his response to the looming imminence of his own death had been prima-rily emotive and existential; the death of his wife, deeply grievous as it was, still allowed him sufficient composure to think and reflect. As a result, he now endeavors not only to persuade himself that immortality exists, but also to explain why it *must* exist as a necessary completion of human life on earth.

Immediately after asking whether he will ever see Masha again, Dos-toevsky thus turns aside from eternity and shifts his gaze to the vicissitudes of the human condition. "To love man like *oneself*, according to the com-mandment of Christ," he declares peremptorily, "is impossible. The law of personality on earth binds. The *Ego* stands in the way" (20: 172). Such a declaration is of course good Christian doctrine: mankind on earth, after the Fall, is subject to the temptations of egoism, and the power of these temptations cannot be gainsaid. Moreover, these words were set down just after Dostoevsky had completed the first part of *Notes from Underground*, where he had portrayed with stunning vehemence the refusal of the hu-man ego to surrender its right to self-assertion and self-expression—its re-jection, even at the price of madness and self-destruction, of any philoso-

---

the text was first officially printed in the Soviet Union. See *PSS*, 20: 362-364; *LN*, 83 (Moscow, 1971), 190-191.

Although this document has been available to Western scholars in German since 1926 and in the original Russian since 1932 (when it was printed in a Russian émigré journal), it has never, so far as my knowledge goes, attracted much attention. See *Der unbekannte Dosto-jewski*, ed. René Fulop-Miller and Friedrich Eckstein (Munich, 1926); and B. Visheslavtsev, "Dostoevsky o Bessmertii," *Sovremennye Zapiski*, 50 (1932), 288-304.

phy that denied its very claim to existence. Dostoevsky, as we shall see, poured into this text everything he had learned in prison camp about the ineradicable need of the human personality to possess a sense of its own autonomy; and even before being transposed into the consciousness of the underground man, this need had already been illustrated by the terrible explosions of frustration in *House of the Dead*.

In fact, Dostoevsky's awareness of the power of egoism goes back much further than his bitter four years as a convict. It was a truth about human nature of which he had become convinced in the 1840s, when the question of egoism had been brought to the fore by the publication of Max Stirner's *The Ego and Its Own* (an impassioned defense of the right of the individual ego to satisfy *its own* needs before all else, and to take precedence over all abstract and general rules of law and morality). The book had been much discussed within the social-cultural circles in which Dostoevsky moved, and egoism had been re-evaluated as a positive force in the human personality by Belinsky and Herzen. Dostoevsky himself had spoken of a lack in the Russian character of a "necessary egoism" (18: 31), attributing to this defect the moral-psychic deformations of personality depicted in his early stories. Such views unquestionably prepared him to perceive, and even to sympathize with, some of the aberrant behavior of the peasant-convicts, which he interpreted as the eruption of an irresistible human need to exert their crushed personalities.

It may thus appear as if Dostoevsky were inclined to agree with Strakhov that human nature was incurably rotten: incapable of fulfilling the law of Christ, mankind was thus doomed to remain sunk in irremediable evil. Such a view would link him with the more pessimistic versions of Christianity, which consider mankind to be largely dependent on God's grace for any possibility of redemption from its wickedness. But Eastern Orthodoxy has always placed more emphasis on man's free will than on grace; and in the very next sentences of his notebook entry, Dostoevsky makes clear that he does not consider any special gift of grace to be necessary: the incarnation of Christ has been sufficient to spur mankind into eternal struggle against its own limitations.

> Christ alone could love man as himself, but Christ was a perpetual eternal ideal to which man strives and, according to the law of nature, should strive. Meanwhile, since the appearance of Christ as *the ideal of man in the flesh*, it has become as clear as day that the highest final development of the personality must arrive at this (at the very end of the development, the final attainment of the goal): that man finds, knows, and is convinced, with the full force of his nature, that the highest use a man can make of his personality, of the full development of his *Ego*—is, as it were, to annihilate that *Ego*, to give it totally and to

everyone undividedly and unselfishly. In this way, the law of the *Ego* fuses with the law of humanism, and in this fusion both the *Ego* and the all (apparently two extreme opposites) mutually annihilate themselves one for the other, and at the same time each attains separately, and to the highest degree, their own individual development. (20: 172)

No mention is made here of any incapacity of mankind to struggle to follow the example of Christ; quite the contrary, it is declared a "law of nature" (an odd phrase in this context; presumably Dostoevsky means human nature) that mankind should do so. Here too one can infer the influence of the prison-camp years, which had shown Dostoevsky that only the traditional Christian morality of the Russian peasant was capable of mollifying and restraining (even if only momentarily) the ravages of egoism. This morality had been the sole ray of hope piercing the moral darkness by which he had been surrounded; and if its light had not been obscured even by the blackness of prison life, then its radiance could be assumed to continue to glimmer in every Christian breast. This is surely one reason why Dostoevsky had declared, in the famous letter he wrote to Mme Fonvizina shortly after quitting the camp, that "if someone proved to me that Christ is outside the truth, and that *in reality* the truth were outside of Christ, then I should prefer to remain with Christ rather than with the truth."[3] Such words have often been taken as an indication that Dostoevsky's Christian faith was less than secure; but this reading overlooks their conditional nature, which is another example of Dostoevsky's ideological eschatology (he is imagining a situation where such a choice might have to be made, not affirming that anyone *had* actually proved to him that the truth was outside of Christ). What he is affirming, rather, is the depth and strength of his existential commitment to Christ—which meant, concretely, to the moral message of love and self-sacrifice that Christ had brought to the world.

Indeed, the sole significance of Christ, as Dostoevsky speaks of him here, is to serve as the divine enunciator of this morality; he fulfills no other purpose, not even the traditional one of redeeming mankind from the wages of sin and death. There is, in fact, not much difference between the Christ of the notebook entry and the Utopian Socialist Christ whom Dostoevsky had defended against Belinsky in 1845-1846, or the Christ he had described earlier as having been sent by God to the modern world, just as Homer had been dispatched to the ancient one, in order to provide "the organization of its spiritual and earthly life."[4] But, in the intervening years, Dostoevsky had acquired a new realization of all the obstacles that prevented Christ's message from being embodied in such an "organization"—the chief one being the human ego itself, with its raging demand for the recognition of its rights.

Five years later, Dostoevsky sketched the plan for what he considered the most important project of his creative career—a series of novels to be called *The Life of a Great Sinner*; and the origins of this conception can already be observed in the words just quoted. For it is only when the egoism of personality has been expanded to its fullest stretch, only when someone has indeed become "a great sinner," that the full sublimity of the *imitatio Christi*—the full grandeur of the voluntary self-sacrifice of the personality out of love—can be most effectively presented. Such a self-sacrifice, in Dostoevsky's view, would unite the law of personality with that of "humanism"; and the use of this term, which had been employed twenty years earlier by Feuerbach and the Left Hegelians to denote the secular and social realization of the Christian law of love, is quite significant. It testifies that Dostoevsky had by no means abandoned his earlier ideals, and was striving to integrate them with his more recently acquired convictions in some coherent fashion. But what had once been conceived as a worldly possibility has now receded into the infinite future, and he goes on to declare that "all history, whether of humanity in part or of each man separately, is only the development, struggle, and attainment of this goal [the fusion of egoism and humanism]." Once having reached it, however, mankind would then truly have arrived at "the Paradise of Christ" (20: 172).

3

What Dostoevsky has begun to do here, in a movement typical of his imaginative manipulation of ideas, is to think them through to the end and envisage the situation resulting from their completion. The "Paradise of Christ" that he foresees, the seamless fusion of the ego and humanism, is thus the final accomplishment of the goal of all human existence. But can this fusion be imagined as literally occurring on earth? And if so, what then would be the position of mankind?

"But if that is the final goal of all humanity," he reasons, "(having attained which it would no longer be necessary to develop, that is, achieve, struggle, continue to glimpse the ideal through all failure and eternally strive toward it)—therefore, it would no longer be necessary to live—then, consequently, when man achieves this, he terminates his earthly existence. Therefore, man on earth is only a creature in development, consequently, someone not finished but transitional." Earthly human nature, with its necessarily unresolved conflict between egoism and the law of love, is not, then, the final state of mankind; and this conviction enables Dostoevsky to answer the question posed at the beginning of his meditations. "It is completely senseless to attain such a great goal if upon attaining it everything is extinguished and disappears, that is, if man will no longer have life when he attains the goal. Consequently, there is a future paradisial life" (20: 172-173).

Here we have Dostoevsky's argument for the necessity of immortality—an argument that contains a number of surprising features. He says nothing, for example, about the resurrection of Christ, which is ordinarily invoked by believers in such a context; nor does he have recourse to the familiar *moral* argument in favor of an afterlife (used by Kant, among others) that immortality rectifies the injustices of an earthly existence in which the good suffer and the evil flourish. Most startling of all, perhaps, is the absence of any reference to the ecstatic "aura" that Dostoevsky sometimes experienced before the onset of an epileptic attack. At such a moment, he felt a direct sensation, if not of Christ, then of a supernatural principle of plenitude; and this fusion "with the highest synthesis of life" enabled him to understand "the extraordinary saying that *there shall be no more time*" (8: 189). Dostoevsky, however, does not appeal either to Christian dogma or to his own mystical raptures; rather, he argues in favor of immortality because, without such a belief, the endless struggle of humanity on earth to fulfill the law of Christ would simply have no point. What motivates Dostoevsky's reflections above all—what he cannot bear to contemplate as a possibility—is the dire prospect that all the toils and turmoils of human life should turn out to be entirely meaningless.

Like another doubt-filled Christian who was also "a child of *his* century," Blaise Pascal, nothing terrified Dostoevsky more than the specter of living in a senseless universe; and *House of the Dead* provides a chilling imaginative evocation of this terror in one of the most self-revealing passages that Dostoevsky ever wrote. The question of immortality is not raised directly in that book; but it contains a haunting depiction of mankind's unquenchable desire to exist in a universe whose infinite spaces, instead of remaining silent, would respond to the longings contained in every human soul. Although Dostoevsky illustrates the point in connection with compulsory labor, his conclusions apply with equal, if not greater, force to the problem of whether human life has any ultimate value or is just "a tale told by an idiot, signifying nothing."

What Dostoevsky postulated (nothing so horrible actually existed in the camp) was a situation in which the convicts were forced to labor "at a task whose character was absolutely useless and absurd." Such a task might be "to pour water from one basin into another, and then from the second into the first, or to pound sand, or to carry a load of earth from one spot to another and vice versa." Anyone faced with the endless repetition of such perfectly useless labor, imposed by what could only be a sadistically vindictive taskmaster, would "hang himself at the end of several days, or he would commit a thousand crimes in order to die perhaps, but to be liberated from such degradation, shame, and torment" (4: 20). It would be an intolerable insult to human dignity for man to live in a world totally deprived of sense; and such a world, from Dostoevsky's point of view, would be one in which death simply meant extinction—a world in which the travails of human life would receive no satisfactory explanation or justification. Here we penetrate to the heart of that intimate connection between psychology and religious metaphysics so typical of Dostoevsky; and this connection explains the rather unexpected nature of his argument in favor of immortality.

4

Once having convinced himself, to his own satisfaction, that a life beyond the grave must exist, Dostoevsky then goes on to imagine what form such a life could possibly assume: "What it is, where it is, on what planet, in what center, that is, in the bosom of the universal synthesis, that is, God?—we do not know." According to Dostoevsky, only one feature of this future life has been revealed to mankind by Christ himself, "the sublime and final ideal of the development of all humanity." The clue is contained in a quotation from St. Matthew: "They neither marry, nor are given in marriage, but are as the angels in Heaven." "A deeply significant feature," Dostoevsky comments, perhaps thinking of the difficulties of his own marriage; but the interpretation he gives this sentence rises far above such personal considerations. Marriage is the means by which the generations succeed each other in time and carry on the eternal struggle to realize the law of love. When this goal has been reached, human reproduction will no longer be required, and thus marriage will end as well. Since the words of Jesus in St. Matthew refer to the Resurrection (Dostoevsky does not cite this part of the sentence), presumably they describe the supernatural state of mankind after the Second Coming.

In any case, Dostoevsky then sets down some remarks on marriage and the family quite surprising in the sharpness of their criticism of these hallowed sources of social stability, and not dissimilar, at least in general import, to what radicals like Chernyshevsky and Dobrolyubov were then saying about the tyranny of familial life in Russia.

> Marriage and the giving in marriage of a woman is, as it were, the greatest deviation from humanism, the complete isolation of the pair from *everyone else* (little remains for everyone else). The family, that is the law of nature, but [it is] all the same abnormal, egotistical, in the full sense of [being] a condition turned away from mankind. The family—this is the most sacred possession of man on earth, for by means of this law of nature man achieves the development of the goal (that is, the succession of generations). But at the same time mankind, also according to the laws of nature, in the name of the final ideal of its goal, must unceasingly negate it. (Duality.) (20: 173)

Primitive Christianity did not hold marriage and the family in very high esteem, and Dostoevsky could well have cited both the words of Christ and St. Paul in support of his views; the original disciples were enjoined to break with the family and follow Christ, while St. Paul reluctantly accepted marriage as an evil preferable only to that of burning with lust. Dostoevsky, all the same, emphasizes the importance of the family as a necessary precondition for the existence of human life itself in its struggle to accomplish the Christian ideal. Yet he sees the family as ineluctably opposed, given its egoistic exclusiveness, to the very essence of this ideal as embodied in the law of love. No passage in Dostoevsky so clearly illuminates why his novels almost always present human life as inextricably embroiled in tragic conflicts. Ordinary human desires, even the most legitimate ones, must inevitably clash with the imperatives of the Christian law of love, and one cannot help but think of the famous declaration of Dimitry Karamazov that "God and the devil are fighting . . . and the battlefield is the heart of man" (14: 100). This formulation, however, simplifies the issue as Dostoevsky presents it here, since "the devil" is not only the temptation to infringe the moral code of society and surrender to the ideal of Sodom but also the duty, through marriage and the family, to fulfill society's most sacrosanct obligations. Whatever else Dostoevsky may have been, he was certainly not an uncritical defender of existing institutions; and these words show how continually he was reaching out in imagination beyond the bounds of *all* earthly establishments.

It is possible that, at this point, the implicit radicalism of his own conjectures made Dostoevsky aware of how close he was coming to his anti-Christian opponents. And, with a sudden shift in perspective, he turns to face those whom he calls the "antichrists," those who think they can refute Christianity by pointing to its failure to transform earthly life. "Why does Christianity not reign on earth if it is true," they ask. "Why do men suffer to this day and not become brothers?" This is the same question that Strakhov had tried to cope with in his controversy with Antonovich, and Dostoevsky now responds to it in terms which, if they had been revealed to the readers of his journal, would certainly have provoked some astonishment.

"It is very clear why," Dostoevsky begins, "because this is the ideal of the future, final life of man, and on earth man is in a transitional state. It will be, but it will be after the attainment of the goal, when man is finally reborn according to the laws of nature into another form which neither marries nor is given in marriage." Dostoevsky then points out that "Christ himself prophesied his teachings only as an ideal, predicted himself that strife and development will continue to the end of the world (the teaching about the sword). . . ." After this reference to St. Mark, who quotes Christ as having said "Not peace I bring but a sword," Dostoevsky contrasts a life on earth doomed to interminable struggle with its quite different heavenly counterpart: "But there—an existence fully synthetic, eternally pleasurable and fulfilled, for which, therefore, 'time will no longer be.' " The quoted phrase, from the Apocalypse of St. John, perhaps alludes indirectly to Dostoevsky's own occasional apprehension of such a state of being (20: 173-174).

Continuing his argument with the "antichrists," and in words that very probably refer to the Crystal Palace ideal he had just been attacking in *Notes from Underground*, Dostoevsky remarks that "atheists, denying god and a future life, are terribly inclined to imagine all this in human form, and in this they sin. The nature of god is exactly the opposite to the nature of man. Man, according to the great findings of science, goes from multiplicity to Synthesis, from facts to their generalization and comprehension. But the nature of god is different. It is the full synthesis of all being scrutinizing itself in multiplicity, in Analysis" (20: 174). By "science" Dostoevsky means philosophy in the sense taken into Russian from German thought, and he seems to be restating the Kantian distinction between the analytic and synthetic understanding. The first is dependent on data furnished by the senses; the second is identical with the *intellectus archetypus*, "the infinite, godly intellect which," as Ernst Cassirer has written, "does not absorb something outside itself but creates the objects of its knowledge."[5] Dostoevsky's conception of God, if we can judge from his remarks here, is noticeably abstract and philosophical, derived more at this stage of his life from German Idealism than from the mystical theology of the Eastern Church. It may be that, in responding to the "antichrists," Dostoevsky deliberately confines himself to arguments that do not appeal to religious experience; or perhaps he was simply not yet as familiar with such theology as some commentators have assumed.[6] In a moment, we shall again see him expressing his ideas in terms that have very little to do with Eastern Orthodoxy.

5

On returning to his main train of thought after this polemical excursus, Dostoevsky continues to scrutinize the mysteries of extraterrestrial being. "But if man is not man—what sort of nature will he have?" he wonders. No answer can be given because "it is impossible to understand on earth, but its law may be intuited by all humanity in immediate emanations (Proudhon, the origin of god) and each particular individual" (20: 174). This appeal to the French revolutionary theorist who identified God as evil ("Dieu, c'est le mal") is unexpected to say the least; and since Proudhon wrote no work specifically on the origin of God, it is difficult to pinpoint Dostoevsky's reference.* In all likelihood, he was thinking of the *Système des contradic-*

---

* "God is stupidity and cowardice; God is hypocrisy and falsehood; God is tyranny and misery; God is evil." P. J. Proudhon, *Système des contradictions économiques*, 2 vols., ed. C. Bouglé and H. Moysset (Paris, 1923), 1: 384.

tions économiques, which he was studying in those years, and where Proudhon speaks of the "hypothesis of God" as being indispensable for his own analysis of human society. Proudhon argued that mankind had not been mistaken in equating the mysterious force making for social cohesion with something called "God"; and perhaps Dostoevsky meant that Proudhon, in sensing this force through such an immediate "emanation," had caught a glimpse of the ultimate harmony of paradisial existence.* For Dostoevsky, such emanations were intimations of immortality in the literal sense, messengers of the complete fulfillment of the law of love: "It is the merging of the whole *Ego,* that is, of knowledge and synthesis *with all. Love everyone like thyself.*" Dostoevsky then repeats that "on earth this is impossible," and concludes this section with a statement finally bringing Christ and immortality into a more customary connection: "Thus everything depends on this: do you take Christ as the final ideal on earth, that is, on the Christian faith. If you believe in Christ, then you believe you will live eternally." Even here, though, Dostoevsky's stress still remains on the incarnated Christ as the heavenly standard-bearer of the law of love, not on the risen Christ come to free mankind from the terror of death (20: 174).

In his final paragraphs, Dostoevsky turns to another question endlessly debated in the history of religions. If we assume that immortality exists, "in that case is there eternal life for every *Ego?*" The answer begins with a reference once again, though without mentioning them explicitly, to the "antichrists": "They say that man is destroyed and dies *completely.*" But such a contention, Dostoevsky retorts, is not even true empirically: "We already know that not completely because, in physically creating a son, man transmits to him a part of his personality, and thus morally leaves a memory of himself to other people." The desire to have one's memory eternally preserved by a funeral service is also a significant expression of a craving to continue to exist after death. The memory of the great benefactors of mankind, as well as the great evildoers, lives on for their successors, and "it is

---

* Despite the words quoted in the preceding footnote, Proudhon also writes, in the same chapter, that the law of love promulgated by Jesus Christ is really the solution to all social problems ("tout est là"); it is only human egoism that prevents this law from being put into practice. Many other passages in the same text also contain sentiments that would have aroused a positive echo in Dostoevsky's sensibility. Proudhon asserts, for example, that while "the contradictions of political economy can be resolved, the intimate contradiction of our nature never will be. . . . Yes, human nature is vicious because it is illogical, because its constitution is only an eclecticism that contains an unending combat between the virtualities of being, independently of the contradictions of society. The life of man is nothing but a continual alternation between work and toil, love and pleasure, justice and egoism; and the voluntary sacrifice of his inferior impulses that man makes to [the ideal of] order is the baptism which prepares his reconciliation with God, which renders him worthy of the beatific union and of eternal felicity."

A few pages later, however, Proudhon rises to a furious attack against God for having created man so imperfectly. Anticipating Ivan Karamazov, Proudhon equally rejects God as unjust and unmerciful toward his creation and cites Job as an instance of God's capricious tyranny. Proudhon's possible relations with Dostoevsky would certainly repay closer study than they have yet received. P. J. Proudhon, *Système des contradictions économiques,* I: 354, 372, 379-380.

the greatest joy for mankind to resemble them" (it is not clear whether this last phrase refers to "the great evildoers" as well) (20: 174).

So far as the greatest of all benefactors, Jesus Christ, is concerned, "Christ entered entirely into mankind, and man strives to transform himself into the *Ego* of Christ as into his own ideal. Having achieved this, he clearly sees that everyone who has achieved this same goal on earth has entered into the condition of his final nature, that is, in Christ. (The synthetic nature of Christ is astonishing. It is, after all, the nature of god, which means that Christ is the reflection of god on earth.)" Dostoevsky then indirectly answers his initial question about eternal life by confessing that it is difficult to understand how all will be received in the general Synthesis, an event he seems to envisage as taking place at the end of time: "But the living, not having died before the final attainment and having been reflected in the final ideal must come to life in the final, synthesized, eternal life" (20: 174). There is no suggestion that the Synthesis will contain a separation of the sheep from the goats, the blessed from the damned; all will participate, so far as one can judge, in the bliss of eternal beatitude.*

A summarizing passage of the utmost importance then returns to Dostoevsky's point of departure, and simultaneously offers a poignant glimpse into the personal roots of these touchingly tentative reflections:

And thus man strives on earth toward an ideal *opposed* to his nature. When a man has not fulfilled the law of striving toward the ideal, that is, has not *through love* sacrificed his *Ego* to people or to another person (Masha and myself) he suffers and calls this condition a sin. And so, man must unceasingly feel suffering, which is compensated for by the heavenly joy of fulfilling the law, that is, by sacrifice. Here is the earthly equilibrium. Otherwise the earth would be senseless.

Dostoevsky's concluding sentences reveal his deep-rooted antipathy to materialism as a doctrine of spiritual death: "The teaching of the materialists—universal stagnation and the mechanism of matter—means death. The teaching of true philosophy—is the destruction of stagnation, that is thought, that is the center and Synthesis of the universe and its outer form—matter, that is god, that is eternal life" (20: 175). What Dostoevsky would seem to mean is that "true philosophy," by means of thought, pierces through to the center of the universe, destroys its stagnant outer form of matter, and arrives at the principle of God and eternal life.

---

* Here Dostoevsky is by no means adhering rigidly to the doctrines of Eastern Orthodoxy. Origen, in the third century A.D., developed a theory of universal salvation that would have included Satan and the fallen angels as well; but it was officially disavowed. Nevertheless, as Ernst Benz remarks, "a hankering for it persisted in Eastern Orthodox religious thought, and Eastern theologians have repeatedly revived it." Dostoevsky seems to take it for granted. See Ernst Benz, *The Eastern Orthodox Church* (New York, 1963), 52.

Despite the many obscurities and ambiguities of these jottings, it should be amply clear by now that they are of inestimable value in the Dostoevsky canon. Nowhere else does he outline so explicitly the lineaments of his tragic universe, where man is endlessly struggling to attain an ideal contrary to the promptings of his individual ego, and where egoism is not only traditionally evil but also embodied in such revered pillars of social cohesion as marriage and the family. No other pages from Dostoevsky's pen cast such a flood of light on some of the most obscure corners of his artistic universe.

Unless we entirely reject their veracity, they reveal Dostoevsky to be a believing Christian in his own way, inwardly striving to accept the essential dogmas of the divinity of Christ, personal immortality, the Second Coming, and the Resurrection. The highest aim of Dostoevsky's Christianity, though, is not personal salvation but the fusion of the individual ego with the community in a symbiosis of love; and the only sin that Dostoevsky appears to recognize is the failure to fulfill this law of love. Suffering arises from the consciousness of such a failure; and Dostoevsky's words help us to grasp not only why suffering plays such a prominent role in his works, but also why it is totally misleading to infer that he believes *any* kind of suffering to be necessarily good. Only that suffering is valuable which, by testifying to an awareness of insufficiency in responding to the example of Christ, also proclaims the moral autonomy of the human personality; and since human egoism will *always* prevent the ideal of Christ from being fully realized on earth, this type of suffering will not (and cannot) cease before the end of time.

It can also hardly escape notice that Dostoevsky's definition of "the Paradise of Christ," if transferred from the theological to the social level, is strikingly analogous to the relation he had portrayed in *Winter Notes* as existing between the ego and the community in the *obshchina*. Evidently, Dostoevsky saw no contradiction between maintaining that the perfect fulfillment of the Christian ideal is impossible on earth and, at the same time, affirming that the Russian nature comes closer to attaining it than a Western culture which had given birth to a rampant individualism and strengthened the baleful hegemony of the law of personality. If Dostoevsky felt an imperative necessity to enter into mortal combat with Western ideas, it was because the radical intelligentsia were attempting to substitute them for those Christian sentiments so deeply embedded (as he firmly believed) in the heart and soul of the Russian people. This passionate defense sometimes leads him, especially in his journalistic writings, into the quagmire of biased and vindictive nationalism; but in his artistic works the fetters of the law of personality are, in most cases, felt much more impartially as an inescapable element of the human condition.

These jottings also help to clarify an aspect of Dostoevsky's creations that has often led to doubts concerning the genuineness of his Christianity. For Dostoevsky never portrays the Christian ideal as a positively beneficent force in human life, and depicts it rather as sometimes having the contrary effect. The appearance of a Christ-like figure in *The Idiot*, for example, only leads to a worsening of conflicts instead of aiding in their appeasement or resolution. But, as we have seen, the major significance that Dostoevsky ascribes to the Incarnation was precisely to exercise such an awakening and quickening function: Christ was sent by God not to give mankind the peace of absolution but to stir it to struggle against the law of personality. Life for Dostoevsky was, as it had been for Keats, "a vale of soul-making," into which Christ had come to call mankind to battle against the death of immersion in matter and to inspire the struggle toward the ultimate victory over egoism.

The theologian John Hick, in an enlightening discussion of the problem of theodicy, has used this famous phrase of Keats to clarify the agonizing issue posed by the existence of evil in a world supposedly created by a God of love.* And though Dostoevsky is not mentioned, it is scarcely a coincidence that Hick believes the Keatsian phrase, which so perfectly defines the attitude expressed in Dostoevsky's notebook, to represent a typically Eastern Orthodox response to this age-old dilemma. Eastern Orthodoxy, unlike the Augustinian tradition of the West, has always regarded man, not as having fallen into irredeemable sin from a state of perfection before the Fall, but rather as having emerged into earthly life still imperfect and unformed; man contains the "image" of God but not his "likeness," which John of Damascus defined as the "assimilation to God through virtue."[7] St. Irenaeus compares man on earth to a child required to grow and develop, and Hick points out that any "theodicy that starts in this way must be eschatological in its ultimate bearings . . . instead of looking to the past for its clue to the mystery of evil, it looks to the future, and indeed to that ultimate future to which only faith can look."[8] For Dostoevsky too, human life was the anvil on which souls were being forged by the hammer blows of fate, and it was only in eternity that this endless process would come to a halt.

---

* Keats's magnificent letter deserves more extensive quotation. "Do you not see how necessary a World of Pains and troubles is to school an Intelligence and make it a soul?" he writes. "A place where the heart must feel and suffer in a thousand diverse ways! Not merely is the Heart a Hornbook, It is the Minds Bible, it is the Minds experience, it is the teat from which the Mind or intelligence sucks its identity—As various as the Lives of Men are—so various become their souls, and thus does God make individual beings, Souls, Identical souls of the sparks of his own essence—This appears to me a faint sketch of a system of Salvation which does not affront our reason and humanity." Dostoevsky would certainly have approved of Keats's view of the relation between the intelligence and the heart. Cited in Walter Jackson Bate, *John Keats* (Cambridge, Mass., 1978), 483.

Only in eternity would the law of personality be finally overcome; and this is surely why Dostoevsky could never effectively imagine such a triumph within the realistic conventions of the nineteenth-century novel to which he remained faithful.

All of Dostoevsky's major works will henceforth be controlled by the framework of values expressed in this notebook entry, and they will dramatize, in one way or another, the fateful opposition between the law of Christ and the law of personality as Dostoevsky understood it. Yet to say this tells us very little that would not be equally true of every great writer in the tradition of European literature beginning with Dante, Shakespeare, and Milton. To understand Dostoevsky, we must try to grasp his *particular* understanding of this great theme, which he fills in, fleshes out, and dramatizes in terms of the social-cultural issues and conflicts of his own day. These conflicts provide him with the living substance of his works; it is through them that he rises to the heights of the great argument that possessed his spirit and inflamed his creative imagination; and his genius consists precisely in the ability to unite these two (at first sight) so very dissimilar levels. But the time has now come to illustrate how he did so in *Notes from Underground*, whose second part, completed sometime in May 1864, was published two months after Marya Dimitrievna's demise.

CHAPTER 21

Notes from Underground

If philosophy among other vagaries were also to have the notion that it could occur to a man to act in accordance with its teaching, one might make out of this a queer comedy.

Søren Kierkegaard, *Fear and Trembling*

Few works in modern literature are more widely read than Dostoevsky's *Notes from Underground* or so often cited as a key text revelatory of the hidden depths of the sensibility of our time. The term "underground man" has become part of the vocabulary of contemporary culture, and this character has now achieved—like Hamlet, Don Quixote, Don Juan, and Faust—the stature of one of the great archetypal literary creations. No book or essay dealing with the precarious situation of modern man would be complete without some allusion to Dostoevsky's explosive figure. Most important cultural developments of the present century—Nietzscheanism, Freudianism, Expressionism, Surrealism, Crisis Theology, Existentialism—have claimed the underground man as their own or have been linked with him by zealous interpreters; and when the underground man has not been hailed as a prophetic anticipation, he has been held up to exhibition as a luridly repulsive warning.

The underground man has thus entered into the very warp and woof of modern culture in a fashion testifying to the philosophical suggestiveness and hypnotic power of this first great creation of Dostoevsky's post-Siberian years. At the same time, however, this widespread notoriety has given rise to a good deal of misunderstanding. It has led critics and commentators to enlist the underground man in the service of one or another contemporary point of view, and then to proclaim their particular emphasis to be identical with Dostoevsky's own (though, even more recently, it has become fashionable to profess a total unconcern about the need to establish any such identification). Most readings, in any case, exhibit a tendency to overstress one or the other of the work's two main aspects: either the conceptual level is taken as dominant (the first part has even been printed separately in an anthology of philosophical texts), or the emphasis has been placed on the perverse psychology of the main character.[1] In fact, however, the text cannot be properly understood without grasping the interaction between these two levels, which interpenetrate to motivate both the underground man's ideas and his behavior.

Notes from Underground attracted very little attention when first published (no critical notice was taken of it in any Russian journal), and only many years later was it brought into prominence. In 1883, N. K. Mikhailovsky wrote his all-too-influential article "A Cruel Talent," citing some of the more sadistic passages of *Notes from Underground* and arguing that the utterances and actions of the character illustrated Dostoevsky's own "tendencies to torture."[2] Eight years later, writing from an opposed ideological perspective, V. V. Rozanov interpreted the work as essentially inspired by Dostoevsky's awareness of the irrational depths of the human soul, with all its conflicting impulses for evil as well as for good. No world order based on reason and rationality could possibly contain this seething chaos of the human psyche; only religion (Eastern Orthodoxy) could aid man to overcome his capricious and destructive propensities. Rozanov, to be sure, comes much closer than Mikhailovsky to grasping certain essential features of the text; but no notice at all is taken of the artistic strategy that Dostoevsky employs—a strategy, as we shall see, that makes the attack on "reason" far more subtle than the sort of head-on confrontation Rozanov thinks it to be. All the same, Rozanov was the first to make the insightful comparison between *Notes from Underground* and Diderot's *Le Neveu de Rameau*, which at least points the way to a better understanding of Dostoevsky's aims.[3]*

Another highly influential view of *Notes from Underground* was the one proposed by Lev Shestov, who read it in the context of Russian Nietzscheanism. The underground man dominates and tyrannizes everyone with whom he comes into contact; and Shestov interprets this as Dostoevsky's personal repudiation of the sentimental and humanitarian ideals of his early work, which have now been replaced by a recognition of the terrible reality of human egoism. Egoism finally triumphs in *Notes from Underground*, thus expressing Dostoevsky's acceptance of a universe of cru-

---

* Considering the intrinsic interest of the question, there has been astonishingly little written about the relation between *Notes from Underground* and *Le Neveu de Rameau*. The only recent Russian article on the subject is informative but quite disappointing so far as any critical insight is concerned. See A. Grigoryev, "Dostoevskii i Didro," *Russkaya Literatura*, 4 (1966), 88-102.

As Grigoryev makes clear, it is impossible to establish whether Dostoevsky read *Le Neveu de Rameau* before writing his own work; but it is very likely that he had done so, given his thorough French education and wide acquaintance with French literature. Diderot's text was published in France in 1823, and there is no reason why Dostoevsky should not have read it just as he read Rousseau, Laclos, and the Marquis de Sade. In any case, the two works spring from much the same moral-philosophical dilemma and employ the same artistic strategy.

Diderot, as Daniel Mornet has argued in an excellent analysis, was himself a partisan of materialism and determinism but found such a philosophy impossible to reconcile with his own moral impulses and values. The character of Rameau's nephew, like the underground man, accepts materialism and carries its teachings, on the plane of personal conduct, to their inevitable end results; and Diderot created him in order to exhibit the nefarious consequences of such beliefs. "If materialism and skepticism are acceptable systems for the reason," Mornet imagines Diderot saying to himself, "are they acceptable as a way of life? . . . Will they not lead to self-abandon, to a cynicism of behavior, to debauchery, to the ferocious lunge of appetites, to the ruin of all and everybody? Perhaps. And *Le Neveu de Rameau* is the demonstration of all this. It is the living study of the consequences of the doctrine, and, because of the horror of the consequences, an attempt to refute the doctrine." Exactly the same device is used, for exactly the same purpose by Dostoevsky in *Notes from Underground*. Daniel Mornet, *Le Neveu de Rameau* (Paris, 1964), 65.

elty, pain, and suffering that no ultimate moral perspective can rationalize or justify. For Shestov, the essence of the work is contained in the underground man's declaration: "Let the world go smash as long as I get my tea every day" (5: 174)—a profession of sublime selfishness in which, according to Shestov, Dostoevsky proclaims his reluctant but courageous acceptance of a philosophy of amoralism "beyond good and evil." Shestov's analysis unquestionably points to an important aspect of the underground man's character; but he simply takes him to be Dostoevsky's mouthpiece, and fails to understand how the figure is used to realize a more complex artistic purpose.[4]

It was evident from the day of publication that Dostoevsky's *Notes from Underground* was an attack, particularly in Part I, on Chernyshevsky's philosophy of "rational egoism"; but interpreters at the turn of the century paid very little attention to this ancient quarrel, which was considered quite incidental and of no artistic importance. Up to the early 1920s, the usual view of *Notes from Underground* assumed that Dostoevsky had been stimulated by opposition to Chernyshevsky, but had used radical ideas only as a foil. Chernyshevsky had believed that man was innately good and amenable to reason, and that, once enlightened as to his true interests, he would be able, with the help of reason and science, to construct a perfect society. Dostoevsky may have also believed man to be capable of good, but he considered him equally full of evil, irrational, capricious, and destructive inclinations; and it was *this* disturbing truth that he brilliantly presented through the underground man as an answer to Chernyshevsky's naive optimism.

Although such a view may seem quite plausible at first reading, it can hardly be sustained after a little reflection. For it would require us to consider Dostoevsky as just about the worst polemicist in all of literary history. He was, after all, supposedly writing to dissuade readers from accepting Chernyshevsky's ideas. Could he really have imagined that anyone in his right mind would *prefer* the life of the underground man to the radiant happiness of Chernyshevsky's denizens of Utopia? Obviously not; and since Dostoevsky was anything but a fool, it may be assumed that the invention of the underground man was not inspired by any such self-defeating notion. In reality, as another line of interpretation soon began to make clear, his attack on Chernyshevsky and the radicals is far more intricate and cunning than had previously been suspected.

2

The first true glimpse into the artistic logic of *Notes from Underground* appears in an article by V. L. Komarovich, who in 1921 pointed out that Dostoevsky's novella was structurally dependent on *What Is To Be Done?*[5] Whole sections of the work in the second part—the attempt of the underground man to bump into an officer on the Nevsky Prospect, for example, or the famous encounter with the prostitute Liza—are modeled on specific episodes in Chernyshevsky's book, and are obvious *parodies* that inverted the meaning of those episodes in their original context. The use of such a literary technique was by no means a novelty for Dostoevsky, who had conceived his first novel, *Poor Folk*, essentially as a reply—though not a mockingly satirical one—to Gogol's *The Overcoat*. His works of the late 1850s and early 1860s, such as *Uncle's Dream*, *The Village of Stepanchikovo*, and *The Insulted and Injured*, are also filled with parodistic echoes and allusions.

The uncovering of such parodies in *Notes from Underground* opened the way to a new approach, and suggested that the relation to Chernyshevsky was far from being merely ancillary to what was, in substance, the portrayal of an aberrant personality. But while Komarovich pointed to the use of parody in the second part of the text, he continued to regard the imprecations of the underground man against "reason" in the first part simply as a straightforward argument with Utilitarianism. The underground man, in other words, was still speaking directly for Dostoevsky and could be identified with the author's own position.

A further decisive advance was made a few years later by another Russian critic, A. Skaftymov, who focused on the problem of whether, and to what extent, the underground man could be considered Dostoevsky's spokesman in any straightforward fashion. Without raising the issue of parody, Skaftymov argued that the negative views of the underground man could in no way be taken to represent Dostoevsky's own position. As Shestov had also pointed out, such an identification would constitute a flagrant repudiation of all the moral ideals that Dostoevsky was continuing to uphold in his journalism. "The underground man in *Notes*," wrote Skaftymov, "is not only the accuser but also one of the accused," whose objurgations and insults are as much (if not more) directed against himself as against others, and whose eccentric and self-destructive existence by no means represents anything that Dostoevsky was approving without qualification. Skaftymov also perceptively remarked (but only in a footnote, and without developing the full import of his observation) that Dostoevsky's strategy is that of destroying his opponents "from within, carrying their logical presuppositions and possibilities to their consistent conclusion and arriving at a destructively helpless blind alley."[6]

These words provide an essential insight into one of the main features of Dostoevsky's technique as an ideological novelist; but Skaftymov does not properly use his own aperçu for the analysis of *Notes from Underground*. Although fully aware that the novella is "a polemical work," he mentions Chernyshevsky only in another footnote and fails to see how this polemical intent enters into the very creation of the character of the underground man. Skaftymov's analysis of the text thus remains on the level of moral-psychological generalities, and while accurate enough as far as it goes, does not penetrate to the heart of Dostoevsky's conception. This can be reached, in my view, only by combining and extending Komarovich's remarks on the parodistic element in *Notes from Underground* with Skaftymov's perception of how the underground man dramatizes within himself the ultimate consequences of the position that Dostoevsky was opposing. In other words, the underground man is not only a moral-psychological type whose egoism Dostoevsky wishes to expose; he is also a social-ideological one, whose psychology must be seen as intimately interconnected with the ideas he accepts and by which he tries to live.

3

Dostoevsky, it seems to me, overtly pointed to this aspect of the character in the footnote appended to the title of the novella. "Both the author of the *Notes* and the *Notes* themselves," he writes, "are of course fictitious. Nonetheless, such persons as the author of such memoirs not only may, but *must*, exist in our society, if we take into consideration the circumstances that led to the formation of our society. It was my intention to bring before our reading public, more conspicuously than is usually done, one of the characters of our most recent past. He is one of the representatives of a generation that is still with us" (5: 99; italics added).

Dostoevsky here is obviously talking about the formation of Russian ("our") society, which, as he could expect all readers of *Epoch* to know—had he not explained this endlessly in his articles in *Time*, most recently and explicitly in *Winter Notes*?—had been formed by the successive waves of European influence that had washed over Russia since the time of Peter the Great. The underground man *must* exist as a type because he is the inevitable product of such a cultural formation; and his character does in fact embody and reflect two phases of this historical evolution. He is, in short, conceived as a parodistic persona, whose life exemplifies the tragic-comic impasses resulting from the effects of such influences on the Russian national psyche. His diatribes in the first part thus do not arise, as has commonly been thought, because of his rejection of reason; on the contrary, they result from his acceptance of *all* the implications of reason in its then-current Russian incarnation—and particularly, all those consequences that advocates of reason such as Chernyshevsky blithely chose to disregard. In the second part, Dostoevsky extends the same technique to those more sentimental-humanitarian elements of Chernyshevsky's ideology that had revived some of the atmosphere of the 1840s.

Dostoevsky's footnote thus attempted to alert his audience to the satirical and parodistic nature of his conception; but it was too oblique to serve its purpose. Like many other examples of first-person satirical parody, *Notes from Underground* has usually been misunderstood and taken straight. Indeed, the intrinsic danger of such a form, used for such a purpose, is that it tends to wipe out any critical distance between the narrator and reader, and makes it difficult to *see through* the character to the target of the satire. A famous example of such a misunderstanding in English literature is Defoe's *The Shortest Way with Dissenters*, in which the dissenter Defoe, ironically speaking through the persona of a fanatical Tory, called for the physical extermination of all dissenters. But the irony was not understood, and Defoe, taken at his word, was sentenced to a term in the pillory as punishment. This danger can be avoided only if, as in *Gulliver's Travels*, the reader is disoriented from the very start by the strangeness of the situation, or if in other ways—linguistic exaggerations or manifestly grotesque behavior—he is made aware that the I-narrator is only a convention and not a genuine character. Although Dostoevsky makes some attempt to supplement his footnote in this direction, these efforts were not sufficient to balance the overwhelming psychological presence of the underground man and the force of his imprecations and anathemas against some of the most cherished dogmas of modern civilization. As a result, the parodistic function of his character has always been obscured by the immense vitality of its artistic embodiment, and it has, paradoxically, been Dostoevsky's very genius for the creation of character that has most interfered with the proper understanding of *Notes from Underground.**

It is not really difficult to comprehend why, in this instance, the passion that Dostoevsky poured into his character should have overshadowed the nature of the work as a satirical parody. Time and again we can hear Dostoevsky speaking about himself through his fictional guise, and he unquestionably endowed the underground man with some of his deepest and most intimate feelings. As the underground man belabors his own self-disgust and guilt, was not Dostoevsky also expressing his self-condemnation as a conscience-stricken spectator of his wife's death-agonies, and repenting of the egoism to which he confessed in his notebook? The self-critical references to the underground man's school years in the second part certainly draw on Dostoevsky's own unhappy sojourn long ago in the Academy of Engineers; and the frenzy of the character's revolt against a world of imprisonment by "the laws of nature" imaginatively revived all the despair

* Wayne Booth, in his illuminating discussion of the misunderstanding about Defoe, makes much the same point. Comparing *The Shortest Way with Dissenters* with Swift's *A Modest Proposal*, he remarks that Defoe is actually superior "in terms of realistic consistency alone," and that, if Defoe's piece is inferior to Swift as satire, "it is certainly more significant as a forerunner of modern fiction." He also cites another critic, Robert G. Rathbun, who observed that "the pamphlet brought Defoe to the pillory, but it also showed his skill in writing from an assumed point of view." One can well say too that in *Notes from Underground* Dostoevsky the novelist tended to overpower Dostoevsky the satirist. See Wayne C. Booth, *The Rhetoric of Fiction* (Chicago and London, 1961), 321.

and torment of the prison years. Besides, what a release it must have been for Dostoevsky, after all his guarded temporizing and cautious qualifying, finally to fling his defiance into the teeth of the radicals and expose the disastrous implications of their "advanced" ideas! No wonder he could not resist the temptation to impart more depth and vitality to his central figure than the literary form he had chosen really required!

These personal taproots of his inspiration, however, all flow into the service of an articulate and coherent satirical conception. *Notes from Underground* has been read as the psychological self-revelation of a pathological personality, or as a theological cry of despair over the evils of "human nature," or as a declaration of Dostoevsky's supposed adherence to Nietzsche's philosophy of "amoralism" and the will to power, or as a defiant assertion of the revolt of the human personality against all attempts to limit its inexhaustible potentialities—and the list can easily be continued. All these readings, and many more, can plausibly be supported if certain features of the text are singled out and placed in the foreground while others are simply overlooked or forgotten. But if we are interested in understanding Dostoevsky's own point of view, so far as this can be reconstructed, then we must take it for what it was initially meant to be—a brilliantly Swiftian satire, remarkable for the finesse of its conception and the brio of its execution, which dramatizes the dilemmas of a representative Russian personality attempting to live by the two European codes whose unhappy effects Dostoevsky explores.[7] And though the sections have a loose narrative link, the novella is above all a diptych depicting two episodes of a symbolic history of the Russian intelligentsia.

PART I

1. The Dialectic of Determinism

The first segment of *Notes from Underground* extends from Chapter I through Chapter VI, and its famous opening tirade gives us an unforgettable picture of the underground man stewing in his Petersburg "corner" and mulling over the peculiarities of his character and his life: "I am a sick man. . . . I am a spiteful man. I am an unpleasant man. I think my liver is diseased." The least one can say, at first contact, is that the underground man is not self-complacent; and we are immediately aware of his acute intelligence. He is ill but refuses to see a doctor, though he respects medicine: "Besides, I am extremely superstitious, let's say sufficiently so to respect medicine." Medicine is of course supposed to be a science—and had indeed become *the* science after Bazarov, Lopukhov, and Kirsanov; but the underground man sarcastically labels excessive respect for medicine as itself just an irrational superstition. He knows he should visit a doctor, but somehow—really for no good reason, simply out of spite—he prefers to stay home, untreated. Why? "You probably will not understand that," he says. "Well, I understand it" (5: 99). Whatever the explanation, there is a clear conflict between a rational course of behavior and some obscure feeling labeled "spite." The underground man's "reason," which would prompt him to seek a doctor out of self-interest, is evidently thwarted by some other motive.

We then learn that the underground man is an ex-civil servant, now retired on a small income, who in the past had engaged in incessant battles to tyrannize the humble petitioners that came his way in the course of business. But while he had enjoyed this sop to his ego, he confesses that "I was not only not spiteful but not even an embittered man. . . . I might foam at the mouth, but bring me some kind of toy, give me a cup of tea with sugar, and I would be appeased." The underground man's nature is by no means vicious and evil; he is more than ordinarily responsive to any manifestation of friendliness; but such responses are carefully kept bottled up no matter how strongly he might feel them: "Every moment I was conscious in myself of many, many elements completely opposed to that [spite]. . . . I knew that they had been teeming in me all my life, begging to be let out, but I would not let them, would not let them, purposely would not let them" (5: 100).

Such a passage should have been sufficient to scotch the prevalent notion that the underground man was perverse and evil "by nature," and that his behavior springs from a character innately deformed and distorted. But alas! The narrator's plain words have been far from enough to prevent precisely such a reading from being widely accepted (and they will no doubt prove as insufficient in the future as in the past). In fact, the underground man is shown as being caught in a conflict between the egoistic aspects of his character and the sympathetic, outgoing ones that he also possesses; but these latter are continually suppressed in favor of the former. At first, we observed a conflict between the underground man's reason and his feelings that might be considered purely psychological (is reason or spite the stronger force?). To this is now added a struggle of a more moral character between egoism and altruism, or at least friendliness. The first conflict dominates Part I, where the underground man essentially talks to himself or to an imaginary interlocutor; the second comes to the fore in Part II, where he is still living (or trying to live) in society and in relation to other people. In both cases, though, we see him torn apart by an inner dissonance that prevents him from behaving in what might be considered a "normal" fashion—that is, acting in terms of self-interest and "reason" in Part I, or giving unhindered expression to his altruistic (or at least amiably social) impulses in Part II. What prevents him from doing so is precisely what Dostoevsky wishes to illuminate and explore.

317

The nature of these impediments becomes clear only gradually in Part I as the underground man continues to expose all his defects to the scornful contemplation of his assumed reader. For it turns out that the contradictory impulses struggling within him have literally paralyzed his character. "Not only could I not become spiteful," he says, "I could not even become anything: neither spiteful nor kind, neither a rascal nor an honest man, neither a hero nor an insect." The underground man's only consolation is that "an intelligent man in the nineteenth-century must and morally ought to be pre-eminently a characterless creature; a man of character, an active man is pre-eminently a limited creature," and he boastfully attributes his characterlessness to the fact that he is "hyperconscious." As a result of this "hyperconsciousness," he was "most capable of recognizing every refinement of 'all the sublime and the beautiful,' as we used to say at one time" (the 1840s). But "the more conscious I was of goodness, and of all that 'sublime and beautiful,' the more deeply I sank into my mire and the more capable I became of sinking into it completely" (5: 100, 102).

This strange state of moral impotence, which the underground man both defends and despises, is complicated by the further admission that he positively *enjoys* the experience of his own degradation. "I reached the point," he confesses, "of feeling a sort of secret, abnormal, despicable enjoyment in returning home to my corner on some disgusting Petersburg night, and being acutely conscious that that day I had again done something loathsome, that what was done could never be undone, and secretly, inwardly gnaw, gnaw at myself for it, nagging and consuming myself till at last the bitterness turned into a sort of shameful accursed sweetness, and finally into real positive enjoyment" (5: 102).

The underground man frankly admits to being an unashamed masochist, and all too many commentators are quite happy to accept this admission as a sufficient explanation of his behavior. To do so, however, simply disregards the relation of the underground man's psychology to his social-cultural formation. For he goes on to explain that his sense of enjoyment derived from "the hyperconsciousness of [his] own degradation," a hyperconsciousness that persuaded him of the impossibility of becoming anything else or of behaving in any other way even if he had wished to do so. "For the root of it all," he says, "was that it all proceeded according to the normal and fundamental laws of hyperconsciousness, and with the inertia that was the direct result of those laws, and that consequently one was not only unable to change but could do absolutely nothing" (5: 102).

What does the underground man mean by this rather baffling assertion? What *are* the "normal and fundamental laws of hyperconsciousness," and why should they lead to immobility and inertia? This passage has often been taken as a reference to the underground man's "Hamletism," which links him with such figures as the protagonists of Turgenev's "Hamlet of the Shchigrovsky District" and "Diary of a Superfluous Man," both of whom are destroyed by an excess of consciousness that unfits them for the possibilities offered by their lives. Such thematic resemblances need not be denied; but this pervasive motif in Russian literature of the 1850s and 1860s is given a special twist by Dostoevsky and shown as the unexpected consequence of the doctrines advanced by the very people who had attacked the "Hamlets" most violently—the radicals of the 1860s themselves. For the pseudo-scientific terms of the underground man's declaration about "hyperconsciousness" are a parody of Chernyshevsky, and the statement is a paraphrase of Chernyshevsky's assertion, in *The Anthropological Principle in Philosophy*, that no such capacity as free will exists or can exist, since whatever actions man attributes to his own initiative are really a result of the "laws of nature." The underground man reveals the effects on his character of the "hyperconsciousness" derived from a knowledge of such "laws," and thus mockingly exemplifies what such a doctrine really means in practice.

Such "hyperconsciousness," based on the conviction that free will is an illusion, leads to a bewildered demoralization dramatized by Dostoevsky with consummate dialectical ingenuity. The underground man, for instance, imagines that he wishes to forgive someone magnanimously for having slapped him in the face; but the more he thinks about it, the more impossible such an intention becomes. "After all, I would probably never have been able to do anything with my magnanimity—neither to forgive, for my assailant may have slapped me because of the laws of nature, and one cannot forgive the laws of nature; nor to forget, for even if it were the laws of nature, *it is insulting all the same*" (italics added). Or suppose he wishes to act the other way round—not to forgive magnanimously, but to take revenge. How can one take revenge when no one is to blame for anything? "You look into it, the object flies off into air, your reasons evaporate, the criminal is not to be found, the insult becomes fate rather than an insult, something like the toothache, for which no one is to blame." This is why, as the underground man asserts, "the direct, legitimate, immediate fruit of consciousness is inertia—that is, conscious sitting on one's hands." Or, if one does not sit on one's hands but acts—say on the matter of revenge—then "it would only be out of spite" (5: 103, 108-109). Spite is not a *valid* cause for any kind of action, and hence it is the only one left when the laws of nature make any justified response impossible.

In such passages, the moral vacuum created by the thoroughgoing acceptance of determinism is depicted with masterly psychological insight. As a well-trained member of the intelligentsia, the underground man intellectually accepts such determinism; but it is impossible for him really to live with its conclusions. "Thus it would follow, as the result of hyperconsciousness, that one is not to blame for being a scoundrel, as though that were any consolation to the scoundrel once he himself has come to realize that he actually is a scoundrel." Or, as regards the slap in the face, it is impossible to forget because "even if it were the laws of nature, it is insulting all the same" (5: 102-103). Dostoevsky thus juxtaposes a *total* human reaction—a sense of self-revulsion at being a scoundrel, an upsurge of anger at the insult of being slapped—against a scientific rationale that dissolves all such moral-emotive feelings and hence the very possibility of a human response. Reason tells the underground man that guilt or indignation is totally irrational and meaningless; but conscience and a sense of dignity continue to exist all the same as ineradicable components of the human psyche.

Here, then, is the explanation for the so-called masochism of the underground man. Why does he refuse to see a doctor about his liver or insist that one may enjoy moaning needlessly and pointlessly about a toothache? It is because, in both instances, some mysterious, impersonal power—the laws of nature—has reduced the individual to complete helplessness; and his only method of expressing a *human* reaction to this power is to refuse to submit silently to its despotism, to protest against its pressure no matter in how ridiculous a fashion. The refusal to be treated is such a protest, self-defeating though it may be; and the moans over a toothache, says the underground man, express "all the aimlessness of your pain, which is so humiliating to your consciousness; all the system of the laws of nature on which you spit disdainfully, of course, but from which you suffer all the same while it does not" (5: 106).

Both these situations are analogous to the shameful "pleasure" that the underground man confesses at keeping alive the sense of his own degradation after his debauches. He refuses to be consoled by the alibi that the laws of nature are to blame; and his dubious enjoyment translates the moral-emotive response of his *human nature* to the blank nullity of the *laws of nature*. Far from being a sign of psychic abnormality, this sensation is in reality—given the topsy-turvy world in which he lives—a proof of the underground man's paradoxical spiritual health. For it indicates that, despite the convictions of his reason, he refuses to surrender his right to possess a conscience or an ability to feel outraged and insulted.

2. The Man of Action

It is only by recognizing this ironic displacement of the normal moral-psychic horizon that we can accurately grasp the underground man's relation to the imaginary interlocutor with whom he argues all through the first part of *Notes from Underground*. This interlocutor is obviously a follower of Chernyshevsky, a man of action, who believes himself to be nothing less than *l'homme de la nature et de la vérité*. The underground man *agrees* with this gentleman's theory that all human conduct is nothing but a mechanical product of the laws of nature; but he also knows what the man of action does not—that this theory makes all human behavior impossible, or at least meaningless. "I envy such a man till my bile overflows," says the underground man. "He is stupid, I am not disputing that, but perhaps the normal man should be stupid—how do you know?" The normal man, the man of action, happily lacks the hyperconsciousness of the underground man; and when impelled by a desire to obtain revenge, for example, he "simply rushes straight toward his goal like an infuriated bull with its horns down, and nothing but a wall will stop him" (5: 103-104). He is totally unaware that whatever he may consider to be the basis for his headlong charge—for example, the need for justice—is a ludicrously old-fashioned and unscientific prejudice that has been replaced by the laws of nature. Only his stupidity allows him to maintain his complacent normality, and to remain so completely free from the paralyzing dilemmas of the underground man.

The men of action sometimes also run up against the stone wall of the laws of nature; but since they do not understand all its implications, the shock of impact has no effect on their convictions or their conduct. "For them a wall is not an excuse, as for example for us, people who think, and consequently who do nothing. . . . The stone wall has for them something tranquilizing, morally determining and final—even something, if you please, mystical. . . ." Confronted by the so-called tenets of natural science—such as, for example, "that in reality one drop of your own fat must be dearer to you than a hundred thousand of your fellow creatures, and that this conclusion is the final solution of all so-called virtues and duties and all such ravings and prejudices"—they stop all their questionings and reasonings (5: 103-105). They simply do not understand that the stone wall of science eliminates their feeling of outraged justice as surely as it eliminates all nonsense about duty. Hence the men of action accept the doctrines of natural science with a smug awareness of keeping up with European progress, while they continue to profess the same moral indignation as people in the "unscientific" past.

The hyperconscious underground man, who lacks this saving grace of stupidity, knows only too well that the stone wall of science and determinism cuts the ground away from *any* type of moral reaction. Hence, when *he* feels aggrieved, he can only nurse a despicable resentment which, as he realizes only too clearly, cannot justly be discharged against anybody. Yet he cannot help behaving *as if* some sort of free human response were still possible and meaningful; "consequently there is only the same outlet left again—that is, to beat the wall as hard as you can." And this gesture of despair at least has the consolation of lucidity and lack of self-deception: "Is it not much better to understand it all, to be conscious of it all, all the impossibilities and stone walls; not to resign yourself to a single one of these impossibilities and stone walls if it disgusts you to be resigned; to reach, by way of the most inevitable logical combinations, the most revolting conclusions on the everlasting theme that you are yourself somehow to blame even for the stone wall, though again it is as clear as day you are not to blame in the least, and therefore, silently and impotently gnashing your teeth, to sink sensuously into inertia, brooding over the fact that there is no one even for you to feel vindictive against?" (5: 109, 106).

Here, we might think, the paradoxes of the underground man reach a paroxysm of psychopathic self-accusation; but psychology by itself does not take us very far in comprehending Dostoevsky's artistic logic. For once we understand the complex inversions of his creation, it is quite clear that no one in the world can be guilty of anything except the underground man. He knows that the idea of guilt, along with all other moral ideas, has been wiped off the slate by the laws of nature; yet he irrationally persists in having moral responses. And since there is nowhere else for him to assign moral responsibility, by the most irrefutable process of deduction he and he alone is to blame for everything. But, at the same time, he knows very well that he is *not* to blame, and he wishes it were possible to forget about the laws of nature long enough to convince himself that he could freely choose to become *anything*—a loafer, a glutton, or a person who spends his life drinking toasts to the health of everything "sublime and beautiful."

This analysis should be enough to illuminate the dialectic of determinism that Dostoevsky dramatizes in these first six chapters of *Notes from Underground*. It would be possible to show how every self-contradictory response of the underground man in these chapters derives from this dialectic, which is driven by the contradiction between the underground man's intellectual acceptance of Chernyshevsky's determinism and his simultaneous rejection of it with the entire intuitive-emotional level of personality identified with moral conscience. As a result, the underground man's self-derision and self-abuse are not meant to be taken literally. The rhetoric of the underground man contains an inverted irony similar to that of *Winter Notes*, which turns back on itself as a means of ridiculing his scornful interlocutor, the man of action. For the life of the underground man is the *reductio ad absurdum* of that of the man of action; and the more repulsive and obnoxious he portrays himself as being, the more he reveals the *true* meaning of what his self-confident judge so blindly holds dear.* It is only the impenetrable obtuseness of the radical men of action that prevents them from seeing the underground man as their mirror image, and from

* This technique of, as it were, mirroring through a warped reflector, whereby a character is confronted with a distorted or degrading image of himself that he refuses to recognize, is one that Dostoevsky has used before and will employ with greater and greater mastery in the future. A situation structurally similar to the one being analyzed here can be found in the early short story *Polzunkov*. See *Dostoevsky: The Seeds of Revolt, 1821-1849* (Princeton, 1976), 322-325.

acknowledging the greeting he might have given them (in Baudelaire's words): "hypocrite lecteur, mon semblable, mon frère!"

3. The Most Advantageous Advantage

The first chapters of *Notes from Underground* present a powerful picture of the existential dilemma of the underground man, whose life illustrates in action the split between reason and the moral-emotive sensibility arising from a total acceptance of *all* the implications of Chernyshevsky's philosophy. After showing the inherent inability of the human psyche to accommodate itself to such a "rational" world, and the strange and seemingly senseless ways in which this refusal can become manifest, the underground man turns more directly to demolish the arguments that Chernyshevsky and the men of action use to defend their position. It may seem as if this refutation contradicts the assertion that he *accepts* the basic tenets of Chernyshevsky's philosophy. But such acceptance has always included a sardonic realization of the total incongruity of those precepts with the norms of human experience; and this incongruity is now formulated more explicitly in the arguments developed throughout Chapters VII-IX.

"Oh, tell me," the underground man asks incredulously, "who first declared, who first proclaimed, that man only does nasty things because he does not know his real interests; and that if he were enlightened, if his eyes were opened to his real, normal interests, he would at once cease to do nasty things . . . he would see his own advantage in the good and nothing else, and since we all know that not a single man can knowingly act to his own disadvantage, consequently, so to say, he would begin doing good through necessity" (5: 110). This was indeed the essence of Chernyshevsky's position—that "rational egoism," once accepted, would so enlighten man that the very possibility of his behaving irrationally, that is, contrary to his interests, would entirely disappear. But this argument, as the underground man points out caustically, has one little flaw: it entirely overlooks that man has, and always will have, a supreme interest, which he will never surrender, in being able to exercise his free will.

The underground man's discourse in these chapters is composed of several strands. One is the repeated presentation of the way in which "statisticians, sages, and lovers of humanity" frequently end up by acting contrary to all their oft-proclaimed and solemnly high-minded principles of rationality. Another is to look at human history and to ask whether man ever was, or wished to be, totally rational: "In short, one may say anything about the history of the world—anything that might enter the most disordered imagination. The only thing one cannot say is that it is rational. The very word sticks in one's throat." A third comes much closer to the present and, in passing, takes a sideswipe at the British historian Henry Thomas Buckle, then very popular with the Russian radicals, who believed that the laws of history could be worked out according to those of the natural sciences. The underground man simply cannot control his merriment over Buckle's assertion "that through civilization mankind becomes softer, and consequently less bloodthirsty, and less fitted for warfare," and he appeals to the reader: "Take the whole of the nineteenth century in which Buckle lived. Take Napoleon—both the Great and the present one. Take North America—the eternal union [then racked by the Civil War]" (5: 111, 116, 112).

These examples show to what extent rationalists and logicians are apt to shut their eyes to the most obvious facts for the sake of their systems; and all these systems, for some reason, always define "human advantages" exclusively "from the average of statistical figures and scientific-economic formulas. Now then, your advantages are prosperity, wealth, freedom, peace—etc., etc. So that a man who, for instance, would openly and knowingly oppose the whole list would be, according to you, *and of course to me as well*, an obscurantist or an absolute madman, no?" (5: 110; italics added). But while the underground man has often been taken for this kind of "absolute madman," such a reading is a clear violation of Dostoevsky's words. The underground man does *not* reject prosperity, wealth, freedom, and peace *in themselves*; he rejects the view that the only way to attain them is by the sacrifice of man's freedom and personality.

"There it is, gentlemen," he says commiseratingly, "does it not seem that something really exists that is dearer to almost every man than his greatest advantage, or (not to violate logic) that there is one most advantageous advantage (the very one omitted, about which we spoke just now) for which, if necessary, a man is ready to go against all laws, that is, against reason, honor, peace, prosperity—in short, against all those wonderful and useful things if only he can attain that fundamental, most advantageous advantage dearer to him than everything else?" (5: 111). The answer to this question, whose parentheses parody some of the more laborious passages in *The Anthropological Principle*, has been given in the first six chapters. The one "most advantageous advantage" for man is the preservation of his free will, which may or may not be exercised in harmony with reason but which, in any case, always wishes to preserve the right to *choose*; and this primary "advantage" cannot be included in the systems of the lovers of humanity because it makes forever impossible their dream of transforming human nature to desire *only* the rational.

4. The Crystal Palace

Chernyshevsky embodied this dream of transformation, as we know, in his vision of the Crystal Palace, and Dostoevsky picks up this symbol to present it from the underground man's point of view. In this future Utopia of plenitude, man will have been completely re-educated so that "he will then voluntarily refrain from erring, and, so to say, by necessity will not want to set his will against his normal interests. More than that: then, you say, science itself will have taught man (though this, I think, is a luxury) that he does not really have either will or caprice and that he never has had them, and that he himself is nothing more than some sort of piano key or organ stop; and that moreover, there are laws of nature in the world; so that everything he does is not at all done by his will but by itself, according to the laws of nature" (5: 112).

The musical imagery here derives directly from Fourier, who believed he had discovered a "law of social harmony," and whose disciples liked to depict the organization of the passions in the phalanstery by analogy with the organization of keys on a clavier. (This latter comparison is made in a widely read work of Victor Considérant, *La Destinée sociale*, whose title Chernyshevsky managed to smuggle into *What Is To Be Done?* as a play on words.)* Also, when the underground man comments that in the Crystal Palace "all human actions will . . . be tabulated according to these laws [of nature], mathematically, like tables of logarithms up to 108,000 and entered in a table" (5: 113), he is by no means exaggerating. Fourier had actually made the effort to work out an exhaustive table of the passions that were, in his view, the immutable laws of (human) nature, and whose needs would have to be satisfied in any model social order. Dostoevsky thus combines Fourier's table of passions with Chernyshevsky's material determin-

---

* The passage in question is a good example of the Aesopian games that Chernyshevsky was playing with his eagle-eyed readers—and with the censorship. Two of his characters are talking about the books being read by the heroine, Vera Pavlovna:

"Look here, Mikhail Ivanych, this one, in French, I have almost made it out myself: 'Gostinaya.' That means a manual of etiquette. And here is one in German; I cannot read it."
"No, Maria Alexevna, it is not 'Gostinaya'; it is 'Destinée.' " He said the word in Russian.
"What, then, is this destiny? Is it a novel, or ladies' oracle, or a dream book?"
"Let's see." Mikhail Ivanych turned over a few pages.
"It deals with series; it is a book for a *savant*."
"Series? I understand. It treats of transfers of money."

The word "series" is a key Fourierist term, which refers to the organization of labor in the phalanstery according to the dominating passions of various types of personalities. The German book—"On Religion," by Ludwig Feuerbach—is taken with equal aplomb to be a work of piety written by King Louis [Ludwig] XIV of France. N. G. Chernyshevsky, *Chto Delat?* (Moscow, 1955), 85.

For some reason, the commentator of *Notes from Underground* in the Academy edition interprets Dostoevsky's imagery as a reference to Diderot, who, in one of his lesser-known texts, spoke of human beings as musical instruments and the human sensibility as a clavier that nature used as its instrument. Fourier is not mentioned at all in this connection. The aim of this reference, and of the commentary in general, seems to be to blunt the sharpness of Dostoevsky's attack on Chernyshevsky, and to identify his target much more vaguely with eighteenth-century materialism. If such a view were accepted, it would of course make the work more easily assimilable in a Soviet Russian context.

It is possible, though highly speculative, that Diderot's image was known to Fourier. But there hardly seems any justification for thinking that Dostoevsky's own musical imagery should be traced back directly to Diderot rather than to Fourier and his disciples such as Considérant. See *PSS*, 5: 384.

ism in his attack on the ideal of the Crystal Palace as involving the total elimination of the personality. For the empirical manifestation of personality is the right to *choose* a course of action whatever it may be; and no choice is involved when one is good, reasonable, satisfied, and happy by conformity with laws of nature that exclude the very possibility of their negation.

Even if one were to imagine attaining this state of perfection, the underground man warns, it might still prove to be terribly tedious. Once man has nothing further to strive toward or hope for, he falls prey to *ennui*; and Dostoevsky at this point falls back on some familiar motifs. *Ennui* immediately recalls the world of Prince Valkovsky and Cleopatra, and it is no surprise to see Pushkin's Egyptian queen turning up to stick gold pins into the breasts of her slave girls for amusement. Luckily, though, the underground man assures us, the Crystal Palace is *not* possible because "man is so phenomenally ungrateful . . . shower upon him every earthly blessing, drown him in bliss so that nothing but bubbles would dance on the surface of bliss, as on water; give him such economic prosperity that he has nothing else to do but sleep, eat cakes, and busy himself with ensuring the continuation of world history—even then man, out of sheer ingratitude, sheer slander, will play you some dirty trick." This "dirty trick" is precisely that he will "even risk his cakes and deliberately desire the most fatal rubbish, the most uneconomical absurdity, simply in order to prove to himself (as if this were so necessary) that men are still men and not piano keys" (5: 116-117).

At this point, the underground man rises to a climactic vision of universal chaos, which parallels, in terms of the socio-historical ideal of the Crystal Palace, the chaos of the underground man's private life in the first six chapters. In both cases, the cause of this chaos is the same: the revolt of the personality against a world in which free will (and hence moral categories of any kind) has no further reason for being. For if the world of the Crystal Palace really existed, "even if man really were nothing but a piano key, even if this were proved to him by natural science and mathematics—he will devise destruction and chaos, will devise sufferings of all sorts, and will insist on getting his way!" And if all this suffering and chaos can also be calculated and tabulated in advance, "then man would purposely go mad in order to be rid of reason and to insist on getting his way!" These words have been endlessly quoted out of context, as if Dostoevsky conceived of ordinary human life as some sort of metaphysical imprisonment that required and justified such a recourse to madness and chaos; but this reading goes against the clear sense of the text. The self-destructive revolt of freedom is not a value in itself; it is envisaged *only* as a last-ditch defense against the hypothetical accomplishment of the Crystal Palace ideal. As the underground man writes in relief: "And after this how is one not to sin by rejoicing that this is not yet, and that for the time being desire still depends on the devil alone knows what!" (5: 117).

Such is the terrible prospect of the proposed completion of the Crystal Palace ideal; and the underground man continues to question the buoyant assurance of Chernyshevsky and his followers that such an ideal is man's true desire. "Man likes to create and build roads, that is incontestable," he concedes, meaning that man wishes to occupy himself with useful and socially productive labor. But he denies that humanity is longing to achieve the static, secular apocalypse of the Crystal Palace, which would signify the end of history and the cessation of all further striving, aspiration and hope. "May it not be that he so loves chaos and destruction (surely this is incontestable, he sometimes loves it very much, that's so), because he instinctively fears to attain his goal and to complete the edifice under construction? How do you know, perhaps he only likes that edifice from a distance, not from close up; perhaps he only likes to build it and not to live in it, leaving it *aux animaux domestiques* such as ants, sheep, etc., etc. Now the ants have an entirely different taste. They have an astonishing edifice of this kind eternally indestructible—the anthill" (5: 118).

This comparison of the Socialist ideal to an anthill was a commonplace in the Russian journalism of the period, but Dostoevsky may have used this image in connection with the end of history as an allusion to Herzen. "If humanity went straight to some goal," Herzen had written in *From the Other Shore*, "there would be no history, only logic; humanity would stop in some finished form, in a spontaneous *status quo* like the animals. . . . Besides, if the libretto existed, history would lose all interest, it would become futile, boring, ridiculous."[8] The obvious similarity of these texts shows how much Dostoevsky had absorbed from the work he admired so greatly; it also reveals how accurately he was thematizing a profound ideological contrast between his own generation and that of the 1860s. For the intellectual and ideological physiognomy of the generation of the 1840s, nourished on Romantic literature and German Idealist philosophy, formed a sharp contrast to that of the 1860s; and Herzen, like Dostoevsky, always staunchly refused to accept Chernyshevsky's material determinism and denial of free will.* It is thus appropriate that the underground man later at-

---

* Very close to the end of his life, Herzen wrote a telling letter to his son Alexander Jr. in which he made the point perfectly clear. The younger Herzen, by this time a noted physiologist, had published a lecture course in which all animal and human activity was interpreted as a function of the nervous reflex system; and he thus concluded, like Chernyshevsky, that free will was an illusion.

His father replied: "At all periods, man seeks his autonomy, his liberty and, though pulled along by necessity, *he does not wish to act except according to his own will*; he does not wish to be a passive gravedigger of the past or an unconscious midwife of the future; he considers history as his free and indispensable work. He believes in his liberty as he believes in the existence of the external world as it presents itself to him because he trusts his eyes, and because, without that confidence, he could not take a step. Moral liberty is thus a psychological or, if one wishes, an anthropological reality." No more expressive statement could be given of Dostoevsky's own existential conception of liberty and moral freedom. See A. I. Gertsen, *Izbrannye Filosofskie Proizvedenia*, 2 vols. (Moscow, 1946), 2: 283.

tributes his opposition to the ideal of the Crystal Palace at least partly to having come of age when he did.

All these arguments are then focused in a final rejection of the Crystal Palace for leaving no room for "suffering." Once again, however, in order to do justice to Dostoevsky, it is necessary to stress the qualified nature of this assertion and the nuance of meaning that he gives it. "After all," the underground man says, "I do not really insist on suffering or on prosperity either. I insist . . . on my caprice, and that it be guaranteed to me when it's necessary." Suffering is no more an end in itself than madness or chaos, and remains subordinate to the supreme value of the assertion of moral autonomy; but it serves as a prod to keep alive this sense of moral autonomy in a world deprived of human significance by determinism: "In the Crystal Palace it [suffering] is even unthinkable: suffering is doubt, negation, and what kind of a Crystal Palace would that be in which doubts can be harbored?" The ability to doubt means that man is not yet transformed into a rational-ethical machine that can behave *only* in conformity with reason. This is why the underground man declares that "suffering is the sole origin of consciousness" (5: 119); suffering and consciousness are inseparable because the latter is not only a psychological but primarily a moral attribute of the human personality.

5. *The Palatial Chicken Coop*

Chapter x of *Notes from Underground* poses a special problem because it was so badly mutilated by the censorship. In this chapter, as we know, Dostoevsky claimed to have expressed "the essential idea" of his work, which he defined as "the necessity of faith and Christ"; but the passages in which he did so were suppressed and never restored in later reprintings. Dostoevsky's failure to return the text to its original form has sometimes been taken to mean that the sense of his initial affirmation could hardly have had any real importance for him and can thus be disregarded; but such an inference fails to take the problem of censorship into account. At no period of his life would Dostoevsky have relished the dangerous and time-consuming prospect of attempting to persuade the censors to reverse an earlier ruling. To have tried to do so would only have imperiled and delayed the publication of the reprints and collected editions of his work on which he counted for badly needed income. Tzvetan Todorov has recently argued, much more interestingly, that Dostoevsky did not restore the cuts for aesthetic reasons: he realized later that the true climax was the end of Part II, and decided it had been a mistake to provide another climax earlier.[9] But even this structural suggestion does not, in my view, offer any conclusive internal reason for Dostoevsky's choice to leave well enough alone.

For the moment, let us examine this "garbled" chapter to see what can still be found that may help us to come closer to Dostoevsky's "essential idea." In the first place, Chapter x brings home quite explicitly how literally unbearable the situation of the underground man has become. Up to this point, he had used his misery mainly as an ironic weapon; but now we realize that the underground revolt of the personality—important and necessary though it may be—cannot ever be taken as an end in itself. Torn between the convictions of "reason" and the revolt of his conscience and feelings, the underground man cries: "Can I have been made simply in order to come to the conclusion that the whole way I am made is a swindle? Can this be the whole purpose? I don't believe it." True, he rejects the Crystal Palace because it is impossible to be irreverent about it and stick out one's tongue at it, but "I did not at all say [this] because I am so fond of putting out my tongue. . . . On the contrary, I would let my tongue be cut off out of sheer gratitude if things could be so arranged that I myself would lose all desire to put it out" (5: 120-121).

Dostoevsky thus indicates that the underground man, far from rejecting all moral ideals in favor of an illimitable egoism, is desperately searching for one that would truly satisfy his spirit. Such an ideal would be one which, rather than spurring the personality to revolt in rabid frenzy, would instead lead to a willing surrender in its favor. Such an alternative ideal would thus be required to recognize the autonomy of the will and the freedom of the personality, and appeal to the moral nature of man rather than to his reason and self-interest conceived as working in harmony with the laws of nature. For Dostoevsky, this alternative ideal could be found in the teachings of Christ; and from a confusion that still exists in the text, we can catch a glimpse of how he may have tried to integrate this alternative into the framework of his imagery.

This confusion arises in the course of a comparison between the Crystal Palace and a chicken coop. "You see," says the underground man, "if it were not a palace but a chicken coop, and it started to rain, I might creep into the chicken coop to avoid getting wet, but all the same I would not take the chicken coop for a palace out of gratitude that it sheltered me from the rain. You laugh, you even say that, in such circumstances, a chicken coop and a mansion—it's all the same. Yes, I answer, if one has to live simply to avoid getting wet." It is not the usefulness of the chicken coop that is impugned by the underground man, but the fact that it is taken for a palace— the fact that, in return for its practical advantages, it has been elevated into mankind's ideal. One recalls Dostoevsky's remark in *Winter Notes* that the desperate English working class prefers the anthill to cannibalism; but the underground man refuses to accept the chicken coop qua palace as *his* ideal: "But what is to be done if I have taken it into my head that this [not to get wet; utility] is not the only object in life, and that if one must live, it may as well be in a mansion? That is my choice, my desire. You will only eradicate it when you have changed my desire. *Well, do change it, tempt me with something else, give me another ideal*" (5: 120; italics added).

The underground man thus clearly opens up the possibility of "another ideal"; and, as the text goes along, he seems to envisage a different sort of Crystal Palace—one that would be a genuine mansion rather than a chicken coop satisfying purely material needs. For he then continues: "And meanwhile, I will not take a chicken coop for a palace. Let the Crystal edifice even be an idle dream, say it is inconsistent with the laws of nature, and I have invented it only as a result of my own stupidity, as a result of *some old-fashioned, irrational habits of my generation*. But what do I care if it is inconsistent? Isn't it all the same if it exists in my desires, or better, exists as long as my desires exist?" (5: 120; italics added). At this point, we observe a shift to a "Crystal edifice" based on the very *opposite* principles from those represented by the Crystal Palace throughout the rest of the text: this new "Crystal edifice" is *inconsistent* with the laws of nature (while the Crystal Palace is their embodiment), and it owes its existence to desire rather than to reason. The change is so abrupt, and so incompatible with what has gone before, that one can only assume some material leading from one type of Crystal building to the other has been excised from the manuscript.

Dostoevsky, we may speculate, must have attempted here to indicate the nature of a true Crystal Palace, or mansion, or edifice (his terminology is not consistent), and to contrast it with the false one that was really a chicken coop. From his letter, we know that he did so in a way to identify a true Crystal Palace with the "need for faith and Christ"; but such an attempt may well have confused and frightened the censors, still terrified out of their wits by the recent blunder over *What Is To Be Done?* and now accustomed to view the Crystal Palace as the abhorrent image of atheistic Socialism. Hence, they would have excised the sentences in which Dostoevsky tried to give his own Christian significance to this symbol, perhaps considering it to be both subversive and blasphemous. These suppositions would explain the strange history of Dostoevsky's text, and account for the flagrant contradiction, clearly evident on close reading, which provoked his indignant outcry that his entire meaning had been distorted.

Although this alternative ideal may have originally been indicated more clearly, Dostoevsky's conception still requires the underground man to remain trapped in the negative phase of his revolt. An alternative is suggested only as a remote and, for the underground man, unattainable possibility; and this is why Todorov's theory explaining the failure to restore the original text does not seem tenable. Each episode was meant to have its own type of climax, and there would have been a distinct gradation between the first and the second. What appears in the underground man's thoughts only as an impossible dream in the first part becomes a living reality in the second, strongly presented in terms of dramatic action. Even if the first climax had been retained in its original form, it would thus not have weakened the second, as Todorov assumes, but rather exemplified its metamorphosis from a hope into a vividly concrete illustration of such a resolution. For the underground man in this first part longs for another ideal; he knows it must exist; but he is so committed to a belief in material determinism and the laws of nature that he cannot imagine what it could be. "I know, anyway, that I will not be appeased with a compromise, with an endlessly recurring zero, simply because it exists according to the laws of nature and *actually* exists. I will not take as the crown of all my desires—a block of buildings with apartments for the poor on a lease for a thousand years, and, for any contingency, a dentist's sign hanging out" (5: 120).

In the final Chapter xi, the underground man continues to oscillate between defiance and despair, both affirming and denying his life and convictions in the space of a few lines: "Though I have said that I envy the normal man to the last drop of my bile, in the conditions in which I see him now I do not wish to be him (though all the same I will not stop from envying him. No, no, the underground is in any case more advantageous!). There, at any rate, one can . . . Bah!, and now here I am lying! I am lying because I know myself, like two times two, that the underground is not at all better, but something else, something I long for but cannot find. To the devil with the underground!" (5: 121). What that something else is, and why the underground man cannot find it, provides the substance for the second part of Dostoevsky's novella.

PART II

1. Apropos of the Wet Snow

The underground man, as we have seen, clings to his ideal of a "true" Crystal Palace because of "some old-fashioned, irrational habits of my generation." Dostoevsky thus locates the psychic-emotive responses of his character in a social-cultural context very clearly delimited in time. The underground man is forty years old in 1864 when he begins to write his *Notes*; he is twenty-four when the events in Part II take place, which would locate them in 1848; and this is the very year that Dostoevsky first assiduously began to attend the meetings of the Petrashevsky circle. These calculations are not intended to suggest that the second part of *Notes from Underground* is about Dostoevsky himself in any literal sense. The underground man is primarily a social-cultural type and must be understood as such; but in the second part, where he becomes a parody of the attitudes of the 1840s, he was certainly nourished by Dostoevsky's judgment of himself as a member of that generation. Evaluating his state of mind at that time, Dostoevsky had written to General E. I. Todleben in 1856: "I believed in theories and Utopias. . . . I was a hypochondriac. . . . I was excessively irritable with an unhealthy susceptibility. I deformed the simplest facts, endowing them with another aspect and other dimensions."[10] This description applies, word for word, to the portrait we are given of the underground man's psychology in his youth.

The period tonality of this second part is also indicated in many other ways besides the precise chronology of dates. The subtitle, "Apropos of the Wet Snow," seems to have no intrinsic relation to the text, and to have been used only to trigger the association recalling the memory of the prostitute Liza. In fact, however, it also helps to set the action firmly in a symbolic setting. P. V. Annenkov had noted in 1849 that the writers of the Natural School were all fond of employing "wet snow" as a typical feature of the dreary Petersburg landscape; and Dostoevsky thus uses his subtitle to bring back an image of Petersburg in the 1840s—an image of what, in the first part, Dostoevsky had called "the most abstract and premeditated city in the world" (5: 101), a city whose very existence (ever since Pushkin's *The Bronze Horseman*) had become emblematic in Russian literature for the violence and inhuman cost of the Russian adaptation to Western culture.

The atmosphere of the 1840s, with all its social-humanitarian exaltations, is also evoked explicitly by the quotation from a poem of N. A. Nekrasov appended as epigraph to the second part. This is the same poem, dating from 1846, that had already been mentioned ironically in *The Village of Stepanchikovo*, the first work in which Dostoevsky explicitly dissociated himself from what he now considered the naive illusions of the Natural School and of his own past. Written from the point of view of the (male) benefactor of a repentant prostitute, who has saved her from a life of sin by his ardent and unprejudiced love, the poem describes her torments of conscience:

> When from the murk of corruption
> I delivered your fallen soul
> With the ardent speech of conviction;
> And, full of profound torment,
> Wringing your hands, you cursed
> The vice that had ensnared you;
> When, with memories punishing
> Forgetful conscience
> You told me the tale
> Of all that happened before me,
> And suddenly, covering your face,
> Full of shame and horror,

You tearfully resolved,
Outraged, shocked . . .
Etc., etc., etc. (5: 124)

By cutting this passage short with three etceteras, Dostoevsky manifestly indicates that the philanthropic lucubrations of the speaker are just so much banal and conventional rhetoric. The redemption of a prostitute theme, taken over by the Russians in the 1840s from French Social Romantics like Eugène Sue, George Sand, and Victor Hugo, and continued up through Tolstoy's *Resurrection* (1899), had indeed become a commonplace by the 1860s. It figures as a minor episode in *What Is To Be Done?*, where one of the heroes salvages a fallen woman from a life of debauchery, lives with her for a time, and turns her into a model member of Vera Pavlovna's cooperative until she dies of tuberculosis. The climactic episode in the second part of *Notes from Underground*—the encounter between the underground man and the prostitute Liza—is an ironic parody and reversal of this Social Romantic cliché.

The second part of *Notes from Underground*, then, satirizes the sentimental Social Romanticism of the 1840s just as the first part satirized the metaphysics and ethics of the 1860s; and Dostoevsky draws for this purpose on the image of the 1840s he had already sketched in the pages of *Time*. It was a period, as he saw it, when the Russian intelligentsia had turned itself inside out so as to conform to the ideological prescriptions coming from abroad: "Everything then was done according to principle, we lived according to principle, and were terribly afraid to do anything not in conformity with the new ideas" (18: 58). Russia thus produced a race of "giants" (as he mockingly calls them), burning with a desire to aid "humanity" but regrettably unable to find any outlet for their vast powers. The 1840s had thus fostered its own kind of egoism and vanity, which allowed the "superfluous men" of the gentry-liberal intelligentsia to live in a dream world of "universal beneficence" while neglecting the simplest and most obvious moral obligations. It was incumbent on them, he had made clear, to live up to their own pretensions, and to turn their abstract love of humanity into a concrete act directed toward a flesh-and-blood individual. This is precisely the theme of the second part of *Notes from Underground*, which has been transposed into the bureaucratic world of Dostoevsky's early work and embodied in a character who is the lowly, but supremely self-conscious, administrative equivalent of the superfluous man.

This shift of theme is reflected in Part II by a very noticeable change of tone. Ultimate issues were at stake in the first part, where the final argument against the world of the "false" Crystal Palace could only be the rage of madness and self-destruction; and Dostoevsky's irony is accordingly bitter and twisted, his tonality harsh and abrasive. No such ultimate issues are involved in the misadventures of the underground man's early manhood, which are all provoked by that standard comic source—overweening vanity. Hence the second part is written in a much lighter tone of burlesque and caricature, and whole sections are nothing but an extended mockery of the underground man's stilted and pedantic responses to the simplest human situations. It is a tribute to the power of received ideas (as well as to the lingering effect of the first part on the reader's sensibility) that Dostoevsky's sharply derisive comedy should so long have gone unnoticed.

2. The Dialectic of Vanity

The opening pages of the second part recall the beginning of the first, where the underground man had spoken of his struggle to tyrannize the humble petitioners who came his way as a low-grade government bureaucrat. We recall that he had also felt more friendly impulses toward other members of the human species, but that "I would not let them, would not let them, purposely would not let them out" (5: 125). This conflict between the impulse to dominate and the desire to enter into a more amicable relation with others was not developed at all earlier; but it now comes to the fore and provides a more intimate background to the relative abstractions of Part I.

Why, we may well ask, did the youthful underground man behave in a fashion so much at variance with the promptings of his own inclinations? The answer once again emerges only gradually, and we first become aware that the underground man, consumed by a boundless vanity, is so acutely self-conscious that he cannot enter into normal social relations with anyone: "All my fellow clerks I, of course, hated from first to last, and I despised them all, and yet at the same time I was, as it were, afraid of them. . . . Somehow it then turned out this way quite suddenly: one moment I despised them, the next I placed them much above me" (5: 125). The underground man's vanity convinces him of his own superiority and he despises everyone; but since he desires such superiority to be *recognized* by others, he hates the world for its indifference and falls into self-loathing at his own humiliating dependence. This is the psychological dialectic of a self-conscious egoism that seeks to conquer recognition from the world and only arouses dislike and hostility in return. Such a dialectic of vanity parallels the dialectic of determinism in the first part, and has the same effect of immuring the ego in a world alienated from any human contact. Just as determinism dissolves the possibility of human response in the first part, so vanity blocks all social fraternity in the second.

Besides portraying this dialectic of vanity in action, Dostoevsky also traces it back to an ideological source—not a specific philosophical doctrine as in Part I, but the general cultural atmosphere of the 1840s, which fostered a forced and artificial Romantic egoism and a sense of superiority to ordinary Russian life that the underground man drank in through every pore. Indeed, what distinguishes him from the very earliest years is his marked intellectual prowess. "Moreover, they [his school fellows] all began to grasp slowly," he writes, "that I was already reading books none of them could read, and understood things (not forming part of our school curriculum) of which they had not even heard." Describing his later life, he says: "In the first place, at home I spent most of my time reading. . . . I tried to stifle all that was continually seething within me by means of external sensations. And the only source of external sensation possible for me was reading. Reading, of course, was a great help—it excited, delighted, and tormented me" (5: 140, 127). Books are thus responsible for keeping the *real* feelings of the underground man bottled up—the feelings, that is, opposed to his vanity and desire to dominate. Books interpose a network of acquired and artificial responses between himself and other people; and since we are in the world of the Russian intelligentsia of the 1840s, these books could only have been the works of the French Utopian Socialists and the Social Romantics and their Russian disciples on which Dostoevsky himself had battened at this period.

Over and over again Dostoevsky stresses the connections between the dialectic of vanity in which the underground man is caught and his intellectual culture. "A *cultivated* and decent man cannot be vain," he remarks, "without setting an inordinately high standard for himself, and without despising himself at certain moments to the point of hatred" (italics added). Comparing his features with those of other clerks in his office, he thinks: "Let my face even be ugly . . . but let it be noble, expressive, and, above all, *extremely* intelligent." Again, while seeking to provoke a quarrel so as to attract attention, he is troubled for a moment by the sordid triviality of the whole business: "Devil knows what I would then have given for a real regular quarrel—a more decent, a more *literary* one, so to speak." And after needlessly insulting a group of old school fellows, he says to them silently: "Oh, if you only knew what thoughts and feeling I am capable of, how cultured I am!" (5: 125, 124, 128, 147). As a result of imbibing the European culture popular in Russia in the 1840s, the underground man, it becomes clear, has lost any capacity for simple and direct human feeling in relation to others. Instead, his vanity and sense of self-importance have become inflated to a degree out of all proportion to his actual social situation; and the conflicts engendered by this discrepancy provide a comic analogue to the fratricidal war of all against all arising in Western European society from the dominance of the principle of egoistic individualism.

Dostoevsky is a master at portraying the psychology of pride and humiliation, and when the humiliation springs from some genuine oppression or suffering, he knows how to make it intensely moving; but it would be a fla-

335

grant misreading to take the underground man as such a victim. For he lives in a purely imaginary world and distorts and exaggerates everything with which he comes into contact. "It is perfectly clear to me now," he says, "that, owing to my unbounded vanity and, probably, to the high standard I set for myself, I very often looked at myself with furious discontent, which verged on loathing, *and so I inwardly attributed the same view to everyone*" (italics added). Anticipating the scorn he might encounter from his old school fellows, on whom he had forced his company, he comments: "I knew, too, perfectly well even then that I was monstrously exaggerating the facts." And, as he confesses, "I always recognized that [exaggeration] was a weak point of mine, and was sometimes very much afraid of it. 'I exaggerate everything, that's where I go wrong,' I repeated to myself every hour" (5: 124, 141, 166).

Very little objective basis thus exists for the underground man's "humiliations," or better, they are all brought on by the excesses of his vanity; but even if his humiliations are entirely self-caused, their effect on him is no less distressing. His inability to enter into human contact with other people plunges him into a savage isolation, and it is only through "petty vice" that he can emerge at all from his everlasting self-preoccupation and self-absorption. At the same time, though, he is acutely aware that his behavior is debasing and degrading: "I indulged my vice in solitude at night, furtively, timidly, filthily, with a feeling of shame that never deserted me, even at the most loathsome moments, and which at such moments drove me to curses. Even then I already had the underground in my soul" (5: 128). In the first part, "the underground" had referred to the revolt of the underground man's personality against his ideas. Here his "feeling of shame" (his ineradicable conscience) once again rises up in revolt—not against a theory that denies the right of conscience to exist, but against an actual indulgence in vice that the underground man cannot help regarding as loathsome even while it offers his only escape from claustrophobic solitude. The reference to vice at this point foreshadows the all-important Liza episode, but in these earlier chapters, filled with comic grotesquerie, the emphasis falls on the underground man's efforts to break out of his solitude through purely social (rather than sexual) intercourse.

All these episodes display the torments and tortures of the underground man as he attempts to assert his existence as an ego who desires above all that someone—anyone—acknowledge his right to be recognized in a fashion compatible with his absurdly inflated self-image. It is for this reason that he becomes involved in the slapstick, mock-heroic farce of trying to summon up enough courage to bump into an officer on the Nevsky Prospect. His preoccupation with this ridiculous problem merely illustrates the picayune obsessiveness of his vanity; but the episode is also a parody of an incident in *What Is To Be Done?* One of the heroes of that book takes a solemn resolution not to yield the right of way in the street to "dignitaries";

and when an outraged gentleman begins to berate the poorly dressed student for bumping into *him*, the dignitary promptly ends up with his face in the mud.

Ironically reversing the scale of values manifested by this democratic protest against the public humiliations of inequality, Dostoevsky depicts the frantic desire of the underground man to assert his "equality" as ludicrous vanity rather than staunchly independent self-respect. The parody of Chernyshevsky is coupled with an allusion to Gogol's *The Overcoat*, which Dostoevsky slips in at the point where the underground man, feverishly preparing the proper costume for his epical encounter, decides to replace the hideous raccoon collar on his overcoat with a more dignified one of beaver. Not only does this detail thicken the period atmosphere (Gogol's story was published in 1842), but it also enriches the ideological implications of the incident, since Gogol's work provided the initial inspiration for the philanthropic thematics of the Natural School of young writers to which Dostoevsky had once belonged.

The theme of "masochism," so prominent in Part I, re-appears again in this first chapter of the second part. For as he walks along the Nevsky Prospect, the underground man experiences "a regular martyrdom, a continual, intolerable humiliation at the thought, which passed into an incessant and direct sensation, that I was a fly in the eyes of this whole world, a nasty, disgusting fly—more intelligent, more cultured, more noble than any of them, of course, but a fly that was continually making way for everyone, insulted and humiliated by everyone. . . . Already then I began to experience a rush of the enjoyment of which I spoke in the first chapter [of the first part]" (5: 130). Once again, however, we must be careful not to take this psychological characterization as self-explanatory. The underground man's masochism is a part of the dialectic of vanity, and it has a more complex function than merely to illustrate a taste for self-abasement. In fact, as we see, the voluntary exposure to humiliation *strengthens* the underground man's sense of inner superiority to all those who look on him with such contempt. At the same time that it makes him painfully aware of his own preposterousness and ignominy, it also sustains him by reinforcing the conviction of his cultural pre-eminence.

Masochism is thus assigned much the same function in both parts of the work—just as it had led to suffering in Part I, and kept alive the faculty of conscience, so in Part II it also acquires a positive significance. The seemingly pathological cultivation of masochistic "enjoyment" by the underground man ultimately buttresses his ego, which refuses to submit docilely to the judgment of the world. The ego thus asserts its independence and autonomy, whatever the price it must pay in indignity and despite all the external pressure to bend to alien authority. Such self-assertion is precisely what enables the underground man, twenty years later, to resist the temptations of a Crystal Palace in which the laws of nature have simply abolished the human personality altogether. Hence, in both parts of the work, Dostoevsky assigns a *relative* value—the value of protecting the autonomy of the personality—to the ideology of the 1840s, regardless of its weaknesses and shortcomings in other respects.

3. Manfred at a Party

Chapter II of the second part finally brings into relief the true target of Dostoevsky's satire. At last we discover—of course, in the form of a carefully distorted caricature—what the underground man has been reading in the books he finds so important. For here he takes on the features of the Romantic "dreamer" whom Dostoevsky had depicted in his early works, and whose literary fantasies had been contrasted with the moral-social claims of "real life" from which he had taken refuge. Dostoevsky's pre-Siberian attitude toward the dreamer had been, on the whole, relatively sympathetic; but he had begun to debunk him more severely in *Uncle's Dream*, and now, in the second part of *Notes from Underground*, the dreamer is manhandled very harshly indeed. Nor is he any longer a purely literary Romantic lost in exotic fantasies of erotic gratification and artistic glory; he has become a Social Romantic filled with grandiose plans for transforming the world. But his new social mission has not really succeeded in altering the dreamer's endemic self-preoccupation, and his failure to meet the moral demands of real life becomes all the more unforgivable in view of the social conscience by which he believes himself to be inspired.

In this chapter, we observe what occurs when, exhausted by the seesaws of the dialectic of vanity, the underground man has recourse "to a means of escape that reconciled everything," that is, when he finds "a refuge in 'the sublime and the beautiful,' in dreams."

> I, for instance, was triumphant over everyone; everyone, of course, lay in the dust and was forced to recognize my superiority voluntarily, and I forgave them all. I, a famous poet and court official, fell in love; I inherited countless millions and immediately sacrificed them for humanity; and at the same time I confessed before all the people my shameful deeds, which, of course, were not completely shameful but also contained an enormous amount of "the sublime and the beautiful," something in the Manfred style. Everyone would weep and kiss me (what idiots they would be if they didn't), while I would go barefoot and hungry preaching new ideas and routing the reactionaries at Austerlitz.* (5: 133)

* The reference to Austerlitz appears to link some of the details of this tirade to Napoleon I, but it also contains a reference to Cabet's *Voyage en Icarie*. The main character of this Utopian novel, a reformer-philanthropist, also defeats a coalition of crowned reactionaries at Austerlitz. Dostoevsky is already suggesting here the tendency of radical social reformers to identify themselves with Napoleon. See *PSS*, 5: 386.

During such delightful interludes, the underground man felt "that suddenly a vista of suitable activity—beneficial, good, and above all *ready-made* (what sort of activity I had no idea, but the great thing was that it should be all ready for me)—would rise up before me, and I should come into the light of day, almost riding a white horse and crowned with laurel." These dreams, of course, replace any actual moral effort on his part; even more, they stifle any awareness that such effort could exist otherwise than in hackneyed, "ready-made" forms. At such moments the underground man felt an overwhelming love for humanity, and, "though it was never applied to anything human in reality, yet there was so much of this love that afterward one did not even feel the impulse to apply it in reality; that would have been a superfluous luxury." Also, these lofty visions of magnanimity happily served as a sop to the stirrings of conscience, because to "an ordinary man, say, it is shameful to defile himself . . . [while] a hero is too noble to be utterly defiled, and so he is permitted to defile himself." The underground man, as he himself remarks, "had a noble loophole for everything" (5: 133).

Yet he cannot long remain content with these delectations of his solitude; inevitably he feels the need to exhibit them (and himself) to the admiring eyes of humanity. After three months of dreaming, his dreams invariably "reached such a state of bliss that it became essential to embrace my fellows and all mankind immediately. And for that purpose I needed one human being at hand who actually existed" (5: 134). These words prelude the lengthy and grotesquely amusing episode (Chapters III and IV) relating the encounter of the underground man with his old schoolfellows. The moment he catches sight of real people, of course, the underground man's exorbitant demands for esteem invariably lead to a rebuff. Only too ready to embrace mankind, he discovers that mankind would rather shake hands and keep a polite distance; and this rejection brings on the dialectic of vanity, with its accompanying duel for domination.

So it has been, it would seem, with the underground man from his earliest years. "Once, indeed, I did have a friend (at school)," he reminisces. "But I was already a tyrant at heart; I wanted to exercise unlimited power over him; I tried to instill into him a contempt for his surroundings . . . but when he submitted to me completely I began to hate him immediately and rejected him—as though all I needed him for was to win a victory over him, to subjugate him and nothing else. But I could not subjugate them all" (5: 140). The surrealistic comedy of the underground man's meeting with his erstwhile comrades, which rises to dizzy heights of hysterical farce, derives from this hopeless yet irresistible impulse to "subjugate them all." After forcing himself on their friendly little party, he insults the guest of honor simply out of resentment and envy, and then parades up and down the room for three solid hours while the others disregard him entirely and continue their festivities.

The intricacies of Dostoevsky's irony are best displayed in the comic pathos of the underground man's bewilderment at the spectacle of stupid, unself-conscious, and tipsy amiability, with its total (even if alcohol-induced) momentary oblivion of self. "It was clear that they were fond of him [the guest of honor]. 'But why? Why?' I wondered. From time to time they were moved to drunken enthusiasm and kissed each other. They talked of the Caucasus, of the nature of true passion, of cards, of cushy jobs in the service; of the income of a hussar named Podkharzevsky, whom none of them knew personally, and rejoiced that he had a large income; of the extraordinary grace and beauty of a Princess D., whom none of them had ever seen either; and finally they reached the point of declaring Shakespeare immortal" (5: 146-147). The underground man's old friends, as Dostoevsky indicates by such a passage, are just as dull-witted and pedestrian a lot as he thinks them to be; but they nonetheless represent a norm of sociability impossible for him to attain or even to comprehend.

The whole group eventually departs for a brothel to finish off the evening, leaving the underground man in solitary possession of the débris of the feast. But, by this time, he has gotten it into his head that only a duel will satisfy his injured honor—and besides, a duel can be the occasion for all sorts of noble reconciliations! "Either they'll all fall down on their knees to beg for my friendship—or I will give Zverkov a slap in the face!" (5: 148). The mention of a duel at once unleashes a flood of literary references (Russian literature is filled with famous duels), and the underground man pursues his companions in a mood that parodies Pushkin's story *The Shot*.

Imagining what might happen if he carries out his plan to insult Zverkov, the guest of honor, the underground man muses:

I will be arrested. I will be tried, I will be dismissed from the service, thrown in prison, sent to Siberia, deported. Never mind! In fifteen years when they let me out of prison I will trudge off to him, a beggar in rags, I shall find him in some provincial city. He will be married and happy. He will have a grown-up daughter. . . . I will say to him: "Look, monster, at my hollow cheeks and my rags! I've lost everything—my career, my happiness, art, science, the woman I loved, and all through you. Here are pistols. I have come to discharge my pistol and—and I . . . forgive you." Then I will fire into the air and he will never hear of me again.

I was actually on the point of tears, though I knew perfectly well at that very moment that all this was out of Pushkin's *Silvio* [Silvio is the hero of *The Shot*] and Lermontov's *Masquerade*. (5: 150)

As might have been expected, these shopworn heroics remain purely imaginary, and everyone has vanished from sight by the time the underground man enters the salon of the "dressmaking establishment."

4. Liza

It is at this point, when the underground man finally encounters another human being more vulnerable than himself, that the comedy changes into tragedy. Dostoevsky was well aware of this shift in tonality, and we have earlier quoted his allusion to it as similar to "a transition . . . in music. . . . In the first chapter, seemingly, there's only chatter; but suddenly this chatter, in the last two chapters, is resolved by a catastrophe."[11] By "the first chapter," Dostoevsky probably means the action leading up to the brothel scene; the brothel scene itself, and Liza's visit to the underground man's home, would then form the remaining two units. But the final text is broken up into smaller chapters, and the catastrophe beginning with Chapter v runs through Chapter x. No part of *Notes from Underground* has been more wrenched out of context to support one or another theory about Dostoevsky, even though the function of this section is surely to drive home the contrast between imaginary, self-indulgent, self-glorifying, sentimental Social Romanticism and a genuine act of love—a love springing from that total forgetfulness of self which had now become Dostoevsky's highest value. By his ironic reversal both of Nekrasov's poem and of the incident in *What Is To Be Done?*, Dostoevsky wished to expose all the petty vainglory lying concealed in the intelligentsia's "ideals," and to set this off against the triumph over egoism that he saw embodied in the spontaneous Christian instincts of a simple Russian soul.

When the underground man arrives in the brothel, the madam, treating him like the old patron that he is, summons a girl. As he goes out with her, he catches sight of himself in a mirror: "My harassed face struck me as extremely revolting, pale, spiteful, nasty, with disheveled hair. 'No matter, I am glad of it,' I thought; 'I am glad that I shall seem revolting to her; I like that' " (5: 151). Not having been able to subdue his companions or to insult them sufficiently to be taken seriously, the underground man typically anticipates revenging himself on the helpless girl; the more repulsive he is to her, the more his egoism will be satisfied by forcing her to submit to his desires. It is not by physical submission alone, however, that the underground man attains a triumph over Liza. For when, after making love, he becomes aware of her hostility and silent resentment, "a grim idea came into my brain and passed all over my body, like some nasty sensation, such as one feels when going into a damp and moldy underground" (5: 152). This idea takes the form of playing on Liza's feelings, with the intention of triumphing over her not only physically but spiritually as well.

The underground man thus proceeds very skillfully to break down the armor of feigned indifference and cynicism by which Liza protects herself against the debasing circumstances of her life. "I began to feel myself what I was saying," he explains, "and warmed to the subject. I longed to expound the cherished *little ideas* I had brooded over in my corner." Mingling horrible details of degradation with images of felicity, whose banality makes them all the more poignant (Balzac's *Le Père Goriot* is parodied in the process), the underground man succeeds in bringing to the surface Liza's true feelings of shame about herself and precipitating her complete emotional breakdown. None of his apparent concern, of course, had been meant seriously; the underground man simply had been carried away by the power of his eloquence and because "the sport in it attracted me most." But Liza is too young, naive, and helpless to see through his falsity, which in this case sounded like truth and was, in fact, even half-true: "I worked myself up to such pathos that I began to have a lump in my throat myself, and . . . suddenly I stopped, sat up in dismay, and bending over apprehensively, began to listen with a beating heart." For Liza had lost control of herself completely, and "her youthful body was shuddering all over as though in convulsions" (5: 155, 156, 161, 162).

The underground man, carried away by his victory, cannot resist attempting to live up to the exalted role of hero and benefactor that he had so often played in his fantasies. When he leaves, he gives Liza his address with a lordly magnanimity, urging her to come and visit him and quit her life of shame. It is this gesture that undoes him and provides Dostoevsky with his dénouement. For the moment the underground man emerges from the self-adulatory haze of his charlatanism, he is stricken with terror. He cannot bear the thought that Liza might see him as he really is—wrapped in his shabby dressing gown, living in his squalid "underground," completely under the thumb of his manservant, the impassive, dignified, Bible-reading peasant Apollon. Never for a moment does it occur to him that he might really try to help her all the same; he is so worried about how *he* will look in *her* eyes that the reality of her situation entirely vanishes from view. Or not entirely: "Something was not dead within me, in the depths of my heart and conscience it refused to die, and it expressed itself as a burning anguish" (5: 165).

After a few days pass and Liza fails to appear, the underground man becomes more cheerful; as usual, "I even began sometimes to dream, and rather sweetly." These dreams all revolved around the process of Liza's re-education, her confession of love for him, and his own confession that "I did not dare to approach you first, because I had an influence over you and was afraid that you would force yourself, out of gratitude, to respond to my love, would try to rouse in your heart a feeling which was perhaps absent, and I did not wish that because it would be . . . tyranny. . . . It would be indelicate (in short, I launch off at this point into European, George-Sandian inexplicably lofty subtleties), but now, now you are mine, you are my creation, you are pure, you are beautiful, you are my beautiful wife" (5: 166-167). And here Dostoevsky throws in two more lines from Nekrasov's poem.

Interspersed with these intoxicating reveries is the low comedy of the underground man's efforts to bend the stubborn and intractable Apollon to his will. Dostoevsky interweaves these two situations adroitly by coordinating Liza's entry with a moment at which the underground man, enraged by the imperturbable Apollon, is giving vent to all his weakly hysterical fury. By this time, he has reached an uncontrollable pitch of frustration and nervous exasperation; at the sight of the bewildered Liza he loses control completely, sobbing and complaining that he is being "tortured" by Apollon. All this is so humiliating that he turns on her in spiteful rage when, by stammering that she wishes to leave the brothel, she reminds him of all that has gone before. His reply is a vicious tirade, in which he tells her the truth about their earlier relation: "I vented my spleen on you and laughed at you. I had been humiliated, so I wanted to humiliate; I had been treated like a rag, so I wanted to show my power." With the typical inversion of his egoist's logic, he shouts: "And I shall never forgive you for the tears I could not help shedding before you just now, like some silly woman put to shame! And for what I am confessing to you now, I shall never forgive *you*, either!" (5: 173-174).

But now an unprecedented event occurs—unprecedented, at least, in the underground man's experience; instead of flaring up herself and hitting back (the only response to which the underground man has been accustomed), Liza throws herself into his arms to console *him*. Both forget themselves entirely and break into tears; but the unconquerable vanity of the underground man, which incapacitates him from responding selflessly and spontaneously to others, soon regains the upper hand: "In my overwrought brain the thought also occurred that our parts were after all completely reversed now, that she was now the heroine, while I was just such a crushed and humiliated creature as she had been before me that night— four days before." And then, not out of love but hate, the underground man takes her on the spot to revenge himself on *her* for having dared to try to console him. To make his revenge more complete and crush her entirely, he slips a five-ruble note into her hand when their embraces are finished. "But I can say this for certain: though I did that cruel thing purposely," he admits, "it was not an impulse from the heart, but came from my evil brain. This cruelty was so affected, so purposely made up, so completely a product of the brain, of *books*, that I could not keep it up for a minute" (5: 175, 177). Dostoevsky could not have stated more explicitly that the heart of the underground man, the emotive core of his nature, had by no means lost its moral sensitivity. It was his brain, nourished by the education he had so thoroughly absorbed—an education based on Western prototypes, and on the images of such prototypes assimilated into Russian literature—that had perverted his character and was responsible for his despicable act.

Liza, however, manages to leave the money on the table unobserved before leaving. Noticing the crumpled bill, the underground man is filled with remorse and runs after Liza into the silent, snow-filled street to kneel at her feet and beg forgiveness. But then, pulling himself up short, he realizes the futility of all this agitation: 'But—what for?' I thought. 'Would I not begin to hate her, perhaps, even tomorrow, just because I kissed her feet today?' " And later at home, "stifling the living pang of [his] heart with fantastic dreams," he conceives the most diabolic rationalization of all for his villainy. "Will it not be better that she carry the outrage with her forever?" he thinks. "Outrage—why, after all, that is purification: it is the most stinging and painful consciousness! Tomorrow I would have defiled her soul and have exhausted her heart, while now the feeling of humiliation will never die in her, and however loathsome the filth awaiting her, that outrage will elevate and purify her—by hatred—h'm—perhaps by forgiveness also. But will all that make things easier for her, though? . . . And, indeed, I will at this point ask an idle question on my account: which is better—cheap happiness or exalted sufferings? Well, which is better?" (5: 177-178).

With this final, stabbing irony, Dostoevsky allows the underground man to use the very idea of purification through suffering as an excuse for his moral-spiritual sadism—exactly as Prince Valkovsky had done to excuse a more vulgar crime. In so doing, Dostoevsky returns to the main theme of the first part and places it in a new light. "Consciousness" and "suffering" had been affirmed as values when the underground man, struggling to preserve his human identity, wished to suffer *himself* rather than to surrender to the laws of nature. But so long as this struggle springs only from the negative revolt of egoism to affirm its existence, so long as it is not oriented by anything positive, it inevitably runs the risk of a diabolic reversal; there is always the danger that the egoist, concerned only with himself, will cause *others* to suffer with the excuse of helping to purify *their* souls. Such a possibility, broached here in passing at the end of *Notes from Underground*, will be brilliantly developed in *Crime and Punishment*, when Raskolnikov tries to convince Sonya that his sacrifice of *another* for a noble end is morally equivalent to *her* self-sacrifice for the same purpose.

5. Conclusion

As the second part of *Notes from Underground* comes to a close, the underground man again returns to the frustrations of his solitude. For one moment he had caught a glimpse of how to escape from the dialectic of vanity: Liza's complete disregard of her own humiliation, her whole-souled identification with *his* torments—in short, her capacity for selfless love—is the only way to break the sorcerer's spell of egocentrism. When she rushes into his arms, thinking not of herself but of him, she illustrates that "something else" which his egoism will never allow him to attain—the ideal of the voluntary self-sacrifice of the personality out of love. In his encounter with Liza, the underground man had met this ideal in the flesh, and his inability to respond to its appeal dooms him irrevocably for the future. Nonetheless, as we look at *Notes from Underground* as a whole, we see that the egoistic Social Romanticism of the 1840s, with its cultivation of a sense of spiritual noblesse and its emphasis on *individual* moral responsibility, does not have a totally negative value. Egocentric though it may be, such sentimental Social Romanticism still stressed the importance of free will and preserved a sense of the inner autonomy of the personality; and without such a sense no truly human life is possible at all. Dostoevsky will continue to portray the relation between the generations in much the same fashion—most explicitly in *The Devils*, where the old Social Romantic Stepan Trofimovich Verkhovensky is morally outraged by the Utilitarian ruthlessness of his Nihilist offspring Peter while ruefully acknowledging the responsibility of his own generation in bringing such a monstrosity to birth.

As a coda to the entire work, Dostoevsky adds some remarks still nominally set down by his narrator, but in which his own voice is heard almost as distinctly as in the prefatory footnote. Indeed, in these final sentences Dostoevsky again endeavors to alert the reader to the nature of his literary technique. "A novel needs a hero," remarks the underground man, "and all the traits for an anti-hero are *expressly* gathered together here, and, what matters most, it all produces an unpleasant impression, for we are all divorced from life, we are all cripples, every one of us, more or less." When the imaginary reader protests angrily at this, begins "shouting and stamping," and tells the underground man to speak only for himself and not for others, the rejoinder lays bare Dostoevsky's use of inverted irony. "As for what concerns me in particular," he retorts, "I have only in my life carried to an extreme what you have not dared to carry halfway, and what's more, you have taken your cowardice for good sense, and have found comfort in deceiving yourselves" (5: 178-179). The full significance of this assertion should by now be clear: Dostoevsky is alluding to his consummate use of satirical exaggeration and parodistic caricature, and his technique of dramatization by what we have called ideological eschatology, that is, by carrying "the logical presuppositions and possibilities of ideas to their consistent conclusion. . . ."

The underground man, hyperconscious as always, knows exactly where the source of the trouble is located: "Leave us alone without books and we shall at once get lost and be confused—we will not know what to join, what to cling to and what to hate, what to respect and what to despise. We are even oppressed by being men—men with *real, our own* flesh and blood, we are ashamed of it, we think it a disgrace and try to be some sort of impossible generalized man" (5: 178-179). It may be inferred, then, that the only hope is to reject all these bookish, foreign, artificial Western ideologies, and to return to the Russian "soil" with its spontaneous incorporation of the Christian ideal of unselfish love.

So ends this remarkable little work, certainly the most powerful and concentrated expression that Dostoevsky ever gave to his genius as a satirist. *Notes from Underground*, it has often been said (and quite rightly), is the prelude to the great period in which Dostoevsky's talent finally came to maturity; and there is no question that with it he attains a new artistic level. For the first time, he motivates an action *entirely* in terms of a psychology shaped by radical ideology; every feature of the text serves to bring out the consequences in personal behavior of certain ideas; and the world that Dostoevsky creates is entirely conceived as a *function* of this purpose. Psychology has now become strictly subordinate to ideology; there is no longer a disturbing tug-of-war, as in *The Insulted and Injured*, between the moral-psychological and the ideological elements of the structure.

Dostoevsky has also at last found the great theme of his later novels, which will all be inspired by the same ambition to counter the moral-spiritual authority of the ideology of the radical Russian intelligentsia (depending on whatever nuance of that ideology was prominent at the time of writing). In this respect, the nucleus of Dostoevsky's novels may be compared to that of an eighteenth-century *conte philosophique*, whose characters were also largely embodiments of ideas; but instead of remaining bloodless abstractions like Candide or Zadig, they will be fleshed out with all the verisimilitude and psychological density of the nineteenth-century novel of social realism and all the dramatic tension of the urban-Gothic *roman-feuilleton*. It is Dostoevsky's genius for blending these seemingly antithetical narrative styles that constitutes the originality of his art as a novelist.*

---

* In the first volume of the present work, reference was made to a considerably different view of Dostoevsky's art expounded by Mikhail Bakhtin, whose work has become very well-known in Western criticism in recent years. Bakhtin claims that Dostoevsky invented a wholly new kind of "polyphonic novel," unlike anything written in the form earlier, which gives each character complete autonomy and makes it impossible (as well as aesthetically undesirable) to attempt to establish any unifying perspective that can be considered Dostoevsky's own.

Bakhtin's book is filled with acute observations concerning Dostoevsky's "dialogic" use of language, which is always oriented in relation to a possible interlocutor; and these observations offer a new insight into an important aspect of Dostoevsky's poetics. But there has been considerable criticism, in my opinion quite justified, of Bakhtin's effort to view him as the creator of a wholly new novelistic form, and to locate him in a tradition of Menippean satire deriving from antiquity rather than maintaining him in the context of the European novel of the eighteenth and nineteenth centuries.

My own ideas on this point coincide with those of René Wellek, who, while also acknowledging the value of many of Bakhtin's insights, has written that "if we look at Dostoevsky's major novels from the point of view of the novelistic tradition, we have to come to the conclusion that he cannot be taken out of the mainstream of the Western novel, out of the company of Balzac and Dickens, with Gogol the early master. . . . One can describe Dostoevsky's difference from his immediate predecessors and contemporaries but one cannot isolate him and claim for him an absolute innovation called 'the polyphonic novel' nor put him into the continuity of the remote 'Menippean satire.' . . . Bakhtin's book has the merit of raising the question of Dostoevsky's dramaticity in a radical manner and suggesting contacts with older genres. But in both cases he grossly overstates his case." René Wellek, "Bakhtin's View of Dostoevsky: 'Polyphony' and 'Carnivalesque,' " *Dostoevsky Studies*, 1 (1980), 31-39; Mikhail Bakhtin, *Problems of Dos-*

Dostoevsky, though, never again attempted anything as hermetic and allusive as *Notes from Underground*. It is very likely that he considered the work a failure—as indeed it was, if we use as a measure its total lack of effectiveness as a polemic. No one really understood what Dostoevsky had been trying to do (with the exception, as we shall see, of Saltykov-Shchedrin); and even though Apollon Grigoryev, with his artistic flair, praised the novella and told his friend to continue writing in this vein, the silence of the remainder of the literary world was positively deafening. We have already quoted Suslova's letter, whose references to Dostoevsky's "scandalous novella" and the "cynical things" he was producing, well convey the general reaction. Since she had not yet read the text, her words manifestly report what she had heard in the literary salon of the novelist Evgenia Tur (which she was then frequenting in Paris), and whose habitués were only repeating the latest literary gossip from Petersburg. Such reactions probably persuaded Dostoevsky that he had perhaps counted too much on the perspicacity of his readers to discern his meaning. He would, in any case, never again place them before so difficult a challenge to their literary and ideological acumen.

toevsky's Poetics, ed. and trans. Caryl Emerson (Minneapolis, 1984); see also, for a close and cogent criticism of Bakhtin, Wolf Schmid, *Der Textaufbau in den Erzählungen Dostoevskijs* (Munich, 1973), esp. 226-228.

CHAPTER 22

The End of *Epoch*

After the interment of Marya Dimitrievna in Moscow, Dostoevsky returned to Petersburg at the end of April and once again began to take an active part in the editorial affairs of *Epoch*. To tide him over financially, he applied for, and obtained, a loan from the Literary Fund; and as if to signal the beginning of a new era in his life, he also ran up a substantial bill at a fashionable Petersburg tailor for a new suit of clothes and a summer overcoat. But if the death of his first wife might be considered a blessing in disguise, whatever the pangs of conscience and the practical disruptions provoked by her long death-agony, he was soon to be confronted with another personal loss that was an unmitigated disaster.

2

Mikhail Dostoevsky and his family had taken up residence for the summer in a *dacha* at Pavlovsk, the fashionable watering place not far from Petersburg whose princely palaces and spacious, tree-shaded, richly adorned park was later to be depicted in *The Idiot*. Feodor was living in Petersburg with his stepson Pasha and making preparations to go abroad again for his health, certainly with the tempting image of a reunion with Suslova never out of his mind. Just before departure, however, he was so struck by his brother's ailing appearance that he decided to delay his voyage. And, in the first week of July, he scribbled a quick note to his stepson from Pavlovsk: "Dear Pasha, send me some linen. My brother is dying. Don't tell anyone about this."[1]

Mikhail Dostoevsky had been overtaxed by the strain of having to cope with the problems of *Epoch* singlehanded, and by the burden of financial obligations that he could meet only by incurring others still more onerous. Not sparing himself physically, and suffering from an intermittent liver ailment, he collapsed on July 6 after hearing that an article on which he had counted could not pass the censorship; three days later he was dead. "How much I have lost with him," Feodor wrote to his brother Andrey some weeks later, "I will not try to tell you. That man loved me more than anything in the world, even more than his wife and family, whom he adored. . . . All the affairs of brother's family are terribly disorganized. The affairs of the journal (an enormous and complicated affair)—all this I will take on

13. Mikhail Dostoevsky, ca. 1864

myself. There are many debts. Not a penny left for the family, and they are
all minors. . . . Naturally, I am at their service. For a brother such as he was,
I will cut off my head and sacrifice my own health."[2]

Mikhail Dostoevsky was buried in the Pavlovsk cemetery on July 13, and
Dostoevsky then faced an agonizing decision. *Epoch* was saddled with a
huge deficit—both long-term debts and more urgent ones, which demanded immediate payment. Matters had been made even worse because
Mikhail, intending to establish his own printing plant, had run up additional obligations with this venture in mind. Dostoevsky explained the situation as he saw it then in a letter written eight months later to his old
friend and confidant Baron Wrangel: "I had to choose between two roads:
abandon the journal, turn it over to the creditors (for a journal, after all, is
a property and worth something) along with all the furniture and belongings, and take in the family. Then get to work, pursue my literary career,
write novels, and provide for the needs of the widow and orphans. Another
possibility: find the money and carry on the publication at whatever cost.

349

What a pity that I did not choose the first!" Instead, the letter continues, "I preferred the second solution. Besides, I am not the only one. All my friends and the old collaborators were of the same opinion."[3]

Dostoevsky obtained ten thousand rubles from his wealthy Kumanin aunt in Moscow, the sum that would have been left him in her will, scraped together additional funds wherever he could, and decided to carry on. He was convinced that, if he could manage to keep publishing until the end of the year, and succeeded in bringing the monthly numbers approximately up to schedule, he would attract enough subscribers to cover expenses and eventually to pay off his debts. His plan was to whip the journal into shape, establish it on a sound financial footing, and then turn it over to Mikhail's family as a source of income when—as he was determined to do in the future—he would withdraw to write his novels. The rapid rise of *Time* had convinced him, quite justifiably, that he was perfectly capable of turning *Epoch* into a flourishing enterprise.

3

If hard work and grim determination had been enough to guarantee success, then Dostoevsky would certainly have succeeded. As it turned out, there were too many obstacles to be overcome even though he literally drove himself to the edge of collapse. "It was necessary to take matters in hand with energy," he explains to Wrangel. "I printed on three presses at the same time, without regard for my health and strength; I alone took on the work of chief editor and the reading of proofs; alone I negotiated with authors and the censorship, corrected articles, raised money, stayed awake until 6 o'clock in the morning, slept five hours a night, and I put the journal on its feet; but it was already too late."[4]

Such an account by Dostoevsky of his own labors may sound a bit hyperbolic, but is fully confirmed by the heartfelt testimony of his youngest brother Nikolay writing to their sister in Moscow. "Brother has given himself entirely to the family [of Mikhail]," he reports, "works all night, never goes to bed before 5 in the morning, works like an ox; all day he does nothing but sit and look after the editorial business of the journal. You have to have lived a long time, and to have gone through a good deal, in order to know just how supremely honorable and noble is that man's soul; and yet I should not like to be in his place. In my opinion, he is the unhappiest of mortals. All his life has been like that. He never complains and says nothing about all that has probably piled up in his heart; that is why I could not help writing these lines."[5]

Despite Dostoevsky's heroic efforts, the needed subscriptions did not flow into the coffers of *Epoch*, and it became financially impossible to continue publication after the first two issues of 1865. In his letter to Wrangel,

Dostoevsky blames the situation on a general fall in subscriptions that had affected all Russian publications, coupled with an economic crisis in the country that made it difficult to obtain credit. But there were, as Dostoevsky well knew, more particular causes for the failure of *Epoch* to attract the necessary readers. Completely drained by his labors as editor and publisher, he was hardly able, after *Notes from Underground*, to do more than write a few articles and one unfinished satirical story (*The Crocodile*). The journal thus was deprived of the cohesion and ideological force given to *Time* by his vigorous contributions on matters of current interest, and it published nothing to match the mass appeal of such works as *The Insulted and Injured* and *House of the Dead*. Dostoevsky had counted on Strakhov to take his place as spokesman for *pochvennichestvo*; but the philosophical journalist was far too cautious and devious a temperament to assume such a role, and he entirely lacked the bellicose verve that made Dostoevsky so effective a polemicist.

Indeed, many people were not even aware that the noted writer Feodor Dostoevsky had any connection with the new journal at all. Some, if we are to believe Strakhov, could not distinguish between the two brothers and thought it was Feodor Dostoevsky who had gone to his grave. Others were confused by the new editor-in-chief, an unknown named A. Y. Poretsky (as an ex-convict, Dostoevsky still could not officially be named as responsible editor), who took charge of the publication in the name of "the family of Mikhail Dostoevsky." Word got back to Petersburg that Turgenev had been considering giving a future story or novel to *Epoch*, but had changed his mind on seeing the name of Poretsky affixed to the masthead. Dostoevsky hastened to explain that Poretsky was only a straw man, whose chief asset was a high rank in the Civil Service. "But it is us, the old contributors," he affirms, "and essentially I myself, who edit."[6] It was clearly impossible to write such a letter to every potential subscriber, or even to state it openly in public; and the journal suffered accordingly.

Dostoevsky says nothing to Wrangel about the changed social-cultural climate in which *Epoch* began to appear, but this too certainly played a part in the failure of the new publication to win back the old readers of *Time*. Much of the attraction of *Time* had been its combination of a liberal or moderately radical social-political position with a Slavophil emphasis that appealed to patriotic and nationalist sentiment. Such an amalgam was no longer feasible; and even if the Dostoevskys had wished to maintain it, the suppression of *Time* had shown them how dangerous it was to risk incurring the displeasure of the authorities by leaning too far leftward. Permission to publish *Epoch* had been granted by the Ministry of Internal Affairs only on condition that the journal maintain an "irreproachable tendency."

Even without such external pressure, if we can judge from a passage in Dostoevsky's notebooks written sometime during 1864-1865, the policy of

Epoch would not have been sensibly different. Here Dostoevsky draws what seems to him the moral of the revolutions of 1848, and applies it to the Russian situation:

> The revolutionary party is bad in that it makes more noise than the results are worth, spills more blood than all the profit received is worth. (By the way, for them blood is cheap.) Every society can accommodate only that degree of progress that it has developed and begun to understand. Why reach further, why reach for the stars in the sky? This can destroy everything because it can frighten everyone. In '48 even the bourgeoisie agreed to demand its rights, but when it was driven further where it could not understand anything (where in fact things were stupid) then it began to defend itself and prevailed. At present in Europe all that is needed is more self-government and freedom of the press. But you will not attain it there. Society is suspicious and not able to bear freedom. All the blood the revolutionaries rave about, all the uproar and underground work will lead to nothing and will come down on their heads. (20: 175)

Such words clearly reveal a hardening of Dostoevsky's opposition to the Russian radicals, who were guilty of the same mistake as their European predecessors. These had been successful so long as the bourgeoisie, and the radicals who led the working class, remained united in their demands for more political and civil liberties; but when the radicals threatened the position of the bourgeoisie, then reaction had triumphed. It was a similar victory for reaction in Russia that Dostoevsky dreaded, and his criticism of the radicals as irresponsibly calling for blood does not at all impugn their aims—only their tactics and judgment. They suffer from the illusions of well-meaning but misguided idealists, unable to gauge the real state of affairs, and will, he fears, only succeed in worsening the social-political situation while bringing down disaster on themselves as well. As a result, he had less and less inclination to curb Strakhov's visceral hostility to radical ideas; and since Strakhov was now a dominating editorial force, his increasing influence shaped the character of the journal. The title of one of his monthly *Notes of a Chronicler*—"The Slavophils Have Triumphed"—conveys the general tenor of his writings, which did much to create the impression that *Epoch* had been transformed into a Petersburg appendage of the Slavophil camp.

To do it justice, however, one should point out that *Epoch* published such notable works as *Notes from Underground*, Turgenev's *Ghosts*, Leskov's *Lady Macbeth of Mtsensk*, and Apollon Grigoryev's splendid memoirs, *My Literary and Spiritual Wanderings*, now recognized as a classic. Also, one new critic made his appearance, whose name is still mentioned in accounts of the period. N. I. Solovyev was an Army doctor who took up his pen to defend art in *Epoch* against Pisarev's "destruction of aesthetics" (initiated by Bazarov), and also to object strenuously when the same critic declared that enlightened capitalists were of more importance for Russian development than all the "philanthropic" endeavors to aid the people directly. The contributors to *The Russian Word*, Solovyev replied, "intend to turn capitalists into the leaders of the labor of the people by giving them an all-round education; and this would be a hundred times more useful than any philanthropy. Is this not a compliment to Rothschild? Capital grows and lives only for itself if it is not moved by a love for humanity. Give capitalists a heart; they already have a head, you need not worry about that."[7] As we shall soon see, this polemic quickly found an echo in Dostoevsky's next story, *The Crocodile*.

Despite the value of such individual contributions, *Epoch* remained more of a collection or anthology than a literary journal expressing a coherent and independent point of view. Nor did Dostoevsky ever quite succeed in catching up with the announced publication schedule, though he came closer and closer as time went on. Born under an unlucky star, *Epoch*'s brief career had a disastrous effect on the whole future course of Dostoevsky's life. When the journal went bankrupt, he was personally saddled with the crushing load of debt he had contracted to keep it afloat, and he struggled for most of the remainder of his life to satisfy his creditors. "Oh, my friend!" he exclaims to Wrangel, "I would voluntarily again go to the prison camp, and for the same number of years, in order to pay off all my debts and feel free again."[8] Such a declaration can hardly be accepted at face value; but it reveals Dostoevsky's genuine desperation at the unfortunate turn taken by his affairs.

4

Two of Dostoevsky's contributions to *Epoch* were brief articles: one an obituary of his brother Mikhail, the other containing comments (the most important of which have already been quoted) elicited by the publication of some letters of Apollon Grigoryev, who had died in September 1864—another loss for Dostoevsky, if not of an intimate, then at least of a valued confederate. Mikhail's memory was celebrated in terms that made his personal history a symbol of the path by which his younger brother too had arrived at the ideals of *pochvennichestvo*. "Long ago, in his youth, he had been a passionate Fourierist, totally devoted to his idea. His conversion from an abstract faith, without contact with the soil, to a communion with the purely Russian faith was the end result of a normal, organic evolution, as is always the case with men genuinely endowed with vitality." That kind of faith, Dostoevsky maintained, was not a new idea invented by an individual thinker (such as, presumably, Fourier's brand of Socialism) but something that had always existed in Russia. His readers would of course understand that he meant a "Russian faith" springing from the social(ist) institutions of the Russian peasantry. As for Grigoryev, he was remembered as an archetypical "Russian Hamlet," inwardly torn by the dissonances of Russian life and culture but nonetheless "a man directly—and even in many ways unconsciously—rooted in the soil, clinging to the pith of his country" (20: 135-136). To Dostoevsky's ear, not a single "false note" marred Grigoryev's "magnificent letters"; and he excused their intemperance, which had not spared the Dostoevsky brothers themselves, as an expression of an inner integrity that refused all compromise with his ideals (20: 135-136).

Much the most important of Dostoevsky's critical contributions to *Epoch* was his biting article "Mr. Shchedrin, or a Schism [*Raskol*] among the Nihilists," written in the form of what he labels "a novel-caricature" (satirical scenes in dialogue form). This work continued the polemics between Dostoevsky and Saltykov-Shchedrin which, it will be recalled, had broken out in the winter of 1863, just before the suppression of *Time*. Dostoevsky had by no means forgotten this exchange, and, at the first opportunity to publish again, had worked some barbed allusions to Saltykov-Shchedrin into *Notes from Underground*. In Part I, Chapter VI of that text, where the underground man dreams his "golden dreams" of defining himself in some way through his own choice (though knowing full well that the notion of choice is an illusion), he imagines that he becomes an aesthete who admires a picture by a painter named Ge and immediately drinks to his health. Similarly, "an author writes *As You Like It*, at once I drink to the health of *As You Like It* because I love all that is 'sublime and beautiful' " (5: 109). Saltykov-Shchedrin had recently written in praise of a picture by the well-known painter N. N. Ge depicting "The Last Supper"; and the "As You Like It" in question is not the play of Shakespeare but a series of articles and sketches by Saltykov-Shchedrin with the same title—a work which Strakhov, just a few months earlier, had also ironically taken to task.[9] The target of Dostoevsky's mockery, using the underground man as his mouthpiece, was thus unmistakable.

Saltykov-Shchedrin picked up the challenge in the next issue of *The Contemporary* with a "dramatic fable" entitled "The Swallows." Previously having affixed this description to the contributors of *Time*, he uses it here again to characterize the staff of a new journal, *Saturn Revived* (*Epoch*), who gather for an editorial conference. The two Dostoevsky brothers, Strakhov, Grigoryev, and others less well-known are portrayed as swallows perched on tubs along the wall of a damp, cavernous cellar (the underground), which is also filled with rats scurrying about the floor. The "first swallow," Mikhail Dostoevsky, constantly utters the complaint, "Why did they insult us?"—an obvious reference to the attacks on *Time* provoked by Strakhov's article. The swallows are all terrified of a mysterious "voice from above" (presumably Katkov), and the "second swallow," Strakhov, affirms: "I offered repentance and received absolution." There are clever parodies of the poetry printed in *Time*, as well as of Grigoryev's meandering prose style, and the hits at the recent past are cruelly funny and effective. The skit ends brutally: "A crash is heard. M. N. Katkov, lit by a tallow candle end, comes down in the cellar. The rats die. The swallows cry 'Excuse us' and fall into the tubs. Odor."[10]

"The Swallows" also contains a parodistic résumé of the first part of *Notes from Underground*, introduced in the course of the editorial conference at which the "fourth swallow, a despondent novelist," tells the others about his new creation:

> The new work I have finished is entitled *Notes on the Immortality of the Soul*. This is a question of the gravest importance for swallows, and as we must first and foremost show that our journal is an organ of swallows that is published by swallows and for swallows, it is completely natural that I took that into account in my choice of subject as well. The *Notes* are written by a sick and spiteful swallow. At first he talks about all sorts of nonsense: that he is sick and spiteful, that everything in the world is topsy-turvy, that his guts hurt, that no one can predict whether there will be plenty of mushrooms next summer, and finally that everyone is trash, and will not become good until he becomes convinced that he is trash, and in conclusion, of course, shifts to the real subject of his meditations. He draws most of his proofs from Thomas Aquinas, but as he does not mention the fact, the reader thinks that the ideas belong to the narrator himself. Then there is the setting of the story. There is neither dark nor light, but some sort of gray in the story; no human voices are heard, only hissing; no human figures are seen, but it is as though bats were flitting about in the dusk. It is not a fantastic world, nor yet a real one, but, as it were, a Cockaigne. Everybody cries, not about anything, but simply because their guts hurt (*sneezes from emotion and falls silent*).[11]

This brilliantly malicious lampoon reveals how clearly Saltykov-Shchedrin had grasped the moral-religious implications of the underground man's tragic ambivalence, which for Dostoevsky could only be overcome by the conquest of egoism and the free self-sacrifice of the personality out of love. Saltykov-Shchedrin was perfectly well aware that such values were, in Dostoevsky's view, a practical realization of the ideal of Christ, and he ridicules the attempt to ground them in an irrational (and ultimately, though Dostoevsky does not express this directly) supernatural Christian faith.*

---

* The title of Saltykov-Shchedrin's parody has recently led to an interesting speculation regarding the censored Chapter x of the first part of *Notes from Underground*. L. M. Rosenblyum, in her valuable study of Dostoevsky's notebooks, suggests that Saltykov-Shchedrin may have

Dostoevsky made no specific reply to this masterly onslaught; instead, he chose to strike back by taking advantage of an ideological free-for-all that had broken out in the radical camp during the preceding year and in which Saltykov-Shchedrin had taken a prominent part. This quarrel between *The Contemporary* and *The Russian Word*, which Dostoevsky dubbed a *"raskol among the Nihilists,"* is still known by that name in histories of Russian culture. The first clash, as we know, had taken place between Pisarev and Antonovich over *Fathers and Children*, but an uneasy truce between the two journals was maintained so long as Chernyshevsky was still at liberty. No such reverence, however, was felt for the revived *Contemporary*, whose chief editors were Nekrasov, Saltykov-Shchedrin, and Antonovich. The second name in particular was heartily disliked by the young zealots of *The Russian Word*. Not long before, Saltykov-Shchedrin had faithfully served the Tsarist régime and risen to the rank of vice-governor of a province; he had published his *Provincial Sketches* in what for the radicals was that sink of abominations, Katkov's *The Russian Messenger*; and it was well known that before joining *The Contemporary* he had tried without success to obtain permission to publish a journal of his own.[12] The "immoderate Nihilists" on *The Russian Word* (as Dostoevsky called them) shared Dostoevsky's own view that Saltykov-Shchedrin's apparent radicalism was only a matter of expediency, and the satirist soon offered them what seemed an irrefutable confirmation of their most damaging suspicions about his principles.

Even though the second phase of this internecine quarrel began after the suppression of *Time* and while Dostoevsky was temporarily absent from the journalistic scene, he was nonetheless intimately involved in its exchanges. For it had flared up again partly as a result of Shchedrin's scathing attacks against the last issues of *Time*, which included his promise to regale his readers with some discussion of, among other topics, "An Exercise in Comparative Etymology, or 'House of the Dead' drawn from French sources. A pedagogical and diverting investigation by Mikhail Zmiev-Mladentsev" (or, in English, Michael Snake Jr.).[13] This insulting reference aroused the wrath of the youthfully belligerent V. A. Zaitsev, who was not only stirred by a comprehensible sympathy for Dostoevsky's sufferings in Siberia but also exasperated by the spectacle of what he considered

learned from the censors themselves that material alluding to such immortality had been cut from Dostoevsky's text. Both *The Contemporary* and *Epoch* dealt with the same censorship office, and gossip of this kind between editors and censors was not uncommon. Whether, as Rosenblyum believes, Dostoevsky referred *explicitly* to immortality in the censored material can only remain an open question. But, as we know from his notebooks, immortality was much on his mind at this time. L. M. Rosenblyum, *Tvorcheskie Dnevniki Dostoevskogo* (Moscow, 1981), 246-247.

Shchedrin's unconscionable political shiftiness. "To make fun of *House of the Dead*," he wrote, "means to run the risk of being told that a work of this kind is written with the author's own blood, and not from the inkwell of a vice-governor's desk."[14] The two journals continued, though in veiled terms, to snipe at each other throughout the remainder of the year; and one unsigned article in *The Russian Word* typically remarked that, while the "general tendency" of *The Contemporary* was sympathetic, readers were having more and more difficulty distinguishing it from *The Russian Messenger* (another dig at Saltykov-Shchedrin's past).[15] The pot boiled over at the beginning of 1864 with the publication of the January installment of Saltykov-Shchedrin's monthly column, "The Life of Our Society."

In the midst of some jeering reflections that, in Aesopian language, took to task the rashness, the intemperance, and the inclination to cherish illusions of those whom he called "the fledglings" (the young radicals of *The Russian Word*), Saltykov-Shchedrin wrote: "When I remember, for example, that *with time* children will give birth to their fathers and the egg will teach the chicken, that *with time* Zaitsevskyish *khlistovshchina* will be universally affirmed [the *khlisty* were a dissident religious sect of orgiastic flagellants], that *with time* cute little Nihilist girls will cut up human corpses with an unfaltering hand while they are dancing and singing 'about nothing, Dunya, do I grieve' (for *with time*, as is well known, no human action will be performed without singing and dancing), then tranquillity settles in my heart, and I busy myself with keeping my conscience pure until that time."[16] These words created an uproar, not so much for the personal reference to Zaitsev, but for what is obviously a contemptuous allusion to the novel that had become the gospel of radicalism.

"How is it well known?" Strakhov asks commiseratingly in his own comment on this passage. "Poor fellow! from where is it well known? It can be well known only from one book, from the novel *What Is To Be Done?*"[17] Indeed, the sneering reference to Chernyshevsky's famous work, whose author was then under arrest and soon to be sent to Siberia, was perfectly plain for all to see. Since Vera Pavlovna pursues medical studies in the later stages of her career, she would have been required to perform autopsies with an unfaltering hand; and since life in the future Crystal Palace, as Chernyshevsky depicts it, images the typical Fourierist union of work and pleasure, singing and dancing are indeed the joyful accompaniment there of hitherto onerous labor. The stab in the back could not be mistaken; nothing in *Notes from Underground* is half as insulting as these sentences in Chernyshevsky's own journal, which had printed the very text now being ridiculed just the year before.

Naturally, this passage provoked a furious riposte from *The Russian Word*, and its February issue contained two articles directed against Saltykov-Shchedrin. Just as Dostoevsky had done earlier, Pisarev's biting "Flowers of Innocent Humor" accused the free-wheeling satirist of practicing "art for art's sake" and being totally irresponsible in his choice of targets; it would be infinitely more useful for society, he suggested, if Saltykov-Shchedrin were to employ his agile pen to popularize the new discoveries of science rather than wasting his time in attempting (unsuccessfully) to create "literature." Zaitsev also joined in by lamenting that *The Contemporary* was now so obviously betraying its old principles.[18] Replying in March, Saltykov-Shchedrin referred to his opponents as "lop-eared" (immature puppies) and also as behaving like *yurodivye* (holy fools, who were traditionally feeble-minded). Like Dostoevsky, he accused them of debasing and degrading the noble ideals in whose name they were presumably speaking;[19] and it is at this point that Dostoevsky himself intervened in the fray, taking advantage of the fact that his own arguments were being used by both sides.

6

Dostoevsky prefaces his skit with a brief introduction summarizing his view of the conflict. "Here, for example, not long ago, not at all long ago," he comments, "a strange commotion occurred. *The Russian Word*, the organ of the immoderate Nihilists, attacked *The Contemporary*, the organ of the moderate Nihilists." The cause of this attack was the strange behavior of Mr. Shchedrin, whose relation to *The Contemporary* had now, Dostoevsky says, aroused the wonder and curiosity of the entire literary world. "In fact, Mr. Shchedrin recently (and God knows why!) took it into his head to express in *The Contemporary* convictions that bluntly and literally contradict the most fundamental convictions of *The Contemporary* in recent years; and it is not surprising that *The Russian Word* even shames *The Contemporary* with Mr. Shchedrin." Rumors are flying thick and fast, and "it has been said that Mr. Shchedrin has been cut in two by Mr. Zaitsev, cut into two separate halves. . . . After which another rumor caused a sensation: the sentiment of his literary dignity awoke in the two halves of Mr. Shchedrin, he refused to be suppressed or to sell to the editorial board his right to have and express his convictions. . . ." But, since he is still writing for *The Contemporary*, does it mean that the journal has begun "to retrogradify"? Or has Mr. Shchedrin promised to behave in the future? All this is very interesting, but unfortunately a total mystery (20: 102-104).

Closely following the manner in which "The Swallows" had been presented, Dostoevsky then presents a text which, luckily, the editors of *Epoch* had found in their portfolio, a "novel" that seems, as if on purpose, to have something to do with a similar affair "and evidently has an allegorical intention." It is so apropos that *Epoch* cannot resist printing a few extracts, which deal with the inner history of another journal called *The Opportunist*

(*Svoevremmenik*). The staff has gathered for an editorial conference and is discussing some of the problems that have recently arisen. "We are in a bad way," begins one of the editors. "You know, gentlemen, that Pravdolyubov [Dobrolyubov] has died, that others—." The unfinished phrase, as everyone would understand, referred to Chernyshevsky's arrest; hence the journal had been deprived of its two leading and most effective contributors. The talk turns on how to proceed in the future, and various alternatives are proposed. "When somebody drives us against a wall," one editor suggests, "and in general in all those cases where a definite and positive opinion is necessary, we will immediately announce that this will all be explained when 'new economic relations have been established'; follow that by a dash, and we're all set" (20: 105). But even this resourceful tactic, it is agreed, will not be sufficient by itself to pull the magazine out of its doldrums.

Stronger medicine is required, and it is agreed that, so far as journals are concerned, "whoever attacks first, barks and bites, brazenly and impudently refuses to answer the most specific inquiries, doesn't give a hang about them, whistles, caricatures, and rushes to abuse everyone indiscriminately—[that journal] will seem powerful and cunning to the common man and the majority." It is decided, as a result, to hire "a barking and biting mutt," who will "sink its teeth into anything we point to and harass it until we yell *Ici!*," and all agree that "our famous humorist and satirist Mr. Shchedrodarov" is just the man for the job (20: 105-106).

Shchedrodarov is accordingly summoned, and carefully instructed in the rigorous conditions of his new employment. He will be obliged to devote his talents "to popularize natural science, presenting it under the guise of stories and tales." He must "respect, screen, and protect all those who declare themselves to be progressives . . . even if they are high school juniors." He must accept as irrefutable truth the principle (established by Chernyshevsky's aesthetics) that "a real apple is better than a painted apple, the more so as one can eat a real apple, but one cannot eat a painted apple"; and from this indisputable axiom follows the Utilitarian inference that "Pushkin is nonsense and luxury." He must read only the "five 'rational' books" (this probably refers to similar advice by Chernyshevsky in *What Is To Be Done?*) and also agree "that for the happiness of all mankind, and equally for the happiness of each separate individual, first and most important of all is the belly, or in other words, the stomach" (20: 107-109).

Inwardly, Shchedrodarov finds all this very hard to accept, and thinks to himself that "perhaps it would be much easier to grab the moon by its horns than to attain satisfied bellies everywhere by the preliminary and intentional paralyzing of all man's other capacities." But, stifling his doubts, he listens to a briefing on how to handle malcontents: "Similarly, if someone should say to you 'I want to think, I am tormented by the eternal unresolved questions, I want to love, I agonize over questions of faith, I search for a moral ideal, I love art,' or anything along those lines, answer him immediately, decisively, and bravely that this is all nonsense, metaphysics, that all that is a luxury, childish dreams, unnecessary" (20: 110-111). But Shchedrodarov, "obliged to read the matter he was instructed to make fun of . . . involuntarily became enlightened, and involuntarily a new light started to shine upon him."

The final section shows him being taken to task by other editors of *The Opportunist*, who accuse him of cribbing from *Time* (*The Russian Word* had said the same about Saltykov-Shchedrin's attack on *them*). Shchedrodarov unabashedly confesses that he has copied from *Time*, "as many others do, too, because it is a good journal"; and at the height of the dispute it is clear that he has become a convert to *pochvennichestvo* ("I do not understand how one can stand on air, without feeling the soil under one"). In the end, the strain of independence is too much and he breaks down and sobs like a baby (20: 112, 114, 115).

Saltykov-Shchedrin wrote a number of appropriately caustic replies to this well-aimed broadside, which unquestionably had drawn blood; but the other editors of *The Contemporary*, for reasons that still remain obscure, did not agree to their publication. Instead, the polemic with *Epoch* was entrusted to Antonovich, who began by confusing the enemy and claiming to have been the author of "The Swallows." Then he proceeded to pen a series of articles that, it is unanimously agreed, mark a nadir of vulgarity and personal vituperation even in the midst of the by no means genteel journalistic exchanges of the mid-1860s. One of these articles, which largely parodied an earlier one of Dostoevsky's in *Time*, depicted him in the throes of a nervous fit and was commonly taken as a mockery of his epilepsy.

Soviet Russian commentators have done their best to make a case for Antonovich, who, after all, had been a favorite of Chernyshevsky and gained his confidence and approbation. The conscientious historian of *The Contemporary* Evgenyev-Maksimov goes to great pains to show that some of the worst passages of Antonovich are transpositions of Dostoevsky's own texts, and merely turn his satirical tactics against himself. But even such an advocate is forced to concede "the quibble" that, if Dostoevsky refers to "an illness" of Saltykov-Shchedrin, this "was an artistic and polemical invention, while Dostoevsky's illness was a real fact."[20] Dostoevsky's notebooks contain numerous indignant passages provoked by Antonovich, and he was particularly incensed at the accusation of being "happy" over the death of Dobrolyubov and the imprisonment of Chernyshevsky. "I feel sorry for the premature death of Dobrolyubov and for the others—both personally and as writers," he jotted down. "But I cannot say, because of this commiseration, that they have not talked nonsense" (20: 200).

In public, Dostoevsky replied to Antonovich only with two brief and dignified editorial comments. Without trying to argue the issues any further, he merely noted that the writer in *The Contemporary*, who indicated that he had met the novelist personally, surely knew where and when Dostoevsky had become a sick man (of course, during his term as a political prisoner in Siberia). The duel between *Epoch* and *The Contemporary* ended at this point, to the general relief of most of the other organs of the Russian press, which had been shocked at the unheard-of coarseness and offensiveness of Antonovich's articles. These certainly left their scars on Dostoevsky, and deepened his suspicions that the radical ideology of the 1860s was bent on destroying all the painfully and (in Russia) recently acquired standards of civilized existence.

7
———

In the very last issue of *Epoch*, Dostoevsky printed the first installment of a never-completed story usually known as *The Crocodile*. (Its original title, dropped on later republication, was *An Extraordinary Event or an Incident in the Arcade, a True Story . . . reported by Semyon Swallow*.) From the name of the supposed author, we see that the work took form as a direct continuation of the polemics carried on by *Epoch* with the radicals; and even though called a "story," *The Crocodile* is closer to a satirical grotesque like *Shchedrodarov* than to *A Nasty Tale*. No attempt is made to attain any psychological verisimilitude; the personal relations between the characters are purely perfunctory; and the point of the story lies in the stereotyped reactions of the figures to the "extraordinary event" that occurs in the Arcade, a covered passageway that served for shows and exhibitions as well as for lectures by well-known representatives of the progressive intelligentsia (such as P. A. Lavrov, mentioned by name in the text). In a preface later omitted along with the original title, Dostoevsky compares the story to Gogol's *The Nose*, which depicts the equally fantastic incident of an official waking up one morning to find that his nose has disappeared. But *The Crocodile* has none of Gogol's bubbling and quick-paced humor, nor does it play the same sort of tricks with narrative technique.

The "extraordinary incident" concerns a rather pretentious and conceited bureaucrat of high rank and his giddy and flirtatious wife, who both go to view a crocodile on exhibition in the Arcade. The gentleman, Ivan Matveich by name, allowing his curiosity to overcome his caution, approaches the reptile too closely and is swallowed alive. To the immense astonishment of the narrator (a rather envious friend), the wife, and the German owner of the crocodile, Ivan Matveich survives, and even settles down comfortably in the belly of the beast. His voice can clearly be heard expressing great satisfaction at what has occurred: it will attract attention, and provide him the leisure to develop his lofty ideas for the betterment of mankind. He will, he assures his listeners, "refute everything and become a new Fourier." Meanwhile, his charming wife, whom all the other men consider "a little sugar-plum," wonders whether to ask for a divorce in view of his inevitably prolonged absence from home. Rejecting an invitation to join him in the crocodile (there appears to be ample room), she seems quite sensible to the attentions of "a certain swarthy gentleman with little moustaches who was something in the architectural line" (5: 194, 201, 202).

Shortly after publishing this text, Dostoevsky was accused, most openly in *The Voice* (*Golos*), of having written an "allegory" deriding Chernyshevsky, who had been publicly degraded and sent to Siberia less than a year before. Since the latter had written and published *What Is To Be Done?* while in prison, it was easy enough to see Dostoevsky's story as a malevolent allusion to that notorious event; and some of the traits of the wife could also be suspected of referring to Mme Chernyshevskaya, whose flirtatious character was well-known and provided a strong contrast with that of her austere husband. Eight years later, in his *Diary of a Writer*, Dostoevsky vigorously denied any allegorical intention and protested against the imputation that "I, myself a former exile and convict, rejoiced in the exile of another 'unfortunate' " (21: 29). Dostoevsky, as we have seen, expressed his regret over Chernyshevsky's fate in his notebooks, and nothing we know about him either then or later would make us doubt the sincerity of these affirmations. He was never in favor of the suppression of ideas, no matter how much he might disagree with them, and always considered it a mistake to hinder their free expression. None of the notebook material bears out any interpretation of the work as a personal attack on Chernyshevsky; quite to the contrary, it indicates that Dostoevsky's target was the radicals of *The Russian Word*. That certain details can be read as cruel references to Chernyshevsky's unhappy fate was probably an unfortunate coincidence; and the most recent Soviet Russian commentators, unlike many of their predecessors, now accept Dostoevsky's disclaimer.[21]

Of course, any attempt to ridicule the radicals at this time inevitably ran the risk of being considered as an attack on Chernyshevsky, whose ideas had established the conceptual framework of the radical ideology of the 1860s. The argument between *The Contemporary* and *The Russian Word* was essentially over how to interpret his heritage; the "immoderate Nihilists" of *The Russian Word* merely considered themselves to be drawing out the full implications of his thought, while their opponents accused them of falsifying and distorting the true doctrines of the Master. Hence, it is not difficult to see allusions to Chernyshevsky everywhere in any satire of the radical position (and, as we have seen, there *were* specific digs against him made in *Shchedrodarov*). But in the case of *The Crocodile*, and despite the reference to Fourier, the ideological thrust can in no way be considered aimed at Chernyshevsky.

The theme of *The Crocodile*, so far as it really has one, centers on the total lack of humanity in all the responses to what is, after all, a distressing occurrence: the swallowing of a human being by a crocodile. No one except the narrator feels sorry for the unhappy victim, and he soon learns that his own instinctive reaction to the plight of a fellow man in distress is totally misplaced. The German owner of the crocodile and his *Mutter* refuse to contemplate the idea of "excavating" the beast to save the living man, since the combination of the two will draw an ever vaster public to their exhibition. Nor is the response of Ivan Matveich himself any different. "They are right," he observes coolly; "the principles of economics"—represented first by the primitive rapaciousness of the German, then by Ivan Matveich's lofty surrender to a higher economic law—take precedence over any spontaneous human reaction of sympathy in the situation.

The satire continues when the narrator of the story goes to seek advice from a mutual friend, the elderly, pedantic bureaucrat Timofey Semyonovich. The latter upholds the position of the German, on the ground that "a crocodile is private property, and so it is impossible to slit him open without compensation." Timofey Semyonovich also repeats some remarks he heard the evening before from an important capitalist, Ignaty Prokofich, which had made a great impression on him. The hard-headed businessman pointed out that Russia is greatly in need of more foreign capital to stimulate industrial development and suggested that communal land should be sold to foreign investors: "When . . . all the land is in the hands of foreign companies, they can fix any rent they like. And so the peasant will work three times as much for his daily bread and he can be turned out at pleasure. . . . But as it is, with the commune, what does he care? He knows he won't die of hunger, so he is lazy and drunken" (5: 189-190).

For this reason, Timofey Semyonovich takes a very dim view of Ivan Matveich's chances of being rescued. "Here we are anxious to bring foreign capital into the country—and only consider: as soon as the capital of a foreigner, who has been attracted to Petersburg, has been doubled through Ivan Matveich, instead of protecting the foreign capitalist we are proposing to rip open the belly of his original capital—the crocodile" (5: 190). Such behavior would be sure to discourage the flow of foreign capital and work against the best interests of the motherland. Timofey Semyonovich even doubts whether Ivan Matveich can get a leave of absence with pay; there is nothing in the regulations about government clerks who take up residence in the belly of a crocodile.

The narrator, who continues to maintain the naive human point of view, is quite upset by this encounter; but not so Ivan Matveich himself. " 'The old man is right,' Ivan Matveich pronounced as abruptly as usual in his conversation with me. 'I like practical people, and I can't endure sentimental milksops!' " He then goes on to sketch a giddy picture of himself holding forth from the stomach of the crocodile before the leaders of mankind and the highest circles of the *beau monde*, who will gather in his sitting room after he is transported there in a tank. Brilliant conversation will reign under the stimulus of his words, "and to be ready for anything let [my wife] buy tomorrow the *Encyclopedia* edited by Andrey Kraevsky, that she may be able to converse on any topic." Meanwhile, Ivan Matveich explains: "I am constructing now a complete system of my own, and you wouldn't believe how easy it is! You have only to creep into a secluded corner or into a crocodile, to shut your eyes, and you immediately devise a perfect millennium for mankind" (5: 195, 197). The rest of the story is taken up with a solemnly ridiculous account of the "scientific" observations he is making in the crocodile's stomach and a close, skillful, and amusing parody of the manner in which the whole incident has been reported (and distorted) in various organs of the Russian press.

It is clear from Dostoevsky's drafts that he intended to continue the story, and his notes contain material for more parodies that lash out at both the right and the left of the Russian social-cultural spectrum. Indeed, to an ordinary reader it would appear as if Dostoevsky is mainly ridiculing the advocates of an unchecked capitalist exploitation of Russia, and these, one would imagine, could scarcely have been the radicals. In fact, however, as noted earlier, the leading publicist of *The Russian Word*, D. I. Pisarev, while still remaining a political radical, was nonetheless a partisan of exactly such rapid capitalist development and large-scale industrialization; only in this way, he believed, would enlightenment spread in Russia and lead to the growth of a class of "thinking people" who could bring about the desired social changes. B. P. Kozmin, one of the best Soviet Russian historians of social thought, has noted that "even in his early writings, Pisarev steps forth as a finished and consistent Westerner, seeking salvation not in strengthening the native principle of the *obshchina*, indigenous, presumably, to Russian life, but in moving it along the road taken by Western Europe, i.e., through capitalism to socialism."[22] Pisarev and his allies were thus laying impious hands on what for Dostoevsky was the holy of holies, and he is already beginning to imagine the possible human consequences of such desecration.*

The Crocodile thus initiates, in my view, a new phase in Dostoevsky's re-

* In a highly informative study of "Economic Development in Russian Intellectual History of the Nineteenth Century," the economic historian Alexander Gerschenkron notes the great discrepancy between the actual course of Russian economic development and what the leaders of Russian radical thought considered likely or desirable for their country.

One notable exception, however, is D. I. Pisarev, who receives high marks for originality despite the "staggering inconsistencies" of his ideas, which allow him to be cited on both sides of the issue in question. "It must suffice here," writes Gerschenkron, "to place on record . . . this [Pisarev's] brief departure from the rut of established [left-wing] thought and the willingness on the part of an important representative of Russia's intellectual history to accept industrial development and the philosophy of economic individualism." See Alexander Gerschenkron, *Economic Backwardness in Historical Perspective* (Cambridge, Mass., 1962), 177.

lationship to radical ideology, a phase in which his attention shifts from Chernyshevsky and his followers (after *Notes from Underground*) to the "inhumanity" of the doctrines propounded by *The Russian Word*. This shift, even though it seems to have gone unnoticed, is sufficiently clear from a straightforward reading of the story, and it has now been amply confirmed by the publication of the notebook material. These writings demonstrate that Dostoevsky's shafts are directed primarily against the particular twist given to radical ideology by Pisarev and Zaitsev—a twist that began with Pisarev's interpretation of Bazarov as a sort of left-wing Superman, whose conscience admitted no "moral regulator," and who thus existed outside the bounds of good and evil.

This glorification of the heroic individual was reinforced, if only for a short while, by Social Darwinism, which Zaitsev invoked to defend the enslavement of the colored races on the grounds of their natural inferiority; and Dostoevsky specifically parodies this opinion in one of the notes for the planned continuation of his satire. Ivan Matveich's skin color darkens in the crocodile, and this is used as an additional reason why he has no right to ask that his interests be put over those of the German owner of the crocodile, a member of the dominating white race (5: 389).* In harmony with such an emphasis, *The Russian Word* also abandoned that Populist strain in Russian radicalism which involved a deep emotional commitment to the values of the people and believed in their immense potential. Zaitsev, for example, minces no words in expressing his lack of regard for the people, whom he called "coarse, stupid, and, as a result, passive; this is of course not their fault, but so it is, and it would be strange to expect any sort of initiative from them."[23] Whatever his disagreements with Chernyshevsky, Dostoevsky had shared with the radical democrats a much more favorable view of the people; and this had created subliminal bonds of sympathy.

Now, however, Dostoevsky sees the inhumanity deriving from the "laws of economics" as endemic on both the left and the right, and he implicitly identifies the two in *The Crocodile* by showing the "progressive" Ivan Mat-

---

* In an article devoted to a book on *The Unity of the Human Race* by the French naturalist Jean Louis Quatrefages, Zaitsev argued that, because of the biological inferiority of the colored races, their only hope of survival in competition with the superior whites was to remain in a position of subordination in which their interests would be safeguarded. Open competition would mean their extinction. The tone of his remarks was sharp and derisive: "Sentimental enemies of lack of freedom," he writes, "are only able to cite texts and sing psalms, but they cannot point to a single fact capable of showing that education and freedom could transform negroes into whites so far as mental capacity is concerned. . . . Only tender-hearted gentlewomen like Mme Beecher-Stowe can insist on brotherhood between the races."

Pisarev came to Zaitsev's defense in the ensuing uproar. "Zaitsev uttered the by no means eccentric thought," he wrote, "that Darwin's law also applies to the human races." Later, he argued that Darwin's law should not stand in the way of the struggle against slavery; but he continued to believe that social inequality was ultimately rooted in biological differences. See the chapter on Zaitsev in V. Ya. Kirpotin, *Publitsisty i Kritiki* (Leningrad, 1932), 158.

This tangential influence of Social Darwinism on Russian radical thought had considerable importance for Dostoevsky, who took it as symptomatic of the overt inhumanity that the radicals (or at least some of their very latest spokesmen) were now willing to accept as legitimate.

CHAPTER 23

"The Vitality of a Cat"

With the failure of *Epoch*, preceded by the death of his first wife and then of his brother, another period of Dostoevsky's life comes to a close. The two people to whom he had been closest in the world were now gone; he was left bereft and alone; and his hopes of establishing himself as a successful editor, who could count on a regular income from a monthly periodical, had finally gone glimmering. Dostoevsky knew that he had reached a watershed in his life; and once again, just as he had done after leaving the prison camp, he marked the occasion with a lengthy letter summing up the past. Writing to his old intimate Baron Wrangel, to whom he could unburden his heart with very little inhibition, Dostoevsky reveals his innermost feelings with unaccustomed frankness.

2

Sometime after Mikhail's death, Wrangel had sent condolences to Feodor over his loss. Not receiving an immediate reply, he had written again; and it is to this second epistle that Dostoevsky finally responds at the end of March. "My dear good friend Alexander Yegorovich," he begins, "I well understand that you must have been surprised and, of course, given your feelings for me, quite annoyed by my silence after your two so very warm and affectionate letters. Do not be surprised, do not be annoyed. I wished to reply to you immediately, but *was not able to do so.*" Dostoevsky promises to explain why in a moment, but first assures Wrangel that the two men are linked together by too many bonds of the past for him ever to forget what they had meant to each other: "Would I have been able to forget you, the friend of a time when I had no friends, the witness of my infinite happiness and my terrible suffering (do you recall that night in the forest, near Semipalatinsk, when we accompanied them?);* the friend who, later in Petersburg, worked so hard for me—could I forget you?"[1]

After such reassurances, Dostoevsky goes on to sketch his life of unre-

---

* This is a reference to the departure of Dostoevsky's first wife and her then husband, Alexander Isaev, from Semipalatinsk at a time when Dostoevsky had already begun to have an affair with her. Wrangel and Dostoevsky accompanied the travelers, as was the Russian custom, on the first leg of their journey; and Wrangel plied Isaev, a notorious drunkard, with champagne in order to allow the lovers a *tête-à-tête* in a separate carriage before they were torn from each other. See *Dostoevsky: The Years of Ordeal, 1850-1859* (Princeton, 1983), chap. 15.

367

mitting literary labor over the past few years and attributes the re-establish-
ment of his literary reputation to *House of the Dead*. He details the financial
problems of *Time* and the moment when success seemed to be within his
grasp; but then came the crushing blow of the interdiction because of
Strakhov's article. "It is true that the writer was partly to blame (one of our
closest collaborators), he made things too complicated and was interpreted
in the opposite sense." Whatever the amity reigning between them on the
surface, Dostoevsky was not able to master the grudge he continued to feel
against Strakhov—and which slips out here—for his catastrophic lack of
clarity. All the more so because the banning of *Time* was the beginning of
the end for Mikhail: "he began to pile up debts; his health was undermined."[2]

Since Wrangel displayed ignorance of the death of Marya Dimitrievna,
Dostoevsky brings him up to date regarding this equally doleful news: "You
pity me because of my fatal loss, the death of my angel, my brother Misha,
but you do not know to what extent destiny has crushed me! Another person who loved me, and whom I loved immeasurably, my wife, died of tuberculosis in Moscow, where she had gone to live last year." Dostoevsky
then conveys to Wrangel the farewell salutations of Marya Dimitrievna
(perhaps invented for this occasion), and evokes an image of their conjugal
life that reveals what complex emotional fibers had united these two beings
amidst all their mutual torments. "She died on April 16th of last year, in full
possession of her faculties, and, in saying good-bye, recalling all those
whom she wished to greet for the last time, she also remembered you. . . .
Oh! my friend, she loved me immeasurably, and I also loved her the same
way, but we were not happy together. I will tell you everything when we see
each other—now I will only say that, despite being positively unhappy together (because of her strange, suspicious, and unhealthily fantastic character)—we could not cease loving each other; the unhappier we were, the
more we became attached to each other. No matter how strange, that is
how it was. She was the most honorable, the noblest and the most magnanimous woman of all those I have ever known in my life."[3]

At the death of his wife and brother, Dostoevsky continues, he suddenly
became aware that the life he had been trying to build, both personally and
professionally, had been shattered. "When she died—even though I was
tortured (all year) watching her death-agony, even though I fully valued
and agonizingly felt all that I was burying with her—still, I could not possibly have imagined to what an extent my life would become empty and
painful when they scattered earth on her grave. And now a year has passed,
and my feeling is the same, not lessening at all. . . . After burying her, I flew
to Petersburg, to my brother—only he was left to me, and in three months
he died as well, having been slightly ill a whole month so that the crisis resulting in his death occurred almost unexpectedly in three days. And thus

I suddenly found myself alone and simply terrified. My entire life at one stroke broke into two. In one half, which I had lived through, was everything I had lived for, and in the other, still unknown half everything was strange and new, and there was not a single heart that could replace those two.

"Literally—I had nothing left for which to live. To establish new relations, to plan out a new life! The very thought of doing so was repellent to me. I, *for the first time*, felt to the marrow of my bones that no one could replace *them*, that it was only *them* that I loved in the world and that a new love not only could not be acquired but should not be. Everything around me became cold and empty. And thus, when I received your warm and kind letter three months ago, filled with previous memories, I became so depressed that I cannot tell you how I felt. But listen while I continue."[4]

3

The first installment of the letter breaks off at this point, and Dostoevsky takes it up more than a week later. "Nine days have passed since I began this letter" he explains, "and in these nine days I have not literally had a moment to finish it."[5] Continuing his account of the problems of *Epoch*, Dostoevsky enters into all sorts of financial details that need not be recorded here. But he stops again after two paragraphs, and only resumes five days later (April 14). The sad story of *Epoch*'s demise is recited once more as Dostoevsky expounds some of the hopes on which he had based his calculations for the future (and that he *did* make calculations is amply proven by the many pages of his notebooks covered with columns of figures).

As a result of having tried to keep *Epoch* afloat, Dostoevsky was now in desperate economic straits: "I owe 10,000 rubles in signed contracts, and 5,000 on my word; 3,000 have to be paid immediately, come what may. In addition, 2,000 are necessary in order to purchase the right to publish my works, a right now held as a guarantee on a loan, so that I can begin to edit myself." Dostoevsky's plan was to write a new novel and issue it in separate installments, "as is done in England"; he also wished to re-edit *House of the Dead* "with illustrations, in a luxury edition," and then, the following year, an edition of his complete works. But the prospect of writing under such desperate pressure, solely to meet his debts, fills him with anguish: "Now I am going to begin writing a novel under the lash, i.e., out of necessity. It will produce an effect, but is that what I need? To work out of necessity, just for money, crushes and destroys me."[6]

Returning to the immediate situation and the grim outlook ahead, Dostoevsky in effect sees his position as practically hopeless: "But in order to begin I need, and right away, at least 3,000. I am beating the bushes trying to get it—otherwise, I am done for. I feel that only an accident can save me.

What remains from all the reserve of strength and energy in my soul is something troubled and disturbed, something close to despair. Worry, bitterness, a completely cold industriousness, the most abnormal state for me to be in, and in addition loneliness—of all my past forty years, nothing remains to me. And yet it still seems to me that I am just now preparing to live. Funny, isn't it? The vitality of a cat."[7]

Nothing could have been more unexpected than this last remark, and yet nothing is more characteristic of the man who had not allowed himself to be crushed by the house of the dead and who, no matter how desperate his situation, had never given way to a paralyzing or crippling despondency. Dostoevsky, after all, believed in the freedom of the will, and in his case, as in that of William James, this conviction sprang from the deepest resources of his personality. There is never a moment in Dostoevsky's life when we can catch him giving up entirely, never a moment when—in the wreckage of whatever hopes he may have been building on, or whatever disaster has overtaken him—he is not making plans for the future and feeling the same surge of energy and expectation to which he so surprisingly gives expression here.

4

Or perhaps it is not so surprising after all if we look a little more carefully at the chronology of Dostoevsky's life. His letter to Wrangel extends through March–April 1865, and while writing it, he had plunged himself emotionally back into the past. Dostoevsky was reliving for Wrangel's benefit everything he had undergone since their parting; and in reporting on his sense of futility at the thought of establishing new emotional ties, he was surely conveying what he must have genuinely felt at Marya Dimitrievna's graveside. Nor would his lacerating experiences with Suslova have made the thought of entering into such new ties any more appealing. But time had already proceeded with its healing work, and just a month or two before his letter to Wrangel, Dostoevsky had probably struck up a liaison—for just how long it is hard to say—with a worldly-wise and emotionally battered woman by the name of Martha Brown (her maiden name had been Panina, and the "Brown" had been acquired, in the course of her European wanderings, from a sailor who may have been American). Her letters to Dostoevsky from the hospital where she was recovering from an illness during January–February 1864-1865 indicate an increasing degree of intimacy, and perhaps the beginning of a love affair about which nothing else is known.

Also, in that very month of April, and just as he was completing his letter to Wrangel, Dostoevsky proposed marriage to the beautiful and rebellious young daughter of a wealthy, highly placed family, Anna Korvin-Krukovskaya, whose short stories he had printed in *Epoch* and whose talent he had encouraged. The sudden shift so noticeable in the letter—the abrupt transition from past to present—may be attributed to such events, when a resurgence of faith in the future suddenly intruded on the melancholy past that he was recalling. Indeed, an entirely new life for Dostoevsky was to begin in a little more than a year, when he would marry another young woman and then flee to Europe for a prolonged exile in order to escape his creditors. A more detailed account of these earlier romantic entanglements, which are a prelude to his remarriage, may be reserved for the next volume.

5

Meanwhile, whatever Dostoevsky's gloom and sadness over the failure of *Epoch*, the end of his impossible labors must nonetheless have come as something of a relief. He knew that his real vocation was to be a novelist; and even when he still believed that *Epoch* could be a success, he had looked forward to the moment when he could return to his essential creative task. Now he was being forced to do so, and for us it is evident that his failure as an editor and journalist was his salvation as an artist. During the next five years, under the pressure of necessity but never at the cost of artistic integrity, he would write three of his greatest novels—*Crime and Punishment*, *The Idiot*, and *The Devils*—and establish his reputation once and for all as belonging in the very front rank of Russian literature. As these works were to prove, his years of participation in the social-cultural ferment of the early 1860s were far from having been spent in vain. For it was in the fierce give-and-take of argument and polemic that he had gradually hammered out his own position, and found the great theme that was to occupy him throughout the remainder of the decade and of his life. It was then that he began to explore, against the background provided by his own confrontation with death and his years in the house of the dead, the moral-psychic dangers involved in the desire of the radical Russian intelligentsia to establish human life on new, "rational" foundations that would replace the God-given order still alive in the Russian moral sensibility.

Notes from Underground was the first work in which Dostoevsky attempted to portray the consequences for the human personality of the attempt to put into practice—but with a full awareness of *all* their implications—the ideas of the progressive and radical ideologies of the 1840s and 1860s; and one can observe him constantly trying to define his own position in relation to such doctrines. Some notes set down for a projected article entitled "Socialism and Christianity," which was never written, show Dostoevsky returning to issues he had grappled with earlier both privately and in public print, and now placing them in the vast historical perspective of the rise and fall of civilizations.

371

In the primitive stages of society, he writes, "God is the collective idea of humanity, the masses, *everyone*. When man lives in masses (in the primitive patriarchal communities, about which legends have been left)—then man lives *spontaneously*." But "then comes the transitional period, i.e., further development, i.e., civilization. (Civilization is a transitional period.) In this further development comes a phenomenon, a new fact, which no one can escape; this is the development of personal consciousness and the negation of spontaneous ideas and laws (authoritarian, patriarchal laws of the masses)." As a result of such individualism, which negates the old law of the masses, man "*always* lost his faith in God as well." All civilizations end in this phase of Godlessness, and Dostoevsky believed that Europe had now reached such a stage of decline. "The disintegration of the masses into personalities, or civilization, is a diseased state" and leads, for the individual, to "the loss of a living idea about God" and to a condition in which "man . . . feels bad, is sad, loses the source of living life, doesn't know spontaneous sensations and is conscious of everything" (20: 189-190).

Presumably (and quite in line with Dostoevsky's usual depiction of the period of Greco-Roman decadence) this was the condition of the world at the time of Christ's incarnation. It was he who provided a new ideal for mankind, one that has retained its validity ever since: "NB. Not one atheist who has disputed the divine origin of Christ has denied the fact that He is the ideal of humanity. The latest on this—Renan. This is very remarkable."* And the law of this new ideal, according to Dostoevsky, consists of "the return to spontaneity, to the masses, but freely. . . . Not forcibly, but on the contrary, in the highest degree willfully and consciously. It is clear that this higher willfulness is at the same time a higher renunciation of the will" (20: 192).

After postulating this paradox, Dostoevsky continues by contrasting the ideal of Christ, which he declares to be "something irresistibly beautiful, sweet, inevitable, and even inexplicable," with that of the Socialists, repeating ideas already familiar from his journalism. "Socialists," he writes, "go no further than the belly. And what all of our 'Young Russia' has been doing for several years is striving with all its powers to prove that there is nothing beyond what the belly contains." For the Socialists, the ideal of total self-sacrifice is viewed only in material terms: "it would mean that there would be no poor, and that everyone would be terribly rich." Willing to

* Ernest Renan's *Vie de Jésus* was published in 1863, and Dostoevsky read it almost immediately. The assertion here could be illustrated with many passages from Renan's book, where he continually speaks of Jesus—even though treating him as a mortal man rather than as the Son of God—as the incomparable ideal of humanity.

"But whatever may be the unexpected events of the future," Renan writes in his final peroration, "Jesus will not be surpassed. His cult will continually be renewed; his legend will provoke tears without end; his sufferings will melt the finest hearts; all centuries will proclaim that, among the sons of men, none was born greater than Jesus." Ernest Renan, *Oeuvres complètes*, 10 vols. (Paris, 1949), 4: 371.

agree that such might be the result, Dostoevsky counters with the objection that "the socialists stop at this point"; for him affluence is only a by-product of the ideal he proclaims, not its final goal. For "the whole infinity of Christianity over socialism consists in the fact that the Christian (ideal), giving up everything, demands nothing [in return]" (20: 192-193).

Until now, Dostoevsky has been thinking in opposition to the Utilitarian generation of the 1860s and its conception of Socialism; but in a rather obscure though highly suggestive passage, he takes notice of the Christian Socialism of the 1840s that he had once greatly admired. And while acknowledging that Christian Socialists may well be "hostile to the idea of rewards, of honorariums," he argues that they do not truly understand the full implications of such hostility. For they continue to ask for rewards all the same, "only from love for the giver or only because he [the Christian Socialist] feels that after this the giver will be even more strongly loved (the new Jerusalem, embraces, the green branches)." Such rewards will evidently be moral-spiritual, not material, and strengthen the bonds of love in the community; but since the notion of a certain expected reciprocity is retained, the self-sacrifice of the Christian Socialist is not *entirely* pure.

In any case, "socialism has not even rationally gotten as far as such an explanation of Christianity, only a few of its representatives have gotten that far, and they were poets" (20: 193). What Dostoevsky means, presumably, is that only a few inspired Christian Socialists have been able to glimpse the true nature of the Christian ideal even to this extent; and they have had no effect on the others. Finally, Dostoevsky summarizes his thoughts: "Patriarchy was the primitive condition. Civilization is the middle, the transitional. Christianity, the third and final degree of man, but at this point development stops, the ideal is attained." As we know from the notebook entry at Marya Dimitrievna's bier, it is impossible fully to attain this ideal on earth; and Dostoevsky thus affirms abruptly that "there is a future life," though without including any of his earlier reasons for drawing such a conclusion (20: 194).

These notes contain Dostoevsky's version of the great culture-myth which, as M. H. Abrams has magisterially shown, dominated so much of the Romantic movement of the first half of the nineteenth century both in England and Germany, and of course came to Russia primarily through the influence of German literature and philosophy. A secularized version of the Judeo-Christian apocalypse, this myth begins with an Edenic state of primal unity between man and the universe, which is then fractured by the rise of consciousness and reason. The acquisition of the power of thought precipitates mankind "from innocent ignorance into knowledge, and from happy obedience to instinct into the misery of being confronted by multiple moral choices";[8] the onset of knowledge is the metaphysical equivalent of the theological fall of man into a state of isolation, self-division, and moral confusion. "Pure reflection, therefore," as Schelling wrote in words that anticipate the underground man, "is a spiritual sickness . . . it is an evil."9 The myth usually culminated in an apocalyptic reconciliation on a higher level between man and the lost state of harmony of which he had once been a part—a reconciliation whose forms differed depending on individual writers and thinkers. Sometimes, as in the case of Fichte or Schiller, such a reconciliation was envisaged only as an infinite and unattainable goal beyond the reach of earthly possibility.

Dostoevsky's appropriation of this myth is marked by a manifestly Christocentric character, which restores some of its original religious significance; and he obviously belongs with those like Schiller—whose works, as he once said, he knew by heart—who could not imagine any genuinely apocalyptic transformation of mankind within the bounds of earthly life. All the same, he does entertain the possibility of what he calls a "return to the masses," a cure for the disease of individualism and civilization, by following the example of Christ and accepting the ideal he has brought to humanity. This would lead to the restoration of whatever unity is still realizable on earth; and such new unity, in accordance with the myth, would also be on a higher level—it would no longer be a unity of instinct, but one achieved freely through a self-conscious surrender of the will.

The emphasis that Dostoevsky places on "freedom" in this new unity to be attained through Christ already prefigures one of the central motifs of the Legend of the Grand Inquisitor. And these reflections also help to illuminate some of the otherwise hermetic imagery of the later novels—Raskolnikov staring with nostalgic envy through the slats of his prison stockade at the tents of the wandering tribesmen of the Siberian steppe; the use of Claude Lorrain's *Acis and Galatea*, with its neo-classical representation of a legendary Grecian Golden Age, in the suppressed chapter of *The Devils* and then in *A Raw Youth*; the idyllic world of spontaneous innocence existing on another planet in *The Dream of a Ridiculous Man*. Such worlds are inevitably doomed to destruction, and within earthly life there is only the hope of their partial restoration through suffering and inner struggle with the help of the ideal proclaimed by Christ.

6

Other notebook entries deal with the more limited issues of what radical ideas might really mean *in practice*, and the self-destructive ways in which they would transform mankind if *seriously* accepted as new paradigms for human conduct and behavior. Sometime toward the end of 1864, for example, Dostoevsky jotted down the following thoughts: "The Socialists want to have man reborn, to *free* him, to imagine him without God and family. They conclude that, having forcibly changed his daily economic life, they will attain their goal. But if man is to be changed, it will not be for *external* reasons and not otherwise than by a *moral* transformation. You will not abandon God until you are convinced by mathematics, and the family until mothers do not wish to be mothers and man wishes to turn love into raw sex. Can you achieve this with weapons? And can one dare to say beforehand, before the experience, that here lies salvation? And with this, risk all of humanity? Western rubbish!" (20: 178-179). The transformation of man was a much more difficult task than "the Socialists" were willing to acknowledge; it would be necessary to change his *moral* nature in order to achieve their goals, and to attempt to do so was to stake the fate of all mankind on a rash gamble on the unknown.

The possible results of such a gamble are described in one of the notes Dostoevsky made for his revision of *The Double*, which had not ceased to preoccupy him even as late as the latter half of 1864. Here he depicts the widening of Mr. Golyadkin's mental horizon as he assimilates the latest discoveries of modern science: "(Mind-shattering news, in the first place) about Garibaldi, and, secondly, about oxygen and hydrogen. Oxygen and hydrogen cause his head to spin. There is no longer a Supreme Being. What will happen to the Ministry and the authorities? *Dream.* Everything is canceled. People are free. Everyone *beats everyone else* on the street in broad daylight. *They are taking care of themselves* (they are saving their kopeks)" (1: 435). The loss of faith in a Supreme Being could thus only result in an explosion of egoism and the reign of universal moral chaos. The same dream, more closely adapted to the thematic symbolism of the book, would in a year or two lead to the conversion of Raskolnikov in *Crime and Punishment*.

Dostoevsky's great novels were thus already beginning to stir in the crucible of his imagination, and the next few years would see them blossom forth in a prodigious burst of creative energy as he observed, with horror and dismay, the drastic worsening of the social-political situation. For during the remainder of the 1860s the radicals became more and more isolated and alienated, more embittered, ingrown and forlorn, more ready to embark on the most reckless and foolhardy adventures. In response, the Tsarist régime became more blindly senseless in its suppression and persecution and struck out wildly in all directions. It was against the background of this truly tragic imbroglio of Russian life, whose manifestations he followed with spellbound and brooding apprehension, that Dostoevsky was to dramatize his personal nightmares and his fears for the future, as well as the saving and healing forces which, he still believed, were contained in the Russian soil and in a Russian national character imbued with the ideal of Christ.

ABBREVIATIONS

Biografiya	Orest Miller and Nikolay Strakhov, *Biografiya, Pisma i Zametki iz Zapisnoi Knizhki F. M. Dostoevskogo* (St. Petersburg, 1883). Preceded by the name of the author of the appropriate section.
DMI	*F. M. Dostoevsky, Materialy i Issledovania*, ed. A. S. Dolinin (Leningrad, 1935).
DVS	*F. M. Dostoevsky v Vospominaniakh Sovremennikov*, ed. A. Dolinin, 2 vols. (Moscow, 1961).
DW	F. M. Dostoevsky, *The Diary of a Writer*, trans. Boris Brasol (Santa Barbara and Salt Lake City, 1979).
LN	*Literaturnoe Nasledtsvo*
Pisma	F. M. Dostoevsky, *Pisma*, ed. and annotated by A. S. Dolinin, 4 vols. (Moscow, 1928-1959).
PSS	F. M. Dostoevsky, *Polnoe Sobranie Sochinenii*, ed. and annotated by G. M. Fridlender et al., 30 vols (Leningrad, 1972-).

NOTES

CHAPTER 1

1. *Literaturnoe Nasledtsvo* [cited hereafter as *LN*], 83 (Moscow, 1971), 310.
2. See *Dostoevsky: The Years of Ordeal,*

1850-1859 (Princeton, 1983), 58.
3. Ibid., 62.

CHAPTER 2

1. *F. M. Dostoevsky v Vospominaniyakh Sovremennikov*, ed. A. Dolinin, 2 vols. (Moscow, 1961), 1: 195. Cited hereafter as *DVS*.
2. F. M. Dostoevsky, *Pisma*, ed. and annotated by A. S. Dolinin, 4 vols. (Moscow, 1928-1959), 1: 579; March 9, 1857. Cited hereafter as *Pisma*. For more details, see *Dostoevsky: The Years of Ordeal, 1850-1859* (Princeton, 1983), 215-216.
3. R. B. Zaborova, "F. M. Dostoevskii i Literaturnii Fond," *Russkaya Literatura*, 3 (1975), 158-170.
4. I. S. Turgenev, *Polnoe Sobranie Sochinenii*, 28 vols. (Moscow-Leningrad, 1960-1968), 8: 174.
5. *Pisma*, 2: 71; January 1/13, 1868.
6. *Dostoevsky, Materiali i Issledovaniya*, ed. G. M. Fridlender, 5 vols. to date (Leningrad, 1971-1983), 4: 243.
7. L. F. Panteleev, *Vospominaniya*, ed. S. A. Reiser (Leningrad, 1958), 231.

8. *Dostoevsky, Materiali*, ed. Fridlender, 4: 243.
9. E. A. Shtakenschneider, *Dnevnik i Zapiski, 1854-1886*, ed. I. N. Rozanova (Moscow-Leningrad, 1934), 269.
10. See *Dostoevsky: The Seeds of Revolt, 1821-1849* (Princeton, 1976), 162-164.
11. *Pisma*, 1: 292; March 14, 1860.
12. Ibid.
13. Ibid.
14. Ibid.; May 3, 1860.
15. Ibid., 1: 296; June 12, 1860.
16. Ibid., 298.
17. Ibid.
18. A. I. Shubert, *Moya Zhizn*, ed. A. Dermana (Leningrad, 1929), 201.
19. *Pisma*, 1: 286; November 12, 1859.
20. Ibid., 294; May 3, 1860.
21. Ibid., 293.
22. Ibid., 299; September 10, 1860.

CHAPTER 3

1. For more information on these circles, see *Dostoevsky: The Seeds of Revolt, 1821-1849* (Princeton, 1976), chaps. 12, 15, 17.
2. Orest Miller and Nikolay Strakhov, *Biografiya, Pisma i Zametki iz Zapisnoi Knizhki F. M. Dostoevskogo* (St. Petersburg, 1883), 170-171. Cited hereafter as *Biografiya*.
3. Ibid., 171.
4. Ibid.
5. A more ample discussion can be found in *Dostoevsky: The Years of Ordeal, 1850-1859* (Princeton, 1983), 61-62.
6. G. M. Fridlender, "U Istokov 'Pochvennichestvo,'" *Izvestiya Akademii Nauk SSSR, Seriya literatura i yazhika*, 5 (1971), 402.
7. *DVS*, 1: 196.
8. Cited in Fridlender, "U Istokov," 402.
9. For Herzen's position and importance during the 1850s, see *Dostoevsky: The Years of Ordeal*, 227-233.
10. Cited in Fridlender, "U Istokov," 406-407.

11. N. A. Dobrolyubov, *Selected Philosophical Essays*, trans. J. Fineberg (Moscow, 1956), 218-373.
12. Cited in Fridlender, "U Istokov," 407.
13. Cited in V. S. Nechaeva, *Zhurnal M. M. i F. M. Dostoevskikh, "Vremya," 1861-1863* (Moscow, 1973), 29.
14. A. P. Mogilyanskii, "K Istorii pervoi publikatsi 'Zapisok iz Mertvogo doma,'" *Russkaya Literatura*, 3 (1969), 179-181.
15. F. M. Dostoevsky, *Stati i Materiali*, ed. A. S. Dolinin, 2 vols. (Moscow-Leningrad, 1922-1925), 1: 361.
16. *Pisma*, 1: 299-300; September 20, 1860.
17. Ibid.
18. E. Lampert, *Sons Against Fathers* (Oxford, 1965), 151.
19. N. G. Chernyshevsky, *Selected Philosophical Essays* (Moscow, 1953), 94.

CHAPTER 4

1. Herzen reiterated this idea in several important essays. "In Russia there has not been a posterity of conquerors," he wrote in one of them, "and thus there cannot be a genuine aristocracy." For other examples, see *PSS*, 18: 236.

2. See *Dostoevsky: The Years of Ordeal, 1850-1859* (Princeton, 1983), 38.

3. V. G. Belinsky, *Selected Philosophical Works* (Moscow, 1948), 363.

4. *Pisma*, 1: 135-136; February 22, 1854.

5. Strakhov, *Biografiya*, 200.

6. For further details on Carus and *Psyche*, see *Dostoevsky: The Years of Ordeal*, 170-174.

7. Cited in A. S. Dolinin, "F. M. Dostoevsky i N. N. Strakhov," in *Shestidesiatye Gody*, ed. N. K. Piksanov and O. V. Tsekhnovitser (Moscow, 1940), 240.

8. Strakhov, *Biografiya*, 225, 195.

9. The quotation is taken from B. F. Egorov, "Apollon Grigoryev—Kritik," *Uchenie Zapiski Tartuskogo Gosudarstvennogo Universiteta*, 98 (1960), 194. A portrayal of Shidlovsky can be found in *Dostoevsky: The Seeds of Revolt, 1821-1849* (Princeton, 1976), 93-100.

10. Cited in A. L. Volynski, *Russkie Kritiki* (St. Petersburg, 1896), 684.

11. V. G. Selitrennikova and I. G. Yakushkin, "Apollon Grigoryev i Mitya Karamazov," *Filologicheskie Nauki*, 1 (1969), 13-24.

12. Andrzej Walicki, *The Slavophile Controversy*, trans. Hilda Andrews-Rusiecka (Oxford, 1975), 510.

13. Apollon Grigoryev, *Sochineniya*, ed. N. N. Strakhov (St. Petersburg, 1876), 247.

14. For the Chernyshevsky-Annenkov controversy on this point, and Dostoevsky's response to it, see *Dostoevsky: The Years of Ordeal*, 250-255.

15. Grigoryev, *Sochineniya*, 618.

16. W. Giusti, "Annotazioni su A. A. Grigorev," *Annali* (Istituto Universitario Orientale, Sezione Slava), 1 (1958), 66. Despite its modest title, this is an extremely perceptive evaluation of the work and personality of Grigoryev.

17. *Pisma*, 1: 165; January 18, 1856.

18. Cited in V. V. Zenkovsky, *A History of Russian Philosophy*, trans. George L. Kline, 2 vols. (New York, 1953), 1: 405.

19. Ibid., 403.

CHAPTER 5

1. Strakhov, *Biografiya*, 223.

2. Ibid., 224.

3. Ibid.

4. Ibid.

5. Ibid., 173.

6. Ibid., 172.

7. Ibid., 220.

8. Ibid., 218-219.

9. V. S. Nechaeva, *Zhurnal M. M. i F. M. Dostoevskikh, "Vremya," 1861-1863* (Moscow, 1973), 65.

10. Strakhov, *Biografiya*, 223.

11. Nechaeva, *Zhurnal "Vremya,"* 68.

12. This is the picture given by Nechaeva, which appears much closer to the actual situation. Ibid., 68-69.

13. Apollon A. Grigoryev, *Materiali dlya biografii*, ed. Vlad. Knyazhnina (Petrograd, 1917), 278.

14. Strakhov, *Biografiya*, 220.

15. Such an idea is strongly advanced by S. Borshchevskii, *Shchedrin i Dostoevskii* (Moscow, 1956), 27-28 and *passim*. But see the remark of a younger Soviet Russian scholar, one of the editors of the new Academy of Sciences edition of Dostoevsky's work,

that "today, one does not write that way any longer either about Dostoevsky, or *pochvennichestvo*, or Shchedrin (particularly [the Shchedrin] of the 1860s)." V. A. Tunimanov, *Tvorchestvo Dostoevskogo, 1854-1862* (Leningrad, 1980), 226.

16. Grigoryev, *Materiali*, 267.

17. Ibid., 278.

18. Strakhov, *Biografiya*, 204.

19. Ibid.

20. *Pisma*, 1: 33; September 8/20, 1863.

21. Grigoryev, *Materiali*, 266.

22. Nechaeva, *Zhurnal "Vremya,"* 69.

23. Mikhail Bakhtin, *Problems of Dostoevsky's Poetics*, ed. and trans. Caryl Emerson (Minneapolis, 1984), 93.

24. For more information, see *Dostoevsky: The Years of Ordeal, 1850-1859* (Princeton, 1983), 243-247.

25. N. A. Dobrolyubov, *Selected Philosophical Essays*, trans. J. Fineberg (Moscow, 1956), 199.

26. Alexander Herzen, *My Past and Thoughts*, trans. Constance Garnett, rev. Humphrey Higgins, 4 vols. (New York, 1968), 4: 154.

CHAPTER 6

1. V. G. Belinsky, *Selected Philosophical Works* (Moscow, 1948), 323-324.

2. For a more extensive discussion of the "vision on the Neva," see *Dostoevsky: The*

Seeds of Revolt, 1821-1849 (Princeton, 1976), 133-136.

3. For an analysis of *Mr. Prokharchin*, see ibid., 316-318.

4. Raymond Williams, *Culture and Society, 1780-1950* (New York, 1983), 87.

5. It was L. P. Grossman who first called attention to *Mary Barton* and wrote an informative article drawing the parallel with *Crime and Punishment*. See L. P. Grossman, "Dostoevskii i chartiski roman," *Voprosy Literaturi*, 4 (1959), 147-158.

6. Jane Delaney Grossman, *Edgar Allen Poe in Russia* (Wurzberg, 1973), 34.

7. E. A. Poe, "The Black Cat," *Complete Works*, ed. James A. Harrison, 17 vols. (New York, 1902; rpt. 1965), 4: 146.

Chapter 7

1. For more details on the reception of *Time*, see *PSS*, 18: 229-236.

2. Ibid.

3. Ibid.

4. Ibid., 18: 280-281.

5. *Pisma*, 1: 183-184; April 13, 1856.

6. N. G. Chernyshevsky, *Selected Philosophical Essays* (Moscow, 1953), 376.

7. N. A. Dobrolyubov, *Selected Philosophical Essays*, trans. J. Fineberg (Moscow, 1956), 542.

8. Chernyshevsky, *Essays*, 317-318.

9. *Pisma*, 1: 142; February 20, 1854.

10. Ibid., 58; January 1, 1840.

11. "I grustnyi vsor ostanovila / Tsaritsa gordaya na nem." A. S. Pushkin, *Sobranie Sochinenii*, 10 vols. (Moscow, 1959-1962), 5: 237.

12. Chernyshevsky, *Polnoe Sobranie Sochinenii*, 15 vols. (Moscow, 1939-1953), 7: 856.

13. Dostoevsky's view of Uspensky turned out to be much more broad-minded than those of the writer's erstwhile left-wing partisans. Three years later, after Chernyshevsky's arrest, *The Contemporary* adopted a much more rigidly Populist line; and when a second edition of Uspensky's stories was published, the critic of the journal wrote: "In his [the author's] relations with the people, one does not hear indifference or impartiality but a mixture of haughtiness and contempt recalling that of an old-time prosperous bailiff of an estate." Uspensky's work rapidly lost favor, and, in his later years, "he became a street buffoon, storyteller and alcoholic, and finally ended his life a suicide." See B. P. Kozmin, *Iz Istoria Revolyutsionnoi Misli v Rossii* (Moscow, 1961), 38; and *A Handbook of Russian Literature*, ed. Victor Terras (New Haven, 1985), 496.

Chapter 8

1. Cited in *PSS*, 18: 281.

2. Wherever possible, references to Dostoevsky's notebooks will be keyed to the texts included in the Academy of Sciences edition of his works. The translations into English are indebted to those in *The Unpublished Dostoevsky*, ed. Carl Proffer, trans. by various hands, 3 vols. (Ann Arbor, Mich., 1973-1976). Individual page references to the English text, however, will not be given.

3. See this citation from Chernyshevsky, and others of the same kind, in *PSS*, 20: 347.

4. For more information on these matters, see V. S. Nechaeva, *Zhurnal M. M. i F. M. Dostoevskikh, "Vremya," 1861-1863* (Moscow, 1973), 155-210, esp. 183, 188.

5. The offending passage is given in *PSS*, 19: 97.

6. Matthew Arnold, *Poems* (London and New York, 1888), 214.

7. *Istoriya Russkoy Kritiki*, 2 vols. (Moscow-Leningrad, 1958), 1: 340.

8. For more information, see *Dostoevsky: The Seeds of Revolt, 1821-1849* (Princeton, 1976), 252-257.

9. Andrzej Walicki, *The Slavophile Controversy*, trans. Hilda Andrews-Rusiecka (Oxford, 1975), 256.

10. Cited in ibid., 256-257.

11. Strakhov, *Iz Istorii Literaturnago Nigilizma* (St. Petersburg, 1890; rpt. The Hague, 1967), 34.

12. Ibid., 39-65.

13. Strakhov's annoyance at this incident is still visible twenty years later in *Biografiya*, 235.

Chapter 9

1. Cited in *PSS*, 3: 529.

2. *F. M. Dostoevsky v Russkoi Kritike*, ed. A. A. Belkin (Moscow, 1956), 42.

3. *Pisma*, 2: 586; November 3, 1857.

4. See the remarks of B. Eikhenbaum, *Lev Tolstoy*, vol. 1 (Leningrad, 1928), 81-82; also G. M. Fridlender et al., *Istoriya Russkogo Romana*, 2 vols. (Moscow-Leningrad, 1962), 1: 426.

5. I. I. Zamotin, *Dostoevsky v Russkoi Kritike, 1848-1881* (Warsaw, 1913), 36-37.

6. *Dostoevsky v Russkoi Kritike*, ed. Belkin, 94-95.

7. Zamotin, *Dostoevsky v Russkoi Kritike*, 41.

8. K. Mochulsky, *Dostoevsky, His Life and Work*, trans. Michael A. Minihan (Princeton, 1967), 210.

9. For more details, see *Dostoevsky: The Years of Ordeal, 1850-1859* (Princeton, 1983), chap. 19.

10. George Steiner, *Tolstoy or Dostoevsky* (New York, 1961), 197.

CHAPTER 10

1. Franco Venturi, *The Roots of Revolution*, trans. Frances Haskell (New York, 1966), 218.

2. Ibid., 199; for more details on the uprising at Bezdna and on Anton Petrov, see 215-219.

3. Abbott Gleason, *Young Russia* (New York, 1980), 215. This extremely insightful study of the 1860s contains a vivid portrait of Shchapov.

4. Leonid Grossman, *Zhizn i Trudy Dostoevskogo* (Moscow-Leningrad, 1935), 116.

5. Venturi, *Roots of Revolution*, 237.

6. N. V. Shelgunov, *Vospominaniya*, 2 vols. (Moscow, 1967), 1: 333-334.

7. Ibid., 338-339.

8. Ibid., 336.

9. Strakhov, *Biografiya*, 232.

10. Shelgunov, *Vospominaniya*, 1: 164.

11. *LN*, 86 (Moscow, 1973), 581.

12. Shelgunov, *Vospominaniya*, 1: 186.

13. These details are taken from the informative article of G. V. Krasnov, "Vystuplenie N. G. Chernyshevskogo s Vospominaniyami o N. A. Dobrolyubove 2 Marta 1862 g. Kak Obshchestvennoe Sobytie," in *Revolutsionnoe Situatsiya v Rossii v 1858-1861*, ed. M. V. Nechkina, vol. 4 (Moscow, 1965), 147.

14. L. F. Panteleev, *Vospominaniya*, ed. S. A. Reiser (Leningrad, 1958), 228.

15. Shelgunov, *Vospominaniya*, 1: 187.

16. Krasnov, "Vystuplenie Chernyshevskogo," 148.

17. Strakhov, *Biografiya*, 232-233.

18. Ibid., 233-234.

CHAPTER 11

1. Cited in Franco Venturi, *The Roots of Revolution*, trans. Frances Haskell (New York, 1966), 292.

2. Ibid.

3. B. P. Kozmin, *Iz Istorii Revolyutsionnoi Misli v Rossii* (Moscow, 1961), 252.

4. Venturi, *Roots of Revolution*, 293.

5. Ibid., 295-296.

6. I. S. Turgenev, *Polnoe Sobranie Sochinenii*, 28 vols. (Moscow-Leningrad, 1960-1968), 8: 258.

7. Strakhov, *Biografiya*, 239-240.

8. Cited in V. S. Nechaeva, *Zhurnal M. M. i F. M. Dostoevskikh "Vremya," 1861-1863* (Moscow, 1973), 302-303.

9. Cited in the informative article by N. G. Rosenblyum, "Petersburgskie Pozhary 1862 g. i Dostoevsky," *LN*, 86 (Moscow, 1973), 30.

10. Chernyshevsky's article is reprinted in *DVS*, 1: 317-321; the citation is on p. 317.

11. See the discussion of this problem in William Woehrlin, *Chernyshevskii, The Man and the Journalist* (Cambridge, Mass., 1971), 306-311.

12. See the citations from his journals in V. A. Tunimanov, *Tvorchestvo Dostoevskogo, 1854-1862* (Leningrad, 1980), 247-248.

13. There exists one other brief account of this meeting. V. N. Shaganov, a fellow exile of Chernyshevsky in Siberia, reports a snatch of conversation about it that took place long before Chernyshevsky's article, probably sometime between 1867 and 1871. As Shaganov recalled: "In May 1862, just at the time of the Petersburg fires, early one morning F. Dostoevsky burst into Chernyshevsky's apartment and abruptly addressed him with the following words: 'Nikolay Gavrilovich, in the name of God, order the fires to be stopped! . . .' It then required much effort, Chernyshevsky said, to clear up the matter with F. Dostoevsky. He refused to believe anything, and, it seems, hurried away finally with such disbelief and with despair in his soul." See V. N. Shaganov, "N. G. Chernyshevskii na katorge i v ssilke," in *N. G. Chernyshevskii v Vospominaniyakh Sovremennikov*, ed. Yu. G. Oksman, 2 vols. (Saratov, 1959), 2: 121.

14. *DVS*, 1: 319-321.

15. N. G. Rosenblyum, "Petersburgskie Pozhary," 39.

16. Ibid., 49.

17. Ibid., 49-54.

18. Ibid., 33.

19. Leonid Grossman, *Zhizn i Trudy Dostoevskogo* (Moscow-Leningrad, 1935), 114.

20. Kozmin, *Iz Istorii*, 272.

21. Ibid.

22. Ibid.

CHAPTER 12

1. Cited in V. S. Nechaeva, *Zhurnal M. M. i F. M. Dostoevskikh, "Vremya," 1861-1863* (Moscow, 1973), 291.
2. Ibid., 292.
3. Cited in *Istoriya Russkoi Literatury XIX v.*, ed. D. N. Ovsyaniko-Kulikovsky, 5 vols. (Moscow, 1915), 3: 45.
4. B. Eikhenbaum, *Lev Tolstoy*, vol. 1 (Leningrad, 1928), 223-224.
5. I. S. Turgenev, *Literary Reminiscences*, trans. David Magarshack (New York, 1958), 194.
6. D. V. Grigorovich, *Polnoe Sobranie Sochinenii*, 12 vols. (St. Petersburg, 1896), 7: 284, 288.
7. Alexander Herzen, *My Past and Thoughts*, trans. Constance Garnett, rev. Humphrey Higgins, 4 vols. (New York, 1968), 4: 1574-1584. The title of this article in English differs slightly from my own.
8. I. S. Turgenev, *Pisma*, 13 vols. (Moscow-Leningrad, 1961), 4: 303.
9. Ibid., 137.
10. Henri Granjard, *Ivan Tourguénev et les courants politiques et sociaux de son temps* (Paris, 1954), 298. This classic work is indispensable for any serious study of Turgenev.
11. Ibid.
12. Turgenev, *Pisma*, 4: 316.
13. Turgenev, *Literary Reminiscences*, 195.
14. Cited in Granjard, *Ivan Tourguénev*, 301.
15. Turgenev, *Pisma*, 8: 152.
16. G. M. Fridlender et al., *Istoriya Russkogo Romana*, 2 vols. (Moscow-Leningrad, 1962), 1: 501.
17. See, for example, the remark in Pisarev's essay "Nineteenth-Century Scholasticism" (1861) that "the Russian peasant has perhaps not yet acquired sufficient stature to realize his own personality and rise to a rea-

sonable egoism and respect for his own individuality" (or, more literally, his own *I*). Dimitry Pisarev, *Selected Philosophical, Social and Political Essays* (Moscow, 1958), 77.
18. "An open manifestation of Turgenev's hatred for Dobrolyubov," Chernyshevsky wrote in 1884, "was, as is well known, his novel *Fathers and Children*." Cited in V. E. Evgenyev-Maksimov, *Sovremennik pri Chernyshevskom i Dobrolyubove* (Leningrad, 1936), 514.
19. P. V. Annenkov, *Literaturnye Vospominaniya* (St. Petersburg, 1909), 549-550.
20. Evgenyev-Maksimov, *Sovremennik*, 548.
21. M. A. Antonovich, *Literaturno-Kriticheskie Stati* (Moscow-Leningrad, 1961), 45.
22. Ibid., 42.
23. Charles Moser, *Anti-Nihilism in the Russian Novel of the 1860s* (The Hague, 1964), 64.
24. Antonovich, *Stati*, 41.
25. Ibid., 81.
26. N. N. Strakhov, *Iz Istorii Literaturnago Nigilizma, 1861-1865* (St. Petersburg, 1890; rpt. The Hague, 1967), 102-103.
27. D. I. Pisarev, *Sochineniya*, 4 vols. (Moscow, 1955), 1: 135.
28. Ibid., 2: 8-9, 10-11.
29. Ibid., 11, 10.
30. Ibid., 15.
31. Ibid., 50.
32. Turgenev, *Pisma*, 5: 12.
33. Ibid., 4: 320.
34. Ibid., 358-359.
35. Ibid., 381.
36. Ibid., 385.
37. Strakhov, *Kriticheskiya Stati*, 2 vols. (Kiev, 1902-1908), 1: 9.
38. Ibid., 201.
39. Ibid., 37.
40. Strakhov, *Biografiya*, 237.

CHAPTER 13

1. Strakhov, *Biografiya*, 237.
2. *Pisma*, 1: 302; July 31, 1861.
3. Strakhov, *Biografiya*, 259.
4. F. M. Dostoevsky, *Materialy i Issledovaniya*, ed. A. S. Dolinin (Leningrad, 1935), 536. Cited hereafter as *DMI*.
5. *Pisma*, 1: 310; June 6/July 8, 1862.
6. Ibid., 310-311.
7. Ibid.
8. E. Dryzhakova, "Dostoevsky i Gertsen," *Sbornik Dostoevsky-Nekrasov* (Leningrad, 1974), 64; A. I. Gertsen, *Polnoe Sobranie Sochinenii*, 30 vols. (Moscow, 1954-1961), 22: 259.
9. Strakhov, *Biografiya*, 240.

10. My depiction of the meeting between Dostoevsky and Herzen is greatly indebted to the researches of Elena Dryzhakova, and I essentially follow her version of the events. My own interpretation, however, differs in some details. See Elena Dryzhakova, "Dostoevsky i Gertsen, Londonskoe Svidanie 1862 Goda," *Canadian-American Slavic Studies*, 3 (1983), 325-348.
11. Gertsen, *Sobranie Sochinenii*, 26: 202, 200, 204.
12. Ibid., 203-204.
13. Ibid., 27: 247.
14. G. F. Kogan, "Razyskania o Dostoevskom," *LN*, 86 (1973), 596.

15. L. P. Grossman and Vyacheslav Polonsky, *Spor o Bakunine i Dostoevskom* (Moscow, 1926). For a recent witty summing up of the opposing arguments, which concludes that Grossman's thesis is a myth, see Jacques Catteau, "Bakounine et Dostoievski," *Bakounine, Combats et Débats* (Paris, 1979), 97-105.
16. Kogan, "Razyskania," 596.
17. *Pisma*, 1: 311; June 26/July 8, 1862.
18. Strakhov, *Biografiya*, 244.

19. Ibid., 243-244.
20. "N. N. Strakhov o Dostoevskom," ed. L. P. Lanskii, *LN*, 86 (1973), 560.
21. Ibid.
22. Ibid., 560-561.
23. Ibid., 561-562.
24. Ibid., 562.
25. For more information, see *Dostoevsky: The Years of Ordeal, 1850-1859* (Princeton, 1983), chap. 9.

Chapter 14

1. Strakhov, *Biografiya*, 245.
2. M. A. Antonovich, *Literaturno-Kriticheskie Stati* (Moscow-Leningrad, 1961), 16, 19-20.
3. Ibid., 31.
4. Strakhov, *Iz Istorii Literaturnago Nigilizma* (St. Petersburg, 1890; rpt. The Hague, 1967), 122-123.
5. Ibid., 122.
6. Reinhold Niebuhr, *An Interpretation of Christian Ethics* (New York, 1956), 146.
7. Cited in V. S. Nechaeva, *Zhurnal M. M. i F. M. Dostoevskikh, "Vremya," 1861-1863* (Moscow, 1973), 235.
8. N. S. Nekrasov, *Polnoe Sobranie Sochinenii i Pisem*, 12 vols. (Moscow, 1948-1953), 10: 479-480.

9. *Pisma*, 1: 312; November 3, 1862.
10. M. E. Saltykov-Shchedrin, *Sobranie Sochinenii*, 20 vols. (Moscow, 1965-1977), 6: 46.
11. Ibid.
12. Strakhov, *Iz Istorii*, 165-182.
13. Cited in Nechaeva, *Zhurnal "Vremya,"* 180.
14. *Pisma*, 1: 317-318; June 17, 1863.
15. Ibid., 318.
16. Strakhov, *Biografiya*, 32.
17. Cited in Nechaeva, *Zhurnal "Vremya,"* 308.
18. Strakhov, *Biografiya*, 247.

Chapter 15

1. Cited in *PSS*, 4: 294.
2. *Pisma*, 2; 605; October 9, 1859.
3. V. A. Zelinskii, *Kriticheskie Kommentarii k Sochineniyam F. M. Dostoevskago* (Moscow, 1901), 42.
4. I. I. Zamotin, *Dostoevsky v Russkoi Kritike, 1846-1881* (Warsaw, 1913), 74.
5. For more information, see *Dostoevsky: The Years of Ordeal, 1850-1859* (Princeton, 1983), chaps. 6-11.
6. Victor Shklovsky, *Za i Protiv* (Moscow, 1957), 101.
7. Cited in V. A. Tunimanov, *Tvorchestvo Dostoevskogo, 1854-1862* (Leningrad, 1980), 75.
8. R. L. Jackson, "The Narrator in Dostoevsky's *Notes from the House of the Dead*," in *Studies in Russian and Polish Literature, in Honor of Wacław Lednicki* (The Hague, 1962), 197.

9. K. Mochulsky, *Dostoevsky, His Life and Work*, trans. Michael Minihan (Princeton, 1967), 186.
10. Jacques Catteau, "De la Structure de la *Maison des Morts* de F. M. Dostoevskij," *Revue des Etudes Slaves*, 54 (1982), 63-72.
11. Shklovsky, *Za i Protiv*, 107.
12. B. M. Eikhenbaum, *The Young Tolstoy*, trans. Gary Kern (Ann Arbor, Mich., 1972), 77.
13. L. N. Tolstoy, *Tales from Army Life*, trans. Louise and Aylmer Maude (London, 1951), 105.
14. I. S. Turgenev, *Pisma*, 13 vols. (Moscow-Leningrad, 1961), 6: 66.
15. Cited in *PSS*, 4: 296.
16. Cited in *PSS*, 4: 297.
17. Tunimanov, *Tvorchestvo Dostoevskogo*, 76-77.

Chapter 16

1. A. S. Dolinin, *Poslednie Romani Dostoevskogo* (Moscow-Leningrad, 1963), 215-230.

2. Roman Jakobson, "Der russische Frankreich-Mythus," *Slavische Rundschau* 3 (1931), 636-642.

3. *Pisma*, 1: 310; June 26/July 8, 1862.
4. The poem is entitled "Mechta" ("Dream"). The closing line calls on "the sleeping East" to "awake" and replace the dying West. *PSS*, 5: 361.
5. Herzen, *My Past and Thoughts*, trans. Constance Garnett, rev. Humphrey Higgins, 4 vols. (New York, 1968), 4: 1688-1689. My

translation differs slightly from that given in this text.
6. *Pisma*, 1: 78; May 4, 1845.
7. For the Westerner arguments against Slavophilism on this point, see Andrzej Walicki, *The Slavophile Controversy*, trans. Hilda Andrews-Rusiecka (Oxford, 1975), chap. 9.

CHAPTER 17

1. *Pisma*, 1: 319; June 19, 1862.
2. Ibid., 318; June 17, 1863.
3. Strakhov, *Biografiya*, 173.
4. *Pisma*, 1: 216-217; March 9, 1857.
5. Aimée Dostoevsky, *Fyodor Dostoevsky* (London, 1921), 105.
6. F. M. Dostoevsky, *The Gambler, with Polina Suslova's Diary*, trans. Victor Terras, ed. Edward Wasiolek (Chicago, 1972), 365. The Russian source for Suslova's diary and letters is A. S. Dolinin, *Gody blizosti s Dostoevskim* (Moscow, 1928).
7. *The Gambler*, 284.
8. Ibid., 208.
9. Ibid., 364.
10. Ibid., 318.
11. L. P. Grossman, *Put Dostoevskogo* (Leningrad, 1929), 154. I am grateful to S. A. Belov of Leningrad for having located this reference for me.
12. *The Gambler*, 257.
13. Strakhov, *Biografiya*, 259.
14. *Pisma*, 1: 323-326; September 1 (new style), 1863.
15. Ibid., 330; September 8/20, 1863.
16. Harvey R. Greenberg, "Psychology of Gambling," in *Comprehensive Textbook of*

Psychiatry, ed. Harold I. Kaplan, Alfred M. Freedman, and Benjamin J. Sadock, vol. 3 (Baltimore and London, 1980), 3279.
17. Otto Fenichel, *The Psychoanalytic Theory of the Neuroses* (New York, 1945), 372-373.
18. Ibid.
19. *Pisma*, 1: 308; June 6, 1862.
20. Ibid., 311; June 26/July 8, 1862.
21. Ibid., 330; September 8/20, 1863.
22. Ibid., 290; dated sometime in 1860.
23. Ibid., 324; September 1 (new style), 1863.
24. *The Gambler*, 202.
25. Ibid., 203.
26. Ibid., 206.
27. Ibid., 206-207.
28. Ibid.
29. For more information, see *Dostoevsky: The Years of Ordeal, 1850-1859* (Princeton, 1983), chap. 15.
30. *The Gambler*, 207.
31. Ibid., 209.
32. Ibid., 210.
33. Ibid., 211.
34. Ibid., 211-212.

CHAPTER 18

1. *Pisma*, 1: 326; September 1 (new style), 1863.
2. F. M. Dostoevsky, *The Gambler, with Polina Suslova's Diary*, trans. Victor Terras, ed. Edward Wasiolek (Chicago, 1972), 213.
3. Ibid., 213-214.
4. Ibid., 213.
5. Ibid., 214.
6. Ibid.
7. Ibid., 215.
8. Ibid., 215-216.
9. Ibid., 214.
10. *Pisma*, 1: 330; September 8/20, 1863.
11. *The Gambler*, 216.
12. *Pisma*, 1: 331; September 8/20, 1863.
13. Henri Granjard, *Ivan Tourguénev et les courants politiques et sociaux de son temps* (Paris, 1954), 325.
14. *DMI*, ed. Dolinin, 543.
15. *Pisma*, 1: 329-331; September 8/20, 1863.

16. Ibid., 331.
17. *The Gambler*, 217.
18. Ibid.
19. *Pisma*, 1: 335; September 18/30, 1863.
20. Ibid.
21. *The Gambler*, 218-220.
22. *Pisma*, 1: 333.
23. Ibid., 336; September 30/October 18, 1863.
24. Ibid., 337; October 18, 1863.
25. *The Gambler*, 222.
26. Ibid.
27. Ibid.
28. A. I. Gertsen, *Polnoe Sobranie Sochinenii*, 30 vols. (Moscow, 1954-1961), 18: 279.
29. *The Gambler*, 223.
30. *Pisma*, 1: 338; October 18, 1863.
31. Ibid.
32. *Pisma*, 1: 339; November 10, 1863.
33. Ibid., 342; November 19, 1863.

CHAPTER 19

1. *DMI*, ed. Dolinin, 543.
2. *Pisma*, 1: 340; November 19, 1863.
3. Ibid., 341.
4. N. G. Chernyshevsky, *Chto Delat?* (Moscow, 1955), 129, 135.
5. *Dostoevsky: The Seeds of Revolt, 1821-1849* (Princeton, 1976), 252-256.
6. Chernyshevsky, *Chto Delat?*, 390.
7. *Pisma*, 1: 343; December 23, 1863.
8. Ibid.
9. Ibid.
10. Ibid., 347; February 9, 1864.
11. Ibid., 345; January 10, 1864.
12. Ibid., 344.
13. L. P. Lanskii, "Dostoevsky v Neizdannoi Perepiske Sovremennikov (1837-1881)," *LN*, 86 (Moscow, 1973), 393; January 1864.
14. *Pisma*, 1: 347; February 9, 1864.
15. Ibid., 349; February 29, 1864.
16. In the magazine, a footnote appended to the title of the work announced that the first installment "should count as an introduction to a whole book, almost a preface." This phrase was eliminated on republication. See the commentary and textual variants in *PSS*, 5: 375, 342.
17. *Pisma*, 2: 608; October 9, 1859. See also *Dostoevsky: The Years of Ordeal, 1850-1859* (Princeton, 1983), 298.
18. Ibid., 612; March 20, 1864.
19. Ibid., 1: 352; March 26, 1864.
20. Ibid., 353.
21. Ibid., 355; April 2, 1864.
22. Ibid., 362; April 9, 1864.
23. Ibid., 365; April 13, 1864.

CHAPTER 20

1. References in the text are to the Academy of Sciences edition of Dostoevsky's work, *PSS*. An English translation of this notebook entry can be found in *The Unpublished Dostoevsky*, trans. by various hands, 3 vols. (Ann Arbor, Mich., 1973), 1: 39-41. This translation, however, should be used with a great deal of caution. The second paragraph on p. 40 is badly mangled by what seems to be a typographical oversight, and there is a serious mistranslation in the sixth paragraph of the same page beginning "NB."
2. For more information, see *Dostoevsky, The Years of Ordeal, 1850-1859* (Princeton, 1983), 55-59.
3. *Pisma*, 1: 142; February 20, 1854.
4. Ibid., 1: 58; January 1, 1840.
5. Ernst Cassirer, *Kant's Leben und Lehre* (Berlin, 1921), 299.
6. In one of the few nonpartisan studies of Dostoevsky's Christology, Ryszard Przybylski links his ideas with those of the seventh-century theologian Maximus Confessor, who exercised an important influence on Eastern Orthodox and Russian Orthodox theology and was himself a disciple of Dionysius the Areopagite. Maximus was a staunch defender of the doctrine that Jesus had two natures, one godly and the other human, which meant that he possessed a human as well as a divine will. Hence, it was possible for mankind to follow Christ's example, and, by assimilating themselves to his nature, to approach that state of "deification" which is mankind's ultimate destiny in Eastern Orthodoxy.

Maximus also saw reason as opposed to the faith of Revelation, and insisted there was no way of reconciling the two; reason was "the enemy of 'man's moral instinct.'" The Slavophils, despite their opposition to Roman Catholicism, shared the conviction of St. Thomas Aquinas that reason and faith could be harmonized, and Ivan Kireevsky championed the idea of a "believing reason." Dostoevsky was, however, closer to the current of Eastern Orthodox thought flowing from Maximus.

Whether Dostoevsky was familiar at first hand with such theological subtleties is a question that cannot be answered; but the analogies are certainly suggestive. He did, however, as Przybylski writes, adopt Christological views of this kind "to oppose the anthropomorphism of Feuerbach and nineteenth-century Socialism." See Ryszard Przybylski, *Dostojewski i "Przęklete Problemy"* (Warsaw, 1964), 219-246.
7. Timothy Ware, *The Orthodox Church* (Baltimore, 1963), 224-225.
8. John Hick, *Evil and the God of Love* (London, 1975), 245. I am indebted to my former student, Professor Shira Wolosky, for having called my attention to Hick's book.

CHAPTER 21

1. *Existentialism from Dostoevsky to Sartre*, ed. Walter Kaufman (New York, 1957), 53-82. For a flat reassertion that the underground man is a universal psychological type, with no social or local coloration, see Wolf Schmid, *Der Textaufbau in den Erzählungen Dostoevskijs* (Munich, 1973), 260.
2. N. K. Mikhailovsky, "Zhestokii Talant," in *F. M. Dostoevsky v Russkoi Kritike*, ed. A. A. Belkin (Moscow, 1956), 306-384.

NOTES

3. V. V. Rozanov, *Dostoevsky and the Legend of the Grand Inquisitor*, trans. Spencer E. Roberts (Ithaca and London, 1972), 35.

4. Lev Shestov, "Dostoevsky and Nietzsche: The Philosophy of Tragedy," in *Essays in Russian Literature, The Conservative View: Leontiev, Rozanov, Shestov*, ed. and trans. Spencer E. Roberts (Athens, Ga., 1968), 3-183.

5. V. L. Komarovich, " 'Mirovaya garmoniya,' Dostoevskogo," in *O Dostoevskom*, ed. Donald Fanger (Providence, R.I., 1966), 119-149.

6. Originally published in a Czech periodical, the essay has been reprinted in A. Skaftymov, *Nravstvennie Iskaniya Russkikh Pisatelei* (Moscow, 1972), 70, 96.

7. In these days of methodological self-consciousness, and so as to avoid the charge of hermeneutical naiveté, it may be advisable to state my own conception of my interpretative task. What I am primarily concerned with is the "meaning" of *Notes from Underground*, using this word in the sense given it by E. D. Hirsch. "Meaning," he writes, "is that which is represented by a text; it is what the author meant by the use of a particular sign sequence; it is what the signs represent." Hirsch distinguishes meaning of this kind from what he calls "significance," which he defines as being "a relationship between that meaning and a person, or a conception, or a situation, or indeed anything imaginable. . . . Significance always implies a relationship, and one constant, unchanging pole of that relationship is what the text means." In my view, the vast majority of commentators of *Notes from Underground* have always been concerned with its significance, and, as a result, its meaning has rather gotten lost in the shuffle.

I am fully aware that Hirsch's ideas have met with massive opposition, and I would agree that in practice meaning and significance cannot be separated as neatly as his definitions would seem to imply. Indeed, in rela-

tion to any work of the past, significance unavoidably enters along with the time gap between past and present. Yet I would also argue that it is empirically possible for a critic to direct his energies either toward meaning or toward significance, and to emphasize one or the other in full awareness of making such a choice—which is precisely what I have chosen to do.

One of the major objections to Hirsch, made by the followers of H.-G. Gadamer, is that the establishment of meaning in Hirsch's sense is a chimerical ideal; it is a false application of the standard of scientific objectivity, which is impossible to attain because of the historicity of human understanding. But my own reading of Gadamer does not persuade me that he is in favor of historical error and illusion, or that he positively *discourages* attempting to obtain as accurate a knowledge of the past as possible. If so, the "fusion of horizons" that he recommends would be nothing more than a series of mythical inventions, and the most delirious reconstruction would have the same value as the work of the most justly reputed scholar.

It thus seems to me that the preliminary establishment of meaning is an indispensable part of the hermeneutic process; and this is enough to justify my own attempt. Dostoevsky's work has already been subject to so much "fusion" that a sober effort to establish meaning can serve a very useful function. See E. D. Hirsch, *Validity in Interpretation* (New Haven and London, 1967), 8; also, for a succinct account of the current debates over hermeneutics, M. H. Abrams, *A Glossary of Literary Terms* (New York, 1981), 84-87.

8. A. I. Gertsen, *Polnoe Sobranie Sochinenii*, 30 vols. (Moscow, 1954-1966), 6: 36.

9. Tzvetan Todorov, "Notes d'un souterrain," in *Les Genres du discours* (Paris, 1978), 158.

10. *Pisma*, 1: 178; March 24, 1856.

11. Ibid., 1: 353; March 26, 1864.

CHAPTER 22

1. *Pisma*, 1: 375; first week of July 1864.
2. Ibid., 4: 272-273; July 29, 1864.
3. Ibid., 1: 399; April 5, 1865.
4. Ibid., 1: 400; April 14, 1865.
5. Cited in V. S. Nechaeva, *Zhurnal M. M. i F. M. Dostoevskikh "Epokha," 1864-1865* (Moscow, 1975), 19.
6. *Pisma*, 1: 378; September 20, 1864.
7. Nechaeva, *Zhurnal "Epokha,"* 198-203.
8. *Pisma*, 1: 401; April 14, 1864.
9. N. N. Strakhov, *Iz Istorii Literaturnago Nigilizma* (St. Petersburg, 1890; rpt. The Hague, 1967), 258-270.
10. "The Swallows" can be found in English appended to the translation of Feodor

Dostoevsky, *Notes from Underground & The Grand Inquisitor*, trans. Ralph E. Matlaw (New York, 1960), 201-209. References will be given to this English version. The Russian text is in M. E. Saltykov-Shchedrin, *Sobranie Sochinenii*, 20 vols. (Moscow, 1965-1977), 6: 488-495.

11. "The Swallows," 207.
12. V. A. Tunimanov, *Tvorchestvo Dostoevskogo, 1854-1862* (Leningrad, 1981), 241. Tunimanov's chap. 5 is a balanced discussion of the relation between Dostoevsky and Saltykov-Shchedrin.
13. Saltykov-Shchedrin, *Sobranie Sochinenii*, 5: 303.

INDEX

Corneille, Pierre, 84
Crisis theology, 312
Crystal Palace (London), 241, 290; in *Notes from Underground*, 327-330, 331, 332; in *Winter Notes on Summer Impressions*, 241, 243, 249; in *What Is To Be Done?*, 291, 306, 326-330, 359
Custine, Astolphe, Marquis de, 56

Dal, V. I., 60
Dante, 178, 310; *The Divine Comedy*, 200
Darwin, Charles, *Origin of Species*, 211
Day, The, 96*n*, 213
Decembrists, 25, 136
Defoe, Daniel, *The Shortest Way with Dissenters*, 317
Determinism, 321-324, 333
Dickens, Charles, 7, 131, 241, 349*n*; *The Old Curiosity Shop*, 112
Diderot, Denis, 313*n*, 327*n*; *Le Neveu de Rameau*, 313
Dobrolyubov, N. A., 6, 12, 27, 47, 59, 71-72, 77, 78-82, 86-90 passim, 95, 108, 109, 145, 149*n*, 165-168, 174, 288, 304, 361, 362; critique of *The Insulted and Injured*, 116; "Downtrodden People," 111; "What is Oblomovism?" 62; "When Will the Real Day Come?" 12*n*
Dolinin, A. S, 235
Don Quixote, 11, 12*n*, 312
Dostoevsky, Anna Grigorievna (FMD's second wife), 89*n*, 254*n*
DOSTOEVSKY, FEODOR MIKHAILOVICH:
    admiration for Herzen, 25-26, 190, 192-194; affair with Suslova, 256-260, 265-274, 281; anti-Catholic prejudice, 187, 190, 271, 275, 276; attitude toward the Jews, 96*n*, 218*n*; epilepsy, 5, 10, 123, 182, 253, 257, 278, 286, 293, 303, 362; European trip in 1862, xi, 181-198; European trip in 1863, 253, 260-284 passim; French, knowledge of, 244; gambling, 185, 260-265, 272-273; literary reputation, 19, 39, 97, 142, 218; meeting with Herzen (London), 190-194; meeting with Herzen (Italy), 278-281; political views, xi, 6, 105, 128-129, 136, 141-142, 146, 150, 209, 310, 333-334; prison experiences, 5, 29, 32-33, 38-39; public readings, 14, 142-143, 144; religious beliefs, 4, 54*n*, 298-311; superstitious nature, 263; views on aesthetics, 46, 75-76, 78-88, 90-96; on Europeans and European culture, 55, 56, 71, 186-187, 235-245, 247, 276; on family and marriage, 304; on human irrationality, 5, 7, 74, 75, 123, 124, 126, 233-234, 248-249, 264, 265, 313, 316; on human psyche, 5, 31-33, 75-76, 100, 127, 248, 322; on meaning of human life, 299, 302, 303, 305, 331. *See also* Men of the 1840s; Men of the 1860s; Slavophils; Westerners
    WORKS, general:
    dialectic of vanity, 238-239, 336-337, 338, 341; fantastic realism, 66-71, 94; humanitarianism, 62-63, 118, 217, 302, 316; ideological eschatology, 31, 250, 302, 315-316, 347-348; imagined interlocutor, 30-31, 54, 56-58, 237-238; inverted irony, 238, 249, 324; sadism in, 126*n*; *skaz* form, 230
    WORKS, individually:
    The Brothers Karamazov, 75, 88*n*, 200, 232; Dimitry, 44, 231, 232; Feodor Karamazov, 88; Grigory, 61; Ivan, 307*n*; "Legend of the Grand Inquisitor," 376
    "A Confession," 295
    Crime and Punishment, 24, 48, 74, 129*n*, 204, 211, 232, 264, 275, 286, 373; Katerina Ivanovna, 254; Luzhin, 368; Raskolnikov, 27, 177, 211-212, 265, 290, 346, 368, 376, 377; Razumikhin, 232; Sonya, 27, 346; Svidrigailov, 73, 88, 98, 127
    Crocodile, 353, 355, 363-368
    The Devils, 24, 90, 95, 137*n*, 143, 145, 152, 163, 204, 296, 373, 376; Kirillov, 102; Lembke, 163; Shatov, 102, 267; Stavrogin, 57, 73, 88, 102, 127, 267; Peter Verkhovensky, 286; Stepan Verkhovensky, 95, 137*n*, 347
    Diary of a Writer, 90, 115, 125*n*, 150, 279, 364; "Peasant Marey," 198
    The Double, 3, 67, 70, 277, 294, 295; Golyadkin, 3, 45, 69, 70, 277, 294, 377
    Dream of a Ridiculous Man, 376
    The Gambler, 261, 268-278 passim
    A Gentle Creature, 24, 298
    The Idiot, 68, 73, 90, 299, 310, 350, 373; Ippolit, 92; Myshkin, 12, 130; Nastasya Filippovna, 129
    The Insulted and Injured, 7, 20-21, 55, 65, 110-131, 161, 215, 315, 348, 353; contemporary reaction, 115; egoism theme, 119, 120, 121-122, 124, 125; forgiveness theme, 115, 120; naive Romanticism, 119-121, 122, 124, 127, 128, 131; social-humanitarianism, 116, 119, 122, 123, 125; structure, 113-115, 119, 122, 131; topical allusions, 115, 116, 117, 126-127; Alyosha, 113, 121, 128-129, 130; Ivan Petrovich, 113-115, 117-119, 121-123, 127, 128; Ikhmenyev, 113-114, 118, 119-121; Masloboev, 113, 114, 117, 122, 127; Natasha, 113, 115, 120-121, 128, 131; Nellie, 113-115, 121-122, 129; Count Nainsky, 114; Nikolay Sergeevich, 113-117; Prince Valkovsky, 88, 113-123 passim, 124*n*, 126-129, 131, 250, 328, 346
    "Letters on Art," 79
    "Life of a Great Sinner," 301
    A Little Hero, 19
    "Mr. -bov and the Question of Art," 78
    "Mr. Prokharchin," 70
    "Mr. Shchedrin or a Schism among the Nihilists," 356, 360, 362
    A Nasty Tale (An Unpleasant Predicament), 201-204, 363
    Netotchka Nezvanova, 3-4, 14
    Notes from the House of the Dead, 7, 19,

LIBRARY OF CONGRESS CATALOGING-IN-PUBLICATION DATA

Frank, Joseph, 1918-
    Dostoevsky: the stir of liberation, 1860-1865.
    Bibliography: p.
    Includes index.
    1. Dostoyevsky, Fyodor, 1821-1881—Biography.
2. Novelists, Russian—19th century—Biography.
3. Soviet Union—Intellectual life—1801-1917.
4. Dostoevsky, Fyodor, 1821-1881—Social and political
views. I. Title.
PG3328.F73   1986   891.73'3 [B]   85-43280
ISBN 0-691-06652-3 (alk. paper)
ISBN 0-691-01452-3 (pbk.)